Computer Communications and Networks

T0140546

For other titles published in this series, go to
http://www.springer.com/series/4198

The **Computer Communications and Networks** series is a range of textbooks, monographs and handbooks. It sets out to provide students, researchers and nonspecialists alike with a sure grounding in current knowledge, together with comprehensible access to the latest developments in computer communications and networking.

Emphasis is placed on clear and explanatory styles that support a tutorial approach, so that even the most complex of topics is presented in a lucid and intelligible manner.

Ajith Abraham • Aboul-Ella Hassanien
Václav Snášel
Editors

Computational Social Network Analysis

Trends, Tools and Research Advances

 Springer

Editors
Prof. Dr. Ajith Abraham
Machine Intelligence Research
   Labs (MIR)
Scientific Network for Innovation
   & Research Excellence
P.O.Box 2259
Auburn WA 98071-2259
USA
ajith.abraham@ieee.org

Václav Snášel
Technical University Ostrava
Dept. Computer Science
Tr. 17. Listopadu 15
708 33 Ostrava
Czech Republic
vaclav.snasel@vsb.cz

Prof. Aboul-Ella Hassanien
Cairo University
Fac. Computers & Information
Dept. Information Technology
5 Ahmed Zewal Street
Orman, Giza 12613
Egypt
a.hassanien@fci-cu.edu.eg

Series Editor
Professor A.J. Sammes, BSc, MPhil, PhD, FBCS, CEng
Centre for Forensic Computing
Cranfield University
DCMT, Shrivenham
Swindon SN6 8LA
UK

ISSN 1617-7975
ISBN 978-1-4471-2532-7   e-ISBN 978-1-84882-229-0
DOI 10.1007/978-1-84882-229-0
Springer Dordrecht Heidelberg London New York

British Library Cataloguing in Publication Data
A catalogue record for this book is available from the British Library

Cover design: SPi Publisher Services

Printed on acid-free paper

Springer is part of Springer Science+Business Media (www.springer.com)

Preface

Social networks provide a powerful abstraction of the structure and dynamics of diverse kinds of people or people-to-technology interaction. Web 2.0 has enabled a new generation of Web-based communities, social networks, and folksonomies to facilitate collaboration among different communities. Social network analysis is a rapidly growing field within the Web intelligence domain. The recent developments in Web 2.0 have provided more opportunities to investigate the dynamics and structure of Web-based social networks. Recent trends also indicate the usage of social networks as a key feature for next-generation usage and exploitation of the Web. This book provides an opportunity to compare and contrast the ethological approach to social behavior in animals (including the study of animal tracks and learning by members of the same species) with web-based evidence of social interaction, perceptual learning, information granulation, the behavior of humans, and affinities between web-based social networks. The main topics cover the design and use of various computational intelligence tools and software, simulations of social networks, representation and analysis of social networks, use of semantic networks in the design, and community-based research issues such as knowledge discovery, privacy and protection, and visualization. This book presents some of the latest advances of various topics in intelligence social networks and illustrates how organizations can gain competitive advantages by applying the different emergent techniques in the real-world scenarios. Experience reports, survey articles, and intelligence techniques and theories with specific networks technology problems are depicted. We hope that this book will be useful for researchers, scholars, postgraduate students, and developers who are interested in intelligence social networks research and related issues. In particular, the book will be a valuable companion and comprehensive reference for both postgraduate and senior undergraduate students who are taking a course in Social Intelligence. The book contains 18 chapters, which are organized into two parts, and all articles are self-contained to provide greatest reading flexibility.

This volume is divided into three parts as detailed below. Part I deals with Social Network Mining Tools and consists of seven chapters.

The increasing achievement of the Web has led people to exploit collaborative technologies in order to encourage partnerships among different groups. The interest in analyzing Virtual Social Networks has grown massively in recent years and it has involved researches from different fields. This led to the development of different methods to study relationships between people, groups, organizations, and other knowledge-processing entities on the Web. In Chapter 1, "An Overview of Methods for Virtual Social Networks Analysis," D'Andrea et al. classify these methods in two categories. The first category concerns methods used for the network data collection, while the second category deals with methods used for the network data visualization. The chapter gives an example of application of these methods to analyze the Virtual Social Network LinkedIn.

The discovery of single key players in social networks is commonly done using some of the centrality measures employed in social network analysis. In Chapter 2, "Discovering Sets of Key Players in Social Networks," Ortiz-Arroyo presents a brief survey of such methods. The methods described include a variety of techniques ranging from those based on traditional centrality measures using optimizing criteria to those based on measuring the efficiency of a network. Additionally, the author describes and evaluates a new approach to discover sets of key players based on entropy measures.

Barton et al. in Chapter 3, "Towards Self-Organizing Search Systems," propose a general three-layer model for designing and implementing a self-organizing system that aims at searching in multimedia data. This model gives developer guidelines about what component must be implemented and how they should behave. The usability of this model is illustrated on a system called Metric Social Network.

Chapter 4, "DISSECT: Data-Intensive Socially Similar Evolving Community Tracker" by Chin and Chignell, examines the problem of tracking community in social networks inferred from online interactions by tracking evolution of known subgroups over time. A variety of approaches have been suggested to address this problem, and the corresponding research literature is reviewed, which include centrality and clustering for identifying subgroup members, and optimization. The main contribution of this chapter is the DISSECT method wherein multiple known subgroups within a social network are tracked in terms of similarity-based cohesiveness over time. The DISSECT method relies on cluster analysis of snapshots of network activity at different points in time followed by similarity analysis of subgroup evolution over successive time periods.

The Blogosphere is expanding at an unprecedented speed, and a better understanding of the blogosphere can greatly facilitate the development of the Social Web to serve the needs of users, service providers, and advertisers. One important task in this process is the clustering of blog sites. In Chapter 5, "Clustering of Blog Sites Using Collective Wisdom," Agarwal et al. illustrate how clustering with collective wisdom can be achieved and compare its performance with respect to representative traditional clustering methods.

In Chapter 6, "Exploratory Analysis of the Social Network of Researchers in Inductive Logic Programming," Lavrač et al. present selected techniques for social network analysis and text mining, and interpret the results of exploratory analysis of the social network of researchers in inductive logic programming (ILP), on the basis of the ILP scientific publications database collected within the ILP-net2 project. In addition the chapter also presents a novel methodology for topic ontology learning from text documents. The proposed methodology, named On-toTermExtraction (Term Extraction for Ontology learning), is based on OntoGen, a semiautomated tool for topic ontology construction, upgraded by using an advanced terminology extraction tool in an iterative, semiautomated ontology construction process.

In Chapter 7, "Information Flow in Systems of Interacting Agents as a Function of Local and Global Topological Features," Andre S. Ribeiro presents the latest results on how a system's structure, namely, its topological features, at global and local levels, affects the flow of information among its elements. It is shown how the topology determines the amount and diversity of information flow, and the ability to cope with noise and uncertainty in the information transmitted. The author uses Boolean Networks as models of dynamical systems of interacting elements whose structure is characterized at a global level by size and average connectivity and at a local level by a generalized clustering coefficient. The dynamics is characterized by the pair-wise mutual information of the time series of the elements states, which quantifies the amount of information flow, and by the Lempel-Ziv complexity, which characterizes the complexity, i.e., diversity of the messages flowing in the system.

Part II consists of eight chapters and deals with Social Network Evolution.

In Chapter 8, "Network Evolution: Theory and Mechanisms," Omidi and Masoudi-Nejad review some of the important network models that are introduced in recent years. The aim of all of these models is imitating the real-world network properties. Real-world networks exhibit behaviors such as small-world, scale-free, and high clustering coefficient.

In Chapter 9, "Vmap-Layout, a Layout Algorithm for Drawing Scientograms," Quirin and Cordón present a drawing algorithm to represent graphically co-citation networks. The proposed method can print real-world networks in an aesthetic way, highlighting the backbone and pushing the less important links to the boundaries. The algorithm is detailed and compared with the classical Kamada-Kawai drawing algorithm on several scientograms.

In Chapter 10, "Nature-Inspired Dissemination of Information in P2P Networks," by Christophe illustrates the dissemination of information within groups of people and aim at answering one question: can we find an effort-less way of sharing information on the web? A nature-inspired framework is introduced as an answer to this question. This framework features artificial ants taking care of the dissemination of information items within the network.

In Chapter 11, "Analysis and Visualization of Relations in e-Learning," Pavla et al. focus on searching of latent social networks in e-Learning systems data. This data consists of student's activity records where latent ties among actors are embedded. The social network studied in this chapter is represented by groups of students who have similar contacts and interact in similar social circles. Different methods of data clustering analysis are applied to these groups and the findings illustrate the existence of latent ties among the group members. The second part of this chapter focuses on social network visualization for monitoring the study activities of individuals or groups, as well as the planning of educational curriculum, the evaluation of study processes, etc.

In Chapter 12, "Interdisciplinary Matchmaking: Choosing Collaborators by Skill, Acquaintance and Trust," Hupa et al. present fundamental concepts on how to score a team based on members' social context and their suitability for a particular project. The chapter represents the social context of an individual as a three-dimensional social network (3DSN), composed of a knowledge dimension expressing skills, a trust dimension, and an acquaintance dimension. Dimensions of a 3DSN are used to mathematically formalize the criteria for prediction of team's performance.

In Chapter 13, "Web Communities Defined by Web Page Content," Kudělka et al. explore the relationship between the intent of web pages, their architecture, and the communities who take part in their usage and creation. The chapter describes techniques, which can be used to extract the mentioned information as well as tools usable in the analysis of this information. Authors define the MicroGenre as a building block of web pages, which is based on social interaction.

In Chapter 14, "Extended Generalized Block Modeling for Compound Communities and External Actors," Radoslaw and Krawczyk consider social communities composed of several cohesive subgroups, which they call compound communities. For such communities, an extended generalized block modeling is proposed in this chapter taking into account the structure of compound communities and relations with external actors. Using the extension, the community protection approach is proposed and used in detection of spam directed toward an e-mail local society.

In Chapter 15, "Analyzing Collaborations Through Content-Based Social Networks," Cucchiarelli et al. present a methodology and a software application to support the analysis of collaborations and collaboration content in scientific communities. High quality terminology extraction, semantic graphs, and clustering techniques are used to identify the relevant research topics. Traditional and novel social analysis tools are then used to study the emergence of interests around certain topics, the evolution of collaborations around these themes, and to identify potential for better cooperation.

Part III deals with Social Network Applications and consists of three chapters.

Grzegorz et al. in Chapter 16 "IA-Regional-Radio – Social Network for Radio Recommendation," present a system based on social network for radio application. This system carries out automatic collection, evaluation, and rating of music reviewers, the possibility for listeners to rate musical hits and recommendations deduced from auditor's profiles in the form of regional Internet radio. First, the system searches and retrieves probable music reviews from the Internet. Subsequently, the system carries out an evaluation and rating of those reviews. From this list of music hits, the system directly allows notation from our application. Finally, the system automatically creates the record list diffused each day depending on the region, the year season, day hours, and age of listeners.

In Chapter 17, "On the Use of Social Networks in Web Services – Application to the Discovery Stage," Maamar et al. discusses the use of social networks in web services with focus on the discovery stage that characterizes the life cycle of these Web services. Traditional discovery techniques are based on registries such as Universal Description, Discovery and Integration (UDDI), and Electronic Business using eXtensible Markup Language (ebXML). Unfortunately, despite the different improvements that these techniques have been subject to, they still suffer from various limitations that could slow down the acceptance trend of web services by the IT community. Social networks seem to offer solutions for some of these limitations, but raise at the same time some issues that are discussed within this chapter.

The friendship relation, a social relation among individuals, is one of the primary relations modeled in some of the world's largest online social networking sites, such as FaceBook. On the other hand, the co-occurrence relation, as a relation among faces appearing in pictures, is one that is easily detectable using modern face detection techniques. These two relations, though appearing in different realms (social vs. visual sensory), have a strong correlation: faces that co-occur in photos often belong to individuals that are friends. Using real-world data gathered from Facebook, which were gathered as part of the FaceBots project, the world's first physical face recognizing and conversing robot can utilize and publish information on Facebook. Mavridis et al. in Chapter 18, "Friends with Faces: How Social Networks Can Enhance Face Recognition and Vice Versa," present methods as well as results for utilizing this correlation in both directions. Both algorithms for utilizing knowledge of the social context for faster and better face recognition are given, as well as algorithms for estimating the friendship network of a number of individuals given photos containing their faces.

We are very much grateful to the authors of this volume and to the reviewers for their tremendous service in critically reviewing the chapters. Most of the authors of chapters included in this book also served as referees for chapters written by other authors. Thanks go to all those who provided constructive and comprehensive reviews. The editors would like to thank Wayne Wheeler and Simon Rees of Springer Verlag, Germany for the editorial assistance and excellent cooperative collaboration to produce this important scientific work. We hope that the reader will share our excitement to present this volume on social networks and will find it useful.

Machine Intelligence Lab (MIR Lab)   *Ajith Abraham*
Cairo University, Egypt   *Aboul Ella Hassanien*
VSB Technical University, Czech Republic   *Václav Snášel*

Contents

Part I
Social Network Mining Tools

Chapter 1
An Overview of Methods for Virtual Social Networks Analysis

Alessia D'Andrea, Fernando Ferri, and Patrizia Grifoni

Abstract The increasing achievement of the Web has led people to exploit collaborative technologies in order to encourage partnerships among different groups. The cooperation can be achieved by Virtual Social Networks that facilitate people's social interaction and enable them to remain in touch with friends exploiting the pervasive nature of information devices and services. The interest in analysing Virtual Social Networks has grown massively in recent years, and it involves researches from different fields. This led to the development of different methods to study relationships between people, groups, organisations- and other knowledge-processing entities on the Web. This chapter classifies these methods in two categories. The first category concerns methods used for the network data collection while the second category deals with methods used for the network data visualisation. The chapter gives an example of application of these methods to analyse the Virtual Social Network LinkedIn.

1.1 Introduction

Social relationships and networking are key components of human life, and they have been historically bound according to time and space limitations; these restrictions have been partially removed because of the Internet evolution and its use diffusion. In particular, the emergence of Web technologies and their evolution towards the Web 2.0 enables people to organise themselves into Virtual Social Networks in the same manner they organise themselves in social networks in the real world.

The difference between both earlier social networks and Virtual Social Networks mainly consists of the mechanism used by the members to communicate each other; the first are based on face-to-face interaction and the latter employ information and communication technologies (ICTi) tools to facilitate interaction and promote communication among people anywhere and anytime.

P. Grifoni (✉)
via Nizza 128, 00198 Rome, Italy, Istituto di Ricerche Sulla Popolazoine e le Politiche Sociali - Consiglio Nazionale delle Ricerche
e-mail: patrizia.grifoni@irpps.cnr.it

A. Abraham et al. (eds.), *Computational Social Network Analysis*, Computer Communications and Networks, DOI 10.1007/978-1-84882-229-0_1,
© Springer-Verlag London Limited 2010

Indeed, Virtual Social Networks are fostered by a blend of hardware and software tools that allow people to easily, immediately, universally, inexpensively, and reliably share information by interacting.

In particular, they are addressed to the possibility to access specific information regarding different areas of interest. Within Virtual Social Networks, individuals can give information (by posting conversations) or get information (by browsing or by posting questions). These information resources are socially helpful because they allow people to easily establish contact among themselves.

The notion of interaction refers to the search of relationship during which people can share, with others, interests and experiences.

The interest in Virtual Social Network Analysis has been growing massively in recent years. Psychologists, anthropologists, sociologists, economists, and statisticians have given significant contributions, making it actually an interdisciplinary research area. This growth matches with an increasing development of methods used to (a) collect and (b) visualise network data in order to analyse relationships between people, groups, organisations- and other knowledge-processing entities on the Net.

The aim of this chapter is to give an overview of these two categories of methods.

In particular, the first category (methods used for network data collection) aims to provide a data set that helps study the effects that Virtual Social Networks have on different aspects of social activities.

To achieve this aim, the following methods are used: (i) Socio-centric: to examine sets of relationships between actors that are regarded for analytical purposes as bounded social collectives. (ii) Ego-centric: to select focal actors (egos), and identify the nodes they are connected to.

The second category (methods used for network data visualisation) aims to render data in easily understood graphical formats, thus making complex information usable.

To achieve this aim, the following are used: (i) graphs: to visualise relationships among members of a narrow Virtual Social Network; (ii) matrices: to visualise large or dense Virtual Social Networks; (iii) maps: to manage a wide amount of data and information; and (iv) a hybrid approach: to integrate different visualisation perspectives according to the user's goal.

The chapter is organised as follows. Section 1.2 provides a short introduction, which deals with some definitions of Virtual Social Networks. Section 1.3 analyses the motivations that lead people to join Virtual Social Networks. Section 1.4 gives a description of methods used for the network data collection and visualisation. Section 1.5 applies the methods for data collection and visualisation to analyse the Virtual Social Network LinkedIn. Finally, Section 1.6 concludes the chapter.

1.2 Background

The term Virtual Social Network indicates a Web-based service that allows individuals to (i) construct a public or semi-public profile, (ii) articulate a list of other people with whom they share a connection, and (iii) view and traverse their list of connections and those made by others within the community [1].

There are many descriptions of the Virtual Social Networks that depend upon the perspective from which they are defined, which may be multi-disciplinary: sociology, technology, business, economic, and e-commerce.

From the sociology perspective, Virtual Social Networks are defined based on their physical features or the strength and type of relationship. Etzioni et al. [2] view Virtual Social Networks from the perspective of bonding and culture and define it as having two attributes namely, a web of affect-laden relationships encompassing a group of individuals (bonding) and commitment to a set of shared values, mores, meanings, and a shared historical identity (culture). Romm et al. [3] define Virtual Social Networks as group of people who communicate with each other via electronic media and share common interests unconstrained by their geographical location, physical interaction, or ethnic origin.

Ridings et al. [4] define Virtual Social Networks as groups of people with common interests and practices that communicate regularly and for some duration in an organised way over the Internet through a common location or mechanism.

The technology perspective refers to Virtual Social Networks based on the software supporting them like list server, newsgroup, bulletin board, and Internet Relay Chat (IRC). These software technologies support the communication within the network and help in creating the boundaries [5].

Hagel and Armstrong [6] take a business perspective and define Virtual Social Networks as groups of people drawn together by an opportunity to share a sense of community with like-minded strangers having common business interest.

Balasubramanian and Mahajan [7] take an economic perspective and define Virtual Social Networks as entities characterised by 'an aggregation of people, who are rational utility-maximizers, who interact without physical collocation in a social exchange process with a shared objective'.

The e-commerce prospective takes a very broad view of Virtual Social Networks on considering what draws people and holds them to buy products and services [8].

In all of these definitions, Virtual Social Networks are described as social entities comprised of individuals who share information and collaborate.

The notion of information refers to the fact that membership of a Social Network is linked to the possibility of gaining access to specific information regarding areas or issues of interest (didactic materials, reports, data bases, etc.), while the notion of collaboration refers to the search for moments of interaction during which one can share, with others, passions, interests, and experiences that are close to one's set of emotions.

As Virtual Social Networks are becoming popular, many studies are performed to investigate their properties in order to understand their practices, implications, culture, and meaning as well as member's engagement with them.

Adamic et al. [9] study an early Virtual Social Network at Stanford University, and find that the network exhibits small-world behaviour, as well as significant local clustering.

Kumar et al. [10] examine two Virtual Social Networks (Flickr and Yahoo) and find that both possess a large strongly connected component.

Girvan and Newman [11] observe that users in Virtual Social Network tend to form tightly knit groups.

Backstrom et al. [12] examine snapshots of group membership in LiveJournal, and present models for the growth of user groups over time.

Finally in a recent work, Ahn et al. [13] analyse complete data from a large South Korean Virtual Social Network (Cyworld), along with data from small sample crawls of MySpace and Orkut.

All these researchers underline that the study of Virtual Social Networks is becoming increasingly important as it allows analysing social, economical, and cultural aspects that are at the basis of decision and planning activities.

1.3   Categorisation of Motivational Factors

The main issue in studying Virtual Social Networks is to analyse motivations that lead people to join them.

One of the obstacles is the vast number of terms and expressions used to describe similar ideas. To unify previous researches and to facilitate the categorisation of motivational factors, we have aggregated similar concepts in order to create several motivational categories (Table 1.1).

As shown in Table 1.1, there are different motivations that lead people to join Virtual Social Networks.

Information exchanging is the most important factor in the success of Virtual Social Networks. The possibility to share a lot of information in Virtual Social Networks, allows discussions on different questions and problems. Individuals can either give information (by posting conversations) or get information (browsing or soliciting information by posting questions or comments). As members interact in a Virtual Social Network, over time the Virtual Social Network emerges as the most authoritative and influential source of knowledge. In fact, Virtual Social Networks provide a more dynamic environment, oriented to innovation and knowledge sharing, than traditional communities. As a consequence, it emerges the increasing 'knowledge profiles' of each member involved into the Virtual Social Network. In this perspective, a Virtual Social Network amplifies openness, interoperability, scalability, and extensibility of a traditional community.

The social aspect represents the second-most popular motivation. This finding suggests that Virtual Social Network members should underline not only the content but also promote the social aspects as well if they wish to increase the success of their network.

People have a need to be affiliated with others because groups give individuals a source of information and help in attain goals and create a social identity.

However, this aspect represents also a negative side. Internet is a very informal medium. Unlike speaking face-to-face, virtual communication does not allow expressing emotion easily. It is necessary to remember that all Social Networks, virtual or real, are based on people, and people are social human beings. It is certain

Table 1.1 Motivational categories

Category	Description	Dimensions	Examples
			To get ideas
		Motivation, skills, digital divide, confidence, well-being	To learn new things
Exchange information	Obtain information about a topic		To learn about new technologies
			To share my successes
			A way for me to express my anger
Social aspect	Obtain emotional support	Education, discussion groups, leisure entertainment, legislation	To get advice
			I can easily let out my emotions
			To support others
Friendship	To made friends	Shared knowledge, collective experience, self-esteem, valuedrole	To talk with people with the same values
			To talk with people similar interests
			Because it is fun
			I enjoy posting in the community
Recreation	For entertainment	Shopping, investments, ordering, bull paying	I like talking about sport
			The interface is easy to use

that Virtual Social Networks allow people to more easily explore their identity and understand their social inhibitions and discuss without the social tensions of real life, but people also need to have a "direct" (face-to-face) social interaction. The absence of this contact can create psychological problems such as neglecting real-life responsibilities. These people who avoid responsibilities may seem invisible and isolated to one another in the physical context but Virtual Social Networks have allowed this culture to develop into an electronic meeting point. They form relationships where deviant views are reinforced through communication with other users who share the same opinions. Problems appear when these groups come into conflict with other groups who hold opposing opinions.

Information exchange and social contact are the central motivation why people join and remain in Virtual Social Networks.

However, some researches suggest that there are other possible reasons; one of these is the possibility people have to seek friendship. Forums, discussions, and chat groups may be established to foster interpersonal exchanges of information.

The expectation of continuing and extending these relationships will encourage members to return frequently to the virtual community. The feeling of being together and being a member of a community comes with the notion of being part of a group, socialising, and spending time together. The interactivity achieved with instant messaging, chat rooms, and bulletin boards, and the different search facilities available on the Web provide a way for people to communicate with others for establishing friendships.

Using the Internet, people have become friends without ever talking or seeing out each other. The structure of the Web makes it easier to find other individuals in similar situations and meet them than it is in real life. With the help of Virtual Social Networks, people meet to share thoughts, ideas, opinions, and feelings about particular problems that they have in common. In fact, it is not uncommon for users to turn to the Web for answers: questions posted to virtual communities, conferences, and mailing lists can gather many experiences within hours.

Many people whose jobs are isolated seek other individuals in Virtual Social Networks not only to exchange opinions, but also just to engage in small talk with persons around the world.

Friendships in virtual space can provide benefits beyond that of information exchange and social aspect.

These responses prove that members of a Virtual Social Network consider networking with other users to be the most significant reason for being involved in cyber space because developing relationships with other people is a key step in transferring knowledge among users. Virtual communication eliminates barriers; people can be everywhere they want to be.

Finally the last motivation is the recreation Virtual Social Networks provide. The use of the Web in general has been much discussed in both the popular press as a new form of recreation similar to that of watching.

A good example of this is MUDS, a Virtual Social Network in which members play games with other users.

1.4 Virtual Social Network Analysis

The Virtual Social Network Analysis indicates the study of the virtual social structure and its effects in order to analyse social and cultural aspects. It conceives a Virtual Social Network as a set of actors (nodes) and a set of relationships connecting pairs of these actors [14].

The analysis allows 'to determine if a Virtual Social Network is tightly bounded diversified or constricted, to find its density and clustering, and to study how the behaviour of network members is affected by their positions and connections' [15].

The objects under observation are not members and their attributes, but the relationships between members and their structure. The advantages of such a representation is that it allows the analysis of social processes as a product of the relationships among social actors.

The formal analysis of a Virtual Social Network can be dealt with two different categories of methods, everyone of them with its own peculiarity, with its different operation.

The first category concerns methods used for the network data collection while the second category deals with methods used for the network data visualisation.

1.4.1 Network Data Collection

The objective of the data collection is to provide a data set that could help analyse the effects Virtual Social Networks have in the different aspects of social activities such as (i) their generation and (ii) their spatial distribution [16].

The generation of social activities considers both the members' (actors') propensity and opportunity to engage in social activities and their interactions with other members in the Virtual Social Network [17].

The spatial distribution describes the activity spaces where members move around when they interact.

The methods used for the Virtual Social Network data collection can be divided into (i) socio-centric and (ii) Ego-centric. The Socio-centric method maps the relations among actors 'that are regarded for analytical purposes as bounded social collectives' [18]. This is most appropriate for tight-bound networks. On the contrary the Ego-centric method maps the relations of a key individual. This is most appropriate for loose-bound networks.

1.4.1.1 Socio-Centric Network Method

The socio-centric Network method is used to analyse virtual social structures. In particular, the method examines sets of relationships among actors that are regarded for analytical purposes as bounded social collectives (Fig. 1.1).

The method is based on the work of Simmel [19] on the configuration of social relationships and the implications of form for the content of interaction. The author argued that 'the size of a social group was key to understanding the interactions among the group's constituents' and he asserted 'dyads are the most basic form of interaction and exchange, involving immediate reciprocity between the two social actors involved'.

The data collection consists of three different steps.

The first step consists in looking at the relationships between each actor in the Virtual Social Network and all other actors.

The types of relationships have to be analysed on considering the nature of the links and in particular with reference to the

- Strength
- Confirmation
- Multiplexity

The strength of a relationship is either given by the frequency and/or duration of the contact and the stability over time [20].

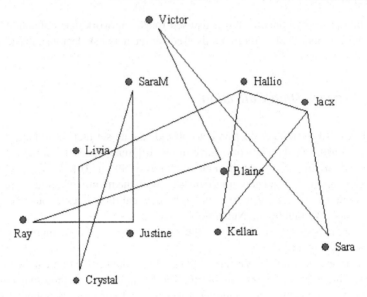

Fig. 1.1 Socio-centric network method: relationships among actors

Table 1.2 Socio-centric network method: measures of key relationships

Focus	Examples of measures
Relationships between actors	Strength, confirmation, multiplexity
Subgroups	Social cohesions, structural equivalence
Characteristics of the Virtual Social Network	Size, Density

The measure of confirmation is determined by the degree to which an actor reports the same relation with others for a content area [21].

The multiplexity refers to the extent to which each actor has different roles and different networks within the Virtual Social Network.

The second step relates to determine if there are subgroups and if certain roles, that each actor takes, have impact on Virtual Social Network.

Finally the last step consists in looking at the overall characteristics of the Virtual Social Network. In particular, the size of the network is important, just as is the density (or connectedness), which is the number of links in a network as a ratio of the total possible links.

The possibilities for the different steps, along with some specific measures of key relationships, are shown in Table 1.2.

These steps require that every actor in the network can answer questions about every other actor of the Virtual Social Network. The questions are about the relationships each actor has with other actors in the Virtual Social Network. The collected answers are transformed in a set of matrices (for each question) for the analysis (as shown in Table 1.3).

Table 1.3 Matrix used for the analysis

	Actor A	Actor B
Actor A	1	4
Actor B	2	3

Each matrix is composed of rows and columns that indicate all the actors in the Virtual Social Network. The cell that is the intersection between a row (one actor) and a column (another actor) reports the answer to the questions given by the first actor about the second actor. The intersection between the second actor and the first reports the answer in the other direction. Each final matrix represents a single kind of relationship.

This kind of survey, if addressed to a small group (20–50 people), allows researchers to request each actor to rate how well they know each of the other actors of the Virtual Social Network.

However, when the group is larger (over 1,000 people), the Socio-centric method has a limited value due to the limitations of computer software and processing power.

1.4.1.2   Ego-Centric Network Method

The Ego-centric Network method focuses on the individual, rather than on the network as a whole. It allows selecting focal actors (egos), and identifies the nodes to which they are connected to (as shown in Fig. 1.2).

The starting point for this method is the location of an actor on a physical plain and his or her activity space that is defined by the actor's connections to key locations. Instead every place of interest to the actor is assigned its own weight, according to the amount of social capital embedded at this place or the utility derived from it.

The number of relationships maintained by an actor can show how central he or she is in the Virtual Social Network.

A high number of relationships indicates that the actor plays an important role in the Virtual Social Network; on the contrary a low number of relationships indicates that the actor is left out of the mainstream of activity (no central actor) and thus is less likely to find what he or she needs.

1.4.2   Network Data Visualisation

Data visualisation can be defined as any technique used to create images, diagrams, or animations in order to communicate a message.

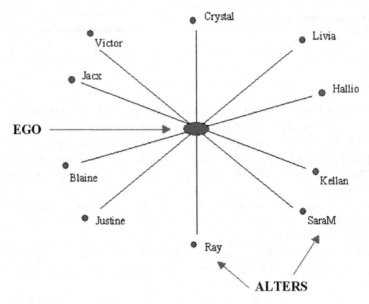

Fig. 1.2 Ego-centric network method

In general, data visualisation is used as a way to aggregate large quantities of data and present them in a way that allows to

- Quickly communicate rich messages (communication).
- Discover new, previously unknown facts and relationships (discovery).
- Get better insight into things we already know (insight).

The visualisation can be performed by using (i) graphs made up of nodes and connection lines and the numbers in each cell stand for specific relationships among these values, (ii) matrices where row and columns stand for actors and properties, (iii) maps, and/or (iv) a hybrid approach.

1.4.2.1 Graphs

In this section, some preliminary notions about graphs and a description of the graph-based network visualisation are given.

A graph is a structure used for modelling information, it is formed by:

 (i) Nodes to represent objects (actors)
(ii) Edges to express relations (communication paths) (Fig. 1.3)

There are different types of graphs:

- Undirected graphs: used to represent (only) symmetric relations (Fig. 1.4).
- Directed graphs: used to represent asymmetric (directed) and symmetric relations (Fig. 1.5).

Fig. 1.3 Graph structure

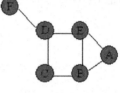

Fig. 1.4 Undirected graph

Fig. 1.5 Directed graph

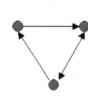

Fig. 1.6 Weighted graph

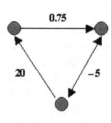

Fig. 1.7 Planar graph

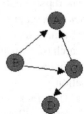

- Weighted graphs: used to represent intensities, distances, or costs of relations (Fig. 1.6).
- Planar graphs: if there are no crossings between the edges (Fig. 1.7).
- Orthogonal graphs: if the edges are drawn using vertical horizontal lines (Fig. 1.8).
- Grid-based graphs: if there is a grid on which the vertexes follow a certain grid the graph (Fig. 1.9).

Different studies have been developed in this field. Moreno [22] introduced direct graphs in order to define characteristics of social actors and variation of point locations to focus on structural data features.

Fig. 1.8 Orthogonal graph

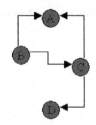

Fig. 1.9 Grid-based graph

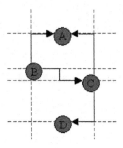

Cyram [23] provides a graph-based network visualisation using various options underlying networks patterns and structures. The graph-based visualisation is used to explore online social networks, providing awareness of community structure; moreover this visualisation is used to support the discovery of people and connections among each person and communities.

Heer and Boyd [24] develop a system that visualises a network through a node-link representation, where each node identifies a member using a name and his or her representative image or picture. The graphic information is integrated by textual information about personal profile; the system offers the possibility to define direct search over profile text.

Figure 1.10 shows an example of graph used for Virtual Social Network visualisation.

The graph, simply looking at who is connected to whom and who is central in the group, allows to indicate the strength and the direction of a relationship, as well as if relationships are strong or weak or if they are one-way or reciprocal.

Strong relationships, indicated by a higher number, are characterised by frequent interaction, feelings of closeness, and multiple types of relationships. For example, a strong relationship may provide actor with emotional support and job-related information.

While weak relationships provide as much social support but, since they are easier to maintain, an actor can have many more of them.

Relationships can also be one-way (if an actor respects someone that doesn't mean that the other person necessarily reciprocates the actor's feelings) or reciprocal (if a relationship goes in both directions). In general, reciprocated relationships tend to be stronger than non-reciprocated relationships.

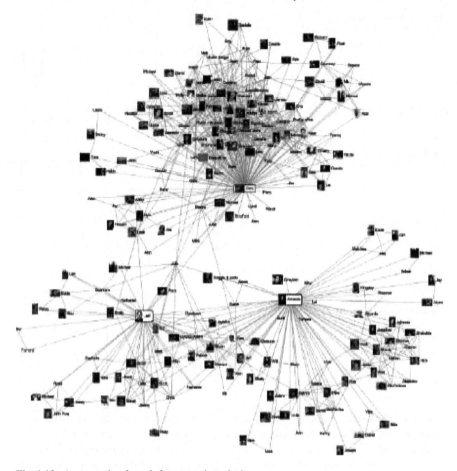

Fig. 1.10 An example of graph for network analysis

1.4.2.2   Matrices

In this section some preliminary notions about matrices and a description of the matrix-based network visualisation are given.

A matrix can be defined as a rectangular array of elements, which can be numbers.

There are different kinds of matrices:

- **Column Matrix** A matrix with only vertical entries (Fig. 1.11).
- **Row Matrix** A matrix with only horizontal entries (Fig. 1.12).
- **Square Matrix** A matrix in which the number of rows equals the number of columns (Fig. 1.13).
- **Identity Matrix** A square matrix in which the main diagonal has all 1s and the remaining elements are all 0s (Fig. 1.14).

Fig. 1.11 Column matrix

$$\underline{b} = \begin{Bmatrix} b_1 \\ b_2 \\ \vdots \\ b_m \end{Bmatrix}$$

Fig. 1.12 Row matrix

$$\underline{a} = \begin{Bmatrix} a_1 & a_2 & \cdots & a_x \end{Bmatrix}$$

Fig. 1.13 Square matrix

$$\underline{A} = \begin{bmatrix} a_{11} & a_{12} & a_{13} \\ a_{21} & a_{22} & a_{23} \\ a_{31} & a_{32} & a_{33} \end{bmatrix}$$

Fig. 1.14 Identity matrix

$$\begin{bmatrix} 1 & 0 & \cdots & 0 \\ 0 & 1 & \cdots & 0 \\ \vdots & & & \vdots \\ 0 & 0 & \cdots & 1 \end{bmatrix}$$

Fig. 1.15 Diagonal matrix

$$\begin{bmatrix} a_{11} & 0 & \cdots & 0 \\ 0 & a_{22} & \cdots & 0 \\ \vdots & & & \vdots \\ 0 & 0 & \cdots & a_{xx} \end{bmatrix}$$

- **Diagonal Matrix** A square matrix in which all entries not on the main diagonal are 0. Those entries on the main diagonal are not restricted to 1 (Fig. 1.15).
- **Symmetric Matrix** A square matrix that it is equal to its transpose (that is defined as a n by m matrix that results from interchanging the rows and columns of the matrix) (Fig. 1.16).
- **Skew-Symmetric Matrix** A square matrix in which its negative is equal to its transpose (Fig. 1.17).
- **Triangular Matrix** A square matrix in which all coefficients below the main diagonal are all zero (Fig. 1.18).
- **Null Matrix** A matrix in which all elements are equal to 0 (Fig. 1.19).

As we said above, generally a matrix is composed of rows and columns that indicate all the actors in the Virtual Social Network. The cell that is the intersection between a row (one actor) and a column (another actor) reports the opinion given by the first actor about the second actor.

The reason for using matrices for visualising Virtual Social Network data is that they allow to see some relationships more easily than verbally describe.

For example, suppose to describe the structure of close friendship in a group of four people: Robert, Sara, Ray, and Justine, we use the values '1' to indicate if an actor likes another, and a '0' if they don't like (see Table 1.4).

Fig. 1.16 Symmetric matrix

$$\begin{bmatrix} 1 & -3 & 2 \\ -3 & 8 & 5 \\ 2 & 5 & 9 \end{bmatrix}$$

Fig. 1.17 Skew-symmetric matrix

$$A = \begin{bmatrix} 0 & -a & -z \\ a & 0 & -c \\ z & c & 0 \end{bmatrix}$$

Fig. 1.18 Triangular matrix

$$\begin{bmatrix} 7 & 3 & 1 \\ 0 & 2 & -5 \\ 0 & 0 & 6 \end{bmatrix}$$

Fig. 1.19 Null matrix

$$\begin{bmatrix} 0 & 0 \\ 0 & 0 \end{bmatrix}$$

Table 1.4 Matrix visualisation

	Robert	Sara	Ray	Justine
Robert	–	1	1	0
Sara	0	–	1	0
Ray	1	1	–	1
Justine	0	0	1	–

On seeing data arrayed in this way, eye is led to scan across each row. In the example it is easy to notice that Robert likes Sara and Ray, but not Justine; Sara likes Ray, but neither Robert nor Justine; Ray likes all three other members of the group; and Justine likes only Ray. Moreover, Ray likes more people than Robert, Justine, and Sara. Is it possible that there is a pattern here? Are men more likely to report relationships of liking than women? Using the matrix representation also immediately highlights a situation: the locations on the main diagonal (e.g., Robert likes Robert, Sara likes Sara) are empty.

1.4.2.3 Maps

Issues connected with wide amount of data and information can be also managed by using maps. They allow visualising each Virtual Social Network element in a 2D plane.

The representation of a map-based networks members is provided by Nardi et al. [25]. It allows visualising a person's social network, defining the central or peripheral position of each contact to her or his work and personal interests. This system provides a visual map of contacts and groups of contacts in the domain of the email communication defining the user's personal social network. In this visualisation, contacts are collected in groups that are differently coloured and positioned in the map; it is similar to a geographic map where the spatial positions represent relationships among contacts. The system offers communication functions and enables the user to retrieve current and archived information associated with contacts. Another example of map-based methods for social network visualisation is socio-mapping implemented by Bahbouh and Warrenfeltz [26]. The method visually expresses information captured by a social map. In this visual representation, each actor has different features according to the goals of the visualisation and she or he is represented as a point in the map. The point height in the map can identify the level of communication, the social position, or the importance of the element in the social structure. The distance between two elements represents the level of the relationship; finally, the quality of the relationship is identified by a set of contour lines or other visual parameters.

1.4.2.4 A Hybrid Approach

An evolution of map-based approach is proposed by Caschera et al. [27]. The authors propose a hybrid and multidimensional method to visualise data and information about social networks and their dynamics considering space, time, and coordinates involving classes of interests. The approach integrates different perspectives of individuals and/or groups of individuals, considering both the Ego-centric and socio-centric point of view. It adopts a graph-based representation approach integrated with a map-based one (hybrid).

The multidimensionality of this approach consists of the opportunity it offers to define visualisations according to coordinates associated with the involved social variables, describing phenomena such as classes of interests (topics) represented by colours, spatial dimension providing the social network elements positions in term's of local coordinates (with the aim to promote face-to-face contacts when possible, and consequently the social ability of the elements), and the temporal dimension that gives the evolution during time.

The spatial dimension identifies each social network element position according to a local/global coordinate system on a 2D space and the different needs of visualisation, while colours identify classes of interest. The temporal dimension helps visualise the social network temporal evolution and to plan individual and group services; this last goal can be viewed as a common temporary issue.

Moreover, the proposed approach allows visualising groups, or individuals, classes of interests using a multidimensional social map. Two dimensions attain to a 2D virtual representation of coloured areas connected to classes of interests. The size of each area is directly proportional to the number of people of the social network involved in the identified class of interests. A third dimension has been introduced to represent the importance of each member of the social network according to his or her classes of interests, given by the number of his or her connections with the other elements of the social network with respect to the specific class of interests. All points of the ovoid with the same height define an isoline, identifying people with the same importance in the social network according to the identified class of interests. Each circle of class of interests is centred in the point that identifies the colour for the specific interest on the colour wheel. Similar colours represent the interests semantic similarity computed.

This representation facilitates social networking because it shows the members' social importance, i.e. the social role of each element; it is a very relevant information for stimulating social networking according to the users goals.

1.5 Application Scenario: The Case of LinkedIn

In the following sections, the methods for data collection and visualisation, described in the previous section, are used to analyse the Virtual Social Network LinkedIn.

LinkedIn is an online network of more than 30 million experienced professionals from around the world, representing 150 industries. The purpose of the site is to allow registered users to maintain a list of contact details of people they know and trust in business. When users join LinkedIn, they have the possibility to create a profile that summarises their professional accomplishments. The profile helps them to find and be found by former colleagues, clients, and partners.

The analysis of LinkedIn consisted of two different phases:

- To find an ex or her classmate and to understand what his group of friends is
- To understand what the social relationships among the members of the group are

The first phase uses the Ego-centric approach while the second phase uses a Socio-centric approach.

1.5.1 Fist Phase

The person that we indented to looking for was Robert. The search engine of LinkedIn allowed us to keep in touch with Robert. Afterward we aimed to identify the nodes to which he was connected to. To achieve our aim, we sent Robert the short questionnaire shown in Table 1.5:

To better illustrate Robert's position within the LinkedIn and the different kinds of relationships he had, we drew a graph (Fig. 1.20).

The graph allows indicating the prevalent directions of relationships that Robert has at LinkedIn. In particular, it is possible to see that he has a one-way relationships with Victor, Jacx, Bleine, Ray, and Livia, while he has reciprocal relationships with Justine, Crystal, Hallio, Kellan, Sara, and SaraM. The graph also shows that Sara is central in the Virtual Social Network, and she has many direct connections and this allows her to be more satisfied with her contacts than Ray who is the less central person. Tracking the number of connections Ray takes to reach Sara is one way

Table 1.5 Questionnaire used to collect Robert personal relationships

Questions	Answers
How many actors have you been in regular contact with in the last 7 days?	11
Please name the actors and indicate the gender and the age	1. Ray – M - 22 2. Crystal – M - 23 3. Livia – F - 30 4. Justine – F - 26 5. SaraM – F - 28 6. Victor – M - 32 7. Hallio – M - 36 8. Blaine – M - 29 9. Kellan – M - 28 10. Jacx – M - 30 11. Sara – F - 27
Of the actors you have regular contact how many are • Sex-partners • Friends • Acquaintances	• Sex-partners: 1 (Sara) • Friends: 8 • Acquaintances: 2 (Blaine; Jacx)
Please indicate which of the actors you have named have been in regular contact with any of the other actors you have named	• Crystal is in regular contact with Victor • Livia has been in regular contact with Sara, Victor, and Justine • Justine: is in regular contact with Livia, Sara, and SaraM • SaraM: is in regular contact with Sara, Justine, Kellan, Bleine, and Hallio • Victor is in regular contact with Crystal, Hallio, and Livia • Hallio is in regular contact with Victor, SaraM, Bleine, and Jacx • Bleine is in regular contact with Hallio, Jacx, Sara, and SaraM • Kellan is in regular contact with SaraM • Jacx has in regular contact with Blaine, Hallio, and Sara • Sara is in regular contact with Livia, Blaine, and SaraM

to monitor the flow of information and opportunities in LinkedIn. In fact, a person who is indirectly linked to many top-level people is more likely to get promoted than someone who is not. This is the proverbial 'small-world problem' that refers to the likelihood that two people who are not directly connected to each other will be able to communicate via indirect connections.

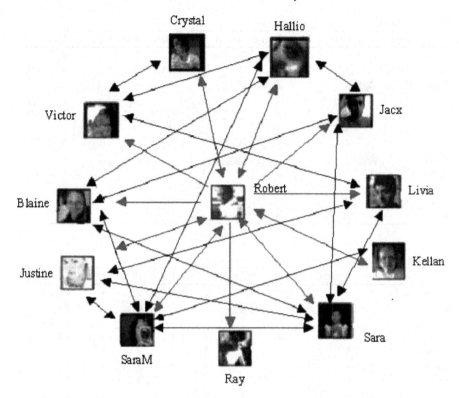

Fig. 1.20 Graph visualisation to illustrate Robert's position

Table 1.6 Questionnaire used to collect Socio-centric date

Questions
How close is … to you?
How comfortable do you feel to discuss with …?
How much do you trust…?

1.5.2 Second Phase

The second phase of the analysis focused on the dynamics of the overall social group in order to understand what the social relationships among the members of the group are. Therefore, we switched from an Ego-centic approach to a Socio-centric one. In particular, we got in touch with Robert's friends to whom we explained the aim of our study. Afterward we sent them the short questionnaire shown in Table 1.6.

Respondents answered questions by using a scale (from 0 to 5). The collected answers were transformed to a set of matrices (for each question) for the analysis (Tables 1.7, 1.8 and 1.9).

With respect to the level of cosiness the matrix shows that while the group is well defined, in fact the middle value resulting from the analysis is 3. While on

Table 1.7 Matrix used to analyse cosiness

	Robert	Ray	Crystal	Livia	Justine	SaraM	Victor	Hallio	Blaine	Kellan	Jacx	Sara
Robert	–	3	3	1	3	3	2	1	2	4	3	5
Ray	3	–	1	3	0	4	3	3	2	2	3	3
Crystal	3	3	–	1	3	3	2	1	0	3	3	4
Livia	3	1	3	–	1	0	3	1	3	1	2	3
Justine	1	0	3	1	–	3	3	3	1	3	3	4
SaraM	3	4	3	4	3	–	3	3	0	3	2	2
Victor	2	3	4	5	3	3	–	3	1	3	3	2
Hallio	2	3	4	2	3	3	4	–	3	2	2	0
Blaine	3	1	2	3	3	2	4	0	–	3	1	4
Kellan	4	5	5	2	3	5	3	1	3	–	3	5
Jacx	3	1	3	5	3	4	2	3	2	1	–	3
Sara	5	1	3	1	3	4	4	3	5	5	3	–

Table 1.8 Matrix used to analyse comfort in discussions

	Robert	Ray	Crystal	Livia	Justine	SaraM	Victor	Hallio	Blaine	Kellan	Jacx	Sara
Robert	–	3	4	4	0	3	4	4	2	4	4	5
Ray	3	–	1	4	4	4	3	3	4	2	4	3
Crystal	4	4	–	4	0	2	2	1	4	3	4	4
Livia	2	1	1	–	4	4	4	1	1	4	4	3
Justine	1	0	4	1	–	2	4	3	3	1	2	4
SaraM	3	4	4	4	3	–	4	5	4	4	2	2
Victor	4	3	0	5	4	0	–	4	4	5	2	2
Hallio	4	4	4	2	0	1	4	–	3	2	3	2
Blaine	3	1	4	3	4	2	4	0	–	4	3	4
Kellan	4	5	4	2	3	5	5	1	4	–	3	4
Jacx	4	4	2	5	4	4	2	3	4	4	–	2
Sara	5	1	4	1	0	4	4	0	5	5	1	–

Table 1.9 Matrix used to analyse trust

	Robert	Ray	Crystal	Livia	Justine	SaraM	Victor	Hallio	Blaine	Kellan	Jacx	Sara
Robert	–	5	4	1	5	5	5	1	3	4	4	5
Ray	5	–	3	5	5	4	3	5	2	2	4	3
Crystal	5	2	–	1	5	2	2	2	5	3	3	5
Livia	2	1	5	–	3	5	5	2	5	4	2	5
Justine	1	2	5	1	–	2	5	5	2	3	2	5
SaraM	5	4	5	4	3	–	3	5	5	5	2	2
Victor	5	3	1	5	5	2	–	2	2	1	2	2
Hallio	5	4	4	2	3	1	4	–	5	5	5	2
Blaine	3	1	2	5	5	5	4	5	–	5	1	4
Kellan	4	5	5	2	2	5	2	5	1	–	3	5
Jacx	4	1	2	5	5	4	3	2	3	3	–	2
Sara	5	1	3	1	3	5	5	2	5	5	1	–

considering the comfort in discussions, the middle value is 4. This suggests that social relationships are well defined. Finally, with respect to the trust the matrix shows that the middle value is 5; this suggests that the group is strongly integrated.

1.6   Conclusion

In the first part of the chapter some definitions of Virtual Social Networks have been provided to consider the sociological, technological, business, economical, and e-commerce perspectives.

Furthermore, the chapter has analysed the motivations that lead people to join Virtual Social Networks.

Information exchange is the most important factor for Virtual Social Networks success. Within Virtual Social Networks individuals can either give information (by posting conversations) or get information (by browsing or soliciting information or by posting questions or comments).

The social aspect represents the second most popular motivation. This finding suggests that members of a Virtual Social Network should underline not only the content but also promote the social aspects as well if they wish to increase the success of their Virtual Social Network.

The possibility to seek friendship represents another reason to join Virtual Social Networks. The interactivity achieved with instant messaging, chat rooms, and bulletin boards and the different search facilities available on the Web provide a way for people to communicate with others for establishing friendships.

Finally, the last motivation is the recreation that Virtual Social Networks provide. The use of the Web in general has been much discussed in both the popular press as a new form of recreation similar to that of face-to-face interactions.

In the second part of the chapter, Virtual Social Network analysis has been described.

The formal analysis of a Virtual Social Network can be dealt with different methods, each one of them with its own peculiarity, with its different operation.

The chapter has classified these methods in two categories. The first category concerns methods used for the network data collection while the second category deals with methods used for the network data visualisation.

The objective of the data collection is to provide a data set that could help to analyse the effects of Virtual Social Networks in the different aspects of social activities such as: (i) their generation, (ii) their spatial distribution, and (iii) their relationship with Information and Communication Technology use. The methods used for the Virtual Social Network data collection can be divided into (i) Socio-centric and (ii) Ego-centric.

The Socio-centric method examines sets of relationships among actors that are regarded for analytical purposes as bounded social collectives. In particular the method

- Looks at the relationships between each actor in the Virtual Social Network, and all other actors.

- Analyses the types of relationships on considering: the frequency and/or duration of the contact, the degree to which actors report the same relation with each other for a content area, and the different networks that actors have within the Virtual Social Network.
- Looks at the overall characteristics of the Virtual Social Network, such as the size of the network and the density (or connectedness), which is the number of links in a network as a ratio of the total possible links.

The Ego-centric Network method focuses on the individual, rather than on the network as a whole. It allows selecting focal actors (egos), and identifying nodes to which they are connected to. In particular, the method analyses the number of relationships maintained by an actor within the Virtual Social Network.

A high number of relationships indicates that an actor plays an important role in the Virtual Social Network. On the contrary, a low number of relationships indicates that an actor is left out of the mainstream of activity (no central actor).

While the objective of the data visualisation is to purge the burden of analysing blocks of data by converting these blocks into figures which can easily suggest what this data means.

The visualisation can be performed by using (i) graphs, (ii) matrices, (iii) maps, and (iv) a hybrid approach that use more than one representation.

Graphs are the most natural solution used to visually represent a social network. They simply and intuitively present all connections between the network elements. However, when managing a large amount of data, matrix visualisation can be more useful, since it can produce a lower user's cognitive overhead.

If social network data and structure are complex and can be organised and visualised according to different points of view and different detail levels, it could be better to use a map representation.

While to visualise data and information about social networks and their dynamics considering space, time, and coordinates involving classes of interests, a hybrid approach could be used.

Finally, in the third part, the chapter applies the methods for data collection and visualisation to analyse the Virtual Social Network LinkedIn. The analysis involved two different phases. In the first phase, we used an Ego-centric approach for data collection and a graph for data visualisation. In the second phase, we used a Socio-centric approach for data collection and a matrix for data visualisation.

References

1. Boyd D, Ellison NB (2007) Social network sites: definition, history, and scholarship. J Comput Mediated Commun 13(1):210–230
2. Etzioni A, Etzioni O (1999) Face-to-face and computer-mediated communities; a comparative analysis. Inform Soc 15(4):241–248
3. Romm C, Pliskin N, Clarke R (1997) Virtual communities and society: toward an integrative three phase model. Int J Inf Manag 17(4):261–270

4. Ridings CM, Gefen D, Arinze B (2002) Some antecedents and effects of trust in virtual communities. J Strategic Inf Syst (11):271–295
5. Lazar JR, Tsao R, Preece J (1999) One foot in cyberspace and the other on the ground: a case study of analysis and design issues in a hybrid virtual and physical community. Web Net J Internet Technol Appl Iss 1(3):49–57
6. Hagel J, Armstrong A (1997) Net gain: expanding markets through virtual communities. Harvard Business School Press, Boston, MA
7. Balasubramanian S, Mahajan V (2001) The economic leverage of the virtual community. Int J Electron Comm 5(Spring):103–138
8. Preece J (2000) Online communities: designing usability, supporting sociability. Wiley, Chichester, UK
9. Adamic LA, Buyukkokten O, Adar E (2003) A social network caught in the Web. First Monday 8(6)
10. Kumar R, Novak J, Tomkins A (2006) Structure and evolution of online social networks. In: Proceedings of the 12th ACMSIGKDD international conference on knowledge discovery and data mining (KDD'06). Philadelphia, PA, pp 611–617
11. Girvan M, Newman EJ (2002) Community structure in social and biological networks. Proc Natl Acad Sci (PNAS) 99(12):7821–7826
12. Backstrom L, Huttenlocher D, Kleinberg J, Lan X (2006) Group formation in large social networks: membership, growth, and evolution. In: Proceedings of the 12th ACMSIGKDD international conference on knowledge discovery and data mining (KDD'06). Philadelphia, PA, pp 44–54
13. Ahn YY, Han S, Kwak H, Moon S, Jeong H (2007) Analysis of topological characteristic of huge online social networking services. In: Proceedings of the 16th international conference on World Wide Web(WWW'07). Ban, Canada, pp 835–844
14. Tindall D, Wellman B (2001) Canada as social structure: social network analysis and Canadian sociology. Can J Sociol 26(2):265–308
15. Scott J (2000) Social network analysis. A handbook. Sage, London
16. Carrasco JA, Hogan B, Wellman B, Miller EJ (2008) Collecting social network data to study social activity-travel behavior: egocentric approach. J Environ Plan B: Plan Des 35(6):961–980
17. Chapin FS (1974) Human activity patterns in the city: things people do in time and in space. Wiley, New York
18. Marsden PV (2005) Recent developments in network measurement. In: Carrington P, Scott J, Wasserman S (eds) Models and methods in social network analysis. Cambridge University Press, Cambridge, pp 8–30
19. Simmel G (1950) On the significance of numbers for social life. In Wolff K (ed) The sociology of Georg Simmel. Free Press, Glencoe, pp 87–104
20. Granovetter M (1983) The strength of weak ties: a network theory revisited. Sociol Theor 1:201–233
21. Tichy NM, Tushman ML (1979) Social network analysis for organizations. Acad Manag Rev 4(4):507–519
22. Moreno JL (1934) Who shall survive? Nervous and Mental Disease Publishing, Washington, DC
23. Cyram (2004) Cyram Net Miner II. Version 2.4.0. Cyram Co. Ltd., Seoul
24. Heer J, Boyd D (2005) Vizster: visualizing online social networks. IEEE symposium on information visualization (Info Vis 2005), 23–25 October. Minneapolis, MN, USA
25. Nardi B, Whittaker S, Isaacs E, Creech M, Johnson J, Hainsworth J (2002) Contact map: integrating communication and information through visualizing personal social networks. Commun ACM 45(4):89–95
26. Bahbouh R, Warrenfeltz R (2004) The application of sociomapping to executive team development. http://www.hoganassessment.com/hoganweb/documents/ApplicationOfSociomapping.pdf. Accessed 11 Nov 2008
27. Caschera MC, Ferri F, Grifoni P (2008) SIM: a dynamic multidimensional visualization method for social networks. PsychNol J 6(3):291–320

Chapter 2
Discovering Sets of Key Players in Social Networks

Daniel Ortiz-Arroyo

Abstract The discovery of single key players in social networks is commonly done using some of the centrality measures employed in social network analysis. However, few methods, aimed at discovering *sets* of key players, have been proposed in the literature. This chapter presents a brief survey of such methods. The methods described include a variety of techniques ranging from those based on traditional centrality measures using optimizing criteria to those based on measuring the efficiency of a network. Additionally, we describe and evaluate a new approach to discover sets of key players based on entropy measures. Finally, this chapter presents a brief description of some applications of information theory within social network analysis.

2.1 Introduction

Social Network Analysis (SNA) comprises the study of relations, ties, patterns of communication, and behavioral performance within social groups. In SNA, a social network is commonly modeled by a graph composed of nodes and edges. The nodes in the graph represent social actors and the links the relationship or ties between them. A graph consisting of n nodes and m edges is defined as $G = \{V, E\}$, where $V = \{v_1, v_2, \ldots, v_n\}$ is the set of nodes or vertex and $E = \{e_1, e_2, \ldots, e_m\}$ is a set of links or edges. In general, graphs where the edges do not have an associated direction are called *undirected graphs*. Graphs that contain no cycles are called *acyclic graphs*. For convenience, in the rest of this chapter, we will use the terms undirected acyclic graph, graph, and network as synonyms. Additionally, we will use indistinctly the term node, player, and actor.

One important issue in SNA is the determination of groups in complex social networks. Groups are disjoint collections of individuals who are linked to each other

D. Ortiz-Arroyo (✉)
Department of Electronic Systems, Esbjerg Institute of Technology, Aalborg University,
Denmark
e-mail: do@aaue.dk

A. Abraham et al. (eds.), *Computational Social Network Analysis*, Computer
Communications and Networks, DOI 10.1007/978-1-84882-229-0_2,
© Springer-Verlag London Limited 2010

by some sort of relation or interaction. Within a group, members have different positions. Some of them occupy central positions, others remain in the periphery, and the rest lies somewhere in between. A group may have one or more key players. While this definition of a group is intuitive, a more mathematical description of a group is required to enable us analyzing systematically social networks. One possible definition of a social group is based on the concept of a *clique*. A clique of a graph G is defined as a subgraph H of G in which every vertex is connected to every other vertex in H. A clique H is called *maximal* if it is not contained in another subgraph of G. While this definition of a clique may be useful to study small social networks,[1] other more complex organizations have been analyzed using *semilattices* and a more recent extension of these mathematical structures called *Galois lattices* [2, 3].

Numerous studies in SNA have proposed a diversity of measures to study the communication patterns and the structure of a social network. One of the most studied measures is *centrality*. Centrality describes an actor's relative position within the context of his or her social network [4]. Centrality measures have been applied in a diversity of research works, for instance, to investigate influence patters in interorganizational networks, to study the power or competence in organizations, analyzing the structure of terrorist and criminal networks, analyzing employment opportunities, and many other fields [5].

The ability that centrality measures have to determine the relative position of a node within a network has been used in previous research work to discover *key players* [6–8] in social networks. Key players are these nodes in the network that are considered "important" with regard to some criteria. In general, the importance of a node is measured in a variety of ways depending on the application. In this chapter, we will define important nodes as those nodes that have a major impact on the cohesion and communication patterns that occur in the network.

One possibility for measuring the importance of a node given the previous criteria is to calculate how many links a node has with the rest of the network's nodes, this is called *degree centrality*. Nodes with high degree centrality have higher probability of receiving and transmitting whatever information flows in the network. For this reason, high degree centrality nodes are considered to have influence over a larger number of nodes and/or are capable of communicating quickly with the nodes in their neighborhood. Degree centrality is a *local* measure [9], as only the connections of a node with its neighbors are taken into account to evaluate node's importance.

Other centrality measures evaluate the degree with which a player controls the flow of information in the network. Messages sent through the network frequently pass through these players; they function as "brokers". A measure that models this property is called *betweenness*.

Another closely related method that has been used to evaluate the importance of a node within a network is based on measuring how close a node is located with respect to every other node in the network. The measure is called *closeness*. Nodes

---

[1] The use of cliques to model social groups has been criticized by some authors (e.g. [1, 2]) due to the strict mathematical definition of cliques.

with low closeness are able to reach (or be reached by) most or all other nodes in the network through geodesic paths.

Some other proposed centrality measures try to evaluate a player's degree of "popularity" within the network, i.e., they represent centers of large *cliques* in the graph. A node with more connections to higher scoring nodes is considered as being more important. The measure that captures this intuition is called *eigenvector centrality*.

Contrarily to a local measure such as degree centrality, metrics like betweenness, closeness, or eigenvector centrality are considered *global* measures [9] since they evaluate the impact that a node has on the global structure or transmission of information within the network.

Degree centrality, betweenness, closeness, and eigenvector centrality are among the most popular measures used in SNA. However, over the years other measures have been proposed in the literature to overcome some of their limitations. Among these measures we can mention *information centrality*, *flow betweenness*, the *rush index*, and the *influence* [10], among others.

In spite of the relative simplicity of the centrality measures we have described, recent research has found that such metrics are robust in the presence of noise. Noise in this case refers to the possibility of including or excluding some nodes and links from a network during its construction due to the use of imprecise or incorrect information. In [11] Borgatti and Carley studied the performance of centrality measures under the conditions of imperfect data. Firstly, they generated random graphs with different densities. Afterward, it was measured the effect that the addition or removal of nodes and edges had on the accuracy of each of the centrality measures employed in the experiments. Borgatti et al. found out that, as expected, the accuracy of centrality measures decreases with an increasing error rate, but surprisingly, it does it in a predictable and monotonic way. This result means in principle that if one were able to estimate the percentage of errors made when a network is built, it could also be possible to estimate bounds on the accuracy of the results obtained by applying centrality measures. The other interesting finding reported in [11] was that all centrality measures performed with a similar degree of robustness. However, it must be remarked that the results of this study apply only to random graphs.

Centrality measures make certain assumptions about the way the information flows in the network. Hence, as described in [10], the type of information flow assumed in the network determines which measure may be more appropriate to be applied in a specific problem. Figure 2.1[2] illustrates some nodes within a network that have different centrality values. This picture clearly illustrates that the type of flow that occurs within a network for an specific application domain must be determined before a centrality measure could be used correctly.

The literature on centrality measures is rather extensive; see for example [4, 6, 7], and [10]. However, very few methods have been proposed to find *sets of key players* capable of optimizing some performance criterion such as maximally disrupting the network or diffusing efficiently a message on the network.

---

[2] A similar figure is used in [12].

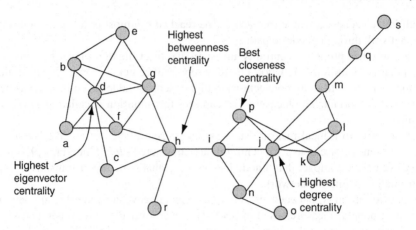

Fig. 2.1 Diverse centrality measures applied on an example network

Methods for discovering a set of key players in a social network have numerous applications. For instance, these methods may help intelligence agencies to disrupt criminal organizations or allocate human resources in a more effective way within formal organizations.

The problem of finding an individual key player is fundamentally different from that of finding a set of k-players. More specifically, the problem of getting an optimal set of k-players is different from the problem of selecting k individuals that are each, individually optimal [12]. For this reason, applying naively centrality measures to find a set of key players will likely fail. A simple example that illustrates why this may happen is the case of a network with a few central nodes that are redundant. Eliminating the redundant nodes will have no effect on the network even if they have high centrality degree. Additionally, it is also possible to find nodes that in spite of not having a high centrality degree have in fact a greater impact in disrupting the network structure when removed. For instance, Fig. 2.1 illustrates that nodes h and i are redundant as the removal of any of them will fragment the network into two or three components. However, as is explained in Sect. 2.3, in this specific example node h is more important than node i.

To simplify analysis, social networks are commonly considered *static* structures. However, most social interactions in reality do not remain static but rather evolve through time. *Dynamic network analysis* is an active area of research [13] that studies models of the evolution of social relations through time. Some of the methods employed to analyze dynamic networks comprise statistical process control and Markov chains among other techniques. Due to lack of space, in this chapter we will only focus on static networks.

This chapter presents a brief survey of methods that have been proposed in the literature recently to discover sets of key players in social networks. Additionally, a new method, based on Shannon's definition of entropy is introduced. To asses the performance of this method we have designed a simulation environment specially built for the purpose. The simulation environment allowed us to perform a comparative evaluation of the results obtained by entropy-based methods with those reported in the literature using other methods. Our preliminary results indicate that the entropy-based methods can be used effectively to identify sets of key players for certain type of networks.

The rest of this chapter is organized as follows. Section 2.2 presents a summary of related work on the use of information theory in SNA. Section 2.3 briefly describes some of the methods that can be used to discover sets of key players. Section 2.4 describes the proposed method based on entropy measures together with an evaluation of its preliminary performance results. Finally, Sect. 2.5 describes some possible research directions and provides some conclusions.

2.2   Information Theory in SNA

Information theory deals with the transmission, storage, and quantification of information. Concepts originally introduced in information theory have been successfully applied in a wide range of fields, ranging from digital communication systems, cryptography and machine learning to natural language processing, neurobiology and knowledge discovery in unstructured data.

One of the fundamental concepts employed in information theory is *entropy*. Entropy was originally proposed by Claude Shannon [14] as a measure to quantify the amount of information that can be transmitted through a noisy communication channel. In a complementary way, entropy is used to quantify the degree of uncertainty in the content of a message or in general the uncertainty within a system. Shannon's definition of entropy of a random variable X that can take n values is presented in Eq. 2.1.

$$H(X) = - \sum_{i=1}^{n} p(x_i) \times \log_2 p(x_i) \tag{2.1}$$

Given its wide applicability, concepts borrowed from information theory have been recently applied in SNA. For instance, in [15] a method capable of measuring centrality on networks that are characterized by *path-transfer flow* is described. In social networks characterized by path-transfer flow, information is passed from one node to other following a path. However, contrary to other patterns of communication, information is contained within a single node at a time, i.e., there is no parallel transfer of information. An example of this type of information flow appears in chain letters where each recipient add its name to the end of the letter and then sends it to other person within the network. Other examples include trading and smuggling networks.

The method introduced in [15] to determine the centrality of nodes in networks characterized by path-transfer flow basically consists in calculating the probability that the flow originated in a node stops at every other node in the network. The basic idea is to model the fact that highly central nodes may be identified by measuring how similar probabilities are that the flow originating in a node will stop at every other node within the network. In a highly central node, such as the one located in the center of a star graph, the probability that the flow starting in the central node ends in any other node in the network is exactly the same. Contrarily, the flow that starts in a node of a graph that is less central will have a more uneven distribution of probabilities. The definition of Shannon's entropy perfectly captures these two intuitions. Entropy is defined in terms of the downstream degree of a vertex, which is the number of eligible vertices to which the transfer can be next made. Then the transfer probability is defined as the inverse of the downstream degree of a node. Using the definition of transfer and stop probabilities in the calculation of Shannon's entropy and then normalizing it, finally provides the centrality measure for a vertex, as is described in [15].

In [16], Shetty and Adibi combine the use of cross-entropy and text-mining techniques to discover important nodes on the Enron corpora of e-mails. The corpora of e-mails is analyzed to create a social network representing the communication patterns among individuals in the company. The email messages in the Enron corpora were analyzed to determine their similarity regarding its contents. The degree of similarity in message content was used as an indication that the people sending these messages were talking about similar topic. Sequences of similar topic e-mails up of length two involving three actors A, B, C sent for instance in the order $A_{sent} B_{sent} C$ were counted. Afterward, a method based on the calculation of cross-entropy for such sequences of messages was used to rank the importance of a node. Nodes that produced the highest impact in reducing the total cross-entropy when removed from the network were selected as the most important ones. The method proposed by Shetty and Adibi was designed specifically to discover the set of key players within the Enron scandal case. Their results show that the method was capable of finding some key players in the Enron company. However, these players were not necessarily participating in the Enron scandal.

The next section discusses other methods that can be used to discover sets of key players in other social networks.

2.3 Methods for Discovering Sets of Key Players

One naive approach that can be used to discover sets of key players is to measure the centrality of every single node in the network. Afterward, nodes are ranked according to their importance as measured by value of the specific centrality measure used. Finally, a subset of size k of these nodes could be selected as the key players.

Another more interesting approach to find key players is described in [17]. This approach is based on measuring the communication efficiency of a network. The efficiency E of a network G was defined in Eq. 2.2:

$$E(G) = \frac{\sum_{i \neq j \in G} \varepsilon_{ij}}{N(N-1)} = \frac{1}{N(N-1)} \sum_{i \neq j \in G} \frac{1}{d_{ij}} \tag{2.2}$$

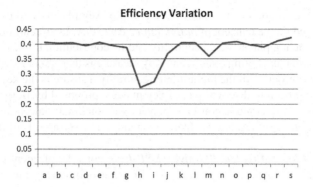

Fig. 2.2 Efficiency variation of a graph taken from Borgatti's examples in [12]

where N is the number of nodes in graph G and ε_{ij} is the communication efficiency, which is proportional to the inverse of d_{ij} (the shortest path length between two nodes i, j). The equation calculates all shortest paths between all pairs of nodes normalized by the number of all possible paths that will be contained in a fully connected graph consisting of N nodes. The method essentially consists in removing nodes one by one, recalculating the drop in network efficiency every time. These nodes that produce the largest impact in reducing the overall efficiency of a network are selected as the key players. The advantage of this method is that it can be easily implemented. Figure 2.2 shows the result of calculating graph efficiency using Eq. 2.2 for the example graph shown in Fig. 2.1.

Figure 2.2 shows that the method based on calculating graph efficiency will detect nodes h, i, and m as being the key players, using an appropriate threshold value. However, the method fails at detecting that nodes h and i are in fact redundant.

The problem of previous two approaches is that they measure the effect that each single node has on the network independently. Hence, as previous example shows they will likely fail at identifying redundant nodes.

Another heuristic approach briefly sketched in [12] consists in selecting the top individual player using whatever centrality measure is appropriated for the task. Then, the nodes that are least redundant are added to the set of key players. The challenge of this approach will be to find an efficient procedure to determine which nodes are the least redundant.

The concept of centrality has been applied not only to single individuals within a network but also to groups of individuals. In [18], measures for degree centrality, closeness, and betweenness are defined for a group. Using these measures, groups having high centrality will be the key players. It must be remarked that group centrality can be used not only to measure how "central" or important a group is, but also in constructing groups with maximum centrality within an organization. For instance, a team of experts can be distributed within an organization in such a way that it has high group centrality. The idea is that this group will provide readily access to the expertise needed by other members of an organization.

In [19] a recent approach to discover a group of key players is presented. The method is based on the concept of *optimal inter-centrality*. Inter-centrality measure takes into account a player's own centrality and its contribution to the centrality of others. The individual optimal inter-centrality measure is then generalized to groups of players. The group with the highest inter-centrality measure is the key group.

Another approach to discover sets of key players, proposed by Borgatti in [12], consists in selecting simultaneously k players via combinatorial optimization. In that work, Borgatti defines two problems related to discovering sets of key players as follows.

The *Key Player Problem Positive (KPP-Pos)* consists of identifying these k-players that could be used as seeds in diffusing optimally some information on the network.

The *Key Player Problem Negative (KPP-Neg)* goal consists of identifying those k-players that, if removed, will disrupt or fragment the network. A more formal definition of the two problems taken from [12] is

"Given a social network(represented as an undirected graph), find a set of k nodes (called a kp-set of order k) such that,

1. *(KPP-Neg) Removing the kp-set would result in a residual network with the least possible cohesion.*
2. *(KPP-Pos) The kp-set is maximally connected to all other nodes."*

Borgatti found that off-the-shelf centrality measures are not appropriate for the task of discovering sets of key players as defined by KPP-Pos and KPP-Neg problems. Hence, he proposes a new method based on combinatorial optimization and greedy heuristics. Additionally, to evaluate the solution to both KPP-Neg and KPP-Pos problems, Borgatti proposes new metrics to measure how successfully both problems are solved. One metric is called the *degree of reachability* described by Eq. 2.3:

$$D_F = 1 - 2 \frac{\sum_{i>j} \frac{1}{d_{ij}}}{N(N-1)} \tag{2.3}$$

where d_{ij} is the distance between nodes i, j, and N the total number of nodes in the graph. The metric D_F captures the fragmentation and relative cohesion of the components in the network.

The other metric proposed by Borgatti is the *weighted proportion* of nodes reached by the set of key players defined in Eq. 2.4:

$$D_R = \frac{\sum_j \frac{1}{d_{Kj}}}{N} \tag{2.4}$$

where d_{Kj} is the distance from any member of the key player set to a node j not in the set. This metric evaluates the degree with which the set of key players is isolated from the rest of the nodes.

The greedy heuristic presented in [12] seeks to select those nodes in the graph that maximize D_F and D_R metrics. The algorithm taken from [12] is presented as Algorithm 2.1.

Algorithm 2.1 (taken from [12])

1: Select k nodes at random to populate set S
2: Set F = fit using appropriate key player metric
3: **for all** nodes u in S and each node v not in S **do**
4:     DELTAF = improvement in fit if u and v were swapped
5: **end for**
6: Select pair with largest DELTAF
7: a. If DELTAF $\leq$ then terminate
8: b. Else, swap pair with greatest improvement in fit and set F = F + DELTAF
9: Go to step 3

Borgatti applied the proposed approach to two data sets, one terrorist network and a network of members of a global consulting company with advice-seeking ties. The results obtained by Borgatti show that the combinatorial optimization together with the use of the success metrics perform well on the two problems considered.

2.4   Discovering Sets of Key Players Using Entropy Measures

A new method aimed at finding sets of key players based on entropy measures that provide a simple solution to both the KPP-Pos and KPP-Neg problems will be introduced in this section.

The method based on entropy measures has some similarities with the method described in [16, 17]. However, contrarily to the approach described in [16], this method relies only on the structural properties of the network, uses Shannon's definition of entropy instead of cross-entropy. Additionally, the method described in [16] was specifically designed to detect important nodes on the Enron corpus, whereas the entropy-based method can be applied in many other problems.

The entropy-based method shares also shares some similarity with the one described in [17]. The main difference lies in the type of measure used which is Shannon's entropy instead of efficiency as defined in Eq. 2.2. Additionally, the entropy-based method is aimed at providing simple alternative solutions to both KPP-Pos and KPP-Neg problems. However, it must be remarked the entropy-based method does not aim at solving both problems optimally as was done in [12], but to provide an alternative simple solution that could be used to tackle both problems.

We first define the connectivity of a node $v_i \in V$ in a graph as:

$$\chi(v) = \frac{\deg(v_i)}{2N}, \quad N > 0 \tag{2.5}$$

where $\deg(v_i)$ is the number of incident edges to node v_i and N the total number of edges in the graph. We can use χ as the stationary probability distribution of random walkers in the graph [20]. This is called the *connectivity probability distribution* of the graph.

Another probability distribution can be defined in terms of the number of shortest or geodesic paths that have v_i as source and the rest of nodes in the graph as targets:

$$\gamma(v) = \frac{spaths(v_i)}{spaths(v_1, v_2, \ldots, v_M)}, \quad spaths(v_1, v_2, \ldots, v_M) > 0 \quad (2.6)$$

where $spaths(v_i)$ is the number of shortest paths from node v_i to all the other nodes in the graph and $spaths(v_1, v_2, \ldots, v_M)$ is the total number of shortest paths M that exists across all the nodes in the graph. This is called the *centrality probability distribution* of the graph.

Using Eqs. 2.5 and 2.6 to define our probability distributions, we can obtain different entropy measures by applying the definition of entropy in Eq. 2.4. This procedure allows us to define *connectivity entropy* H_{co} and *centrality entropy* measures H_{ce} of a graph G in the following way:

$$H_{co}(G) = -\sum_{i=1}^{n} \chi(v_i) \times \log_2 \chi(v_i) \quad (2.7)$$

$$H_{ce}(G) = -\sum_{i=1}^{n} \gamma(v_i) \times \log_2 \gamma(v_i) \quad (2.8)$$

It must be noticed that Eqs. 2.7 and 2.8 should be normalized to enable us to compare the centrality or connectivity entropies obtained from different types of networks. However, this is not done here since we will not be comparing different networks.

The connectivity entropy measure provides information about the connectivity degree of a node in the graph. In a fully connected graph, the removal of a node will decrease the total entropy of the graph in the same proportion as when any other node is removed. All nodes will have the same effect on the graph entropy leaving it still densely connected after a node is removed. However, in a graph with lower density, the removal of nodes with many incident edges will have a larger impact in decreasing the total connectivity entropy of the system, compared to the case when a node with a smaller connectivity degree is removed. This effect is illustrated in Figs. 2.3 and 2.4.

Centrality entropy provides information on the degree of reachability for a node in the graph. In a fully connected graph the removal of any node will have the same effect on centrality entropy as when any other node is removed. All nodes are equally important for the flow of information. This effect is illustrated in Fig. 2.4. Contrarily, in partially connected graphs, those nodes whose removal will split the graph in two or more parts or that will reduce substantially the number of geodesic paths available to reach other nodes when removed, will have a higher impact in decreasing the total centrality entropy. This effect is illustrated in Figs. 2.5 and 2.6 where the removal of node v_5 causes the disconnection of node v_6, and this event produces the largest change in centrality entropy for the graph.

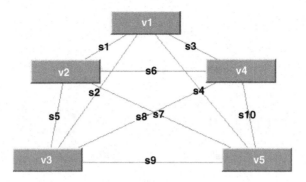

Fig. 2.3 Fully connected graph

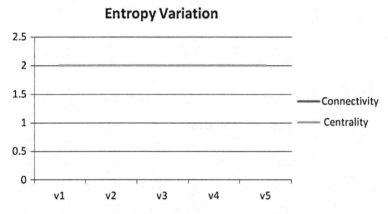

Fig. 2.4 Entropy variation of a fully connected graph

Note that Figs. 2.4 and 2.6 also show that there is either perfect or very high correlation between the connectivity and centrality entropy measures when applied to the fully connected and partially-connected graph examples, respectively. This happens due to the fact that these graphs are very symmetric. Homogeneity is the strongest form of symmetry that a graph can posses. Therefore, the correlation among these two measures will decrease as the network becomes more and more heterogeneous. This fact will be illustrated in the following example graphs.

In general, centrality and connectivity entropies provide an average measure of network *heterogeneity* since they measure either the diversity of paths to reach the nodes within the graph or the diversity of link distribution in the graph, respectively. Heterogeneity in complex networks is identified by looking at the degree distribution P_k, which is the probability of a node having k links [21]. The method introduced in this section additionally to degree distribution adds path distribution, which is the probability P_l that a node is being reached by other nodes through l different geodesic paths.

The entropy-based method introduced in this chapter is presented in Algorithm 2.2. In summary, the algorithm attempts to solve KPP-Pos and KPP-Neg

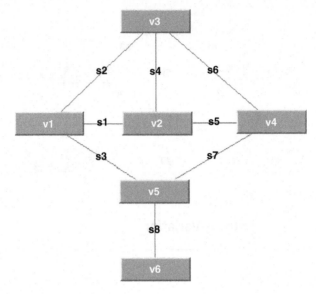

Fig. 2.5 Partially connected graph

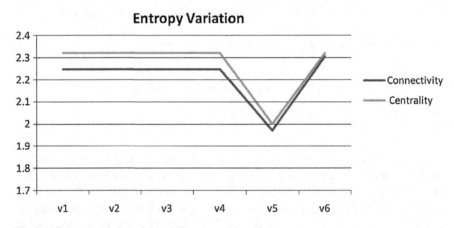

Fig. 2.6 Entropy variation of a partially connected graph

problems using connectivity entropy and centrality entropy. The basic idea is to find
those nodes that produce the largest change in connectivity or centrality entropy
when removed from the graph. These nodes should be included in the set of key
players as they have the largest impact in the structure (information content) of the
network. The value of δ_i, allows us to control how many players should be included
in the set.

Since centrality entropy is based on the calculation of all the unweighted shortest
paths in the network, it has the highest effect in the complexity of Algorithm 2.2.
The complexity of Dijkstra's shortest path algorithm (from a single source node to

all others) is $O(n^2)$.[3] However, given that Algorithm 2.2 needs to calculate all the shortest paths from every single node in the graph its overall complexity is $O(n^3)$.

Algorithm 2.2 Entropy-based method

1: Calculate initial total entropy $H_{co_0}(G)$ and $H_{ce_0}(G)$
2: **for all** $nodes \in$ graph G **do**
3:    Remove node v_i, creating a modified graph G'
4:    Recalculate $H_{co_i}(G')$ and $H_{ce_i}(G')$, store these results
5:    Restore original graph G
6: **end for**
7: To solve the KPP-Pos problem select those nodes that produce the largest change in graph entropy $H_{co_0}\text{-}H_{co_i} \geq \delta_1$
8: To solve the KPP-Neg problem select those nodes that produce the largest change in graph entropy $H_{ce_0}\text{-}H_{ce_i} \geq \delta_2$

Figure 2.8 shows the results of applying Algorithm 2.2 to the graph in Fig. 2.7. The graph is provided as an example by Borgatti in [12]. Our results show that centrality entropy is capable of detecting redundant nodes such as h and i. Node i is redundant as its removal will not have any impact on the number of partitions

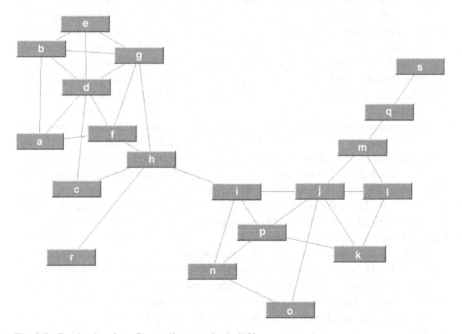

Fig. 2.7 Graph taken from Borgatti's examples in [12]

---

[3] The complexity is calculated assuming that an adjacency matrix is used to represent the graph, other implementations using other more efficient data structure representations perform better.

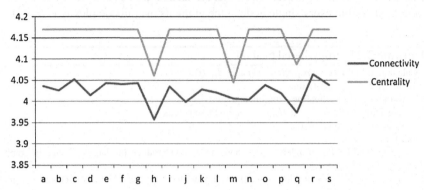

Fig. 2.8 Entropy variation of a graph taken from Borgatti's examples in [12]

created, once h has been removed. This happens in spite of i having a high centrality value. The reason this occurs is that when node h is disconnected it leaves node r isolated from the rest of the graph, fragmenting the network into three components. The paths that go from r to the rest of the nodes contribute significantly to the overall centrality entropy of the graph. Contrarily, when node i is removed, the graph will be fragmented into two components. However, as node r will remain connected it will still be able to communicate with the subnetwork to which it is attached, contributing with these paths to the total entropy calculation. In this simple example, the algorithm will find the set of key players consisting of $\{h, m, q\}$. By adjusting the value of δ_i we can control how many nodes we will include in the final set of key players.

It must be noted that in a graph similar to the one in Fig. 2.7, but where node r is eliminated, our algorithm will still be able to determine that node h is more important than node i. This is due to the fact that there are more nodes in that part of the graph where node i is the "gatekeeper" and therefore more paths leading to that subnetwork. Figure 2.9 shows the result of applying the entropy-based algorithm to a graph similar to the one in Fig. 2.7 but not containing node r. The set of key players in this case will still be $\{h, m, q\}$ as these are the nodes that produce the largest change in centrality entropy.

Figure 2.9 also shows that node h has the largest impact on connectivity entropy when removed from the graph. Interestingly, the same graph also shows that node q has more effect on connectivity entropy, when compared to node m. The reason is that removing m leaves still a connected graph composed of nodes q and s, which contributes to the total entropy. Contrarily, removing q leaves the single node s isolated.

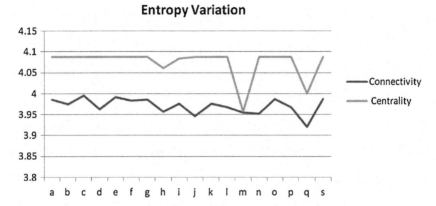

Fig. 2.9   Entropy variation of modified graph taken from Borgatti's examples in [12]

2.4.1   Applying Entropy Measures to More Complex Social Networks

Figure 2.11 shows the results of applying Algorithm 2.2 using centrality and connectivity entropy to the terrorist graph in Fig. 2.10. The graph is a simplification of the graph provided by Krebs in [7]. Figure 2.11 shows that centrality entropy identifies a set of key players consisting of {*atta, nalhazmi, darkazalni*}, since these are the nodes that produce the biggest changes in entropy when removed, with *atta* producing the largest change. It must be noticed that nodes *nalhazmi* and *darkazanli* have the same effect on centrality entropy. This is because if we look at Fig. 2.10 we can see that both nodes will disconnect a single node if removed. However, removing *nalhazmi* will also cause a major impact in connectivity entropy, contrarily to the case when *darkazanli* is removed. This indicates that *nalhazmi* may be indeed more important than node *darkazanli*, even if both produce a similar effect on centrality entropy. This factor can also be used to grade the importance of a node in the graph.

Removing the set consisting of {*atta, nalhazmi, darkazalni*} causes the network to be fragmented into five components. The optimization algorithm proposed by Borgatti produces a fragmentation of seven components.

Our Algorithm 2.2 finds that the set of nodes in Fig. 2.10 that solves KPP-Pos problem consists of {*nalhazmi, halghamdi, salghamdi, atta*}, as these are the nodes that will have the biggest impact on connectivity entropy when removed from the graph. The optimization algorithm proposed by Borgatti found that only three nodes are needed to reach 100% of the graph.

Previous results show that when entropy measures are applied to the terrorist network we can find similar results as those obtained by Borgatti. However, it must be remarked that the graph used by Borgatti in his experiments (derived from the one made available by Krebs in [7]) contains 63 nodes, whereas the network employed in our experiments (also derived from Krebs graph) contains only 34 nodes.

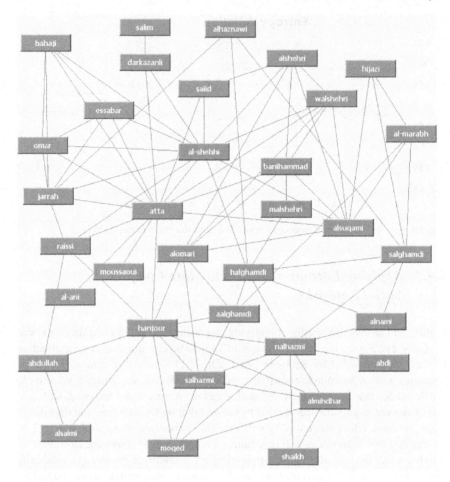

Fig. 2.10 Terrorist network

Figure 2.12 shows the result of calculating the efficiency of the terrorist network in Fig. 2.10. The figure illustrates that the key players detected by the graph efficiency calculation are {*atta, nalhazmi, darkazalni, hanjour*}. The graph efficiency calculation finds *hanjour* as key player contrarily to centrality entropy measure. However this node does not cause a fragmentation in the network. Interestingly, it is connectivity entropy which also finds *hanjour* as key player since this node will cause a major disruption in the connectivity of the key players with the rest of the network.

In a different example of social network, Fig. 2.14 shows the result of applying centrality and connectivity entropy to the graph in Fig. 2.13. The graph describes the advise-seeking ties between members of a company and was obtained from [12].

Applying Algorithm 2.2 to this network, we found that the set of most important players for solving KPP-Neg consists of {*HB, BM, WD, NP, SR*}. In this same

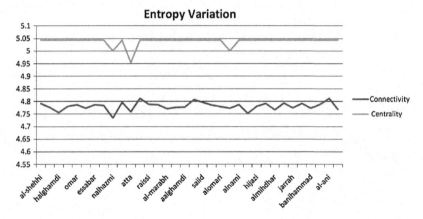

Fig. 2.11 Entropy variation of terrorist network

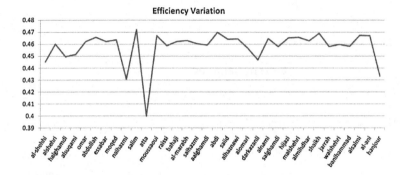

Fig. 2.12 Efficiency variation of terrorist network

example, Borgatti obtained a set of key players consisting of $\{HB, BM, WD\}$ [12]. This is the set of players that if removed will divide the network into six components. Our algorithm finds the same elements additionally to NP and SR. However, it must be remarked that contrarily to [12], the centrality entropy-based algorithm does not try to optimize any specific metric.

In KPP-Pos problem, we are asked to find the smallest set of nodes that are well connected to the entire network. This set of players are the ones that if used as "seeds" will reach 100% of the network.

If we look only at the connectivity entropy chart in Fig. 2.14 we notice that Algorithm 2.2 will select nodes $\{BM, DI, HB, BW, CD, BS', NP, TO, BS\}$ as the key players when a set of size $k = 9$ is selected. These are the nodes that when removed will produce the largest changes in connectivity entropy. This list indicates that connectivity entropy allows us to get 89% of the key players found by Borgatti for a similar set size. However, if we add to the set, the 10th node that produces the next largest change in connectivity entropy, we will obtain a set consisting of $\{BM, DI, HB, BW, CD, BS', NP, TO, BS, PS\}$. This new set contains 100% of the nodes that Borgatti found as the key players in [12].

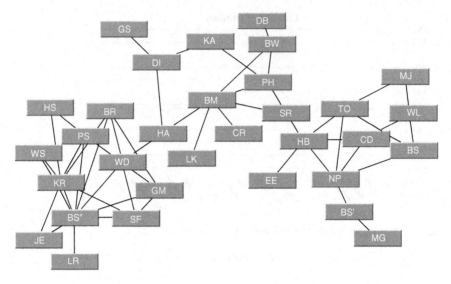

Fig. 2.13 Company ties network

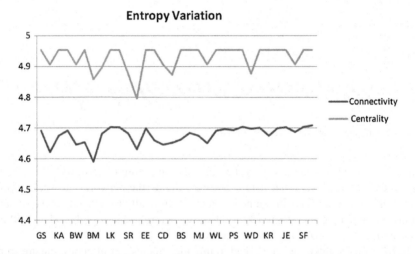

Fig. 2.14 Entropy variation of company ties network

In this last example it must be noted that the graph used in these experiments is exactly the same that represents the "company ties" problem described in [12].

Finally, Fig. 2.15 shows the result of calculating the efficiency of the company ties network in Fig. 2.14. The figure illustrates that the key players discovered by the graph efficiency calculation are $\{HA, SR, HB, WD\}$. In this case the efficiency calculation finds two of the three key players that were also found by Borgatti's optimization method and our centrality entropy-based calculations.

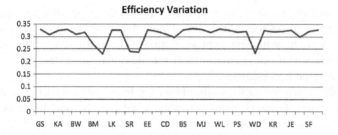

Fig. 2.15 Efficiency variation of company ties network

It must be remarked that being connectivity and centrality entropies average measures of the heterogeneity of a graph, these measures will not be useful when applied to more homogeneous graphs. This fact is partially shown in Fig. 2.4 for the fully connected graph shown in Fig. 2.3. When a network obtained from Enron's e-mail corpora was constructed, it was found that the network was very homogeneous. Because of this, results showed that the entropy-based centrality measure had very little variations when nodes were removed from the graph.

2.5   Conclusions and Future Work

In this chapter we have described methods aimed at discovering sets of key players in social networks. A new method that finds the set of key players within a network using entropy measures was introduced. The method provides a simple solution to the KPP-Pos problem, selecting the set of nodes that produce the largest change in connectivity entropy when removed from a graph. Similarly, to solve KPP-Neg centrality entropy is used, measuring how the overall entropy changes when a node is removed from the graph. The main advantage of this method is its simplicity. We have shown the application of an entropy-based method in discovering sets of key players to two examples of social networks: a terrorist organization and a company. Our experimental results show that these methods are capable of obtaining comparable results with those described in [12], where combinatorial optimization algorithm and special performance metrics are used. However, one of the disadvantages of entropy-based methods is that these methods only work on non-dense heterogeneous networks.

We created a special simulation environment to asses the performance of the some of the methods presented. The simulation environment accepts as input the description of a graph in the standard XML-based file format for graphs called GraphML. The development process of the simulation environment was substantially reduced by using open source libraries. To create the mathematical models and representation of a graph we use the jGraphT library. JGraphT is an extension to jGraph, a popular graphic visualization library that has been optimized to handle several data models and algorithms. The algorithms provided by jGraphT allow us to traverse and analyze the properties of a graph. To show the simulation results we used jChart and jFreeChart. Finally, as jGraph does not provide a free graph layout algorithm we have implemented a variation of the well-known spring algorithm [22]. The whole simulation environment was designed using design patterns and was written in the Java language.

A possible extension to the study of entropy-based measures of centrality is to investigate their robustness, using a method similar to the one described in [11] on both random and real graphs. The entropy-based approach may also be extended with heuristics targeted at optimizing some specific metrics, similarly as it was done in [12]. Other measures borrowed from information theory such as mutual information may be used to provide insights into the dependencies between the nodes in the graph.

Finally, we plan to investigate techniques aimed at reducing the current overall complexity ($O(n^3)$) of the algorithms employed to find all the shortest paths within the network more efficiently. This is one of the weaknesses not only of the entropy-based measures described in this chapter but also of other similar methods that require to find all possible shortest paths between pairs of nodes within a network. In this regard we are exploring a simple approach that finds simultaneously all the shortest paths within the nodes in the graph on the multicore shared memory personal computers that are widely available today. The entropy-based algorithms will be implemented in the programming language Erlang, a functional language that provides parallel-processing capabilities based on the message passing model.

References

1. Wasserman S, Faust K (1994) Social network analysis. Cambridge University Press, Cambridge.
2. Freeman LC (1996) Cliques, galois lattices, and the human structure of social groups. Social Networks 18(3):173–187
3. Falzon L (2000) Determining groups from the clique structure in large social networks. Social Networks 22(2):159–172
4. Friedkin NE (1991) Theoretical foundations for centrality measures. Am J Sociol 96(6):1478–1504
5. Borgatti SP, Everett MG (2006) A graph-theoretic framework for classifying centrality measures. Social Networks 28(4):466–484
6. Freeman LC (1977) A set of measures of centrality based on betweenness. Sociometry 40(1):35–41
7. Krebs V (2002) Uncloaking terrorist networks.First Monday 7(4). http://firstmonday.org/htbin/cgiwrap/bin/ojs/index.php/fm/article/view/941/863
8. Borgatti SP (2003) The key player problem. In: Breiger R, Carley K, Pattison P (eds) In dynamic social network modeling and analysis: workshop summary and papers. National Academy of Sciences Press, Washington, DC, pp 241–252
9. Scott J (2000) Social network analysis: a handbook. Sage, London
10. Borgatti SP (2004) Centrality and network flow. Social Networks 27(1):55–71
11. Borgatti SP, Carley K, Krackhardt D (2006) Robustness of centrality measures under conditions of imperfect data. Social Networks 28:124–1364
12. Borgatti SP (2006) Identifying sets of key players in a network. Comput Math Organ Theory 12(1):21–34

13. McCulloh IA, Carley KM (2008) Social network change detection. Technical report, Carnegie Mellon University
14. Shannon C (1948) A mathematical theory of communication. Bell Syst Tech J 17:379–423, 623–656
15. Tutzauer F (2006) Entropy as a measure of centrality in networks characterized by path-transfer flow. Social Networks 29(2):249–265
16. Shetty J, Adibi J (2005) Discovering important nodes through graph entropy the case of enron email database. In: LinkKDD '05: Proceedings of the 3rd international workshop on Link discovery. ACM, New York
17. Latora V, Marchiorib M (2003) How the science of complex networks can help developing strategies against terrorism. Chaos Soliton Fract 20(1):69–75
18. Everett MG, Borgatti SP (2005) Extending centrality. In: Carrington P, Scott J, Wasserman S (eds) Models and methods in social network analysis. Cambridge University Press 28:57–76
19. Ballester C, Calvo-Armengol A, Zenou Y (2005) Who's Who in Networks Wanted – The Key Player. CEPR Discussion Paper No. 5329. Centre for Economic Policy Research, London. Available at http://ssrn.com/abstract=560641
20. Doyle PG, Snell LT (1984) Random walks and electric networks. Mathematical Association of America, Washington, DC
21. Solé RV, Valverde S (2004) Information theory of complex networks: on evolution and architectural constraints. In: Lecture notes in physics, vol 650, pp 189–207. Springer, Berlin/Heidelberg
22. Kamada T, Kawai S (1989) An algorithm for drawing general undirected graphs. Inform Process Lett 31:7–15

Chapter 3
Toward Self-Organizing Search Systems

Stanislav Barton, Vlastislav Dohnal, Jan Sedmidubsky, and Pavel Zezula

Abstract The huge amount of images, videos, and music clips produced everyday by various digital devices must be processed. Firstly, this kind of data calls for content-based search or similarity search rather than keyword-based or text-based search. Secondly, new scalable and efficient methods capable of storing and querying such data must be developed. Although many distributed approaches exist, one of the most suitable and flexible is provided by self-organizing systems. These systems exhibit high resistance to failures in dynamically changing environments. In this chapter, we propose a general three-layer model for designing and implementing a self-organizing system that aims at searching in multimedia data. This model gives a developer guidelines about what component must be implemented, and how they should behave. The usability of this model is illustrated on a system called Metric Social Network. The architecture of this system is based on the social network theory that is utilized for establishing links between nodes. The system's properties are verified by organizing and searching in 10 million images.

3.1 Introduction and Motivation

In recent years, the growing demand for search within multimedia on the Web scale escalated a very popular scientific field of content-based information retrieval. In this area, the exact match is becoming insufficient as the search criteria and rather very close objects to the query are desired. The problem is that the multimedia data are binary data by orders of magnitude more voluminous than textual data. In order to transform such data objects to a more convenient form, various techniques

S. Barton
Conservatoire National des Arts et Metiers, CC 432292, Rue Saint-Martin, 75141 Paris, Cedex 03, France
e-mail: stanislav.barton@cnam.fr

V. Dohnal (✉), J. Sedmidubsky, and P. Zezula
Faculty of informatics, Masaryk University, Botanicka 68a, 60200 Brno, Czech Republic
e-mail: [dohnal;xsedmid;zezula]@fi.muni.cz

A. Abraham et al. (eds.), *Computational Social Network Analysis*, Computer Communications and Networks, DOI 10.1007/978-1-84882-229-0_3,
© Springer-Verlag London Limited 2010

to extract only characteristic features have been introduced. The extracted characteristic features are used for indexing and searching instead of the raw (binary) data. However, the metadata, which are usually represented as vectors, cannot be ordered in the natural way in contrast to numbers or strings. Therefore, they cannot be indexed by traditional indexing structures, e.g., B-tree.

The most general approach to similarity search, still allowing construction of index structures, is modeled as a *metric space*. Thus, a *metric function* is used to measure the distance of any pair of objects from a dataset. The higher the distance is, the less similar the objects are. Many index metric structures were developed and surveyed recently [43,58]. With the exponential growth of the data volume, the problem of *scalability* must be tackled. Thus, search algorithms should be constant in time, or logarithmic at most, to be applicable on huge data volumes. For these volumes, the centralized approaches to index metric spaces such as M-tree [18] and D-index [21] do not suffice anymore, so a straightforward shift from centralized toward distributed index structures has been made.

Distributed systems are characterized by nearly unlimited storage resources and significant computational power in contrast to centralized applications. A query is usually processed in parallel by several nodes in the network and, therefore, the size of a dataset practically does not influence their searching costs. Examples of such systems that build on the metric-space model, are GHT* [5] and M-Chord [39]. Nevertheless, such structures define a global data-assignment protocol, so data changes lead to large data reorganizations among the peers.

Current research trends focus on the shift toward systems with much looser structure like self-organizing systems. Unlike structured peer-to-peer (P2P) networks, self-organizing systems are resistant to node failures and data changes because there is no global data-assignment protocol defined and each node organizes its own data and rules itself. Moreover, self-organizing systems are able to control and evolve autonomously. On the other hand, their searching performance is usually worse in comparison to the structured networks. Figure 3.1 illustrates increasing scalability while shifting from centralized solutions to distributed systems. Nevertheless, the

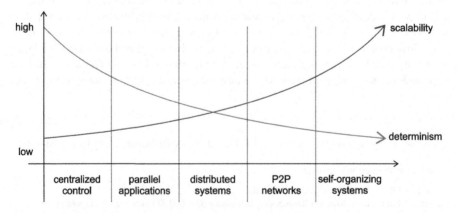

Fig. 3.1 Trade-off between scalability and determinism in system control

improved scalability comes at the expense of determinism [34]. The decreasing determinism may be expressed by several properties. The most characteristic one is the transition from complete answers to approximate answers. In general, centralized applications are usually exploited for indexing small amounts of data and provide precise answers to queries. On the other hand, self-organizing systems are capable of indexing huge amounts of data, but computing complete answers is infeasible. Centralized applications are well established, distributed networks become a cutting-edge technology, and self-organizing systems are under research.

In this chapter, we focus on a general approach for building unstructured P2P networks having their loose structure created and maintained through self-organization. Main contribution of this chapter is the three-layer model proposed as a successful design method for this kind of systems. To prove the concept of the design method, an example of a self-organized system for similarity search in multimedia is presented and tested.

The remaining part of the chapter is organized as follows. In Sect. 3.2, related work and basics of self-organizing systems are summarized. In Sect. 3.3, a three-layer architecture model is introduced. In Sect. 3.4, we present Metric Social Network (mSN) as an instance of a self-organizing system implemented using the three-layer model. Experimental trials with this system are presented in Sect. 3.5. Section 3.6 concludes the chapter and draws future research directions.

3.2 Self-Organizing Search Systems

We aim at developing a search system that will allow users to query large data collections on similarity. Thus, we survey existing systems suitable for large-scale similarity search. Next, principles of self-organizing systems are overviewed.

3.2.1 Similarity Search Systems

Many systems for similarity search that can be applied on large data archives have been proposed. However, only some of them are able to process complex data types, such as images or video clips. All these systems exploit a distributed computational environment, but they differ mainly in the aspect of distributing data within the system. First, we survey structured systems that define a global data partitioning schema. Next, we focus on unstructured systems.

A P2P structure that indexes text documents transformed to a vector space model is called pSearch [51]. This system uses the CAN structure [41] internally to distribute the documents over the network. When a query consisting of terms is posed, the query's position in the space is determined, and it is then forwarded to the peer responsible for the position. Finally, the query is spread to neighboring peers that may contain other relevant documents. Distributed Quadtree [52] is a P2P index for spatial data (Euclidean space). This structure manages a virtual global quad-tree [42]. The leaves (data blocks) of the tree are assigned to individual peers by means of the Chord [48] protocol. This protocol defines a hashing function that maps the blocks into a linear domain. The authors of the SWAM approach [3] generally formalize the issue of similarity search in vector data and define the similarity in terms of L_p metrics. All these systems exploit specific properties of the data domain that organize, so their applicability to other data is cumbersome.

In the following, we focus on structured systems that use a metric space to model similarity. The metric space offers the required generality and extensibility to the systems. GHT* [5] and VPT* [6] structures capitalize on the metric space model and create a distributed tree structure based on generalized-hyperplane [54] and vantage-point [57] partitioning schema of the metric space, respectively. On the other hand, M-Chord [39] maps the metric space into a one-dimensional domain exploiting a set of selected pivots. It employs a standard P2P technique called Skip Graphs [2] to divide the one-dimensional domain among the peers and to provide the routing algorithm. MCAN [24] transforms the metric space using a set of selected pivots into n-dimensional vector spaces and applies the CAN partitioning and routing protocol. A disadvantage of MCAN is that it becomes inefficient for a larger number of dimensions.

All the structures surveyed above define a global protocol for distributing data over the network, which leads to two main disadvantages. Firstly, data has to be migrated to the peer identified by the protocol, which is not suitable for large and dynamically changing networks containing a huge number of data objects. Secondly, these structures are vulnerable to peer failures because of the assumption that target peers function properly, but this disadvantage can be addressed using node or data replication.

Systems operating in unstructured P2P networks would solve the problems of peer failures and data migration. In contrast to structured P2P networks, the peers of an unstructured network do not exchange the data with one another in order to efficiently process queries. MRoute [25] is an unstructured P2P network for indexing and searching in multimedia data. The data is considered as objects of a metric space. MRoute transforms the objects to binary vectors using preselected pivots. Then, Routing Index [19], originally developed for organizing text documents, is applied to index these binary vectors. SIMPEER [23] introduces a super-peer architecture where the super-peers collect information about the content of peers connected to the particular super-peer. This approach uses a metric technique iDistance [30] for clustering data and creating a concise representation of a peer stored at a super-peer. However, the super-peers can be observed as a bottleneck of the whole system due to their centralized-control nature. Another work [33] presents preliminary results on Metric Overlay Networks (MONs), inspired by the idea of Semantic Overlay Networks (SONs [20]). The basic idea of SONs is that peers in an unstructured network are joined into semantically close groups. However, the scalability issue of MON is unclear. The authors used a dataset of 68,000 images. From our experience [44], such systems applied to small networks exhibit good results, but on a large scale the results deteriorate radically.

Current research directions in searching in large data archives exhibit shift from hierarchical and centralized structures to network-like and distributed systems that are autonomous and do not need any centralized control. However, such a novel approach requires scalable, distributed, and robust algorithms with self-adaptive and self-organizing mechanisms [34]. Therefore, systems utilizing these algorithms organize themselves usually without any human intervention. In the following, we summarize basic principles of self-organizing systems.

3.2.2 Self-Organizing Systems

A self-organizing system consists of many entities interacting with each other in order to create a desired outcome. In other words, the structure of a self-organizing system often appears without an explicit pressure from outside the system, so the constraints on organization are internal to the system and result from interactions among the entities. The system can evolve in time or space and show various organizations [34].

The essence of self-organizing systems is that organization is achieved in a distributed manner, thus there is no need for centralized control. Individual entities communicate and exchange information locally, so there is no global view of the entire system. High-level, but simple, rules defined in the individual entities lead to sophisticated functionality of the overall system.

A very important property of self-organizing systems is their ability to exploit positive and negative *feedback*. Based on the feedback, the system is able to decide what action is more useful for a specific context. The positive feedback permits the system to evolve and support the creation of the desired outcome, whereas the negative feedback aims at regulating the influence of previous bad adaptations and preventing the system to get stuck in local solutions [14, 34]. Every good self-organizing system should satisfy the following properties.

- *Scalability* With an exponential increase of entities and their interactions, the system must be able to finish operations within acceptable bounds, e.g., expressed in computational costs, communication costs, or in time.
- *Adaptability* Resources of the system change over time, which can degrade system's performance and cause operation interruption. In order to preserve performance and operation accessibility in dynamic environments, systems must provide mechanisms to adapt to changes in a coordinated manner.
- *Robustness* There is no single point of failure. Systems usually rely on fluctuations and randomness which provides them with several solutions that come into account when critical errors occur. The entities of the systems can automatically detect and recover from failures caused by internal errors or external inconsistencies. Increasing damage will decrease performance, but the degradation will be graceful – the quality of the output will deteriorate gradually, without any sudden loss of function in contrast to common systems where removing a random number of components cause systems' breakdown [34].

The entities and their mutual communication should be resistant to errors and malicious attacks. When self-organization is applied to computer systems, a crucial aspect is how security, privacy, and trust are maintained. A lot of research in the area of trust management covering security policies, credentials, relationships, and authorization has been already done. Various works describe algorithms for decentralized security [8,9], rights delegation [32], trust measurement and defense against malicious attacks [50], and trust management and authorization [10, 11].

The field of self-organization seeks general rules about the growth and evolution of system's structure and methods which should predict the future organization. It is expected that the results will be applicable to all other systems exhibiting similar characteristics. However, self-organization has also its limits and some self-organizing processes cannot be directly mapped to computer systems.

3.2.2.1 Application Areas

Current research tends to exploit the properties of self-organizing systems such as scalability, adaptability, or robustness for modern network designs. However, such behavior forms the basis of many natural systems, e.g., in human society or animal behavior, the process of self-organization forms the essence of individual survival. In the following, we introduce examples of self-organization from various disciplines.

Biology

The behavior of most biological systems is based on self-organization. For example, ants looking for food employ quite a simple self-organizing behavior. They are able to find a very short path from the nest to the food source and back owing to their pheromone trails [31]. Dorigo [22] employed this method to optimize finding the shortest path in a graph. Michlmayr [36] applied the same to search in unstructured P2P networks. The authors of [16] optimized routing in mobile networks. Another example is a school of thousands of fish moving together as a coordinated unit. When the school changes direction, all its members rapidly respond [53].

Sociology

Human society represents a large self-organizing system of people forming *social network*. Social network is the term used in sociology since the 1950s and refers to a social structure of people related either directly or indirectly to each other through a common relation or interest [55]. In 1967, the social psychologist Stanley Milgram presented the *small-world phenomenon* [37], sometimes referred as *six degrees of separation*. The experiment revealed that most pairs of people in USA are reachable by the chain of five intermediates on average. Other examples of self-organization are an economy, a brain, or a city [26].

Computer Science

The process of self-organization may be seen in computer systems. Especially Internet Protocol (IP) gives many examples of such behavior, e.g., auto-configuration of IP addresses, router auto-configuration, or service discovery. Devices attaching to a network configure their address themselves with the help of a router. Using Dynamic Host Configuration Protocol (DHCP) devices are able to automatically obtain an IP address from the router, which allows devices to adapt to changes in their environment (e.g., to obtain a new IP address when they move to a different network) [40]. Neural networks aim at recognizing patterns and are capable of returning good results even if some their nodes or links are removed [29]. In robotic systems, stand-alone robots self-organize their activities, and they are able to dynamically adapt to a changing environment [13, 15]. For example, in case of a robot's breakdown, other robots try to self-organize and take over all its tasks. The idea of self-tuning databases keeping performance at a satisfactory level automatically was proposed in [56].

Physics

Magnetization is one of the simplest process of self-organization. Magnetic material consists of many tiny magnets, each of them with a particular orientation. The molecules in the tiny magnets randomly move resulting in their disorganized behavior. With the growing temperature, random movements are stronger which makes the tiny magnets more difficult to arrange [28]. Crystallization is a self-organizing process where molecules randomly move and create a symmetric pattern of dense matter. Lasers, ideal gas, and most dynamical systems are self-organizing [1, 7, 38].

The process of self-organization includes many disciplines not mentioned above, such as information theory, mathematics, philosophy, chemistry, and others. Various disciplines show a totally different form of self-organization, so we usually choose a concept, e.g., ant colony system, and apply similar principles to the system being designed and implemented. The model we introduce can guide system developers throughout the whole development process and can identify possible hitches in early stages.

3.3   Three-Layer Model of Self-Organizing Search Systems

In this section, we propose a three-layer model of self-organizing search systems. The purpose of this model is to help in all development stages of a system being created. The guidelines given in the model should prevent from missing an important part of the system that would lead to the system that is not scalable, robust, or adaptable. In order to accept various theories of self-organization, the model is very general but it still gives clear guidelines.

Fig. 3.2 Influence graph of
the components of a node

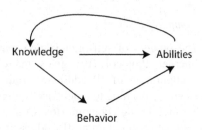

The model consists of three layers: (1) *abstract layer* specifies basic strategies
and the way of behavior that the target system has to satisfy; (2) *conceptual layer*
extends the abstract layer and defines principles of the self-organization theory selected; (3) *implementation layer* focuses on specific algorithms that implement the
principles defined on the conceptual layer.

A self-organizing system lacks a firm structure, so the system is described
through the entities it comprises of and by the means of their mutual interaction.
From the computer science point of view, the system will usually operate in a P2P
network, so from now on, we will refer to the entities of the system as *nodes*.

Each node consists of three logical components:

- *Knowledge* is the node's repository that stores data and information about the
  neighboring parts of the system.
- *Abilities* are actions the node can carry out, such as query processing.
- *Behavior* denotes strategies that are used by the abilities.

The node's components influence each other and cannot be conceived as isolated
parts of the design. For instance, the knowledge is used to determine the current
behavior of the entity for the incoming impulses, and on the other hand the behavior
substantially influences the way the abilities are conducted. Figure 3.2 depicts the
individual influences.

3.3.1 Abstract Layer

The abstract layer serves as a platform for general description of a node of the
system being designed. The description concerns the logical design of the node
including the means of communication with other nodes: querying, behaving, and
self-managing. As mentioned before we recognize three main logical components
of the node. In the following, we give more detail description of them.

3.3.1.1 Knowledge

This component functions as the node's repository. An important part of it is the
node's local data. Another part stores the links to other nodes in the system (the
node's neighbors).

- *Data repository* is where the searchable local data is kept.
- *Semantic links* represent the node's awareness about the system – links to other nodes. Semantic information can be associated with these links. Notice that the links are logical connections between nodes. The information is actually exchanged between the nodes using an underlying physical network, where a link can lead to a path of individual physical interconnections.
- *Statistics* or summary information gathered from the local data, the queries processed so far, or the system's dynamism subjectively observed by the node.

3.3.1.2 Behavior

The behavior represents strategies that are chosen to conduct the algorithms recognized as abilities of the node. The way the node behaves depends on node's *self-confidence* that can be influenced by the query being processed. In particular, the self-confidence is an indicator of certainty about the node's knowledge, e.g., the recency of the knowledge or its completeness. We distinguish two possible strategies:

- *Exploitation* Deterministic decisions made upon certain parts of the node's knowledge toward looking for the most relevant parts of the system. It is applied when the self-confidence is high.
- *Exploration* Decisions made upon the node's current knowledge toward discovering unvisited or unseen parts of the system. It can also include randomness. It is applied when the self-confidence is low.

3.3.1.3 Abilities

The node's abilities are algorithms that evaluate requests received by the node. The execution of the algorithms often depends on the value of self-confidence. On the abstract layer of the model, the algorithms state their aims and purpose rather than how the goals are achieved.

3.3.1.4 Query Processing

As the primary goal of the system is searching, the foremost ability is query processing. The aim is to find the best community (group) of nodes that carry the answer to the query. According to the node's knowledge, the node is able to forward the query, or process it directly on its own data. The general query-processing algorithm can be characterized as follows:

1. The user poses a query at a node. We refer to this node as the *query-issuing node*.
2. The node's self-confidence is computed.
3. Outgoing links are selected based on the exploitation or exploration strategy. In particular, when self-confidence is high the exploitation strategy locates the most

promising nodes directly and the exploration is employed moderately. On the other hand, when self-confidence is low, the exploration is prevalent and explores the system to locate the relevant data.

4. The contacted nodes return their answers to the query-issuing node.

3.3.1.5 Announcement or Advertising

An ability usually used for knowledge dissemination. The node is able to communicate with other nodes without requiring any response (one-way communication). For instance, this ability can be used for the knowledge update in the system after query processing. This is called *announcement* and can be seen as the exploitation strategy because the nodes where the knowledge should be updated were identified at the query-processing stage. On the other hand, *advertising* stands for the exploration strategy. For example, the node can asynchronously notify random nodes in the system with the knowledge update.

3.3.1.6 Node Management

The node is also capable of managing the data it governs. This obviously includes inserting new data, deleting, and updating existing data. The node is also able to manage itself which includes updating statistics gathered through out the system's lifetime. The dynamicity of the self-organizing system expresses the volatility of nodes and data, which is ubiquitous in huge systems. The data volatility means modifying (adding, deleting) data stored on individual nodes, whereas the node volatility represents joining of new nodes and leaving of existing nodes. This is in P2P networks referred to as *peer churn* [49]. By monitoring the number of advertisement coming from new nodes or existing nodes and by analyzing changes in answers during query evaluation, the self-confidence of the node can be influenced. In highly dynamic systems, the self-confidence should decrease in time, which causes the system to behave more exploratively.

3.3.2 Conceptual Layer

In the proposed model, the conceptual layer lists and describes concepts used to achieve the self-organization of the system. Firstly, a general concept has to be chosen (e.g., social networking or ant colony). Next, the abstractions from the abstract layer are instantiated using this selected concept. In particular, semantics is given to the individual node's components and their parts. However, the implementation of a specific part can still be ambiguous on this layer.

To be successful with the design of a self-organizing search system, the designer has to consider the following recommendations:

- *Completeness of the instantiation* Not necessarily the constructed system has to have a concept for all abstractions described on the abstract layer. For example, the system does not need to know how to actively spread knowledge in a push model (advertise). Yet, if the main concern of the design is searching, the inability to process queries would be inappropriate.
- *Completeness of the conceptual design* Usually some of the concepts imply an existence of another. Therefore the conceptual description of the search system should be complete in the sense of transitive enclosure. For instance, if self-confidence is based on relevance of node's links related to a query, relevance must be defined on this layer.
- *Particular concept selection* The general concept sometimes allows various approaches to the instantiation. In that case, this level may contain a list of possible instantiations under consideration and may specify which of them were selected for implementation.

3.3.3 Implementation Layer

Finally, on this layer, the semantic and conceptual description get their exact specification. It comprises of functions and algorithms implementing the concepts from the conceptual layer. All the concepts on the above layer must be implemented.

3.4 Building a Social-Network Search System

In this section, we show how the proposed three-layer model can be utilized for designing a self-organizing search system. Firstly, the selected concepts of social network and metric space along with their principles are presented. Secondly, the implementation of instantiated parts on the abstract and conceptual layer is described.

3.4.1 Conceptual Layer

In our experimental system design, we have chosen to tailor the system according to the concept of *social network*. The term refers to a structure of people related by social ties that allow communicating among people or searching for desired information. The social ties (semantic links) are usually divided to

- *Strong (Friend) Links* A person has a close connection with friends; they usually share interests similar to the person's interests for a certain activity; most of them are in touch with one another.

- *Weak (Acquaintance) Links* A person knowing another person as an acquaintance gives him or her an opportunity to contact outside world from the person's interests point of view; the acquaintances serve to get new information; few of them can know each other.

Granovetter [27] discovered that in many activities, such as finding a job, getting news, launching a restaurant or spreading the latest fad, week links are more important than strong links.

Real social networks are governed by two laws: dynamism and preferential connectivity. Each network starts from a small nucleus and expands with the addition of new nodes. Then these new nodes first link to another nodes in an existing network practically at random, but through consequent communication they find better and better friends and acquaintances. However, the connectivity process is also dynamic as good friends and acquaintances disappear or become less friendly and other better friends and acquaintances show up. Once a network is created, there are usually many paths between a starting and target node. However, an important question is how to select among many acquaintances the correct node to form the next link in the chain so that the resulting path becomes as short as possible.

We adapt this concept to computer systems where the nodes (computers) of the system act on behalf of their users and create a self-organizing search system. According to the small-world experiment [37], any node of the system should be reachable in a small, preferably constant, number of hops.

3.4.1.1 Knowledge

The knowledge consists of the three components defined on the abstract layer. The data-repository module is influenced by the metric space model chosen and the concept of social networks requires to determine and store two kinds of semantic links. At this stage, we do not need to keep any additional statistics about the local data or queries processed.

3.4.1.2 Data Repository

Extensibility is another notion that has started to play an important role because it ensures that a system can be applied to various and quite different in nature data without any fundamental change in the system's design or implementation. The notion of *metric space* offers this kind of extensibility [43]. We decided to adopt the metric space, so the data items stored in the system are actually objects in the metric space.

Formally, a metric space $\mathcal{M} = (\mathcal{D}, d)$ is defined for a *domain* of objects $\mathcal{D}$ and a total function d that evaluates a *distance* between a pair of objects. The properties of this function are: non-negativity, symmetry, and triangle inequality. In particular, the distance expresses *dissimilarity* between two objects. Examples of distance functions are L_p metrics (City-block (L_1) or Euclidean (L_2) distance), the edit distance, or the quadratic-form distance. The distance function is not typically applied directly to a binary form of data, but it is rather applied to some features extracted from it. For instance, a color histogram can be extracted from an image or a photo.

The way of modeling data is closely related to the form of querying. In the metric space, similarity queries are usually represented as *nearest-neighbors* and *range* queries. The nearest-neighbors query is specified by a query object $q \in \mathcal{D}$ and a positive integer k. From a database $X \subset \mathcal{D}$, the query returns k most similar objects to q. The range query $R(q, r)$ is specified by a query object $q \in \mathcal{D}$ and a radius r as the distance constraint. From the database X, it retrieves all objects found within the distance r from q. There are also other types of queries, for example similarity joins or combinations of basic queries [58].

3.4.1.3 Semantic Links

We define semantic links between nodes in the system based on results of querying. During query processing, some nodes that are likely to contain data relevant to a query are contacted. These nodes evaluate the query on their local data and return their answers to the node which posed the query. The query-issuing node decides which nodes become friends and which become acquaintances on the basis of results received. Thus new semantic links are created. These links are accompanied with the metadata about this processed query. The metadata consist of items defining the query (e.g, query object and radius in case of the range query), time when the query was issued, and a *quality* of the answer (defined below).

Formally, the node P_{start} issues a query Q and the routing algorithm locates the most promising nodes $P_1, \ldots, P_n$ in the system. These nodes process the query on their local data and return their answers (*partial answers*) $A_{P_i}(Q)$ to the query-issuing node P_{start}. This node merges the partial answers and returns the *combined answer* $A(Q) = \bigcup_{i=1}^{n} A_{P_i}(Q)$ to the user. Note that the combined answer is approximate. The node that answered as best is denoted as the acquaintance. Whereas the nodes that answered similarly become friends. The decision is based on the definition of *quality* of a partial answer. It is a function $Qual(A_{P_i}(Q))$, returning a *quality object* Q_i scoring the partial answer $A_{P_i}(Q)$ passed in the argument. A linear ordering $\preceq_Q$ is defined on the quality objects: $Q_1 \preceq_Q Q_2$ iff Q_2 is worse than Q_1. As a result, the best answer and the most similar answers can be easily determined. A specific algorithm for evaluating the quality as well as the ordering is defined on the implementation layer.

Semantic links can be created upon other concepts that the selected one. For example, friends can become

- Nodes posing similar queries, which can express similar tastes of their users
- Nodes maintaining similar local data

3.4.1.4 Behavior

To select the correct behavior strategy, each node must be able to compute its self-confidence. We define self-confidence using *relevance* of links. Relevance expresses the link's usability with respect to the query being evaluated. In particular, the metadata of the query is compared with the metadata of the query associated with the link. Relevance of the link is then the similarity of these two metadata. The links having high relevance are used to compute the node's self-confidence. Specific algorithms that evaluate self-confidence and relevance of links are defined on the implementation layer.

3.4.1.5 Abilities

The node's abilities on the conceptual layer include a more specific query-routing algorithm which exploits the acquaintance and friend links. These links may also be used for advertising when new nodes join the system or for announcing when the node's knowledge has been updated. The social network concept does not concern itself about data management routines, i.e., they remain unchanged.

3.4.1.6 Query Processing

Query processing represents looking for the most promising acquaintances because it is supposed that acquaintance links lead to the communities of friends that manage the queried data. In other words, the acquaintance links are followed during query forwarding. When the best acquaintance is contacted, it evaluates the query on its data and asks its query-related friends for the evaluation as well. Finally, the partial answers are sent back. The friend links are used for further improving the query result. The procedure is summarized as follows.

1. The user poses a query at the query-issuing node.
2. Each node contacted computes self-confidence:
   a. Relevance of each link to the query is computed
   b. The most relevant links are used to compute self-confidence
3. The value of self-confidence influences the selection of the exploitation or exploration strategy.

   - Exploitation (high self-confidence) – the query is forwarded using the most relevant acquaintance links.
   - Exploration (low self-confidence) – the query is sent to the nodes that are targets of the links that have small probability to contain data relevant to the query. This corresponds to an attempt to locate unvisited parts of the system that can be relevant to the query.

Query forwarding stops when a better acquaintance cannot be found.
4. The best acquaintances evaluate the query on their local data and ask all their query-related friends to do it too.
5. All partial answers are returned to the query-issuing node.

3.4.1.7   Announcement

Semantic links maintained by each node have to be updated continuously in order to allow the system to evolve and adapt to changes in data or users' requirements. Since these links are related to a query, a straightforward algorithm is to update them immediately after the query is processed. Partial answers returned by nodes during query processing are analyzed and the information about newly identified acquaintances and friends is spread to the system. However, the spreading is controlled and the information is announced to identified acquaintances and friends as well as the nodes contacted by the exploration strategy.

3.4.1.8   Advertisement

A node usually advertises its content when it joins the system, i.e., a bootstrap protocol. We use the procedure that selects representatives from the locally stored objects and queries the system for similar objects to these representatives. Because the node is new in the system, it has poor knowledge about the system, so the exploration strategy prevails during the query evaluation. When the node updates its data, it can also use advertising messages to propagate the changes but we do not use this mechanism yet.

3.4.2   Implementation Layer

In this section, we describe specific algorithms for the notions drawn in the previous section. The algorithms implement all the functionality required at a node, so the nodes together create a whole self-organizing search system. In particular, we describe the algorithms that mSN [44] consists of mSN is a self-organizing system for searching in image or photo collections shared by individual users of the system. Only range queries are supported by the system, however algorithms of existing distributed indexes implement nearest-neighbors queries using repeating a range query and varying the query radius. In the following, we present the algorithms separately for each of the node's components.

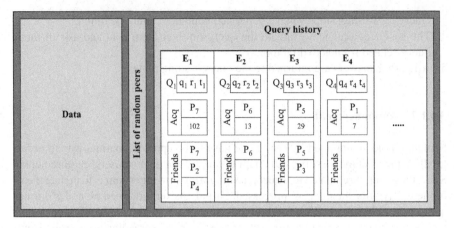

Fig. 3.3 Schema of an mSN node

Knowledge

The particular components of node's knowledge are depicted in Fig. 3.3. The data repository describes the way of storing individual objects within this component. The semantic links are kept in a structure of processed queries. A list of random nodes is maintained in the statistics. This list is later used by an exploration strategy.

Data Repository

Each node organizes a user's collection of images. Thus, a specific metric space must be defined. The domain of the metric space is formed by five characteristic features extracted from the images. All the features are stored as one 280-dimensional vector. These features are standard MPEG-7 [35] descriptors: *color structure* (CS), *color layout* (CL), *scalable color* (SC), *edge histogram* (EH), and *homogeneous texture* (HT). In detail, CS, CL, and SC express the spatial distribution of colors in an image. The EH captures local density of edge elements and their directions (sometimes called the *structure* or *layout*); it acts as a simple and robust representation of shapes. Finally, HT is a texture descriptor. The MPEG-7 standard also defines the distance functions for comparing the individual features. Table 3.1 summarizes them. There are five distinct distance functions, but we need just one. So, it is defined as a weighted sum where the weights are given in the table.

Semantic Links

Semantic links in the system are maintained by a structure called *query history*. This structure keeps links to other nodes and allows storing semantic information

Table 3.1 Summary
of extracted features

MPEG-7 Feature	Metric	Weight
Scalable Color	L_1 metric	2
Color Structure	L_1 metric	3
Color Layout	Sum of L_2	2
Edge Histogram	Special	4
Homogeneous Texture	Special	0.5

associated with each link. In detail, the query history $H = \{E_1, \ldots, E_n\}$ consists of individual *entries* E_i, where the entry represents information about a query processed by the system. The entry E is a tuple $E = (Q, Acq(Q), Qual(A_{Acq(Q)}(Q)), Fri(Q))$, where $Q = R(q, r, t)$ denotes the regular range query enriched with the time when the query was issued, $Acq(Q)$ is the acquaintance, $Qual(A_{Acq(Q)}(Q))$ is its quality, and $Fri(Q)$ is the set of identified friends. The quality of the acquaintance is important in the query routing algorithm because the stop condition of query forwarding is based on this quantification.

The links are created upon scoring the partial answers returned by the nodes contacted during processing the query Q. The quality of partial answer is measured as the number of retrieved objects:

$$Qual(A_{P_i}(Q)) = |A_{P_i}(Q)| \tag{3.1}$$

The linear ordering is straightforward since the quality is integer. The better the partial answer is, the higher number of objects it contains. The acquaintance is then the node returning the highest number of objects:

$$Acq(Q) = P \Leftrightarrow \forall P_i : |A_P(Q)| \geq |A_{P_i}(Q)| \tag{3.2}$$

where P_i are all the nodes that participated in the evaluation of the query Q. The other kind of link (friend link) connects nodes that returned similar answers, i.e., the nodes returning a significant number of objects compared to the combined answer size:

$$Fri(Q) = \{P_i : |A_{P_i}(Q)| \geq |A(Q)|/n\} \tag{3.3}$$

where n denotes the number of answering nodes.

Statistics

We do not keep any special statistics about the system dynamicity. However, each node maintains a list of random nodes that are employed in the exploration strategy of query routing. It helps find the new and previously unvisited parts of the system efficiently. An experiment that compares the evolution speed of mSN system when random nodes are used and are not used was undertaken. The results in terms of recall are depicted in Fig. 3.4. One identical query was repeatedly issued from different nodes in the system. Observe that some nodes were unable to locate any

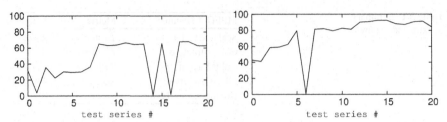

Fig. 3.4 Progress of recall when the query is not (*left*) routed to random nodes and when it is (*right*)

relevant objects when the list of random nodes was not used. Moreover, the answer size was increasing slowly as compared to the system using the list of random nodes. Notice that the recall was obtained by dividing the size of answer returned by the query routing algorithm of mSN by the size of *total answer*. The total answer was determined by asking all nodes in the system just for this purpose.

Each node manages the list of random nodes as follows. Initially, when it joins the network, the list of random nodes is empty and must be filled. Despite this, the node must know at least one another node because it has joined the system successfully. The new node sends a special request to all known nodes and waits for response. Upon receiving a response, it adds the responding node to the list. Any node receiving such a request decides with a random function whether to respond to the node that originated this request or not. In either case, the node forwards this request further to all its random nodes. To avoid flooding the system, the forwarding is repeated until time-to-live (TTL) is zero. We empirically verified that TTL set to four is sufficient to obtain a list of 30–50 random nodes. In the situation of having the list empty, any node can end up since the list of random nodes can get underfilled or invalidated due to the nodes leaving the system or expelling nodes that were identified as acquaintances or friends.

Behavior

Before presenting the procedure for computing self-confidence of a node, we define the concept of *confusability* of two queries.

Confusability

We present *confusability* of queries [45, 46] that extends the universal law of generalization [17, 47] by taking into account the extent of queries and the time. The confusability of two range queries $Q = (q, r, t)$ and $Q_i = (q_i, r_i, t_i)$ is defined as a weighted sum of the distance (D), intersection (I) and time (T) confusability:

$$C(Q, Q_i) = w_D \cdot D(Q, Q_i) + w_I \cdot I(Q, Q_i) + w_T \cdot T(Q, Q_i) \qquad (3.4)$$

The weights must satisfy: $w_{D,I,T} \geq 0$ and $w_D + w_I + w_T = 1$. The resulting confusability returns a value between zero and one as the individual components do.

The confusability is usually used to retrieve entries from the query history when a query is evaluated, thus Q stands for the query being processed and Q_i for the query stored in an entry E_i in the query history. The partial confusabilities are defined as follows:

- Distance confusability $D(Q, Q_i)$ is Shephard's confusability [47] applied to the query objects of queries Q and Q_i:

$$D(Q, Q_i) = e^{-B \cdot d(q, q_i)} \tag{3.5}$$

The parameter B is data- and distance-function-dependent. From our experience, a convenient value of B is the inverted value of the most frequent distance in the dataset (refer to Fig. 3.5b). In our setting, $B = 2.1^{-1} = 0.476$.
- Intersection confusability $I(Q, Q_i)$ expresses the volume of space covered by the intersection of the query regions (ball-like regions). We define it in two-dimensional space:

$$I(Q, Q_i) = \frac{|region(Q) \cap region(Q_i)|}{|region(Q)|} \tag{3.6}$$

This helps in selecting similar queries by the size and overlap of their regions.
- Time confusability $T(Q, Q_i)$ expresses the similarity of queries Q and Q_i with respect to their timestamps in wall clock time:

$$T(Q, Q_i) = \max\left(0, \frac{t_{max} - |t - t_i|}{t_{max}}\right) \tag{3.7}$$

The parameter t_{max} stands for the time interval after which a query is considered to be archaic. In real systems, this value should correspond to data volatility. Due to experimenting with the system, we used 5 min only, which corresponds to 600 queries processed in the system.

We empirically verified that the weights $w_D = 0.38$, $w_I = 0.38$, and $w_T = 0.24$ are suitable for our system searching in the image database. In particular, we give three times higher preference to the query shape than to the time aspect.

Self-Confidence

On the conceptual layer, we outlined that the computation of self-confidence uses relevance of links. We define relevance of a link as the confusability of the query being processed and the query associated with the link. As a result the node's confusability is defined as

1. Compute *confusability* for each entry in the query history (i.e., take the query associated with the entry and the query being processed).
2. Take the five entries $E_1, \ldots, E_5$ having the highest confusability. *Self-confidence* (SC) is the mean value of these confusabilities, i.e., $SC = avg_{i=1..5}(E_i)$.

Abilities

In the following, query-processing steps are summarized in a routing algorithm. Secondly, a procedure to update node's knowledge called announcement is presented. Next, the actions that a new node joining the system must do are outlined. Finally, a technique to index local data for efficient searching is mentioned as a part of node management.

Query Processing

Each node proceeds the following steps when it receives a range query $Q = R(q, r, t)$. Complete specification of the query-routing algorithm is available in Algorithms 3.1 and 3.2. The first algorithm is used for locating the best acquaintance and the second algorithm contacts all friends of the best acquaintance. Initially, a user poses the query Q at the node P_{start} (query-issuing node). Next, the node proceeds the steps of Algorithm 3.1:

1. Node's self-confidence (SC) is computed.
2. Depending on the value of SC, the ratio of exploitation and exploration strategy is determined, so the algorithm can adapt to a new query (unseen before) fast:

   - Exploitation – the query Q is forwarded to acquaintances of n entries having the highest confusability. The number of entries (*flooding factor*) is decided by the value of SC:

$$Flooding\ factor(SC) = \begin{cases} 1 & if SC \in [0.90, 1.00] \\ 2 & if SC \in [0.65, 0.90) \\ 3 & if SC \in [0.40, 0.65) \\ 4 & if SC \in [0.15, 0.40) \\ 5 & if SC \in [0.00, 0.15) \end{cases} \qquad (3.8)$$

   Notice that different entries can have the same acquaintance, hence the query is forwarded only once.
   - Exploration – the query Q is forwarded to a random node with the probability p inversely proportional to the value of self-confidence, i.e., $p = 1 - SC$. A random node is always contacted when the node has less than five entries in its query history. To avoid an infinite loop during contacting random nodes, the forwarding is stopped after a predefined number of hops is reached.

Algorithm 3.1 Routing Algorithm `forwardQueryAdapt`

Input: sender P_S, contacted node P_C, range query $Q = R(q, r, t)$, previous answer size pas, query-issuing node P_{start}

1: $V \leftarrow$ five most similar entries $E_1, \ldots, E_5$ to Q from the query history respecting $C(Q, Q_i)$, where $E_i = (Q_i, Acq(Q_i), |A_{Acq(Q_i)}(Q_i)|, Fri(Q_i))$
2: $V \leftarrow$ ordered entries of V by decreasing confusability
3: $SC \leftarrow$ the average confusability value of the entries of V (self-confidence)
4: $n \leftarrow$ floodingFactor(SC)
5: $W \leftarrow$ first n entries of V
6: $useRandomNode \leftarrow$ decide whether a random node will be used with a probability $1 - SC$
7: **if** ($useRandomNode$ **or** $|V| < 5$) **then**
8: $\quad P^{rand} \leftarrow$ a node randomly chosen from the list of random nodes
9: $\quad$ forwardQueryAdapt(P_C, P^{rand}, Q, pas, P_{start})
10: **end if**
11: **for** each entry $E_i \in W$ **do**
12: $\quad$ /* $E_i = (Q_i, Acq(Q_i), |A_{Acq(Q_i)}(Q_i)|, Fri(Q_i))$ */
13: $\quad P \leftarrow Acq(Q_i)$
14: $\quad$ **if** $|A_P(Q_i)| > pas$ **then**
15: $\quad\quad$ forwardQueryAdapt(P_C, P, Q, $|A_P(Q_i)|$, P_{start})
16: $\quad$ **else**
17: $\quad\quad$ **for all** $P_j \in Fri(Q_i)$ **do**
18: $\quad\quad\quad$ answerQuery(P_j, Q, P_{start})
19: $\quad\quad$ **end for**
20: $\quad\quad$ retrieve all objects from the local data that satisfy Q
21: $\quad\quad$ send retrieved objects back to P_{start}
22: $\quad$ **end if**
23: **end for**

Algorithm 3.2 Friend-of-Friend Answering `answerQuery`

Input: contacted node P_C, range query $Q = R(q, r, t)$, query-issuing node P_{start}

1: /* $E_i = (Q_i, Acq(Q_i), |A_{Acq(Q_i)}(Q_i)|, Fri(Q_i))$ */
2: $V \leftarrow \{E_i \mid E_i \in$ query history of node $P_C \wedge d(q, q_i) \leq r\}$
3: **for all** $E_i \in V$ **do**
4: $\quad$ **for all** $P_j \in Fri(Q_i)$ **do**
5: $\quad\quad$ answerQuery(P_j, Q, P_{start})
6: $\quad$ **end for**
7: **end for**
8: retrieve all objects from the local data that satisfy Q
9: send retrieved objects back to P_{start}

Remark. The adaptability of this algorithm is wired in the automatic increase or decrease of the flooding factor. The process of query forwarding can be repeated more times to locate the nodes that are the most promising to hold the searched data. The forwarding stops when the contacted node's quality (*pas* value in Algorithm 3.1) is higher than any of its acquaintances to which the node can forward the query. The node P_{start} sets $pas = 0$.

3. If this node is the most promising acquaintance (i.e., forwarding has stopped), the query Q is evaluated on the local data and the partial answer is returned to P_{start}. Simultaneously, the query-related friends of this node are contacted to evaluate the query on their local data and Algorithm 3.2 is called. This algorithm locates all close entries E_i in this node's query history (having its query object q_i close to the current query, i.e., $d(q, q_i) \leq r$) and asks the friends associated with these entries to evaluate the query on their local data too. It is supposed that these friends hold substantial parts of the total answer $A(Q)$.

Announcement

After processing a query Q, the node P_{start} analyzes the partial answer received and identifies the acquaintance and friends. As a result, the new entry $E = (Q, Acq(Q), |A_{Acq(Q)}(Q)|, Fri(Q))$ is created. This entry is stored in the query history of: P_{start}, the friends identified, and also nodes $P_i{}^{rand}$ that were contacted by the exploration strategy. In this way, a new acquaintance link from P_{start} to the node $Acq(Q)$ as well as acquaintance links between all random nodes $P_i{}^{rand}$ and $Acq(Q)$ get instantiated. Also friend links between each pair of nodes in $Fri(Q)$ are established.

Advertisement

A node joining the system needs to be incorporated in the structure fast. After the node obtains the list of random nodes, it runs a k-means algorithm on its local data to identify ten good representatives of data, i.e., the node creates its data profile. Next, the node forms range queries for each of the representative and poses them to the system. This way the node's data profile is spread into the system. In case the node does not share any data, just the list of random nodes is obtained, which is crucial for the routing algorithm functionality.

Node Management

The node internally stores its data in M-tree [18]. M-tree is a hierarchical index structure that supports secondary storage. The algorithms in M-tree inserts new and queries existing data efficiently.

3.4.3 Implementation Summary

In this section, we summarize why our approach satisfies conditions for being a good self-organizing system. The system has no single point of failure because all nodes are equal from the functionality point of view. The self-organization of mSN is achieved by mutual interaction of its nodes. No global rule is defined nor imposed, so the nodes' behavior is affected by their current knowledge only. In detail, the system fulfills following properties.

- *Scalability* The system is able to answer similarity queries within predefined costs. Communication costs can be bounded by an appropriate setting of (i) the maximum number of hops, (ii) the flooding factor intervals determining the number of nodes to which a query is forwarded, and (iii) the maximum number of friends contacted. Computational costs are influenced by the index structure managing local data and the size of query history. To speed up query processing on local data, we utilize an approximate search algorithm in M-tree. The size of query history should be kept in certain bounds to identify useful links efficiently, so the capacity of query history is 100 entries in mSN. When the query history overflows, the oldest entry gets removed.
- *Adaptability* mSN adapts to a dynamic environment in terms of changing data and user tastes. Firstly, new nodes joining the system advertise their data efficiently by executing several queries. Secondly, randomness in the routing algorithm ensures fast location of unvisited parts of the system, so even the first answer is of a satisfactory quality and it further improves. Due to aging of entries in the query history, the system also adapts to changes in nodes' local data.
- *Robustness* The nodes do not depend on any other node. When a node asks another node to do a task (to process or forward a query, to update its query history, etc.) and the node does not respond within a predefined timeout, all links pointing to this faulty node can be removed and a different node can be asked to complete the task. After a massive physical communication network failure, the system can split into two systems, each of them continuing their existence independently.

Our system is implemented based on the proposed three-layer model for self-organizing search systems but the real use of mSN is not possible because we do not deal with security issues, trust management, and resilience against malicious attacks.

3.5 Experimental Evaluation of mSN

To proof the concept of the proposed three-layer model, the functionality of implemented mSN was tested. Descriptive features of 10 million images taken from the CoPhIR [12] collection were used as a dataset. The description of the extracted features and the distance function used to define the metric space is given in Sect. 211. Recall that the features of each image forms a 280-dimensional vector. The distance distribution of the dataset is quite uniform and such a high-dimensional data space is extremely sparse. Figure 3.5b depicts distance density of this dataset.

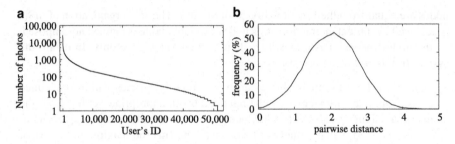

Fig. 3.5 (**a**) Number of photos per user. (**b**) Distance density of the image dataset

With respect to the nature of indexed data, there are two different approaches to the method of assigning the data to nodes in the network. Firstly, the data can be assigned to a node regarding the objects mutual distances. Thus, the objects being close to each other are assigned to the same node. The method implemented by us incorporated the transformation of the vector into one-dimensional space and afterwards an data assignment algorithm for P2P networks based on M-Chord [39]. Secondly, since each image contains information about the owner, the nodes can represent the users and the data the images they own. Figure 3.5a demonstrates the photo count per user in the image data set. As can be seen a substantial number of users have a really small photo count. Since we have been limited by hardware to a certain maximum number of nodes, we had to group users with small photo count to fit the whole database to the available nodes.

3.5.1 Measures

The properties of the answer to the processed query have been quantified using following measures. The *approximate* answer corresponds to the combined answer gained by mSN and the *total* answer corresponds to the precise answer.

- *Recall* – A ratio of the size of the approximative answer gained from mSN to the size of the total answer in percent.
- *Costs* – A number of nodes contacted by the routing algorithm in order to either forward the query or to process it on local data.
- *EOPP* – A normalized error on nodes' positions gaining values from the interval [0, 1]. It expresses the accuracy of approximate search. The approximate and the total answer are ordered lists of nodes (that participated in answering) by the distance of node's nearest object to the query object. The formula is defined as:

$$EOPP = \frac{\sum_{i=1}^{|Approx|} Total[Node_i] - Approx[Node_i]}{|Approx| \cdot |Total|} \tag{3.9}$$

where *Approx* stands for the approximate answer and *Total* for the total answer. The *Approx[Node]* denotes the position of the node *Node* in the ordered list *Approx*. If *EOPP* = 0, the approximate and the total answer are equal. The higher value *EOPP* has, the more inaccurate the answers are. If the approximate answer was found on 10 nodes, and the total is located on 20 nodes and *EOPP* = 0.1, the first two nodes from the total answer are missed. In the case of *EOPP* = 0.5, the first half of nodes from the ordered total answer is missed.

- *mSN-NER* – A number of nodes that returned a non-empty answer to a query processed by mSN.
- *Total-NER* – A number of all relevant nodes to a processed query – non-empty answering nodes in the total answer.
- *NER-ratio* – A ratio of *mSN-NER* and *Total-NER*.

Concerning the legibility purposes, notice that the measured values are in some figures multiplied by a constant – usually 10 or 1,000.

3.5.2   Analysis of Self-Adaptability

The self-adaptability of the proposed network represents the ability to process unseen queries that have not been processed before, well and to improve response to repeatedly processed queries. Ideally, the recall of the newly processed query should not be lower than the random access and should be acquired with considerable costs. As for repeatedly processed queries, their recall should rise together with lowering costs.

To analyze the self-adaptability of the network to newly coming and repeated queries, the following experiment has been conducted. The methodology is to iteratively execute a series of testing queries whose metadata is stored to the particular nodes' query history. After such executed series, a subset of this series is used to measure the adaptability of the network. This processing does not affect the state of the network since the metadata is not stored to nodes' query history. Moreover, for each particular query regardless to the state of the network, P_{start} was chosen randomly from all nodes in the network. The distance density of the set of testing queries is in Fig. 3.6.

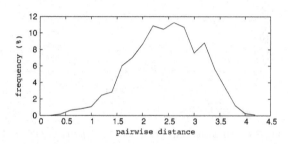

Fig. 3.6 Distance density of the set of 50 testing queries

To give the reader the insight into the dependence of the network size onto the
self-adaptability, two sizes of network were used for each data assignment approach,
their properties are summarized in Table 3.2. In the case of the similarity clustering
assignment method, the smaller dataset was acquired by randomly selecting 500
nodes of the larger network. In the case of the data owner assignment method, the
smaller network was acquired by taking the 2.5-million dataset and distributing it
over nodes according to the original owner.

3.5.3 Clustered-Data Assignment Evaluation

Figure 3.7 depicts the results measured on the two networks where data were assigned to the nodes using the method of similar distances. The settings used for
these networks varied in the number of maximal hops in the query routing algorithm. In the smaller network, the maximal number of hops was four and in the
larger one it was set to five. All the processed queries were range queries with the
radius $r = 1$. The average total answer comprised of 1,708 objects on the smaller
network and 6,880 on the large one.

The progress of the recall curve in both cases has the same ascending trend. The
zeroth measuring was obtained after all nodes joined to the system using the bootstrap protocol. The smaller network accessed a half of its nodes and retrieved about
40% of the total answer whereas the larger network accessed about 18% of its nodes
and achieved recall of 17%. After 20 iterations, the achieved maxima are 90% on the
smaller network and 84% on the larger one. Yet, concerning the adaptability, after
second iteration the recalls were 60% and 52%, respectively. Notice that in Fig. 3.6 it
is illustrated that most queries from the testing set have their mutual distance greater
than one. From the routing algorithm point of view, the presence of metadata about
such queries in nodes' query history does not affect the routing itself – it seems that
the queries are processed independently on each other.

Table 3.2 Properties of analyzed networks	Network size	Object count
	500 nodes	2,500,000
	2,000 nodes	10,000,000

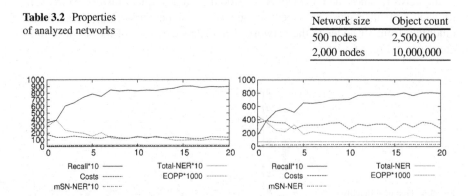

Fig. 3.7 Self-adaptability of the 500 nodes (*left*) and 2,000 nodes (*right*) networks where the data
is assigned according to similar distances

As for the costs, the primary expectations were that the costs will diminish with each iteration dramatically. This trend can be observed for both networks, yet its progress is not as fast as expected. This is due to contacting random nodes in order to achieve the consistency of the combined answer and for exploration reasons. Still, the reader can observe certain drop in costs accompanied with considerable rise of recall.

We also compared our results to the results of M-Chord – a structure whose data clustering method was used. The idea of clustering is to divide the data set into groups using the iDistance method [30]. Thus, each group corresponds to the data assigned to one node. We processed the same 20 measuring queries by M-Chord and monitored the costs. Since M-Chords always retrieves the total answer, 266 nodes were contacted on average in order to process the query on the smaller network and 945 nodes on the larger network. Therefore, we can state that for instance, after processing of five identical queries in the network, we get 65% of the total answers with 33% of costs of the M-Chord structure. This difference increases hand in hand with further processing of the same or similar queries.

Another way to express the quality of mSN's answer is to study the EOPP coefficient. Ideally, the EOPP should remain in low numbers which would mean that the routing algorithm contacted nodes that contain the most similar parts of the total answer. As can be observed in Fig. 3.7 for both networks, the progress is auspicious. In case of the larger network, the lowest values are actually higher than the values of the smaller one. This is caused by the smaller ratio of *mSN-NER* and *Total-NER* and by the fact that the routing algorithm favors the nodes with larger amounts of relevant objects rather than those with closer objects. This error propagates more into evaluation of the EOPP.

3.5.4 Data-Owner Assignment Evaluation

The results gained by the data-owner clustering method have already been presented in [4]. Figures 3.8 and 3.9 depict the averages measured on the smaller and larger networks. All the queries used were the same as in the clustered-data experiments.

Again, the progress of the recall curve in both cases has the same ascending trend. The initial recall in the smaller network is larger than in the larger one – the

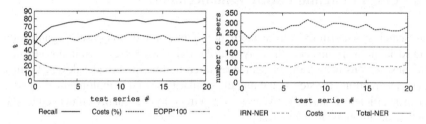

Fig. 3.8 Self-adaptability of the smaller network

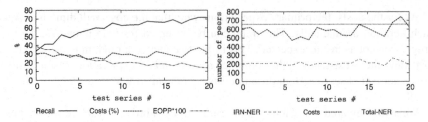

Fig. 3.9 Self-adaptability of the larger network

smaller network accessed 52% of its nodes and retrieved about 47% of the total answer whereas the larger network accessed about 28% of its nodes and achieved recall of 32%. After 20 iterations, the achieved maxima of recall are 80% in the smaller network and 71% in the larger one.

To compare the costs, the total answer to each of the training queries was obtained by flooding the whole network. The average value measured is depicted in Fig. 3.8 as the Total-NER. As can be observed in the case of the smaller network, the total answer is spread on average over 36% of the total amount of nodes. The image retrieval network has to contact on average 55% of the network after ten iterations to locate 77% of the total answer. In the case of the larger network, see Fig. 3.9, the total answer is spread on 33% of the nodes in the network, and the search algorithm contacted on average after ten iterations 30% of the network to reach 60% of the recall. After 20 iterations, the recall on the larger network is on average 72%. The recall achieved grows slower on the larger network which is due to the slower learning ability and lower proportions of nodes contacted in order to locate the answer.

As we see, the numbers measured are proving the scalability of the proposed system, since the spread of the answer among nodes grows linearly, the recall does not degrade significantly and still, we observe a decrease in the costs. The quality of approximation is again studied by the EOPP coefficient. The results are depicted in Figs. 3.8 and 3.9, where the progress is again auspicious. The trends should be strictly decreasing, which means that the algorithm retrieves from the network in each step more relevant parts of the answer. As we see the EOPP of mSN follows such progress.

3.6 Conclusion and Future Enhancements

Our search system (mSN) whose nature lies in the combination of self-organization and social networking is not the only contribution of work presented in this chapter. The abstractions behind the presented research outline the broader design leading toward a creation of systems enabling the similarity search in multimedia data with intrinsic efficiency (and effectiveness), yet being only marginally influenced by the Web-scale amounts of indexed data.

As is proven in the practical part of this work, such design addresses problems coming along efforts of building large-scale distributed databases – the problem of limited or even lacking control of the data distribution over nodes in the built system. Such a setting demands modern adaptive approaches whose design is supported by the rules given in this chapter.

mSN, developed using the universal design guidelines, is an example of a strict system in which every participating entity conducts in a good will. Although one of the experimental evaluation scenarios presents a real-life deployment of this structure, the real life use is not possible because the issues regarding trust as partially mentioned in Sect. 3.2.2 are not implemented.

Since the proposed three-layer model allows a combination of multiple self-organization concepts, the future work will focus on the study of these concepts and their suitability for various tasks in a good self-organizing search system. For instance, this means the combination of social networking for discovery of the desired resources and the ant-colony approach facilitating the lookup of the shortest path to such resources and the path's aging, like the pheromones do. These issues also lead to the management of query history in general, which is omitted in the presented version of mSN. Other improvements that are under investigation comprise of the efficiency in node communication like piggy-backing during query evaluation and agents trading information in order to improve search results.

Acknowledgments Partially supported by the EU IST FP6 project 045128 (SAPIR), the Czech Science Foundation projects 201/07/P240 and 102/05/H050.

References

1. Ashby WR (1962) Principles of the self-organizing system. In: Principles of Self-Organization, Pergamon Press, New York, NY, pp 255–278
2. Aspnes J, Shah G (November 2007) Skip graphs. ACM Trans Algor 3(4):37:1–37:25
3. Banaei-Kashani F, Shahabi C (2004) SWAM: a family of access methods for similarity-search in peer-to-peer data networks. In: Proceedings of the 13th ACM conference on information and knowledge management (CIKM 2004). ACM, Springer-Verlag Heidelberg, Margherita di Pula, Cagliari, Italy, pp 304–313
4. Bartoň S, Dohnal V, Sedmidubský J, Zezula P (2008) Building self-organized image retrieval network. In: Proceedings of the 6th workshop on large-scale distributed systems for information retrieval (LSDS-IR 2008). ACM, New York, USA, pp 51–58
5. Batko M, Gennaro C, Zezula P (2005) Similarity grid for searching in metric spaces. In: DELOS workshop: digital library architectures. Lecture notes in computer science, Springer-Verlag Heidelberg, Margherita di Pula, Cagliari, Italy, vol 3664/2005:25–44
6. Batko M, Novak D, Falchi F, Zezula P (2006) On scalability of the similarity search in the world of peers. In: Proceedings of the 1st international conference on scalable information systems (INFOSCALE 2006). ACM, Hong Kong, May 30–1 June, pp 1–12
7. Beer S (1966) Decision and control: the meaning of operational research and management cybernetics. Wiley, New York
8. Blaze M, Feigenbaum J, Lacy J (1996) Decentralized trust management. In: Proceedings of the IEEE symposium on security and privacy. IEEE Computer Society, pp 164–173

9. Blaze M, Feigenbaum J, Strauss M (1998) Compliance checking in the policymaker trust management system. In: Proceedings of the 2nd international conference on financial cryptography (FC 1998). Springer, London, UK, pp 254–274

10. Blaze M, Feigenbaum J, Ioannidis J, Keromytis AD (1999) The role of trust management in distributed systems security. In: Secure internet programming. Springer, Berlin, pp 185–210

11. Blaze M, Ioannidis J, Keromytis AD (2002) Trust management for IPsec. ACM Trans Inform Syst Secur 5(2):95–118

12. Bolettieri P, Esuli A, Falchi F, Lucchese C, Perego R, Piccioli T, Rabitti F (2009) CoPhIR: a test collection for content-based image retrieval. CoRR abs/0905.4627. http://cophir.isti.cnr.it/

13. Bonabeau E, Dorigo M, Theraulaz G (1999) Swarm intelligence: from natural to artificial systems. Oxford University Press, New York, NY, USA

14. Camazine S, Franks NR, Sneyd J, Bonabeau E, Deneubourg JL, Theraula G (2001) Self-organization in biological systems. Princeton University Press, Princeton, NJ, USA

15. Cao UY, Fukunaga AS, Kahng AB (March 1997) Cooperative mobile robotics: antecedents and directions. Auton Robot 4(1):7–27

16. Caro GD, Ducatelle F, Gambardella LM (2005) Anthocnet: an adaptive nature-inspired algorithm for routing in mobile ad hoc networks. Eur Trans Telecommun 16:443–455

17. Chater N, Vitanyi PM (2003) The generalized universal law of generalization. J Math Psychol 47(3):346–369

18. Ciaccia P, Patella M, Zezula P (1997) M-tree: an efficient access method for similarity search in metric spaces. In: Jarke M, Carey MJ, Dittrich KR, Lochovsky FH, Loucopoulos P, Jeusfeld MA (eds) Proceedings of the 23rd international conference on very large data bases (VLDB 1997). Morgan Kaufmann, Athens, Greece, pp 426–435, 25–29 August 1997

19. Crespo A, Garcia-Molina H (2002) Routing indices for peer-to-peer systems. In: Proceedings of the 22nd international conference on distributed computing systems (ICDCS 2002). IEEE Computer Society, Washington, DC, USA, p 23

20. Crespo A, Garcia-Molina H (2004) Semantic overlay networks for p2p systems. In: Proceedings of the 3rd international workshop on agents and peer-to-peer computing (AP2PC 2004), New York, NY, USA, 19 July 2004. Lecture notes in computer science, vol 3601. Springer, pp 1–13

21. Dohnal V, Gennaro C, Savino P, Zezula P (2003) D-Index: distance searching index for metric data sets. Multimed Tool Appl, 21(1):9–33

22. Dorigo M, Stützle T (2004) Ant colony optimization. MIT, Cambridge, MA

23. Doulkeridis C, Vlachou A, Kotidis Y, Vazirgiannis M (2007) Peer-to-peer similarity search in metric spaces. In: Koch C, Gehrke J, Garofalakis MN, Srivastava D, Aberer K, Deshpande A, Florescu D, Chan CY, Ganti V, Kanne CC, Klas W, Neuhold EJ (eds) Proceedings of 33rd international conference on very large data bases (VLDB 2007), 23–27 Sept 2007, University of Vienna. ACM, Austria, pp 986–997

24. Falchi F, Gennaro C, Zezula P (2007) A content-addressable network for similarity search in metric spaces. In:Databases, information systems, and peer-to-peer computing. International workshops, DBISP2P 2005/2006, Trondheim, Norway, 28–29 August 2005, Seoul, Korea, 11 Sept 2006. Revised selected papers. Lecture notes in computer science, vol 4125. Springer, August 2007, pp 98–110

25. Gennaro C, Mordacchini M, Orlando S, Rabitti F (2007) MRoute: A peer-to-peer routing index for similarity search in metric spaces. In: Proceedings of the 5th international workshop on databases, information systems and peer-to-peer computing (DBISP2P 2007). VLDB Endowment, pp 1–12, September 2007

26. Gershenson C, Heylighen F (2005) How can we think the complex? In: Richardson K (ed) Managing organizational complexity: philosophy, theory and application, chap 3, pp 47–61. Information Age Publishing

27. Granovetter M (May 1973) The strength of week ties. Am J Sociol 78(6):1360–1380.

28. Heylighen F (2001) The Science of Self-organization and Adaptivity. In: Kiel LD (ed) Knowledge Management, Organizational Intelligence and Learning, and Complexity. In: The Encyclopedia of Life Support Systems ((EOLSS), (Eolss Publishers, Oxford). [http://www.eolss.net]

29. Holland JH (1992) Adaptation in natural and artificial systems. MIT, Cambridge, MA, USA
30. Jagadish HV, Ooi BC, Tan KL, Yu C, Zhang R (2005) iDistance: an adaptive B^+-tree based indexing method for nearest neighbor search. ACM Trans Data Base Syst (TODS 2005) 30(2):364–397
31. Johnson S (2002) Emergence: the connected lives of ants, brains, cities, and software. Scribner, September 2002
32. Kagal L, Cost S, Finin T, Peng Y (2001) A framework for distributed trust management. In: Proceedings of IJCAI-01 workshop on autonomy, delegation and control, Seattle, August 6, 2001
33. Linari A, Patella M (2007) Metric overlay networks: processing similarity queries in p2p databases. In: Proceedings of the 5th international workshop on databases, information systems and peer-to-peer computing (DBISP2P 2007). VLDB Endowment
34. Mahmoud Q (2007) Cognitive networks: toward self-aware networks. Wiley-Interscience
35. Manjunath B, Salembier P, Sikora T (eds)(2002) Introduction to MPEG-7:multimedia content description interface. Wiley, New York, NY, USA
36. Michlmayr E (2007) Ant algorithms for self-organization in social networks. PhD thesis, TU Wien, May 2007
37. Milgram S (1967) The small world problem. Psychol Today 2(1):60–67
38. Nicolis G, Prigogine I (1977) Self-organization in nonequilibrium systems. Wiley, New York
39. Novak D, Zezula P (2006) M-Chord: a scalable distributed similarity search structure. In: Proceedings of first international conference on scalable information systems (INFOSCALE 2006). IEEE Computer Society, Hong Kong, May 30–1 June, pp 1–10
40. Prehofer C, Bettstetter C (2005) Self-organization in communication networks: principles and design paradigms. Commun Mag 43(7):78–85
41. Ratnasamy S, Francis P, Handley M, Karp R, Schenker S (2001) A scalable content-addressable network. In: Proceedings of the 2001 conference on applications, technologies, architectures, and protocols for computer communications (SIGCOMM 2001). ACM, San Diego, CA, 27–31 August 2001, pp 161–172
42. Samet H (1984) The quadtree and related hierarchical data structures. ACM Comput Surv (CSUR 1984) 16(2):187–260
43. Samet H (2006) Foundations of multidimensional and metric data structures. The morgan kaufmann series in data management systems. Morgan Kaufmann
44. Sedmidubský J, Bartoň S, Dohnal V, Zezula P (2007) Querying similarity in metric social networks. In: Proceedings of the 1st international conference on network-based information systems (NBIS 2007), Regensburg, Germany, 3–7 September 2007. Lecture notes in computer science, vol 4658. Springer, pp 278–287
45. Sedmidubský J, Bartoň S, Dohnal V, Zezula P (2008) Adaptive approximate similarity searching through metric social networks. In: Proceedings of the 24th international conference on data engineering (ICDE 2008), Extended abstract, pp 1424–1426. IEEE Computer Society, Los Alamitos, CA
46. Sedmidubský J, Bartoň S, Dohnal V, Zezula P (2008) A self-organized system for content-based search in multimedia. In: Proceedings of the IEEE international symposium on multimedia (ISM 2008). IEEE Computer Society, Los Alamitos, CA 90720-1314, pp 322–327
47. Shepard RN (1987) Toward a universal law of generalization for psychological science. Science 237(4820):1317–1323
48. Stoica I, Morris R, Karger DR, Kaashoek FM, Balakrishnan H (2001) Chord: a scalable peer-to-peer lookup service for internet applications. In: Proceedings of the 2001 conference on applications, technologies, architectures, and protocols for computer communications (SIGCOMM 2001). ACM, San Diego, CA, 27–31 August 2001, pp 149–160
49. Stutzbach D, Rejaie R (2006) Understanding churn in peer-to-peer networks. In: Proceedings of the 6th ACM SIGCOMM conference on Internet measurement (IMC 2006). ACM, New York, NY, USA, pp 189–202
50. Sun YL, Han Z, Yu W, Liu KJR (2006) A trust evaluation framework in distributed networks: Vulnerability analysis and defense against attacks. In: Proceedings of 25th IEEE international

conference on computer communications. Joint conference of the IEEE computer and communications societies (INFOCOM 2006), 23–29 April 2006, IEEE, Barcelona, Catalunya, Spain, pp 230–236

51. Tang C, Xu Z, Dwarkadas S (2003) Peer-to-peer information retrieval using self-organizing semantic overlay networks. In: Proceedings of the 2003 conference on applications, technologies, architectures, and protocols for computer communications (SIGCOMM 2003). ACM, New York, NY, USA, pp 175–186

52. Tanin E, Harwood A, Samet H (2005) A distributed quadtree index for peer-to-peer settings. In: Proceedings of the 21st international conference on data engineering (ICDE 2005), 5–8 April 2005, IEEE Computer Society, Tokyo, Japan, pp 254–255

53. Treherne J, Foster W (August 1981) Group transmission of predator avoidance behaviour in a marine insect: the trafalgar effect. Anim Behav 29(3):911–917

54. Uhlmann JK (1991) Satisfying general proximity or similarity queries with metric trees. Inform Process Lett 40(4):175–179

55. Wasserman S, Faust K, Iacobucci D (November 1994) Social network analysis : methods and applications (structural analysis in the social sciences). Cambridge University Press

56. Weikum G, Mönkeberg A, Hasse C, Zabback P (2002) Self-tuning database technology and information services: from wishful thinking to viable engineering. In: 28th international conference on very large databases (VLDB 2002). Morgan Kaufmann, Hongkong, China, pp 20–31

57. Yianilos PN (1993) Data structures and algorithms for nearest neighbor search in general metric spaces. In: Proceedings of the 4th annual ACM symposium on discrete algorithms (SODA 1993). ACM, Austin, TX, USA, 25–27 January 1993, pp 311–321

58. Zezula P, Amato G, Dohnal V, Batko M (2005) Similarity search: the metric space approach, vol 32. Advances in database systems. Springer, New York, NY, USA

Chapter 4
DISSECT: Data-Intensive Socially Similar Evolving Community Tracker

Alvin Chin and Mark Chignell

Abstract This chapter examines the problem of tracking community in social networks inferred from online interactions by tracking evolution of known subgroups over time. Finding subgroups within social networks is important for understanding and possibly influencing the formation and evolution of online communities. A variety of approaches have been suggested to address this problem and the corresponding research literature on centrality, clustering, and optimization methods for finding subgroupings is reviewed. This review will include a critical analysis of the limitations of past approaches. The focus of the chapter will then turn to novel methods for tracking online community interaction. First, the method proposed by Chin and Chignell called SCAN will be briefly introduced, where a combination of heuristic methods is used to identify subgroups in a manner that can potentially scale up to very large social networks. Then, we present the DISSECT method where multiple known subgroups within a social network are tracked in terms of similarity-based cohesiveness over time. The DISSECT method relies on cluster analysis of snapshots of network activity at different points in time followed by similarity analysis of subgroup evolution over successive time periods. The DISSECT method can be supplemented with behavioral measures of sense of community where administration of a questionnaire is feasible. Finally, we conclude the chapter with a discussion on possible applications and use of the DISSECT method.

A. Chin (✉)
Nokia Research Center, Building 2, No. 5 Donghuan Zhonglu, Economic and Technological Development Area, Beijing 100176, China
e-mail: alvin.chin@nokia.com

M. Chignell
Department of Mechanical and Industrial Engineering, University of Toronto, 5 King's College Road, Toronto, Ontario, M5S 3G8, Canada
e-mail: chignell@mie.utoronto.ca

A. Abraham et al. (eds.), *Computational Social Network Analysis*, Computer Communications and Networks, DOI 10.1007/978-1-84882-229-0_4,
© Springer-Verlag London Limited 2010

4.1 Introduction

For many people and organizations, the Internet has become a place where communication interactions occur, supplanting part of the functionality of face-to-face meetings and group interactions. With the growth of social networking on the Internet and Web 2.0 functions such as blogging, social tagging, and video sharing, more and more information is becoming available online about how people interact and with whom. Vast social hypertexts [36] are forming on the World Wide Web as networks of documents are increasingly being connected explicitly and implicitly to networks of people, and on a grand scale. Rich online social networks may be inferred relatively easily from blogs, Web forums, e-mail, and the emergence of Web 2.0 [86]. Web sites incorporating around tags, social bookmarks, podcasts, and mashups are examples of social hypertexts, where Web pages are nodes in a social network and hyperlinks between pages form links (relationships) between the nodes [21]. Feedback on Web pages foster online conversation, creating explicit links between authors and readers. It is now possible to infer social behavior from studying the relationships between nodes and patterns of communication that are formed from these communication media, using social network analysis [46]. As people communicate with each other through networks of interconnected Web pages, common ties may be established and social interactions may develop [8, 31, 38, 61, 93, 115], leading in some cases to a sense of virtual community [8] that may sometimes be analogous to the sense of community that people develop in physical environments [17].

When analyzing the social networks formed from online interaction, the focus can be on using graph structure (nodes and links) or on semantics (content analysis and text analysis). Previous research has shown that cohesive subgroups form communities of interest [29], have weak ties [46], and have cohesive bonds that bring people together [90]. Research on finding cohesive subgroups of online interactions within social networks remains an interesting and open issue.

Finding cohesive subgroups can be used as a first step to identify communities of interest that people belong to. Tags can then be assigned to the subgroups by using semantic analysis to form meta-tags that describe the interests or the expertise of a group of people. The assigned tags can then be used for activities such as marketing research, advertising, and expertise location. For instance, someone who seems to be actively involved in a number of communities involving Linux and its applications is likely to have expertise that is relevant to Linux problems, or to know someone else who has that expertise.

Online social networks evolve over time, and research has looked into the temporal aspects of social networks changing over time (e.g. [72, 100]). It has been found that groups discovered in social networks differ in their cohesiveness or bonding [90], which can be in time or space. Since online social networks have time inherent in their structure, cohesive subgroups can be defined as those that are similar over time based on Social Identity Theory [103] where group members feel closer if they are similar to each other. Cohesive subgroups can also be considered as optimum subgroups by calculating the optimum number of clusters [62], modularity [85], or optimizing graphs [104]. Similarity measures are used in our research to assess the cohesiveness of subgroups. Since they explicitly consider changes in subgroupings over time, similar measures take into account network membership dynamics in the social network. Different types of similar measures can be constructed depending on the particular network dynamics observed.

This chapter addresses the problem of tracking community in social networks inferred from online interactions, by expanding on the problem of finding subgroups initially explored through the SCAN method [22] and addressing the limitations of the SCAN method. The first section of the chapter provides the literature review of research that can be used for finding subgroups for tracking community. This forms the basis for the creation and explanation of our SCAN method in the second section, which addresses the drawbacks of previous research. In addition, we describe the applications and limitations of the SCAN method. This results in the creation of a new framework called Data-Intensive Socially Similar Evolving Community Tracker or DISSECT as described in the third section, where multiple known subgroups within a social network are tracked in terms of similarity-based cohesiveness over time. We also discuss the implications of DISSECT for community evolution, and the evaluation of DISSECT using behavioral measures. Practical applications of the DISSECT approach in expertise location, marketing, and information search are discussed in the conclusions section of the chapter.

4.2   Finding Subgroups for Tracking Community

In this section, we review previous literature on finding subgroups in social networks. This work can be differentiated according to the different types of measure or structure that are targeted: centrality, cohesive subgroups and clustering, and similarity.

4.2.1   Centrality

Network centrality (or centrality) [44] is used to identify the most important/active people at the center of a network or those that are well connected. Numerous centrality measures such as degree [40, 45, 79, 116], closeness [19, 70, 75], betweenness [30, 47, 49, 57, 76, 85, 106, 108], information [25, 26, 42], eigenvector [37, 84, 95], and dependence centrality [78, 79] have been used for characterizing the social behavior and connectedness of nodes within networks. The logic of using centrality measures is that people who are actively involved in one or more subgroups will generally score higher with respect to centrality scores for the corresponding network.

Researchers have compared and contrasted centrality measures in various social networks (e.g. [19, 34, 66, 80]), however three centrality measures which have been referred to the most with respect to subgroup membership are degree, closeness, and betweenness centrality.

Degree centrality [44] measures the number of direct connections that an individual node has to other nodes within a network. Nodes with high degree centrality have been shown to be more active [45] and influential [79]. Degree distribution has been used to visualize the role of nodes within subgroups [116]. *Closeness centrality* [44] measures how many steps on average it takes for an individual node to reach every other node in the network. In principle, nodes with high closeness centrality should be able to connect more efficiently or easily with other nodes, making them more likely to participate in subgroups. Closeness centrality has been used to identify important nodes within social networks [26, 70, 75], and identify members with a strong sense of community [19,20]. *Betweenness centrality* measures the extent to which a node can act as an intermediary or broker to other nodes [44]. The more times that a particular node lies on paths that exist between other pairs of nodes in the network, the higher the betweenness centrality is for that node. Nodes that have a high betweenness centrality may act as brokers between subgroups and they may have stronger membership in surrounding communities [30, 47]. Betweenness centrality has been used to reveal the hierarchical structure of organizations [49, 106, 108], and to identify opinion leaders [76] and influential members with a strong sense of community in blogs [19,20].

Betweenness centrality is mostly used to find and measure subgroup and community membership [47–49, 76, 85, 106, 108], whereas degree and closeness centrality are used for characterizing influential members. Although network centrality measures are easy to calculate using computer programs such as Pajek [28] and UCINET [9], there has been no consensus among researchers as to the most meaningful centrality measure to use for finding subgroup members [25]. In extremely large social networks, computational efficiency may become an issue in selecting which centrality measure to use. With respect to three commonly used centrality measures, degree centrality is the easiest to calculate, closeness centrality is more complex, and betweenness centrality has the highest calculation complexity [18].

4.2.2   Cohesive Subgroups and Clustering

Finding cohesive subgroups within social networks is a problem that has attracted considerable interest (e.g. [42, 92, 102, 114]), because cohesive subgroups can indicate the most active members within a community. There are two types of approaches to finding cohesive subgroups. In the first approach, clique analysis and related methods look directly at the links that occur in a network and identify specific patterns of connectivity (e.g., subgroups where everyone in the subgroup has a direct connection to everyone else). In the second approach, clustering and partitioning methods are used which are less direct (but more computationally efficient) in that they base their groupings (clusters) on proximity measures (similarities or distances) derived from the connection patterns between network nodes.

4.2.2.1   Clique and k-Plex Analysis

Cliques and k-plexes have been used to characterize groupings in social networks [2, 5, 21, 32, 92, 102, 113]. Cliques are fully connected subgroups [113] where each member has a direct connection to every other member in the subgroup, thus forming a completely connected graph within the subgroup. Pure cliques tend to be rare in social networks [102] because the criterion of full connectedness tends to be overly strict, thus pure clique analysis will miss many meaningful subgroupings [2, 5, 113].

In a subgroup of n members, the full connectedness requirement of cliques (where every person in the clique is connected to $n - 1$ other members in the clique), may be relaxed by requiring fewer connections to other group members. In the *k-plex* approach, connectedness is expressed as the minimum number $n - k$ of connections that each person in the group must have to the other group members. In a k-plex, as the parameter k increases, the connectedness requirement is relaxed [54]. k-Plex analysis has been used for finding subgroup members [5, 21, 82, 102] in a network. However, as with clique analysis, finding k-plexes in large networks is a computationally expensive and exhaustive process because it scales exponentially with the number of nodes in the network and is an NP-complete problem [5]. An additional issue with k-plex analysis is that the most appropriate value of k for subgroup analysis in a particular social network may not be obvious.

4.2.2.2   Clustering and Partitioning

Clustering and other techniques such as link analysis [10, 65] and co-citation analysis [1, 41, 64, 67–69] can be used to detect subgroups within social hypertext networks. Hierarchical clustering automates the process of finding subgroups by grouping nodes into a cluster if the nodes are similar and then successively merging clusters until all nodes have been merged into a single remaining cluster. Techniques based on hierarchical clustering have been used to quantify the structure of community in Web pages [24, 30, 47, 73], blogs [88, 89], and discussion groups [50]. Hierarchical clustering (using such algorithms as in [55, 118]) results in a hierarchy (tree) being formed where the leaves of the tree are the nodes that are clustered and can be visualized as dendrograms. Nested clusters within the derived hierarchy may then be inferred to be subgroups.

In contrast to hierarchical cluster analysis, the groups formed in partitioning methods are not nested. Partitioning methods are relatively efficient, but they require that the number of subgroups in the partition be defined prior to the analysis. On the other hand, hierarchical cluster analysis does not yield a partition, and the hierarchy (dendrogram) that is output needs to be cut in order to identify a particular set of subgroups. For partition analysis, the method is run using a number of different values of k (i.e., number of groups in the partition) and the selection criterion is used to define which of the possible partitions should be chosen as the best subgrouping. For hierarchical clustering, the selection criterion is used to decide at which point the dendrogram should be cut in order to obtain a non-nested set of subgroups.

Orford [87] described a range of criteria for determining where to partition a dendrogram; however, the best criterion to use will generally vary with the problem context. Recent research has tended to assess specific measures for obtaining an optimal partition (e.g. [62]), using modularity (designated as Q) proposed by Newman and Girvan [85] for finding community structure in [7, 27, 33, 91, 94], vector partitioning [111] or normalized cut metrics [71, 97, 98, 117]. However, as noted by Radicchi et al. [91], it is not clear whether the "optimal" partitions are representative of real collaborations in the corresponding online communities. Van Duijn and Vermunt [110] noted that it is difficult to determine which measure is the most appropriate to use across a range of applications.

4.2.2.3 Summary

Hierarchical clustering has been shown to produce similar subgroupings as k-plex analysis and is less computationally intensive [22]. Modularity has been proposed as an optimizing method for partitioning dendrograms obtained from hierarchical clustering into subgroupings. Researchers (such as Lin et al. [74] and Traud et al. [105]) have combined clustering and partitioning algorithms together in order to identify subgroups instead of relying on one alone. However, relatively little evaluative research has been carried out thus far on which methods of unsupervised subgroup formation work well in subgroup analysis of social networks, and under what conditions.

4.2.3 Similarity

Cohesive subgroups should have a core group of people that remain the same over different time periods, because we hypothesize that subgroups will be cohesive to the extent that their members remain together based on "common fate" [109] where objects are more likely to be part of a grouping if they move together over time. However, subgroups may split or merge, so that cohesiveness is not necessarily a property of a single subgroup, but may sometimes relate to a family of one or more related subgroups. In general, cohesive families of subgroups at one time period should be similar to corresponding subgroups at a different time period.

Mathematically, similarity may be viewed as a geometric property involving the scaling or transformation necessary to make objects equivalent to each other. Several mathematical similarity measures have been defined such as Euclidean distance [35] and the cosine distance or dot product [112]. Other models of similarity are based on comparison of matching and mismatching features using a set-theoretic approach such as Tversky's feature contrast model [107], Gregson's content similarity model [51], and the Jaccard coefficient [59], which is defined as the size of the intersection divided by the size of the union of the objects being compared.

For assessing cohesion within subgroups, Johnson [60] proposed the ultrametric distance as a way of measuring distance within a hierarchy. For comparing two different clustering hierarchies, one heuristic method for estimating similarity consists of converting each hierarchy to a matrix of ones and zeros where the ones represent the parent–child links in each hierarchy. The similarity between two hierarchies is then estimated as the correlation between the two corresponding matrices of ones and zeroes. A more formal approach is to use quadratic assignment [58] to assess the similarity between two partitions. Other related work by Falkowski et al. [39] focused on finding community instances using similarity.

From the preceding review, it can be seen that there are a number of similarity assessment approaches that may be applied to the problem of measuring the cohesiveness of subgroups over time. Unlike previous similarity methods, our method addresses the strength of cohesiveness of subgroups over time using a custom-built measure of similarity to meet the demands of identifying subgroups in a dynamic social network based on the content model of similarity [51].

4.3   Tracking Online Community Interactions Using the SCAN Method

A number of methods already exist for finding subgroups and clusters, but there is as of this writing no method that can potentially scale up to handle large social networks, or can identify subgroups that remain cohesive over time using an unsupervised learning approach. In this section, we explain the SCAN method and use an example to illustrate how to track online community interactions.

4.3.1   Social Cohesion Analysis of Networks (SCAN) Method

The Social Cohesion Analysis of Networks (SCAN) method was developed for automatically identifying subgroups of people in social networks that are cohesive over time [22]. The SCAN method is to be applied based on the premise that a social graph can be obtained from the online community interactions where the links are untyped (i.e., there are no associated semantics). In the social graph, each link represents an interaction between two individuals where one individual has responded to the other's post in the online community. The SCAN method has been designed to identify cohesive subgroups on the basis of social networks inferred from online interactions around common topics of interest. The SCAN method consists of the following three steps:

1. Select: Selecting potential members of cohesive subgroups from the social network.
2. Collect: Grouping these potential members into subgroups.
3. Choose: Choosing cohesive subgroups that have a similar membership over time.

4.3.1.1 Select

In the first step, the possible members of cohesive subgroups are identified. We set a cutoff value on a measure that is assumed to be correlated with likelihood of being a subgroup member, and then filter out people who fail to reach the cutoff value on that measure. We use betweenness centrality as this cutoff measure, since prior research has found that it does a fairly good job of identifying subgroup members although other centrality measures such as degree and closeness centrality could also be used. By selecting a cutoff centrality measure, we obtain a subgraph of the original social graph where all members that have a centrality below the cutoff centrality measure are removed, resulting in a list of potential active members of subgroups.

4.3.1.2 Collect

In the second step of the SCAN method, the objective is to recognize active subgroups from the subset of network members identified in the Select step. This is accomplished by forming subgroups of the selected members using cluster analysis, specifically weighted average hierarchical clustering. In general, hierarchical cluster analysis is more computationally efficient than k-plex analysis [22], and weighted average hierarchical clustering is a relatively efficient approach that has been used frequently by researchers. The output of hierarchical clustering is a set of nested, non-overlapping clusters, i.e., a tree, or dendrogram (a visual representation of a tree that is frequently used to represent a hierarchy of nested clusters visually). The extraction of the hierarchy shows potential cohesive subgroups, but it does not actually partition the people into a particular set of non-nested subgroups.

4.3.1.3 Choose

In the third step of the SCAN method, we identify the most cohesive subgroups over periods of time by computing the similarity of the possible cohesive subgroups between pairwise consecutive periods of time, and then selecting the cohesive subgroupings that result in the highest similarity. In comparing subgroups between pairwise consecutive periods of time, we need to consider networks in each period where membership is either fixed, where new members enter but existing members do not leave the network, or where new members enter and existing members leave the network at different time periods. The present version of the SCAN method only considers constant membership and new members that enter the network, through the application of two similarity measures.

For the first similarity approach (as described in detail in [22]), the cohesion across all subgroups between two consecutive time periods T_1 and T_2 can be calculated according to Eq. 4.1:

$$Sim_{T_1,T_2} = \frac{2 * N(T_1 \cap T_2)}{N(T_1 \cup T_2)} , \qquad (4.1)$$

where $N(T_1 \cap T_2)$ is the number of pairs where both members are in the same cluster in T_1 and in T_2. $N(T_1 \cup T_2)$ is the total number of pairs who are in the same cluster in either (or both) T_1 and T_2. The parameter 2 is added as a multiplier to the numerator of this expression so that the resulting similarity measure is scaled between 0 and 1.

The second similarity approach (as detailed in [18]) measures the cohesion of the largest individual subgroup. This examines all the possible pairwise relationships between members of the subgroup, and determines how many of the pairs still exist (i.e., are inside a subgroup) in the second time period. The similarity can then be calculated using the following formula according to Eq. 4.2:

$$Sim_{T_1,T_2} = \frac{N(S_1 \cap T_2)}{N(S_1)} ,$$

(4.2)

where S_1 is the largest subgroup in T_1, $N(S_1 \cap T_2)$ is the number of common pairs from the largest subgroup S_1 that still exist in T_2, and $N(S_1)$ is the number of pairs in the largest subgroup S_1. As an example, if there was a subgroup of five people which then split into a group of two and a group of three, then there would be a combination of five choose two or ten pairs from the first time period and after that there would be three choose two or three pairs remaining together in one of the spin-off groups plus one pair together in the second spin-off for a total of four pairs remaining together in the second time period, so the similarity between the two time periods would then be $4/10 = 0.4$. It can be seen that this approach results in an intuitive measure that is easy to calculate.

These measures of similarity can then be used to assess cohesiveness over time with a betweenness centrality cutoff being chosen that maximizes this measure of similarity in the sample. The clusters for each time period T_1 and T_2 that are obtained from the highest similarity using the selected betweenness centrality cutoff, then form the cohesive subgroups, with the level of measured similarity between adjacent time periods providing an indicator of the amount of cohesiveness.

4.3.2 Application and Limitations of the SCAN Method

The SCAN method was tested on the TorCamp Google group (as explained in [22]) and a set of YouTube vaccination videos and its comments (as explained in [23]). The SCAN method was able to find a cohesive subgroup in the TorCamp Google group case study even though semantics of the links between members in the social network were not utilized in this task. In general, the cohesiveness criterion using similarity and the SCAN method worked well with the TorCamp Google group because the dataset reflected online interactions of topics of common interest, from which the discussions had clearly identifiable active members based on the number of responses.

However, the method was unable to distinguish between two types of activist groups (anti-vaccination and pro-vaccination) in a set of YouTube vaccination

Table 4.1 Content analysis of the comments made on anti-vaccination and pro-vaccination videos (using the anti- and pro-labeling of videos provided by Keelan et al. [63])

Network	Number of videos	Number of anti-comments	Number of pro-comments
Anti-vaccination	34	76	6
Pro-vaccination	66	67	13

videos because the conversational threads contained mixtures of people from those two types of activist groups (anti- and pro-vaccination) as shown in Table 4.1 [23].

In datasets where online interactions revolve around debate and activism, the SCAN method will not be able to find particular classified subgroups, because these types of people are intertwined within the discussions around social media (such as the YouTube vaccination videos) and many of the comments may not be related to the discussion.

One of the remaining challenges in applying the SCAN method concerns the selection of time periods across which subgroup cohesion is compared. It seems likely that the appropriate time period will depend on how quickly a subgroup evolves or grows, and also on the size of the subgroup and the rate of interaction that occurs within the subgroup. Within each time period selected for analysis, there needs to be social interaction to allow application of the SCAN method, while it should also be possible to construct multiple periods where there is a reasonable expectation that sufficient cohesion will occur across time periods to make similarity assessment viable. While past research has examined cohesion between pairs of time windows, it is possible that in long-lasting subgroups comparison of cohesion across multiple time windows may also provide more accurate estimates of cohesion within subgroups.

4.4   Data-Intensive Socially Similar Evolving Community Tracker (DISSECT)

In this section, we outline a framework for a new method for tracking community evolution based on the SCAN method. This method is referred to as the Data-Intensive Socially Similar Evolving Community Tracker (DISSECT). The steps in this method are listed and possible techniques for implementing each step are discussed. Detailed implementation of the steps in the DISSECT method are left as topics for future research.

In the SCAN method, the problem of finding cohesive subgroups across different time periods using similarity was addressed. The DISSECT methodology provides a framework for more extensive analysis of community formation in online interactions. The DISSECT method addresses the following shortcomings of the SCAN method:

1. The SCAN method only focused on betweenness centrality; other centrality measures may be useful.
2. The SCAN method only looked into two types of similarity measures (constant membership and members entering the network); there is a need to examine for other types.
3. The time periods used in the SCAN method were defined ad hoc as a matter of convenience, without any systematic evaluation.
4. The SCAN method fails if semantic properties determine subgroup membership.

4.4.1 Framework for the DISSECT Method

The DISSECT method addresses the shortcomings identified in the SCAN method, and uses the following steps:

1. Find the initial time periods for analysis.
2. Label subgroups of people from the network dataset using content analysis and semantic properties. If possible, individuals are also labeled so as to facilitate later similarity analysis between subgroups at different time periods.
3. Select the possible members of known subgroups to be tracked using the Select step from the SCAN method.
4. Carry out cluster analysis of interaction data taken at snapshots in time and involving known subgroups of people (using the Collect step from the SCAN method).
5. Repeat steps 3 and 4 for different values of centrality (note that the DISSECT approach is agnostic in terms of which of the many available measures of centrality should be used).
6. Calculate similarity of subgroups for the designated time periods from step 1 using the clustering results of the previous step. In this case, the similarity measure can be augmented to take into account semantic labels assigned to different people. The advantage of using similarity measures that include semantics as well as link structure is that they can identify non-cohesive groups of people with heterogeneous viewpoints and affiliations who may yet have bursts of interaction during specific periods of debate.
7. Repeat steps 2 through 6 for different time period intervals and combinations.
8. Construct a chronological view of each subgroup showing how it changes over time (as the assigned semantic labels change), and also showing how subgroups merge and split in response to the changing interests of their members.

The ultimate goal in a DISSECT analysis is to trace the evolution of subgroups into communities. The DISSECT method does not stand as a theory of how communities form. However, logically it would seem that if communities do emerge out of online interactions then they are likely to evolve, initially, from smaller subgroups.

Some of the steps in the DISSECT method are now described further below.

4.4.1.1 Find the Initial Time Periods for Analysis

Here, the objective is to divide the dataset into time periods (which may be equal or unequal in duration) in order to track subgroups in the network over time. Time periods should be long enough so that there is enough data to distinguish potential subgroups, and there should be a sufficient number of them to estimate cohesion over time. Further research is needed to determine guidelines concerning what lengths and numbers of time periods should be used for different types of online interaction.

4.4.1.2 Label Subgroups of People from the Network Dataset Using Content Analysis and Semantic Properties

For each time period defined from the previous step, content analysis may be performed to label the links and/or individuals within the network. Techniques such as noun-phrase analysis [52] and other natural language-processing techniques that analyze content of the posts [53] can be used for classifying the links and the nodes. For example, in the YouTube vaccination video study as mentioned in the previous section, people were labeled based on the comments they made, and videos were labeled based on whether they were anti-vaccination or pro-vaccination in viewpoint.

4.4.1.3 Select the Possible Members of Known Subgroups that You Want to Track (from the Previous Step)

While betweenness centrality appears to be a useful filter for screening potential subgroup members, further research is required to assess when and how other centrality measurement methods might be used. In addition, more rigorous criteria (other than simple inspection of the frequency distribution) are needed for choosing the appropriate cutoff centrality in the Select step of the SCAN method. As a starting point, degree centrality may be a better criterion with which to screen potential subgroup members because it deals with direct interactions where the ties have stronger bonds that indicate stronger cohesion, and also because it has lower computational complexity than the betweenness, and closeness centrality measures.

4.4.1.4 Cluster Analysis to Infer Possible Subgroups

Once the network is screened for potential subgroup members, hierarchical clustering (e.g., weighted average hierarchical clustering) is used to group the potential members into subgroups. The output of the cluster analysis is a hierarchy (dendrogram) that contains nested subgroups of people. The nested nature of these subgroups means that hierarchical cluster analysis does not yield unambiguous subgroups (i.e., a partition) directly. In order to create a subgroup partition, the dendrogram has to be cut at a particular similarity value. Further research is needed on how best to cut dendrograms in order to obtain partitioned subgroups.

The issue of how to create subgroup partitions is likely to be particularly important in situations where multiple subgroups are expected. Orford [87] made the point that the best method for partitioning a dendrogram will depend on the type of data. It is suggested that while modularity has received recent attention in partitioning community data into subgroups, further research is needed that compares its effectiveness in this context to other potentially useful measures that have been proposed in the literature. For example, random walks have been suggested as an alternative approach for finding community structure [101].

4.4.1.5 Repeat the Steps in Sects. 4.4.1.3 and 4.4.1.4 for Different Values of Centrality

There are a number of ways in which centrality measurement and clustering or partitioning can be carried out. If we treat maximization of the subgroup similarities across time periods as the objective (criterion), then the problem of choosing the particular methodology to be used can be envisioned as a parameter search (maximization) problem where the goal is to obtain subgroupings that are maximally cohesive (self-similar) over time.

4.4.1.6 Calculating Similarity

As noted in the preceding subsection, similarity (as an indicator of cohesiveness) can be treated as an objective function to be maximized. Further research is needed to determine which similarity measures are best for finding cohesive subgroups, since Eqs. 4.1 and 4.2 were formulated from first principles and their use in this context is not, as yet, backed by research evidence. As noted elsewhere, the similarity measures that were developed in SCAN have to be modified to take into account incoming and outgoing actors from different time periods. When pairwise similarities are calculated, for each pairing of people, the pair should only be included in the analysis if both people in the pair were part of the social network for both time periods being assessed.

Other issues concern the problem of making the SCAN or DISSECT methodology scalable to very large online social networks. Subgroupings can be represented as matrices of ones and zeros (where an edge with one between two people indicates some kind of interaction with the challenge being to implement the set-theoretic similarity measure as a sequence of relatively simple operations on the two matrices of binary data). Block modeling may be one way of accomplishing this by identifying blocks of structurally similar actors within an adjacency matrix derived from social network data [3, 11, 99]. While blocks may indicate the presence of cohesive subgroups, Frank [43] has argued that blocks differ from cohesive subgroups since blocks of actors engage in common patterns of interaction throughout the network, but do not necessarily engage in the direct interactions that occur between members of cohesive subgroups. Nonetheless, block modeling could be applied to the adjacency matrix to construct possible subgroups in an alternative fashion.

4.4.1.7 Repeat Steps in Sects. 4.4.1.2 Through 4.4.1.6 for All Possible Time Period Intervals and Combinations

How do we know that the time periods that are selected initially in step 1 provide the most optimum cohesive subgroups? We need to study the effect of varying the number of time periods and the size of each time period on subgroup cohesion and similarity. There are many other methods that can be used for analyzing networks over time such as probabilistic stochastic models, time windows, and time graphs and burst analysis. For example, SIENA [100] is a network package that uses stochastic, actor-oriented models for the evolution of social networks which could be used to take all the possible configurations of the network ties and then model the observed network dynamics (the actual ties that happened in different time periods). The results could then be compared with that found from the similarity analysis in order to evaluate its performance. In addition, time windows can be defined such as in Social Networks Image Animator (SoNIA) in order to visualize the subgroups [81] and sliding time windows can be used for varying the time window to determine their effect on the formation of subgroups and their cohesiveness [39]. By representing the social interactions as time graphs that have time added to the link indicating when the social interaction happened (forming typed links), burst analysis can be used in order to discover subgraphs of bursts that indicate cohesive subgroups around a specific event [67] and to study the formation of groups [4].

No matter which method is used to define the time periods, we need to repeat the steps in Sects. 4.4.1.2 through 4.4.1.6 for each time period selected in order to determine which one provides the optimal subgroup cohesion.

4.4.2 Using DISSECT to Identify Community Evolution

As motivation for identifying community evolution, we previously used the results of our SCAN method [22] to track the subgroups within the TorCamp Google group for 2 years. Figure 4.1 visualizes the cohesive subgroups from the TorCamp Google group and shows how members in the TorCamp Google group move in and out of subgroups at different time periods. The movement of the members into clusters in different time periods is indicated by the arrows, whereas the shades of the nodes indicate (as shown in the legend) in which time period the member first appeared as a member of the subgrouping.

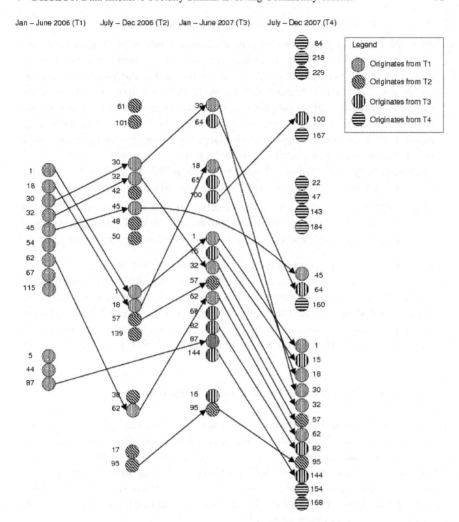

Fig. 4.1 Visualizing cohesive subgroupings in the TorCamp Google group from 2006 to 2007

Similarly, from the results of DISSECT, Communities might evolve in a number of ways. For instance:

1. A core subgroup growing until it becomes a highly centralized community

   By computing the degree and closeness centralities of each of the people in the network in each time period, we can see if the centralities and the number of members increase. This will determine which people from the core subgroup become more tightly connected to the group. If the number of members increases within the core subgroup is growing and the members are becoming more tightly connected, therefore forming into a highly centralized community.

2. A number of subgroups coalescing into a multipolar community

   At a specific time period, we can have various numbers of subgroups within an online community. These subgroups can combine to form a multipolar community in which various subgroups can be connected to each other. During the merging and community formation process, leaders or activity members within the contributing (merging) subgroups will act as bridge connectors, and the betweenness centrality of these members will likely be the highest in the overall network. One can then follow how the subgroups change with time, and track which members are more central at different times as the network evolves.

3. Coalesced subgroups forming clusters which then become affiliated in a multi-layered community which may have both centralized and multipolar aspects

   The community formed can have a core subgroup that is highly centralized but with subgroups that coalesce into a multipolar community. To find these types of subgroups, we can use techniques based on the previous steps as starting points.

Presumably many different methods of community formation occur online. The unsolved problem is how to come up with reliable and flexible algorithms for tracking a broad range of community evolution processes. To determine how well the algorithms find subgroups and the central members, we can use behavioral measures such as Sense of Community, Social Network Questionnaire, and Frequency of Ties [18] for evaluating the subgroups found in the DISSECT method.

4.4.2.1 Behavioral Measures for Evaluating Subgroups

The Sense of Community inventory [77] assesses the internal perceptions that a person has about his or her role in a community. The inventory consists of four components: membership, need, influence, and shared emotional connection. Chavis [16] created the Sense of Community Index to provide a quantitative measure for sense of community and its components. Members of cohesive subgroups have been shown to have high scores of sense of community (calculated in [16]) from our case study of the TorCamp Google group [21].

The Social Network Questionnaire (developed by Chin and Chignell [18]) is based on the Social Network List (SNL) developed by Hirsch [56] and the Social Support Questionnaire (SSQ) developed by Sarason et al. [96]. These tools are based on name generator techniques [6, 12–14, 113] in which participants are asked to name all the people that they know or communicate with (considered as ties). The Social Network Questionnaire is designed to obtain a social network of acquaintances that participants have by asking them which members that they know from the subgroups identified in DISSECT and how close their relationship is with those members.

The Frequency of Ties questionnaire (also developed by Chin and Chignell [18]) is designed to provide a more quantitative interpretation of the frequency of communication for each network tie. Participants are asked the frequency of communication using approximate number of exchanges that they have with a list of members identified as part of subgroups from the DISSECT method. This helps to determine which members of the subgroups are the most influential based on communication with other members in the network.

All three measures described above can be used to characterize the behavior of cohesive subgroup members by making correlations with centrality and the edge weights in the network (number of interactions between two members). For example, we performed correlations between sense of community, number of ties known with other members and network centrality. Table 4.2 summarizes these results.

Figure 4.2 shows that degree centrality in the TorCamp Google group tends to increase as the number of ties known increases.

According to the TorCamp Google group case study that we conducted [18], cohesive subgroup members have higher centrality scores, send more messages, have weak ties, have greater number of known ties, and have a higher sense of community

Table 4.2 Pearson correlations between Sense of Community subscales, number of ties known, and network centrality ($N = 9$) in the TorCamp Google group

Sense of community subscale	Number of ties known	Degree centrality	Betweenness centrality	Closeness centrality
Membership	0.737	0.589	−0.408	0.542
Emotional connection	0.634	0.292	−0.552	0.453
Influence	0.211	0.096	−0.398	0.182
Needs	0.089	0.173	−0.563	0.196

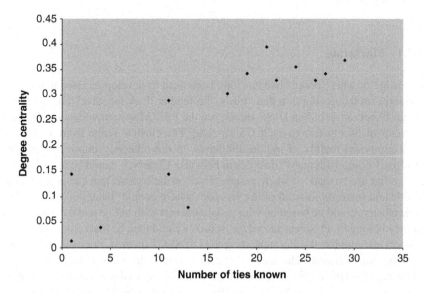

Fig. 4.2 Association of number of ties known on degree centrality

than other members that are not part of cohesive subgroups. Further research, however, is still needed to show how the results generalize to other data sets.

4.5 Conclusion

In this chapter, we propose a framework for tracking community evolution in an online community called DISSECT or Data-Intensive Socially Similar Evolving Community Tracker. This framework is an expanded and enhanced version of the SCAN method [22], for finding cohesive subgroups in online interactions. The framework is designed to be a step-by-step process to track the evolution of community members. This chapter has discussed the steps in the framework, and has raised research issues that need to be considered.

4.5.1 Applications

Given that a method now exists for tracking cohesive subgroups from large networks (of at least 200 nodes) automatically, there are many applications to which it can be used of which three examples will be briefly mentioned here

1. Marketing
2. Expertise location
3. Information search

4.5.1.1 Marketing

Knowledge of where people live has long been used to develop targeted marketing campaigns on the assumption that "birds of a feather flock together." For instance, Claritas Corporation of San Diego developed the PRIZM system which assigns one or several of 66 clusters to each US zipcode. The clusters range from #1 Upper Crust, composed mainly of multimillionaires, to the relatively impoverished #66 Low-Rise Living, with many lifestyles in between. Clearly, it would be beneficial to have similar online maps of where people "live" on the Internet that can predict their lifestyle and interests. Instead of the zipcodes where people "hang out" physically, online clusters could be based on who people interact with online and the subgroups that they belong to. Products and advertisements could then be marketed to relevant members and interested subgroups using the DISSECT method. For example, based on a subgroup of friends who are avid watchers of the television series *Lost* (identified through the DISSECT method), and given that some of those friends also watch another television series called *Heroes*, then the system would recommend the user to watch *Heroes*.

4.5.2   Expertise Location

Well-cataloged and organized maps of online communities and subgroups would also facilitate tasks such as expertise location, either by inferring expertise directly based on subgroup membership, or else by asking relevant subgroups to nominate a suitable expert who could respond knowledgeably to an inquiry once irrelevant members such as spammers have been removed. For many applications, finding the right neighborhood may be the main problem (after which "locals" can act as guides to detailed information) and labeled subgroups can serve as entry points into neighborhoods. An example of such an application could be an expert-finding application for finding experts and leaders in online environments using the SCAN method (such as blogs, video, and social networking platforms such as Facebook and MySpace). This would then allow users to contact and connect to those experts to grow their social network and engage in constructive debate and conversation.

4.5.3   Information Search

The DISSECT method may also be useful for enhancing information search practice, including search within a social network and community-based search. The first approach deals with searching for content or searching for people, using a social network as a form of filtered or targeted network compared to the broad search that is carried out today on search engines such as Google. This approach is needed because according to Cervini, "without the ability to execute directed searches, through a social network, the transition cost of finding other users within the system is simply too high to warrant using the system" [15]. Applications such as Social Network and Relationship Finder (SNARF) [83] have been created for visualizing and ranking the most relevant contacts to the user based on contact interactions in e-mail, for example. However, these types of applications are very general and do not take into account how to identify the experts within the social network and how to recommend specific people to the user. The DISSECT method can be used to find the "expert" people within the social network. A contact search application could be created as an interface to search for information from relevant people and subgroups in a user's social network, obtained from e-mail or some other online collaborative medium or even people's search histories.

The second approach is community-based search and involves the development of community-based search engines that use knowledge of labeled subgroups to improve search performance. This can be done both by labeling information (e.g., blogs or Web pages) in terms of the subgroups that authors and readers belong to, and also in terms of modifying queries based on the subgroups that the people composing those queries belong to. Pages that reflect matching communities or interests could then be ranked higher in search results, and could be labeled according to the communities that they are associated with.

Acknowledgements We would like to thank the TorCamp group for allowing us to use their Google Groups site for data analysis and the participants for completing the behavioral surveys. The authors would also like to thank Jennifer Keelan and Kumanan Wilson for providing us with the content analysis information from the YouTube vaccination videos shown in Table 4.1.

References

1. Adar E, Li Z, Adamic LA, Lukose RM (May 2004) Implicit structure and the dynamics of blogspace. In: Workshop on the weblogging ecosystem, 13th international World Wide Web conference
2. Alba RD (2003) A graph-theoretic definition of a sociometric clique. J Math Sociol 3:113–126
3. Anderson CJ, Wasserman S, Faust K (1997) Building stochastic blockmodels. Social Networks 14:137–161
4. Backstrom L (2006) Group formation in large social networks: membership, growth, and evolution. In: KDD 06: Proceedings of the 12th ACM SIGKDD international conference on knowledge discovery and data mining, ACM Press, pp 44–54
5. Balasundaram B, Butenko S, Hicks I, Sachdeva S (2007) Clique relaxations in social network analysis: the maximum k-plex problem. Technical report, Texas A and M Engineering
6. Bass LA, Stein CH (1997) Comparing the structure and stability of network ties using the social support questionnaire and the social network list. J Soc Pers Relat 14:123–132
7. Bird C (2006) Community structure in oss projects. Technical report, University of California, Davis
8. Blanchard AL, Markus ML (2004) The experienced "sense" of a virtual community: characteristics and processes. SIGMIS Database 35(1):64–79
9. Borgatti SP, Everett GM, Freeman CL (2002) Ucinet for windows: software for social network analysis. Analytic Technologies, Harvard, USA
10. Brin S, Page L (1998) The anatomy of a large-scale hypertextual web search engine. In: WWW7: Proceedings of the 7th international conference on World Wide Web 7. Elsevier Science BV, Amsterdam, the Netherlands, pp 107–117
11. Burt R (1982) Toward a structural theory of action: network models of social structure, perception, and action. Academic, New York
12. Burt R (1984) Network items and the general social survey. Social Networks 6:293–339
13. Campbell KE, Barret AL (1991) Name generators in surveys of personal networks. Social Networks 13:203–221
14. Carrington PJ, Scott J, Wasserman S (2006) Models and methods in social network analysis. Cambridge University Press, New York, NY, USA
15. Cervini AL (2003) Network connections: An analysis of social software that turns online introductions into offline interactions. Master's thesis, New York University, New York, NY
16. Chavis DM (2008) Sense of community index. http://www.capablecommunity.com/pubs/ Sense%20of%20Community%20Index.pdf. Accessed 30 September 2008
17. Chavis DM, Wandersman A (1990) Sense of community in the urban environment: a catalyst for participation and community development. Am J Commun Psychol 18(1):55–81
18. Chin A (January 2009) Social cohesion analysis of networks: a method for finding cohesive subgroups in social hypertext. PhD thesis, University of Toronto
19. Chin A, Chignell M (2006) A social hypertext model for finding community in blogs. In: Proceedings of the 17th international ACM conference on hypertext and hypermedia: tools for supporting social structures. ACM, Odense, Denmark, pp 11–22
20. Chin A, Chignell M (2007) Identifying communities in blogs: roles for social network analysis and survey instruments. Int J Web Based Commun 3(3):345–363
21. Chin A, Chignell M (2007) Identifying subcommunities using cohesive subgroups in social hypertext. In: HT '07: Proceedings of the 18th conference on hypertext and hypermedia. ACM, New York, NY, USA, pp 175–178

22. Chin A, Chignell M (2008) Automatic detection of cohesive subgroups within social hypertext: A heuristic approach. New Rev Hypermed Multimed 14(1):121–143
23. Chin A, Keelan J, Pavri-Garcia V, Tomlinson G, Wilson K, Chignell M (2009) Automated delineation of subgroups in web video: A medical activism case study. Journal of Computer-Mediated Communication. In Press
24. Clauset A (2005) Finding local community structure in networks. Phys Rev E 72:026132
25. Costenbader E, Thomas WV (October 2003) The stability of centrality measures when networks are sampled. Social Networks 25:283–307
26. Crucitti P, Latora V, Porta S (2006) Centrality measures in spatial networks of urban streets. Phys Rev E 73:036125
27. Danon L, Duch J, Diaz-Guilera A, Arenas A (2005) Comparing community structure identification. J Stat Mech Theor Exp: P09008
28. de Nooy W, Mrvar A, Batagelj V (2005) Exploratory social network analysis with Pajek. Cambridge University Press, New York, USA
29. Dixon J (1981) Towards an understanding of the implications of boundary changes – with emphasis on community of interest, draft report to the rural adjustment unit. Technical report, University of New England, Armidale
30. Donetti L, Munoz AM (2004) Detecting network communities: a new systematic and efficient algorithm. J Stat Mech Theor Exp 2004(10):P10012
31. Driskell BR, Lyon L (2002) Are virtual communities true communities? Examining the environments and elements of community. City and Community 1(4):373–390
32. Du N, Wu B, Pei X, Wang B, Xu L (2007) Community detection in large-scale social networks. In WebKDD/SNA-KDD '07: Proceedings of the 9th WebKDD and 1st SNA-KDD 2007 workshop on Web mining and social network analysis. ACM, New York, NY, USA, pp 16–25
33. Duch J, Arenas A (2005) Community detection in complex networks using extremal optimization. Phys Rev E (Stat Nonlinear Soft Matter Phys) 72(2):027104
34. Dwyer T, Hong HS, Koschutzki D, Schreiber F, Xu K (2006) Visual analysis of network centralities. In: APVis '06: Proceedings of the 2006 Asia-Pacific symposium on information visualisation. Australian Computer Society, Darlinghurst, Australia, pp 189–197
35. Elmore LK, Richman BM (March 2001) Euclidean distance as a similarity metric for principal component analysis. Month Weather Rev 129(3):540–549
36. Erickson T (1996) The world-wide-web as social hypertext. Commun ACM 39(1):15–17
37. Estrada E, Rodriguez-Velazquez AJ (2005) Subgraph centrality in complex networks. Phys Rev E 71:056103
38. Etzioni A, Etzioni O (2001) Can virtual communities be real? In: Etzioni A (ed) The Monochrome Society, Princeton University Press, Princeton, pp 77–101
39. Falkowski T, Bartelheimer J, Spiliopoulou M (2006) Community dynamics mining. In: Proceedings of 14th European conference on information systems (ECIS 2006). Gteborg, Sweden
40. Fisher D (2005) Using egocentric networks to understand communication. IEEE Internet Comput 9(5):20–28
41. Flake WG, Lawrence S, Giles LC, Coetzee MF (2002) Self-organization and identification of web communities. IEEE Computer 35(3):66–71
42. Fortunato S, Latora V, Marchiori M (2004) Method to find community structures based on information centrality. Phys Rev E (Stat Nonlinear, Soft Matter Phys) 70(5):056104
43. Frank AK (1997) Identifying cohesive subgroups. Social Networks 17(1):27–56
44. Freeman CL (1978) Centrality in social networks: Conceptual clarification. Social Networks 1:215–239
45. Frivolt G, Bielikov M (2005) An approach for community cutting. In: Svatek V, Snasel V (eds) RAWS 2005: Proceedings of the 1st International workshop on representation and analysis of Web space, Prague-Tocna, Czech Republic, pp 49–54
46. Garton L, Haythornthwaite C, Wellman B (1997) Studying online social networks. J Comput Mediated Commun 3(1):1–30
47. Girvan M, Newman EJM (2002) Community structure in social and biological networks. Proc Natl Acad Sci USA 99:7821

48. Gloor AP (2005) Capturing team dynamics through temporal social surfaces. In: Proceedings of the 9th international conference on information visualisation (InfoVis 2005). IEEE, pp 939–944

49. Gloor AP, Laubacher R, Dynes BCS, Zhao Y (2003) Visualization of communication patterns in collaborative innovation networks – analysis of some w3c working groups. In: CIKM '03: Proceedings of the 12th international conference on information and knowledge management, ACM Press, New York, NY, USA, pp 56–60

50. Gómez V, Kaltenbrunner A, López V (2008) Statistical analysis of the social network and discussion threads in slashdot. In: WWW '08: Proceedings of the 17th international conference on World Wide Web. ACM, New York, NY, USA, pp 645–654

51. Gregson AMR (1975) Psychometrics of similarity. Academic, NY, USA

52. Gruzd A, Haythornthwaite C (2007) A noun phrase analysis tool for mining online community. In: Proceedings of the 3rd international conference oncommunities and technologies, East Lansing, Michigan, USA, pp 67–86

53. Gruzd A, Haythornthwaite C (2008) Automated discovery and analysis of social networks from threaded discussions. Paper presented at the International Network of Social Network Analysis, St. Pete Beach, FL, USA

54. Hanneman AR, Riddle M (2005) Introduction to social network methods (online textbook). University of California, Riverside, CA

55. Hartigan J (1975) Clustering algorithms. Wiley, New York, NY, USA

56. Hirsch JB (1979) Psychological dimensions of social networks: A multimethod analysis. Am J Commun Psychol 7(3):263–277

57. Hoskinson A (2005) Creating the ultimate research assistant. Computer 38(11):97–99

58. Hubert JL, Schultz J (1976) Quadratic assignment as a general data analysis strategy. Brit J Math Stat Psychol 29:190–241

59. Jaccard P (1901) Distribution de la flore alpine dans le bassin des dranses et dans quelques rgions voisines. Bulletin del la Socit Vaudoise des Sciences Naturellese, 37:241–272

60. Johnson CS (1967) Hierarchical clustering schemes.Psychometrika, 32

61. Jones Q (1997) Virtual-communities, virtual settlements and cyber-archaeology: A theoretical outline. J Comput Supported Coop Work 3(3)

62. Jung Y, Park H, Du DZ, Drake LB (2003) A decision criterion for the optimal number of clusters in hierarchical clustering. J Global Optim 25(1):91–111

63. Keelan J, Pavri-Garcia V, Tomlinson G, Wilson K (2007) Youtube as a source of information on immunization: a content analysis. JAMA: J Am Med Assoc 298(21):2482–2484

64. Kleinberg J (2002) Bursty and hierarchical structure in streams. In: KDD '02: Proceedings of the 8th ACM SIGKDD international conference on knowledge discovery and data mining. ACM, New York, NY, USA, pp 91–101

65. Kleinberg MJ (1999) Authoritative sources in a hyperlinked environment. J ACM 46(5): 604–632

66. Koschtzki D, Schreiber F (2004) Comparison of centralities for biological networks.In: Giegerich R, Stoye J (eds) Proceedings of the German conference on bioinformatics (GCB'04), Bielefield, Germany, pp 199–206

67. Kumar R, Novak J, Raghavan P, Tomkins A (2003) On the bursty evolution of blogspace. In: WWW '03: Proceedings of the 12th international conference on World Wide Web. ACM, New York, NY, USA, pp 568–576

68. Kumar R, Novak J, Raghavan P, Tomkins A (2004) Structure and evolution of blogspace. Commun ACM 47(12):35–39

69. Kumar R, Raghavan P, Rajagopalan S, Tomkins A (1999) Trawling the web for emerging cyber-communities. Computer Networks 31(11–16), pp 1481–1493

70. Kurdia A, Daescu O, Ammann L, Kakhniashvili D, Goodman RS (November 2007) Centrality measures for the human red blood cell interactome. Engineering in Medicine and Biology Workshop. IEEE, Dallas, pp 98–101

71. Leskovec J, Lang JK, Dasgupta A, Mahoney WM (2008) Statistical properties of community structure in large social and information networks. In: WWW '08: Proceedings of the 17th international conference on World Wide Web. ACM, New York, NY, USA, pp 695–704

72. Leydesdorff L, Schank T, Scharnhorst A, de Nooy W (2008) Animating the development of social networks over time using a dynamic extension of multidimensional scaling
73. Li X, Liu B, Yu SP (2006) Mining community structure of named entities from web pages and blogs. In: AAAI Spring Symposium Series. American Association for Artificial Intelligence
74. Lin RY, Chi Y, Zhu S, Sundaram H, Tseng LB (2008) Facetnet: a framework for analyzing communities and their evolutions in dynamic networks. In: WWW '08: Proceedings of the 17th international conference on World Wide Web. ACM, New York, NY, USA, pp 685–694
75. Ma W-H, Zeng PA (2003) The connectivity structure, giant strong component and centrality of metabolic networks. Bioinformatics 19(11):1423–1430
76. Marlow C (2004) Audience, structure and authority in the weblog community. In: International communication association conference, New Orleans, LA
77. McMillan WD, Chavis DM (1986) Sense of community: a definition and theory. J Commun Psychol 14(1):6–23
78. Memon N, Harkiolakis N, Hicks LD (2008) Detecting high-value individuals in covert networks: 7/7 London bombing case study. In Proceedings of the 2008 IEEE/ACS International Conference on computer systems and applications. IEEE Computer Society, Washington DC, USA, 4–31 April 2008, pp 206–215
79. Memon N, Larsen LH, Hicks LD, Harkiolakis N (2008) Detecting hidden hierarchy in terrorist networks: Some case studies. Lect Notes Comput Sci 5075:477–489
80. Mizruchi SM, Mariolis P, Schwartz M, Mintz B (1986) Techniques for disaggregating centrality scores in social networks. Sociol Methodol 16:26–48
81. Moody J, McFarland AD, Bender-deMoll S (2005) Visualizing network dynamics. Am J Sociol: Jan 2005
82. Mukherjee M, Holder LB (2004) Graph-based data mining on social networks. In: Proceedings of the 10th ACM SIG conference on knowledge discovery and data mining, ACM, Seattle, USA, pp 1–10
83. Neustaedter C, Brush AJ, Smith AM, Fisher D (2005) The social network and relationship finder: Social sorting for email triage. In: Proceedings of the 2nd conference on E-mail and anti-spam (CEAS 2005), California, USA
84. Newman EJM (2006) Modularity and community structure in networks. Proc Nat Acad Sci 103(23):8577–8582
85. Newman EJM, Girvan M (2004) Finding and evaluating community structure in networks. Phys Rev E 69:026113
86. O'Reilly T (2005) What is web 2.0? http://www.oreillynet.com/pub/a/oreilly/tim/news/2005/09/30/what-is-web-20. Accessed 30 September 2008
87. Orford DJ (1976) Implementation of criteria for partitioning a dendrogram. Math Geol 8(1):75–84
88. Paolillo CJ, Wright E (2004) The challenges of foaf characterization. http://stderr.org/~elw/foaf/. Accessed 30 September 2008
89. Paolillo CJ, Wright E (2005) Social network analysis on the semantic web: Techniques and challenges for visualizing foaf. http://www.blogninja.com/vsw-draft-paolillo-wright-foaf.pdf. Accessed 30 September 2008
90. Piper EW, Marrache M, Lacroix R, Richardsen MA, Jones BD (1983) Cohesion as a basic bond in groups. Hum Relat 36(2):93–108
91. Radicchi F, Castellano C, Cecconi F, Loreto V, Parisi D (2004) Defining and identifying communities in networks. Proc Natl Acad Sci USA 101(9):2658–2663
92. Reffay C, Chanier T (2003) How social network analysis can help to measure cohesion in collaborative distance learning. In: Proceedings of computer supported collaborative learning 2003. Kluwer, ACM, Dordrecht, NL, pp 343–352
93. Rheingold H (1993) The virtual community: homesteading on the electronic frontier. Addison-Wesley, Toronto, ON, Canada
94. Ruan J, Zhang W An efficient spectral algorithm for network community discovery and its applications to biological and social networks. In: Seventh IEEE international conference on data mining (ICDM 2007), Omaha, Nebraska, USA, 28–31 October 2007, pp 643–648

95. Ruhnau B (October 2000) Eigenvector-centrality – a node-centrality? Social Networks 22(4):357–365
96. Sarason GI, Levine HM, Basham BR, Sarason RB (1983) Assessing social support: the social support questionnaire. J Pers Social Psychol 44:127–139
97. Schaeffer ES (2007) Graph clustering. Comput Sci Rev 1(1):27–64
98. Shi J, Malik J (2000) Normalized cuts and image segmentation. IEEE Trans Pattern Anal Mach Intell 22(8):888–905
99. Snijders ABT, Nowicki K (1997) Estimation and prediction for stochastic block models for graphs with latent block structure. J Classif 14:75–100
100. Snijders AB Tom, Christian EG Steglich, Schweinberger M (2007) Modeling the co-evolution of networks and behavior. In: Kees van Montfort, Han Oud, Albert Satorra (eds) Longitudinal models in the behavioral and related sciences, Routledge Academic, England, pp 41–71
101. Steinhaeuser K, Chawla VN (2008) Is modularity the answer to evaluating community structure in networks. In: International workshop and conference on network science (NetSci'08), Norwich Research Park, UK
102. Sterling S (2004) Aggregation techniques to characterize social networks. Master's thesis, Air Force Institute of Technology. Ohio, USA
103. Tajfel H, Turner CJ (1986) The social identity theory of inter-group behavior. In: Worchel S, Austin LW (eds) Psychology of intergroup relations. Nelson-Hall, Chicago, USA
104. Tantipathananandh C, Berger-Wolf YT, Kempe D (2007) A framework for community identification in dynamic social networks. In: KDD '07: Proceedings of the 13th ACM SIGKDD international conference on knowledge discovery and data mining. ACM, New York, NY, USA, pp 717–726
105. Traud LA, Kelsic DE, Mucha JP, Porter AM (2009) Community structure in online collegiate social networks, American Physical Society, 2009 APS March Meeting, March 16–20, pp 1–38
106. Tremayne M, Zheng N, Lee KJ, Jeong J (2006) Issue publics on the web: Applying network theory to the war blogosphere. J Comput Mediated Commun 12(1), article 15. http://jcmc.indiana.edu/vol12/issue1/tremayne.html
107. Tversky A (1977) Features of similarity. Psychol Rev 84(4):327–352
108. Tyler RJ, Wilkinson MD, Huberman AB (2005) E-mail as spectroscopy: Automated discovery of community structure within organizations. Inform Soc 21(2):143–153
109. Uttal RW, Spillmann L, Sturzel F, Sekuler BA (2000) Motion and shape in common fate. Vision Res 40(3):301–310
110. van Duijn1 AJM, Vermunt KJ (2005) What is special about social network analysis? Methodology 2:2–6
111. Wang G, Shen Y, Ouyang M (2008) A vector partitioning approach to detecting community structure in complex networks. Comput Math Appl 55(12):2746–2752
112. Wang H, Wang W, Yang J, Yu SP (2002) Clustering by pattern similarity in large data sets. In: SIGMOD '02: Proceedings of the 2002 ACM SIGMOD international conference on management of data. ACM, New York, NY, USA, pp 394–405
113. Wasserman S, Faust K (1994) Social network analysis: methods and applications. Cambridge University Press, United Kingdom
114. Wellman B (2003) Structural analysis: from method and metaphor to theory and substance. In: Wellman B, Berkowitz SD (eds) Social structures: a network approach, Cambridge University Press, UK, pp 19–61
115. Wellman B, Guilia M (1999) Net surfers don't ride alone: virtual communities as communities. In: Wellman B (ed) Networks in the global village: life in contemporary communities, Westview Press, Colorado, US
116. Welser TH, Gleave E, Fisher D, Smith M (2007) Visualizing the signatures of social roles in online discussion groups. J Soc Struct 8, http://www.cmu.edu/joss/content/articles/volume8/Welser

117. Zahn TC (1971) Graph-theoretical methods for detecting and describing gestalt clusters. IEEE Trans Comput C-20(1):68–86
118. Zhao Y, Karypis G (2002) Evaluation of hierarchical clustering algorithms for document datasets. In: CIKM '02: Proceedings of the 11th international conference on information and knowledge management. ACM, New York, NY, USA, pp 515–524

Chapter 5
Clustering of Blog Sites Using Collective Wisdom

Nitin Agarwal, Magdiel Galan, Huan Liu, and Shankar Subramanya

Abstract The blogosphere is expanding at an unprecedented speed. A better understanding of the blogosphere can greatly facilitate the development of the social Web to serve the needs of users, service providers, and advertisers. One important task in this process is the clustering of blog sites. Although a good number of traditional clustering methods exist, they are not designed to take into account the blogosphere's unique characteristics. Clustering blog sites presents new challenges. A prominent feature of the social Web is that many enthusiastic bloggers voluntarily write, tag, and catalog their posts in order to reach the widest possible audience who will share their thoughts and appreciate their ideas. In the process, a new kind of collective wisdom is generated. The objective of this work is to make use of this collective wisdom in the clustering of blog sites. As such, we study how clustering with collective wisdom can be achieved and compare its performance with respect to representative traditional clustering methods. Here contain, we will present statistical and visual results, report findings, opportunities for future research work, and estimated timeline, extending this work to many real-world applications.

5.1 Introduction

The advent of Web 2.0 [17] has created a surge of content via online media such as blogs, wikis, social bookmarking such as del.icio.us, online photo sharing such as Flickr, and other such services. Although blogging is not a new phenomenon, it has been there for the past 7–8 years, Web 2.0 has helped make it more accessible and permeate the society rapidly. Journalism "by the people" or *citizen journalism* began to flourish. In 2006, *Time* named "You" as Person of the Year, due to the growth of user-generated content.

People not only generate content but also enrich the existing media (both text and non-text). A popular example is Google's image labeler, which is a social game that involves human subjects labeling images and retaining the most commonly used

N. Agarwal (✉), M. Galan, H. Liu, and S. Subramanya
Arizona State University, Tempe, AZ 85287, USA
e-mail: [Nitin.Agarwal.2;Magdiel.Galan;Huan.Liu;Shankara.Subramanya]@asu.edu

A. Abraham et al. (eds.), *Computational Social Network Analysis*, Computer
Communications and Networks, DOI 10.1007/978-1-84882-229-0_5,
© Springer-Verlag London Limited 2010

tags for a particular image. Other examples include tagging blog sites or posts with relevant labels, providing feedback for search results, etc. This results into what is known as a new form of *collective wisdom*. Collective wisdom (also known as group wisdom, wisdom of crowds, open source intelligence, and co-intelligence) is defined as the shared knowledge arrived at by a group of individuals, used to obtain the best possible approximation to the perfect solution.

With an explosive and continuous growth of the blogosphere, there is a need for automatic and dynamic organization of the blog sites. Clustering of these blog sites is a promising way to achieve the automatic organization of the content. In this work we focus on the challenges involved in clustering blog sites by leveraging the available collective wisdom.

Blog site clustering not only helps better organize the information, but also aids convenient accessibility to the content. Clustering blog sites helps in optimizing the search engine by reducing the search space. As such, we would only need to search the relevant cluster and not the entire blogosphere.

Blogosphere follows a scale-free model and obeys Long Tail distribution [2]. A vast majority of bloggers reside in the Long Tail and cannot be well targeted for otherwise potential business opportunities (i.e., niches). To do better, it requires a good number of bloggers who can provide more data for targeted marketing. This warrants a need for aggregating the Long Tail bloggers. Clustering various Long Tail bloggers to form a critical mass will not only potentially expand a blogger's social network, but also increase participation so as to move them from the Long Tail toward the Short Head. This could help the search engines to expand their result space and include results beyond just the Short Head. Including relevant clusters from the Long Tail in the search space would help in identifying those niches.

Clustering blog sites will invariably lead to connecting the bloggers. Connecting the bloggers in the Long Tail helps in identifying *familiar strangers* [1]. The underlying concept of familiar strangers is that they share some patterns and routines (or commonalities), although they are not directly connected. Clustering blog sites also helps promote the Web 2.0 new marketing 4Ps [16]: personalization, participation, peer-to-peer, and predictive modeling.

5.2 Related Work

5.2.1 Blog Clustering

Blogs have increasingly become a subject of research. Authors in [5, 13, 18, 21] explore clustering of the blogs to identify communities. Such blog community-based clustering relies on user-induced connections in the underlying blog network to identify communities. However, such blog clusters only identify the community structure of the blogosphere and may not necessarily help in clustering blogs of similar contents. A closer attempt to contents is done by Brooks and Montanez [4] utilizing the blog tags for hierarchical clustering.

Though content- or topic-based clustering of Web documents and text has been widely studied, content-based clustering of blogs has not been studied widely. Work by Bansal et al. [3] performs semantic analysis in order to discover topic trends, with the goal of identifying clusters that persist over time. The clusters are based on identifying biconnected components in a graph. In [24, 26], Web document clustering has been done based on the k-Means algorithm [14]. Apart from k-Means, agglomerative and hierarchical clustering has also been used for document clustering. Such is the case for [25], which uses a hierarchical structure for linkage-based clustering measured as by similarities of other objects linked to a pair of objects, where objects can refer to authors, papers, links, and Web sites. Similar work is accomplished by Li and Liu [22], where the authors use hierarchical clustering to try to identify communities by establishing connections per the co-occurrance of words and entities in entities such as Web pages and blogs. Authors in [9] present a review of the clustering algorithms and both [6, 20] have provided reviews of document-clustering techniques.

The mentioned clustering algorithms can be directly applied to blogs by considering blogs as Web documents. The adopted vector space model can be used to encode the blogs represented as term frequency vectors for the similarity matrix using Singular Value Decomposition (SVD), to which apply a clustering technique such as some form of k-Means or hierarchical clustering and/or variations of them. However, by doing this, we would be ignoring the many unique characteristics of blog which would aid us in obtaining a better clustering. A significant consideration is that blog sites are not as rich in text as Web documents. Most blog sites are personal accounts, opinions, ideas, thoughts, and expressions that have less content and not well authored. However, labels or tags assigned by humans (both bloggers as well as readers), also known as the collective wisdom, make them special and different from Web documents. As such, traditional Web documents keyword clustering algorithms mentioned above would fail to return good results due to blog's sparsity and curse of dimensionality. Therefore, novel techniques are required that leverage the enormous collective wisdom available.

5.2.2 Leveraging Tag Information

The tags and labels provided by humans, which represent our case for Collective Wisdom, have been previously used for various tasks like search and retrieval, and recommender systems. The human annotation provided for Web pages and blogs provide valuable metadata for use in search. Web sites like "del.icio.us," "Flickr," and "YouTube" use such user-provided metadata in the form of collaborative tagging for search and retrieval. Since large amount of such metadata is available even in the blogosphere, it can be leveraged for search and retrieval operations. Authors in [11] provide an algorithm to search using the tag information. In [10] the authors have used the tag information for a blog recommendation algorithm.

Though the use of "collective wisdom" has been studied as just mentioned, there is still opportunity for improvements in terms of using a greater variety of user-generated data (like user-provided labels in blogs) and for more kinds of applications in the blogosphere (like clustering of the blogs in the blogosphere) and the Web in general.

5.3 Problem Definition

The focus of this work is of the clustering of blog sites. More formally, given m blog sites, $S_1, S_2, \ldots, S_m$, we construct k disjoint clusters of the m blog sites, such that $k \leq m$. We exploit the collective wisdom while forming clusters of these blog sites. The collective wisdom that is available and we make use is in the form of predefined labels for each blog site. A single blog site could be tagged under multiple such labels.

With the proposed new framework for clustering, based on the predefined labels, we intend to explore new ways for clustering. We also show that the clusters thus obtained are more meaningful as compared to traditional ways for clustering. Moreover, conventional approaches for clustering have inherent shortcomings such as:

- Text clustering suffers from the curse of dimensionality and sparsity [8].
- The similarity measure does not capture the semantic similarity very well [12].
- The clusters thus obtained are sometimes not very meaningful [12].
- User needs to specify the number of clusters a priori which could be hard to anticipate [19].

Based on these shortcomings, we propose a novel clustering approach that leverages collective wisdom and tackles the challenges of the conventional clustering approaches listed above.

5.4 Generating Similarity for Blog Clustering

5.4.1 Wisdom: Leveraging Collectivism

We leverage the label information available with each blog site in clustering them. A naive approach would be to treat all the blog sites that have same label as one cluster but that would result in as many clusters as there are labels. We may also then find, upon analysis, that some of the clusters thus obtained might be related and would be better if they were to be merged into one representative cluster. An even greater challenge is in regards to blog sites that may be tagged under multiple labels, which makes it difficult to form clusters in the naive way, since it would be difficult to decide with certainty to which of the multiple labels the blog should be clustered upon. While the naive approach struggles in this scenario, it is precisely in this type of scenario, of multiple labels, that our approach excels the most.

Our goal in clustering is to cluster similar labels. Clustering the similar labels can be formulated as an optimization problem. Assume we have t labels, $l_1, l_2, \ldots, l_t$ and are clustered into k clusters, $C_1, C_2, \ldots, C_k$, then optimal clustering is obtained if, for any two labels l_i and l_j,

$$\min \sum d(l_i, l_j), \forall (l_i, l_j) \in C_m, \quad 1 \le m \le k, \ i \ne j \tag{5.1}$$

$$\max \sum d(l_i, l_j), \forall l_i \in C_m, \forall l_j \in C_n, \quad 1 \le (m, n) \le k, \ m \ne n \tag{5.2}$$

Here $d(l_i, l_j)$ refers to a distance metric between the labels l_i and l_j. Formulation 5.1 minimizes the within-cluster distance between the cluster members and Formulation 5.2 maximizes the between-cluster distance. Finding efficiently an optimal solution for the above min–max conditions is infeasible.

Existing work like [23] proposes a method for clustering based on maximum margin hyperplanes through the data by posing the problem as a convex integer program. The hard clustering constraint is relaxed to a soft clustering formulation that can be feasibly solved with a semidefinite program. In a probabilistic approach, data is considered to be identically and independently drawn from a mixture model of several probability distributions [15]. An expectation maximization (EM) based approach is used to first estimate conditional probabilities of a data point (x) given a cluster (C) by $(P(x|C))$ and then find an approximation to a mixture model given the cluster assignments. k-Means is an approximation to EM-based clustering approach. Another approach to cluster the blog sites is based on the tags assigned to the blog posts and the blog site. Each blog site can be profiled based on these accumulated tags. A simple cosine similarity distance metric could be used to find similarity between different blog sites. However, the vector space model of the blog sites based on the tags is high-dimensional and sparse. We use a SVD-based clustering algorithm as the baseline to avoid the curse of dimensionality. This is discussed in greater detail in Sect. 5.4.2.

There are also instances in which bloggers include hierarchical labels in their labeling. Also in this case, one intuitive solution is to cluster the blogs by the labels. However, this naive clustering approach may not be suitable for clustering the blogs since, as illustrated in Fig. 5.1, bloggers often use Personal as the label descriptor for varied interests. Using this naive approach may not be helpful in capturing the nuances of bloggers' interests and we need to refine the label descriptor by identifying and aggregating the related labels. This is also referred as the *topic irregularity problem* where bloggers use the same label descriptor to define their blog which in fact contains blog posts of varied interests. That would require that different labels with similar themes be connected even when a blogger does not list his or her blog under all these labels. For example, a blog named "Words From Iraq" is labeled as Iraq and Society; another blog, "Iraq's Incovenient Truth," is labeled as Political, and News and Media. Although they are related blogs, they are annotated by completely different labels. Connecting these labels through some sort of link or relation would make more sense.

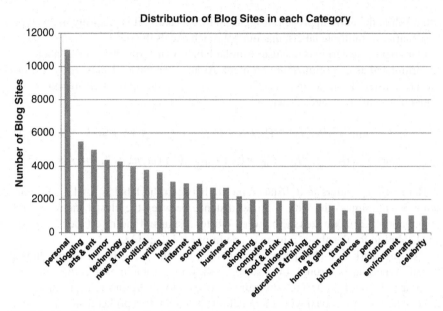

Fig. 5.1 Distribution of blog sites with respect to the labels

Based on the above discussion and limitations with the vector space model, we propose an approach to achieve blog site clustering leveraging the "collective wisdom" of the bloggers. Often bloggers specify more than one predefined labels for a particular blog site or post. When a blogger assigns multiple of these predefined labels, the blogger imposes a level of similarity between the selected labels. In this context, we can make the assertion that the labels are related, or that a relation exists between the labels due to the commonality to the blog as interpreted by the blogger in his wisdom. As such, this action has the effect of establishing a link between these predefined labels, or that a link has been imposed, between the labels. When additional bloggers create the same relation between the same predefined labels within their blog, they validate the notion that a relation does exists between said labels. The greater the number of bloggers that, in their wisdom, generate the same relation, the greater the notion that the labels are strongly related. We record the level of the relation, as measured by the number of bloggers who made the same link or connection.

The number of blog sites that create the links between various labels is termed as *link strength*, which could be treated as the edge weights of the label relation graph. It is the *link strength* that becomes the basis of our collective wisdom approach of creating clusters of strongly linked interrelated labels. We capitalize upon this interpretation and translate into a *label relation graph* for the labels associated to a blog, an instance of which is depicted in Fig. 5.2. For example, predefined labels like Computers and Technology; Computers and Internet; Computers

Fig. 5.2 An instance of label relation graph

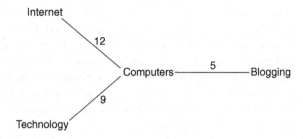

and Blogging were linked by the bloggers. Using the label relation graph, different labels can be clustered or merged. We will refer to this collective wisdom-based

---

Algorithm 5.1 *WisColl*

1: Record label-pairs for first blog/blogger
2: **Repeat**:
3:     Record label-pairs for next blog/blogger.
4:     Increment *link strength* for common label-pairs to previous blog/bloggers.
5: **Until**: all blogs/bloggers.
6: Remove label pairs whose *link strength* less than threshold.

---

approach, as *WisColl*. The steps necessary for *WisColl* are illustrated in Algorithm 5.1. The algorithm assumes the pre-processing steps, such as stemming, stop words, and other related preprocessing steps has already been completed.

We experiment with different thresholds for the link strength in Sect. 5.5. We visualize the label relation graph thus obtained using a visualization and analysis tool, Pajek.[1] Once the label relation graph is computed after thresholding, we perform label clustering using k-Means and Hierarchical clustering algorithms and compare their results. The results are presented in Sect. 5.5.2.

The following short example can help better illustrate the relation of *link strength* and threshold. In this example of five blogs and seven labels, a "1" indicates that the label l was selected by the blogger for the blog b for the respective label.

blog/label	l_1	l_2	l_3	l_4	l_5	l_6	l_7
b_1	0	1	1	1	0	0	0
b_2	1	0	0	0	1	1	0
b_3	1	0	0	0	0	1	0
b_4	0	0	0	0	0	1	1
b_5	0	0	1	1	0	0	1

In the example, the linked labels, and their respective *link strength* (LS) are: l_1–l_5 (LS = 1 since the link between the two labels was only made once by blog b_2), l_1–l_6 (LS = 2 since the link between the two labels was made twice, first by

---

[1] http://vlado.fmf.uni-lj.si/pub/networks/pajek/

blog b_2, and secondly, by blog b_3), l_2–l_3 (LS = 1: b_1), l_2–l_4 (LS = 1: b_1), l_3–l_4 (LS = 2: b_1, b_5), l_5–l_6 (LS = 1: b_2), and l_6–l_7 (LS = 1: b_4). Initially, in this set-up, all labels are connected together in a single cluster, as seen in Fig. 5.3. Linked labels with link strength of "1" are quickly removed, as they indicate they were linked only once among all the blogs. After the removal, two clusters emerge: l_1–l_6 (LS = 2: b_2, b_3) and l_3–l_4 (LS = 2: b_1, b_5) as shown in Fig. 5.4. It should be noted that the removal of nodes or labels that are below the threshold, it is in effect reducing the vector space "dimensionality."

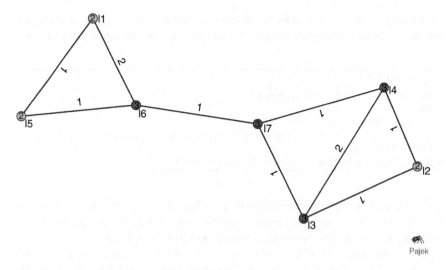

Fig. 5.3 Link strength example: initial setup

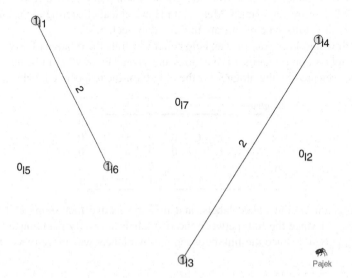

Fig. 5.4 Link strength example. After removal of linked labels with link strength of '1'

WisColl is time-sensitive and adaptive to the current interests, since the labels of a blog site could change depending on what the blogger is blogging about. This results in dynamic, as well as adaptive, clustering. Every time new blog posts appear, either there will be new edges appearing in the *label relation graph* and/or link strength changes, as blogger specifies different labels. As such, the clustering results would change.

5.4.2   A Conventional Approach

As a clustering algorithm for the baseline, we cluster the blogs using the blog post text and then find the predominant label for each cluster. The "Vector Space" model is used to encode the blogs with each blog being represented as a term frequency vector. SVD and the cosine similarity measure are then used to obtain the similarity matrix for clustering.

The vector space representation for each blog is constructed to find the term frequencies in the blog posts of each blogger. For each blogger up to five blog posts are available and thus extracted and using these posts a 'blog-term' matrix is constructed. The following preprocessing steps are applied to the terms obtained by blog posts before constructing the matrix:

1. Trim white spaces and punctuation marks, token scrubbing is performed on the blog post text.
2. All the terms are *stemmed* using the portal stemmer to obtain their morphological roots.
3. The stop words are removed from the remaining list of terms.

After the preprocessing steps, using the resulting normalized terms, the blog-term matrix B ($m \times t$ matrix, with m bloggers/blog sites and t terms) is constructed. Latent semantic analysis [7] is performed on this matrix to obtain the lower dimensional semantic representation of each blog. This involved decomposing the blog-term matrix using SVD [7].

$$B = USV^T \qquad (5.3)$$

The blogger-term vectors were then projected into the semantic feature space by selecting the top k singular values and the corresponding singular vectors from U and V. The reconstructed blog-term matrix is of rank k.

$$B_k = U_k S_k V_k^T \qquad (5.4)$$

In our experiments we achieved the best performance by selecting top 25 eigenvectors. In the resulting matrix B_k each row corresponds to one blog and is represented by the vector $d_i = (d_{i1}, d_{i2}, \ldots, d_{it}) 1 \leq i \leq m$. The $m \times m$ similarity matrix S was then constructed by finding "cosine similarity" between term vectors corresponding to each pair of blogs. The (i, j)th element of S gives the similarity between blogs i and j and is given by

$$S(i, j) = (d_i \times d_j)/(\|d_i\| \times \|d_j\|) \tag{5.5}$$

Once we have the similarity matrix, clusters of bloggers/blogs can be easily visualized. Clustering is achieved by setting a threshold τ for similarity. A link between two nodes is considered weak if the similarity is less than τ. When the weak links are removed, clusters emerge. By identifying the predominant labels for the nodes in each cluster, we identify the cluster labels.

5.5 Experiments and Discussion

Figure 5.5 illustrates our approach to data collection and experimentation. We initiate our technique by drawing from a pool of bloggers. To this set of bloggers, we apply typical baseline clustering approach (Sect. 5.4.2). We also apply our approach to draw from wisdom collectivism that identifies commonality among bloggers. To evaluate the two approaches: baseline vs. collective wisdom, we implement agglomerative Hierarchical and k-Means clustering techniques to make possible comparison between the two approaches, as well as Pajek, to help visualize the results.

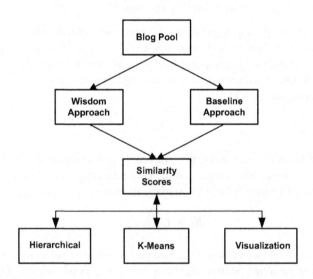

Fig. 5.5 Analysis tree

5.5.1 Design and Methodology

We test WisColl with sample data collected from a blog site directory available at BlogCatalog,[2] which will serve as template to further test other blog sources. BlogCatalog is a directory of blog sites that allows bloggers to label the blog sites under a given hierarchy. The directory structure of BlogCatalog is relatively shallow, with 33 nodes having no children. The maximum depth of the hierarchy is three and only two nodes have that depth. We experiment with varying granularity of structural information. Bloggers submit the blog sites to BlogCatalog. Each site is authored by a blogger. Each blog site contains some blog posts of which last five are displayed on the BlogCatalog.

To collect the BlogCatalog, data we started with four bloggers from different labels as the starting points and crawl their social networks, recursively in a breadth-first fashion. These bloggers belong to the most popular labels (i.e., having largest number of blog sites) at BlogCatalog. For each blogger thus crawled (uniquely identified by their blogger IDs), we collect their blog site's URL, title, and labels, the blog post tags, snippets, title, and permalink, and the blogger's social network information, i.e., his or her friends.

Along with evaluating collective wisdom, we also evaluate the structural properties of the labels, i.e., since the labels have a nested hierarchical structure, what level gives the best clustering results. To perform this we construct three different datasets:

1. *Top-Level* The hierarchical structure of the labels is known a priori. For this dataset we abstract the labels of all the blog sites to their parent level labels. For example, `Family` is a child of `Personal`. So all the blog sites that are labeled `Family` are relabeled as `Personal`, thus abstracting their labels to the parent level. Note that the maximum depth of this hierarchical structure of labels is three and we abstract the labels to the highest parent level label. There are in total 56 labels.
2. *All-Label* This variant of the dataset does not abstract the label information. It considers the full hierarchical structure of the labels. There are in total 110 labels at all the levels of the hierarchy.
3. *One Node-Split* According to the distribution of blog sites in various top level labels, illustrated in Fig. 5.1, `Personal` has the largest number of blog sites.[3] Hence, we split `Personal` into its child labels, to reduce the skewed distribution.

Note that the approach presented here would work for any blog dataset with user-specified metadata like labels or tags.

---

[2] http://www.blogcatalog.com/

[3] For the sake of space constraint and the analysis presented here, we limit the labels in this chart that have at least 1,000 blog sites.

5.5.2 Results and Analysis

In this section, we present the experiments' results and analyses. The experiments are designed to evaluate the following:

- What granularity of label hierarchical structural information generates best clustering? For this we study the clustering results for the three variants of the dataset mentioned in Sect. 5.5.1.
- Which one of the two clustering approaches: (a) link-based clustering approach (that leverages collective wisdom), or (b) the baseline approach performs best per k-Means, Hierarchical, or Visualization clustering?

Before we delve into the parameter tuning of various clustering methods issues, we study the effect of different thresholds for link strength on WisColl. Based on the results of this study, we fix the threshold for link strength for rest of the experiments. For threshold experiments, we use the All-label variant of the dataset (Sect. 5.5.1).

5.5.2.1 Link Strength

We experiment with different thresholds for the All-label link strengths range of values. These values have been captured in Table 5.1. The table shows the range of values, and their distribution, for all of the 456 line pair values, for all of the 110 All-label nodes.

Each *link strength*, or threshold selection, results in a network restructuring and reduction. The restructuring occurs as a result of removing those links whose line values are below the threshold value, which can cause a cluster to transform or break into smaller clusters. The reduction occurs by removing those nodes that are no longer connected to any other node as a result of their links being removed.

Table 5.1 Link strength statistics for ALL labels

Line Value	Frequency	Freq%	CumFreq	CumFreq%
1	320	70.1754	320	70.1754
2	62	13.5965	382	83.7719
3	33	7.2368	415	91.0088
4	15	3.2895	430	94.2982
5	7	1.5351	437	95.8333
6	7	1.5351	444	97.3684
7	6	1.3158	450	98.6842
8	0	0.0000	450	98.6842
9	2	0.4386	452	99.1228
10	1	0.2193	453	99.3421
11	3	0.6579	456	100.0000
Totals	456	100.0000		

Figure 5.6 illustrates the dependency of threshold value, and the distribution of clusters by cluster size and frequency. The figure is for the range of All-label threshold values, corresponding to those values in Table 5.1. This figure shows for example that after selecting a threshold value of 2, this will result in a network structure consisting of two clusters, one of size 2, as containing two nodes, and the other of size 72, as being formed by 72 nodes. For the case that the threshold is set to 3, this results in three clusters: two of them of size 2, one of size 48. In looking at the data from Fig. 5.6, the plot shows that as we increase the threshold, the number of smaller size clusters increases, and the larger size clusters decreases, up to a certain transition point, after which also the smaller cluster size decreases, as the total number of remaining nodes in the network decreases. For the All-label case, this transition point is centered around a threshold value of 5 as illustrated by Fig. 5.7.

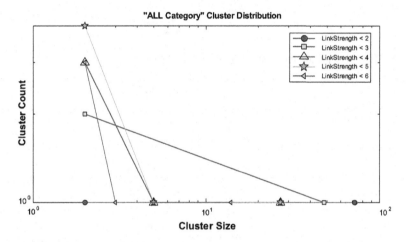

Fig. 5.6 All-label cluster frequency by cluster size per corresponding threshold value

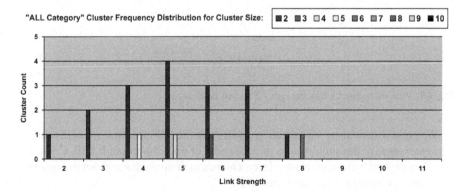

Fig. 5.7 All label cluster histogram for small size clusters per corresponding threshold value

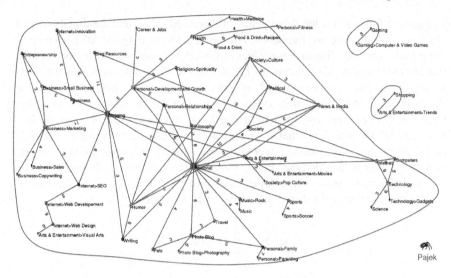

Fig. 5.8 WisColl results for link strength ≥ 3 for All-label dataset

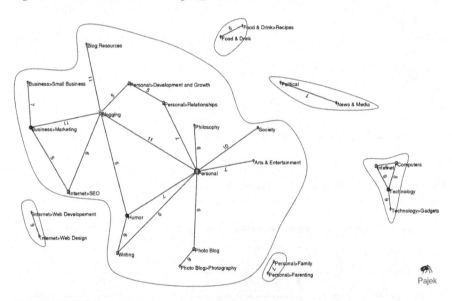

Fig. 5.9 WisColl results for link strength ≥ 5 for All-label dataset

We present the cluster visualization results[4] for the All-label link strength range, for representative threshold values of 3, 5, and 7 in Figs. 5.8 through 5.10. Contour lines highlight the clusters. Node placement was maintained throughout the figures to facilitate visualizing clusters transitions.

---

[4] Pajek was used to create the visualizations.

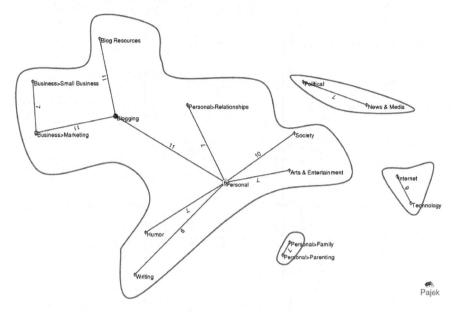

Fig. 5.10 WisColl results for link strength ≥7 for All-label dataset

In the figures, link strength is denoted by the values on the edges. Names of the nodes depict the labels assigned by the bloggers to the blog sites. A cluster of labels would represent a cluster of all the blog sites that are labeled with one of these labels. Some nodes like `Internet>Web Design` depict the hierarchical structure of labels. Here the blog sites are labeled `Web Design` which is a child of `Internet`. We present detailed statistics for clustering results for all the threshold values in Table 5.2. For threshold >= 3, total coverage is highest but we have a single large cluster and two very small clusters depicted by the cluster coverages. Similar is the case for threshold >= 4, 7, and 10. This indicates that highly unbalanced clusters are achieved at other thresholds as compared with threshold >= 5. This value coincides with our previous notion that this is the transition point as shown in Figs. 5.6 and 5.7. Hence we set threshold = 5 for remainder of the experiments.

5.5.2.2 Label Hierarchy

Next we study the effect of structural information of labels on WisColl. For this experiment we consider all the three variants of the dataset, i.e., Top-level, All-label, and One node-split.

A sample of the clustering results for Top-level is shown in Fig. 5.11. This option performs the worst among all the three variants. The cluster size is highly unbalanced. There is a single cluster to which all the nodes belong. This is the case throughout all threshold levels. No contour lines are drawn since no additional clusters are generated at any level. A sample clustering results for One node-split is

Table 5.2 Various statistics to compare clustering results for different threshold values for WisColl

	Number of clusters	Highest degree	Lowest degree	Largest cluster size	Smallest cluster size	Coverage Total %	Coverage 1st cluster %	Coverage 2nd cluster %
All-categories, >= 3	3	17	1	48	2	79.78	76.98	1.76
All-categories, >= 4	5	11	1	27	2	67.57	58.05	4.31
All-categories, >= 5	6	8	1	15	2	54.76	42.3	6.375
All-categories, >= 7	4	6	1	10	2	44.63	33.64	4.61
All-categories, >= 10	1	3	1	5		21.67	21.67	

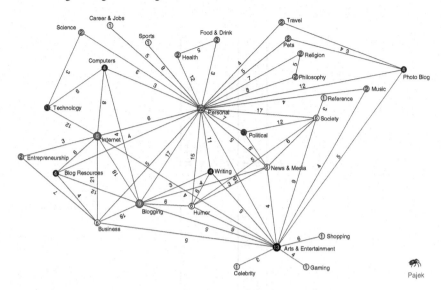

Fig. 5.11 WisColl results for link strength ≥3 for Top-level label dataset

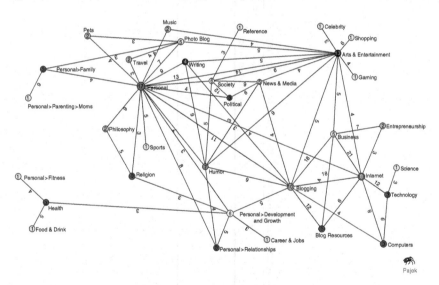

Fig. 5.12 WisColl results for link strength ≥3 for Personal label dataset

shown in Fig. 5.12. The results are a slightly better than Top-level but still the clustering quality is poor with unbalanced cluster size, as only in a couple of instances, more than a single cluster is present. As such, best clustering results are obtained with All-label as shown in Figs. 5.8 through 5.10.

We compare the statistics of clusters obtained from WisColl for different versions of datasets in Table 5.3. Although the total coverage is maximum for Top-level

Table 5.3 Various statistics to compare clustering results for different label structure for WisColl

Category	Number of clusters	Highest degree	Lowest degree	Largest cluster size	Smallest cluster size	Coverage Total %	Coverage 1st cluster %	Coverage 2nd cluster %
All-categories, >= 5	6	8	1	15	2	54.76	42.3	6.375
Top-level	1	16	1	22	2	100	100	
One node-split	3	9	1	21	2	82.87	76.44	3.88

label structure, there is only one cluster that connects all the labels. This results in 100% coverage for the first cluster. As such, there is no search space reduction for this case. Every time a query comes the results are returned from the 1st and only cluster and since it contains all the labels, whole dataset would need to be searched. Similarly, results for One node-split show that the cluster size is highly unbalanced. There are only three clusters with the first cluster having majority of coverage (=76.44%) and the difference between 1st and 2nd cluster is very small. This largely affects the search space reduction. Results for All-labels has the lowest coverage but the cluster sizes are not as unbalanced. Moreover, the difference between the coverage for first and second clusters is larger than One node-split. This leads to better search space reduction. This shows that leveraging the complete structure of collective wisdom gives best results as compared to exploiting a part of it. This demonstrates the contributions of collective wisdom in improving the search space.

5.5.2.3 Visualizations – Pajek

Here we visualize the results of WisColl algorithm (e.g. Fig. 5.9) and baseline algorithm to study the advantages of collective wisdom. Results for the baseline clustering were generated in an analogous fashion as to what was collected for the WisColl approach. As such, we first studied the Baseline's link strengths range of values. These values are shown in Table 5.4. The table shows the range of values, and their distribution, for all of the $346, 921$ edge line pair values, corresponding to 842 baseline nodes.

Figure 5.13 illustrates the dependency of threshold value, and the distribution of edge-connected clusters by size and frequency, for the Baseline range of threshold values, corresponding to those values in Table 5.4. This figure shows a similar behavior as was observed for Fig. 5.6, that as we increase the threshold, the number of smaller size clusters increases, and the larger size clusters decreases, up to a certain transition point, after which the total number of remaining nodes in the network decreases. For the Baseline case, this transition point is centered around a threshold value of 0.75 to 0.80. This is illustrated by Fig. 5.14 which shows cluster size distribution and the transition, with increasing threshold value, for the smaller size clusters. Figure 5.15 presents the edge-connected cluster visualization results for the Baseline link strength range, for representative threshold value of 0.80.

Best visualization of cluster type clustering forming results for baseline approach were achieved with the threshold $\tau = 0.9$ for Fig. 5.16. Here, nodes represent the blog sites or bloggers. For easier comparison, we also display the labels of their blog sites besides their name. For example, a node label like, emom=Small Business:Moms, tells us that the blogger emom has a blog site with labels Small Business and Moms. Cluster quality for both the approaches could be compared by looking at the labels of the cluster members. However, we do not use

Table 5.4 Baseline link strength statistics

Line	Value	Range	Frequency	Freq%	CumFreq	CumFreq%
0.0000	...	0.0417	53288	15.3603	53288	15.3603
0.0417	...	0.0833	51239	14.7696	104527	30.1299
0.0833	...	0.1250	47085	13.5723	151612	43.7022
0.1250	...	0.1667	40021	11.5361	191633	55.2382
0.1667	...	0.2083	33588	9.6817	225221	64.9200
0.2083	...	0.2500	27705	7.9860	252926	72.9059
0.2500	...	0.2917	22250	6.4136	275176	79.3195
0.2917	...	0.3333	18505	5.3341	293681	84.6536
0.3333	...	0.3750	14759	4.2543	308440	88.9078
0.3750	...	0.4167	11054	3.1863	319494	92.0942
0.4167	...	0.4583	8581	2.4735	328075	94.5676
0.4583	...	0.5000	6052	1.7445	334127	96.3121
0.5000	...	0.5417	4290	1.2366	338417	97.5487
0.5417	...	0.5833	2823	0.8137	341240	98.3625
0.5833	...	0.6250	2382	0.6866	343622	99.0491
0.6250	...	0.6667	1364	0.3932	344986	99.4422
0.6667	...	0.7083	851	0.2453	345837	99.6875
0.7083	...	0.7500	488	0.1407	346325	99.8282
0.7500	...	0.7917	279	0.0804	346604	99.9086
0.7917	...	0.8333	167	0.0481	346771	99.9568
0.8333	...	0.8750	79	0.0228	346850	99.9795
0.8750	...	0.9167	33	0.0095	346883	99.9890
0.9167	...	0.9583	23	0.0066	346906	99.9957
0.9583	...	1.0000	15	0.0043	346921	100.0000
Totals			346921	100.0000		

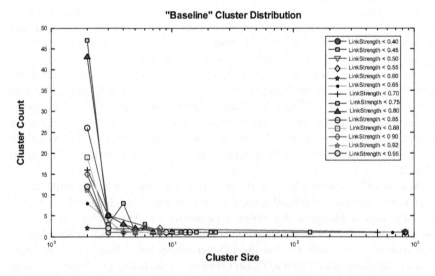

Fig. 5.13 Baseline cluster frequency by cluster size per corresponding threshold value

"Baseline Category" Cluster Frequency Distribution for Cluster Size: ■2 ■3 □4 □5 ■6 ■7 ■8 □9 ■10

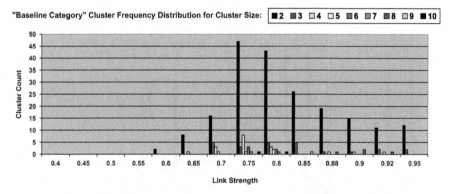

Fig. 5.14 Baseline cluster histogram for small size clusters per corresponding threshold value

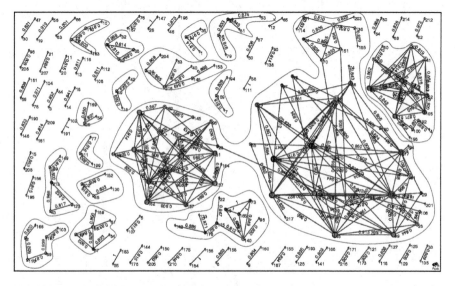

Fig. 5.15 Results for link strength ≥0.80 for baseline dataset

the label information while clustering in baseline approach. We report the differences between the two approaches based on the results as follows:

1. There are too many clusters obtained from baseline approach and many have very small size (most of them are two-member clusters). However, this is not the case with WisColl.

2. As a result of too many small-sized clusters, clusters are too focused. This affects the insertions of new blog site later on. Cluster configurations are highly unstable in such a focused clustering. For example cozimono = Music:Rock:Pop and billiam = Music:Rock:Pop are clustered together. This group is highly focussed and if a new blog about Music comes is added then it would not be assigned to this group.

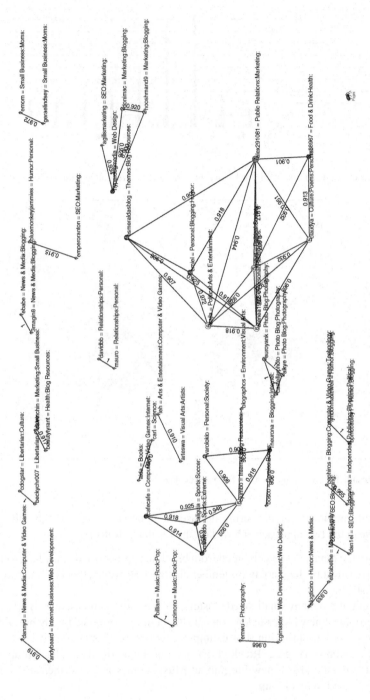

Fig. 5.16 Results for link strength ≥0.90 for baseline dataset; labels included

3. Close analysis shows that some clusters obtained from baseline clustering, have members whose blog site labels are not semantically related. For example, `bluemonkey jammies` = `Humor:Personal` and `emperoranton` = `SEO: Marketing` are clustered together. However, the labels are totally different and are not at all semantically related. There are several such clusters obtained from baseline clustering approach. This demonstrates that baseline clustering does not give semantically coherent clusters. This is because vector space clustering using blog posts are susceptible to text noise, and blogs are usually noisy. Also blogs are dynamic in nature with the blogger occasionally posting about different topics. Such off topic posts affect the clustering using vector space methods. However WisColl gives high-quality, semantically coherent clusters. For example, clusters having members like `Internet>` `Web Design` and `Internet>` `Web Development`; `Food & Drink` and `Food & Drink>` `Recipes`; `Internet, Computers, Technology,` and `Technology>` `Gadgets`, etc. are semantically related.

4. Several clusters obtained from baseline approach have members that have exactly same labels. For example, the cluster with bloggers `emom` and `geraelindsey` have the same labels, i.e., `Small Business` and `Moms`. This does not help in identifying relationships between blog sites that have different themes. Clustering blog sites that have different yet related theme/topics are more helpful. WisColl generates clusters that have blog sites with topics like, `Technology`, `Computers`, `Internet`, and `Technology>` `Gadgets`. Such a cluster serves a better purpose for various applications like search, organization of information, etc.

5.5.2.4   *k*-Means vs. Hierarchical Results

A Hierarchical clustering was generated for the 27 labels identified by WisColl for Link Strength five or greater, (see Fig. 5.9). The clustering was achieved using Pajek's Hierarchical Ward method, and is illustrated in Fig. 5.17. From the hierarchical diagram, we selected seven major clusters, as illustrated by Table 5.5. We then generated a *k*-Means clustering for $k = 7$ for the labels to analyze how well *k*-Means and Hierarchical clustering compared between the two methods.

   In order to compare how WisColl-based clustering fares with regards to the baseline blogger clustering, we generated similar Hierarchical and *k*-Means clusters for the baseline's blogger space as follows. In order to be able to compare between the results obtained from the label space, into the blogger space, we "map" each vector in the label space to its corresponding vector(s) in the blogger space. This was accomplished by associating the bloggers to each of the labels in the label cluster, given the blogger had used that label in his or her blog. This transforms the clusters in the label space to an equivalent cluster made out of bloggers in the blogger space. The mapping was generated for both Hierarchical and *k*-Means results. Since many of the bloggers had used more than one label for a blog, if the between-cluster distance is computed using single link, then many of these distances would be 0.

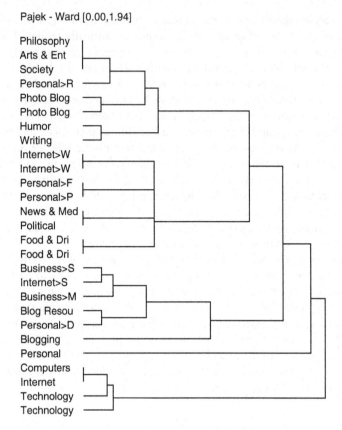

Fig. 5.17 Hierarchical clustering for link strength ≥ 5 for All-label dataset

This will skew the distribution of the cluster distances. Therefore we calculate the between-cluster and within-cluster distances using the average link. The mapping generates same number of clusters in the blogger space as the number of clusters obtained in label space. Since we selected seven clusters for hierarchical clustering in the label space, after mapping we get seven clusters of bloggers.

Next we try to observe the best value for K in k-Means. For the analysis and comparison, we followed the premise discussed in Sect. 5.4.1, where we presented the min and max criteria based on Formulation 5.1, which minimizes the within-cluster distance between the cluster members (i.e., more cohesive clusters) and Formulation 5.2 with regards to maximizing the between-cluster distance (i.e., well separated clusters). Figure 5.18 shows these results for the blogger clusters. To asses the value of K, we take advantage from the results obtained from Fig. 5.13, which suggests that based on link-strength analysis, the highest cluster count is for link strength 0.75, which is slightly above 60. Hence, we use 60 as the maximum value of K. We perform clustering of bloggers for $K = 5$ to 60. As shown in the figure, we

Table 5.5 Hierarchical clustering table with clustering assignment for link strength ≥5 for All-label

Index	Clus ID	Cluster Component
1	1	Philosophy
2	1	Arts & Entertainment
3	1	Society
4	1	Personal>Relationships
5	1	Photo Blog
6	1	Photo Blog>Photography
7	2	Humor
8	2	Writing
9	3	Internet>Web Design
10	3	Internet>Web Development
11	3	Personal>Family
12	3	Personal>Parenting
13	3	News & Media
14	3	Political
15	3	Food & Drink
16	3	Food & Drink>Recipes
17	4	Business>Small Business
18	4	Internet>SEO
19	4	Business>Marketing
20	4	Blog Resources
21	4	Personal>Development and Growth
22	5	Blogging
23	6	Personal
24	7	Computers
25	7	Internet
26	7	Technology>Gadgets
27	7	Technology

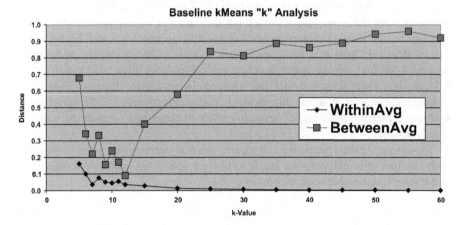

Fig. 5.18 k-Means k-analysis for baseline dataset

Table 5.6 Comparing WisColl with baseline approach using k-Means and hierarchical clustering

Type	Method	Within	Between
(a) Baseline-Blogger space	k-Means	0.0363 ± 0.1264	0.2194 ± 0.1301
	Hierarchical	0.0890 ± 0.1186	0.3644 ± 0.0903
(b) WisColl-label space	k-Means	0.0615 ± 0.1643	0.2860 ± 0.0536
	Hierarchical	0.0857 ± 0.1672	0.2761 ± 0.0571
(c) WisColl-Blogger space	k-Means	0.0844 ± 0.0995	0.7090 ± 0.0143
	Hierarchical	0.0849 ± 0.0943	0.8118 ± 0.0047

observe a lot of fluctuations in the range $K = 5$ to $K = 12$. Upon deeper analysis it shows that we obtain lowest within-cluster distance for $K = 7$. This results is in accordance to the hierarchical clustering as it also generated seven clusters. Note that for $K > 25$ even though it looks that the clustering is better (large between-cluster distance and small within-cluster distance) but in reality we obtain a lot of two member clusters for higher value of K, just like in Fig. 5.15.

The results comparing Hierarchical and k-Means clusters are summarized in Table 5.6. The table shows three categories: (a) "Baseline - Blogger Space" refers to the clustering generated by clustering in the blogger's space; (b) "WisColl – label Space", evaluates the clustering generated using label relation graph in the label's space; and (c) In "WisColl – Blogger Space," we transformed the label space clusters into the blogger space as described previously. It is in this last case, since we project the labels into the bloggers space, we can then make a fair comparison between the methods.

From the results in Table 5.6, we make two observations. First, WisColl performs better than Baseline in both clustering algorithms, k-Means and hierarchical (i.e., categories "a" and "c" in the table). Although we get lower within-cluster distance for baseline approach than the WisColl, the between-cluster distance is higher for baseline as compared to WisColl. This means that though we have cohesive clusters from baseline approach but they are not well separated. Also, the variance in the between-cluster distance of baseline approach is much higher than that of WisColl. Note that this comparison is made in blogger space to be fair. Second, k-Means performs better than hierarchical for WisColl in label space, since k-Means has lower within-cluster and higher between-cluster distance. However, in blogger space for WisColl, hierarchical clustering performs a little better than k-Means clustering with higher between-cluster distance and comparable within-cluster distance.

To summarize the results, we can clearly see that our method, when compared with baseline after mapping the labels to blogger space, has a better "separation" and tighter variation between the clusters.

5.6   Conclusions and Future Work

Clustering blog sites is a challenging task with many real-world applications. Classic clustering methods are not designed to take advantage of some of the characteristics of the blogosphere, like user-specified metadata. In this research, we propose to cluster blog sites by employing collective wisdom. We investigate various types of information available in a blog catalog site like user-specified tags and labels. We propose to leverage collective wisdom to generate graph that represents similarity between labels. We call this collective wisdom-based approach, WisColl, which is further used to perform clustering using conventional clustering approaches such as k-Means and hierarchical clustering algorithms. We compare WisColl with a representative SVD-based approach that does not use collective wisdom to discern their differences. Since WisColl mainly relies on the label information by the bloggers, it is poised to automatically adapt to the dynamic changes of the label information. Furthermore, in search of an effective clustering algorithm with collective wisdom, we evaluate different values of link strengths and various levels of directories, present results statistically and visually, and summarize findings.

Future work includes the integrative use of multiple types of information such as labels, tags, and posts in clustering, and use of the clustering results to help focused search in the blogosphere. We will also analyze the cluster's transitions with subsequence adjustments to link strength threshold values, and explore the possibility of defining rules to manage them, such as to the cases when numerous pair-wise clusters are generated, and others deleted, even though the seem to belong; may be sampling related. Our tests will include an expanded base beyond the original data collected from BlogCatalog, and analyze how well our methods conform with the newer data set. In the long term, subsequent to this work, we will explore how effectively bloggers belonging to the Long Tail are aggregated and represented as part of the critical mass. This corresponds to understanding how much we can close the gap with respect to the Short Head, which would result in a more effective target search space.

References

1. Agarwal N, Liu H, Salerno J, Yu PS (2007) Searching for 'Familiar Strangers' on blogosphere: problems and challenges. In: NSF symposium on next-generation data mining and cyber-enabled discovery and innovation (NGDM), Baltimore, MD
2. Anderson C (2006) The long tail: why the future of business is selling less of more. Hyperion, New York
3. Bansal NKN, Chiang F, Tompa FW (2007) Seeking stable clusters in the blogosphere. In: Proceedings of VLDB-07, University of Vienna, Austria, pp 806–817
4. Brooks C, Montanez N (2006) Improved annotation of the blogosphere via autotagging and hierarchical clustering. In: Proceedings of the WWW 2006. ACM, Edinburgh, UK, pp 625–632
5. Chin A, Chignell M (2006) A social hypertext model for finding community in blogs. In: HYPERTEXT '06: proceedings of the 17th conference on hypertext and hypermedia. ACM, New York, NY, USA, Odense, Denmark, pp 11–22

6. Cutting D, Karger D, Pedersen J, Tukey JW (1992) Scatter/gather: a cluster-based approach to browsing large document collections. In: Proceedings of the SIGIR, pp 318–329
7. Deerwester S, Dumais S, Furnas G, Landauer T, Harshman R (1990) Indexing by latent semantic analysis. J Am Soc Inform Sci 41(6):391
8. Devaney M, Ram A (1997) Efficient feature selection in conceptual clustering. In: Proceedings of ICML, pp 92–97
9. Dubes RC, Jain AK (1988) Algorithms for clustering data. Prentice Hall, Englewood Cliffs, NJ, USA
10. Hayes C, Avesani P, Veeramachaneni S (2007) An analysis of the use of tags in a blog recommender system. In: Proceedings of the IJCAI, Hyderabad, India, pp 1–20
11. Hotho A, Jaschke R, Schmitz C, Stumme G (2006) Information retrieval in folksonomies: Search and ranking. In: Proceedings of ESWC, Budva, Montenegro, pp 411–426
12. Huang JZ, Ng M, Jing L (2006) Text clustering: algorithms, semantics and systems. PAKDD Tutorial, Singapore
13. Lin Y-R, Sundaram H, Chi Y, Tatemura J, Tseng B (2006) Discovery of blog communities based on mutual awareness. In: www'06: 3rd annual workshop on webloging ecosystem: aggreation, analysis and dynamics
14. MacQueen JB (1967) Some methods for classification and analysis of multivariate observations. In: Proceedings of the 5th symposium on mathematics, statistics, and probability, pp 281–297
15. McLachlan GJ, Basford KE (1988) Mixture models. Inference and applications to clustering. Statistics: textbooks and monographs. Dekker, New York
16. Mootee I (2001) High intensity marketing. SA Press
17. O'Reilly T (September 2005) What is web 2.0 – design patterns and business models for the next generation of software. http://www.oreillynet.com/pub/a/oreilly/tim/news/ 2005/09/30/ what-is-web-20.html
18. Qamra A, Tseng B, Chang EY (2006) Mining blog stories using community-based and temporal clustering. In: Proceedings of the CIKM, pp 58–67
19. Song W, Park SC (2006) Genetic algorithm-based text clustering technique:automatic evolution of clusters with high efficiency. In: Proceedings of the 7th international conference on web-age information management workshops (WAIMW), Hong Kong, China, p 17
20. Steinbach M, Karypis G, Kumar V (2000) A comparison of document clustering techniques. Technical report TR-00-034, Department of Computer Science and Engineering, University of Minnesota
21. Tseng BL, Tatemura J, Wu Y (2005) Tomographic: clustering to visualize blog communities as mountain views. In: Proceedings of the World Wide Web
22. Xin Li PSY, Liu B (2006) Mining community structure of named entities from web pages and blogs. In: Proceedings of AAAI-06
23. Xu L, Neufeld J, Larson B, Schuurmans D (2004) Maximum margin clustering. In: Proceedings of the neural information processing systems conference (NIPS), Vancouver, Canada
24. Xu S, Zhang J (2004) A parallel hybrid web document clustering algorithm and its performance study. J Supercomput 30:117–131
25. Yin X, Han J, Yu PS (2006) Linkclus: efficient clustering via heterogeneous semantic links. In: VLDB'2006: proceedings of the 32nd international conference on very large data bases. VLDB Endowment, pp 427–438
26. Zamir O, Etzioni O (1998) Web document clustering: a feasibility demonstration. In: Proceedings of SIGIR, Melbourne, Australia, pp 46–54

Chapter 6
Exploratory Analysis of the Social Network of Researchers in Inductive Logic Programming

Nada Lavrač, Miha Grčar, Blaž Fortuna, and Paola Velardi

Abstract In this chapter, we present selected techniques for social network analysis and text mining and interpret the results of exploratory analysis of the social network of researchers in inductive logic programming (ILP), based on the ILP scientific publications database collected within the ILPnet2 project. Part of the analysis was performed with the Pajek software for large (social) network analyses, where the central entity of the analysis was the author, related to other authors by coauthorship links, weighted by the number of his or her publications registered in the ILPnet2 database. The chapter presents also a novel methodology for topic ontology learning from text documents. The proposed methodology, named OntoTermExtraction (Term Extraction for Ontology learning), is based on OntoGen, a semiautomated tool for topic ontology construction, upgraded by using an advanced terminology extraction tool in an iterative, semiautomated ontology construction process. The approach was successfully used for generating the ontology of topics in Inductive Logic Programming, learned semiautomatically from papers indexed in the ILPnet2 publications database.

6.1 Introduction

In social sciences, social network analysis has become a powerful methodology, complementing standard statistical approaches. Network concepts have been defined, tested, and applied in research traditions throughout the social sciences, ranging from anthropology to business administration and history. Social network

N. Lavrač, M. Grčar, and B. Fortuna
Jožef Stefan Institute, Jamova cesta 39, 1000 Ljubljana, Slovenia
e-mail: [nada.lavrac;miha.grcar;blaz.fortuna]@ijs.si

N. Lavrač
University of Nova Gorica, Vipavska 13, 5000 Nova Gorica, Slovenia

P. Velardi (✉)
Universita di Roma "La Sapienza", 113 Via Salaria, Roma RM 00198, Italy
e-mail: velardi@di.uniroma1.it

A. Abraham et al. (eds.), *Computational Social Network Analysis*, Computer
Communications and Networks, DOI 10.1007/978-1-84882-229-0_6,
© Springer-Verlag London Limited 2010

analysis focuses on interpreting patterns of social ties among people, groups of people, organizations, or countries [9,12,14]. A typical domain is a group of individuals and their characteristics and the structure of their ties. Social network analysis tools have recently gained much popularity; these include a specialized professional tool for social network analysis, named Pajek [9].

Exploratory analysis of social networks can be made more powerful if complemented by the use of data mining tools [4], and text mining [1] in particular. A frequently used approach is to use clustering techniques [6] for clustering of text documents. In order to complement social network analysis, a particularly interesting goal is to automatically detect the main topics addressed by the community of actors of a social network, e.g., topics of papers written by researchers of a specific research area.

In order to detect the document topics, and cluster the documents according to these topics, the OntoGen tool [2] for semiautomated, data-driven ontology construction can be applied, focused on the construction and editing of topic ontologies. In a topic ontology, each node is a cluster of documents, represented by keywords (topics), and nodes are connected by relations (typically, the SubConceptOf relation). The system combines text mining techniques with an efficient user interface aimed to reduce user's time and the complexity of ontology construction. In this way, it presents a significant improvement in comparison with present manual and relatively complex ontology editing tools, such as Protégé [13], the use of which may be hindered by the lack of ontology engineering skills of domain experts constructing the ontology.

Concept naming suggestion (currently implemented through describing a document cluster by a set of relevant terms) plays one of the central parts of the OntoGen system. Concept naming helps the user to evaluate the clusters when organizing them hierarchically. This facility is provided by employing unsupervised and supervised methods for generating the naming suggestions. Despite the well-elaborated and user-friendly approach to concept naming, as currently provided by OntoGen, the approach was until now limited to single-word keyword suggestions, and by the use of very basic text lemmatization in the OntoGen text preprocessing phase. This chapter proposes an improved ontology construction process, employing improved concept naming by using terminology extraction as implemented in the advanced TermExtractor tool [11].

The domain we analyzed was the social network of authors of scientific publications, stored in the publications database of the ILPnet2 Network of Excellence in Inductive Logic Programming [5, 10]. ILPNet2 consisted of 37 project partners composed mainly of universities and research institutes performing research in the area of Inductive Logic Programming [8]. Our main entity for the analysis were individual authors, related to other authors by coauthorship relationships. The database includes 589 authors, 1,046 coauthorships, and most ILP-related papers published in 1970–2003. We first performed social network analysis experiments, aimed at answering some questions such as: Who are the most important authors in the area? Are there any closed groups of authors? Is there any person in-between most of these groups? Is this person also very important? Social network analysis was followed by text mining experiments, performed on ILPNet2 documents, aimed at semiautomatically building a topic ontology of the domain of Inductive Logic Programming.

The chapter presents the ILPNet2 domain and data preprocessing in Sects. 6.2 and 6.3. Analysis of the social network of ILP authors, performed by the Pajek tool in terms of cohesion (density, degree, components), brokerage (degree, closeness, betweenness), and ranking (prestige, acyclic decomposition) techniques used for ILPNet2 analysis, is presented in Sect. 6.4. Section 6.5 describes text mining technologies, as implemented in the OntoGen and TermExtractor tools, and their use in ILPNet2 data analysis. Section 6.6 presents the improved methodology, through a detailed description of the individual steps of the advanced ontology construction process. In Sect. 6.7 the approach is illustrated by the results achieved in the analysis of the ILPnet2 database. The chapter concludes with a summary in Sect. 6.8.

6.2   The ILPnet2 Database

The analyzed domain is the scientific publications database of the ILPnet2 Network of Excellence in Inductive Logic Programming [5]. ILPnet2 consisted of 37 project partners composed mainly of universities and research institutes. The entities for our analysis are ILP authors and their publications. The ILPnet2 database is publicly available on the Web and contains information about ILP publications between 1971 and 2003. The data about publications were in the BibTeX format, available in files at http://www.cs.bris.ac.uk/~ILPnet2/Tools/Reports/Bibtexs/2003,...(one file for each year 2003, 2002, ...).

The first stage of the exploratory data analysis process is data acquisition and preprocessing. The data were acquired with the *wget* utility and converted into the XML format. A part of the shell script that collects the data from the Web is shown below.

```
$for ((i=1971;i<2004;i++)); do
wget
http://www.cs.bris.ac.uk/~ILPnet2/Tools/Reports/Bibtexs/$;
done
```

To simplify data manipulation and analysis, it was convenient to store the data also into a relational database format, using the Microsoft SQL Sever. The resulting ILPnet2 database (see its database schema in Fig. 6.1) contains the following tables:

- *Authors*: ID (key), name of the author
- *AuthorOf* (relates authors to publications with a many-to-many relation): ID (key), ID of the author, ID of the publication
- *Publications*: ID (key), title, abstract, institution, year, month

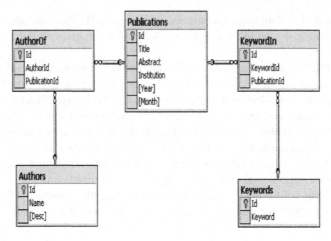

Fig. 6.1 The ILPnet2 database schema

- *KeywordIn* (related keywords to publications with a many-to-many relation): ID (key), ID of the keyword, ID of the publication
- *Keywords*: ID (key), keyword

One of the tasks accompanying the database construction was the normalization of authors' names. Due to the simplicity of our heuristics, some names were not normalized correctly hence the same author was given several different identifiers. Such false normalizations were corrected manually by reviewing the table of mappings between authors' names and their identifiers. While this was crucially needed for social network analysis, this step was not needed for the experiments in ontology construction, as ontology construction uses only document titles and abstracts, preprocessed using a predefined list of stop-words and the Porter stemmer.

6.3 Data Preprocessing for Social Network Analysis

We converted the data into the Pajek compatible input file (.net) which contain the following mandatory elements:

- *Vertices* Each vertex represents an author and is described with an ID (in our case this is the sequential number of the author in the Authors table), a short string (in our case this is the normalized name of the author), and some other parameters. We have also set the vertex size (parameters x and y fact) which denote the author's productivity.
- *Edges* Each edge is described with two IDs corresponding to the two vertices that define the edge (i.e., the two vertices connected by this edge). Furthermore, each edge is characterized with a weight that corresponds to the degree of collaboration (i.e., coauthorship) between the two authors.

Fig. 6.2 A network
converted to bond by
coauthorship

For certain types of analyses, our undirected social network of authors was converted to a directed network, using *bond by coauthorship*. We first created a *complete directed network* (i.e., a network based on a graph containing no loops and multiple arcs but connecting each and every pair of vertices both ways) based on the vertices representing the authors. We weighted each arc according to the *trust* of the source author in the target author; as suggested in [9] trust is modeled as a linear combination of the number of joint publications and the number of target author's publications as illustrated in Fig. 6.2.

In our application, we applied the logarithm to the number of individual's publications and the number of joint publications (i.e., w_A and $w_{A\&B}$ in Fig. 6.2) when calculating arc weights. With the logarithm we achieved a near-linear growth in the "logarithmized" productivity from the least to the most productive author. This in effect prevented the few hyper-productive authors from getting all the highest in-arc weights as soon as α was set to somewhat less than 1. The values of the number of joint publications were treated equally. Furthermore, both types of values were normalized with respect to their corresponding maximum value so that "high productivity" was able to compete with "high level of collaboration" (both were represented with a value close to 1 after the normalization).

The next step was to remove some of the arcs from our complete directed network. We decided to allow each author to keep at most k outgoing arcs – the ones with the highest weights. With the so-obtained directed network (directed graph to be more specific) we were able to calculate the structural prestige of authors (see Sect. 6.4.3).

6.4   ILPNet2 Social Network Analysis

Several techniques for social network analyses on ILPnet2 database were used: cohesion, brokerage, and ranking.

6.4.1   Cohesion

Cohesion is an attractive force between the individuals (network nodes). Solidarity, shared norms, identity, collective behavior, and social cohesion are considered to emerge from social relations. Therefore, the first concern of social network analysis is to investigate which individuals are related and which are not. A general hypothesis is that people who match on social characteristics will interact more often, and people who interact regularly will foster a common attitude or identity. The ultimate goal is to test whether structurally delineated subgroups differ with respect to other social characteristics, for instance, norms, behavior, or identity. For the purpose of our analysis we used the following techniques to detect cohesive subgroups in our ILPnet2 network: density, degree, and components.

Density In network analysis density represents the number of lines in a simple network, expressed as a proportion of the maximum possible number of lines. It is inversely related to network size: the larger the social network, the lower the density because the number of possible lines increases rapidly with the number of vertices, whereas the number of ties which each person can maintain is limited.

Degree The degree of a vertex is the number of lines incident with the vertex. Degree is a discrete attribute of a vertex (it is always an integer).

Figure 6.3 shows the distribution of the degree of coauthorships ILPnet2. Almost 150 authors have two coauthorships and only few authors have more than ten.

Since the visualization of our network (Fig. 6.4) showed no specific characteristics, we looked for vertices with the highest degree. The removal of the lines with value less than 10 and the reduction of the vertices with degree less than 1 resulted in the visualization shown in Fig. 6.5. Note that 24 authors which have more than 10 coauthorships are grouped together in seven subgroups, mostly consisting of researchers from the same country.

Components Components identify cohesive subgroups in a straightforward manner: each vertex belongs to exactly one component. Networks are connected weakly or strongly. A network is weakly connected if all vertices are connected by a semi-path. A semi-path is a semi-walk in which no vertex in between the first and last vertex of the semi-walk occurs more than once. A semi-walk from vertex u to vertex v is a sequence of lines such that the end of one line is the starting vertex of the next line and the sequence starts at vertex u and ends at vertex v. Figure 6.6 shows 110

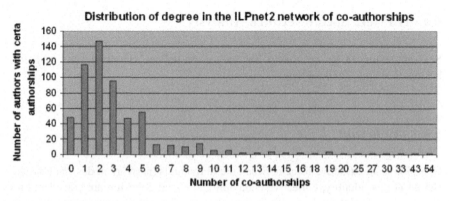

Fig. 6.3 The distribution of the degree of coauthorships

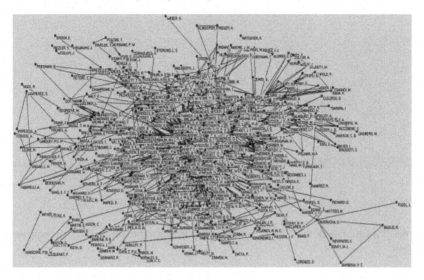

Fig. 6.4 Connections in ILPnet2, visualized by Pajek

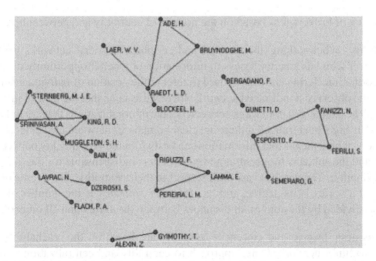

Fig. 6.5 Visualization of the ILPnet2 network after removal of the lines with value less than 10 and the reduction of the vertices with degree less than one

components of the ILPnet2 network. Having analyzed the individual components we have observed that the individuals in smaller components are mostly grouped according to the country, whereas the biggest component includes different individuals connected with each other.

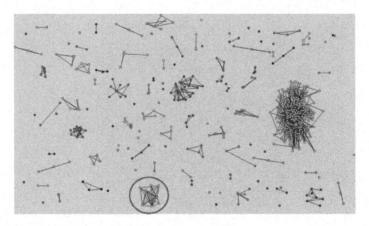

Fig. 6.6 Visualization of the ILPnet2 network using the algorithm for discovering components in Pajek

6.4.2 Brokerage

The notion of brokerage is based on the notions of centrality and betweenness.

Centrality When talking about center and periphery in social networks we want to discover who has a better access to information or a better opportunity to spread the information. Term *centrality* is used to refer to the position of individual vertices within the observed nondirected network where we assume that the flow of information may be exchanged both ways between people or organizations that are linked. A network is highly centralized if there are clear boundaries between the center and the periphery, which means that information can be distributed very quickly between the center and the subjects (noncentral nodes), which is indispensable for the transition of information. The vertices vary with respect to their centrality. The *degree of centrality* of a vertex is its degree, and its *closeness centrality* is the number of other vertices divided by the sum of all distances between the vertex and all others.

Betweenness Degree and closeness centrality are based on the reachability of a vertex within a network. Other approach to centrality and centralization is based on an idea that vertex is more important as an intermediary in the communication network. This approach is based on the notion *betweenness*, where *betweenness centrality* of a vertex is measured by the proportion of all shortest path between pairs of other vertices that include the given vertex. See the visualization of this notion in Fig. 6.7.

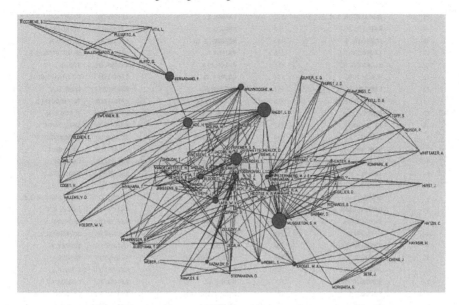

Fig. 6.7 Betweenness in ILPnet2 shown in Pajek, where larger vertices represent people that have more direct or indirect connections (i.e., have a better ability to disperse information)

6.4.3 Ranking

Ranking deals with the notions prestige and ranking through acyclic decomposition.

Prestige In social networks there are many techniques to calculate the so-called *structural prestige* of a person. Note, however, that structural prestige is not identical to the concept of *social prestige* (or *social status*), but depends on the data from which we are able to infer a structure so that the structural prestige of a person only reflects his or her actual social prestige.

- The *in-degree* of a vertex represents the *popularity* of the person represented by the vertex. To measure popularity, we need to have a directed network.
- *Domains* represent extend prestige to indirect in-links so that the overall structure of the network is taken into account. The *input domain* of a vertex is defined as the number or percentage of all other vertices that are connected by a path to this vertex. A *restricted input domain* restricts the maximum paths length. In well-connected networks it is recommended to limit the input domain to direct neighbors (i.e., to use popularity instead) or to those at a predefined maximum distance (e.g., 2).
- *Proximity prestige* of a vertex is defined as the proportion of all vertices (except itself) in its input domain divided by the mean distance from all vertices in its input domain. It ranges from 0 (no proximity prestige) to 1 (highest proximity prestige).

Input degree		Unrestricted input domain size		Proximity prestige	
28	MUGGLETON, S. H.	152	LAMMA, E.	0.082030307	RAEDT, L. D.
21	RAEDT, L. D.	152	RIGUZZI, F.	0.077044151	DZEROSKI, S.
20	DZEROSKI, S.	152	PEREIRA, L. M.	0.068453862	LAVRAC, N.
17	LAVRAC, N.	152	RAMON, J.	0.066777042	MUGGLETON, S. H.
17	BLOCKEEL, H.	152	FLACH, P. A.	0.064046309	ADE, H.
12	FLACH, P. A.	152	LAVRAC, N.	0.06462585	BRUYNOOGHE, M.
12	SRINIVASAN, A.	152	STRUYF, J.	0.063683172	LAER, W. V.
11	GYIMOTHY, T.	152	BLOCKEEL, H.	0.060918631	TODOROVSKI, L.
10	JACOBS, N.	152	DEHASPE, L.	0.057783113	FLACH, P. A.
10	BERGADANO, F.	152	LAER, W. V.	0.054504505	SRINIVASAN, A.
9	WROBEL, S.	152	BRUYNOOGHE, M.	0.054346497	GAMBERGER, D.
9	STEPANKOVA, O.	152	DZEROSKI, S.	0.052812523	SABLON, G.
9	ITOH, H.	152	RAEDT, L. D.	0.051974229	DEHASPE, L.
9	ADE, H.	152	GAMBERGER, D.	0.051837094	BLOCKEEL, H.
8	KING, R. D.	152	LACHICHE, N.	0.048245614	KING, R. D.
8	OHWADA, H.	152	TODOROVSKI, L.	0.048015873	STERNBERG, M. J. E.
8	BRUYNOOGHE, M.	152	KAKAS, A. C.	0.047743034	KAKAS, A. C.
8	BOSTROM, H.	152	JOVANOSKI, V.	0.047283414	LACHICHE, N.
8	KRAMER, S.	152	TURNEY, P.	0.044957113	JOVANOSKI, V.
8	FURUKAWA, K.	152	ADE, H.	0.044957113	TURNEY, P.
8	CSIRIK, J.	152	DIMOPOULOS, Y.	0.043609897	RAMON, J.
7	HORVATH, T.	152	SABLON, G.	0.043226091	STRUYF, J.
7	ESPOSITO, F.	77	KING, R. D.	0.040507749	RIGUZZI, F.
7	SHOUDAI, T.	77	MUGGLETON, S. H.	0.040341393	DIMOPOULOS, Y.
7	DEHASPE, L.	77	SRINIVASAN, A.	0.035082604	LAMMA, E.

Fig. 6.8 Top 25 authors in the ILP domain according to the three structural prestige measures, namely input degree, unrestricted domain size, and proximity prestige

Ranking We now discuss a technique for extracting discrete ranks from social relations. A recipe for determining the hierarchy, named *acyclic decomposition*, is presented. Once we have determined the nature of our network, we can start discovering the clusters and/or the hierarchy. The first approach we discuss is the so-called *acyclic decomposition*. While cyclic subnetworks (i.e., strong components) represent clusters of equals, acyclic subnetworks perfectly reflect the hierarchy. The recipe for determining the hierarchy is as follows:

1. Partition the network into strong components (i.e., clusters of equals, described in Sect. 6.4.1).
2. Create a new network in which each vertex represents one cluster.
3. Compute the maximum depth of each vertex to determine the hierarchy.

Figure 6.9 shows the hierarchy in the ILPnet2 network. Each vertex represents one strong component (cluster of equals), each labeled by a random representative (e.g., #KING, R. D.). If we then "extract" individuals from each of the components, we get the network shown in Fig. 6.10. The size of the vertex denotes the author's productivity (the number of publications). Once the hierarchy has been established, we remove the intercluster arcs (i.e., arcs that were interconnecting the strong components), and convert the bi-directed intra-cluster arcs (arcs within a strong component) into edges. After removing all the remaining arcs, we are left with the network shown in Fig. 6.11. With this procedure we have fine-grained each

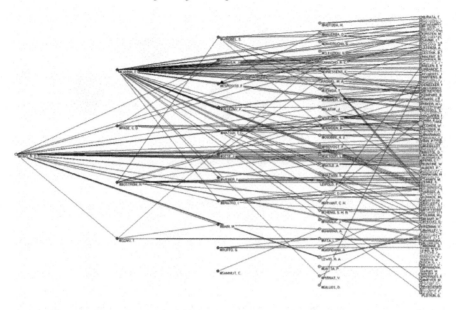

Fig. 6.9 The hierarchy in the ILPnet2 network

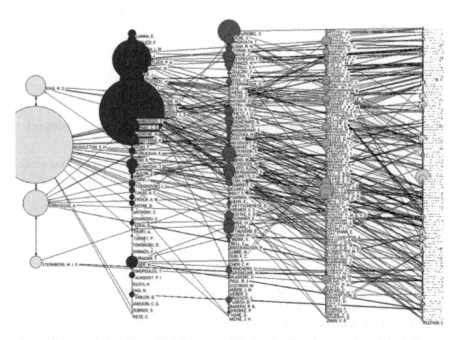

Fig. 6.10 The hierarchy in the ILPnet2 network. The individuals were "extracted" from the strong components

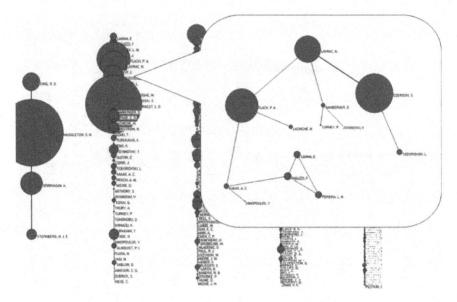

Fig. 6.11 The hierarchy in the ILPnet2 network. The strong components were fine-grained into smaller clusters of bidirectional connected individuals

strong component into smaller clusters of people that are interconnected (see an enlarged cluster in Fig. 6.11).

6.5 Document Analysis: Background Text Mining Technologies

This section describes the background technologies used in ILPNet2 publications analysis: semiautomated topic ontology generation tool OntoGen, and term extraction tool TermExtractor.

6.5.1 OntoGen

The two main design goals of the ontology construction tool OntoGen [2, 3] were to enable (1) the visualization and exploration of existing concepts from the ontology, and (2) addition of new concepts or modification of existing concepts using simple and straightforward machine learning and text mining algorithms. These goals are supported by the following two main characteristics of the OntoGen system:

• *Semiautomatic* The system is an interactive tool that aids the user during the topic ontology construction process. It suggests concepts, relations between the concepts, and concept names, automatically assigns instances to the concepts, visualizes instances within a concept and provides a good overview of the ontology to the user through concept browsing and various kinds of visualizations. At the same time, the user is always in full control of the system and can affect topic ontology construction by accepting or rejecting the system's suggestions or manually editing the ontology.

- *Data-Driven* Most of the aid provided by the system is based on the underlying data provided by the user typically at the start of the ontology construction process. The data affect the structure of the domain for which the user is building the topic ontology. The data are usually a document corpus, where ontological instances are either documents themselves or named entities occurring in the documents. The system supports automated extraction of instances (used for learning concepts) and co-occurrences of instances (used for learning relations between the concepts) from the data.

The main window of the system provides multiple views on the ontology. A tree-based view on the ontology, which is intuitive for most users, presents a natural way to represent a topic ontology as a concept hierarchy. This view is used to show the folder structure and as a visualization offering a one-glance view of the whole topic ontology. Each concept from the ontology is further described by the most informative keywords, automatically extracted (employing unsupervised and supervised learning methods) from the cluster of documents defining the concept.

A sample topic ontology in the form of a tree-based concept hierarchy, constructed from the ILPnet2 documents, is shown in Fig. 6.12. Both the first and the second level of the concept hierarchy were constructed using the k-Means clustering algorithm, where the first level was split into seven concepts and each of these concepts was further split into three sub-concepts. The hierarchical structuring is user-triggered. At each single level, k-Means is invoked for various user-defined values of k, then selecting the preferred k and dividing all the documents into k-subclusters, consequently.

While this procedure of topic ontology construction is elegant and simple for the user, quite some effort is needed to understand the contents and the meaning of the selected concepts. This is especially striking when comparing the second-level concepts, for example the sub-concepts of the concept named *logic _program, program,* and *inductive _logic* in Fig. 6.12 with the sub-concepts of the concept *logic program* in Fig. 6.13, which shows the concept hierarchy developed by the novel concept naming methodology based on TermExtractor, proposed in the next section.

6.5.2 TermExtractor

The TermExtractor tool [11] for automatic extraction of terms (possibly consisting of several words, as opposed to single keywords) from documents works as follows.

Given a collection of documents from the desired domain, TermExtractor first extracts a list of candidate terms (frequent multi-word expressions). In the second

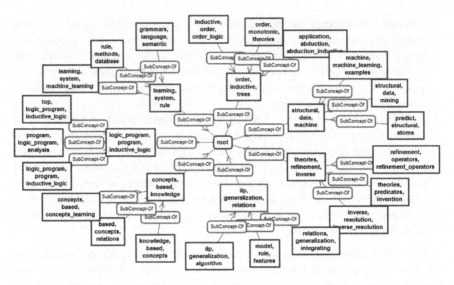

Fig. 6.12 Ontology constructed by the standard OntoGen approach, constructed from the ILP-net2 publications data, using the k-Means clustering algorithm without using the pre-calculated vocabulary extracted by TermExtractor

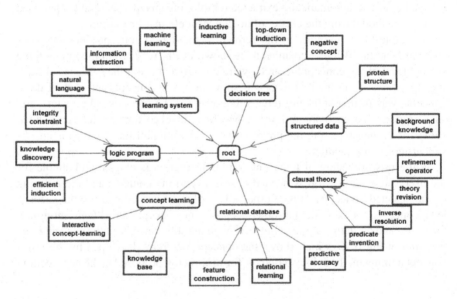

Fig. 6.13 Ontology constructed from the ILPnet2 documents using the pre-calculated terminology

step it evaluates each of the candidate terms using several scores which are then combined and the candidates are ranked according to the combined score. The output is a set of candidates whose score exceeds a given threshold. Documents from contrast domains are used as extra input for term evaluation and serve as a control group for measuring the term significance. The following scores are used to evaluate candidate terms in the second step (normalized score values are in the [0,1] interval):

- *Domain relevance* is high if the term is significantly more frequent in the domain of interest than in other domains.
- *Domain consensus* is high if the term is used consistently across the documents from the domain.
- *Lexical cohesion* is high if the words composing the term are more frequently found with the term than alone in the documents.
- *Structural relevance* is high for terms that are emphasized in the documents (e.g., appear in the title).
- *Miscellaneous* set of heuristics is used to remove generic modifiers (e.g., large knowledge base).

The combined score is a weighted convex combination of the individual scores.

6.6 The OntoTermExtraction Methodology

There are several ways in which a vocabulary can be acquired. In some domains there already exist established vocabularies (e.g., EUROVOC used for annotating European legislation, AGROVOC used for annotating agricultural documents, ASFA used within UN FAO, DMOZ created collaboratively to categorize Web pages, etc.). Another option is automatic extraction of terms from documents, which is especially attractive for the domains where there is no established vocabulary.

Concept and concept name suggestions play a central part in every ontology construction system. OntoGen provides unsupervised and supervised methods for generating such suggestions [2, 3]. Unsupervised learning methods automatically generate a list of sub-concepts for a currently selected concept by using k-means clustering and latent semantic indexing (LSI) techniques to generate a list of possible sub-concepts. On the other hand, supervised learning methods require the user to have a rough idea about a new topic[1] – this is identified through a query returning the documents. The system automatically identifies the documents that correspond to the topic and the selection can be further refined by the user–computer interaction through an active learning loop using a machine learning technique for semiautomatic acquisition of user's knowledge.

While OntoGen originally used only the input documents for proposing concept suggestions and term extraction techniques for providing help at naming the concepts, it should be noted that the whole process can be significantly improved by constructing a predefined vocabulary from the domain of the ontology under

---

[1] Hereafter, we name *concepts* the document clusters generated by the k-Means clustering algorithm, while a *topic* is a description of the concept, e.g., a term of a set of terms that best identify the document cluster.

construction. The vocabulary can be used to support the user during hierarchical ordering of concepts, and to create concept descriptions, thus helping concept evaluation.

The rest of this section presents the proposed OntoTermExtraction methodology, through a detailed description of the individual steps of this ontology construction process.

6.6.1 Steps in the Proposed OntoTermExtraction Methodology for Concept Naming

The advanced ontology construction process, proposed in this chapter, consists of the following steps:

(a) Document clustering to find the nodes in the ontology
(b) Terminology extraction from document clusters using TermExtractor
(c) Populating the term vocabulary and keyword extraction
(d) Choosing the concept name (topic) by comparing the best-ranked terms with the extracted keywords

6.6.2 Populating the Terms and Keyword Extraction

For each term from the vocabulary, a classification model is needed which can predict if the term is relevant for a given document cluster. In this chapter we use a centroid-based nearest neighbor classifier which was developed for fast classification of documents into taxonomies. We use this approach since it can scale well to larger collections of terms (hundreds of thousands of terms). A training set of documents is needed to generate a classification model. In some cases vocabularies already come with a set of documents annotated by the terms. In this case these documents can be used for training the term models. When no annotated documents are available, information retrieval can be applied for finding documents to populate the terms.

In this chapter we propose using two different techniques to populate terms extracted by TermExtractor.

Let T be the set of terms automatically extracted from document clusters:

- The first technique used the ILPnet2 collection. Each term $t \in T$ was issued in turn as a query and the top-ranked documents (according to cosine similarity, using TFIDF word weighting) were used to populate the term.
- The second technique did not use the ILPnet2 collection and relied on Google Web search instead. A query was generated from each term t by taking its words and attaching an extra keyword "ILP" to limit the search to ILP-related Web

pages. For example, if *t* is *inductive logic programming*, the query is *ILP inductive logic programming*. The query was then sent to Google and snippets of the returned search results were used to populate the term.

The ILP vocabulary prepared in this way was used as an extra input to OntoGen, besides the collection of the articles. We tried both approaches but in this chapter we only show the results of the second technique, because the retrieval from the whole Web turned out to be a richer resource than just the ILPnet2 collection. Details on how the vocabulary looked and how it was applied in the ILP ontology construction are described in Sect. 6.5.

6.7   ILPnet2 Vocabulary and Ontology Construction

In this section, the approach is illustrated by the results achieved in the analysis of the ILPnet2 publications database.

6.7.1   Vocabulary Extraction

As described in the previous section, we used TermExtractor to automatically extract the vocabulary for the ILP domain from the ILPnet2 collection of ILP publications. Table 6.1 shows the 11 top-ranked terms (out of 97) extracted from ILPnet2 documents.

All the terms were populated using Google Web search. As an example, here are the top five snippets that were returned for the query "ILP predictive accuracy":

- *Boosting Descriptive ILP for Predictive Learning in Bioinformatics* – General, this means that a higher predictive accuracy can be achieved. Thirdly, although some predictive ILP systems may produce multiple classification ...

Table 6.1 Top-ranked terms extracted by TermExtractor from ILPnet2 documents

Top-10 terms extracted from ILPnet2	Term weight	Domain relevance	Domain consensus	Lexical cohesion
Inductive logic	0.928	1.000	0.968	0.557
Logic programming	0.924	1.000	0.988	0.293
Inductive logic programming	0.893	1.000	0.966	0.181
Background knowledge	0.825	1.000	0.737	0.835
Logic program	0.824	1.000	0.867	0.203
Machine learning	0.785	1.000	0.777	0.221
Data mining	0.776	1.000	0.691	0.672
Refinement operator	0.757	1.000	0.572	1.000
Decision tree	0.742	1.000	0.613	0.714
Inverse resolution	0.722	1.000	0.557	0.894
Experimental result	0.718	1.000	0.594	0.684

- *Imperial College Computational Bioinformatics Laboratory (CBL)* – Results on scientific discovery applications of ILP are separated below ... Progol's predictive accuracy was equivalent to regression on the main set of 188....
- *Evolving Logic Programs to Classify Chess-Endgame Positions* – Indicate that in the cases where the ILP algorithm performs badly, the introduction of either union or crossover increases predictive accuracy....
- *Estimating the Predictive Accuracy of a Classifier* – The predictive accuracy of a classifier. We present a scenario where meta-.... Workshop on Data Mining, Decision Support, Meta-Learning and ILP, 2000....
- -*-BibTeX ... – An outline of the theory of ILP is given, together with a description of Golem.... Performance is measured using both predictive accuracy and a new cost....

For each query the snippets of the first 1,000 results were used. The snippets served as input for term modeling, while the models generated for each term, using this data, were then used for generating the concept suggestions and name suggestions in OntoGen.

6.7.2   Ontology Learning

First the ILPnet2 collection and vocabulary were loaded into the program. The collection was imported in OntoGen as a directory of files, where each document was a separate ASCII text file (File → New ontology → Folder). The vocabulary was loaded using the Tools → Context menu.

After experimenting with different numbers and with the help of concept visualization, a partition into seven concepts using the k-Means clustering algorithm was chosen. For all the seven concepts the first-ranked term suggested from the vocabulary suggested by TermExtractor was selected. This means that the term extraction and population have indeed succeeded to rank the terms in a meaningful way. This is illustrated also by the following list of discovered concepts, with best-ranked concept names proposed by TermExtractor, followed by the second best-ranked concept name (in parentheses), and the list of most important keywords, as chosen originally by OntoGen:

- Learning system (learning algorithm) – learning, system, rule, language, methods, machine_learning, machine, approach, ilp, grammars
- Decision tree (logical decision tree) – order, inductive, trees, order_logic, discovery, decision, application, decision_trees, database, experiments
- Structured data (chemical structure) – structural, data, machine, predict, examples, relations, machine_learning, mining, definitions, knowledge
- Clausal theory (theory revision) – theories, refinement, inverse, resolution, predicates, operators, inverse_resolution, invention, refinement_operators, revision
- Relational database (inductive learning) – ilp, generalization, relations, model, algorithm, constraints, integrating, rule, agent, evaluation

By checking the publication years of articles from different concepts it was possible to analyze the *evolution* of topics. For example, we can notice that most frequent years in concepts clausal theory, concept learning and logic program were around 1994, concepts structured data and learning system were most frequent around year 2000, and concepts decision tree and relational database appear to be most recent in years following 2000. Each of the concepts was further split into sub-concepts using suggestions from the vocabulary which resulted in the two-level taxonomy shown in Fig. 6.13.

6.8 Summary

We have presented specific techniques for social network analyses and text mining, applied to the discovery of regularities in the ILPNet2 scientific publications database. Using the social network analysis software Pajek, the graphical presentations give us an insight into the relational ties between the ILPNet2 authors. Moreover, this chapter presents the results of text analysis techniques, and a novel concept naming methodology applicable in semiautomated topic ontology construction, and illustrates the improved concept naming facility on the ontology of topics extracted from the ILPnet2 scientific publications database. Concept naming supports the user in the task of concept discovery, concept naming, and keeps the constructed topic ontology more consistent and aligned with the established terminology in the domain. Further work will be devoted to the evaluation of the constructed ontologies [7].

Acknowledgments This work was supported by the Slovenian Ministry of Higher Education, Science and Technology project Knowledge Technologies, and the 7FP EU project Bisociation Networks for Creative Information Discovery (BISON). The authors are grateful to S. Sabo, D.A. Fabjan and P. Ljubi who have transformed the ILPNet2 database into the XML format and contributed to the results of experiments in social network analysis with Pajek.

References

1. Feldman R, Sanger J (2007) The text mining handbook: Advanced approaches in analyzing unstructured data. Cambridge University Press, New York, pp 1–424
2. Fortuna B, Mladeni D, Grobelnik M (2006) Semi-automatic construction of topic ontologies. In: Ackermann et al (ed) Semantics, web and mining. LNCS (LNAI), vol 4289. Springer, Berlin, pp 121–131
3. Grobelnik M, Mladeni D (2005) Simple classification into large topic ontology of web documents. In: Proceedings of the 27th international conference information technology interfaces, Dubrovnik, Croatia, pp 188–193
4. Han J, Kamber M (2006) Data mining: Concepts and technique, 2nd edn. Morgan Kaufmann, San Francisco, CA
5. ILPNet2 publications database. Available online at http://www.cs.bris.ac.uk/~ILPnet2/
6. Jain K, Murty M, Flynn P (1999) Data clustering: A review. ACM Comput Surveys 31(3):264–323

7. Mladeni D, Grobelnik M (2007) Evaluation of semi-automatic ontology generation in real-world setting. In: Proceedings of the 29th international conference information technology interfaces, Dubrovnik, Croatia, pp 547–551

8. Muggleton S (ed) Inductive logic programming. Academic Press, London

9. de Nooy W, Mrvar A, Batagelj V (2005) Exploratory social network analysis with Pajek. Cambridge University Press, New York, See also http://vlado.fmf.uni-lj.si/pub/networks/pajek/

10. Sabo S, Grar M, Fabjan DA, Ljubi P, Lavra N (2007) Exploratory analysis of the ILPnet2 social network. In: Proceedings of the 10th international multi-conference information society, Ljubljana, Slovenia, pp 223–227

11. Sclano F, Velardi P (2007) TermExtractor: A web application to learn the common terminology of interest groups and research communities. In: Proceedings of the 9th conference on terminology and artificial intelligence, Sophia Antipolis, France. See also http://lcl2.uniroma1.it/termextractor

12. Scott J (2000) Social network analysis. Sage, London

13. The Protégé project 2000. Available online at http://protege.stanford.edu

14. Wasserman S, Faust K (1994) Social network analysis: Methods and applications. Cambridge University Press, New York

Chapter 7
Information Flow in Systems of Interacting Agents as a Function of Local and Global Topological Features

Andre S. Ribeiro

Abstract Information flow between elements of a system determines the system's functioning. This flow depends on the topology of the system. This chapter presents the latest results on how a system's structure, namely, its topological features, at global and local levels, affect the flow of information among its elements. It shows how the topology determines the amount and diversity of information flow, and the ability to cope with noise and uncertainty in the information transmitted.

We use Boolean Networks as models of dynamical systems of interacting elements whose structure is characterized at a global level by size and average connectivity and at a local level by a generalized clustering coefficient. The dynamics is characterized by the pairwise mutual information of the time series of the elements states, which quantifies the amount of information flow, and by the Lempel–Ziv complexity, which characterizes the complexity, i.e., diversity of the messages flowing in the system. With these measures, we relate structure and dynamics.

7.1 Introduction

Increase in complexity of organizations such as in the diversity of its agents' knowledge and tasks is forcing hierarchical structures to be replaced by clustered structures. Groups of agents are required to perform unique tasks and thus are given the power of decision, which are no longer made by a single or a few agents of the system [1]. Such organizational structures require complex information flow among its agents [2, 3] to maintain their cohesion and allow the execution of joint complex tasks, due to the variety of unique specialties and responsibility sharing. A system's structure, i.e., how elements of a system are interconnected, is a key factor for

A.S. Ribeiro (✉)
Department of Signal Processing, Computational Systems Biology Research Group,
Tampere University of Technology, Finland
and
Center for Computational Physics, Coimbra University, P-3004-516 Coimbra, Portugal
e-mail: andre.sanchesribeiro@tut.fi

A. Abraham et al. (eds.), *Computational Social Network Analysis*, Computer
Communications and Networks, DOI 10.1007/978-1-84882-229-0_7,
© Springer-Verlag London Limited 2010

information retention and transmission through its elements. This chapter presents the recent results and new insights on information flow among agents of systems as a function of the system's local and global structure.

A system's behavior, when not fully explainable by the individual behavior of its elements, is said to be emergent. Such emergent behaviors occur in many complex systems, such as brains, ecosystems, societies, and gene regulatory networks.

Emergence of new behaviors, not present in the behavior of the individual elements that compose the system, occurs when elements are connected such that information flows between them. One simple example is the toggle switch, a small gene network of two genes, which repress one another via their expression products, the proteins. This interaction allows information flow between the two genes. For example, when one of the two proteins' is present in high amounts, it is able to repress the other gene's expression. The proteins' temporal expression pattern observed in a toggle switch cannot be explained without the repression interactions between the two genes [5]. These two interactions are the channels by which the information, about the proteins levels of each gene, flows between the two genes. From this information flow emerges a characteristic stochastic toggling behavior where, at each moment, only one of the two genes has a high expression level [4].

The behavior of systems thereby depends, to a great extent, on its structure. How the structure determines the system's dynamics is what is addressed in this chapter. First, we focus on how global topological features regulate the flow of information among elements of a system [2]. Next, we address the effects of local topological structures on this information flow [6, 7]. Finally, introducing noise in the dynamics, which models events such as information loss and errors in transmission, we study how the information flux can be optimized as a function of global and local topologies and of path length between the elements of a system.

Importantly, the model system is dynamical, based on Boolean networks (BNs), and not only topological, which allows measuring the effects of the structure on the dynamics of information flow. The efficiency of this flow is measured by the temporal mutual information between the elements of the system. This allows measuring to what extent the information flow is able to generate coordinated complex behaviors.

7.2 Methods

7.2.1 Boolean Networks as Models of Systems of Interacting Elements

The theory of the dynamics of complex networks such as gene regulatory networks began with the study of the simplest model systems able to exhibit complex behaviors: Random Boolean Networks (RBNs) [8]. A BN is a directed graph with N nodes. Nodes represent elements of the system, and graph arcs represent interactions between the elements. Each node is assigned a binary output value and a Boolean function, whose inputs are defined by the graph connections. The network's state at a given moment is the vector of nodes' state at that moment. In a synchronous BN, all nodes are updated simultaneously. By running the network over several time steps starting from an initial state, a trajectory through the network's state space can be observed (referred to as a "time series").

RBNs can be drawn randomly from an ensemble of networks in which the inputs to each node are chosen at random from among all of the nodes in the system, and its Boolean rule can be selected at random from a specified distribution over all possible Boolean rules. These two assumptions of randomness allow analytical insights of the behavior of large networks. RBNs were used as the first model of GRN [8]. Each node is a gene and is assigned a Boolean function from the set of possible Boolean functions of k variables. In the RBN model studied here, time is discrete and nodes update their states synchronously. Thus, a state of the network passes to a unique successor state at each moment. Over time, the system follows a trajectory that ends on a state cycle attractor. In general, an RBN has many attractors.

One important feature of RBNs is that their dynamics can be classified as ordered, disordered, or critical. As the dynamics of an RBN is simulated some nodes become "frozen", meaning that they no longer change their state, while others remain dynamic, meaning that the state periodically changes from one state to the other. The fractions of frozen and dynamic nodes depend on the dynamical regime.

In ordered RBNs, the fraction of nodes that remain dynamical after a transient period vanishes like $1/N$ as the system size N goes to infinity; almost all of the nodes become "frozen" on an output value (0 or 1) that does not depend on the initial state of the network. In this regime, the system is highly stable against transient perturbations of individual nodes, meaning that externally imposing a change in one node state does not cause significant changes in other nodes states. In disordered (or chaotic) RBNs, the number of dynamical or unfrozen nodes scales like N, and the system is unstable to many transient perturbations, meaning that a perturbation will spread through many nodes.

We consider ensembles of RBNs parameterized by the average indegree K (i.e, average number of inputs to the nodes in the network) and the bias p (i.e., the fraction of inputs states that lead to an output with value "1") in the choice of Boolean rules. The indegree distribution is Poissonian with mean K, and at each node the rule is constructed by assigning the output for each possible set of input values to be 1 with probability p, with each set treated independently. If $p = 0.5$, the rule distribution is 'unbiased'. For a given bias, the critical connectivity, K_c, is [9]:

$$K_c = [2p(1 - p)]^{-1}. \tag{7.1}$$

For $K < K_c$, the ensemble of RBNs is in the ordered regime; for $K > K_c$, the disordered regime. For $K = K_c$, it is in the ensemble exhibits critical scaling of the number of unfrozen nodes; the number of unfrozen nodes scales like $N^{2/3}$. The order–disorder transition in RBNs has been characterized by several quantities, including fractions of unfrozen nodes, convergence or divergence in state space, and attractor lengths.

7.2.2 Mutual Information as a Measure of Information Flow

The mutual information contained in the time series of two elements measures how their dynamics are coordinated in time [10]. In a large, complex network of interacting elements, I is a global measure of how well the system coordinates with the dynamics of its elements. I is defined as follows. Let s_a be a process that generates a 0 with probability p_0 and a 1 with probability p_1. We define the entropy of s_a as

$$H[s_a] \equiv -p_0 \log_2 p_0 - p_1 \log_2 p_1. \tag{7.2}$$

For a process s_{ab} that generates pairs xy with probabilities p_{xy}, where $x, y \in \{0, 1\}$, the joint entropy is defined as

$$H[s_{ab}] \equiv -p_{00} \log_2 p_{00} - p_{01} \log_2 p_{01} - p_{10} \log_2 p_{10} - p_{11} \log_2 p_{11}. \tag{7.3}$$

If any of the probabilities in the entropy formulas is zero, its contribution to the entropies is zero as well, i.e., in this context, we assume: $0 \log_2 0 = 0$. Ideally, for a particular RBN, we would run the dynamics starting from all possible initial states and observe the time series for infinite time steps. However, the state space of even modestly sized RBNs is prohibitively large for such approach. Instead, the network is started from random initial states, and is run for a certain number of time steps, from which one attains an unbiased sample of the network dynamics.

The fraction of steps for which the value of node i is x gives p_x for the process s_i. The value of p_{xy} for the process s_{ij} is given by the fraction of time steps for which node i has the value x and *on the next time step* node j has the value y. The I between the time series of the pair ij is then defined as [2]

$$I_{ij} = H[s_i] + H[s_j] - H[s_{ij}]. \tag{7.4}$$

With this definition, I_{ij} measures the extent to which information about node i at time t influences node j one time step later, at $t + 1$. Note that the propagation may be indirect; a nonzero I_{ij} can result when i is not an input to j but both are influenced by a common node through previous time steps. To quantify the efficiency of information propagation through an RBN, we use the average pairwise mutual information, defined as

$$I = N^{-2} \sum_{i,j} I_{ij}. \tag{7.5}$$

The efficiency of information propagation in an ensemble of networks is given by the *average* pairwise mutual information of the ensemble, $\langle I \rangle$, where $\langle \cdot \rangle$ indicates the mean value over the members of the ensemble.

In general, since usually the networks' connectivity is relatively low ($K \leq 5$), one does not expect an element to be strongly correlated with more than a few other elements in the network, so the number of pairs ij that contribute significantly to the sum in Eq. 7.5 is expected to be at most of order N. It is therefore convenient to work with the quantity $\mathscr{I}_N \equiv N\langle I \rangle$, which may approach a nonzero constant in the large N limit. The symbol $\mathscr{I}_\infty$ denotes the $N \to \infty$ limit of $\mathscr{I}_N$.

We estimate the average mutual information of RBNs by a mean-field analytical calculation of $\langle I \rangle$ (for this one assumes sparse, tree-like structures), and by numerical measurements of the $\langle I \rangle$ of quenched networks. In this latter case, we calculate the $\langle I \rangle$ of the time series of RBNs for a given time interval.

Two arguments show that $\mathscr{I}_\infty$ is zero both in the ordered regime and deep in the disordered regime. First, M_{ij} is zero whenever s_i or s_j generates only 0s or only 1s. In the ordered regime almost all nodes remain frozen on the same value on all attractors, so the number of nonzero elements M_{ij} remains bounded for large N. Thus $\langle I \rangle$ must be of order N^{-2} and $\mathscr{I}_\infty = 0$ *everywhere in the ordered regime*.

Second, if s_{ij} is the product of two independent processes s_i and s_j, then $M_{ij} = 0$. When the system is highly disordered, where K is large and the Boolean rules are drawn from uniformly weighted distributions over all possible rules, the correlation between the output of a node and any particular one of its inputs becomes vanishingly small. That is, all pairs of nodes will mostly have independent time series, thus, $\mathscr{I}_\infty$ vanishes in the limit of large K.

Given that $\mathscr{I}_\infty = 0$ for all network parameters that yield ordered ensembles, one might expect that it rises to a maximum somewhere in the disordered regime before decaying back to zero in the strong disorder limit. However, this is *not* the case [2]. Fixing the bias parameter p at $1/2$ and allowing K to vary, $\mathscr{I}_\infty$ exhibits a jump discontinuity at the critical value $K = 2$, then decays monotonically to zero as K is increased. For example, in ensembles of unbiased RBNs, $\langle I \rangle$ is maximized for critical ensembles [2].

Mean-field calculations are commonly used in the theory of RBNs. The most common ones are within the realm of the annealed approximation where one assumes that the rules and the inputs are randomized at each time step. This approach is sufficient, for example, to calculate the average number of nodes that change value at each time step. To understand the propagation of information, a more elaborate mean field model is needed, based on the assumption that the state of a node in a large disordered network is independent of its state at the previous step, but that its rule remains fixed [2].

Additionally, an important feature characterizing the propagation of information in a network is the distribution of local biases. The local bias at a given node is determined by the rule at that node and the local biases of its inputs. When the bias of the output value is stronger than the bias of the inputs, information is lost in transmission through the node. In the meanfield model of RBN used here, each node takes the value 1 with a given probability b, the local bias. In the annealed approximation all local biases are equal since rules and inputs are redrawn randomly at each time step, so the system is characterized by a single global bias. In the extended mean field model used here and first presented in [2], it is considered a distribution of local biases. To determine $\mathscr{I}_\infty$, one has to determine the distribution of local biases, b, and then use it to analyze the simple feed forward structures that provide the non-vanishing contributions to $\mathscr{I}_\infty$ in the disordered regime.

7.2.3 Generalized Clustering Coefficient

In general, real large-scale gene networks are not locally tree-like [11], although they are sparse. Thus, it is of importance to investigate how local topological features affect the dynamical behavior, i.e., the differences in the dynamics of tree-like and non tree-like structures. Also, it was observed that RBNs with large and small number of nodes, while having the same average connectivity, exhibited different dynamical behavior [3]. Differences in the clustering coefficient (C) [12] of those networks was hypothesized as a possible cause.

We investigate this further and show that it is not sufficient to account for the original C to characterize networks' local structure. Other local structures besides triangles, also play a role. Thus, to characterize the local topological structure of finite networks we introduce the "generalized clustering coefficient", C_p. This measure allows quantifying the dependence of I on the degree of global clustering. We show that C_p accounts for all local effects by simulating RBNs where the C_p is zero, and showing that $\langle I \rangle$ of the network ensemble becomes independent of network size.

The original clustering coefficient (C) measures the fraction of connections between the first nearest neighbors of a node in an undirected graph, out of the total number of possible connections [12]. If E_i is the number of connections between the k_i nodes connected to a node i, the network's average C is

$$C = \frac{1}{N} \sum_{i=1}^{N} \frac{2E_i}{k_i(k_i - 1)}. \tag{7.6}$$

Notably, the $\langle I \rangle$ of small RBNs (approximately $N < 250$) with an imposed $C = 0$ (no triangles) is still dependent on N, but not as much as when $C \neq 0$.

An annealed approximation can predict the $\langle I \rangle$ of ensembles of RBN given k [2], if N is large enough and the networks have relatively low connectivity ($k < 5$) (resulting in locally tree-like topologies) but fails otherwise.

Small RBNs (or highly connected ones) are usually not locally tree-like structures when randomly generated, even for small k values. The existence of self-inputs, bidirectional connections, triangles, and other small structures (e.g., squares), destroy the tree-likeness of a structure, and hence affect $\langle I \rangle$.

To generate an ensemble of RBNs whose dynamics (characterized by $\langle I \rangle$) is independent of N, one must impose to the RBNs an equal value of some generalized version of C that accounts for all non-tree-like local structures. This procedure can also be used to study the dynamics of specific networks using an ensemble approach.

This generalized clustering coefficient (C_p) is, as the original C, computed for each node and averaged over all the nodes. For simplicity, connections directionality is not accounted for in C_p's calculation. The coefficient p denotes the following: C_p is the clustering coefficient of a network due to local structures of order p (here, only up to order 5 is considered). $C_{(i,j)}$ is the clustering coefficient of a network from order i up to order j (inclusively).

Let α be the node index and $\kappa_{i,j}^{\alpha}$ the amount of connections between the nodes at distance i and the nodes at distance j from node α. $T_{i,j}^{\alpha}$ is the possible maximum amount of such connections. C_p (for order $p > 2$) is defined as

$$C_p = \frac{1}{N} \sum_{\alpha=1}^{N} \left(\frac{\sum_{r=1}^{p-2} \kappa_{r,p-r-1}^{\alpha}}{\sum_{r=1}^{p-2} T_{r,p-r-1}^{\alpha}} \right). \qquad (7.7)$$

For $p < 3$, we define C_1 as the fraction of nodes with self inputs and C_2 as the mean ratio of connections that are bidirectional connected to each node. If a node has 3 connections and one of them is bidirectional, then its contribution to C_2 is $\frac{1}{3}$. Note that C_3 equals the original C [12]. The generalized clustering coefficient of a RBN, from order i up to order j, is thus defined as

$$C_{(i,j)} = \sum_{p=i}^{j} C_p. \qquad (7.8)$$

In the numerical simulations presented in the results section, we consider local structures only up to order 5, due to computational limitations in determining higher orders of C_p and because this was sufficient to account for all local structure effects in RBNs of 25 nodes or more. Notice that the value of C_p for each p value is computed independently, and the set of C_p values for each p is what characterizes the network topology. For simplicity, so that network topologies can be characterized by a single value, rather than a sequence of values, we opt to sum the values of each C_p into a single quantity, the "network C_p". Other ways of combining each of the C_p values into a single quantity could also be considered.

This quantity is sufficient to characterize, from a global point of view, the effects of the local structures in the dynamics, at the level of detail observed here. A more exact procedure to compare the local structure features of two RBNs is to compare their values of C_p, for each order p, independently.

Also, the algorithm that computes C_p only recognizes substructures in which each node is unique so that, e.g., self-inputs (order 1) are not accounted for again when counting bidirectional connections (order 2), and so forth. The same principle is followed when imposing a C_p value to a RBN.

To test if the $\langle I \rangle$ of RBNs with $C_p = 0$ (or another imposed value), is independent of the network size N, one must generate RBNs with random topology which are then rewired to impose a target C_p. The rewiring procedure must not change other properties of the topology and logic of the network. Namely, the in- and out-degree distributions must remain unchanged.

In- and Out-Degree Distributions and Rewiring

To compare networks with a different generalized clustering coefficient we need to generate networks in which other affecting factors are unchanged. Most importantly, we want to compare networks in which the in- and out-degree distributions of the nodes are the same but which differ only in their local clustering structure. To do this, we use the following iterative algorithm.

First, a network is generated with desired in- and out-degree distributions with no local clustering by selecting an in-degree and out-degree for each node to approximate the desired distributions and then drawing the connections randomly so that the constraints created by the degrees are fulfilled. The resulting network is likely to have a low C_p. Starting from a network generated as described, we then use an iterative optimization method to increase or decrease C_p without changing the degree distributions. At each iteration, we determine if the C_p of the network is higher or lower than desired. If it is higher, then we search the network for the loop structures corresponding to the order of the C_p that we want to reduce, and one of the connections that forms the loop is removed in such a way that the number of nodes with a given in- or out-degree does not change. This means that if we remove a connection that goes out from a node with out-degree m and connects to a node with in-degree n we will use the connection to link some node with out-degree $m - 1$ and a node with in-degree $n - 1$. To ensure that the loops are searched for in an unbiased manner, the indices of the nodes are shuffled at each iteration.

Likewise, if C_p is lower than desired, loops must be introduced. The network is searched for a chain of length $p + 2$, where the direction of the first connection corresponds to the direction of the last. The first and last connections are then moved so that the first node becomes an input of the last node in the chain, and the second-last becomes an input of the second node. This forms a loop of length p and maintains the nodes' in- and out-degree distributions. Again, the indices of the nodes are shuffled at each iteration to ensure that the loops are generated uniformly throughout the network.

Both the destruction and construction of loops involves moving connections in the network. This can have unintended side effects such as increasing or decreasing C_p of other orders than we were intending to modify. Thus, the algorithm must be re-run for other orders until the target C_p values have been reached. In some cases, the search for a possible rewiring can be extremely long. For practical purposes we limit that search. Namely, after a specified number of attempts, if the algorithm is unable to find a rewiring scheme which imposes the desired C_p value, it simply discards this network, and starts all over with a newly created network.

Since the cost of finding loops grows exponentially with p, this becomes an expensive operation to perform at higher orders. We limit ourselves to order 5, but show that this is enough to account for almost all local structure effects in the dynamics.

7.2.4 Lempel–Ziv Complexity

We focus on how networks can be optimized for information transfer. Besides the correlation between nodes dynamics, it is also important to be able to maximize the complexity of the information sent via the existing communicating channels between the system's elements.

Lempel–Ziv (LZ) [13] is a measure of the complexity of a sequence over a finite alphabet (here $\{0,1\}$) counting the number of new sub-strings (words) found as the sequence is read from left to right. The algorithm separates the sequence into shortest words that have not occurred before, and the complexity equals the number of such unique words, except the last word, which may not be unique [14].

For example consider the sequence 0110010110110010011 0 [14]. The first digit, 0, is a new word since it hasn't been seen before. So is the second digit, 1. The third digit, also a 1, has been seen before, so one must increase the length of the word by one, resulting in a new word "10", and so on. Repeating this process, the sequence gets parsed as follows: 0.1.10.010.1101.100100.110, where the dots delimit new words. Thus, the LZ complexity of this word is 7. All words, except the last one, are unique and, using this definition of LZ complexity, the search for previous occurrences of a word can span across previously seen word boundaries [14]. Repetitions leads to lower LZ. For example, the complexity of the sequence 01010101010101010101 is only 3. In general, time series with repetitive or simple patterns have low LZ, whereas series with complex pattern structures have high LZ.

It has been shown [14] that "networks in the ordered or critical regimes exhibit lower LZ complexities of the sequences generated by each node due to their pattern-like behavior over time, as compared to networks in the chaotic regime, which give rise to more random gene behavior". We measured the average LZ complexity ($\langle LZ \rangle$) of the time series of elements states, using the algorithm suggested in [15].

7.3 Results

7.3.1 Mutual Information as a Function of the Global Topology

In this section we study, using a meanfield approximation and numerical calculations, how the global topological features of RBNs, e.g., average connectivity, affect the average flux of information between its nodes.

Mutual Information in Feed-Forward Structures

To develop a meanfield approximation of information flow in RBNs we first study how $<I>$ propagates in feed-forward structures such as the one shown in Fig. 7.1 [2]. Given a well-defined distribution of local biases, one can calculate the $<I>$ between pairs of nodes in feed-forward structures that are relevant in the large network limit in the disordered regime. This technique assumes that the state of a given node at time $t + n$ is statistically independent of the state at t for $n \neq 0$, in which case the behavior of the inputs to a feed-forward structure can be fully determined from the distribution of local biases.

The most direct contribution to $\langle I \rangle$ between t and $t + 1$ comes from pairs of nodes where one is the input to a third node, and the other is an output of that same

Fig. 7.1 Schematic structure
assumed for the mean-field
calculation of $\mathscr{I}_\infty$. *Black
nodes* exemplify directly
linked pairs. *Light grey nodes*
exemplify a pair that
contributes to $\mathscr{I}_\infty$ due to a
shared influence (i_0).
Information from i_0 takes one
time step longer to reach the
light grey node on the *right*
than to the one on the *left*.
Hatching indicates frozen
nodes

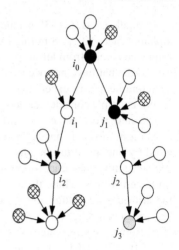

Fig. 7.2 The large system
limit $\mathscr{I}_\infty$ for $N\langle I\rangle$ (*solid
line*) and the contribution to
$\mathscr{I}_\infty$ from direct information
transfer through single nodes
(*dashed line*). The *empty
circles* at the discontinuity of
$\mathscr{I}_\infty$ indicate that we do not
know the value of $\mathscr{I}_\infty$ for
$K = 2$. The size of sample
vectors is $S = 10^4$

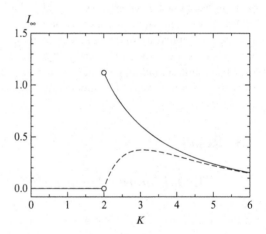

third node. Other significant contributions to $\langle I\rangle$ come from chains of nodes that
share a common starting point. From the analysis in [2] of these structures it was
shown that the critical point occurs at $K = 2$, with ordered networks arising for
$K < 2$ and disordered networks for $K > 2$.

The Large System Limit. Meanfield Approach

The results of the analytical estimation of $\mathscr{I}_\infty$ for $K > 2$ and for $\lim_{K \to 2+} \mathscr{I}_\infty$
using a meanfield analysis are shown in Fig. 7.2 [2]. It is interesting to note that
the direct links alone are not responsible for the peak at criticality. Rather, it is
the correlations between indirectly linked nodes that produce the effect, and in fact
dominate $\mathscr{I}_\infty$ for K at and slightly above the critical value ($K = 2$).

Because as the network becomes more chaotic (as K increases) the dashed and solid lines converge, one can conclude that the loss of correlation between the long chains is the cause for loss of criticality of the RBN. Also, one can conclude that critical networks are the only ones where such long chains starting from the same node exist. This topological feature is unique to critical networks and is responsible for the maximization of $\langle I \rangle$ in this regime.

Distribution of Local Biases

The distribution of local biases affect $\mathscr{I}_\infty$. Biases significantly different from $b = 1/2$ are important for networks with K that is not deep into the disordered regime, and the distribution of local biases is highly nonuniform. Dense histograms of biases distributions for various K are shown in Fig. 7.3. Singularities at $b = 0$ and $b = 1$ occur for K in the range $2 < K < 3.4$, and for all $K > 2$ there is a singularity at $b = 1/2$.

Meanfield Estimation of the Effect of Noise in the Dynamics

When uncorrelated noise is added to each node at each time step, $\mathscr{I}_\infty$ may decrease due to the random errors, but may also *increase* due to the unfreezing of nodes. It is therefore of interest to analyze how these effects combine.

The results of an analytical analysis of this problem is shown in Fig. 7.4 for the case where each output is inverted with probability ε on each time step [2]. In the following section are shown the results using a numerical analysis.

As ε is increased from zero, the peak at which $\mathscr{I}_\infty$ is maximized shifts to the disordered regime and broadens. The increase of $\mathscr{I}_\infty$ due to random unfreezing is visible on the ordered side ($K < 2$). In the critical regime, where indirect contributions dominate $\mathscr{I}_\infty$, there is a strong decrease as correlations can no longer be maintained over long chains. This is the main reason why noise causes a shift in the

Binned probability density

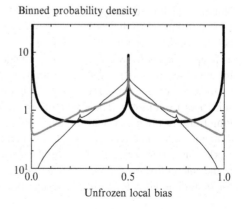

Fig. 7.3 Histograms for the distributions of unfrozen local biases b for $K \to 2_+$ (*bold black line*), $K = 3$ (*bold grey line*), and $K = 4$ (*thin black line*). Bins of width 10^{-4} were used to estimate the probability density from a sequence of 10^6 sample vectors drawn after 10^3 steps for convergence. The size of the sample vectors is $S = 10^4$

Unfrozen local bias

Fig. 7.4 The large system limit $\mathscr{I}_\infty$ as a function of K for various noise levels ε in the updating. The *thin solid line* shows $\mathscr{I}_\infty$ for networks without noise. The other lines represent $\varepsilon = 0.001$ (*thick solid line*), 0.01 (*dashed line*), and 0.1 (*dotted line*). The size of the sample vectors is $S = 10^4$

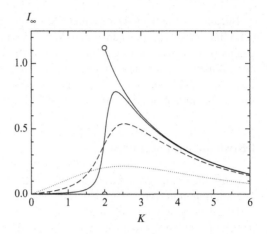

value of connectivity that maximizes mutual information and is confirmed by the numerical simulations. Deep in the disordered regime, there is a slight decrease expected due to the added randomness. For $\varepsilon > 0.1$, the maximum of $\mathscr{I}_\infty$ shifts back toward $K = 2$. In fact, it can be shown that as ε approaches $1/2$, which corresponds to completely random updating, the $\mathscr{I}_\infty$ curve approaches:

$$\mathscr{I}_\infty = \frac{K}{\ln 2}\left(\frac{1}{2} - \varepsilon\right)^2 \exp(-K/2). \tag{7.9}$$

In this limit, the maximum mutual information occurs at $K = 2$ and the peak height scales like $(1/2 - \varepsilon)^2$. Interestingly, the fact that the critical K is recovered in the strong noise limit is coincidental, since it does not occur for other choices of Boolean rule distributions.

Finite Size Effects

Numerical simulations on finite networks [3] reveal an important feature near the critical value of K that is not analytically accessible using the above techniques because of the difficulty of calculating $\mathscr{I}_\infty$ at the critical point. In [2] only the limit as K approaches K_c was computed, not the actual value at K_c. $\langle I \rangle$ is now computed by sampling from pairs of nodes of many networks.

In collecting numerical results to compare to the $\mathscr{I}_\infty$ calculation, there are some subtleties to consider. The calculations are based on correlations that persist for long times in the mean-field model. To observe these, one must disregard transient dynamics and also average over the dynamics of different attractors of each network. The latter average should be done by including data from all the attractors in the calculation of $\mathscr{I}_N$, *not* by calculating separate mutual information calculated for individual attractors. For the results presented here, a satisfactory convergence was observed both for increasing lengths of discarded transients and for increasing numbers of initial conditions per network. Finally, an accurate measurement of $\mathscr{I}_N$ requires sufficiently long observation times; short observation times cause systematic overestimations. In the figures below, the size of the spurious contribution due to finite observation times is smaller than the symbols on the graph.

Figure 7.5 shows that the peak in $\mathscr{I}_N$ extends well above the computed $\mathscr{I}_\infty$ value. The figure shows $\mathscr{I}_N$ as a function of K for several system sizes N. As N increases, the curve converges toward the infinite N value both in the ordered and disordered regimes. In the vicinity of the critical point, however, the situation is more complicated. The limiting value at criticality will likely depend on the order in which the large size and $K \to K_c$ limits are taken.

One can also study $\mathscr{I}_N$ as a function of the bias p, while holding K fixed at 4. Figure 7.6 shows that $\mathscr{I}_N$ again peaks at the critical point $p = (2 - \sqrt{2})/4$; the qualitative structure of the curves is the same as that for varying K.

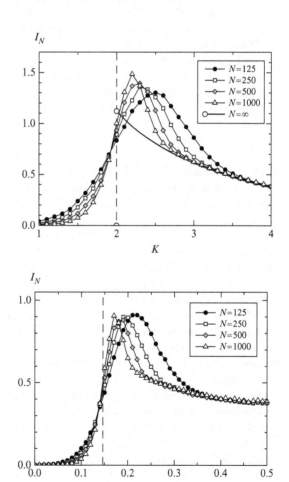

Fig. 7.5 $\mathscr{I}_N$ as a function of K for several different system sizes. For these calculations we use 10^4 networks with 40 runs from different initial states per network and a discarded transient of length 10^4 updates for each run. The sequences of states were recorded for a sample of $10N$ pairs of nodes in each network. The *vertical dashed line* indicates the critical value of K

Fig. 7.6 $\mathscr{I}_N$ as a function of p for several different system sizes. For these calculations we use 10^3 to 10^4 networks with 40 runs from different initial states per network and a discarded transient of length 10^4 updates for each run. The sequences of states were recorded for a sample of $10N$ pairs of nodes in each network. The *vertical dashed line* indicates the critical value of p

7.3.2 Effects of Local Topology on Global Dynamics

Local topological features affect I in RBNs. Using the definition of generalized clustering coefficient, C_p, we show that this quantity captures the effects of local structures on the global dynamics of networks. Namely, the variation of $\langle I \rangle$ (I averaged over an ensemble of RBNs with the number of nodes N and average connectivity k) with N and k is caused by the variation of $\langle C_p \rangle$. Also, the variability of I between RBNs with equal N and k is due to their distinct values of C_p.

Consequently, we use the described rewiring method to generate ensembles of BNs, from ordinary RBNs, with fixed values of C_p up to order 5, while maintaining in- and out-degree distributions. Using this methodology, the dependency of $\langle C_p \rangle$ on N and k and the variability of I for RBNs with equal N and k are shown to disappear in RBNs with C_p set to zero. The $\langle I \rangle$ of ensembles of RBNs with fixed, non zero C_p values, also becomes almost independent of N and k. In addition, it is shown that $\langle C_p \rangle$ exhibits a power-law dependence on N in ordinary RBNs, suggesting that the C_p affects even relatively large networks.

The method of generating networks with fixed C_p values is useful to generate networks with small N whose dynamics have the same properties as those of large scale networks, or to generate ensembles of networks with the C_p of a specific network, and thus comparable dynamics. The results show how a system's dynamics is constrained by its local structure, suggesting that the local topology of biological networks might be shaped by selection, e.g., towards optimizing coordination between its components.

First, we quantify the $\langle I \rangle$ and standard deviation ($\sigma(I)$) over an ensemble of RBNs, each independently simulated, as N and k vary. A network's I is computed from a time series starting at a random state, and corresponds to the average $I_{i,j}$ between all pairs of nodes. The values of the standard deviation show how variable the I of networks with the same k and N can be, due to having different C_p values.

Next, we measure the average and standard deviation of C_p, up to order 5, of that ensemble of networks which confirm that these quantities behave similarly to the average and standard deviation of I as N varies, respectively. Also, it is shown that the differences in C_p between RBNs, with equal k and N values, cause the differences in behavior between them, i.e., in $\langle I \rangle$.

After, we show that as C_p is set to zero for increasing values of p, $\langle I \rangle$ becomes less dependent on the size N. For $p > 3$ no dependency is observed. Importantly, the same is true for the standard deviation of I, indicating that RBNs built according to this procedure have a more predictable dynamics.

Finally, we show that $\langle I \rangle$ of an ensemble of RBNs, generated imposing a fixed value of C_p up to order 3, does not depend on network size either. This shows that the ensemble approach can be used to explore the dynamical properties of real networks with a non-zero C_p value, as long as the same value of that quantity is imposed to the networks of the ensemble.

In all following results, each data point corresponds to the average, or standard deviation, of either I or the generalized C_p, computed respectively from a 1,000 time step time series, and topology of 100 independent simulations. Each simulation consists of generating an RBN, with a given k and N. In some cases, the network C_p is fixed as well (when explicitly stated). Then, from a random initial state, we extract a time series of 1,000 consecutive time steps, from which I is calculated.

We do not discount initial transients in the time series. Although, in 1,000 time steps, most of the time the RBN will be in an attractor (representing "long term behavior"), we aimed to observe the effects of $\langle C_p \rangle$ also in transients. In all cases, the BNs have random topology. Connections are placed following a Poisson distribution of in-degrees with a random selection of inputs resulting in a Poissonian out-degree distribution also. Strictly speaking, the degree distribution is binomial, which for large networks, sparsely connected, is a good approximation of a Poisson distribution.

The update rules are random Boolean functions with a p_{bias} of 0.5. This means that for each combination of input values, the output value is selected randomly (independently with respect to other input combinations) with probability p_{bias} of obtaining a 1. In the case a given C_p value is imposed on the topology, this is done according to the method previously described.

Mutual Information of Finite Size BNs

The detailed analysis of I as a function of k for RBNs with large N [2] assumes that the networks are locally tree-like structures. To analyze the effects "non-tree-like" local structures on I, we start by measuring the variation of $\langle I \rangle$ with network size and connectivity. In Fig. 7.7, the $\langle I \rangle$ of the time series of RBNs is plotted as a function of k and N. The most important observation from this figure is that the

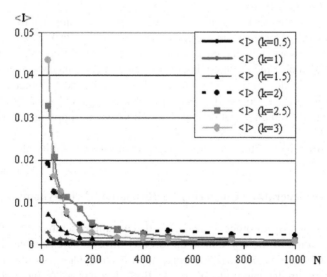

Fig. 7.7 $\langle I \rangle$ of RBNs of time series of length $T = 10^3$. Each data point is the average of 100 independent RBNs. Effects of local structures are most prominent for small N and large k

local structure of the networks randomly generated must change as N increased, causing the differences in dynamics (expressed in the average correlation between all nodes in the time series).

$\langle I \rangle$ is highly dependent on k and N. As N increases, as expected, local structural effects play a less relevant role since maintaining k constant and increasing N creates structures which are locally more tree-like, resulting in a significant decrease of $\langle I \rangle$ as N increases. For $N > 250$ and low connectivity values ($k < 2$), the $\langle I \rangle$ becomes almost invariant for further increases of N.

All curves in Fig. 7.7 follow the same trend as N increases, except for $k = 2$ which corresponds to the critical regime of RBNs ($k = 2$ and $p_{\text{bias}} = 0.5$), as previously shown. For $N < 250$, RBNs with $k = 2$ do not have the highest $\langle I \rangle$, exemplifying the relevance of local structure effects in the dynamics of these networks.

As k increases, the number of local structures increase, thus $\langle I \rangle$ increases. Importantly, for $k = 3$, e.g., only for $N > 500$ do local effects appear me negligible. This is another indication that the main cause for the difference between predictions using the annealed approximation and numerical simulations is the existence of local structures.

We note that the results of the simulations (Fig. 7.7) are consistent, in the sense that lowering k and/or increasing N always decreases $\langle I \rangle$, indicating that numerically sampling 100 networks per data point is sufficient to obtain the average behavior. The only two exceptions to these trends are the RBNs with $N > 500$ and $k = 2$, and the RBNs with $100 < N < 300$ and $k = 2.5$. Both cases are explained by the fact that these networks are in the critical regime [2]. The maximization of $\langle I \rangle$ at $k = 2.5$, when $100 < N < 300$, is due to the values of C_p. As shown in subsequent results, these networks $\langle I \rangle$ is maximized at $k = 2$ if the C_p of these networks is fixed to zero.

In Fig. 7.8, the standard deviation of I ($\sigma(I)$) is plotted, computed from the same set of RBNs and respective time series used to obtain $\langle I \rangle$ in Fig. 7.7. The $\sigma(I)$ captures how networks with the same values of N and k can differ in their dynamics, if the construction of the topology is not restricted in any other way but fixing N and k. The results in Fig. 7.7 confirm that as N decreases and/or k increases, $\sigma(I)$ increases and is very large, i.e., of the same order of magnitude as I, for small N, which indicates the high variability of I in RBNs when sampling networks with equal N and k.

We now investigate if the variation of C_p explains the variability of I.

Effects of the Generalized Clustering Coefficient on RBNs Dynamics

Figure 7.9 shows, up to order 5, the $\langle C_p \rangle$ of the same ensembles of RBNs. The standard deviation of the C_p values, up to order 5, of these ensembles is plotted in Fig. 7.9. Given Figs. 7.6 to 7.8, a correlation is clear. One sees that I and C_p vary in a very similar way with N and k. Both decrease as N increases. After,

$\sigma(I)$

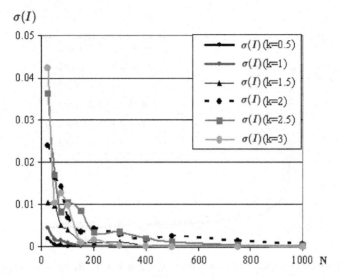

Fig. 7.8 Standard deviation of I of RBNs from time series of length $T = 10^3$. Each data point is the average of 100 independent RBNs, varying N and k. The diversity of dynamical behavior is higher for small N and large k

$<C(1,5)>$

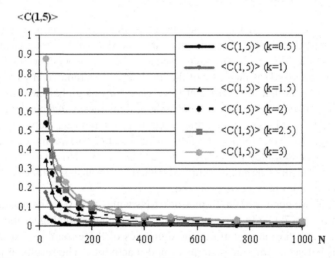

Fig. 7.9 C_p up to order 5, averaged over 100 networks, for networks with random topology (RBN), varying k and N. For lower values of N and higher k more nodes become part of highly interconnected local structures

approximately $N \simeq 400$, the two quantities decrease very slowly as they converge to the values estimated in [2], dependent only on the average connectivity. A similar correlation exists between the standard deviation of these two quantities (Figs. 7.8 and 7.10).

$\sigma(C(1,5))$

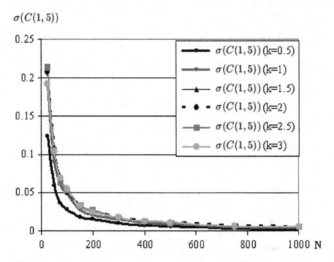

Fig. 7.10 Standard deviation of C_p up to order 5, averaged over 100 RBNs, varying k and N. The diversity of topological features is higher for small N and large k

Removing the Dependence of $\langle I \rangle$ on $\langle C_p \rangle$

To observe if the $\langle C_p \rangle$ of RBNs explains the dependence of $\langle I \rangle$ on N, we measured the $\langle I \rangle$ for RBNs with $k = 2$, removing various orders of C_p by rewiring maintaining in- and out-degree distributions unchanged. If the dependence of $\langle I \rangle$ on N is completely removed (as the order of the local structures removed by rewiring increases) it indicates that it is sufficient to account for this global measure of local structures to generate ensembles of RBNs whose dynamics is independent of N.

Additionally, if this is true, then the variability of I between networks of same N and k, ought to be due to the variability in values of C_p between those networks. Thus, the $\langle I \rangle$ of ensembles of networks whose C_p is imposed to a fixed value should become independent of N and its standard deviation diminish significantly, in comparison to the values previously observed.

To test this, we generated ensembles of RBNs with $C_p = 0$, of increasing order, up to order 5 (Fig. 7.11). In agreement with the hypothesis, the higher the order of C_p fixed to zero, the more uniform the dynamics of the ensemble is in terms of correlations between temporal patterns of nodes activities. The results in Fig. 7.12 agree with the hypothesis as well, by showing that $\sigma(I)$ when $C(1,5) = 0$ is much smaller than $\sigma(I)$ when C_p is not imposed, given equal N and k (converging only for $N > 800$ where local structures are no longer present in networks of either ensembles).

Based on the simulation results with the ensembles of networks used here, it is necessary to account for C_p only up to order 5. Higher order terms, difficult to account for computationally, did not significantly affect the dynamics of RBNs. For higher values of k than the ones considered here, it might become necessary to account for higher orders of C_p. However, it is increasingly difficult to find rewiring

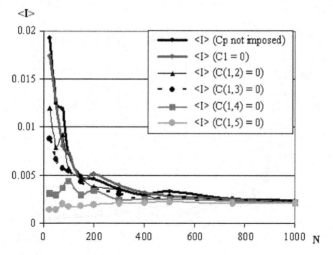

Fig. 7.11 $\langle I \rangle$ of RBNs from time series of length $T = 10^3$. The topologies are built such that up to various p the $C_p = 0$. Each data point is an average of 100 independent RBNs, varying N and with $k = 2$

schemes to remove increasing orders in high-k networks, maintaining in- and out-degree distributions unchanged. We also note the consistency in the results in the sense that as higher orders of C_p are fixed to zero by rewiring, the dependence of $\langle I \rangle$ on N decreases further. Another observation from Fig. 7.11, in the case of C_p removed up to order 5, the $\langle I \rangle$ of networks with $N < 100$ is slightly smaller than for larger RBN. This difference is of the order of 10^{-4}, whereas the variation in $\langle I \rangle$ due to C_p variation is on the order of 10^{-2}. This weak dependency of $\langle I \rangle$ on N, only visible when removing C_p up to order 5, is addressed ahead.

It is now of importance to determine if one can generate RBNs whose dynamics is independent of N by imposing a uniform C_p value up to order 5. If C_p can capture local structure effects on the global dynamics of networks, the $\langle I \rangle$ of networks of an ensemble with an imposed non-zero value of C_p should be independent of N.

In Fig. 7.12 the $\langle I \rangle$ is shown for ensembles of RBNs with increasing size N. The topologies of these networks were generated by fixing C_p of orders 1, 2, 4 and 5 to zero, while C_3 is imposed such that $0.09 \leq C_3 \leq 0.11$. C_3 is allowed an interval of values since setting it to a specific unique value makes the generation of such RBN topologies very time consuming.

As shown in Fig. 7.13, the $\langle I \rangle$ is virtually independent of N, for $N \geq 100$. Also, in comparison to the $\langle I \rangle$ of RBNs where C_p is not fixed, for large values of N, the networks with fixed values of C_p ought to have a higher $\langle I \rangle$, because, for large values N, the first ones have $C_p = 0$. Finally, for small values of N, the situation should invert, i.e., the RBNs whose C_p is not fixed, ought to have a higher $\langle I \rangle$ because they will have a higher C_p. In addition, interestingly, networks with fixed C_p and $K = 2$ still maintain the property of maximizing the value of $\langle I \rangle$ [2]. This property does not appear to be significantly affected by the procedure of imposing

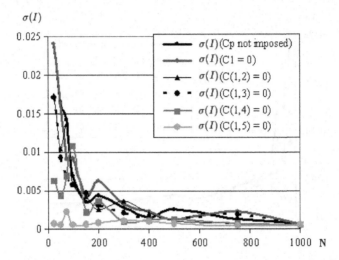

Fig. 7.12 Standard deviation of I of RBNs from time series of length $T = 10^3$. The topologies are built such that up to various p the $C_p = 0$. Each data point is an average of 100 independent RBNs, varying N and with $k = 2$

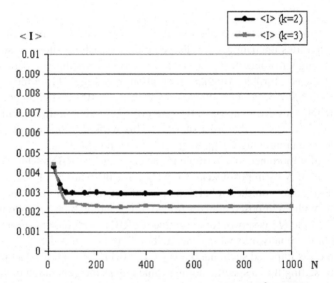

Fig. 7.13 $\langle I \rangle$ of RBNs computed from time series of length $T = 10^3$. The RBN topologies are built such that C_3 is imposed to be between 0.09 and 0.11, while other orders of C_p are fixed to zero up to order 5. Each data point is the average result of 100 independent RBNs, varying N and with $k = 2$ and $k = 3$. The $\langle I \rangle$ of these RBNs shows virtually no dependency on N

values to the C_p of the RBNs, which explains the difference between the values of $\langle I \rangle$ for $K = 2$ and 3. Other factors, such as the average path length are almost negligible, otherwise one would expect the opposite results, namely, $\langle I \rangle$ of networks with $K = 3$ is bigger than $\langle I \rangle$ of networks with $K = 2$.

In [2] it was shown that $\langle I \rangle$ is maximized for critical RBNs whose C_p is not fixed. These results [6] indicate that this holds true for RBNs with an imposed value of C_p. Also, for large N, both for $k = 2$ and $k = 3$, networks with fixed C_p have higher $\langle I \rangle$ than otherwise, since if C_p is not fixed it approaches zero for large N.

Additionally, networks with higher C_p will have, given equal values of k and N, higher $\langle I \rangle$. Importantly, and in agreement with the goals of applying a constraint in the C_p of the networks of the ensemble, the increase of $\langle I \rangle$ as N decreases was reduced by two orders of magnitude, and only starts increasing at $N < 100$, while previously, the increase occurred at $N < 250$.

Here we have mostly focused on the effects of varying N in RBNs where the C_p is imposed up to a certain order. Varying k and maintaining N fixed has the same effects, that is, imposing C_p constant up to order 5 to this ensemble also results in removing the dependency of $\langle I \rangle$ of k (data not shown).

7.3.3 Dynamics of Lattice Structures

This section investigates the influence of lattice geometry in network dynamics, using a cellular automaton with nearest-neighbor interactions and two admissible local states. We show that there are significant geometric effects in the distribution of local states and in the distribution of clusters, even when the connection topology is kept constant. Moreover, we show that some geometric structures are more cohesive than others, tending to keep a given initial configuration. To characterize the dynamics, we determine the distributions of local states and introduce a cluster coefficient. The lattice geometry is defined from the number of nearest neighbors and their disposition in 'space', and here we consider four different geometries: a chain, a hexagonal lattice, a square lattice, and a cubic lattice [7].

We consider periodic lattice structures, all with the same topological features, average path length and clustering coefficient, and investigate what differences prevail in their dynamics when only the lattice geometry is varied.

To this end, we model four lattice geometries with k nearest neighbors: chain ($k = 2$), hexagonal lattice ($k = 3$), square lattice ($k = 4$), and cubic lattice ($k = 6$), and impose a dynamics of a cellular automaton as a prototype model of dynamical systems with spatiotemporal complexity (Fig. 7.14).

Model

We consider a two-state cellular automaton, whose local states $s = 0$ and $s = 1$ evolve according to a nearest-neighbor homogeneous coupling: for each node $\mathbf{r}$ the present state $s_t(\mathbf{r})$ influences, with the same weight, the future state $s_{t+1}(\mathbf{r})$ as its neighborhood, and the neighborhood contributes to that future state as a mean field of the k nearest neighbors. The equation of evolution of the model is

$$s_{t+1}(\mathbf{r}) = \mathcal{H}\big(S_t(\mathbf{r}) - 1\big), \tag{7.10}$$

Fig. 7.14 Several lattices considered

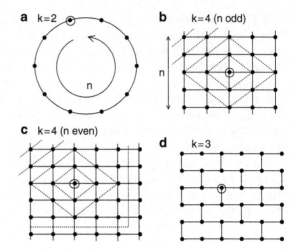

where $\mathscr{H}(x)$ is the Heaviside function, guaranteeing that $s_{t+1}(\mathbf{r})$ assumes only the values 0 and 1, and the quantity $S_t(\mathbf{r})$, that varies between -1 and 1, is

$$S_t(\mathbf{r}) = s_t(\mathbf{r}) + \frac{1}{k} \sum_{\mathbf{r}',k} s_t(\mathbf{r}'),\qquad(7.11)$$

with $\mathbf{r}'$ representing the coordinates of the k nearest neighbors. Given these equations, each future local state tends to be at the same state as the majority part of the sites $\mathbf{r}$ and $\mathbf{r}'$. The particular case $S_t(\mathbf{r}) = 1$, for which $s_{t+1}(\mathbf{r})$ has a discontinuity, occurs only when all neighbors of node $\mathbf{r}$ are at the same state, different from the state of $\mathbf{r}$, and, in this case, is assume that $\mathbf{r}$ changes to the state of its neighbors.

This model has the property that for any geometry, i.e. for any value of k, the number of combinations of local states and neighboring states evolving toward a future state $s_{t+1}(\mathbf{r}) = 0$ equals the number of combinations evolving toward $s_{t+1}(\mathbf{r}) = 1$. Also, for $k = 2$, i.e., in the case of one-dimensional cellular automaton with nearest-neighboring coupling, the model reduces to the Wolfram's rule number 232. Periodic boundary conditions are imposed.

With this framework and fixing the average path length and the clustering coefficient one guarantees that all differences in the dynamics are due to differences in the lattices geometry.

Comparing Different Lattice Geometries

We study state and cluster distributions for each lattice geometry mentioned above, considering the cellular automaton ruled by Eq. 7.10. We determine the fraction R_s of states at $s = 0$ and measure a cluster coefficient R_c which quantifies the tendency for cluster formation. Here, we use the usual definition of cluster [16], i.e., a set of adjacent nodes at the same state, and therefore, the cluster coefficient R_c is defined from the fraction of adjacent nodes at different states, namely

$$R_c = 1 - \frac{1}{kN} \sum_{r,N} \sum_{r',k} |s_t(\mathbf{r}) - s_t(\mathbf{r'})| . \tag{7.12}$$

The cluster coefficient ranges from 0, when any two adjacent nodes have different amplitudes, i.e., the number of clusters equals the number of nodes, and 1, when all nodes have the same amplitude, i.e., the entire lattice is part of a single cluster.

For each lattice geometry, Table 7.1 gives the expression of the average path length $\langle \ell \rangle$ as a function of the number N of nodes. These expressions are obtained either from the corresponding adjacency matrix or from geometric procedures [7]. For the four geometries the clustering coefficient is always 0. Thus, to impose the same value of the topological quantities one just needs to determine the number of nodes in each case, namely for the chain of nodes we choose $N = 143$, for the hexagonal lattice $N = 12$, for the square lattice $N = 72$, and for the cubic lattice $N = 48$. For these choices one finds approximately the same average path length, $\langle \ell \rangle \simeq 36$, for all lattices.

Figure 7.15a shows for each geometry the distribution F of fraction R_s of states at $s = 0$, from a sample of 10^6 random initial configurations, while Fig. 7.15b shows the same distribution after a transient of 10^3 time-steps, beyond which the system is thermalized. While for $k = 2$ the unit interval where fraction R_s is defined was divided always in 100 subintervals, for the other geometries the number of divisions depends on the total number N of nodes. Therefore, although the four distributions have apparently different 'integrals', they are in fact all equal to 1.

From Fig. 7.15a one observes Gaussian-like distributions of the initial configurations, centered at $R_s = 0.5$, whose widths ω_s^0 depend on the geometry, decreasing when k increases. After thermalization (Fig. 7.15b) all distributions remain centered at $R_s = 0.5$, but now have a different width ω_s than the initial one. Since the width of the distribution of initial random configurations depends on the total number N of nodes used for each geometry, to compare geometric effects in the final state distribution, one must compare the ratio ω_s/ω_s^0. Here, one finds $\omega_s/\omega_s^0 \sim 3.4$ for the chain, $\omega_s/\omega_s^0 \sim 2.6$ for the hexagonal lattice, $\omega_s/\omega_s^0 \sim 2.1$ for the square lattice and $\omega_s/\omega_s^0 \sim 0.8$ for the cubic lattice. Thus, different geometries correspond to different state distributions.

Figure 7.16 displays the distributions of the clustering coefficient R_c for the same sample of initial configurations, after thermalization, while in the inset are the corresponding initial distributions of R_c. When changing the geometry, one observes a distribution of R_c not only with a different width, but also with a different mean value μ_c. After thermalization the mean values are quite different: $\mu_c = 0.84$ for the chain, $\mu_c = 0.78$ for the hexagonal lattice, $\mu_c = 0.61$ for the square lattice, and $\mu_c = 0.54$ for the cubic lattice. In other words, the mean value of cluster distributions decreases when the number of k nearest neighbors increase. Subtracting from this final mean μ_c, the mean value μ_c^0 of the corresponding initial distribution, one finds a measure of the 'cohesion' in the system, i.e., a measure of the ability of the

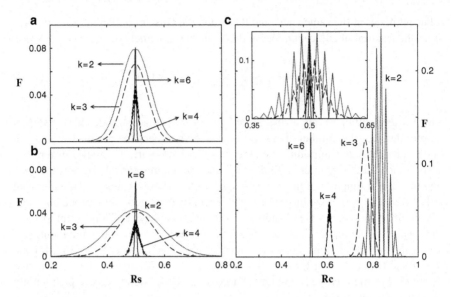

Fig. 7.15 Different lattice geometries have different widths of the distribution $F(R_s)$, where R_s is the fraction of states at $s = 0$. For each geometry: (**a**) the distribution $F(R_s)$ of a sample of 10^6 initial configurations and (**b**) the same distribution after a transient of 10^3 time-steps after which the system is thermalized. The ratio ω_s/ω_s^0 of both distribution widths, before and after thermalization, depends on the lattice geometry, i.e., on k. While the mean value $F(R_s)$ is always $\mu_s = 0.5$, (**c**) the distribution $F(R_c)$ of the cluster coefficient R_c shows a 'shifting' of the mean values when compared to the one of the initial configurations (see *inset* ($\mu_c^0 = 0.5$))

system to change a given initial state configuration. In this sense, from Fig. 7.15c, the cubic lattice is the most cohesive one, while the chain allows more variation of state configurations with respect to the initial system's configuration.

The particular feature observed for the chain ($k = 2$), whose cluster distribution has zero and non-zero values, is due to the fact that for this geometry $N \times R_c$ must be an even number. In the chain the product $N \times R_c$ equals precisely the number of clusters in the lattice and, since one has only two admissible local states, the number of clusters must be even. For all other geometries, R_c varies monotonically with the number of clusters, being still a suitable measure of the number of clusters and consequently a suitable measure of their average size. The results in Fig. 7.15 were obtained for a specific average path length $\langle \ell \rangle$. In Fig. 7.16 we show how the width ratios ω_s/ω_s^0 and ω_c/ω_c^0 and the mean difference $\mu_c - \mu_c^0$ vary with the average path length. Horizontal lines indicate the linear fitting obtained for each geometry. The fittings correspond to different values, depending on the geometry one is considering. Note that, this fitting was computed from a wider spectrum of $\langle \ell \rangle$ than the one shown in the figure. Therefore, for the hexagonal lattice ($k = 3$), since the average path length increases fastly with N, only one data point is visible in the range shown (see Table 7.1).

As seen from Fig. 7.16, each geometry has specific values of the width ratios and mean differences. In fact although these quantities vary significantly with the

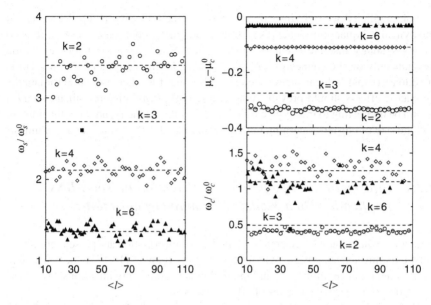

Fig. 7.16 *Left*: Ratio ω_s/ω_s^0 between the widths of final and initial state configurations distributions as a function of the average path length $\langle \ell \rangle$. *Right*: The ratio ω_c/ω_c^0 and the mean difference $\mu_c - \mu_c^0$ of the cluster distribution $F(R_c)$. *Horizontal dashed lines* indicate the linear fitting for each geometry, that characterizes it

Table 7.1 The average path length $\langle \ell \rangle$ for four different geometric structures with k nearest neighbors: a chain ($k = 2$), a hexagonal lattice ($k = 3$), a square lattice ($k = 4$), and a cubic lattice ($k = 6$)

Chain ($k = 2$)	Hexagonal ($k = 3$)	Square ($k = 4$)	Cubic ($k = 6$)
$\dfrac{N+1}{4}$ (n odd)		$\dfrac{\sqrt{N}}{2}$ (n odd)	$\dfrac{3(N + N^{2/3})}{4(N^{2/3} + N^{1/3} + 1)}$ (n odd)
	$\dfrac{7}{12}N^{3/2} - \dfrac{1}{3}N^{1/2}$		
$\dfrac{N^2}{4(N-1)}$ (n even)		$\dfrac{N^{3/2}}{2(N-1)}$ (n even)	$\dfrac{3(N^{4/3} + N^{1/3})}{4(N-1)}$ (n even)

average path length, oscillating around the horizontal fitting lines, for each geometry these variations occur in particular ranges of values. Therefore, lattice structure is well characterized by any of these quantities.

Discussion

The ratio between width of the final state distribution and width of the corresponding set of initial configurations characterizes each geometry. The measurement of the number of clusters showed that, even for a constant average path length, some geometries are more prone to cluster than other. In particular, the ability for cluster formation decreases significantly with the number of nearest neighbors.

For simplicity, we only investigated two-state cellular automaton. However, all the dynamical quantities, state distribution, and cluster coefficient can be extended to any spatially discrete extended systems. Moreover, since the lattice evolution depends only on the connections between elements (topology) and not on specific functions (maps) of local states, one can expect that for other cellular automata the geometric effects should prevail. As a final remark, from this preliminary study it would be interesting to investigate for each particular geometry, not only the number and the size of clusters emerging in the system, but also their shape and dynamics.

7.3.4 Information Propagation and Retention in Noisy BNs. Implications to a Model of Human Organizations

Structures where knowledge creation and flow of information are present are inherently dynamic and adaptive to external and internal changes [17,18] to be resistant to environmental uncertainty [19] and internal noise. Human organizations have these capacities, with variable degrees of effectiveness.

We focus on organizations' topology of interactions between elements [20] and quantify mutual information and L-Z complexity to study which structures optimize information propagation and retention through its elements. While in the previous sections we studied the dynamics of information flow assuming noiseless communication, now we consider the existence of noise in the interactions between the elements of the system.

We explore how this noise affects the mutual correlations between the elements of the system and global knowledge acquirement, quantified with the LZ complexity of each element, averaged over all elements.

Distinction between information and knowledge is not trivial [17]. Information is understood as flow of signals [10], while knowledge is not just the storing of information, but depends on the receiver's interpretation of the messages. Here, we do not deal with the problem of converting information into knowledge, which has been extensively studied (see e.g. [17]). Rather, we focus in information propagation and retain from which, consequently, knowledge arises, e.g., in human organizations.

Optimizing information propagation and retention between the elements of a system is a complex but important task since the knowledge an organization retains is a fundamental resource, affecting how efficient is the organization.

Several mechanisms allow communication among people within an organization. Usual communication mechanisms, such as face-to-face meetings, provide the opportunity to share knowledge, create empathy and trust, and focus explicitly on common problems and their solutions have been studied [21]. Even features such as the building structure play a role in the efficiency of a work environment. The process of transfer of learning, both among its members and with outsiders, allows organizations to develop their competitiveness. Several studies suggest that organizational structure is fundamental for enhancing learning and affects performance [22].

Most previous works on optimizing knowledge sharing in organizations focused on the individuals' characteristics and how information sharing can be improved given human behavior. Here we focus on the effects of the global topological structure, defined by direct work relations such as employer-employee and between co-workers. We model the structure as a directed graph between elements. The dynamics is Boolean, as in a synchronous BN.

Each message, sent from one element to another, has an information content (either 0 or 1). There is a probability that the message will not be accurately perceived, which we refer to as "noise". Its content, either correctly or wrongly perceived, acts upon the receiving element, according to its internal properties (mimicking individual perception), modeled by assigning to each element a random Boolean function which, given the combination of inputs values, determines the output value at the next time moment.

Each element of the system has memory, where it is stored the states that element experienced over time. This binary array of the internal states time series constitutes the information received, from which knowledge is acquired. Information can be lost due to the noise in transmission and/or perception, modeled by introducing a probability that an element will, at each time step, do the opposite of what the inputs states and its Boolean function determine.

We measure this system's ability to propagate information through the elements and store information in each element from the time series of the elements' states, for various levels of noise and average connectivity.

Note that an element's state doesn't necessarily change each time step, even if the information is correctly perceived. For example, in a real setting, when someone receives an information, his "internal state" changes provided that the message contains information that requires a change in behavior, i.e., messages can be irrelevant given previous knowledge.

The elements that send the information (inputs) and the receiver (output) should be dynamically correlated if the information is relevant, which occurs by the state change of output when the inputs' state changes, or by maintenance of state in the opposite case. The temporal mutual information, I, captures this correlation, since its zero between two elements if one of the elements' time series is "frozen" (no relevant information being propagated, thus, no state change), and for uncorrelated time series (no information being propagated in such a way that the elements states become correlated). When inputs and output states change over time in a correlated manner, their pairwise mutual information ought to be high.

Regarding the diversity of messages sent, it should be maximized in a system that desires effective information transmission between its elements with relevant meaning (messages from which the receiver can extract new knowledge). To measure the diversity of messages sent, we compute the normalized (also called relative) L-Z complexity (LZ) of each element's time series since this quantity increases with the diversity of messages sent.

These two measures complement one another in the present setting. Imagine that an element has a periodic or nearly periodic time series. While $\langle I \rangle$ will be high, in a long time scale perspective, this element is not actually transmitting diverse

Fig. 7.17 Average LZ for various average connectivity values k in 1,000 time steps. One hundred networks per data point, each with 1,000 nodes

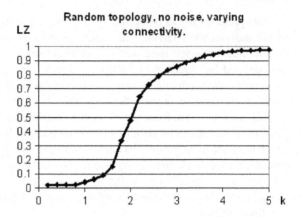

information to its outputs. This is observed in the value of LZ, which in these cases is low. For noiseless RBNs, we already studied the variation of $\langle I \rangle$ with the average connectivity k of an RBN. The variation of $\langle LZ \rangle$ with k is shown in Fig. 7.17.

The $\langle LZ \rangle$ goes through a phase transition for the same connectivity value that maximizes mutual information ($k = 2$). Thus, critical networks are not only optimal for transmitting information, but also, the content of the information transmitted suffers a dramatic increase as the network connectivity reaches the critical regime. These results indicate that, assuming no noise, the structures optimal for information transfer and for maximizing messages content diversity is critical or slightly chaotic.

Variation of Mutual Information with Noise Level

Mutual information of a noiseless RBN is maximized in the critical regime. Given noise in the dynamics, one expects that this will change. It is not, however, straightforward to predict if noise increases or decreases the value of the average connectivity for which $\langle I \rangle$ is maximized. On one hand, increasing noise reduces the number of frozen nodes in the RBN, thus noise increase is expected to increase mutual information. However, noise also decreases the correlation between inputs and outputs states causing the opposite effect.

To address the effects of noise in the global dynamics, we measured $\langle I \rangle$ and $\langle LZ \rangle$ of RBNs with average connectivity of 1, 2, and 3, with various levels of noise. The results, in Fig. 7.18, can be summarized as follows. When introducing very small noise levels, $\langle I \rangle$ grows significantly due to a drastic decrease of the fraction of frozen nodes (notice that unfreezing a node causes many of its outputs to unfreeze as well). Above 0.02 noise level, $\langle I \rangle$ starts decreasing due to the generalized decrease of correlation between all inputs and its outputs. Because at this noise level, most nodes are already, most of the time, unfrozen, increasing noise further causes only decreasing of $\langle I \rangle$.

Importantly, given noise, the $\langle I \rangle$ of RBNs with $k = 1$ is much higher than of $k = 2$ networks. Noise causes a decrease of the average connectivity that maxi-

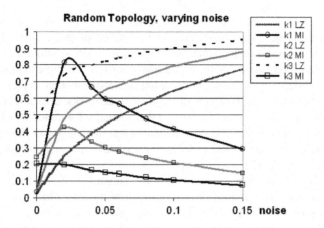

Fig. 7.18 $<I>$ and LZ for networks with $k = 1, 2, 3$ in 1,000 time steps, with various levels of noise. One hundred networks per data point, each with 1,000 nodes

mizes mutual information. The LZ always increases with the increase of noise. This increase however, is not beneficial to information transmission between the elements of the system, since while the messages are more complex, its complexity is due to noise, thus, its storing is not beneficial.

Finally, it is interesting to notice that the RBNs whose $\langle I \rangle$ was least affected by noise were those with $k = 3$, implying that the best way to cope with noise is to have redundancy in the topology. Imagine that someone is transmitting a message of N bits to someone else. The message has a probability of arriving with errors in some bits. If the errors appear always in randomly located bits, one way to detect them is to send the same message three times at least, and infer the "correct message" with the majority rule. If position j, was equal to '1' two times and equal to '0' one time, the true value for that position is, with some certainty, '1'. One cannot, however, be 100% certain that in fact the correct value is '1', since there is a small probability that is '0'. The larger the number of repetitions, the less likely it is for the majority rule to fail. In general, one can estimate, from the value of the probability of error per bit, the number of repetitions of the message and the message length, the probability that the message obtained by applying the majority rule has no errors, 1 error, etc.

7.4   Conclusions

On Systems' Global Topological Properties

Eukaryotic cells may be dynamically critical [23]. Our calculations indicate that, *within the class of RBNs with Poissonian degree statistics and typically studied rule distributions*, critical networks provide an optimal capacity for coordinating dynamical behaviors. This coordination requires the presence of substantial numbers of dynamical (unfrozen) nodes, the linking of those nodes in a manner that allows long-range propagation of information while limiting interference from multiple propagating signals, and a low error rate. To the extent that evolutionary fitness depends on such coordination and RBN models capture essential features of the organization of genetic regulatory networks, critical networks are naturally favored. Thus, it was conjectured that mutual information is optimized in critical networks for broader classes of networks that include power-law degree distributions and/or additional local structure such as clustering or over-representation of certain small motifs [2].

A key insight from these studies is that the maximization of average pairwise mutual information is achieved in RBNs by allowing long chains of effectively single-input nodes to emerge from the background of frozen nodes and nodes with multiple unfrozen inputs. The behavior of the average pairwise mutual information in RBNs with flat rule distributions is nontrivial and somewhat surprising. This is due largely to the fact that the network of unfrozen nodes in nearly critical systems does indeed have long single-input chains. By choosing a rule distribution carefully, however, one can enhance the effect and produce arbitrarily high values of $\mathscr{I}_\infty$ even deep in the disordered regime. Whether real biological systems have this option is less clear. The interactions between transcription factors and placement of binding sites required to produce logic with high sensitivity to many inputs appear difficult (though not impossible) to realize with real molecules.

Maximization of pairwise mutual information may be a sensible proxy for maximization of fitness within an ensemble of evolutionarily accessible networks: we suggest that systems based on high-$\langle I \rangle$ networks can orchestrate complex, timed behaviors, possibly allowing robust performance of a wide spectrum of tasks. If so, the maximization of pairwise mutual information within the space of networks accessible via genome evolution may play an important role in natural selection of real genetic networks. We have found that maximization of pairwise mutual information can be achieved deep in the disordered regime by sufficiently non-uniform Boolean rule distributions. However, in the absence of further knowledge, a roughly flat rule distribution remains the simplest choice, and in this case pairwise mutual information is maximized for critical networks. Given the tentative evidence for criticality in real genetic regulatory networks [23–26], these results may be biologically important.

It is an attractive hypothesis that cells' genetic regulatory networks are critical or perhaps slightly in the ordered regime [27]. Critical networks display an intriguing balance between robust behavior in the presence of random perturbations and flexible switching induced by carefully targeted perturbations. That is, a typical attractor of a critical RBN is stable under the vast majority of small, transient perturbations (flipping one gene to the "wrong" state and then allowing the dynamics to proceed as usual), but there are a few special perturbations that can lead to a transition to a different attractor. This observation forms the conceptual basis for thinking of cell types as attractors of critical networks, since cell types are both homeostatic in general and capable of differentiating when specific signals (perturbations) are delivered.

Recently, some experimental evidence has been shown to support the idea that genetic regulatory networks in eukaryotic cells are dynamically critical. In [24], the microarray patterns of gene activities of HeLa cells were analyzed, and the trajectories in a HeLa microarray time-series data characterized using a L-Z complexity measure on binarized data. The conclusion was that cells are either ordered or critical, not disordered. In Ref. [25], it was deduced that deletion of genes in critical networks should yield a power law distribution of the number of genes that alter their activities with an exponent of -1.5 and observed data on 240 deletion mutants in yeast showed this same exponent. In [26], microarray gene expression data following silencing of a single gene in yeast was analyzed. Again, the data suggests critical dynamics for the gene regulatory network. These results suggest that operation at or near criticality confers some evolutionary advantage.

On Systems' Local Topological Properties

The results show that C_p is an appropriate global measure of the "degree" of effects of local structures in network dynamics. Importantly, we show that the original clustering coefficient [12] (here corresponding to C_3) is insufficient to explain the effects of local structures. This was shown by the fact that in RBNs with $C_{1,3} = 0$, the $\langle I \rangle$ still varies with N. Namely, it increases as N decreases which means that the local structures of these networks still play a role in the dynamics. By removing the fourth and fifth order C_p, this dependency of $\langle I \rangle$ on N is removed and even the smallest networks behave identically to the larger "tree-like" networks (i.e., have identical $\langle I \rangle$). Additionally, the values of the standard deviation of C_p over the ensemble explain the diversity in the dynamics of RBNs where only the values of N and k are constrained.

The $\langle I \rangle$ of RBNs with zero or some other fixed value of C_p, becomes almost independent of N. The dynamics of RBNs of equal N and k also become far more uniform. Finally, the higher the order of C_p removed, the more the networks behave like "infinite" (tree-like) structures. This means that the method of network construction proposed here allows constructing RBNs with a small number of nodes to which mean field approximations can be applied, since these usually assume tree-like structures ($C_p = 0$). It also allows the generation of large networks with a given C_p, which might be of importance especially when using the ensemble approach [27] to study the dynamics of biological networks such as GRNs, since these rarely have locally tree-like structures.

Overall, the results show that "non-tree-like" local structures cause a significant increase in the dynamical correlation between nodes in an RBN. This agrees with one of its topological consequences, the decrease of the average path length [12]. Also, it suggests that networks, such as biological ones, subject to selection, are most likely not tree-like structures, if high correlation between the functioning of its elements is required.

If a network is to be selected based on its $\langle I \rangle$, our results indicate that this can be done by selecting a certain C_p. Moreover if the maximization of the expected range of variability of I is what is being selected, then the range of variability of C_p should be maximized. This range is most likely bounded by the necessity of maintaining all nodes connected to a single network, and perhaps also by the necessity of minimizing the network's average path length.

While critical networks maximize $\langle I \rangle$ in RBNs [2] assuming tree-like RBNs, these results suggest that the value of C_p of the networks in the ensemble cannot be neglected, and perhaps the notion of criticality could be extended to incorporate this topological feature.

Networks with a high C_p might be naturally favored since they maximize $\langle I \rangle$. Interestingly, studies of the structure of natural networks [28] suggest that their C (as originally defined [12]) is higher than expected by chance. If this holds true, it necessarily implies that the same is true for C_p.

Our conclusions suggest that when applying the ensemble approach [27] to study biological networks, such as genetic networks, the networks of these ensembles ought to have similar C_p values as the biological network in question, if they are to properly mimic the global dynamical properties as well. Moreover, our measurements of the standard deviation of C_p and the distribution of I values of networks with equal N and p, show that for those networks to have uniform dynamical properties, it is not sufficient to impose an average C_p over the ensemble. Instead, the C_p of each individual network must be fixed to the same value.

These results are an example of how a system's structure affects its dynamics regardless of the nature of the components and interactions [20]. Boolean network dynamics are highly constrained by their local topological structure. Changing the local topological features while maintaining update rule distributions results in significant changes in average global coordination. We expect that these results are extendable to a wide variety of systems, including stochastic delayed genetic networks [29].

Finally, we note that the results may be of biological relevance, by suggesting that large networks, including genetic networks, might follow local and global topological constraints, such as criticality and high C_p, if they are to maximize the coordination between their components. Namely, the results are another tentative evidence that one should not expect to find biological networks with random topology at local or global level.

On the Effects of Noise in Information Flux

Finally, it is of interest to note that a small increase in the networks' average connectivity is sufficient to cope with high levels of noise. This observation may be of importance, for example, to understand how gene regulatory networks, which have been shown to be stochastic [29, 30], may cope with its internal stochasticity. Also of interest is the fact that a small amount of noise causes a significant decrease of the fraction of frozen nodes in a system, and thus, the high increase of the global mutual information between all the elements dynamics, indicating that proper wiring schemes between genes might take of the underlying noise to maximize constant information flow.

Acknowledgments This work was supported by the Academy of Finland, proj. no. 213462 (Finnish Centre of Excellence program 2006-11). I thank my co-authors of the articles where many of the results here described were first presented, especially Stuart Kauffman, Jason Lloyd-Price, Bjorn Samuelsson, Juha Kesseli, Antti Hakkinen, Olli Yli-Harja, Pedro Lind, and Josh Socolar.

References

1. Ribeiro AS, Almeida M (2006) Acta Astronautica 59(8–11):1086–1092
2. Ribeiro AS, Kauffman SA, Lloyd-Price J, Samuelsson B, Socolar J (2008) Phys Rev E 77(1):011901
3. Ribeiro AS, Este RA, Lloyd-Price J, Kauffman SA (2006) WSEAS Trans Syst 12(5):2935–2941
4. Ribeiro AS, Zhu R, Kauffman SA (2006) J Comput Biol 13(9):1630–1639
5. Ribeiro AS (2007) Phys Rev E 75(1):061903
6. Ribeiro AS, Lloyd-Price J, Kesseli J, Hakkinen A, Yli-Harja O (2008) Phys. Rev. E 78(5):056108
7. Ribeiro AS, Lind PG (2005) Physica Scripta T118:165–167
8. Kauffman SA (1969) J Theor Biol 22:437–467
9. Derrida B, Pomeau Y (1986) Europhys Lett. 1:45–49
10. Shannon CS (1948) Bell Syst Tech J 27:379–423 and 623–656
11. Davidson EH (2006) The regulatory genome: gene regulatory networks in Development and evolution. Academic Press, San Diego, CA, USA
12. Watts D, Strogatz S (1998) Nature 393:440–442
13. Lempel A, Ziv J (1976) IEEE Trans Inform Theory 22:75–81
14. Shmulevich I, Kauffman SA, Aldana M (2005) PNAS 102(38):13439–13444
15. Borowska M, Oczeretko E, Mazurek A, Kitlas A, Kuc P (2005) Annu Proc Med Sci 50(Suplement 2)
16. Boccaletti S, Kurths J, Osipov G, Valladares DL, Zhou CS (2002) Phys Rep 366:1–101
17. Bhatt GD (2000) Learn Organ 7(2):89–99
18. Hopfield JJ (1982) Proc Natl Acad Sci USA 79:2554–2558
19. Nonaka I (1994) Organ Sci 5(1):14–37
20. Von Bertalanffy L (1968) General Systems Theory. Braziller, New York
21. Darr E, Argote L, Epple D (1995) Manage Sci 41:1750–1762
22. Capron L, Mitchell W (1998) Ind Corp Change 7:453–484
23. Shmulevich I, Kauffman SA, Aldana M (2005) PNAS 102:13439–13444
24. Shmulevich I, Kauffman SA (2004) Phys Rev Lett 93:048701
25. Ramo P, Kesseli J, Yli-Harja O (2006) J Theor Biol 242:164–170
26. Serra R, Villani M, Semeria A (2004) J Theor Biol 227(1):149–157
27. Kauffman SA (1993) The origins of order: self-organization and selection in evolution. Oxford University Press, Oxford
28. Barabasi A-L (2002) Linked: the new science of networks. Perseus, Cambridge, MA
29. Ribeiro AS, Zhu R, Kauffman SA (2006) J Comput Bio 13(9):1630–1639
30. Arkin A, Ross J, McAdams H (1998) Genetics 149:1633–1648

Part II
Social Network Evolution

Chapter 8
Network Evolution: Theory and Mechanisms

Saeed Omidi and Ali Masoudi-Nejad

Abstract In this chapter, we intend to give a review on some of the important network models that are introduced in recent years. The aim of all of these models is to imitate the real-world network properties. Real-world networks exhibit behaviors such as small-world, scale-free, and high clustering coefficient. One of the significant models known as Barabási–Albert model utilizes preferential attachment mechanism as a main mechanism for power-law networks generation. Ubiquity of preferential attachment in network evolution has been proved for many kinds of networks. Additionally, one can generalize functional form of the preferential attachment mathematically, where it provides three different regimes. Besides, in real-world networks, there exist natural constraints such as age or cost that one can consider; however, all of these models are classified as global models. Another important family of models that rely on local strategies attempt to realize network evolution mechanism. These models generate power-law network through making decisions based on the local properties of the networks.

8.1 Introduction

Network and graph are synonymous conceptions. Accordingly, the first well-known model was Erdös–Rényi random graph model that was introduced in the 1950s [1,2]. One of the important properties of this model is the degree distribution among graph vertices that obeys approximately Poisson distribution [3]. Nevertheless, empirical results have confirmed that many kinds of real-world networks follow power-law

S. Omidi and A. Masoudi-Nejad (✉)
Laboratory of Systems Biology and Bioinformatics (LBB), Institute of Biochemistry
and Biophysics & COE in Biomathematics, University of Tehran, Tehran, Iran
e-mail: amasoudin@ibb.ut.ac.ir

S. Omidi
Department of Algorithms and Computations, College of Engineering, University of Tehran,
Tehran, Iran
e-mail: saeedomidi@ut.ac.ir

A. Abraham et al. (eds.), *Computational Social Network Analysis*, Computer
Communications and Networks, DOI 10.1007/978-1-84882-229-0_8,
© Springer-Verlag London Limited 2010

degree distributions with relatively high clustering coefficient [4, 5]. Furthermore, the majority of real-world networks is dynamic systems and evolves in time. The evolution implies continued addition of new vertices into the network [6]. Accordingly, Barabási and Albert [5] proposed a network model that composed of two components. That is growth and preferential attachment mechanism. Preferential attachment means that degree of each vertex determines its attractiveness. This principle is similar to the one introduced in renowned Simon model used to explain power-law distribution in various social and economic systems [7]. Albeit this model could generate power-law networks, still there exist other global properties that this model is unable to fulfill them. For example, average clustering coefficient that measures the clumpiness or cliquishness of the real-world networks [8] is much higher than BA model. Nevertheless, Barabási–Albert model was a significant step toward finding the actual mechanisms for growing real-world networks. Therefore, this model has provided the foundation for theoretical networks researches and offered an important inspiration source for new network models. As a result, many network models generalized the Barabási–Albert model to enhance the conformity to the real-world networks.

Another important model is the model that relies on the local strategies for evolving networks [9–12]. This model tries to mimic the behavior of real-world networks by proposing local strategies that act upon a vertex and its neighbors. This is a pragmatic approach to the network evolution since, when a vertex enters into the network, it does not have to know the overall topology of the network; still, many of these local models implicitly display the preferential linking behavior by the local rules.

In this chapter, we aim to review some of the significant network models and briefly examine their features. We are trying to provide an essential basis for theoretical researches on the networks theory. In Sect. 8.2, we present the preliminary concepts briefly. We give an introduction to the Erdös–Rényi random graph model in Sect. 8.2.2; then we present the Barabási–Albert model in detail in Sect. 8.3. In Sects. 8.4 and 8.5, we will present the generalizations of the Barabási–Albert model such as aging and fitness models; in Sect. 8.6, we will study some of the important local models to produce networks by using local rules. In Sect. 8.7, self-similarity in real-world networks and a model that generates fractal networks are considered; after that, deterministic models as a means to approximating properties of the stochastic models are demonstrated in Sect. 8.8; and finally, we give a brief review on models that are relying on the self-organization criteria in Sect. 8.9.

8.2 Preliminary Concepts

In this section, we intend to investigate some basic concepts that will be used throughout this chapter. A graph is a pair $G = (V, E)$ of sets that the elements of V are the vertices (or nodes) of the graph G and the elements of E are two-element subsets of V referred to as edges (or, links or connections) satisfying $E \subseteq V \times V$.

The vertex set of a graph G is referred to as $V(G)$, and its edge set as $E(G)$. Let $N = |V|$ and $M = |V|$ are the number of vertices and edges, respectively. Hence, $V(G) = \{v_1, v_2, \ldots, v_N\}$ and $E(G) = \{e_1, e_2, \ldots, e_M\}$. Each element of $E(G)$ consists of two vertices $\langle v_i, v_j \rangle$, where v_i and v_j are called initial and final vertices, respectively. It is possible to categorize graphs as directed and undirected. For an undirected graph, the order of initial and final vertices in each edge is considered trivial, but, for directed graphs, the order is strictly necessary.

A vertex v_k is incident with an edge e_l if $v_k \in e_l$. Two vertices v_i and v_j of G are adjacent, or neighbors if $\langle v_i, v_j \rangle \in E(G)$. Degree d_i of vertex v_i is the number of neighbors of v_i, or in other word defined as the number of edges incident to v_i. A vertex of zero degree is called *isolated vertex*, or simply *isolated*. For directed graphs, we can definitely take apart degree value for each vertex into in-degree and out-degree values. If all the vertices of G have the same k, then G is k-regular, or simply regular. The number $\langle k \rangle_G$ for graph G is defined as follows.

$$\langle k \rangle_G = \frac{1}{|V(G)|} \sum_{\forall v_i \in V} k_i \tag{8.1}$$

This is the average degree of G. In fact, if we sum up all the vertex degrees in G, we count every edge exactly twice, so that we can deliberately rewrite Eq. 8.1 as follows

$$\langle k \rangle_G = \frac{2M}{N} \tag{8.2}$$

For instance, the average degree of the Internet at router level was about 2.57 at 1999 [13] and had grown to 2.66 up to 2000 [14]. Therefore, the average degree is not a fixed value for many real-world networks. We won't take into account the dynamism of average degree, since this matter is extensively discussed in [15]. This model called *accelerating growth* is proposed by Dorogovtsev and Mendes [16] and generalized by Gagen and Mattick [17].

A *path* is a sequence of vertices such that each vertex in the sequence being adjacent to its immediately next and previous vertices in the sequence. A graph is called *connected* if there is at least a path between any pair of vertices in the graph. A maximal connected subgraph of a graph is called a *component*. The number of edges of a path is its length ℓ. An important quantity of a graph is *average path length* $\langle \ell \rangle_G$. The shortest path length between two vertices v_i and v_j in graph G is called distance and is shown by $dis(v_i, v_j)$. The *diameter* d_G of graph G is the longest distance between any pair of vertices in graph. Clearly, $\langle \ell \rangle_G \leq d_G$, but in most cases $\langle \ell \rangle_G$ is not much smaller than d_G [15]. Network with relatively low $\langle \ell \rangle_G$ and d_G is called *small-world* network. When in particular network with $\langle \ell \rangle_G \propto \ln N$ is called small-world network.

In real-world networks, not all vertices have the same degree. Distribution function $P(k)$ indicates the probability that a randomly picked vertex has degree k and is called *degree distribution*, which deals with the spread of vertices degrees in network. There are some well-known degree distributions such as *Poisson*, *power-law*, and *exponential* distribution. Network with power-law degree distribution is called *scale-free*. Scale-free networks are also small-world network [4]. What is the degree distribution for generated networks by the model is the first question that arises when one suggests a new network model.

Clustering coefficient $C(v_i)$ measures the number of edges between the neighbors of the v_i, or in other words 'what proportion of the acquaintances of a person (vertex) know each other'. The root of the clustering coefficient concept is from sociology [6] and first, suggested by Watts and Strogatz [18] in the context of networks. Formally, the clustering coefficient of v_i is defined as the ratio between the number of existing edges between neighbors of the vertex, say ϵ_i, and its maximum possible value, $k_i(k_i - 1)/2$, as follows

$$C(v_i) = \frac{2\epsilon_i}{k_i(k_i - 1)} \tag{8.3}$$

As a result of this formulation, $0 \leq C(v_i) \leq 1$. The *average clustering coefficient* $\langle C \rangle_G$ of the graph G is the average of $C(v)$ over all vertices in the graph,

$$\langle C \rangle_G = \frac{1}{n} \sum_{\forall v \in V(G)} C(v) \tag{8.4}$$

Thus, it measures the degree of transitivity of a graph that implies neighbors of a vertex themselves likely to be neighbor. Transitivity occurs when triangles exist in the graph. Consequently, this can be used to reformulate Eq. 8.4 as we get

$$\langle C \rangle_G = \frac{3 \times \text{number of triangles in the graph}}{\text{number of connected triples in the graph}} \tag{8.5}$$

Average clustering coefficient of a network is another significant global (or macroscopic) property of the networks that must be addressed by network growing models. Empirical results have shown that average clustering coefficient for many real-world networks is comparatively higher than average clustering coefficient of produced networks by existing network growing models. For example, for Math co-authorship network obtained from all relevant journals in the field of mathematics and published in 1991–1998 [19], $\langle C \rangle_{\text{math}} = 0.46$, but for the corresponding random graph of the same size and average degree, $\langle C \rangle_{\text{rand}} = 5.9 \times 10^{-5}$.

The first model, which tries to capture the small-world phenomena, as well as high average clustering coefficient in real-world networks, was proposed by Watts and Strogatz [18] in 1998. Watts–Strogatz (WS) model postulates many real-world networks that tend to have small diameter in addition to large average clustering coefficient [15]. WS model interpolates between an ordered finite diameter lattice and a random graph through rewiring. The algorithm of this model briefly consists of two successive steps: (1) start from a lattice, and (2) with probability p rewire each edge and exclude self-loops at the end.

Another important global property of the networks is *degree correlation*. Correlation between degrees of the nearest neighbors in a network is naturally described

by the joint distribution of the degrees for end vertices of edges in graph, $\Pr(k|k')$
(35) $\Pr(k|k')$ indicates the probability of a vertex with degree k, being adjacent to
another vertex of degree k'.

8.2.1 Power-Law Distribution

Before introducing Barabási–Albert model, it would be advantageous to explain
power-law distribution. Let us start with a simple example [20]. Fig. 8.1 shows the
histogram of the US city population distribution, which is plotted from the 2000 US
census.

The left panel of the Fig. 8.1 shows a highly right-screwed diagram that means
most US cities have small population; however, there is a small number of cities,
which have higher population than mean value. Surprisingly, the right panel of
Fig. 8.1 replotted left panel with logarithmic horizontal and vertical axes. As you
can see, this diagram (right hand) follows nearly a straight line with negative
slope.in Regardless of logarithmic axes, converting this straight line to functional
form named P(k) is simple, as follows on

$$P(k) = -\gamma k + c \qquad (8.6)$$

Now, deal with logarithmic nature of right-hand histogram. We can simply times
two sides of Eq. 8.6 with the a logarithm function,

$$\ln P(k) = -\gamma \ln k + c \qquad (8.7)$$

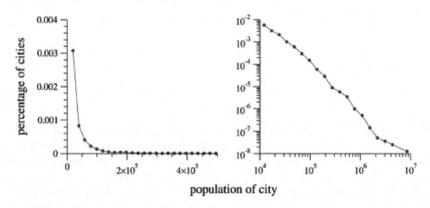

Fig. 8.1 *Left*: histogram of the populations of all US cities with population of 10,000 or more.
Right: another histogram of the same data, but plotted on logarithmic scales. The approximate
straight-line form of the histogram in the right panel implies that the distribution follows a power-
law (Data from the 2000 US Census [20])

Taking the exponential of both sides, this is equivalent to

$$P(k) = C \times k^{-\gamma} \tag{8.8}$$

where, $C = \exp(c)$. Equation 8.8 indicates the probability of finding a city with population k, in other word, it is distribution function of population of US city. Distributions of the form of Eq. 8.8 are said to follow a power-law distribution. The constant γ is called the exponent of the power-law. Constant C in Eq. 8.8 provides normalization requirement of distribution function $P(k)$ and calculate as follows:

$$1 = \int_{k_{min}}^{\infty} P(k)\,dk = C \int_{k_{min}}^{\infty} k^{-\gamma}\,dk = \frac{C}{1-\gamma}[k^{-\gamma+1}]_{k_{min}}^{\infty} \tag{8.9}$$

$$C = (\gamma - 1)k_{min}^{\gamma-1} \tag{8.10}$$

From Eq. 8.9 the restriction $\gamma > 1$ emerges as a result. In addition, there is a restriction on value k, if $k = 0$ the distribution function $P(k)$ diverges. Furthermore, scaling exponent must be $\gamma > 1$ since for $k \to \infty$ when $\gamma = 1$, $P(k)$ diverges. The moments of distribution are defined by

$$M_n(P_k) = \int_{k_{min}}^{k_{max}} k^n \cdot P(k)\,dk \tag{8.11}$$

where the first moment of degree distribution is equivalence to $\langle k \rangle$, or average degree of the network Eq. 8.2. Note that, for constant value of the first moment of degree distribution the average degree of the network does not change in time.

Power-law distribution for discrete variables is different. For discrete variables for finding the value of C, instead of integration in Eq. 8.9, we have to use summation operator and this yields

$$P(k) = \frac{k^{-\gamma}}{\zeta(\gamma)} \tag{8.12}$$

or, equivalency

$$P(k) = C \frac{\Gamma(k)\Gamma(\gamma)}{\Gamma(k+\gamma)} \tag{8.13}$$

where $\zeta(x)$ and $\Gamma(x)$ are the Riemann zeta and Gamma functions, respectively.

In networks, we are only interested in the behavior of the degree distribution in large degrees. Therefore, we need not worry about the low degree region. The cut in degree distribution may be emerging and the position that this cut-off appears called k_{cut} and one should estimate this value for particular network model [15]. One interesting point about power-law degree distributions or scale-free networks is robustness against error and random perturbations [21]. This is reasonable, since the number of vertices of low degrees is higher rather than the number of hubs and this means that the chance of removing hubs is relatively low and the chance of removing low degree vertices is high. Removing low degree vertices is not dangerous and hubs keep the network connected. However, the Achilles's heel of scale-free networks is vulnerability against the intentional attacks. An intentional attack tries to remove most connected vertices to make the network disconnect [15].

8.2.2 Erdös–Rényi Random Graph Model

The theory of random graphs was founded by Erdös and Rényi in 1959–1961 after Erdös had discovered the ability of probabilistic methods to tackle the problems in graph theory [1, 2, 22]. Random graph theory studies the properties of the probability space associated with the graphs at infinitive graph size. Its main goal is to determine threshold probabilities that a particular property of graph will most likely reveal at above threshold and disappear below the threshold. We are not discussing random graph theory here; but we found it useful before starting the other models and only focused on properties of graphs that we need them later on in this chapter. For comprehensive information about this topic, refer to "Random Graphs" from Bollobás [3].

Let N be a positive integer, and $0 \leq p \leq 1$. The random graph $\mathcal{G}_{N,p}$ is a probability space over the set of graphs on the vertex set $V = \{v_1, v_2, \ldots, v_N\}$ and present of each edge determined by

$$P(\langle v_i, v_j \rangle \in E) = p \tag{8.14}$$

Note that, existences of edges are mutually independent. In other word, p determines whether any pair of vertex set is connected or not and is fixed for all pairs. The value of p determines properties such as density, average degree, and clustering coefficient of the graph. From the algorithmic perspective, this model starts from a set of isolated N vertices, and connect each of two vertices with the constant probability p. Therefore, it is clear that

$$|E(G)| = p \times \frac{N(N-1)}{2} \tag{8.15}$$

Moreover, because $\langle K \rangle = 2M/N$, we can find average degree as follow when $N \to \infty$

$$\langle K \rangle = p \times N \tag{8.16}$$

The observations have shown that many real-world networks are scale-free. However, ER model (that stands for Erdös–Rényi random graph model) is unable to generate graphs with power-law degree distribution. Let, k_i is a random variable that indicates degree of vertex v_i. For random graph $\mathcal{G}_{N,p}$ the k_i follows a binomial distribution $bin(k_i, N-1, p)$ as follow

$$P(k_i) = \binom{N}{k_i} p^{k_i} (1-p)^{N-k_i} \tag{8.17}$$

For two different vertices v_i and v_j, $P(k_i)$ and $P(k_j)$ are almost independent. For finding the degree distribution of graph $\mathcal{G}_{N,p}$, we utilize generating function method [32]

$$G_0(s) = \sum_{k=0}^{N} P(k)\, s^k \tag{8.18}$$

By substituting Eq. 8.17 into Eq. 8.18, we will get

$$G_0(s) = \sum_{k=0}^{N} \binom{N}{k} p^k (1-p)^{N-k}\, s^k$$
$$G_0(s) = (1 - p + ps)^N \tag{8.19}$$

Now, suppose $p = \lambda/N$, we can approximate Eq. 8.19 as the following, which is close to it in limit $N \gg 1$. These assumptions make Eq. 8.19 as

$$G_0(s) = e^{\lambda(s-1)} \tag{8.20}$$

$G_0(s)$ is truly normalized because, $G_0(1) = 1$. Furthermore, average degree $\langle k \rangle = G_0'(1) = \lambda$. Now, let us compute degree distribution of $\mathcal{G}_{N,p}$ with $p = \lambda/N$,

$$P(k) = \frac{1}{k!} \frac{d^k G_0}{ds}^k \Big|_{s=0} = \frac{\lambda^k e^{-\lambda}}{k!} \tag{8.21}$$

which is the Poisson distribution, and for $N \gg 1$, $P(k)$ is approximately Poissonian. Therefore,

$$\lim_{N \to \infty} P(k) = \frac{\lambda^k e^{-\lambda}}{k!} \tag{8.22}$$

Therefore, Erdös–Rényi model generates networks that obey from Poisson degree distribution.

Another important property is average path length between all pairs of vertices in the graph, which increase logarithm in graph size [23],

$$\langle \ell \rangle_{\text{ER}} = \frac{\ln(n)}{\ln(\langle k \rangle)} \tag{8.23}$$

Therefore, ER model generates small-world graphs. In addition, ER random graphs are uncorrelated [33].

8.3 Barabási–Albert Model

Power-law distributions have emerged in an extraordinary diverse of phenomena and are widespread in real-world networks. In [4–6] there are many examples of power-law, and hence scale-free networks. The origin of the power-law degree distribution was explained first in seminal paper of Barabási and Albert [5], and they found this feature as a consequence of two generic mechanisms: (1) networks grow continuously by the addition of new vertices, and (2) new vertices attach preferentially to vertices that have relatively high degree. A model based on these two ingredients reproduces the observed stationary scale-free distributions.

Most real-world networks are an open system that means new vertices can be inserted to them by passing time, therefore set V is dynamic and increase its cardinality. For example, emergence of new web sites in the Internet, or addition of new topics to the Internet Wikipedia [24]. In Barabási–Albert, the number of vertices in the network will grow linearly by time. Therefore, rate of addition in Barabási–Albert model is constant and is equal to 1.

Preferential attachment mechanism has been adopted as a crucial assumption in growing networks since 1999 when Barabási–Albert model was introduced. This principle is similar to the one introduced in well-known Simon model used to explain power-law distribution in various social and economic systems [7]. In fact, the existing vertices that are more "attractive" will have a higher chance to receive new connections, and hence increase their degrees; as a result, this mechanism leads to "popularity is attractive" in networks. Barabási and Albert proposed the vertex degree as a measure of attractiveness. Ubiquity of preferential attachment in network evolution has been proved for many kinds of networks [25]. A good illustration of this is the influence of preferential attachment in protein network evolution that has been confirmed via cross genome comparison [26]. To formulate preferential attachment we assume that the probability $\prod(k_i)$ that a new vertex will be connected to existing vertex v_i depends on the degree k_i of that vertex, such that

$$\Pi(k_i) = \frac{k_i}{\Sigma_{\forall j} k_j} \tag{8.24}$$

Therefore, as opposed to the ER random graph model that connection probability is a fixed value, the connection probability $\Pi(k)$ of BA model (stands for Barabási–Albert model) is not a predefined constant value for all vertices in the network. The algorithm of the Barabási–Albert model is the following:

1. **Growth** Starting with fixed number m_o of vertices, at every time step, we add a new vertex with $m(\leq m_o)$ edges that connect the new vertex to m different vertices that have already presented in the system.
2. **Preferential Attachment** The probability of connecting new vertex to existing vertices follows Eq. 8.24.

After t time steps the above algorithm generates a network with $n = m_o + t$ vertices and mt edges. Numerical simulations indicated that this network evolves into power-law degree distribution with a scaling exponent $\gamma \approx 3$. Barabási and Albert, also, demonstrated that for generating scale-free networks, the existence of both growth and preferential attachment are indispensable; in other words, without one of them the generated networks will not be definitely scale-free [5,6].

8.3.1 Master-Equation Approach

The dynamic properties of the BA model can be characterized by using various analytical approaches. Here we are going to introduce master equation approach and its continuous limits which was used by Dorogovtsev et al. [27]. For the sake of simplicity, suppose $m_o = m = 1$. Let function $p(k_i, v_i, t)$ indicates the probability that the vertex s has degree k at time t. Hence, $p(k, t)$ is total degree distribution of network in time t and $p(k) = p(k, t \to \infty)$ is stationary degree distribution of network that does not change in time. Now, it is possible to write the following master equation for degree probabilities of an individual vertex [27, 28]

$$p(k, v_i, t + 1) = \frac{k - 1}{\Sigma_{j \le t} k_j} p(k - 1, v_i, t) + \left(1 - \frac{k}{\Sigma_{j \le t} k_j}\right) p(k, v_i, t) \quad (8.25)$$

The first term in the above equation accounts for connecting new edge to vertex v_i, where its degree is $(k - 1)$ at time t and the second term conveys nonincreasing of degree k of vertex v_i at time t. Clearly, $\Sigma_{j \le t} k_j = 2t$ when $m = 1$, which means number of edge endpoints. Rearranging Eq. 8.25 gives

$$2t \left[p(k, v_i, t + 1) - p(k, v_i, t)\right] = (k - 1)p(k - 1, v_i, t) - dp(k, v_i, t) \quad (8.26)$$

Passing to the continuous limit in t and k, we get

$$2t \frac{\partial p(k, v_i, t)}{\partial t} + \frac{\partial [dp(k, v_i, t)]}{\partial t} = 0 \quad (8.27)$$

In addition, average connectivity of an individual vertex v_i at time t is equal

$$\overline{k}(v_i, t) = \sum_{k=1}^{\infty} k \times p(k, v_i, t) = \int_0^{\infty} k \times p(k, v_i, t) \, dk \quad (8.28)$$

Now, by applying $\int_0^{\infty} k \, dk$ to Eq. 8.27 and integrating its right, we get

$$\frac{\partial \overline{k}(v_i, t)}{\partial t} = \frac{\overline{k}(v_i, t)}{\int_0^t \overline{k}(v, t) \, dv} \quad (8.29)$$

The meaning of Eq. 8.29 is fairly obvious; each new edge is distributed homogeneously among all vertices by considering the preferences. By above modeling, one can find degree distribution of a network analytically. Assuming that $P(k)$ and $\overline{k}(v, t)$ exhibit scaling behavior, that is $P(k) = k^{-\gamma}$ and $\overline{k}(v, t) = v^{\theta}$. Consequently, we obtain the following scaling relation

$$\gamma = 1 + \frac{1}{\theta} \quad (8.30)$$

That means the scale-free nature of generated networks in BA model, (Fig. 8.2).

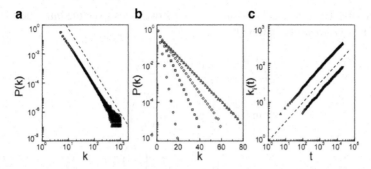

Fig. 8.2 (**a**) The power-law connectivity distribution at t = 150,000 (o) and t = 200,000 (2) as obtained from the model, using $m_0 = m = 5$. The slope of the dashed line is $\gamma = 2.9$. (**b**) The exponential connectivity distribution for model A, in the case of $m_0 = m = 1$ (o), $m_0 = m = 3(\square)$, $m_0 = m = 5(\lozenge)$ and $m_0 = m = 7(\triangle)$. (**c**) Time evolution of the connectivity for two vertices added to the system at $t_1 = 5$ and $t_2 = 95$. The *dashed line* has slope 0.5 [5]

8.3.2 Properties of the BA Model

As we have empirically seen, networks that generated by BA model obey a power-law degree distribution and in asymptotic $t \to \infty$ the scaling exponent approaches to 3; nonetheless, there are other properties that a model should fulfill: clustering coefficient, average path length, network diameter, degree correlation are examples of some of the important global properties of networks. Thus, we need to examine whether the global properties of generated networks by the model are fairly close to the real-world networks properties. In this section, we consider some of these properties.

8.3.2.1 Degree Distribution of BA Model: Continuum Approach

Another important analytical method to inspect properties of the networks is continuum theory that was proposed by Barabási and Albert [5] that is chiefly focused on the dynamics of the vertex degree. Let unknown function $k_i(t)$ indicates degree of vertex v_i at time t. Due to the preferential attachment, a vertex that acquired more connections than another vertex will increase its degree at relatively higher rate; thus an initial difference in the degree between two vertices will increase further as the network grows. As demonstrated by Barabási and Albert [5], the rate at which a vertex acquire edges is

$$\frac{dk_i(t)}{dt} = \frac{k_i(t)}{2t} \qquad (8.31)$$

rearranging Eq. 8.31 gives

$$\frac{dk_i(t)}{k_i(t)} = \frac{dt}{2t} \qquad (8.32)$$

We can solve Eq. 8.32 easily by integrating its two sides from the introduction time t_i of vertex v_i, to arbitrary time t.

$$\int_{k_i(t_i)}^{k_i(t)} \frac{dk_i(t)}{k_i(t)} = \int_{t_i}^{t} \frac{dt}{2t}$$

$$\ln\left(\frac{k_i(t)}{k_i(t_i)}\right) = \frac{1}{2} \ln\left(\frac{t}{t_i}\right)$$

$$k_i(t) = k_i(t_i) \left(\frac{t}{t_i}\right)^{1/2} \tag{8.33}$$

By assumptions of BA model, each new vertex initially has m edges, so $k_i(t_i) = m$,

$$k_i(t) = m\left(\frac{t}{t_i}\right)^{1/2} \tag{8.34}$$

Using above equation we can find the probability that a vertex has degree smaller than k, as

$$\Pr(k_i(t) < k) = \Pr\left(t_i > \frac{m^2 t}{k^2}\right) \tag{8.35}$$

From basic probability, we can rewrite Eq. 8.35 as

$$\Pr\left(t_i > \frac{m^2 t}{k^2}\right) = 1 - \Pr\left(t_i \le \frac{m^2 t}{k^2}\right)$$

$$= \frac{m^2 t}{k^2(t + m_0)} \tag{8.36}$$

The degree distribution $P(k)$ can be obtained using

$$P(k) = \frac{\partial \Pr(k_i(t) < k)}{\partial k} = \frac{2m^2 t}{m_0 + t} \times \frac{1}{k^2 + 1} \tag{8.37}$$

In asymptotically $t \to \infty$, $P(k)$ will be

$$P(k) \sim 2m^2 \times k^{-3} \tag{8.38}$$

Therefore, scaling exponent of a network that is generated by BA model when $t \to \infty$ will be $\gamma = 3$.

In addition, we can find the degree distribution by solving Eq. 8.27 and finding unknown function $p(k, v_i, i)$. The solution of Eq. 8.26 is

$$p(k, v_i, t) = \delta\left(k - \sqrt{t/i}\right) \tag{8.39}$$

We can find the stationary degree distribution in the continuous approximation by following equation

$$P(k) = P(k, t \to \infty) \lim_{t \to \infty} = \frac{1}{t} \int_0^t p(k, v, t) dv \qquad (8.40)$$

Hence, by inserting $p(k, v_i, t)$ in Eq. 8.39 into the Eq. 8.40 we will get approximately

$$P(k) \sim 2k^{-3} \qquad (8.41)$$

This is close to the solution Eq. 8.38, which is obtained by means of the continuum theory.

8.3.2.2 Clustering Coefficient

As we mentioned in Sect. 8.2, real-world networks exhibit a large degree of clustering. For classical random graph with fixed connection probability p, connecting two neighbors of a vertex is same as connecting two vertices without any common acquaintance. Hence, in average, there will be $p \times \frac{k(k-1)}{2}$ edges among k neighbors of every vertex. Therefore, the average clustering coefficient of random graphs is corresponding to the value of p and hence,

$$\langle C \rangle_{ER} = p = \frac{\langle k \rangle}{N} \qquad (8.42)$$

The important point is that the average clustering coefficient in ER model is dependent on reverse network size. Conversely, in many real-world networks average clustering coefficient is nearly independent of the network size; so by increasing network size this value will be almost stable.

Figure 8.3 shows the clustering coefficient of a network that is generated by BA model with average degree $\langle k \rangle = 4$ and different sizes, comparing with the clustering coefficient of ER random graph model.

It is clear from Fig. 8.3 that clustering coefficient of BA networks diminishes slower than ER random graph as the network size increases. Clustering coefficient of the real-world networks is about five times higher than ER random graph, and decreases gradually as network size increases even in many of real-world networks that is independent of the network size [6]. Numerical simulations [6] have shown that the average clustering coefficient of the BA model is approximately $\langle C \rangle_{BA} \approx N^{-0.75}$, which asserts that clustering coefficient of BA networks decays slower than ER model with $\langle C \rangle_{ER} \approx N^{-1}$. Nevertheless, it is still much different from the behavior of real-world networks.

Xu et al. [9] analytically have shown that

$$\langle C \rangle_{BA} = \frac{m \ln^2 N}{8N} \qquad (8.43)$$

Fig. 8.3 Clustering coefficient versus size of the BA model with $\langle d \rangle = 4$, compared with the clustering coefficient of ER random graph, with $\langle C \rangle_{random} = \langle d \rangle / N$ [6]

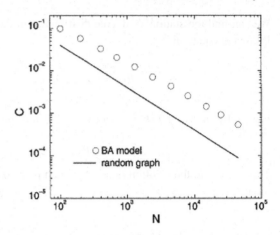

So, as N grows by time, the clustering coefficient scales as $\ln^2 N / N$. Note that, we can substitute t in the above equations instead of N, since $N = t$ when $t \gg 1$.

Notice that the average clustering coefficient value dramatically decreases when there are isolated and leaf vertices in the network; because, by definition of Eq. 8.3 the clustering coefficient value for isolated and leaf vertices is zero. Hence, these zero values decrease the average clustering of the network. Kaiser [29] excludes this effect from Eq. 8.3. This exclusion leads to calculating average clustering coefficient values that are up to 140% higher than the traditional values.

8.3.2.3 Average Path Length

Another important property to characterize a network model is the average path length or the network diameter. Analytically, the average path length of BA model grow logarithmically with the increase of graph size and observations demonstrate that the average path length in real-world networks is generally small too. These networks thus exhibit small-world effect. For instance, despite the large number of vertices, the World Wide Web demonstrates the small-world property. The most popular manifestation of small-world is the "six degrees of separation" concept, which is uncovered by the social psychologist Stanley Milgram in 1967, who concluded that there was a path of acquaintances with a typical length of about 6 between most pairs of people in the USA [30].

Analytical results [31] have shown that average path length of BA model is equal to

$$\langle \ell \rangle_{BA} = \frac{\ln(n)}{\ln \ln(n)} \tag{8.44}$$

The average path length of BA model is typically lower than the average path length of real-world networks and ER random graphs of the same size [6]. Scale-free networks with scaling exponent $2 < \gamma < 3$ possess a diameter $d \sim \ln \ln(n)$, smaller than ER random graph. Similar result was found by generating function formulation [32].

Due to high clustering coefficient we can reach any desired vertex in the network by passing through a very small step or intermediate vertices. In addition, there is another reason that is emergence of high degree vertices in the scale-free networks, namely "hubs", which connect different parts of networks. Hubs efficiently decrease average distance path in the networks. Apparently, existence of hubs is the factor that leads to average path length in BA networks being smaller than ER random graph of the same size.

8.3.2.4 Degree Correlations

Krapivsky and Redner [33] have shown analytically that there is a untrivial correlation between the degrees of connected vertices. This means that the joint distribution does not factorize. As Krapivsky and Redner claimed that this is the most important distinction between ER random graphs and BA model, Barrat and Pastor-Satorras [34] analytically studied this property for BA model.

8.3.3 Generalization of Preferential Attachment: Rate Equation Approach

As demonstrated in the previous section the probability of connecting a new vertex to existing ones is linearly proportional to the degree of those vertices; in other words, the probability of connecting to vertex v_i is equal to,

$$\Pi k_i \propto k_i$$

We can, however, generalize this mechanism by allowing $\Pi_k \propto k^\alpha$, where it was found that the degree distribution $P(k)$ crucially depends on the value of α [35]. For $\alpha = 1$ this model will reduce to classical BA model with connecting probability Eq. 8.14. For $\alpha < 1$, connecting probability grows weakly with the vertex degree (or popularity) and $P(k)$ decreases as an exponential distribution in k. The case of $\alpha > 1$ leads to *gelation* phenomenon, that means a single *gel* vertex connects to nearly all other vertices in the network [33]; consequently, it absorbs almost all of the edges in the network. Only in the borderline case of an asymptotically linear connecting probability (equation above) is particularly intriguing as it leads to $P(k) \sim k^{-\gamma}$ with the tunable scaling exponent γ to any value larger than 2, which is depending on the detail of connecting probability formula. Specifically, the strictly linear connecting probability, $\Pi_k = k$, leads to $\gamma = 3$ as we have shown in Sect. 8.3.2 by continuum theorem approach. Now, let us portray this generalization via rate equation approach that employed by Krapivsky et al. [33, 35]. The rate equations for $N_k(t)$ are

$$\frac{dN_k}{dt} = \Pi^{-1}[\Pi_{k-1}N_{k-1} - \Pi_k N_k] + \delta_{k,1} \qquad (8.45)$$

The first term on the right-hand side of Eq. 8.45 accounts for the process in which a vertex of degree $k - 1$ connects to the new vertex and consequently N_k increases. The second term accounts for N_k reduction since a vertex of degree k connects to the new vertex and causes to increase its degree to $k + 1$, hence leads to reduce N_d. Note that, $\Pi(t) = \sum_{k \geq 1} \Pi_k N_k(t)$ is for normalization purpose. In every step our model adds a new vertex with single edge; therefore, $N_1(t)$ grows by time or $N_1(t) = t$. Accordingly, rate of change in $N_1(t)$, (or dN_1/dt) is equal to 1, and the last term on the right-hand side of Eq. 8.45 deals with this. Also, $N_0 \equiv 0$, so Eq. 8.45 applies for $k \geq 1$.

It will be useful to define the moments of degree distribution as

$$M_n(t) = \sum_{k \geq 1} k^n N_k(t) \tag{8.46}$$

The first two moments of degree distribution are trivial and equal to $M_0(t) = t + M_0(0)$ – total number of vertices – and $M_1(t) = 2t + M_1(0)$ – total number of endpoints of edges. Noticeably, the first two moment are independent of connecting probability Π_k; higher order of moments, however, are reliant upon Π_k.

At this time, we are going to find N_k by solving Eq. 8.45 for variant types of connecting probability Π_k. For solving Eq. 8.45, we need an initial condition where in long-time behavior $t \to \infty$ this initial condition vanishes, and we do not take into account initial condition in asymptotical regime $t \to \infty$.

First, let us consider linear case $\Pi_k = k$ for which $\Pi(t)$ is equal to $M_1(t)$; as a result, normalization constant is $\Pi(t) = 2t$. Equation 8.45 when $\Pi_k = k$ is equivalent to

$$\frac{dN_k}{dt} = \frac{1}{2t}[(k - 1)N_{k-1} - dN_k] + \delta_{k,1} \tag{8.47}$$

for $k = 1$ will be

$$\frac{dN_1}{dt} = \frac{-1}{2t} N_1 + 1$$

A guess to solve above equation is $N_1 = n_1 t$, so

$$n_1 + \frac{1}{2} n_1 = 1$$

$$n_i = \frac{2}{3}$$

Therefore, $N_1 = \frac{2}{3}t$. Furthermore, $N_2 = \frac{1}{6}t$ and we can simply find N_3, N_4, etc. for Eq. 8.47. The linear functional form of N_k implies that it grows linearly with time. In general form,

$$N_k(t) = n_k \times t \tag{8.48}$$

Now, substituting Eq. 8.48 in Eq. 8.47, yields the simply recursion $n_k = n_{k-1} (k - 1)/(k + 2)$. Solving it for n_k will provide,

$$n_k = \frac{4}{k(k+1)(k+2)} \tag{8.49}$$

As a result, $n_k \approx 4k^{-3}$ continuously. When $k \to \infty$, we can estimate this result discretely by Gamma-function $\Gamma(x)$, which we know $\Gamma(x+1) = x!$ and hence, $\lim_{x \to \infty} \frac{\Gamma(x)}{\Gamma(x-y)} = x^y$ which gives

$$n_k = \frac{4 \, \Gamma(k)}{\Gamma(k+3)} \tag{8.50}$$

Then, by substituting $N_k(t) = n_k \times t$ and $\Pi(t) = \mu \times t$ into Eq. 8.45 we obtain the recursion relation $n_{k-1} = n_{k-1}\Pi_{k-1}/(\mu + \Pi_k)$ and $n_1 = \mu/(\mu + \Pi_1)$. Solving for n_k brings forth

$$n_k = \frac{\mu}{\Pi_k} \prod_{j=1}^{k} \left(1 + \frac{\mu}{\Pi_1}\right)^{-1} \tag{8.51}$$

To complete the solution we need to calculate μ. Combining the definition $\mu = \sum_{k \geq 1} \Pi_k n_k$ and Eq. 8.51 we obtain the implicit relation

$$\sum_{k=1}^{\infty} \prod_{j=1}^{k} \left(1 + \frac{\mu}{\Pi_j}\right)^{-1} = 1 \tag{8.52}$$

Thus the value μ always depends on the entire connecting probability Π_k. For $\Pi_k \sim k^\alpha$, when $0 < \alpha < 1$, substituting this asymptotics into Eq. 8.51 and writing the product as the exponential of a sum and converting the sum to an integral expression, finally perform the integration, we will achieve

$$n_k \sim \begin{cases} k^{-\alpha} \, \exp\left[-\mu\left(\dfrac{k^{1-\alpha} - 2^{1-\alpha}}{1-\alpha}\right)\right] & \dfrac{1}{2} < \alpha < 1 \\[2ex] k^{\mu^2-1/2} \, \exp[-2\mu\sqrt{k}] & \alpha = \dfrac{1}{2} \\[2ex] k^{-\alpha} \exp\left[-\mu\dfrac{k^{1-\alpha}}{1-\alpha} + \dfrac{\mu^2}{2}\dfrac{k^{1-2\alpha}}{1-2\alpha}\right] & \dfrac{1}{3} < \alpha < \dfrac{1}{2} \end{cases} \tag{8.53}$$

To complete the solution we need to determine the value of μ. We are to find an explicit expression for μ, even if the connecting probability is strictly homogeneous (we'll take into account nonhomogeneous in Sect. 8.5). However, numerical techniques shows that $\mu(\alpha)$ varies smoothly between 1 and 2 as α increases from 0 to 1. From (Fig. 8.4) it is clear that when $\alpha = 1$, $\mu = 2$ and accordingly $n_k = k^{-3}$- original BA model by Eq. 8.24.

For the asymptotically linear connecting probability $\Pi_k \sim k$, expanding the product in Eq. 8.51 and following step by step the approach that led to Eq. 8.53 now gives the power-law asymptotic behavior,

Fig. 8.4 The amplitude
of μ versus α [33]

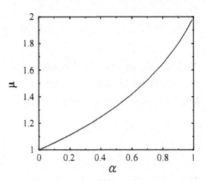

$$n_k \sim k^{-\nu} \quad \text{with } \nu = 1 + \mu \tag{8.54}$$

An important feature of this result is that the scaling exponent ν can be tuned to any value larger than 2, since $\mu = \sum_{k \geq 1} \Pi_k n_k \sim \sum_{k \geq 1} k n_k$ must converge, which leads to $2 < \nu < \infty$.

For example, consider the connecting probability $\Pi_k = k$ for $k \geq 2$, while $\Pi_1 \equiv \alpha$ is an arbitrary positive number. It is convenient to separately treat Π_1 and Π_k for $k \geq 2$ in Eq. 8.52, hence

$$\mu = \Pi_1 \sum_{k=2}^{\infty} \prod_{j=2}^{k} \left(1 + \frac{\mu}{\Pi_j}\right)^{-1} \tag{8.55}$$

$$\mu = \alpha \Gamma(2 + \mu) \sum_{k=2}^{\infty} \frac{\Gamma(1+k)}{\Gamma(1+\mu+k)} \tag{8.56}$$

The summation term can be evaluated by employing

$$\sum_{i=2}^{\infty} \frac{\Gamma(\alpha+i)}{\Gamma(\beta+i)} = \frac{\Gamma(\alpha+2)}{(\beta-\alpha-1)\Gamma(\beta+1)} \tag{8.57}$$

As a result, Eq. 8.56 is converted into

$$\mu = \alpha \left(\frac{2}{\mu-1}\right) \tag{8.58}$$

$$\mu^2 - \mu - 2\alpha = 0 \tag{8.59}$$

$$\mu = \frac{1 \pm \sqrt{1 + 8\alpha}}{2} \tag{8.60}$$

By omitting negative result for μ in the above equation, it is impossible to $\sum_{k \geq 1} \Pi_k n_k$ being negative. For that reason, by substituting μ into the scaling exponent ν in Eq. 8.54 is

$$v = \frac{3 + \sqrt{1 + 8\alpha}}{2} \tag{8.61}$$

Eventually, by Eq. 8.52 the degree distribution for instance model $\Pi_1 = \alpha$ and $\Pi_k = k$ for $k \geq 2$ is

$$n_1 = \frac{\mu}{\mu + \alpha}, \quad n_k = \frac{\mu \alpha}{\mu + \alpha} \frac{\Gamma(2 + \mu)\Gamma(k)}{\Gamma(1 + \mu + k)} \quad \text{for } k \geq 2 \tag{8.62}$$

For $\alpha > 1$, we have $v > 3$; in particular, $v \to \sqrt{2\alpha}$ as $\alpha \to \infty$. For $\alpha = 1$ we get classical BA model. For the superlinear connecting probability $\Pi_k = k^\alpha$, with $\alpha > 1$. In superlinear connecting probability, "gelation" or "winner-take-all" phenomena arises [36]. when $\alpha > 2$ there is nonzero probability that the initial vertex is connected to almost every other vertex of the network. First, suppose the model in which at every discrete time step a new vertex would be introduced and through a single edge connected to the presented vertices of the network by connecting probability $\Pi_k = k^\alpha$. Therefore, after N time step where there are N vertices in the network the probability that a new vertex makes a connection to initial vertex is equal to

$$\Pi(k_1) = k_1^\alpha \bigg/ \sum_{i=1}^{N} k_i^\alpha \tag{8.63}$$

Without loss of generality, we are suppose to at Nth step every vertex except initial vertex connected to the initial vertex and their degree is only one, this is equivalent to *star* topology on the network with N vertices. Hence, $k_1 = N$ and $k_i = 1$ for $2 \leq i \leq N$ which we can rewrite Eq. 8.63 as,

$$\frac{N^\alpha}{N^\alpha + N} = \frac{1}{1 + N^{1-\alpha}} \tag{8.64}$$

Now, we can easily determine the probability of emergence star like topology in the network with initial vertex centrality, as follows,

$$\mathcal{P} = \prod_{N=1}^{\infty} \frac{1}{1 + N^{1-\alpha}} \tag{8.65}$$

Clearly, $\mathcal{P} = 0$ when $\alpha \leq 2$ and $\mathcal{P} > 2$ when $\alpha > 2$. Thus, for superlinear connecting probability with $\alpha > 2$ there is a nonzero probability that the initial vertex absorbs all other vertices of the network. For $3/2 < \alpha < 2$, the number of vertices with two edges grows as $t^{2-\alpha}$, while the number of vertices with more than two edges is finite. Generally, for $(m + 1)/m < \alpha < m/(m - 1)$, the number of vertices with more than m edges is finite, while $N_k \sim t^{k-(k-1)\alpha}$ for $k \leq m$. At the end, Krapivsky and Redner [33] asserted that the correlation between the degrees of neighboring connected vertices exist for any functional form of connection probability Π_i.

8.4   Network Growing with Aging

In previous section we have seen connecting probability $\Pi_k \propto k$, which means Π_k depends only on the degree of vertex. As demonstrated by [33] although in the BA model there is no explicit aging, in which the connection probability depends on the age of the target vertex, older vertices will be much better connected than younger vertices. Let $c_k(t, a)$ be the average number of vertices of age a (their born time is $t - a$ that called t_i) which have degree k. Noticeably, number of vertices at time t of degree k is related to $c_k(t, a)$ through $N_k(t) = \Sigma_{a \leq t} c_k(t, a)$. The joint distribution for linear preferential attachment evolves according to the following rate equation,

$$\left(\frac{\partial}{\partial k} + \frac{\partial}{\partial a} \right) c_k = \frac{(k-1)}{2t} c_{k-1} - \frac{k}{2t} c_k + \delta_{k,1} \delta(a) \qquad (8.66)$$

By solving Eq. 8.66 we will get

$$c_k(t, a) = \sqrt{1 - \frac{a}{t}} \left\{ 1 - \sqrt{1 - \frac{a}{t}} \right\}^{k-1} \qquad (8.67)$$

As a consequence, the degree distribution of vertices with fixed age decays exponentially with degree. Young vertices ($a/t \to 0$) typically have smaller degree than old vertices ($a/t \to 1$) as you can see in Fig. 8.5. It is the slow decay of the degree distribution for old vertices that ultimately leads to a power-law degree distribution.

However, in most real-world networks, there is an aging factor that exerts direct influence over connection probability Π_k; and hence, the evolution of network. A well-known example of the networks is the network of citations of scientific papers [37] in which each paper is a vertex and direct edges exhibit references to the cited papers. Indeed, we rarely cite old papers, and the citation rate of an article decreases in time; yet the reduction rate of citations for different papers is not identical.

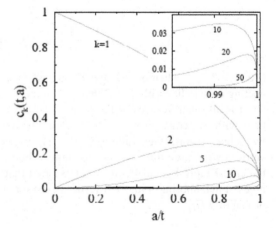

Fig. 8.5 Age-dependent degree distribution in the BA model. Low-degree nodes tend to be relatively young while high-degree nodes are old [33]

For that reason, one should incorporate the effect of age factor in preferential attachment mechanism. Aging model that studied by Dorogovtsev and Mendes [38], in which each new vertex of the network will be attached to one (this means, $m = 1$) already existed vertex with a probability proportional to (i) the connectivity of the old site as in the Barabási–Albert's models and (ii) $a^{-\beta}$ where a is the age of the vertex and equal to $(t - t_i)$, where t_i is the vertex introduction time. Theoretically, the exponent β may be of any value $-\infty < \beta < +\infty$. Obviously, for negative value of β, the attractiveness of vertices increases with aging; and hence many edges are connected to the oldest vertices. In practice, however, we must accurately determine β that guarantees to generate networks, which explicitly conform to observations in real-world networks.

By means of continuum approach in Sect. 8.3.2 we can immediately model aging [38] by following equation

$$\frac{\partial \bar{k}(v_i, t)}{\partial t} = \frac{\bar{k}(v_j, t)(t - t_i)\beta}{\int_0^t \bar{k}(v_j, t)(t - t_j)^{-\beta} \, dv_j}, \quad \bar{k}(t, t) = 1 \tag{8.68}$$

We are interested to solve Eq. 8.68 in the scaling form

$$\bar{k}(v_i, t) \equiv k(s/t), \quad s/t \equiv \zeta \tag{8.69}$$

Then by substituting Eq. 8.69 into Eq. 8.68, one can get the following equitation

$$-\zeta(1 - \zeta)^\beta \frac{d \ln k(\zeta)}{d\zeta} = \left[\int_0^1 k(\zeta)(1 - \zeta)^\beta \, d\zeta \right]^{-1} \equiv \theta \tag{8.70}$$

where θ is the scaling unknown constant for $\bar{k}(v_i, t)$ and initial condition of Eq. 8.70 is $k(1) = 1$. By solving Eq. 8.70 we find for $-\infty < \beta < 1$, $\theta(\beta)$ when $\beta \to 0$ will be,

$$\theta \cong \frac{1}{2} - (1 - \ln 2)\beta \tag{8.71}$$

Finally, through $\gamma = 1 + 1/\theta$, we get

$$\gamma \cong 3 + 4(1 - \ln 2)\beta \tag{8.72}$$

When $-\infty < \beta < 1$. In the limit case $\beta \to 1$, we find

$$\theta \cong c_1(1 - \beta), \quad \gamma \cong \frac{1}{c_1} \frac{1}{1 - \beta} \tag{8.73}$$

Here, $c_1 \cong 0.8065$, $c_1^{-1} \approx 1.2400$. As it should be, we get the values $\gamma = 3$ and $\theta = 1/2$ for $\beta = 0$ (BA model without aging). In brief, at $\beta > 1$, degree distribution of network obeys exponential distribution, while β changes from 0 to 1, γ grows from 3 to ∞, and θ decreases from 1/2 to 0 (Fig. 8.6). Simulations demonstrate also that γ has a tendency to decrease from 3 to 2, and θ grows from 1/2 to 1 when β decreases from 0 to $-\infty$.

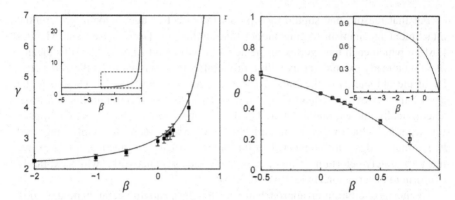

Fig. 8.6 *Left*: Scaling exponent γ versus aging exponent β, the inset depicts the analytical solution in the range $-5 < \beta < 1$. *Right*: Exponent θ of the mean connectivity ($\bar{k}(v, t) \propto v^{-\theta}$) versus aging exponent β. The inset shows the analytical solution in the range $-5 < \beta < 1$. Note that points are obtained from the simulations and line is analytical solution [38]

8.5 Fitness Model

Bianconi and Barabási [36] pointed out that in real-world networks there is a competitive aspect, and each vertex has an intrinsic ability to collect edges in evolution process of network. For example, on the World Wide Web, the web pages compete for URLs to augment their visibility and consequently their attractiveness, also in the scientific community, scientists and publications compete for citations. The dynamics and outcomes of this competition emerge itself on the global structures of the network. In addition, by the preferential attachment formula Eq. 8.24 of BA model there is no chance to receive edges by an isolated vertex (attractiveness of an isolated vertex is noting), or in other word $\Pi_0 = 0$. However, there should be a finite chance to collect edges by even isolated vertices.

The reasonable linear form of the connection probability Eq. 8.24, as well as an additive value together offers the broader attachment probability $\Pi = \Pi = \eta k + \zeta$. The coefficient η may be called "strength" or "multiplicative fitness" of vertex and ζ is "initial attractiveness" or "additive fitness" of vertex. In relation to η and ζ there would be multiple cases. In this section, we will aim to investigate the models that deal with these issues.

8.5.1 Pure Additive Fitness

Dorogovtsev and Mendes [38] demonstrate a directed graph model that connection probability of the model is proportional to constant additive fitness and vertex indegree (number of incoming links). The algorithm of the model is: at each time step, a new vertex is added which has n incoming edges. These edges go out from arbitrary vertices. Simultaneously, m extra edges are distributed with preference. This means that again, they go out from random vertices but target end of each of them is attached to a vertex with probability that is proportional to $k_{in} + \zeta$ (note that, $\eta = 1$ in this model). In that ζ is a predefined constant and is identical for all vertices in the network. Here, we are going to study only in-degree distribution, and it is possible to generalize the method for undirected networks [39]. By continuous approach (Sect. 8.3.2), we may assume m and n are real values and not necessary integer values. The equation for average in-degree is of the form

$$\frac{\partial \bar{q}(v_i, t)}{\partial t} = m \frac{\bar{q}(v_i, t) + \zeta}{\int_0^t [\bar{q}(v, t) + \zeta] dv} \tag{8.74}$$

Through the initial condition $\bar{q}(0, 0) = 0$, and the boundary condition $\bar{q}(t, t) = n$. The solution of Eq. 8.74 can be

$$\bar{q}(v, t) = (n + \zeta) \left(\frac{v}{t}\right)^{-m/(m+n+\zeta)} - \zeta \tag{8.75}$$

Hence, the scaling exponent for average in-degree is

$$\theta = \frac{m}{m + n + \zeta} \tag{8.76}$$

And from Eq. 8.30 we have

$$\gamma = 2 + (n + \zeta)/m \tag{8.77}$$

Because $n + \zeta > 0$ the exponent γ is in the range $2 < \gamma < \infty$ while θ is in the range $0 < \theta < 1$. Notice, by the setting of $n = 0$ and $\zeta = m$, this model will be reduced to classical BA model.

Now, we consider a network where an additive fitness ζ, chosen from a probability distribution $f_A(\zeta)$, is assigned to each vertex's connection probability. However, the answers do not change crucially. Merely we need to substitute the average value, $\langle f_A(\zeta) \rangle$ or simply $\langle \zeta \rangle$, instead of ζ, in to Eq. 8.30 to obtain scaling exponent as following on

$$\gamma = 2 + \frac{n + \sum_{v\zeta} [\zeta f A(\zeta)]}{m} \tag{8.78}$$

In addition, we can choose n and m randomly and we can find scaling exponent by substituting $\langle n \rangle$ and $\langle m \rangle$ into Eq. 8.77, instead of n and m. Ergün and Rodgers [39] proposed an undirected model for additive fitness and solve it analytically through rate equation approach, which is consistent across the obtained results.

8.5.2 Pure Multiplicative Fitness

Bianconi and Barabási [40] proposed a model in which, for each vertex, a multiplicative fitness parameter η_i is assigned, which does not change in time, and chosen from a distribution function $\rho(\eta)$. Their model exhibits the competition aspect in classical BA model. But, instead of preferential attachment Eq. 8.24 here we have

$$\Pi_i = \frac{\eta_i k_i}{\sum_{\forall j} \eta_j k_j} \tag{8.79}$$

The continuum theory approach (mentioned before that for study the BA model) predicts that the change rate of degrees [40] is equivalent to

$$\frac{\partial k_i}{\partial t} = m \frac{\eta_i k_i}{\sum_{\forall j} \eta_j k_j} \tag{8.80}$$

The solution of Eq. 8.80 is

$$k_i(t, t_i) = m \left(\frac{t}{t_i}\right)^{g(\eta_i)} \tag{8.81}$$

Equation 8.81 indicates that vertices with higher η_i increase their degree faster than those with lower fitness even older ones. The dynamic exponent satisfies

$$c = \int \rho(\eta) \frac{\eta}{1 - g(\eta)} d\eta \tag{8.82}$$

$$g(\eta_i) = \frac{\eta}{c} \tag{8.83}$$

The degree distribution of the model is a weighted sum of the different power-law distributions

$$P(k) \sim \int \rho(\eta) \frac{C}{\eta} \left(\frac{m}{k}\right)^{\frac{C}{\eta}+1} \tag{8.84}$$

which depends on the fitness distribution $\rho(\eta)$.

In addition, if we let $\eta_i = (t - t_i)^{-\beta}$, where t_i is introduction time for vertex v_i, our model will be aging model (Sect. 8.4).

8.5.3 Mixed Multiplicative and Additive Fitness

In this section, we will follow the rate equation formulation by Ergün and Rodgers [39] in which network is built by connecting vertices with probability proportional to vertex degree, random additive fitness ζ, and random multiplicative fitness η as follows

$$\Pi_i = \eta(k_i - 1) + \zeta \tag{8.85}$$

where ζ and η are chosen from a distribution function $f_A(\eta, \zeta)$. This model is a generalization of renowned BA model. The rate equation of this model, which describes unknown function $N_k(\eta, \zeta, t)$ that indicates number of vertices of degree k at time t, is

$$\frac{\partial N_k(\eta, \zeta, t)}{\partial t} = A^{-1}[(\eta(k-2) + \zeta)N_{k-1} - (\eta(k-1) + \zeta)N_k]$$
$$+\delta_{k,1} f_A(\eta, \zeta) \tag{8.86}$$

The first term on the right-hand side of Eq. 8.86 characterizes the increase in the number of vertices with k edges when a vertex of degree $k-1$ gains an edge. The second term accounts the decrease in the number of vertices of degree k. The last term expresses the continuous addition of vertices of degree one and fitness values ζ and η with probability $f_A(\eta, \zeta)$. Moreover, the normalization factor is

$$A(t) = \sum_{k,\eta,\zeta} [\eta(k-1) + \zeta]N_k(\eta, \zeta, t)$$
$$= \int \int \int [\eta(k-1) + \zeta]N_k(\eta, \zeta, t) dk \, d\eta \, d\zeta \tag{8.87}$$

To solve Eq. 8.16, we would define the moment of $N_k(\eta, \zeta, t)$ as follow

$$M_{i,j,l} = \sum_{k,\eta,\zeta} k^i \eta^j \zeta^l N_k(\eta, \zeta, t) \tag{8.88}$$

We can obtain $N_k(\eta, \zeta, t)$ via lowest moments of $N_k(\eta, \zeta, t)$, and it also gets all of moments as linear function of time. Therefore, we define $M(t) \equiv mt$ and $N_k(\eta, \zeta, t) \equiv \eta_k \, t$. Now, we can find m as follow

$$m = \frac{1}{m} \sum_{k,\eta,\zeta} \eta[\eta(k-1) + \zeta]n_k + \langle \zeta \rangle \tag{8.89}$$

where $\langle \zeta \rangle$ is the average additive fitness. So, from Eq. 8.86 obtain

$$[\eta(k-2) + \zeta + m]n_k(\zeta, \gamma) = [\eta(k-1) + \zeta]n_{k-1}(\zeta, \gamma) + m\delta_{k,1} f_A \tag{8.90}$$

We obtain $n_k(\zeta, \eta)$ from Eq. 8.90 as

$$n_k(\zeta, \eta) = \left[\frac{\Gamma\left(k + \frac{\zeta}{\eta} - 1\right)}{\Gamma\left(k + \frac{\zeta + m}{\eta}\right)}\right] \times \frac{\Gamma\left(\frac{\zeta + m}{\eta}\right)}{\Gamma\left(\frac{\zeta}{\eta}\right)} \frac{m}{\eta} f_A(\eta, \zeta) \tag{8.91}$$

Equation 8.91 in asymptotical regime $k \to \infty$, the first term in above equation becomes approximately $k^{-\left(\frac{m}{\zeta} + 1\right)}$ and hence by take out the last term

$$n_k(\zeta, \eta) \sim k^{-\left(1 + \frac{m}{\eta}\right)} \tag{8.92}$$

Therefore, the degree distribution of the model for triple $\langle k, \zeta, \gamma \rangle$ obtains as a power-law distribution with scaling exponent $\gamma = 1 + m/\eta$. From Eq. 8.92 it is clear that for different values of multiplicative fitness, the model generates networks with different power-law distributions. To gain m in Eq. 8.92 we need to solve

$$\iint f_A(\eta, \zeta) \frac{\zeta}{m - \eta} d\eta \, d\zeta = 1 \qquad (8.93)$$

To obtain the degree distribution of the model with respect to different values of ζ and γ that obey from distribution function $f_A(\eta, \zeta)$, we need to solve the following equation

$$n_k = \iint k^{-\left(1 + \frac{m}{\zeta}\right)} \frac{\Gamma\left(\frac{\zeta + m}{\eta}\right)}{\Gamma(\zeta/\eta)} \frac{m}{\eta} f_A(\eta, \zeta) d\zeta d\eta \qquad (8.94)$$

where the integrations are performed in predetermined regions for both ζ and η. For instance, for $f_A(\eta, \zeta) = 1$ and $0 \le \eta, \zeta \le 1$, by solving Eq. 8.93 we will get

$$m = \frac{1}{1 - e^{-2}} \approx 1.156 \qquad (8.95)$$

Then, in the course of substituting m from Eq. 8.95 into Eq. 8.94 and applying region [0,1] for integration in Eq. 8.94, we will get

$$n_k \sim \frac{1}{\ln k} k^{-2.156} \qquad (8.96)$$

which is power-law distribution with exponent $\gamma = -2.156$.

8.5.4 Bose–Einstein Condensation

Bianconi and Barabási [36] mapped the network evolution into an equilibrium Bose gas, which is extremely studied in statistical mechanics. In their model vertices correspond to energy levels, and each edge represents two particles in different energy levels (or perhaps same, if the growth model permits self-loops) (Fig. 8.7). This model allows to assign an energy level ϵ_i to each vertex that is determined by its multiplicative fitness η_i through the following relation

$$\epsilon_i = -\frac{1}{\nu} \ln \eta_i, \quad \nu = 1/T \qquad (8.97)$$

where T indicates system's temperature. An edge between two vertices ν_i and ν_j corresponds to two particles on the energy levels ϵ_i and ϵ_j. The addition of a new vertex in the evolution process introduces a new energy level ϵ_i, as well as $2m$ particles in which m of these particles land at energy level ϵ_i and other m particles

Fig. 8.7 Mapping between the network model and Bose gas [36]

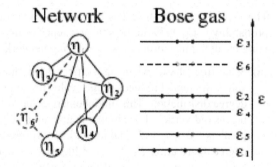

land on each energy level by probability given by Eq. 8.79 with $\eta_j = \exp(-\nu\epsilon_j)$. The rate at which energy level ϵ_i acquires new particles will be obtained by solving equation

$$\frac{\partial k_i(\epsilon_i, t, t_i)}{\partial t} = m\frac{e^{-\nu\epsilon_i}k_i(\epsilon_i, t, t_i)}{Z_t} \tag{8.98}$$

where $k_i(\epsilon_i, t, t_i)$ indicates the number of particles on energy level ϵ_i at time t, and Z_t is defined as

$$Z_t = \sum_{j=1}^{t} e^{-\nu\epsilon_j}k_j(\epsilon_j t, t_j) \tag{8.99}$$

We assume that each vertex increases its degree following power-law distribution

$$k_j(\epsilon_i, t, t_i) = m\left(\frac{t}{t_i}\right)^{f(\epsilon_i)} \tag{8.100}$$

One can find $f(\epsilon)$ as

$$f(\epsilon) = e^{-\nu(\epsilon-\mu)} \tag{8.101}$$

where $f(\epsilon_i)$ is the energy-dependent dynamic exponent and μ plays the role of the chemical potential, which fulfill the equation

$$I(\nu, \mu) = \int g(\epsilon)\frac{1}{e^{\nu(\epsilon-\mu)} - 1} = d\epsilon = 1 \tag{8.102}$$

where $g(\epsilon)$ is the degeneracy of the energy level ϵ, since η is chosen from the distribution $\rho(\eta)$, the energy levels are chosen from the distribution $g(\epsilon) = \nu e^{-\nu\epsilon}e^{-\nu\epsilon}$. Equation 8.102 indicates that in the thermodynamic limit $t \to \infty$ the fitness model maps into the Bose gas. As a result, the occupation number follows the Bose statistics

$$n(\epsilon) = \frac{1}{e^{\nu(\epsilon-\mu)} - 1} \tag{8.103}$$

The mapping into a Bose gas in fitness network model in which its connection probability is Eq. 8.79 predicts the existence of three distinct phases that characterizing the dynamical properties of evolving networks.

(a) Scale-free phase: when all vertices have the identical multiplicative fitness value, the model reduces to the scale-free model. Hence, it obeys a power-law degree distribution. This model emerges the "first-move-winner" behavior; this means old vertices have higher degree than younger vertices. Indeed, Eq. 8.100 predicts $f(\epsilon) = 1/2$. Therefore, Eq. 8.100 reduces to Eq. 8.33 and this yields degree distribution $P(k) \sim k^{-3}$ likewise the classical BA model.

(b) Fit-get-rich phase: when different vertices in the network have different multiplicative fitness values and Eq. 8.102 has a solution (i.e., $I(v, \mu) = 1$). Equation 8.100 indicates that each vertex increases its degree in time, but the growth rate of degree for vertices with higher multiplicative fitness is relatively higher than vertices with lower fitness. This allows fitter vertices that added to the network later than the older but less fit vertices acquire more edges along the network evolution process. This phase exhibits the "fit-get-rich" phenomenon. It is important to note that, the vertex with the highest fitness is not an absolute winner at the end. Again, in this phase degree distribution obeys power-law $P(k) \sim k^{\gamma}$, where γ can be calculated if fitness distribution $\rho(\eta)$ is known and well-defined.

(c) Bose–Einstein condensate: Bose–Einstein condensation appears when Eq. 8.102 has no solution. In this phase, the vertex with the highest multiplicative fitness is absolute winner. Thus, Bose–Einstein condensation predicts a real "winner-take-all" phenomenon. In this phase, despite the continuous addition of new vertices, vertex with the highest fitness always maintains a finite fraction of the total number of edges. Notice that, we have seen the "winner-take-all" behavior in Sect. 8.3.3 that the super-linear connection probability $\Pi_k \propto k^{\alpha}$ for $\alpha > 2$ leads to emergence of "gelatin" phenomena in evolving network.

8.6 Local Strategy

Up to now, we have considered network growing strategies that are based on the global features of networks. For example, in BA model when a new vertex enters into the network it makes its connection decisions based on the overall degrees of the network. This statement is true for other mechanisms that try to generalize BA model such as, aging and fitness. Therefore, these models only consider the macroscopic configuration of the network. However, this is a crude interpretation of networks evolution. For instance, when someone decides to add a router to the Internet he or she must know about the whole topology of the Internet! Actually, there are local or microscopic events that occur in real-world networks and thereby collection of these local actions shapes the network global structure. In this section, we want to introduce "local" or "microscopic" strategies that are another family of strategies that endeavor to mimic growing behavior of real-world networks. The term local or microscopic expresses evolution rules that involve a vertex and its neighbors (a local area in the network). Ultimately, these local rules influence the overall network structure such as the network degree distribution.

8.6.1 Rewiring Model

Albert and Barabási [41] first tried to extend the well-known BA model by incorporating local strategies into the model. Their extended model encompasses from rewiring of existing edges, adding new edges to the network without addition of new vertices, and adding vertices with predetermined degree. Their model predicts existence of two regimes: the scale-free and exponential regimes. Albeit, many of the real-world networks are scale-free, but still there exist a number of networks that obey exponential degree distributions [4].

The algorithm of this new model starts from m_0 isolated vertices, and at each iteration performs one of the following three operations:

(i) With probability p add m ($\leq m_0$) new edges: for doing this, randomly select a vertex and connect the selected vertex to another vertex with probability

$$\Pi_i = \frac{k_i + 1}{\Sigma_j (k_j + 1)} \tag{8.104}$$

Repeat this operation m times for m distinct edges. In the continuum theory the growth rate for degree of vertex v_i is given by

$$\left(\frac{\partial k_i}{\partial t}\right)_i = pm\frac{1}{N} + pm\frac{k_i + 1}{\Sigma_j (k_j + 1)} \tag{8.105}$$

where N is the network size. The first term on the right-hand side of Eq. 8.104 accounts of random selection of v_i as an end point of the new edge, while the second term reflects the preferential attachment Eq. 8.104 for another end point of the new edge.

(ii) With probability, q rewire m edges: remove a randomly selected edge $e = \langle v_i, v_j \rangle$ and replace with another edge $e_{rew} = \langle v_i, v_j' \rangle$, where vertex v_j' is selected with preferential probability Eq. 8.104 (note that, rewiring operation is a composite operation that consists of remove and replace operations, concurrently). Repeat this operation m times. Therefore, it gives

$$\left(\frac{\partial k_i}{\partial t}\right)_{ii} = -qm\frac{1}{N} + qm\frac{k_i + 1}{\Sigma_j (k_j + 1)} \tag{8.106}$$

(iii) With probability, $1 - (p + q)$ add one vertex to the network: the new vertex has m edges that connect new vertex to already available vertices in the network with probability Π_i from Eq. 8.104.

$$\left(\frac{\partial k_i}{\partial t}\right)_{iii} = (1 - p - q)m\frac{k_i + 1}{\Sigma_j(k_j + 1)} \tag{8.107}$$

Note that, purpose of $k_i + 1$ in Eq. 8.104 is to give a finite chance to isolated vertices to acquire edges, same as additive fitness or initial attractiveness that leads to $\Pi(0) \neq 0$ (Sect. 8.5.1). In addition, it is clear that extended model reduces to Barabási–Albert model when $p = q = 0$.

Now, by gathering the contributions of the three mentioned operations that are formulated by Eqs. 8.105–8.107, we will obtain

$$\frac{\partial k_i}{\partial t} = (p - q)m\frac{1}{N} + m\frac{k_i + 1}{\Sigma_j(k_j + 1)} \tag{8.108}$$

Expected number of vertices at time t is equal to $N(t) = m_0 + (1 - p - q)t$. Solution of Eq. 8.108 will be

$$k_i(t) = [A(p,q,m) + m + 1]\left(\frac{t}{t_i}\right)^{\frac{1}{B(p,q,m)}} - A(p,q,m) - 1 \tag{8.109}$$

where

$$A(p,q,m) = (p - q)\left(\frac{2m(1 - q)}{1 - p - q} + 1\right) \tag{8.110}$$

$$B(p,q,m) = \frac{2m(1 - q) + 1 - p - q}{m}$$

The degree distribution has the generalized power-law form that obtained from continuum theory

$$P(k) \propto [k + \kappa(p,q,m)]^{-\gamma(p,q,m)} \tag{8.111}$$

where $\kappa(p,q,m) = A(p,q,m) + 1$ and $\gamma(p,q,m) = B(p,q,m) + 1$.

Equation 8.111 is valid only when $A(p,q,m) + m + 1 > 0$, which for fixed p and m we must take into account the value of q. If $q < q_{max}$, the degree distribution $P(k)$ obey power-law distribution and hence generated networks are scale-free. However, for $q > q_{max}$, Eq. 8.111 is not feasible which indicates that continuum theory fails to predict the behavior of "rewiring model". In [41], it is demonstrated that in this regime $P(k)$ shifts to an exponential distribution. Therefore, there would emerge two phases in network evolution and the boundary between scale-free and exponential phases is determined by a function of m.

Another rewiring strategy is proposed by Krapivsky and Redner [33] named GNR, which is a generalized model of Eq. 8.45. The GNR model incorporates a simple form of edge rewiring into the model that is specified by Eq. 8.45. In GNR model, the newly created edge can be redirected to the "ancestor" vertex (the vertex that is pointed by particular vertex is called its ancestor) of the original target vertex. Generated networks by this model are directed and resulting networks have a simple tree-like topology – they posses no cycles. At each time step, a new vertex

Fig. 8.8 Illustration of the
main processes in the GNR
model. The new vertex (*solid*)
selects a target **x**,
haphazardly. with probability
$1 - r$ a link is established to
the **x**, while with probability
r the link is redirected to the
ancestor of **x** [33]

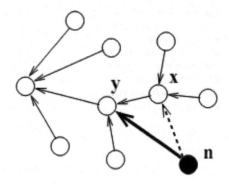

n is added and an earlier vertex **x** is selected randomly. With probability $1 - r$, a
link from **n** to **x** is created and with probability r, the link is redirected to the vertex
x ancestor – vertex **y** (Fig. 8.8).

We can analyze GNR model in the rate equations framework, as following:

$$\frac{dN_k}{dt} = \delta_{k,1} + \frac{1-r}{M_0} [N_{k-1} - N_k]$$
$$+ \frac{r}{M_0} [(k-2)N_{k-1} - (k-1)N_k] \tag{8.112}$$

The two first terms on the right-hand side of Eq. 8.112 for $r = 0$ are equivalent to
Eq. 8.47 and the last two terms characterize the change in N_k due to redirection. By
solving Eq. 8.112 we can find the degree distribution of generated networks, which
obey power-law distribution with scaling exponent $\gamma = 1 + \frac{1}{r}$ and one can tune it
to any arbitrary value larger than 2. For $r = 1/2$ this model will be reduced to BA
model. As a result of the tree-like structure for produced networks by GNR model
(Fig. 8.8), the average clustering coefficient of the generated networks is absolutely
zero. Hence, this model cannot bring a good explanation about the real-world networks that commonly possess high average clustering coefficient.

It would be possible in GNR that whenever a new vertex connects to more
than one vertex the resulting networks possess cycles that leads to nonzero average clustering coefficient. The model that generalized GNR model was proposed by
Rozenfeld and Avraham [42]. Their model makes it possible that a newly added vertex connects to more than one vertex. In every step, the model introduces one vertex
to the network and connects it to m already presented vertices, with probabilities
$\{p_m\}$ for $m = 1, 2, \ldots$, and each of the m target vertices selected randomly and for
each of them with probability $1 - r$ makes a connection, or redirect to an "ancestor" of the vertex. One can recognize that the GNR model corresponds to the choice
$P_m = \delta_{m,1}$ in Rozenfeld and Avraham model. Let $N_k^{(l)}$ indicates number of vertices
of degree k that have exactly l ancestor. In rate equation framework we have

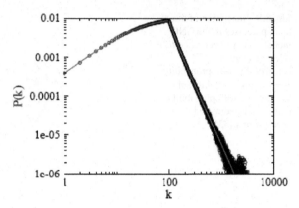

Fig. 8.9 Degree distribution of network constructed with $p_m = 1/100$ for $m = 1, 2, \ldots, 100$ (uniform probability), and $r = 0.5$. The solid line shows analytical prediction yield from Eq. 8.113 [42]

$$\frac{dN_k^{(l)}}{dt} = \sum_m m p_m \left\{ \frac{(1-r)}{M_0} \left[N_{k-1}^{(l)} - N_k^{(l)} \right] \right.$$

$$\left. + \frac{r}{M} \left[(k-l-1)N_{k-1}^{(l)} - (k-l)N_k^{(l)} \right] \right\} + p_l \delta_{k,l}, \ k \geq l$$

$$N_k^{(l)} = 0, \quad k < l \tag{8.113}$$

This model exhibits scale-free behavior with scaling exponent $\gamma = 1 + 1/r$. Notice that, the scaling exponent γ is independent of $\{P_m\}$, despite it influences on other properties such as average degree of network. Empirically, the degree distribution for small k values is determined by the particular choice of the $\{p_m\}$ (Fig. 8.9).

In addition, this model generates networks with nonzero average clustering coefficient in comparison with the GNR model that produces tree-like networks with zero average clustering coefficients.

8.6.2 Random Walk Model

In this section, we aim to study the growing strategy that relies on the random exploration of the sub-networks via vertices, which are recently entered into the network. This model, which is proposed by Vázquez [11, 43] is inspired from the information discovery in citation and WWW networks. There are different ways to obtain information about documents (articles, web pages) in citation and WWW networks, such as following the references (citations, hyper-links) from the other known documents. In the case of citation networks, we often find new articles through the following references for an article. In addition, people find out new web pages by following hyper-links of the other web pages. This model characterizes the network surfing (random walking) by new vertices. Let us assume that the walk starts from a vertex selected in random fashion and with probability, q_e it decides to follow one edge on that vertex or otherwise select another vertex. Then the probability of visiting vertex v_i will be,

$$p_i = \frac{1 - q_e}{N} + q_e \sum_j j_{ij} \frac{p_j}{K_j^{out}} \tag{8.114}$$

where J_{ij} is the ith row and jth column of network's adjacent matrix and is equal to 1 if, there exist edge $\langle v_i, v_j \rangle$ in network, or otherwise is zero. In a mean-field approximation, one can replace the sum term in Eq. 8.114 by Θd_i^{in}, and it gives

$$p_i = \frac{1 - q_e}{N} + q_e \Theta d^{in} i \tag{8.115}$$

where Θ indicates the average probability of visiting a vertex that points to vertex v_i. When we visit a vertex, we can make a connection to that vertex and new vertex with probability q_v and hence increase the degree of that vertex. So, we can obtain *Theta* as

$$\Theta = \frac{v_a}{q_v v_s N} \tag{8.116}$$

where v_s and v_a are number of surfers (walker) and number of newly added vertex per unit time, respectively. Now, the probability of that the in-degree of a vertex of in-degree k^{in} increase by 1 is $A(k^{in}) = q_v p(k^{in})$ which from Eqs. 8.115 and 8.116 we obtain it as follows

$$A(k^{in}) = \frac{1}{N} \left[q_v(1 - q_e) + q_e \frac{v_a}{v_s} k^{in} \right] \tag{8.117}$$

The degree distribution corresponding to this attachment rate can easily be obtained by following rate equation

$$\frac{dN_{k^{in}}}{dt} = v_s [A_{k^{in}-1} N_{k^{in}-1} - A_k^{in} N_k^{in}] + v_a \delta_k^{in}, 0 \tag{8.118}$$

As a result, Eq. 8.118 yields a power-law in-degree distribution with scaling exponent $\gamma = 1 + /q_e$, for large in degrees (Fig. 8.10). Hence, the random walk model produces in-degree power-law networks that their exponent can be tuned to any value upper than 2. Note that, scaling exponent γ is independent of q_v. In addition, one can compute the average clustering coefficient of networks that are generated by random walk model. Independent of directed form of networks in random walk model we suppose $k = k^{in} + k^{out}$. The average clustering coefficient of random walk model is equivalent to [11]

$$\langle C \rangle_k \approx \frac{2(1 + q_e)}{K} \tag{8.119}$$

Thus, we obtain an inverse proportionality between the clustering coefficient and the vertex degree (Fig. 8.10).

Note that, random walk on the network leads to an effective linear preferential attachment. In the random walk model, a surfer follows only an edge from a vertex.

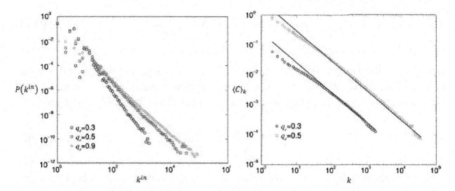

Fig. 8.10 *Left*: In-degree distribution of random walk model for different q_e values for $N = 10^6$. *Right*: Clustering coefficient as a function of vertex degree in the random walk model from Eq. 8.119 [43]

However, one may consider a recursive schema for connecting to neighbors of a vertex by connecting to each of the vertex neighbors with probability q_e. As this is done by Vázquez [11] when surfer visits a vertex follows all of its edges and connects to each of its neighbors with probability q_e. This new model called "Recursive Search model" allows exploring larger portion of the network. For limiting cases, $q_e = 0$ the degree distribution is exponential and for $q_e = 1$ is power-law for large k^{in} with scaling exponent $\gamma = 2$.

8.6.3 Copying Mechanism

Kumar et al. [44] proposed a model for growing web graphs by copying mechanism. Their model is motivated by existing commonality between certain pages. The primary idea of this model is based on copying mechanism in evolving WWW network in which new web pages will copy links from existing pages link lists in the same subject. Alas, copying the references lists in the context of citation networks is even more commonplace. In this model in each stage, a new vertex with a single edge enters to the network. Then, arbitrarily select a vertex u and with probability α connect to this vertex or with probability $1 - \alpha$ connect to the ancestors of u. This leads to implicit preferential attachment, because vertices with higher degrees have relatively higher chance to receive new edges than low connected vertices. In fact, since u selected randomly, the probability that a vertex (web page) of degree k receives a new edge (hyperlink) is proportional to $(1 - \alpha)k$, indicating that the copying mechanism is similar to the linear preferential attachment mechanism in Sect. 8.3.3 Kumar et al. proved that the expectation of in-degree distribution is

$$P(k^{in}) = k^{-(2-\alpha)/(1-\alpha)} \tag{8.120}$$

Fig. 8.11 Illustration of
GNC model. The new vertex
attaches to randomly selected
target vertex, as well as to all
of its ancestors [45]

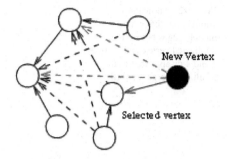

Thus, scaling exponent γ can be tuned between 2 and ∞. Another network model
that utilized copying mechanism is proposed by Krapivsky and Redner [45], named
GNC. In this model, at each step a new vertex enters into the network and connects
to a randomly selected vertex and ancestors of the target vertex (Fig. 8.11).

If the target vertex is the initial root vertex, resulting graph will be *star* and if
target is the recently added vertex into the network, the final graph will be complete
graph of order N. As Krapivsky and Redner [33] have shown analytically, average degree of the GNC networks grows logarithmically with the system size N.
The GNC model can be extended. For instance, instead of connecting to single
vertex connect to m vertices. Furthermore, we can connect to each target vertex
with probability p and its ancestors with probability q. The in-degree distribution
of GNC model obeys a power-law distribution $P_{\text{in}}(k) \propto k^{-2}$ and out-degree distribution follows Poisson distribution. However, out-degree distribution does not obey
commonly presumed power-law form, but the analysis of [46] that is based on latest
data on the structure of the Web [47] convincingly shows that power-law distributions do not fit to actual out-degree distribution. In addition, Dorogovtsev et al. [48]
proposed a growing network model in which preferential linking is combined with
partial inheritance of edges of the target vertex by newly introduced vertex. The
degree distribution of this model depends on the network size. When the size of
network tends to infinity, the degree distribution behaves as power-law with scaling
exponent $\gamma = \sqrt{2}$.

Another kind of model that reveals copying mechanism is Duplication-
Divergence model that is employed to illustrate the evolution mechanisms in
biological networks such as Protein networks and Gene Regulation networks.

8.6.4 Duplication-Divergence Model

The evolution of some real-world networks such as protein interaction network,
gene regulation network is given by replication (copying) or partial replication of
its local structures. Gene duplication is considered the main evolutionary source
of new functions. The protein interaction network is commonly defined as an
evolving network with vertices and edges corresponding to proteins and their interactions, respectively. Mainly, two processes can influence the growing protein

Fig. 8.12 An instance of
duplication divergence
model. Edges between
duplicated vertex and vertices
3 and 4 disappeared as a
result of divergence [50]

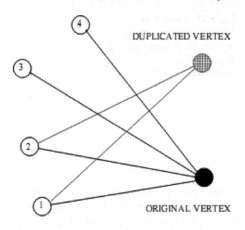

interaction networks: addition and elimination of interactions among proteins, and
gene duplications increase number of proteins and interactions [49]. The rate of
these processes can be estimated from available genome data and are sufficiently
high to affect network structure on short time scales. For instance, more than 100
interactions may be added to the *yeast* network every million years. Thus, single
gene duplication leads to addition of new vertex (that is, copy of an existing vertex)
into the network, which is initially connected to all of the original vertex's neighbors. Later, some edges between each of the duplicates and their neighbors vanish
as a result of mutation (Fig. 8.12).

Duplication and divergence can occur simultaneously or separately. Here,
we analyze the separated version of duplication-divergence model and follow
Vázquez analysis [11,43] by continuum theorem. In this model, we assume that the
creation and deletion of edges take place randomly and independent of the vertices
degrees at the edge both ends, or any other topological properties. Hence, growth of
a vertex degree is given by

$$\frac{\partial k_i}{\partial N} = v_D k_i + v_c (N - k_i) - v_L k_i \tag{8.121}$$

where, v_D, v_C and v_L are the rates per unit of vertex added to duplications, edge
creation, and edge lost, respectively. Each duplication implies the addition of a new
vertex and, therefore,

$$v_D = \frac{1}{N} \tag{8.122}$$

We will further assume that

$$v_c = \frac{\mu_0}{N}, \quad v_L = \frac{\mu_1}{N} \quad \text{for } \mu_1 < 1 \tag{8.123}$$

Substituting Eqs. 8.122 and 8.123 into Eq. 8.121 yields

$$N\frac{\partial k_i}{\partial N} = \mu_0 + (1 - \mu_1)k_i \tag{8.124}$$

Note that, the linear dependency of the growth rate in Eq. 8.124 and degree k_i manifested again the existence of linear preferential attachment. Solving Eq. 8.124 give

$$k_i(N) = \left(k_i(N_i) + \frac{\mu_0}{1 - \mu_1}\right)\left(\frac{N}{N_i}\right)^{\beta} - \frac{\mu_0}{1 - \mu_1}, \quad \beta = 1 - \mu_1 \qquad (8.125)$$

where N_i and $k_i(N_i)$ are the graph size and degree of vertex v_i when vertex v_i is added to the graph. From Eq. 8.125, one can find $\Pr(k_i < k)$ as we have seen in continuum theory approach and then find the degree distribution $N \gg 1$ for as follows

$$P_k = \frac{\partial \Pr(k_i > k)}{\partial k} \sim \left(\frac{\mu_0}{1 - \mu_1} + k\right)^{-\gamma} \qquad (8.126)$$

In addition, Ispolatov et al. [50] inspected duplication-divergence model in another fashion. Another model in this family is Deletion and Duplication model that was proposed by Farid et al. [51]; their model intended to capture the essential features of the evolution of protein interaction networks. In [52, 53], the used duplication-divergence approach to model protein interaction evolution. Additionally, Teichmann and Babu [54] investigate the role of gene duplication in network transcriptional regulatory network evolution and define possible duplication scenarios as evidence on how duplication mechanism shapes the genetic networks. Enemark and Sneppen [55] studied existence duplication models and extend them to achieve conformity with the gene regulatory networks.

8.7 Self-Similarity in Growing Networks

Emergence of self-similarity in many real-world networks raises a fundamental question: "What are the mechanisms that lead to these structures?". However, there is a contradiction. If we rewrite Eq. 8.44 as follows

$$N \approx e^{\langle \ell \rangle} \qquad (8.127)$$

The form of Eq. 8.127 that indicates small-world in network implies that real-world networks are not self-similar, because self-similarity requires a power-law relation between N and ℓ. Therefore, there is a paradox between small-world and self-similar properties in real-world networks [56]. However, many real-world networks are self-similar as proposed by Song et al. [56, 57] in which they calculate the fractal dimension by borrowing the concept of large-scale renormalization from critical phenomena. The renormalization schema tiles a network of N vertices with $N_B(\ell_B)$ boxes (Fig. 8.13a) through box-covering algorithm. The boxes contain vertices separated by a distance ℓ_B, measured as a length of the shortest path between them. Next, replace each box with a vertex and this process repeats until the whole network is reduced to a single vertex. For more information about box-covering algorithm, refer to [58].

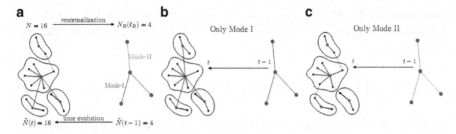

Fig. 8.13 Self-similar dynamical evolution of networks. (**a**) $\tilde{N}(t) = 16$ vertices are renormalized with $N_B(\ell_B) = 4$ boxes of size $\ell_B = 3$. (**b**) Analysis of Mode I alone, which leads to hub–hub attraction. This model generates scale-free although non-fractal networks. (**c**) Model II alone produces scale-free and fractal network together. Mode II exhibits hub–hub repulsion [56]

As a result of preceding algorithm, fractal networks can be characterized by the following scaling relations

$$\frac{N_B(\ell_B)}{N} \sim \ell_B^{-d_B}, \quad \frac{k_B(\ell_B)}{k_{\text{hub}}} \sim \ell_B^{-d_k} \tag{8.128}$$

where k_{hub} and $k_B(\ell_B)$ are the degree of the most connected vertex inside each box and that of each box, respectively. Two exponents d_B and d_k in Eq. 8.128 are the weak version of the fractal dimension and the scaling exponent of the box, respectively. For the non-fractal networks like the Internet or BA model decay rate of $N_B(\ell_B)$ is exponential, indicating either infinity d_B or not a well-defined value for fractal dimension. At this time, one can suggest a growing strategy by reversing above algorithm that leads to growing fractal networks in predefined dimension. A present time network with $\tilde{N}(t)$ vertices had $\tilde{N}(t-1) = N_B(\ell_B)$ vertices at previous step. In [56], authors studied degree correlation profiles of various kinds of networks that include fractal and non-fractal networks. Observations of correlation profiles of fractal and non-fractal networks that offered persuasive evidence that fractal networks pose a high degree of anticorrelation – vertices of high degree tend to connect to low degree vertices. Therefore, in fractal networks there is a strong repulsion between the most connected vertices (or, hubs) on all length scale. On the other hand, non-fractal networks such the Internet is less anticorrelated.

Mathematical framework that addresses the mechanism for fractal network

$$\tilde{N}(t) = n\tilde{N}(t-1),$$
$$D(t) + D_0 = a(D(t-1) + D_0) \tag{8.129}$$
$$\tilde{k}(t) = s\tilde{k}(t-1)$$

growth could be where $n > 1$, $s > 1$, and $a > 1$ are constants and $\tilde{k}(t)$ indicates the maximum degree of the vertices inside a box at time t and $D(t)$ is the diameter of the network. The first term in Eq. 8.129 accounts to growth rate, the second term is analogous to the linear preferential attachment mechanism and the last term describes the growth of the diameter, which determines whether the network is small-world and/or fractal. The scaling exponents in Eq. 8.128 will be equal to $d_B = \ln n / \ln a$, $d_k = \ln s / \ln a$. The scaling exponent γ will be

$$\gamma = 1 + \frac{\ln n}{\ln s} \qquad (8.130)$$

In addition, it would be suitable to incorporate different growth modes for box connectivity into Eq. 8.129. Mode I with probability e connects two boxes through an edge between their hubs leading to hub–hub attraction (Fig. 8.13b). Mode II with probability $1 - e$ connects two boxes through non-hub vertices leading to hub–hub repulsion (Fig. 8.13c). Mode I bears the non-fractal and small-world networks, whereas Mode II leads to fractal networks without small-world effect. Simultaneous appearance of both small-world and fractal properties in scale-free networks is due to a linear combination of modes I and II. Therefore, we can combine these two modes into the growing mechanism by set $0 < e < 1$.

8.8 Deterministic Growth Models

Up to now, we have considered stochastic growing mechanisms in which growing networks obey probabilistic rules. This randomness causes difficulty in understanding what shapes networks as scale-free. As we have seen, retrieving the characteristics from these models is so difficult or even impossible. When one faces to complex problems in a random network model, it would be helpful to make a conformable tractable model and then acquire interested properties from this simpler model and lend the results to the corresponding random model. A kind of simplification in random models is to construct deterministic models that generate networks by simple deterministic rules and obey properties of their random counterparts like, degree distribution, clustering coefficient, etc. Therefore, it would be of major theoretical interest to construct models that lead to scale-free networks in a deterministic fashion. In general, analytical investigation of deterministic models is much easier than stochastic models owing to their definite nature. The first deterministic model was proposed by Barabási et al. [59]. Another significant deterministic model was proposed by Dorogovtsev et al. [60].

8.8.1 Barabási–Ravasz–Vicsek Model

The construction of BRV model that follows a hierarchical rule commonly used in deterministic fractals [59], is shown in Fig. 8.14.

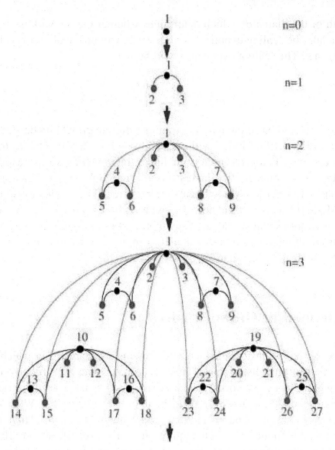

Fig. 8.14 Deterministic scale-free network generated by BRV model. Red vertices indicate rim vertices and black ones specify hubs. Actually, the graph is a bipartite graph [61]

The network was built in iterative manner and in each iteration reuses the elements from the previous step as follow:

Step 0: start from an isolated vertex, called root

Step 1: Add two other vertices and connect them to the root, hence root gain two edges

Step 2: Add two unit graphs identical to the graph in step 1 and connect all of the four rim (bottom) vertices in these two graphs to the root vertex hence, root gain four edges and its degree enhances to six

Step 3: Add two unit graphs identical to the graph in step 2 and connect all the eight rim vertices in these two graphs to the root vertex, hence root gain eight edges and its degree increases to 14....

Step n: Add two unit graphs (with 3^{n-1} vertices each of them) identical to the graph in step $n-1$ and connect all 2^n rim vertices in these two graphs to the root vertex

In this model, the total number of vertices $N(n)$, the total number of edges $L(n)$, and the degree of maximum connected vertex $k_{max}(n)$ are given by [61]

$$\begin{cases} N(n) = 3^n \\ L(n) = 3L(n-1) + 2^n = 2(3^n - 2^n) \\ k_{max}(n) = 2 + 2^2 + \cdots + 2^n = 2(2^n - 1) \end{cases} \tag{8.131}$$

The average degree at time n is equivalent to

$$\langle k \rangle_n = \frac{1}{N(n)} \sum_{i=1}^{N(n)} k_i = \frac{2L(n)}{N(n)}$$

$$= \frac{4(3^n - 2^n)}{3^n} = 4 \left(1 - \left(\frac{2}{3} \right)^n \right)_{n \gg 1} \approx 4 \tag{8.132}$$

Now, let us determine the degree distribution of this model. Thanks to its deterministic and discrete nature, the model can be solved exactly. To show scale-free nature of this model we should show the tail of the degree distribution determined by the most connected vertices, or hubs [59]. In the ith step the degree of root is $2^{i+1} - 2$. In addition, after n steps there are $2 \cdot 3^{n-i-1}$ vertices of degree $2^{i+1} - 2$ in the network. At this time, we can derive the scaling exponent for hubs. Let $k = 2^{i+1} - 2$ and $P(k) = 2 \cdot 3^{n-i-1}$ and by supposing $P(k) \propto k^{-\gamma}$ we can derive γ as follows

$$\gamma = \frac{\ln 3}{\ln 2} \approx 1.585 \tag{8.133}$$

This shows a scale-free nature of the hubs in the network. For bottom (rim) vertices, in the ith step there exist 2^i vertices of degree i. In nth step, there are $2^i.3^{n-i-1}$ bottom vertices of degree i in the network. Let $P(k) = 2^i \cdot 3^{n-i-1}$ and $k = i$, we find

$$P(k) \propto \left(\frac{2}{3} \right)^k = e^{-\gamma' k} \tag{8.134}$$

where

$$\gamma' = \ln(3/2) \approx 0.405 \tag{8.135}$$

Therefore, the scaling of bottom vertices follows an exponential degree distribution.

8.8.2 Pseudofractal Scale-Free Web

The PSW (Pseudofractal Scale-free Web) model is another deterministic model that proposed by Dorogovtsev et al. [60]. The PSW can be considered as a process of edge multiplication [62]. In this model, the growth starts from a single edge connecting two vertices at $t = -1$. At each time step, for every edge of the network, a new vertex is added and connected to the both end vertices of the edge (Fig. 8.15).

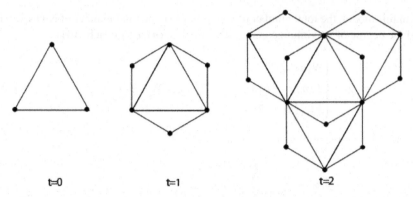

t=0   t=1   t=2

Fig. 8.15 Deterministic scale-free network generated by PSW model. At each time step, every edge generates a new vertex that is attached to both end vertices of the edge. Note that, the graph at time $t + 1$ can be made by connecting together the three t-graph [62]

The total number of vertices at time t is $N(t) = 3(3^t + 1) / 2$, and the total number of edges is $L(t) = 3^{t+1}$. Therefore, the average degree is

$$\langle k \rangle_t = \frac{4}{1 + 3 + {}^{-t}} \tag{8.136}$$

The degree spectrum of the graph is discrete, which means there are no some degrees in the graph. At time t, the number $m(t, k)$ of vertices of degree $k = $ gree $k = 2, 2^2, 2^3, \ldots, 2^t, 2^{t+1}$ is equal to $3^t, 3^{t-1}, \ldots, 3^2, 3$, respectively. Apparently, for large t, $m(t, k)$ decreases as a power of k, so the network can be called scale-free. The space between degrees of the spectrum grows with increasing k. Therefore, to relate the exponent of this discrete degree distribution for stochastic scale-free networks, we use a cumulative distribution $P_{\text{cum}}(k) = \sum_{k' \geq k} m(k', t) / N(t) \sim k^{1-\gamma}$. Thus, we obtain

$$\gamma = 1 + \frac{\ln 3}{\ln 2} \approx 2.585 \tag{8.137}$$

In addition, in [60] authors analytically compute the distribution of clustering and average clustering of the network, which is equal to $\langle C \rangle = 4/5$ when $t \to \infty$. Therefore, the clustering of PSW model is high. The extreme simplicity of PSW model allows us to obtain a number of results that we could not compute for stochastic models easily.

8.8.3 Geometric Fractal Growth Model

This model introduced by Jung et al. [63] is based on exponentially growing number of vertices in scale-free networks. In this model at each time step, each already existing vertex generates its offspring. The number of offspring vertices for a vertex is proportional to the vertex degree and constant $m - 1(m > 1)$. For making connection to offspring, there are two cases: first, each offspring vertex connects to its parent vertex and second, connects to its parent and grandparent vertices. In first case, generated network has tree-like structure and in second case, has loop structure. Here we analyze only the first case.

Let $k_i(t)$ be the degree of vertex v_i at time t. In this model, number of offspring at time t for vertex v_i is equal to $(m - 1)k_i(t - 1)$, where m is a constant. Therefore, degree of vertex v_i at time t is

$$k_i(t) = m \cdot k_i(t - 1) \tag{8.138}$$

For $t \geq 2$. The degree of vertex, born at $t = 0$ ($t = 1$), at time $t = 1$ is $k_0(1) = m(k_1(1) = 1)$. Then the degree of vertex v_i (at time t) that is born at time t_i is

$$k_i(t) = m^{t - t_i} \tag{8.139}$$

Let $L(t)$ be the total number of vertices newly born at time t, we have

$$L(t) = \Sigma_{j=0}^{t-1}(m - 1)m^{t-1-j}L(j) \tag{8.140}$$

For $t \geq 2$ with $L(0) = 1$ and $L(1) = m$ we have $L(t) = 2m(m - 1)(2m - 1)^{t-2}$. Accordingly, the total number of vertices $N(t)$ at time t is

$$\begin{aligned} N(t) &= \Sigma_{i=0}^{t}L(i) \\ &= 1 + m(2m - 1)^{t-1} \end{aligned} \tag{8.141}$$

For $t \geq 2$. The degree distribution of this model from [63] is equal to $P(k) \propto k^{-\gamma(m)}$, where

$$\gamma(m) = 1 + \ln(2m - 1)/\ln m \tag{8.142}$$

where for $m \to 1$, we get $\gamma(1) = 3$ and for asymptotic $m \to \infty$, $\gamma(\infty) = 2$. Thus, we can tune the scaling exponent as $2 < \gamma < 3$.

8.9   Self-Organization Network Models

Another family of network models tries to employ self-organizing criteria into the model. Self-organizing process plays a major role in many real-world networks such as collaboration networks, social networks, and so on. Generally, models that based on self-organization generate networks with higher average clustering coefficient than BA model. The self-organization defines processes that some simple rules occur locally between constituent entities of a system and the global results will be sophisticated. So, one can categorize self-organized network models in local strategies that we considered in Section 8.6.

We can categorize models in two main categories as recommended by Kim et al. [64]: first, models that rely on preferential attachment mechanism that we have extremely investigated up to now. Second, models that generate scale-free networks as a result of a balance between modeled tendencies to form hubs against an entopic pressure towards a random network with an exponential degree distribution and based on rewiring algorithms [65], or in other word, interplay between regularity and irregularity. However, what is the underlying mechanism leading to power-law degree distribution is still at issue [66]. These models have successfully explained the origin of complexity in some networks, but it is recognized that another, equally large number of cases cannot be accounted by either class of models [67].

In this section, we considered network models that try to generate scale-free networks by self-organization rules.

8.9.1 Self-Organization of Communication and Topology

The model was proposed by Rosvall and Sneppen [68], which is the simplest in a family of models based on interplay between communication and dynamical changes of topology in social networks. Actually, it is an information game based on social links and communication rules that present the dynamics of human organization. In this model, each agent (vertex) tries to find out network's parts by getting information from its acquaintances (neighbors) by means of communication. This model allows agents to establish new links to facilitate access to other parts of the network, based on the information they gathered through communication with their acquaintances. This model is defined as follows:

- *Communication* Select a random link and let two vertices at the ends of this link communicate about an arbitrary agent. The two agents also update their information about each other.
- *Rewiring* Select a random agent and let it use its information to establish a connection to shorten its distance to an arbitrary agent. Subsequently, a randomly chosen agent loses one of its links. Therefore, this model conserves number of links in the network.

Communication allows agents to build their own perception of where they are relative to other agents in the network. Each agent has its own perception list that contained agent's knowledge about the entire network (Fig. 8.16). Agents try to update their perception lists through communication that negotiate about their information. The information packet contains an agent name, time stamp and the name agent from which that information has come from.

The quality of the information is determined by its age. Recent information possesses higher quality than the old information. Hence, there should be a time stamp to each information entry in perception list that determines information quality. Therefore, in each communication about a randomly chosen third agent between two agents one of them adapts its viewpoint to the agent with the newest (higher quality) information.

Fig. 8.16 *Left*: communication between both end points of randomly chosen edges. In each communication, two agents negotiate about arbitrary third agent. Each communication leads to an update of perception lists. In addition, when an agent updates one of its information entry it stores the agent id that is the origin of information. *Right*: a randomly chosen agent decides to shorten its distance to another randomly chosen agent by introducing a new connection and using its own information. This new connection, points to the agent that is origin of the information (**A** points to **E**). Creation of new connection balanced with random removes of a connection (for example, **C** to **D**) [68]

Then, an arbitrary agent (agent **A** in right side of Fig. 8.16) is interested in shorting its distance to another randomly chosen agent (agent **H** in right side of Fig. 8.16) in the system. Agent **A** establishes a connection to the agent that has newest information about **H**, here is agent **E**. These creations of new connection randomly balanced remove of other connections. As we have seen, rewiring consists of creating and removing a connection concurrently. If rewiring takes place after a few communication, it will be random instead of being based on the actual network topology.

The presented model describes a social game where the aim is to be central, and a winner is an agent with many connections that provide reliable information to other agents. In addition, the authors incorporate different tricks to win the game into the model. They studied strategies: Chatting (allow some agents communicate twice as much as other agents), Cheating (when some agents use a clock with relatively lower clock-speed than other agents), one Lying (allow some agents lie on the time stamps of their information and pretend a piece of information is fresh).

In this model, lying strategy causes obliterate of reliability in the network and even one liar is enough to collapse the trustworthiness in the network. In this situation, there is no winner in the network.[1]

---

[1] Finally, you can see a nice applet of the model at http://cmol.nbi.dk/models/inforew/inforew.html

8.9.2 Merging and Regeneration

The model proposed by Kim et al. [64] was associated with the phenomena of aggregation with injection suggested in the context of astrophysical systems. Two main components of this model are (1) merge pairs of already existed vertices, and (2) growth via introducing a new vertex. Formally, update rules of this model are:

- At each time step, choose an edge and merge both end points of the edge together. This operation substitutes one vertex of degree $(k_i-1)+(k_j-1)-n_{common}$ instead of two vertices of degree k_i, and k_j respectively. Notice that n_{common} indicates number of common neighbors between two vertices that merged together. Recall, degree of the new vertex was obviously found by the set theory relation. $|A \cup B| = |A| + |B| - |A \cap B|$.
- At the same time, introduce a new vertex of degree K_{new}, which is determined randomly. This new vertex selects its K_{new} neighbors arbitrarily. This step is similar to the BA model without preferential attachment mechanism.

Obviously, this model incorporates preferential attachment implicitly by first updating rule, since chance of merging for each vertex is linearly proportional to its degree. As a result, this updating rule causes the generated networks being scale-free. However, the authors showed this model even by selecting two random vertices instead of an edge, again generate power-law network with different scaling exponents.

Recently, Perotti et al. [67] introduced another model that is based on self-organization. In their model, membership of each new agent (vertex) to the network is determined by the agent's effect on the network global stability. Despite, this model does not possess preferential attachment implicitly, but generates scale-free networks with scaling exponent $\gamma \approx 2.4$.

8.10 Conclusion

The main goal of this chapter is briefly review to some of important network models that are suggested in recent years. The aim of all of these models is imitating the real-world network properties. Real-world networks exhibit behaviors such as small-world, scale-free, high clustering coefficient, non-trivial degree correlation, and self-similar topology. Erdös–Rényi's model was the first model that was proposed in 1959. Although, this model possesses relatively simple mechanism, or the model generates networks that cannot fulfill essential conditions to be analogous to the real-world networks.

The most important model was proposed Barabási and Albert in 1999, which incorporates linear preferential attachment mechanism into the network growth. Preferential attachment was inspired from well-known Simon model that used to explain power-law distribution in various social and economic systems. Analytically, this model produces power-law networks with scaling exponent $\gamma = 3$ when, size of the network is very large. However, the average clustering of this model is reversely dependent to the network size, which is opposite of the real-world networks. Another important observation is emerging non-trivial degree correlation in the networks that are produced by the model. In addition, one can generalize functional form of the preferential attachment. Superlinear form exhibits "winner-take-all" phenomena in which a central vertex is connected to almost all of the remaining network vertices.

In real-world networks there exist natural constraints like age or cost. The aging model generalize Barabási–Albert model to mimic age constraint. By changing parameters, aging model generates scale-free networks with arbitrary scaling exponent between 2 and ∞. Additionally, fitness models as a generalization of Barabási–Albert model, tries to incorporate other natural factors. Fitness models introduce two factors: multiplicative fitness and additive fitness.

Another important family of models that rely on local strategies attempt to realize network evolution mechanism. These models are used to portray the evolution of cellular networks, for instance, protein interaction networks. Local term conveys strategies that rely on a vertex and its neighbors. Some of the important models of these kind are random walk, rewiring, duplication-divergence, and copying models. Self-similarity is another property of the majority of real-world networks and fractal model proposed by Song et al. aims to produce fractal networks. Self-organization in some real-world network growth is a further mechanism that leads to produce power-law networks with comparatively high clustering coefficient.

All of the above models utilized stochastic growth. However, analytical study of these stochastic models is tough or even impossible. Hence, there should be a kind of models that are analytically easy to deal with. Deterministic models, that are simplification of the stochastic models, let us to approximate properties of the stochastic models straightforwardly.

References

1. Erdős P, Rényi A (1959) On random graphs. Publ Math 6:290–297
2. Erdős P, Rényi A (1959) Graph theory and probability. Can Math Soc CJM 11:34–38
3. Bollobas B (2001) Random graphs, 2nd edn. Cambridge University Press, Cambridge (0521797225)
4. Amaral LA, Scala A, Barthelemy M, Stanley HE (2000) Classes of small-world networks. Proc Natl Acad Sci USA (PNAS) 97:11149–11152, 0027-8424
5. Barabási A-L, Albert R (1999) Emergence of scaling in random networks. Science 286: 509–512
6. Albert R, Barabási A-L (2002) Statistical mechanics of complex networks. Am Phys Soc Rev Modern Phys 74(1):47–97
7. Simon HA (1955) On a class of skew distribution functions. Biometrika 42:425–440
8. Chakrabarti D, Faloutsos C (2006) Graph mining: Laws, generators and algorithms. ACM Comput Surv 38:1–69
9. Xu X, Liu F, Liu L (2005) Mechanism for linear preferential attachment in growing networks. Physica A 356:662–672

10. Albert R, Barabási A-L (2000) Topology of evolving networks: Local events and universality. Phys Rev Lett 85:5234–5237
11. Vázquez A (2003) Growing network with local rules: Preferential attachment, clustering hierarchy, and degree correlations. Phys Rev E 67:056104.5
12. Rozenfeld HD, Avraham DB (2004) Designer nets from local strategies. Phys Rev E 70:056107
13. Faloutsos M, Faloutsos P, Faloutsos C (1999) On power-law relationships of the Internet topology. ACM Press, In: SIGCOMM '99: Proceedings of the conference on applications, technologies, architectures, and protocols for computer communication, vol 29, pp 251–262
14. Govindan R, Tangmunarunkit H (2000) Heuristics for Internet map discovery. In: INFOCOM 2000. Nineteenth annual joint conference of the IEEE computer and communications societies. Proc IEEE 3:1371–1380
15. Bornholdt S, Schuster HG (2003) Handbook of graphs and networks: From the genome to the internet. Wiley-VCH, Berlin (3-527-40336-1)
16. Dorogovtsev SN, Mendes JFF (2001) Effect of the accelerated growth of communications networks on their structure. Phys Rev E 63:025101
17. Gagen MJ, Mattick JS (2005) Accelerating, hyperaccelerating, and decelerating networks. Phys Rev E 72:016123
18. Watts DJ, Strogatz SH (1998) Collective dynamics of 'small-world' networks. Nature 393:440–442
19. Barabási A-L, Jeong H, Neda Z, Ravasz E, Schubert A, Vicsek T (2002) Evolution of the social network of scientific collaborations. Phys A Statist Mech Appl 311:590–614
20. Newman MEJ (2005) Power laws, Pareto distributions and Zipf's law. Contemp Phys 46:323–351
21. Albert R, Jeong H, Barabási A-L (2000) Error and attack tolerance of complex networks. Nature 406:378–482
22. Erdős P, Rényi A (1960) Random graphs. Publ Math Inst Hung Acad Sci 5:17–61
23. Chung F, Lu L (2002) The average distances in random graphs with given expected degrees. Proc Natl Acad Sci USA (PNAS) 99:15879–15882
24. Capocci A, Servedio VDP, Colaiori F, Buriol LS, Donato D, Leonardi S, Caldarelli G (2006) Preferential attachment in the growth of social networks: The case of Wikipedia. Phys Rev E 74:036116
25. Jeong H, Néda Z, Barabási A-L (2003) Measuring preferential attachment in evolving networks. Europhys Lett 61:567–572
26. Eli E, Erez YL (ed) (2003) Preferential attachment in the protein network evolution. Ame Phys Soc Phys Rev Lett 91:1387 01
27. Dorogovtsev SN, Mendes JFF, Samukhin AN (2000) Structure of growing networks: Exact solution of the Barabási–Albert model. Phys Rev Lett 85:4633–4636
28. Dorogovtsev SN, Mendes JFF (2001) Scaling properties of scale-free evolving networks: Continuous approach. Phys Rev E 63:056125
29. Kaiser M (2008) Mean clustering coefficients: The role of isolated nodes and leafs on clustering measures for small-world networks. Inst Phys Publ New J Phys 10:083042
30. Milgram S (1967) The small world phenomenon. Psychol Today 2:60–67
31. Bollobás B, Riordan O (2004) The diameter of a scale-free random graph. Combinatorica 24:5–34
32. Newman MEJ, Strogatz SH, Watts DJ (2001) Random graphs with arbitrary degree distributions and their applications. Phys Rev E 64:026118
33. Krapivsky PL, Redner S (2001) Organization of growing random networks. Phys Rev E 63:066123
34. Barrat A, Pastor-Satorras R (2005) Rate equation approach for correlations in growing network models. Phys Rev E 71:036127
35. Krapivsky PL, Redner S, Leyvraz F (2000) Connectivity of growing random networks. Phys Rev Lett 85:4629+
36. Bianconi G, Barabási A-L (2001) Bose–Einstein condensation in complex networks. Phys Rev Lett 86:5632–5635

37. Redner S (1998) How popular is your paper? An empirical study of the citation distribution. Eur Phys J B 4:131–134
38. Dorogovtsev SN, Mendes JFF (2000) Evolution of networks with aging. Phys Rev E 62:1842–1845
39. Ergün G, Rodgers GJ (2002) Growing random networks with fitness. Phys A 303:261–272
40. Bianconi G, Barabási A-L (2001) Competition and multiscaling in evolving networks. Europhys Lett 54:436–442
41. Albert R, Barabási A-L (2000) Topology of evolving networks: Local events and universality. Phys Rev Lett 85(24):5234–5237
42. Rozenfeld HD, Avraham DB (2004) Designer nets from local strategies. Phys Rev E 70:056107
43. Vázquez A (2002) Degree correlations and clustering hierachy in networks: Measures, origin and consequences. PhD thesis, Institute for Advanced Study, Einstein Drive Princeton, New Jersey 08540, USA
44. Kumar R, Raghavan P, Rajagopalan S, Sivakumar D, Tomkins AS, Upfal E (2000) The Web as a graph. In: Proceedings of the nineteenth ACM SIGMOD-SIGACT-SIGART symposium. ACM, Dallas, TX, pp 1–10
45. Krapivsky PL, Redner S (2005) Network growth by copying. Phys Rev E 71:036118
46. Donato D, Laura L, Leonardi S, Millozzi S (2004) Large scale properties of the webgraph. Eur J Phys B 38:239–243
47. [Online] STANFORD DIGITAL LIBRARIES TECHNOLOGIES. http://www-diglib.stanford.edu
48. Dorogovtsev SN, Mendes JFF, Samukhin AN (2000) Growing network with heritable connectivity of nodes. http://arxiv.org/abs/cond-mat/0011077v1
49. Wagner A (2003) How the global structure of protein interaction networks evolves. Roy Soc Publ Proc Roy Soc B Biol Sci 270:457–466, 1514
50. Ispolatov I, Krapivsky PL, Yuryev A (2005) Duplication-divergence model of protein interaction network. Phys Rev E 71:6
51. Farid N, Christensen K (2006) Evolving networks through deletion and duplication. New J Phys 8:1367–2630
52. Evlampiev K, Isambert H (2007) Modeling protein network evolution under genome duplication and domain shuffling. BMC Syst Biol 1:49
53. Vázquez A, Flammini A, Maritan A, Vespignani A (2003) Modeling of protein interaction networks. Complexus 1:38–44
54. Teichmann SA, Babu MM (2004) Gene regulatory network growth by duplication. Nat Genet 36:492–496
55. Enemark J, Sneppen K (2007) Gene duplication models for directed networks with limits on growth. Journal of Statistical Mechanics: Theory and Experiment: P11007. doi: 10.1088/1742-5468/2007/11/P11007
56. Song C, Havlin S, Makse HA (2006) Origins of fractality in the growth of complex networks. Nat Phys 2:275–281
57. Song C, Havlin S, Makse HA (2005) Nature 433:392–395
58. Kim JS, Goh K-I, Kahng B, Kim D (2007) Fractality and self-similarity in scale-free networks. New J Phys 9:177
59. Barabási A-L, Ravasz E, Vicsek T (2001) Deterministic scale-free networks. Physica A 299:559–564
60. Dorogovtsev SN, Goltsev AV, Mendes JFF (2002) Pseudofractal scale-free web. Phys Rev E 65:066122
61. Iguchi K, Yamada H (2005) Exactly solvable scale-free network model. Phys Rev E 71:036144
62. Zhang Z, Rong L, Zhou S (2007) A general geometric growth model for pseudofractal scale-free web. Physica A 377:329–339
63. Jung S, Kim S, Kahng B (2002) Geometric fractal growth model for scale-free networks. Phys Rev E 65:056101
64. Kim BJ, Trusina A, Minnhagen P, Sneppen K (2005) Self organized scale-free networks from merging and regeneration. Eur Phys J B 43:369–372

65. Baiesi M, Manna SS (2003) Scale free networks from a Hamiltonian dynamics. Phys Rev E 68:047103
66. Yan G, Zhou T, Jin Y-D, Fu Z-Q (2004) Self-organization induced scale-free networks. http://arxiv.org/abs/cond-mat/0408631
67. Perotti JI, Billoni OV, Tamarit FA, Chialvo DR, Cannas SA (2009) Emergent self-organized complex network topology out of stability constraints. Phys Rev Lett 103:108701
68. Rosvall M, Sneppen K (ed) (2006) Modeling self-organization of communication and topology in social networks. Phys Rev E 74:016108

Chapter 9
Vmap-Layout, a Layout Algorithm for Drawing Scientograms

Arnaud Quirin and Oscar Cordón

Abstract We present in this chapter a drawing algorithm to represent graphically co-citation networks (scientograms). These networks have some interesting and unusual topological properties, which are often valuable to be visualized. In general, these networks are pruned with a network scaling algorithm and then visualized using a drawing algorithm (J Vis Lang Comput 9:267–286, 1998). However, typical drawing algorithms do not work properly, especially when the size of the networks grows. Edge crossings appear while the drawing space is not adequately filled, resulting in an unsightly display. The approach presented in this chapter is able to print the networks filling all the available space in an aesthetic way, while avoiding edge crossings. The algorithm is detailed and compared with the classical Kamada–Kawai drawing algorithm on several scientograms.

9.1 Introduction

Social networks have some interesting and unusual topological properties, which are often valuable to be printed graphically. However, the raw networks cannot be often visualized easily, especially when their size grows proportionally with the number of data to be dealt with, and thus specific algorithms for simplifying such large networks have been developed. Network scaling algorithms, the goal of which is to take proximity data and to obtain structures revealing the underlying organization of those data, use similarities, correlations, or distances to prune a network based on the proximity between a pair of nodes. One of the most known, the Pathfinder algorithm [11], is used frequently because of its various mathematical properties, including the conservation of the triangle inequalities among a path of any number of links, the capability of modeling asymmetrical relationships, the representation of the most *salient* relationships present in the data, and the fact that hierarchical constraints in most cluster analysis techniques do not apply to Pathfinder Networks (PFNETs) [11].

A. Quirin (✉) and O. Cordón
European Centre for Soft Computing, Edf. Científico Tecnológico, Mieres, Spain
e-mail: [arnaud.quirin;oscar.cordon]@softcomputing.es

A. Abraham et al. (eds.), *Computational Social Network Analysis*, Computer
Communications and Networks, DOI 10.1007/978-1-84882-229-0_9,
© Springer-Verlag London Limited 2010

The resulting network could then be graphically represented using a network drawing algorithm. This methodology ensures that the network is represented in an aesthetic way, usually by adding several spatial constraints, such as the minimization of the edges crossings, the optimal distribution of the nodes over the space, and the minimization of the length of the edges. The final goal of this methodology is to generate a network having some properties. If the network represents the complex tissue of relationships between individuals or organizations, and if its goal is the comprehension of these relationships by a domain expert, we may be interested by some specific properties. For instance, the backbone could be better highlighted if it is drawn in the center, and minor links could be represented in the border of the map. The Kamada–Kawai [15] or the Fruchterman–Reingold [13] algorithm are usually applied for this task.

There are some kinds of Social Network Analysis (SNA) applications that could benefit from such methodology, giving to the domain expert or even a simple user a simple access to the information contained in these networks. One of these applications is co-citation network analysis. Co-citation network models depict the complex tissue of relationships occurring in the scientific literature. The graphical representation of these kinds of networks while preserving their information is still a challenge. However, some work has been done using *scientograms* [8, 9], visual representations showing the spatial distribution of the scientific actors in a given domain, wherein these actors can be as diverse as scientific categories, authors, journals, or papers. They show also additional information about the relationships between them, for instance, the proximity between two scientific authors. Because of the complexity of the domain they aim to represent and, more specifically, the fact that virtually all the scientific actors are connected together, these maps usually contain a large number of links and are really dense and hard to be directly represented.

The said methodology has already been described in the literature in the case of the scientograms [27]. But this methodology suffers from some drawbacks. First, the Pathfinder algorithm is very slow, avoiding the representation of the maps in an online way. Secondly, even if the Kamada–Kawai algorithm is the most used network drawing algorithm in this topic [19], it suffers from some aesthetic problems. In fact, this algorithm does not have an explicit procedure, either to avoid edge crossings, or to fill properly the full space allocated for the drawing. In the literature, the slowness of the Pathfinder algorithm has already been solved using a fast variant [24], but no algorithm has yet been proposed to overcome the drawbacks of the visualization of the Kamada–Kawai algorithm.

In fact, for the analysis of scientograms, the drawbacks of the Kamada–Kawai algorithm could prevent an expert from an optimal interpretation of the relationships taking place inside the considered scientific domain. For instance, edge crossings can make a node, and its labels overlap, thus avoiding a good reading of the map. Another point is the absence, in the Kamada–Kawai algorithm, of specific spatial constraints to avoid the links going back to the center of the map. Spatial artifacts, such as nodes appearing close together even if they are spatially separated by several links, could convey false or misinterpreting information.

In this chapter, we propose a new drawing algorithm to overcome these drawbacks. The structure of the current contribution is as follows. In Section 2, we review the existing methodology to design scientograms. In Section 3, we describe our proposal. In Section 4, some experiments will be shown. Finally, some concluding remarks are pointed out in Section 5.

9.2   A Methodology to Generate Scientograms

The achievement of a vast scientogram is a recurrent idea in the modern age. In 1998, Chen [8, 9] was the first researcher to bring forth the use of PFNETs in citation analysis. This is due to the fact that scientograms are the most appropriate means to represent the spatial distribution of research areas, while also affording information on their interactions [26]. Taking the latter as a base, Moya-Anegón et al. [21] proposed a method for the visualization and analysis of vast scientific domains using the ISI[1]-JCR category co-citation information. They represented it as a social network, simplified that network by means of the Pathfinder algorithm considering $q = n-1$ and $r = \infty$, and graphically depicted its layout using the Kamada–Kawai algorithm [15], thus getting a structural model of the scientific research in a vast domain. Note that $r = \infty$ and $q = n - 1$ are the common parameter values when Pathfinder is used for large domains scientogram generation. These values are very advantageous for large network pruning [10].

The different method stages are briefly described as follows. The last step is the one replaced by our proposal.

9.2.1   Category Co-citation Measure

Co-citation is a widely used and generally accepted technique for obtaining relational information about documents belonging to a domain. Because we strive to represent and analyze the structure of vast domains, whether they be thematic, geographic, or institutional, we fall back on ISI-JCR co-citation categories [21] as a tool.

Hence, once the rough information of the ISI-JCR co-citation for the categories present in the domain to be analyzed is obtained, a co-citation measure CM is computed for each pair of categories i and j as follows:

$$CM(ij) = Cc(ij) + \frac{Cc(ij)}{\sqrt{c(i) \cdot c(j)}} \qquad (9.1)$$

where Cc is the co-citation frequency and c is the citation frequency.

---

[1] Currently registered as *Thomson Scientific*.

Notice that the aim of this scientogram generation method is that the final scientogram obtained is a tree. Hence, in order to avoid the existence of cycles in the pruned network, the considered measure of association adds the normalized co-citation (divided by the square root of the product of the frequencies of the co-cited documents' citations [25]) to the rough category co-citation frequency. In this way, the network weights become real numbers, allowing us to create small differences between similar values for the co-citation frequency, thus avoiding the occurrence of cycles and achieving the optimal prune of each link considering the citing conditions of each category.

9.2.2 Network Pruning by Pathfinder

Then, the Pathfinder algorithm is applied to the co-citation matrix to prune the network. We should take into account the fact that the networks resulting from citation, co-citation, or term co-occurrence analysis are usually very dense, when the categories are used as the unit for each node. Because of this fact, and especially in the case of vast scientific domains with a high number of entities (categories in our case) in the network, Pathfinder is parameterized to $r = \infty$ and $q = n - 1$, in order to obtain a schematic representation of the most outstanding existing information by means of a network showing just the most salient links. In general, the weights of the links of the co-citation matrix belong to $\mathbb{R}$ and are all different, so the final result of the Pathfinder algorithm is a tree. To perform this step, the MST-Pathfinder algorithm, a quick version of the original Pathfinder algorithm based on *Minimum Spanning Trees*, is used [24].

9.2.3 Network Layout by Kamada–Kawai

Kamada–Kawai algorithm [15] is then used to automatically produce representations of the pruned network resulting from the Pathfinder run on a plane, starting from a circular position of the nodes. It generates social networks with aesthetic criteria such as common edge lengths, forced separation of nodes, building of balanced maps, etc. Nevertheless, some criteria are not directly satisfied in the Kamada–Kawai algorithm. This is the case of a number of crossed links: in fact many links crossings appear making a lot of nodes overlap, and making the reading of the map harder. Another point is the fact that edges can go backwards to the center of the map, putting close two nodes linked by a long path. This can give a false impression of closeness to the expert because of the spatial distribution of the nodes. These are two of the main drawbacks we observed while using the Kamada–Kawai visualization applied to co-citation networks.

An example of the render of the Kamada–Kawai applied on the co-citation network of Europe is shown in Fig. 9.1.

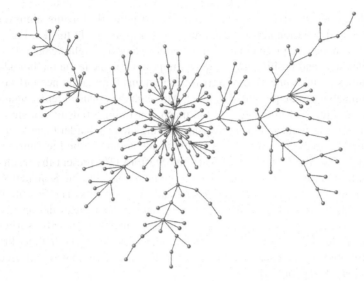

Fig. 9.1   An example of a scientogram corresponding to the Europe scientific domain in 2002

9.2.4   Advantages and Drawbacks of Our Methodology

Since its proposal in 2004, this methodology has been applied to compare the structure of vast scientific domains [20, 27], to the macro and microstructural analysis of a specific domain [18, 19], and even to study their evolution through time [28, 29].

Hence, it is actually a very powerful tool due to its summarization capability as well as its simplicity to represent the relational information linked through a series of intelligible sentences that make easier the comprehension, analysis, and interpretation of a scientific domain. However, the critics that can be made on the Kamada–Kawai algorithm about the crossed links make it difficult to apply for the generation of scientograms in an automatic way, as a human post-processing is currently needed to avoid the crossings and move the labels in order so that they can be read clearly. We aim to solve these drawbacks using a new visualization algorithm, as we will see in the remainder of this chapter.

9.2.5   The Use of Other Network Layout Algorithms
for Social Networks Drawing

Apart from the Kamada–Kawai algorithm, an extensive number of graph drawing algorithms have been already published in the literature [2, 3]. But very few of them have been devoted to the drawing of social networks because of the high complexity of this kind of networks [19].

In [6], the authors have chosen a radial-based network drawing algorithm to represent a collaboration network, and they named it *Visone*. In this kind of radial drawing, the nodes are placed in concentric circles, thus highlighting the role of the central elements and pushing away the less important elements on the boundaries. Other studies on the same kind of drawing algorithms for citation networks or co-authorship networks are presented in [5, 7]. Although the obtained representation is nice, the placement of the nodes are too much constrained, thus the length of the links can suffer from meaningless growing, making the map harder to understand.

In general, force-directed layout algorithms are studied in the literature to deal with social networks. The study of Katz and Stafford [16] present the results obtained with the Fruchterman–Reingold algorithm compared to the Kamada–Kawai algorithm to visualize the American Federal Judiciary network. The Fruchterman–Reingold algorithm is also used in [12] for the visualization of the evolution of social networks over time. In general, this algorithm gives interesting results as it reveals clusters of nodes. For our application to the co-citation networks, both force-directed layout algorithms were tested, but the Kamada–Kawai algorithm was preferred due to its aesthetic behavior [19].

In conclusion, a few different drawing algorithms are studied in the literature, while the need of a comprehensible and aesthetic drawing algorithm is growing as social networks become more and more complex.

9.3 Overview of the Algorithm

This section describes our drawing algorithm. As said, our methodology ensures that the result of the Pathfinder algorithm, the network we have to draw, is a tree. Thus, to develop our algorithm, we took as a base the tree visualization algorithm presented in [22], and extend it to make it applicable on scientograms. The basic version of the algorithm is first presented, then several variants are discussed for the specific case of scientogram design.

9.3.1 Main Algorithm

To ease the understanding of our proposal, some preliminary terminology is first introduced. In the following, we consider an ordered tree T, in which each node N has a parent $P = \text{PARENT}(N)$, except the root node $R = \text{ROOT}(T)$. CHILDREN(N) is the set of nodes having node N as their parent. ASCENDANT(N) is the chain of nodes from node N to the root node R, defined as $\{ N, \text{PARENT}(N), \text{PARENT}(\text{PARENT}(N)), ..., R \}$. SUBTREE$(N)$ is the subtree having node N as its root. SIZE(N) is equal to the number of nodes in SUBTREE(N), including its own root. For instance, SIZE(N) is equal to 1 for a node having no children; 2 for a node having one child; etc. LEVEL(N) is the number of nodes in the set

ASCENDANT(N). For instance, LEVEL(N) is equal to 1 for the root node; 2 for any of the children of the root node; etc. DEPTH(N) is the maximum value for LEVEL(M) for any node M in the tree SUBTREE(N). For instance, DEPTH(N) is equal to 1 for a node having no child; 2 for a node having any number of children, with none of them having children; etc. By convention, we will also use the notation ROOT(T) to define the node having the lowest level in a subtree T.

The algorithm is named *Vmap-Layout* because of the kinds of maps it draws, i.e., *Visual Science Maps*, another name for scientograms. It is divided itself into three sub-functions, which are called in a sequential way. The first sub-function, *Attribute Computation*, computes for each node the attributes needed for the remainder of the algorithm. The second subfunction, *Node Positioning*, is a recursive function aiming to compute the coordinates of each node. The third one, *Node Relocation*, adjusts the location of the nodes according to some specific criteria, thus improving the final visualization. The different sub-functions are detailed in the following sections.

9.3.2 Attribute Computation

Within the first sub-function, we compute several attributes assigned to each node: SIZE(N), LEVEL(N), and DEPTH(N). These attributes will be used later to facilitate the generation of the coordinates of each node and to improve the runtime of the algorithm. The first step is to select a root node, the one that will be printed in the center of the map. It will be used to compute some specific attributes that cannot be computed without the definition of a root node. The network generated by the Pathfinder algorithm does not selfcontain any root node; hence we have to use an additional technique to select one. There are many ways to select a center in a graph. Many of them are described by Bavelas [4] and Parlebas [23]. The one used here, that gives good visual results, is the *deliverer criterion*: we compute the sum of the distances between any node and all the others, and we take as the root the one having the smaller value. Once we have selected the root node R, a number of other attributes can be computed. Giving R, we can assign to each node N the values corresponding to SIZE(N), LEVEL(N), and DEPTH(N). As the tree is represented in memory using lists of children, the time complexity of all these operations is $O(n)$ where $n = SIZE(R)$. The complexity of *Attribute Computation* is thus $O(n)$. The sub-function is outlined in Fig. 9.2.

---

1. Compute the root node using the *deliverer criterion*: compute the sum of the distances between a node and all the others, and take as a root the one having the smaller value.
2. Assign to each node N the values given by SIZE(N), LEVEL(N) and DEPTH(N).

Fig. 9.2 The *Attribute Computation* sub-function

9.3.3 Node Positioning

Using the second sub-function, the algorithm fixes the location of each node as a pair of 2D coordinates. To do so, the global idea is to fill as much space as possible. The tree is drawn from the root node to the leaves, and the algorithm runs in a recursive way: the root node is drawn in the center of the map and at each iteration the algorithm draws all the nodes N having the same level L = LEVEL(N). The algorithm starts by selecting a region of the empty space in which it can draw the tree (we will call this region *initial polygon* in the following). Then, it assigns the root node to the center of this polygon, it divides the initial polygon into several slices (as many as the number of children in the root node), and it assigns one child of the root node to each slice. After the application of this function, the coordinates of the center of the polygons are assigned to each node.

There are several ways to design the initial polygon. As the whole tree will lie inside the initial polygon, the later will determine the final shape of the full map. This shape could be a square, a circle, or any other n-sided polygon. Figure 9.6 shows some possibilities for the initial polygon. The assignation of a center C to a given polygon could also be done in several ways. Some techniques are shown in Fig. 9.8. Lastly, the division of a given polygon into different slices can also been done in several ways, which are detailed in the next sections.

Once the coordinates of the first level of the tree are fixed, the algorithm starts again, considering each of the slices as a new polygon and the corresponding node N as the root of a new subtree S = SUBTREE(N). Once no child has been found, the algorithm stops. The sub-function is outlined in Fig. 9.4. As we are using a recursive function based on the children on a given node, the complexity of *Node Positioning* is thus $O(n)$.

At the end of this sub-function, all the nodes of the tree have been assigned to a pair of coordinates in the 2D-space. An example of the execution of this sub-function on a tree is shown in Fig. 9.3.

9.3.4 Node Relocation

The goal of the third sub-function is only aesthetic. At the end of the application of the previous sub-function, some graphical elements, such as the nodes or the text labels, can overlap. By relocating the nodes, we improve the placement of the overlapping elements. Here, having the coordinates of the nodes generated previously, the algorithm fixes the final location of each node to avoid these overlaps as much as possible. We say that two nodes overlap when they are too close to each other, according to a distance defined by the expert, and we call them *problematic* nodes. Problematic nodes cause text labels not to be read in a clear way, and reduces in general the readability of the map. The main idea of this function is to apply a node relocation process in which the problematic nodes are moved according to a repulsive force depending on the surrounding nodes, like if they were connected with

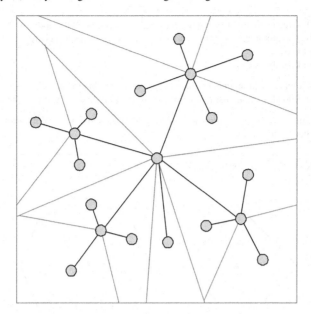

Fig. 9.3 An example of the execution of the *Node Positioning* sub-function

---

1. Let P, a 2D-space region in which to draw the tree, and T, a tree.
2. Choose a central point C in P and assign to this point the root of the tree $R = \text{ROOT}(T)$.
3. If $\text{CHILDREN}(R)$ is empty, stop.
4. Divide P in different slices (*sub-polygons*), giving as many sub-polygons that the number of children of R. Let R_i be a child of R, the area of the corresponding sub-polygon P_i should be proportional to $\text{SIZE}(R_i)$.
5. For each child R_i of R, run *Node Positioning* on the region P_i and the tree R_i.

Fig. 9.4 The *Node Positioning* sub-function

repulsive springs. To avoid deadlocks in some cases (e.g., when a node is located exactly between other two nodes and at an equal distance), the problematic nodes are also slightly moved in a random direction, until they met a criterion set by the expert.

The sub-function is outlined in Fig. 9.5. As the time complexity of the KD-Tree preprocessing is $O(n \cdot \log(n))$ and the time complexity of the KD-Tree search for one node is $O(\log(n))$ [1], the time complexity of *Node Relocation* is $O(n \cdot \log(n))$. Thus, the complexity of the full algorithm is $O(n \cdot \log(n))$.

At the end of the third function, the final coordinates of the nodes have been computed. During the final drawing of the nodes, additional improvements could be made in order to improve the aesthetic aspect of the map. For instance, nodes and label sizes can be varied depending on their depth in the tree to better highlight the center of the map.

1. Apply a KD-Tree technique to compute the distance between all the nodes of T.
2. Select only the problematic nodes, i.e., the nodes close enough according to a criterion defined by the expert.
3. For each node of this set, do:

   - Apply a repulsive strength δ and move the node along this force.
   - Move it around its final position using a small random distance in the interval $[-\sigma,\sigma]$.

4. Execute again the *Node Relocation* sub-function until a given amount of iterations defined by the expert has been reached.

Fig. 9.5 The *Node Relocation* sub-function

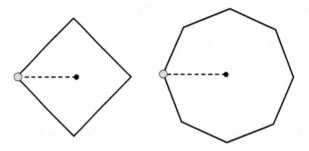

Fig. 9.6 Initial polygons with four or eight sides

9.3.5 Selecting Different Initial Polygons

During the initialization of the Vmap-Layout algorithm, we have to select the initial polygon, within which the full tree has to be drawn. This polygon encloses all the layout and its shape will determine the global shape of the drawing.

In order to improve the general aspect of the final map and to customize the result for several uses (paper or online drawing), several options can be used. The definition of this shape is controlled by an expert parameter, giving the number of sides the initial polygon should have (see Fig. 9.6). The larger this value, the more circular the shape will be, but the slower will the algorithm run. This is due to the fact that, as at later stages, the computation of the areas and the angles of a sub-polygon would be more complex. This number of sides does not change in any manner the further execution of the algorithm but has only an aesthetic aspect.

Once the initial shape is designed, it is used to draw the initial tree, composed of its root and of all its first-level children (see Fig. 9.7). Any shape surrounding the graph could be used. For the application to co-citation networks, we opted by a circle because the SCImago Research Group[2] experts, with whom we collaborate, prefer this shape. Thus, in order to have a good compromise between time and aesthetic,

---

[2] http://www.scimago.es/

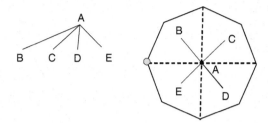

Fig. 9.7 On the *left*, the tree to draw. On the *right*, the initial polygon and the *center* in black. The polygon is first divided into four slices, because the node *A* has four children, and then we assign the corresponding nodes to the corresponding sub-polygons. The little circle is the starting point giving the direction of the polygon assignment

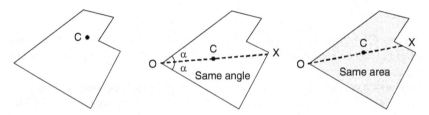

Fig. 9.8 Centers positioned with the *Center of Mass*, the *Angle-Based Central Point* and the *Area-Based Central Point* methods

a value of 15 sides seems to be well suited. Larger values than 30 will unnecessarily increase the run-time and smaller values than 12 would give an impression of discontinuity.

9.3.6 Selecting Different Ways to Compute the Central Point of a Polygon

For each polygon, a central point has to be selected to become the starting point of the next sub-tree to print (see step 2 in Fig. 9.4). We have explored at least three different methods to choose the central point *C* of a polygon *P* (see Fig. 9.8). The first method, called "*Center of Mass*," takes for *C* the center of gravity of *P*. This center is defined in any case, but suffers from two problems: it could be outside of the polygon (this can occur when the polygon is nonconvex) and a polygon with a lot of segments could attract the center far away from the *natural* center of the polygon. The second method, called "*Angle-Based Central Point*," uses the angle to compute the central point. For a given polygon *P*, we first select a point on its border, that we call origin *O*. This origin *O* has itself to be defined by some methods. For instance, the origin could be the center of the parent polygon (the one used to generate the current polygon), or the left-most point of the polygon. We then draw a line dividing the angle *O* in two equal parts. Then we take the middle point of this line as

Fig. 9.9 A problem that can
occur with the *Area-Based
Central Point* method: the two
areas cannot be made equal

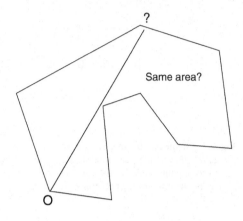

the center C of the polygon. The third method, called "*Area-Based Central Point*,"
applies the same procedure, but by dividing the polygon into two parts having the
same area.

Our tests have shown that the *Area-Based Central Point* is the best method. However, some problems could occur for some specific shapes of polygons in which it is
impossible to divide a sub-polygon into two areas of equal sizes, pushing the central
point C outside the polygon. This can happen when the polygon has internal angles
greater than pi (see Fig. 9.9), when the chosen initial polygon is nonconvex or when
the structure of the tree is quite uncommon. That is why other methods are provided.

For the *Angle-Based Central Point* and the *Area-Based Central Point* methods,
once the line dividing the polygon in two parts has been determined, we still have
to place the point C over this line. The usual way is to use the middle of the line,
as described in the first paragraph of this section. But other values for the measure
of the distance OC have been explored. This distance has a direct influence on the
length of the edges and the location of the next sub-polygons, and playing with
this value can lead to interesting results on the final drawing. An expert parameter
has been set for this measure and is named *Cutpoint Value*. It is the ratio between
the distance OC and the distance OX (see Fig. 9.8). With a small value for this
parameter, we get maps where the centers are close among them, and with a larger
value, we get maps where the centers are more far away among them. Several values
for this parameter have been tried, such as 0.25, 0.5, and 0.6. The best results have
been obtained with values lower or equal to 0.5.

9.3.7 Selecting Different Dividing Slice Methods

The way to divide a polygon into different slices (see step 4 in Fig. 9.4) will determine the respective areas for the drawing of the next sub-polygons. Small areas
should be allocated to small sub-trees, whereas larger areas should be allocated
to larger sub-trees. This operation can be achieved by at least two methods (see

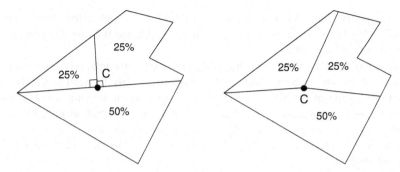

Fig. 9.10 The result of the dividing using the *Angle-Based Dividing* (*on the left part*) and the *Area-Based Dividing* (*on the right part*) methods

Fig. 9.10). With the first method, called *Angle-Based Dividing*, the algorithm defines the size of the slices in order the angle around the center C is proportional to the size of each sub-tree R_i. With the second method, called *Area-Based Dividing*, the algorithm defines the size of the slices in order the area around the center C is proportional to the size of each sub-tree R_i. In many scientograms generated using real world data, the second method does not work properly because the non-convex shapes of the polygons make the finding of a percentile using the area an impossible problem (see Fig. 9.9). Therefore, in our application, we always used the *Angle-Based Dividing* method.

Any use of the two previously described methods needs a measure defined for each node in order to compute the proportion in percentage allocated to the corresponding sub-polygon. The simplest way, called the *Sub-Size-Based Ratio Computation*, is to take the size of each node (defined by the SIZE(T) attribute), i.e., the number of nodes in a subtree T, to compute a proportional ratio assigned to the children of T. Then, this ratio is used as a percentage to compute the size of all the slices of the corresponding sub-polygons. Nevertheless, this method suffers from a lack of customization possibilities by the expert.

Another method called the *Sub-Depth-Based Ratio Computation* has been explored. It uses the depth of the trees, defined by the DEPTH(T) attribute, to modify the proportion allocated to each slice depending on whether they are close or far away from the center of the map. The expert has to set two additional parameters, the proportion given for the allocation of the slice of the lowest level, corresponding to the initial root of the tree (this value has been named "START"), and the proportion given for the allocation of the slice of the deepest level, corresponding to a given leaf of the tree (this value has been named "END"). Because only these two values, START and END, have to be specified by the expert, the remaining values used to fix the proportion of the intermediate levels are computed using a linear regression. Using another point of view, the START value fixes the behavior of the nodes close to the center of the map (or the backbone), which are the most important ones, and the END value fixes the behavior of the minor nodes shown in the periphery. These parameters are thus useful for our application of co-citation networks. We have obtained the best results using 0.5 and 0.25 for the respective values of START and END.

The behavior of the *Sub-Depth-Based Ratio Computation* method is very simple. It allows us to constrain the angle of the links to go only forward when we are close to the center of the map (see Fig. 9.11). In fact, when drawing scientograms, having edges going mainly forward gives a better representation as nodes located far away in terms of number of edges are spatially dissociated. That is why we selected the *Sub-Depth-Based Ratio Computation* method as the default one for our experimentations.

To show how the proportion of the slices are computed using the *Sub-Size-Based Ratio Computation* and the *Sub-Depth-Based Ratio Computation* methods, an example is presented in Fig. 9.12 using a small tree. For some selected nodes, the values are computed for both methods. The proportion is always computed as a

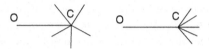

Fig. 9.11 On the left, the normal behavior in which all the space is used to compute the size of each slice. On the right, a modified behavior in which a constraint is applied before computing the size of each slice, allowing us to direct the network in a given way

Tree

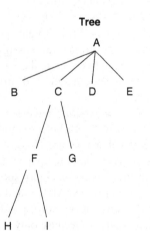

(1) Normal behavior

Measure : the 'sub_size' attribute

Node	Measure	Proportion
B	1/8	12.5%
C	5/8	62.5%
F	3/4	75%
H	1/2	50%

(2) Modified behavior

Measure : the 'sub_depth' attribute

Node	Measure	Proportion
B	2/2	the value 'START'
C	2/4	0.5 'START' + 0.5 'END'
F	3/4	0.25 'START' + 0.75 'END'
H	4/4	the value 'END'

Fig. 9.12 Different ratio computation methods for dividing the slices: an example of a tree (*left*); the proportions obtained using the *Sub-size-Based Ratio Computation* method (*top*); and the proportions obtained using the *Sub-Depth-Based Ratio Computation* method (*bottom*)

ratio between two numbers, the current attribute of the node (respectively the SIZE and the DEPTH) and the maximum value for this attribute (so, the maximum size of the current sub-tree or the maximum depth if the second measure is considered). Note that the ratio computation method is totally independent from the method of dividing these slices, i.e., the ratio can be used independently with the *Area-Based Dividing* or the *Angle-Based Dividing* methods.

9.3.8 *Details on the* Node Relocation *Function*

Once the coordinates of the nodes have been found by the *Node Positioning* sub-function (see Fig. 9.4), a node relocation stage occurs in order to improve the location of the overlapping nodes. This stage is done by the *Node Relocation* sub-function (see Fig. 9.5).

The goal of this sub-function is to identify the nodes that are too close, according to an expert criterion, and to move them randomly in order to avoid the overlapping of the nodes. The process is iterated several times until a perfect configuration is found by the algorithm. Because of the cost of the computation of the distance between nodes, and since this process has to be iterated, we use a KD-Tree technique to compute these distances. A KD-Tree allows the computation of the distance between a set of nodes in order that we can quickly know which set of nodes is closer to any given node.[3]

The *Node Relocation* sub-function works as follows. A parameter named *radius* is defined by the expert to specify the minimum allowed distance between two nodes. Only the coordinates of any node having a smaller or equal distance to this radius will be modified by the algorithm, while the coordinates of the nodes located at a greater distance will not be changed. Two additional parameters are defined, the *spring-strength* δ giving the strength of the movements during the relocation of the nodes and the *random-strength* σ giving the quantity of randomness applied to the nodes that have to be relocated.

From each node N of the set defined by the *radius* parameter, we apply a force defined as the sum of all the repulsive forces generated by the nodes close to N, multiplied by the value defined by the *spring-strength* δ parameter (a repulsive strength), and add a random value chosen into the interval $[-\sigma, \sigma]$ to it. Figure 9.13 shows how the repulsive forces generated by all the surrounding nodes are applied on a given node, and how this node is moved. This is done until a given number of iterations have been completed. A higher value for this parameter can be used to establish the convergence of the coordinates of the nodes, but at the cost of slowing down the process. We have obtained good and fast results with a value of 100 iterations.

---

[3] The library we have used for this process is called the ANN Library [17]. The advantage of this library is that an approximate distance computation is used in order to speed up the process, provided the fact that knowing the exact values of the distances is not important, which is the case in our application.

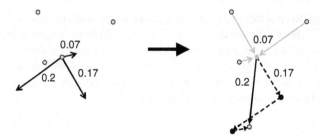

Fig. 9.13 An example of the modification of the coordinates of a node after applying the *Node Relocation* function

The *spring-strength* δ parameter is used to define the step size of movement applied to the node. A small value moves the nodes slowly through the iterations of the algorithm, while a bigger value allows sudden changes of the coordinates of the nodes. A value of 0.10 was used in our experiments. The *random-strength* defines the quantity of randomness applied to the location of the node at the end of each iteration. A value of 0 disables any randomness during the movement of the nodes. A value of 0.05 was used.

9.4 Experiments

In this section, we will show the results obtained on some scientograms. The data are directly extracted from a database of co-citation measures for Europe, generated in 2002. Some specific criteria are set in order to select a subset of the whole database restricted to four world regions: Europe, the USA, Spain, and Cuba. The resulting file encodes a fully connected network, with labeled nodes and weighted links, ready to be pruned. Thus, the first step is to use the MST-Pathfinder algorithm to prune these networks in order to get trees. The computing time for this step is roughly 9 ms on an Intel dual-core Pentium 3.2 GHz with 2 GB of memory.

The next step is to print the maps using the Vmap-Layout algorithm. The algorithm has been written in C++, and compiled on Linux with the GNU GCC compiler with the -O3 option. The computing time using the Vmap-Layout algorithm is roughly 71 ms. The main parameters used are as follows. The initial polygon has 15 sides. The central point has been computed using the Angle-Based Central Point method. The Cutpoint Value has been set to 0.5. The slices have been divided using the Angle-based dividing method. Finally, the Sub-Depth-Based Ratio Computation has been used to position the central point in the polygon.

A comparison has been performed using the Kamada–Kawai algorithm. For this purpose, we have used the GraphViz library. GraphViz is an open source network drawing software, freely provided by AT&T Labs, and available at: http://www.graphviz.org/. It integrates the Kamada–Kawai algorithm in the form of the *neato* utility. This utility exports in diverse graphical formats a description of a network done with a proprietary language, the DOT language [14]. Thus, the second step was to convert the previous network in the format accepted by this library. The computing time using the Kamada–Kawai algorithm is 0.6 ms.

The last step is to generate the graphical output from the DOT description using *neato*. Actually, as these maps are designed for on-line consultation, the Scalable Vector Graphics (SVG) format was chosen. The time to generate the SVG image is 1,300 ms. The following command was used to generate this map, once the library is installed:

```
dot -Kneato -Tsvg -o Europe.svg Europe.dot
```

The final results, for the Vmap-Layout and the Kamada–Kawai algorithms are shown in Figs. 9.14 and 9.15 for Europe; in Figs. 9.16 and 9.17 for the USA; in Figs. 9.18 and 9.19 for Spain; and in Figs. 9.20 and 9.21 for Cuba.

Fig. 9.14 The scientogram of Europe in 2002, drawn with the Kamada–Kawai algorithm

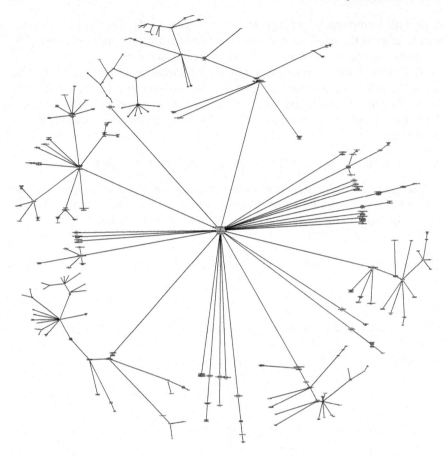

Fig. 9.15 The scientogram of Europe in 2002, drawn with the Vmap-Layout algorithm

Several remarks can be made from these pictures. First, we have to notice that the Vmap-Layout algorithm avoids the edge crossings as expected, as each sub-tree is drawn in its own sub-space. Secondly, the nodes connected to the central node are properly spaced, and aligned on its own circle, allowing an expert to read properly the labels. In the case of the Kamada–Kawai maps, the reading of the top-level labels is not so clear. Finally, all the space available in the figure is properly filled with the Vmap-Layout, giving more space to the larger sub-trees.

9.5 Conclusion

The Vmap-Layout algorithm is an effective and a fast technique for the representation of co-citation networks. Our algorithm can print real-world networks in an

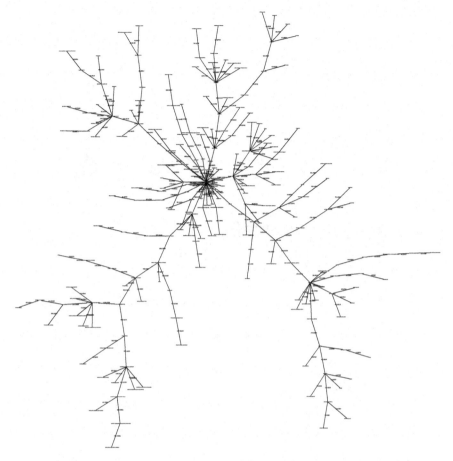

Fig. 9.16 The scientogram of the USA in 2002, drawn with the Kamada–Kawai algorithm

aesthetic way, highlighting the backbone and pushing the less important links to the boundaries. Several variants have been described, allowing an expert to tune the representation depending on his needs.

We are currently investigating other improvements of this algorithm. One option is to allow it to use extra space over the polygons in order to reduce the white space between the edges. Another option is the use of different techniques for the node relocation, for instance, based on the simulated annealing metaheuristic, to find a better positioning of the nodes. We are also planning some experiments on other kinds of real data sets, including larger networks.

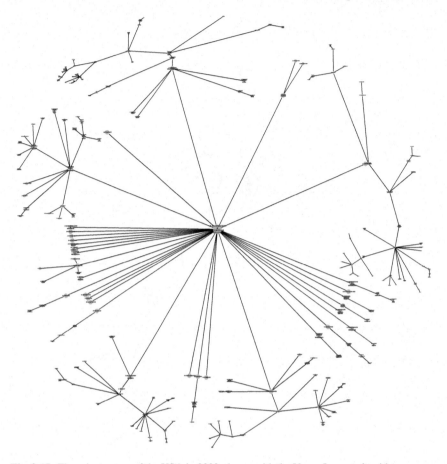

Fig. 9.17 The scientogram of the USA in 2002, drawn with the Vmap-Layout algorithm

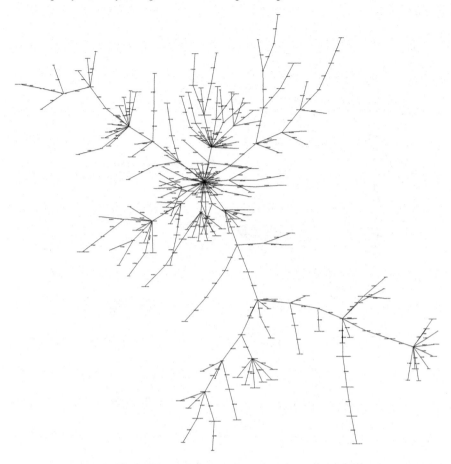

Fig. 9.18 The scientogram of Spain in 2002, drawn with the Kamada–Kawai algorithm

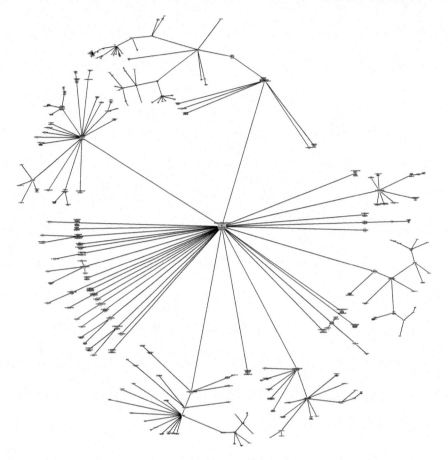

Fig. 9.19 The scientogram of Spain in 2002, drawn with the Vmap-Layout algorithm

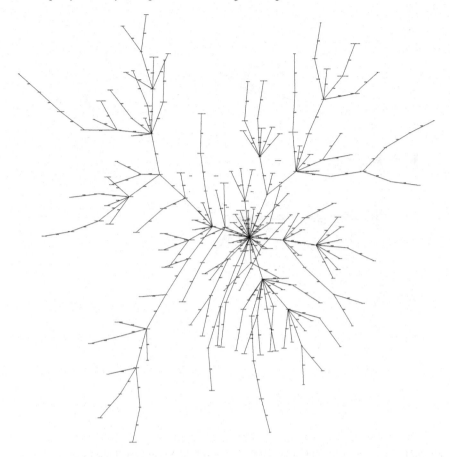

Fig. 9.20 The scientogram of Cuba in 2002, drawn with the Kamada–Kawai algorithm

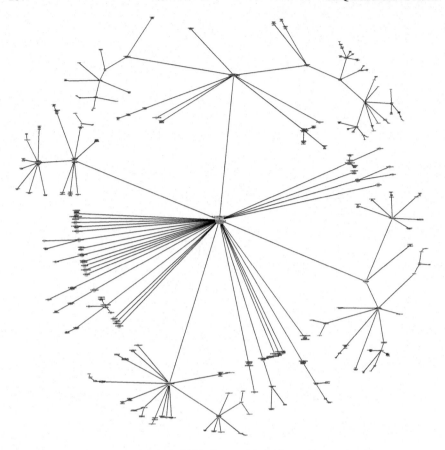

Fig. 9.21 The scientogram of Cuba in 2002, drawn with the Vmap-Layout algorithm

References

1. Arya S, Mount DM, Netanyahu NS, Silverman R, Wu AY (1998) An optimal algorithm for approximate nearest neighbor searching fixed dimensions. J ACM 45(6):891–923
2. Battista GD, Eades P, Tamassia R, Tollis I (1994) Algorithms for drawing graphs: An annoted bibliography. Comp Geo Theor Appl 4(5):235–282
3. Battista GD, Eades P, Tamassia R, Tollis I (1999) Graph Drawing. Prentice Hall, Upper Saddle River, NJ
4. Bavelas A (1951) Réseaux de communications au sein de groupes placés dans des conditions expérimentales de travail, Les sciences de la politique aux États- Unis. Armand Colin, Paris
5. Brandes U, Erlebach T (2005) Network analysis: Methodological foundations, Vol. 3418 of Lecture Notes in Computer Science. Springer, Berlin
6. Brandes U, Kenis P, Wagner D (2003) Communicating centrality in policy network drawings. IEEE Trans Vis Comput Gr 9(2):241–253
7. Brandes U, Wagner D (2003) Graph drawing software, Visone – analysis and visualization of social networks. Berlin, pp 321–340
8. Chen C (1998) Bridging the gap: The use of pathfinder networks in visual navigation. J Vis Lang Comput 9:267–286
9. Chen C (1998) Generalised similarity analysis and pathfinder network scaling. Interact Comput 10:107–128
10. Chen C (2004) Information visualization: Beyond the horizon. Springer, Berlin, Germany
11. Dearholt D, Schvaneveldt R (1990) Properties of pathfinder networks. In: Pathfinder associative networks: Studies in knowledge organization. Ablex Publishing Corporation, Norwood, NJ, pp 1–30
12. Dynes SBC, Gloor PA, Laubacher R, Zhao Y, Dynes S (2004) Temporal visualization and analysis of social networks. In: North American Association for Computational Social and Organizational Science Conference (NAACSOS), Pittsburgh
13. Fruchterman TMJ, Reingold EM (1991) Graph drawing by force-directed placement. Software Pract Exper 21(11):1129–1164
14. Gansner ER, North SC (2000) An open graph visualization system and its applications to software engineering. Software Pract Exper 30(11):1203–1233
15. Kamada T, Kawai S (1989) An algorithm for drawing general undirected graphs. Info Process Lett 31(1):7–15
16. Katz DM, Stafford DK (2008) Hustle and flow: A social network analysis of the american federal judiciary. In: Annual Meeting of the The Law and Society Association, Montreal, Canada
17. Mount DM, Arya S (2006) ANN: A library for approximate nearest neighbor searching, version 1.1.1, online software available on http://www.cs.umd.edu/~mount/ANN/, released the 4/8/2006
18. Moya-Anegón F, Vargas-Quesada B, Chinchilla-Rodríguez Z, Corera-Álvarez E, González-Molina A, Muñoz-Fernández F, Herrero-Solana V (2006) Vis. y Anal. de la Estr. Sci. Esp.: ISI web of science 1990–2005 (in Spanish). El Profesional de la Información, 15(4):258–269
19. Moya-Anegón F, Vargas-Quesada B, Chinchilla-Rodríguez Z, Corera-Álvarez E, González-Molina A, Muñoz-Fernández F, Herrero-Solana V (2007) Visualizing the marrow of science. J Am Soc Info Sci Technol 58(14):2167–2179
20. Moya-Anegón F, Vargas-Quesada B, Chinchilla-Rodríguez Z, Corera-Álvarez E, Herrero-Solana V, Muñoz-Fernández F (2005) Domain analysis and information retrieval through the construction of heliocentric maps based on ISI-JCR category cocitation. Info Process Manage 41:1520–1533
21. Moya-Anegón F, Vargas-Quesada B, Herrero-Solana V, Chinchilla-Rodríguez Z, Corera-Álvarez E, Muñoz-Fernández F (2004) A new technique for building maps of large scientific domains based on the cocitation of classes and categories. Scientometrics 61(1):129–145
22. Nguyen QV, Huang ML (2002) A space-optimized tree visualization. In: IEEE symposium on information visualization (InfoVis 2002), pp 85–92
23. Parlebas P (1972) Centralité et compacité d'un graphe. Math. et Sci. Hum. 39:5–26

24. Quirin A, Cordón O, Guerrero-Bote VP, Vargas-Quesada B, Moya-Anegón F (2008) A quick MST-based algorithm to obtain pathfinder networks. J Am Soc Info Sci Technol 59(12):1912–1924
25. Salton G, Bergmark D (1979) A citation study of computer science literature. IEEE Trans Prof Commun 22:146–158
26. Small H, Garfield E (1985) The geography of science: Disciplinary and national mappings. J Info Sci 11:147–159
27. Vargas-Quesada B, Moya-Anegón F (2007) Visualizing the structure of science. Springer, New York
28. Vargas-Quesada B, Moya-Anegón F, Chinchilla-Rodríguez Z, Corera-Álvarez E, González-Molina A, Muñoz-Fernández FJ, Herrero-Solana V (2008) Evolución de la estructura científica española: ISI web of science 1990–2005 (in Spanish). El Profesional de la Información 17(1):22–37
29. Vargas-Quesada B, Moya-Anegón F, Chinchilla-Rodríguez Z, González-Molina A (2007) Showing the essential science structure of a scientific domain and its evolution. Info Vis (in press)

Chapter 10
Nature-Inspired Dissemination of Information in P2P Networks

Christophe Guéret

Abstract After having first been used as a means to publish content, the Web is now widely used as a social tool for sharing information. It is an easy task to subscribe to a social network, join one of the Web-based communities according to some personal interests and start to share content with all the people who do the same. It is easy once you solve two basic problems: select the network to join (go to hi5, facebook, myspace,...? join all of them?) and find/pick up the right communities (i.e., find a strict label to match non-strict centers of interest). An error of appreciation would result in getting too much of useless/non-relevant information. This chapter provides a study on the dissemination of information within groups of people and aim at answering one question: can we find an effortless way of sharing information on the Web? Ideally, such a solution would require neither the definition of a profile nor the selection of communities to join. Publishing information should also not be the result of an active decision but be performed in an automatic way. A nature-inspired framework is introduced as an answer to this question. This framework features artificial ants taking care of the dissemination of information items within the network. Centers of interest of the users are reflected by artificial pheromones laid down on connections between peers. Another part of the framework uses those pheromone trails to detect shared interests and creates communities.

10.1 Introduction

In this chapter, we discuss the problem of information exchange in networks. A particular focus is set on solutions and algorithms aimed at taking advantages of the social interaction underlying message exchanges. During the first section, some general concepts about networks and communication paradigms are introduced. The two following sections are aimed at introducing patterns of communication

C. Guéret (✉)
Vrije Universiteit, Amsterdam, The Netherlands
e-mail: cgueret@few.vu.nl

A. Abraham et al. (eds.), *Computational Social Network Analysis*, Computer
Communications and Networks, DOI 10.1007/978-1-84882-229-0_10,
© Springer-Verlag London Limited 2010

paradigms observed in nature and algorithms based on them. Finally, we conclude this chapter with the definition of a general framework for network-level communications using stigmergy.

10.2 Networks and Communication Schemes

10.2.1 Network Structures

Let us consider an undirected graph $G(V, E)$ with a set of nodes $V = \{v_1, v_2, \ldots, v_n\}$ and a set of arcs $E \subseteq V \times V$. Two nodes v_i and v_j are connected if $e_{ij} \in E = \{e_{ij} | v_i, v_j \in V\}$. The distance between two nodes v_i and v_j will be denoted as $D(i, j)$. Depending on the context, this distance can be chosen to be related to the topology or to any other abstract measure, for instance, choosing to set the distance to the number of nodes between two nodes (Eq. 10.1) or choosing it to be equal to the latency of a message transfer.

$$D(i, j) = \min \left(\|\{e^1, \ldots, e^k | e^1 = e_{i\bullet}, e^k = e_{\bullet j}, e^\bullet \in E\}\| \right) \tag{10.1}$$

Definition 10.1. The neighbourhood N_i of a node v_i is the set of nodes located at a unit distance from v_i.

$$N_i = \{e_{ik} \in E | D(i, k) = 1\} \tag{10.2}$$

Definition 10.2. The degree k_i of a node v_i is equal to its number of neighbours.[1] The distribution of the degree values will be referenced to as $P(k)$

$$k_i = \|N_i\| \tag{10.3}$$

The distance separating two nodes and the respective degrees are used to compute two coefficients: the average path length and the clustering coefficient of the network.

Definition 10.3. Let C_n^2 be the number of possible pairs of two nodes in the network. The average path length $\mathcal{L}$ is the average distance separating pairs of nodes.

$$\mathcal{L} = \frac{1}{C_n^2} \sum_{i,j \in V} D(i, j) \tag{10.4}$$

Definition 10.4. Let v_i be a node in the graph G. The clustering coefficient C_i of v_i is given by the ratio between the number of existing neighbours among N_i and the total number of possible connections.

---

[1] Note that in case of a directed graph, a distinction would be made between the *in* and *out* degrees.

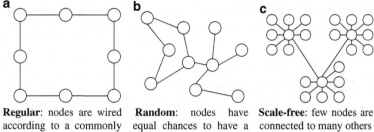

Regular: nodes are wired according to a commonly agreed-upon strategy

Random: nodes have equal chances to have a few or many neighbours

Scale-free: few nodes are connected to many others

Fig. 10.1 Examples network topologies depending on the degree distribution and the distance between nodes

$$C_i = \frac{\|E(N_i)\|}{k_i * (k_i - 1)} \tag{10.5}$$

The clustering coefficients are averaged in order to get the global coefficient C for the network

$$C = \frac{1}{\|V\|} \sum_{i \in V} C_i \tag{10.6}$$

According to the values of the average path length and the clustering coefficient, it is possible to identify three types of networks: regular, random and scale-free (see Fig. 10.1). Those different topologies can be found in several types of networks. Mobile ad-hoc networks (MANETs) made of several entities having an high churn rate are typically a random network. Social graphs and Web graphs have been proved to follow scale-free topologies. The characteristics of those networks are as follows:

Regular   This first category of networks can also be referenced as lattice, grid or mesh. Almost all the nodes have the same degree. This can be observed in networks wired according to a predefined, regular, pattern.

Random $P(k)$ follows a poison law with a parameter proportional to k. This indicates that in those graphs, nodes have equal chances to have a few or many neighbours. Such a graph will thus be homogeneous. This is the exact opposite of the regular graph.

Scale-free The distribution of degree in a scale-free network follows a power law [3]. Those networks have a high clustering coefficient and a low average path length. A few nodes have a lot of short links to other nodes, and long links connect those clusters to each other.

A distinction can be made between the physical structure of the network and its logical topology. The logical topology is a new network structure, commonly referred to as an *overlay*, making an abstraction of the physical one. The physical structure of a network is sometimes hard to know and very often hard to change. Overlays do not have those limitations and can be tailored to particular needs. It can be interesting to adapt the overlays to take into account more of the underlying network, for instance, taking advantage of some small world behaviours of the exchanges. This aspect will be the main focus of Section 10.4.3.

10.2.2 Communication Schemes

A communication scenario consists of a setup of a channel between the sender and the receiver and the transmission of the message. Back in 1997, Franklin proposed to describe this scenario according to three criteria [11]:

Push vs. Pull   The initiator of the transfer is an important characteristic. When the sender establishes the channel, the message is "pushed" to the receiver, whereas a receiver may open the connection in order to "pull" the message from the server. The difference is an essential role for the receiver. A push-type communication allows him to receive messages he did not explicitly request.

Unicast vs. broadcast   The cardinality of a transfer precises how many nodes are concerned. From the sender's point of view, a transfer can be unicast, broadcast or multicast, respectively, when it concerns one, many or a set of receivers. As opposed to multicast transfers that can be seen as a set of unicast the sender does not precisely know who will receive a broadcasted message.

Aperiodic vs. periodic   The periodicity allows to differentiate communications following a precise schedule from those performed on demand.

Based on those criteria, fetching a Web page from a Web server can be identified as an aperiodic, unicast pull transfer. This is a basic client/server communication scheme, the main disadvantage of which is the need for a client to explicitly ask for something precise. Publish/subscribe communication offers a more flexible alternative. In these systems, receivers can express needs to a server (subscribe) and automatically receive relevant messages later on published by the server. This is a combination of an aperiodic, unicast, pull (subscription) from the subscriber to the server followed by periodic and multicast pushes (publication) from the server to all its subscribers. By the way, subscription can be seen as an equivalent to constant queries [12]. In the mechanism coined by Cheriton [8], the sender and the receiver never explicitly establish a new connection to transfer a message. Instead, they rely on an already existing communication channel, usually described as a 'bus'. Every message sent on a bus is received by all the connected receivers. See Fig. 10.2 for an illustration of those basic schemes.

Among those three mechanisms, the "pull-free" dissemination appears to provide many advantages for both servers and receivers [12]. Because messages are just pushed on a common communication channel, indirect transfers can be made.

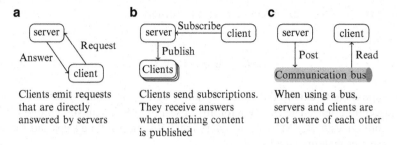

Fig. 10.2 Three basic communication schemes showing different combinations of initiator, cardinality and periodicity

Clients getting messages from the bus do not need to reveal their identity to the servers. Furthermore, the servers do not need to keep track of a potentially large list of clients.

In the following section, some of the dissemination schemes observed in nature are introduced along with their computational models.

10.3   Nature-Inspired Communication Paradigms

10.3.1   Epidemic and Rumour Spreading

Diseases feature an interesting way to diffuse information. Given a population, the model is pretty simple: each individual is assigned a status corresponding to its sensitivity against the disease, for instance, being "infected" or "susceptible". Starting from an initial status, the individuals may change to another status when they are in contact with the virus. It is possible to identify several types of epidemic systems depending on the number of states and the probabilities for going from one state to another.

The simplest system, known as SI, is based on two states: *Susceptible* – the individual is healthy and can be contaminated and *Infected* – the individual is sick and contagious. A susceptible individual may become infected with a probability β and, unfortunately for him or her, there is no chance of recovery. Let us consider a discrete model,[2] and let S_t and I_t be the number of susceptible and infected individuals, respectively, at timestamp t. The population is assumed to be of a constant size $N = S_t + I_t$ (which means nobody dies). At every time step, every infected may only contaminate one other. This means that the probability of becoming sick is β times the probability of being in contact with someone infected (I_n/N). The evolution of the population sizes is described by equation system 10.7. In those

---

[2] Under the assumption that Δt is very short, continuous models can be derived from discrete equation systems [1].

equations, $r = \frac{\beta \Delta t}{N}$ is the infection rate of the disease.

$$S_{t+1} = S_t - rS_t I_t$$
$$I_{t+1} = I_t + rS_t I_t \tag{10.7}$$

It is possible to extend this model by allowing infected individuals to return to the susceptible state. The equation for this Susceptible-Infected-Susceptible system (SIS) introduces $b = \gamma \Delta t$ as the recovery rate between two time steps and γ as the recovering probability (see Eq. 10.8).

$$S_{t+1} = S_t - rS_t I_t + bI_t$$
$$I_{t+1} = I_t + rS_t I_t - bI_t \tag{10.8}$$

Following the same reasoning scheme, several other epidemic systems can be designed. The Susceptible-Infected-Removed (SIR) model introduces a third state *Removed* for individuals who either die or become immune after having been infected once. The Susceptible-Exposed-Infected-Removed (SEIR) model extends SIR with a state *Exposed* used to make a distinction between susceptible individuals who may become infected and the others not exposed to the epidemic. In SIRS and SEIRS the removed state is limited in time by the introduction of a loop to the susceptible state [23].

Several phases can be taken into account with a combination of epidemic models. As an example, the Progressive-Susceptible-Infected-Detected-Removed (PSIDR) model [33] takes into account the delay needed for the identification of a virus. An initial SI proliferation phase is followed by an SIDR declination phase once the virus is identified and specific antivirus is introduced into the system.

The models can be even more flexible by using a non-constant population [24] and/or non-constant propagation rates [22].

Contagious Dissemination of Information

The use of dissemination of information was initiated by Demers in 1988. He designed a "gossip" protocol aimed at keeping up to date a distributed database [9]. The principle is simple and follows a SI mechanism: every time a node receives a message for the first time (he is susceptible), it transmits to a probabilistically chosen subset of nodes he is connected to (infect them according to an infection rate r). The information may also be altered by the nodes before they diffuse it (the epidemic mutates). Because all the nodes may either be infected (server) or susceptible (client), gossiping is a P2P protocol. An important element of Gossip algorithms is the transfer of state from the sender to the receiver. At the end of the communication, the client is infected just as the sender was. On an implementation point of view, this prevents a client from sending back the information to the server that just sent it to him. There is also an anti-entropy mechanism used in case an individual joins the network after the epidemic phase.

Since then, several gossip algorithms have been proposed. Depending on the strategy used to set the propagation rate, these algorithms are assigned to three categories [5]:

Fixed   The rate is set to a specific, constant, value. Noteworthy is that this value is set to 1, that is, if every neighbour receives the message, there is a flooding of the message. An example of such an approach is the original algorithm from Demers.

Adaptive   This latest category can be described as dynamic + learning. The probability is changed according to a local information and some feedback from previous transfers. The Smart Gossip protocol [42], taking into account the topology of the network and the reliability of the nodes to compute its propagation rate, is an example of adaptive gossip.

Dynamic   A local information is used to dynamically adjust the coefficient. The directional gossip [34] protocol is an example of this category. This protocol uses the size of the neighbourhood as an estimation for the network clustering value. Isolated, distant, peers will have higher chances to get the messages.

Another interesting example of adaptive gossip has been shown by the study of fireflies by Wokoma et al. [49]. When isolated, those insects have a particular capacity to emit a light signal at a frequency proper to each individual. Once in a group context, their reaction is to modify this frequency in order to have the same as their neighbours. Such a behaviour can be translated into an adaptive gossip protocol for the diffusion of updates. A peer willing to communicate an update will have to blink more rapidly; that is transmit messages in a more active rate.

10.3.2   Stigmergy

Stigmergy is an indirect communication system. Traces left in the environment by some entity are consequently used by the same or another entity. Such a behaviour has been first observed in ants. Although being independent from each other and acting without the presence of a global supervisor, they are all collectively able to find the shortest path linking the nest to a source of food.

Meta-heuristics based on artificial ants appeared in the 1990s, with the work of Dorigo [10]. A model of ants behaviour can be established making an analogy of the traveling salesman problem. This problem is expressed as such: a salesman has to visit several cities with the constraints of visiting each city only once and minimising the total travel distance. The task for the salesman, as well as for the ants, is to find the shortest path going through all the nodes of a weighted, undirected, graph.

Let us consider a set of N cities. The weight x_{ij} associated to an arc between two cities i and j denotes the distance separating them. A set of m artificial ants are initially randomly set at different cities in the graph. The goal for an artificial ant is then to complete a tour of all the cities following three rules:

1. The selection of the next city to go to depends on the quantity of pheromones laid down on the road.
2. It is not allowed to return to a previously visited city. To that, a tabu list $T(k)$ is used.
3. Once a complete tour is finished, it returns to the starting point and leaves pheromones on the way back.

Let $\tau_{ij}(t)$ be the amount of pheromones on a link between i and j at time t. The action of moving from one city to another is performed within t and $t+1$. During that time, pheromones will evaporate. New ones will also be added by ants having completed their tour. The final quantity after N moves is found at $t+N$

$$\tau_{ij}(t+N) = (1-\rho)\tau_{ij}(t) + \Delta\tau_{ij} \tag{10.9}$$

ρ is the persistence factor of the pheromones, $1-\rho$ represents the amount of pheromones evaporated between t and $t+N$. In the meantime, the amount of pheromones is increased by $\Delta\tau_{ij}$.

$$\Delta\tau_{ij} = \sum_{k=1}^{m} \Delta\tau_{ij}^k \tag{10.10}$$

In this later formulation, τ_{ij}^k is the amount of pheromones added by the ant k. This quantity depends on the quality of the tour. The goal being to find the shortest tour, this quantity will be inversely proportional to the length L_k of the tour.

$$\Delta\tau_{ij}^k = \begin{cases} \dfrac{Q}{L_k} & \text{if the ant used the arc } (i,j) \\ 0 & \text{otherwise} \end{cases} \tag{10.11}$$

Some other variations can be considered, for instance, attributing an equal quantity of pheromones to each part of the tour whatever be its length or taking into account the distance between cities rather than the total length of the tour.

Artificial ants moves are managed by transition probabilities. The probability for the ant k, at a time t, to go from the city i to the city j is equal to $p_{ij}^k(t)$.

$$p_{ij}^k(t) = \begin{cases} \dfrac{[\tau_{ij}(t)]^\alpha [\eta_{ij}]^\beta}{\sum_{l\in N\setminus T(k)} [\tau_{il}(t)]^\alpha [\eta_{il}]^\beta} & \text{if } j \in N\setminus T(k) \\ 0 & \text{otherwise} \end{cases} \tag{10.12}$$

This formulation is based on a trade-off between the pheromones and the attractiveness of the path. Some path with a lot of pheromones may not be so attractive if no one else is currently using it – or the inverse. This attractiveness can, for instance, be used to force diversification (avoid path were other ants are). In the case of the traveling salesman, this parameter is set to the inverse of the distance: $\eta_{ij} = \frac{1}{d_{ij}}$. The shorter a path is, the more attractive it will be. The two coefficients α and β allow for adjusting the relative importance of those two decision parameters.

Because every entity has the opportunity to alter a common environment, indirect communication can take place. The messages sent are the modifications made to that environment. In the specific example of the TSP, this information is the distance between a pair of cities.

10.3.3 Immune System

The immune system is a complex mechanism of self-defense that develops during the evolution of living organisms. This system is animated by the rivalry between two types of entities: antigens and antibodies. Within an organism, antibodies are in charge of chasing and destroying antigens. This defense system is characterised by its proliferation and mutation mechanisms. Under stimulation by an antigen, B cells (a particular type of lymphocytes) start the production of matching antibodies (proliferation). Though antibodies are specialised, the system can mutate to adapt itself to new antigens.

In the context of communication, messages are embodied into the antibodies. Those antibodies walk through the network and undergo proliferation when the environment is favourable for it.

10.3.4 Comparison

When the goal is to achieve a good coverage of the network, epidemic algorithms are among the best choices. Those algorithms can cope with churns. They are also best suited for dissemination without explicit targets. Ant-based algorithms are generally more suited to routing problems. Taking the TSP problem as an example, the goal is to deliver a message to a given destination. The quality of the decision can be assessed by different means and used to modify further decisions. This implies learning and improvement over time (Table 10.1).

Table 10.1 Comparison of interaction elements within different nature-inspired paradigms

	Epidemic	Stygmergy	Immune
Channel	Connections between peers	A global environment every individual can freely interact with	Hosting peer
Servers	Peers in infected state	All entities	Antibodies
Clients	Peers in susceptible state	All entities	Antigens
Information	Individuals status	Modification in the environment	Genotype of cells

10.4   Nature-Inspired Algorithms for Communication

10.4.1   Information Querying

Search, and the associated query problem, is certainly the most well-known of the communication problems. Examples of it are the quest for a particular data on the WWW or for a file on a P2P file-sharing network. This search process can be described by three, consecutive, sub-processes addressing a particular question each [30]:

1. *What?* The first step consists of the identification of the seek content. This process may consist of: computing the identifier associated to the request (in case of DHTs), finding some meta-data related to keywords provided (for search sites providing advanced search features), ...
2. *Where?* Once the goal of the search is known, search itself has to be done. That part is the most tricky. Among other specific points, the difficulty of the task depends on the complexity of the network and the quality of the previous step.
3. *How?* When the document as been identified, it can be retrieved.

In this model, the first and the second steps may eventually be merged if the query already represents the document requested, for instance, if some provided keywords are the only meta data available to perform the search. The latest step, the one on the retrieval of the document will not be detailed further as few different solutions exist to it. The typical approach consists of establishing a standard client/server exchange between the (know identified) server and the client. In the case where multiple servers have been found, it may also be possible to fetch part of the document from each of them.

The content provided by servers is registered in an index. A list of files to be shared is an example of such an index associating file names to content. When a request for a particular file is received, the corresponding content is sent back as an answer. Those indexes may be local, central or distributed. In the following, we present some strategies associated with the use of those three types of indexes. For a complete overview of search strategies, the interested reader can refer to [40].

10.4.1.1   Centralised Indexes

A central index is a unique entity containing the information from all the indexes. Every peer getting connected to the network sends its index to this central authority. All the requests are then sent to that central point.

After being the first approach used by P2P system, in the form of the file sharing software Napster, this centralisation of information has been proved not to scale. The biggest central indexes are now the search engines, such as Google, that crawl the Web and index part of its content. They are able to provide a reasonable answer to the "where" question, as long as the "what" is correctly expressed.

10.4.1.2   Local Indexes

In non-structured networks, the placement of information for that of peers follows a particular scheme. Under this context, it becomes impossible to know in advance the destination for a request and therefore routing cannot be achieved. Instead, the strategy consists of sending the query to some peers *hopping* they will either be able to answer or to forward it to another peer more likely to answer.

In the context of forward, a message is transferred from peer to peer until its objective is fulfilled. The most straightforward strategy for forwarding messages is the random walk: the receiver is randomly selected, and the message is sent. But some more clever strategies can be applied. For their routing algorithm REMINDIN' [47], Tempich et al. choose to take in account five aspects of information exchange visible in human interaction: (1) a question is usually sent to someone likely to answer it. (2) by answering this question, this person proves he has some relevant knowledge. (3) someone knowledgeable about a particular domain is likely to have some information about a similar or broader topic. (4) every individual has its own domain of expertise. (5) the estimation of the wisdom of someone is a measure relative to the personal wisdom of someone. In REMINDIN, those points are taken into consideration thanks to two essential aspects of the algorithm: the memorisation of the provenance of information and a given notion of confidence among the peers. In particular, whenever a peer answers a request, it memorises the name of the asking peer. This is commonly referred to has referral networks.

An epidemiological strategy can be considered in order to duplicate the messages when they reach a node. In that case, a SIR model is typically applied. The best example of this type of information dissemination is the protocol used in Gnutella, a file-sharing software developed in 2006 by Nullsoft. A request for a particular file received by a peer is duplicated and sent to some other peers.

The ImmuneSearch [13] system avoids the flooding behaviour of gossip algorithms by using a communication model inspired from the humoral immune system. Each peer has to define an information profile describing the content of its local index and a search profile describing what it is interested in. Search profiles are turned into antibodies tracking the antigens (information profiles). Aging of antibodies limits the propagation of the requests in the network and their proliferation allows to query more peers when the environment is favourable to it (when some solutions have been found).

10.4.1.3   Distributed Indexes

A distributed index is a distributed structure aimed at storing the content of all the local indexes provided by the peers. It is itself an index on top of which two functions `insert(identifier,content)` and `fetch(identifier)` are, respectively, used for the insertion and the retrieval of elements.

Fig. 10.3 Examples of
distributed indexes used on
top of two different index
spaces. In both examples, the
dotted line represents a look
up operation. *Grey circles* are
the positions of the nodes.
Dashed elements are parts of
the addressing space

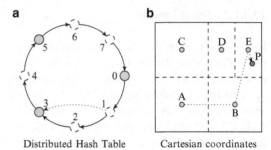

Distributed Hash Table   Cartesian coordinates

The identifier associated to the element being inserted/retrieved depends on the representation space used for the distributed index. The most common types of identifiers are hash codes, prefix-based names and Cartesian coordinates:

Hash   Distributed Hash Tables (DHT) are an example of structured network topologies. A unique identifier is associated to each node and data in the overlay. This identifier is drawn from an hash function. In Chord [46], the best-known example of DHT, each node is connected to the following node and to the previous one in a ring topology.

Prefix   In a prefix-based strategy, the code associated to each identifier is such that the distance between a query and a matching answer is related to the edit distance between their respective identifiers [38]. Tapestry [50] and Pastry [41] are two other systems making use of a prefix encoding.

Cartesian   The content-addressable network CAN [39] features an identifier space based on cartesian coordinates. The entire addressing space is divided among the peers. The routing operations are designed to bring a request closer to the matching answers.

The Fig. 10.3 shows an illustration of hash codes and cartesian coordinates identifiers.

Distributed indexes are commonly used on top of structured networks. But they can also be designed to use non-structured topologies. As an example, the Anthill system designed by Babaoglu et al. [2, 35] uses two types of artificial ants to take care of insertion and lookup operations. On insertion operations, an "insertAnt" walks from peer to peer until it finds a suitable place to store the element. "searchAnt" can then browse the network for an identifier and turn themselves into "replyAnt" when they are successful.

10.4.2 Dissemination of Information

The problem stands as this: a server has an information it is willing to send to a client yet to be determined among all the nodes in the network. Some concrete examples of this scenario are load-balancing problems (the server wants to get rid of some tasks) and daily use of mails (the server – a user – wants to inform other users about something he found).

10.4.2.1   Selective and Directed Dissemination

Messages can be sent to a specific group of nodes or routed towards promising destinations in the network.

The publish/subscribe mechanism is the most straightforward way of performing selective dissemination. With such a system in place, messages only have to be sent to the subscribers. However, it can be hard to manage the subscriptions, particularly in non-structured P2P networks where every peer is a potential publisher. The solutions proposed in Elvin4 [44], Siena [6, 7] and P2P-DIET [31, 32] is to extend the pub/sub with the third type of message. This new message allows for a client to precise what it expects and for a server to precise the type of messages it is likely to publish in the future. This information can then be used to route subscription and publication messages through the network.

Directed diffusion [27] uses gradients of interests to route pushed messages. Periodically, peers broadcast the list of the messages they are interested in. In turn, peers forward every list they receive and update a radiant to the source.

More recently, Web 2.0 Web sites appeared as a new way to achieve directed dissemination of information. Such Web sites, for instance, the free encyclopedia Wikipedia, allow anyone to publish information and temper with what other users published. The Web sites are turned into an environment upon which a stigmergic communication takes place among all the visitors.

10.4.2.2   Blind Dissemination

Blind dissemination has to be achieved when a server wants to send a message but has no clue on potential recipients. The load-balancing problem, where the task consists of distributing tasks over a set of nodes, is one of the potential application domains for blind dissemination. The tasks are the messages an overloaded server will want to send to an underloaded server.

The circulation of messages can be in charge of moving around the network, taking messages from overloaded servers they visit and dropping them on underloaded places. In the Messor [36] system, this get/put process is separated into two steps: an ant first looks for an underloaded server and then goes finding an overloaded server willing to transfer a task. This approach avoids having to move tasks along with the ants, thus reducing the bandwidth.

10.4.3   Modification of the Topology

The objective is to take into account some social behaviours in order to adapt to the network. Such social behaviour has been proved to appear, in the form of small world networks, in the case of file sharing among researchers [26]. It as also been reported than taking into account such social topologies can improve communication [37]. Two strategies can be applied: either modify the network or add another overlay providing added information.

10.4.3.1 Rewiring

Rewiring algorithms consists of dynamically adjusting the topology of the network. The general skeleton of such an algorithm is simple. Using some satisfaction measure, a peer evaluates the quality of its neighbourhood. If this quality appears not to be sufficient, then connections are dropped and new ones are established. The choice of the satisfaction estimation and rewiring rules dictates different algorithms.

In the model proposed by Schmitz [43], a peer periodically initiate searches in the network in order to find new peers having a similar profile. When the satisfaction of the peer for its neighbourhood falls below a given threshold, a random walk is started. The expertise of every visited peer is recorded. After a fixed number of visits, the result is returned back to the original peer who then re-adjusts its connections.

The T-Man algorithm [28, 29] uses a different approach based on addressbook exchanges. Periodically, a peer selects one of its neighbour and sends him the list of profiles of the peers it is currently connected to. In return, it receives a similar message from the receiver. Then, both peers merge, sort and truncate the result of the merge from their respective current list and the one they just received. When the sorting function is based on the neighbourhood, this auto-catalyst process allows for the rapid identification and clustering of peers having a similar neighbourhood.

10.4.3.2 Adding Shortcuts

The addition of shortcuts can be used as an alternative solution to rewiring when modifying the network is not possible (for instance with DHTs). Because shortcuts are added "on top" of the existing structure, they can also appear as a most flexible alternative. For every peer, shortcuts are stored as a list of peer to contact in priority before using the normal communication strategy.

The small-world overlay protocol [25] (SWOP) adds shortcuts on top of the Chord distributed hash table. The added layer is made of "head" and "inner" nodes connected through "long" or "cluster" links. Long links are established between head nodes. Within a particular cluster, clusters links connect the inner nodes to the cluster's head node. The clusters are of predefined size. Before using the normal Chord lookup, a node will first refer to the head node of its group. The SWAN algorithm [4] is a similar approach aimed at CAN-based networks.

In the case of networks with changing topologies (ad hocs, for instance), the shortcuts have to be dynamically adapted. Assuming that a peer answering to a request is likely to answer to further requests, Sripanidkulchai proposes to update the shortcuts whenever the network is queried [45] – in that case, a Gnutella network.

When the query message returns back to its sender with the list of potential servers, some names are kept and added to the shortcut list. Later, those peers will be queried in priority. The popularity of a particular item and the answering history of a peer can also be considered in the decision process [48].

10.5   Achieving Network-Level Stigmergy

In the previous sections, we presented various schemes for the exchange of information in a network. Those schemes differ according to the initiator of the transfer and the network type. But the actual communication is still based on the client/server paradigm, meaning that either the sender or the receiver has to be active at some point and decide to establish the communication. This action can consist of sending a mail or browsing a wiki, for instance. This section investigates another approach for the network layer. The main idea is to provide a selective dissemination layer separated from the application layer.

10.5.1   General Objectives

As proven by the success of Web 2.0 Web sites, stigmergy is a communication scheme allowing an easy publication of information. Unfortunately, this is currently limited to some specific places (e.g., the Web sites). On the network side, the is no such content-focused stigmergy possible. The closest models based either on gossip algorithms or distributed publish subscribe rely on a the (partial) flooding of the network with information or the description of centers of interest (define profiles). Recommender systems, such as the one used by the Web site Amazon.com for buying suggestion, free the user from having to define a profile. But, because the two activities are performed on two different environments, their recommendation system cannot suggest a book to a user based on a paper he or she is currently writing for a conference.

The framework proposed in this section is aimed at providing a common environment prone to stigmergy among various applications used by different nodes.

10.5.2   Architecture

The communication metaphors used to design communication algorithms within that framework is that of a group of people talking in an open space. In this context, the underlying communication channel allows for any individual to hear what others are saying – providing they are not to far away. All the persons are also free to move around the space. Typically, those moves would be targeted towards three objectives: get closer to an acquittance, reach the source of an interesting discussion or just walk randomly, hoping to stumble upon some interesting conversations. As people are moving and talking, interest-based clusters are emerging from the initial, unstructured, crowd. In order to establish a nature-inspired algorithm, those rules have to be interpreted in terms of peers and messages.

Peers

The architecture proposed is a multi-agent system. Each peer in the network is an agent who is able to discuss with its siblings and move around the network by changing its connections. Air, the communication channel used to speak in the natural model, is replaced by network connections between the peers. In order to mimic the non-directed nature of the initial support and enable overhearing from other peers, all of the received messages may be directly forwarded.

Within the agent, three essential elements have to be managed:

Stocks   The stack of messages is divided into two, according to where they come from the application layer or the network layer. Message added to the application stack are meant to be distributed in the network. The ones set in the network stack will be used by end-user applications. Things arriving at the network stack are automatically pushed to the application stack so that the user can see them. Messages forwarded from the application to the network are triggered by the user.

Connections   Communications are restricted to a set of connected peers. In order to reflect the creation of clusters based on interests, this set of peers has to be dynamically adjusted according to the communications. An addressbook is kept and progressively filled.

Communications   The circulation of messages compromises the selection of a message to send and the selection of a receiver. The general efficiency of the system will depend on those choices. Particularly, a compromise will have to be made between exploration and exploitation: trying to investigate new areas of the network or keep up sending only to peers known to be interested.

As illustrated by Fig. 10.4, the communication system of an individual lies between his brain and his ears + mouth. The brain decides the things to say while the ears and the mouth act, respectively, as an input and output device. The equivalent agent is an interface between end-user applications and the Internet.

Messages

The content of messages sent from a peer to another can be of any kind (Web site address, document, sound file, ...). The main information used by the algorithm

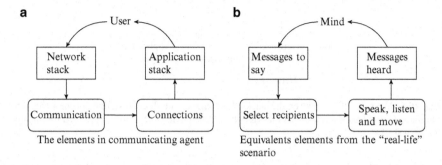

Fig. 10.4 Comparison of messages flow within a peer according to the metaphore (**b**) and the architecture proposed (**a**). Only the user may (re)inject messages into the network. Arriving messages are directly sent to the application stack

is a pheromone trace associated to the message considered to represent its content. Given a message I, this pheromone vector is $\tau(I)$. Using a similar notation, the pheromones associated to a connection $i \leftarrow j$ from the node n_j to n_i are defined as $\tau_{i \leftarrow j}(t)$. We also assume the existence of a similarity function sim, which can be used to compare two pheromones trails.

Users

In contrary to other systems, there is no profile defined for the users. Those profiles are replaced by the pheromones associated to the connection between peers. Every message published or forwarded by a peer will be perceived by the receiver as a hint about its center of interests.

10.5.2.1 Management of Stacks

Not every information a peer is willing to publish will be interesting all the time. The more outstanding example of this limit would be the publication of news. To take this into account, and in addition to the pheromones marking, a validity limit is associated to every message. The messages are then considered to be perishable goods ants have to move before the date expires.

Locally on each peer, the messages are stored in two distinct stacks. There are three transfer rules that regulate exchanges of messages between the stacks (Fig. 10.5):

1. User action: Messages are moved from the application stack to the network stack on explicit user action. This transfer assumes an interest from the user to the message he or she picked up from the application stack.
2. Automatic: The objective of this automatic transfer is to make messages gathered from the network visible to the user.

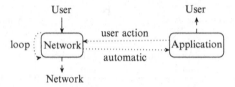

Fig. 10.5 Messages flow between the stacks. *Solid arrows* are direct insertions of messages into the stack. *Dashed arrows* represents messages being taken out. *Dotted arrows* are used for transfer between stacks

3. Loop: Under special conditions, a message from the network stack may be taken out of the stack and added back. This loop transfer is used by communications when the decision is to keep a given message instead of forwarding it.

A message published by a peer will go into the network stack and then be pushed into the network. Later on, a user browsing the content of the application stack of its peer may stumble upon this message and have a look at it. Doing so, a new copy of the message is added to the network stack and diffused into the network. This scenario acts in favour of the most important messages: the more seen a message is, the more visible it will be for the entire network. Non-interesting messages are prone to rapidly disappear.

10.5.2.2 Management of Communications

The algorithm proposed is based on messages are seen as perishable goods transferred from nest to nest. Artificial pheromones associated to each connection keep track of the messages exchanged, thus creating a global and network-based memory.

Transfer of a Message

The selection of a destination consists of two steps. First, all the connected peers $V_i(t)$ are separated into two groups depending on whether they are likely to be interested by the information I or not. Those groups are respectively defined as $V_i(I,t)$ and $\overline{V_i}(I,t)$. The decision is based on the similarity between the message to be sent and the traces left by those previously received. Every connection for which the similarity is above the threshold $s_{\min}$ is assumed to lead to interested peers. According to a probability η, the ant will decide which group to pick up a destination from.

$$V_i(I,t) = \{n_j \in V_i(t) \mid s(\tau_{i \leftarrow j}(t), \tau(I)) \geq s_{\min}\} \setminus T_i(I,t) \qquad (10.13)$$

$$\overline{V_i}(I,t) = \{n_j \in V_i(t) \mid n_j \notin V_i(I,t)\} \setminus T_i(I,t) \qquad (10.14)$$

A tabu list $T_i(I,t)$ is used to remove some connections from the two groups, for instance, to avoid sending back a message to its previous sender. If the objective is to force diversification in send, this list may be associated to the peer. In doing so, peers to which the message had just been sent to will not be available for a new send. This list can also be associated to the message to avoid message loops or to the memory of the ants to avoid them doing loops as in [15, 16].

Then, a probability of being selected ρ_j is associated to every destination n_j. The equation used to compute this probability depends on the group (interest or not) the destination belongs to. Within the group of interested peers, the chances of being selected are proportional to the similarity of the connection, whereas all of the non-interesting destination are assumed to be equally non-interested (see Eq. 10.15). The possibility of a loop transfer, as introduced in the previous section, is materialised by the addition of $1 + n^+$ peers to the computation of the probability for destinations in $\overline{V_i}(I, t)$. The probability associated to this choice complements the other choices within $\overline{V_i}(I, t)$. That is, $\rho_i = 1 - |\overline{V_i}(I, t)| \cdot \rho_j$. Choosing to put back the message into the network stack will be n^+ times more important than the other possibilities.

$$
\rho_j = \begin{cases} \dfrac{\text{sim}(\tau_{i \leftarrow j}(t), \tau(I))}{\sum_{z \in V_i(I,t)} \text{sim}(\tau_{i \leftarrow z}(t), \tau(I))} & \text{if } n_j \in V_i(I, t) \\[4mm] \dfrac{1}{|\overline{V_i}(I, t)| + 1 + n^+} & \text{if } n_j \in \overline{V_i}(I, t) \end{cases} \tag{10.15}
$$

As shown in Fig. 10.6, the decision of sending the message I over the connection $i \to j$ at a time t is taken as the result of a combination of choices. The probability $P_{i \to j}^{\text{send}}(I, t)$ is a product of the probabilities associated to each of those choices (cf. Fig. 10.6 for a graphical representation).

Once $P_{i \to j}^{\text{send}}(I, t)$ has been computed for every $n_j \in V_i(t)$ and the special case $i = j$, the ant randomly selects a destination and leaves the nest to go delivering the message.

Actualisation of Pheromones Level

On its way from the peer n_i to the peer n_j, the ant carries a message. Pheromones are updated to reflect the content of this message. On the way back to its nest, the ant lays down no pheromones – as the ant is returning with empty hands to its nest.

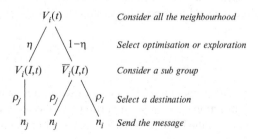

Fig. 10.6 Decision tree. Starting from the entire neighbourhood, the ant first decides to send the message to a potentially interested or not interested destination. Then, the actual destination is selected

10.5.2.3 Management of Connections

The topology of the network is modified according to its perceived quality. Connections leading to a poor traffic are cut down and new connections are established based on the addressbook. If this addressbook only contains unusable peers. Requests for recommendation can be sent to other peers. This helps feeding the addressbook.

Rewiring of the Neighbourhood

The utility of a connection $i \rightarrow j$ depends on the number of times it has been evaluated as an interesting destination for forwarding a message over the last X decisions. The rationale is not to stay connected to peers that appear not to be interested by the current content of the stacks. The lower X is, the faster the system will adjust the neighbourhood to cope with changes in the stacks.

$$S_{i \rightarrow j}^{\text{drop}}(t) = -\log \left(\frac{U_{i \rightarrow j}(t) + \epsilon}{1 + \epsilon} \right), \quad n_j \in V_i(t) \tag{10.16}$$

The probability $P_{i \rightarrow j}^{\text{drop}}(t)$ is then computed to be proportional to dropping scores. This decision process can be improved by the introduction of a minimum utility β. Instead of considering all the neighbourhood as potentially removable connections, only those having a score below this threshold will be considered. If none of the current connection falls under the limit, that is if the peer is satisfied by its neighbourhood, none of them will be dropped.

Addition of Peers to the Addressbook

Every peer receiving a recommendation request answers giving the name of a peer grabbed from its own neighbourhood. The selection of the peer to recommend is based on the pheromone traces left on the connections.

Let us consider the case of a peer n_j receiving a request from the peer n_i. At time t when the request is received, n_j will decide to recommend to n_i a peer $n_k \in V_j(t)$ based on a recommendation score $S_{j \rightarrow i}^{\text{reco}}(k, t)$. Because it would be meaningless to recommend to a peer to get connected to itself, n_i is excluded from the possible choices

$$S_{j \rightarrow i}^{\text{reco}}(k, t) = \text{sim}(\tau_{j \leftarrow i}(t), \tau_{j \leftarrow k}(t)), \quad n_k \in V_j(t) \setminus \{n_i\} \tag{10.17}$$

The probability $P_{j \rightarrow i}^{\text{reco}}(k, t)$ to send a recommendation for the peer n_k over the connection $j \rightarrow i$ is proportional to the recommendation scores. The higher this score is, the better the chances of a peer to be recommended.

10.5.3 Results and Applications

In order to validate the algorithms, this framework has been implemented in a test case using a cosine distance for the similarity and a weighted keyword vector for the pheromones [17–21].

The expected applications are the dissemination of information and the identification of underlying social behaviours. Following design principles similar to that of the semantic desktop, this system could be implemented as part of a file system to ease sharing of information. In that specific case, semantic data would have to be considered for the pheromones trails.

Another application domain we started to investigate in [14] is the non-supervised classification task. Messages published by the peers are elements of the data set to be sorted. After some iterations of the algorithms, peers publishing similar messages (e.g., elements of the same class) will get connected to each other.

10.6 Conclusion

This chapter discussed the problem of information exchange in a P2P setting. In that context, sharing information requires an extra amount of work from the sender in order to identify the potential receivers of a message. Picking up some global dissemination platform, such as a Web 2.0 Web site, can partially solve this issue (through indirect communication) but still implies for a specific Web site to be chosen. And, if the information is to be sent to different groups of people, duplicate the message over several of those information-sharing platforms.

This chapter introduced another approach fostering stygmergic behaviour of artificial ants to Web scale. In the proposed model, every peer emits messages that are moved over the network, from peer to peer, by artificial ants. Those messages are flavoured by the keywords they contain, leaving traces on all the connections they take upon. Those smelling traces constitute a global memory used by the ants to route messages efficiently towards areas of interest. This relaying mechanism is complemented by an epidemic model on the contamination of the peers by the messages they received. Once contaminated, a peer can in turn become a sender of the message.

This generic framework can be used for the dissemination of information and the identification of social behaviours underlying discussions between peers. It has been implemented and used as such in a test prototype.

References

1. Allen L (1994) Some discrete-time si, sir and sis epidemic models. Math Biosci 124(1):83–105
2. Babaoglu O, Meling H, Montresor A (2002) Anthill: A framework for the development of agent-based peer-to-peer systems. In: Proceedings of the 22th international conference on distributed computing systems (ICDCS '02), Vienna, Austria

3. Barabasi AL, Albert R (1999) Emergence of scaling in random networks. Science 286:509
4. Bonsma E (2002) Fully decentralised, scalable look-up in a network of peers using small world networks. In: Proceedings of the 6th multiple conference on systemics, cybernetics and informatics, Orlando
5. Burmester M, Le TV, Yasinsac A (2006) Adaptive gossip protocols: Managing security and redundancy in dense ad hoc networks. J Ad Hoc Networks 4(3):504–515, DOI 10.1016/j.adhoc. 2005.11.007
6. Carzaniga A, Rosenblum DS, Wolf AL (2000) Achieving expressiveness and scalability in an internet-scale event notification service. In: Proceedings of the 19th ACM symposium on principles of distributed computing (PODC2000), Portland, Oregon
7. Carzaniga A, Rosenblum DS, Wolf AL (2001) Design and evaluation of a wide-area event notification service. ACM Trans Comput Syst 19(3):332–383
8. Cheriton D (1992) Dissemination oriented communication systems. Tech. Rep., Stanford University, Computer Science Department
9. Demers AJ, Greene DH, Hauser C, Irish W, Larson J, Shenker S, Sturgis HE, Swinehart DC, Terry DB (1988) Epidemic algorithms for replicated database maintenance. Oper Syst Rev 22(1):8–32
10. Dorigo M, Maniezzo V, Colorni A (1996) The Ant System: Optimization by a colony of cooperating agents. IEEE Trans Syst Man Cybernet Part B Cybernet 26(1):29–41
11. Franklin M, Zdonik S (1997) A framework for scalable dissemination-based systems. In: Proceedings of the 12th ACM SIGPLAN conference on object-oriented programming, systems, languages, and applications (OOPSLA'97), ACM, New York, NY, USA, pp 94–105, DOI 10.1145/263698.263725
12. Franklin M, Zdonik S (1998) Data in your face: Push technology in perspective. In: Proceedings of the 1998 ACM SIGMOD international conference on Management of data (SIGMOD'98), ACM, New York, NY, USA, pp 516–519, DOI 10.1145/276304.276360
13. Ganguly N, Canright G, Deutsch A (2005) Design of a robust search algorithm for p2p networks. In: Heidelberg SB (ed) High performance computing – HiPC 2004, Lecture Notes in Computer Science, vol 3296, pp 222–231, DOI 10.1007/b104576
14. Guéret C (2006) Navigateurs internet intelligents: Algorithmes de fourmis artificielles pour la diffusion d'informations dans un réseau p2p. PhD thesis, Université François Rabelais Tours, Laboratoire d'Informatique, 64, Avenue Jean Portalis – 37200 Tours
15. Guéret C, Monmarché N, Slimane M (2004) Spreading information within a p2p network using artificial ants. In: Proceedings of the 8th annual meeting on health, science and technology
16. Guéret C, Monmarché N, Slimane M (2005) Aide à la navigation sur internet: Utilisation de fourmis artificielles pour l'échange d'informations dans un réseau p2p. In: Actes du congré de la ROADEF
17. Guéret C, Monmarché N, Slimane M (2006) Automonous gossiping of information in a P2P network with artificial ants. In: Dorigo M, Gambardella LM, Birattari M, Martinoli A, Poli R, Stützle T (eds) Proceedings of the 5th international workshop on ant colony optimization and swarm intelligence (ANTS'2006). Springer, Bruxelles, Belgium, Lecture Notes in Computer Science (LNCS), vol 4150, pp 388–395
18. Guéret C, Monmarché N, Slimane M (2006) A self-organizing ant-based information gossiping algorithm for P2P networks. In: Proceedings of the 6th international workshop on innovative Internet community systems (I2CS'2006), German Society of Informatics, Neuchâtel, Lecture notes in informatics (LNI), p 10
19. Guéret C, Monmarché N, Slimane M (2006) Sharing resources with artificial ants. In: Proceedings of the 9th international workshop on nature inspired distributed computing (NIDISC'06), at the 20th IEEE international parallel and distributed processing symposium (IPDPS'2006), Rhodes Island, p 8
20. Guéret C, Monmarché N, Slimane M (2007) A biology-inspired model for the automatic dissemination of information in p2p networks. Nature-inspired systems for parallel, asynchronous and decentralised environments (NISPADE), Special issue of multiagent and grid systems (MAGS) 3(1):87–104

21. Guéret C, Monmarché N, Slimane M (2007) Sharing resources in a p2p network with artificial ants. J Math Model Algorithms (JMMA) 6:345–360, DOI 10.1007/s10852-007-9062-9
22. Hethcote HW, van den Driessche P (1991) Some epidemiological models with nonlinear incidence. J Math Biol 29:271–287
23. Hethcote HW, van den Driessche P (1995) An sis epidemic model with variable population size and a delay. J Math Biol 34:177–194
24. Hethcote HW, Levin S (1989) Periodicity in epidemiological models. Appl Math Ecol 1:193–211
25. Hui KYK, Lui JCS, Yau DKY (2004) Small world overlay p2p networks. In: Proceedings of IEEE international workshop on quality of service (IWQoS), Montreal, Canada
26. Iamnitchi A, Ripeanu M, Foster IT (2002) Locating data in (small-worlds?) peer-to-peer scientific collaborations. Lecture Notes in Computer Science, Revised papers from the 1st international workshop on peer-to-peer systems 2429:232–241
27. Intanagonwiwat C, Govindan R, Estrin D (2000) Directed diffusion: A scalable and robust communication paradigm for. Sensor networks. In: Proceedings of the 6th annual ACM/IEEE international conference on mobile computing and networking (MobiCOM00), Boston, MA, USA, pp 56–67
28. Jelasity M, Babaoglu O (2004) T-Man: Fast gossip-based construction of large-scaleoverlay topologies. Tech. Rep. UBLCS-2004-7, University of Bologna, Department of Computer Science, Bologna, Italy
29. Jelasity M, Babaoglu O (2005) T-man: Gossip-based overlay topology management. In: Brueckner S, Serugendo GDM, Hales D, Zambonelli F (eds) Engineering self-organising applications (ESOA'05), Utrecht, The Netherlands
30. Joseph S, Hoshiai T (2003) Decentralized meta-data strategies: Effective peer-to-peer search. IEICE Trans Commun E86-B(6):1740–1753
31. Koubarakis M, Tryfonopoulos C (2004) Distributed resource sharing using self-organized peer-to-peer networks and languages from information retrieval. In: Invitational workshop on self-*properties in complex information systems, Bertinoro, Italy
32. Koubarakis M, Tryfonopoulos C, Idreos S, Drougas Y (2003) Selective information dissemination in p2p networks: Problems and solutions. SIGMOD Record, Special Issue on Peer-to-Peer Data Management 32(3):71–76
33. Leveille J (2002) Epidemic spreading in technological networks. Tec. Rep. HPL-2002-287, Information infrastructure laboratory, HP Laboratories Bristol
34. Lin M, Marzullo K (1999) Directional gossip: Gossip in a wide area network. Tech. Rep., La Jolla, CA, USA
35. Montresor A (2001) Anthill: A framework for the design and analysis of peer-to-peer systems. In: Proceedings of the 4th European research seminar on advances in distributed systems, Bertinoro, Italy
36. Montresor A, Meling H, Babaoglu O (2002) Messor: Load-balancing through a swarm of autonomous agents. Tech. Rep. UBLCS-02-08, Departement of Computer Science, University of Bologna, Bologna, Italy
37. Palau J, Montaner M, López B (2004) Collaboration analysis in recommender systems using social networks. In: Proceedings of the 8th international workshop on cooperative information agents (CIA'04), Erfurt (Germany)
38. Plaxton CG, Rajaraman R, Richa AW (1997) Accessing nearby copies of replicated objects in a distributed environment. In: Proceedings of the ninth annual ACM symposium on parallel algorithms and architectures (SPAA'97), ACM, New York, NY, USA, pp 311–320, DOI 10.1145/258492.258523
39. Ratnasamy S, Francis P, Handley M, Karp R, Schenker S (2001) A scalable content-addressable network. In: SIGCOMM '01: Proceedings of the 2001 conference on applications, technologies, architectures, and protocols for computer communications, ACM, New York, NY, USA, pp 161–172, DOI 10.1145/383059.383072
40. Risson J, Moors T (2004) Survey of research towards robust peer-to-peer networks: Search methods. Tec. Rep. UNSW-EE-P2P-1-1, University of New South Wales, Australia

41. Rowstron A, Druschel P (2001) Pastry: Scalable, distributed object location and routing for largescale peer-to-peer systems. IFIP/ACM international conference on distributed systems platforms (Middleware)
42. Roy CR, Kyasanur P, Gupta I (2006) Smart gossip: An adaptive gossip-based broadcasting service for sensor networks. In: Proceedings of the IEEE MASS
43. Schmitz C (2004) Self-organization of a small world by topic. In: Proceedings of the 1st international workshop on peer-to-peer knowledge management (P2PKM)
44. Segall B, Arnold D, Boot J, Henderson M, Phelps T (2000) Content based routing with elvin4. In: Proceedings of AUUG2K
45. Sripanidkulchai K, Maggs B, Zhang H (2003) Efficient content location using interest-based locality in peer-to-peer systems. In: Proceedings of IEEE Infocom, San Francisco, p 11
46. Stoica I, Morris R, Liben-Nowell D, Karger DR, Kaashoek MF, Dabek F, Balakrishnan H (2003) Chord: a scalable peer-to-peer lookup protocol for internet applications. IEEE/ACM Trans Netw 11(1):17–32, DOI 10.1109/TNET.2002.808407
47. Tempich C, Staab S, Wranik A (2004) Remindin: Semantic query routing in peer-to-peer networks based on social metaphors. In: Proceedings of the 13th World Wide Web conference (WWW2004), New York, USA, pp 640–649
48. Voulgaris S, Kermarrec AM, Massoulie L, van Steen M (2004) Exploiting semantic proximity in peer-to-peer content searching. In: Proceedings of the 10th IEEE international workshop on future trends in distributed computing systems (FTDCS 2004), Suzhou, China
49. Wokoma I, Sacks L, Marshall I (2002) Biologically inspired models for sensor network design. In: Proceedings of the London communications symposium 2002 (LCS 2002)
50. Zhao BY, Kubiatowicz JD, Joseph AD (2001) Tapestry: An infrastructure for fault-tolerant wide-area location and Tech. Rep., Berkeley, CA, USA

Chapter 11
Analysis and Visualization of Relations in eLearning

Pavla Dráždilová, Gamila Obadi, Kateřina Slaninová, Jan Martinovič, and Václav Snášel

Abstract The popularity of eLearning systems is growing rapidly; this growth is enabled by the consecutive development in Internet and multimedia technologies. Web-based education became wide spread in the past few years. Various types of learning management systems facilitate development of Web-based courses. Users of these courses form social networks through the different activities performed by them. This chapter focuses on searching the latent social networks in eLearning systems data. These data consist of students activity records wherein latent ties among actors are embedded. The social network studied in this chapter is represented by groups of students who have similar contacts and interact in similar social circles. Different methods of data clustering analysis can be applied to these groups, and the findings show the existence of latent ties among the group members. The second part of this chapter focuses on social network visualization. Graphical representation of social network can describe its structure very efficiently. It can enable social network analysts to determine the network degree of connectivity. Analysts can easily determine individuals with a small or large amount of relationships as well as the amount of independent groups in a given network. When applied to the field of eLearning, data visualization simplifies the process of monitoring the study activities of individuals or groups, as well as the planning of educational curriculum, the evaluation of study processes, etc.

11.1 Introduction

With the rapid development of new Internet and computer-based technologies, Web-based education, especially eLearning, became very popular in education. This is a form of computer-aided instruction that virtually does not depend on the need for a specific location or any special hardware platform [12]. eLearning systems,

P. Dráždilová, G. Obadi (✉), K. Slaninová, J. Martinovič, and V. Snášel
FEECS, Department of Computer Science, VŠB, Technical University of Ostrava, Ostrava, Czech Republic
e-mail: pavla.drazdilova@vsb.cz; gamila.ahmed.obadi.st@vsb.cz; slaninova@opf.slu.cz; jan.martinovic@vsb.cz; vaclav.snasel@vsb.cz

A. Abraham et al. (eds.), *Computational Social Network Analysis*, Computer Communications and Networks, DOI 10.1007/978-1-84882-229-0_11,
© Springer-Verlag London Limited 2010

also called learning management systems (LMS) or computer management systems (CMS) are used to provide maintenance of particular courses and facilitate communication between educators and students within the student community. Users of these courses are members of the social network with specific attributes resulting from the eLearning environment.

Networks stemming from real life are concerned with relations among real objects and have become a significant part of modern life. Important examples include links between Web pages, citations of references in scientific papers, power grids, social networks of relatives, or other connections between individuals in various environments, e.g., Web-based or eLearning systems. The word "network" is usually used for what mathematicians and some computer scientists call graphs [71]. A network (graph) is a set of items called vertices with connections between them (edges). The amount of data required to describe even small social networks can be quite large, which makes the analysis of these data collections very complicated. This process can be simplified by using some mathematical and graphical tools, which makes the study of the graph theory one of the fundamental pillars of discrete mathematics.

Users of LMS can be specified as members of a community, which has one target – achieving learning goals. This community (consisting of students) shares the typical characteristics of a social network. There is a set of people connected through information exchanged in an LMS environment. Hence, data mining techniques described in this chapter specialize in eLearning with relation to social networks and social network analyses.

The main problem, which researchers solve in data collection and data preprocessing, is the large amount of obtained data from LMS. The second part of this chapter is dedicated to data storage and data processing of large data collections, using selected techniques of matrix decomposition and other matrix processing, data clustering, and conceptualization and reduction of dimension in large matrices. In the next section, learning management system environment with relation to data mining techniques and other aspects is described.

Section 11.4 explicates recent work focused to social networks. Environment of Web-based (or on-line social) networks, which is comparable with majority environment of LMS, is described. Large-scale social networks and social networks are generally in permanent progress. Hence, we must regard the social networks with context of their evolution. Section 11.5 is dedicated to social network analysis (SNA), especially with relation to eLearning and the subsection is focused on the software used for SNA.

Results of social network analysis are often presented by visualization instruments used for comprehensible description of network structure and for visualization of relations between nodes (e.g., students and instructors in eLearning). This area is mentioned in Section 11.6.

In Section 11.7, our experiment provided on LMS Moodle data collections obtained from eLearning environment of Silesian University, Czech Republic, is presented. This case study is aimed to pattern retrieval of students behavior in educational process.

Modern applications, information systems and others including Web applications or LMS generate huge amounts of data collections. These data collections are sorted in various forms, from text-based data sources such as logs (pure text), through HTML, XML and other formats to semi-structured data sources such as multimedia sources (images, audio, or video files). These collections of data are maintained in databases, data warehouse, or simply in data or log files.

Log file analysis has been enjoying a growing attention in every area of human activities. This domain is very interesting both for research area and for software developers in the commercial sphere. There are various disciplines which are considered to analyze the data sources for achieving worthy information, often represented as knowledge. These information (or knowledge) is often used for management, maintenance, and improvement of systems being produced for these data sources, or for other purposes. Among others, we must mention disciplines like machine learning, data mining, knowledge discovery, and data warehouse, which were blended together and are generally derivated from the original discipline called data mining, which is well known in research area.

11.2   Data Mining

There are various definitions of data mining presented in the research area. In [30] Data mining is presented as the nontrivial extraction of implicit, previously unknown, and potentially useful information from data. Benoit [7] offers the definition of relative discipline knowledge discovery in databases (KDD), which he refers to as data mining: Data mining is a multistage process of extracting previously unanticipated knowledge from large databases, and applying the results to decision making. Data mining tools detect patterns from the data and infer associations and rules from them. The extracted information may then be applied to prediction or classification models by identifying relations within the data records or between databases. Those patterns and rules can then guide decision making and forecast the effects of those decisions. Principle of Data Mining [41] defines thus: Data mining is the analysis of (often large) observational data sets to find unsuspected relationships and summarize the data in novel ways that are both understandable and useful to the data owner.

Many researchers presented basic phases of data mining. Detailed description of particular phases is stated in [28]: learning the application domain, creating a target dataset, data cleaning and preprocessing, data reduction and projection, choosing the function of data mining, choosing the data mining algorithm(s), data mining, interpretation and using discovered knowledge. A more pregnant description of data mining phases is mentioned by Schuman [95]: Collection of data, Data preprocessing, Data analysis, Data visualization and Data interpretation. In the same paper, unified definition of data mining and novel interesting view to data mining phases with relation to chemical states of aggregation is proposed.

Common widely used data mining methods include classification, regression, clustering, summarization, dependency modeling, change and deviation detection proposed in [28]. Among the well-known classification algorithms we must mention Bayesian Classification, decision trees, neural network and backpropagation, k-nearest neighbor classifiers and genetic algorithms [21]. Clustering techniques include partitioning (often based on k-means algorithm) and hierarchical methods, grid, model and density-based methods [40] and others. Change and deviation detection, also called as sequential analysis and sequence discovery [21], is oriented to discovering the most significant changes in data sets or relationships based on time.

Data mining methods are applied in various domains such as software engineering, system management, Web analysis, information retrieval and others. There are many purposes for Data mining of data collections. Among others, we must mention domains such as crisis analysis, system maintenance and quality management (oriented to usability or power management), design of recommended systems (software development, Web applications, etc.), analysis of relations among users or inferring social networks or groups in various environments (Web searching, call systems, mailing, Web social networks, citation networks, health care and medical research, etc.).

The analysis of system data collections in commercial sphere is wide-spread. Information systems and software applications of various types become more complex and are obliged to cooperate with heterogeneous software and hardware components. The data mining and analysis is oriented to easier monitoring, management, and maintenance of such systems. In [82], automatic mining of system log files regarding new aspects of log data such as data complexity, short log messages, and temporal characteristics of log data are presented. There are proposed mining methods specialized in automated categorization of messages in system logs, to incorporate temporal information with visualization tools to evaluate interesting temporal patterns for system management.

Another field of data mining research is Web searching and information retrieval from the World Wide Web. The research is oriented to data mining of logs available from search engines for further recommendation of results or queries. Query recommendation of related queries for search engine users using past queries stored in large-scale Web access logs and Web page archives is presented in [80]. Method for weighted social networks construction based on information on the Web and search engines such as Google is described in [62]. Some search engines have integrated social bookmarking services, individual search history information, or statistics of search activities (e.g., Google [108], Google Trends [109], Yahoo Buzz, Ask IQ [104]).

Data mining research oriented to Web is very similar to Web-based systems used in majority of the LMS. Data mining techniques used for data processing in eLearning are presented in Section 11.3.

The main problem, which researchers solve during data collection from LMS is the huge amount of obtained data sets. In the next subsection, selected techniques suitable for data reduction, which can be used in the data preprocessing phase of data collections obtained from LMS, is presented.

11.2.1 Data Reduction

Experts agree that singular value decomposition (SVD) is one of the most important instruments used in linear algebra. Additional information relevant to SVD can be found in [25, 34]. Now we will provide a basic theorem with relevance to SVD.

Theorem (SVD) Any $m \times n$ matrix A, with $m \geq n$, may be factorized as

$$A = U \Sigma V^T, \tag{11.1}$$

where $U \in R^{m \times m}$ and $V \in R^{n \times n}$ are orthogonal, and $\Sigma \in R^{n \times n}$ is diagonal,

$$\Sigma = \text{diag}(\sigma_1, \sigma_2, \ldots, \sigma_n), \tag{11.2}$$

$$\sigma_1 \geq \sigma_2 \geq \cdots \geq \sigma_n \geq 0. \tag{11.3}$$

The columns U and V are called singular vectors and the diagonal elements σ_i singular values. The SVD appears in various other scientific fields under different names. In statistical and data analysis, the singular vectors are closely related to principal components, and in image processing the SVD goes by the name Karhunen-Loewe expansion. Let us consider the following notation for designating singular values: $\sigma_i(A) =$ the ith largest singular value of A.

SVD serves as a very useful tool when searching for the approximation matrix A using B with a lower rank. Informally, it can be stated that SVD enables us to reduce dimensions within which we solve problems. Another effect of this reduction is the elimination of static. Formally, these ideas may be formulated by the following statement:

Theorem Assume that matrix $A = R^{m \times n}$ has rank$(A) = r > k$. The matrix approximation problem

$$\min_{\text{rank}}(Z) = k |A - Z|_2 \tag{11.4}$$

has the solution

$$Z = A_k = U_k \Sigma_k V_k^T, \tag{11.5}$$

where $U_k = (u_1, \ldots u_k)$, $V_k = (v_1, \ldots, v_k)$, and $\Sigma = \text{diag}(\sigma_1, \sigma_2, \ldots, \sigma_k)$. The minimum is

$$|A - A_k|_2 = \sigma_{k+1}(A). \tag{11.6}$$

11.2.2 Cluster Analysis

Data mining methods generally used were presented in the previous part. In this chapter, there is not enough space to describe each of them. The subsection is dedicated to a widely used data mining technique called cluster analysis, which is a representative. This technique was used in the experiment presented in Section 11.7 of this chapter.

Cluster analysis is the process of separating objects, with the same or similar properties, into groups that are created based on specific issues. We will call these groups of objects *clusters* [48]. Clustering may be applied to objects in various research areas, mainly in text processing and working with documents in information retrieval (IR) systems. The term clustering can be in this sphere used for creating a thesaurus. In eLearning, we can think of students as objects. The similarity of students is set on the basis of their activities in the LMS system. Cluster analysis is in this subsection presented with relation to IR systems. However, base principles are conformable to eLearning systems.

Joining similar documents to a cluster may be done by increasing the speed level for searching in search engines. The reason for carrying out a cluster partitioning is explained in the *hypothesis about clusters* [49, 84]:

When documents are in close proximity, they are relevant to the same information.

The process that searches for the ideal cluster partitioning in sets of documents and within which there are mutually similar documents is called *clustering*. The cluster is then formed mutually by a set with similar documents.

In an ideal situation, the clustering procedure should accomplish two goals: correctness and effectivity [27, 84]. The criteria for correctness are as follows:

- Methods should remain stable, while collections grow, or, in other words, distribution into clusters should not drastically change the addition of new documents.
- Small errors in document descriptions should be carried over as small changes in cluster distributions into clusters.
- A method should not be dependent on its initial document ordering.

Conventional cluster distribution methods [9, 32, 49] are split into two categories:

Partitional methods – the goal is to employ a partition that best maintains clustering criteria.

Hierarchal methods – These methods are based on matrix similarities in documents. The goal of this method is to create a cluster hierarchy (tree cluster).

Sets of clustering algorithms being used and developed today are too large. A similar view can be found in publications such as [32, 49].

Due to the fact that most clustering methods work with mutual similarities between clusters, it is necessary to convey this similarity by using *cluster similarity partitioning coefficient*.

Let us have a twin cluster c_i a $c_j \in \{c_1, c_2, \ldots, c_l\}$, where l is the amount of all calculated clusters. Then, similarity coefficient $\text{sim}(c_i, c_j)$ fulfills these conditions:

$$\text{sim}(c_i, c_j) \geq 0 \tag{11.7}$$

$$\text{sim}(c_i, c_j) = \text{sim}(c_j, c_i) \tag{11.8}$$

$$\text{sim}(c_i, c_i) = \text{max}_{\text{sim}} \tag{11.9}$$

where max_{sim} is the maximum value of the similarity coefficient. Similarity between clusters is defined the same way as the similarity between two documents or between a document and a query.

11.2.2.1   Hierarchical Methods

These methods utilize the matrix similarity C, which can be described as follows for the document collection n :

$$C = \begin{pmatrix} \text{sim}_{11} & \text{sim}_{12} & \dots & \text{sim}_{1n} \\ \text{sim}_{21} & \text{sim}_{22} & \dots & \text{sim}_{2n} \\ \vdots & \vdots & \ddots & \vdots \\ \text{sim}_{n1} & sim_{n2} & \dots & \text{sim}_{nn} \end{pmatrix} \qquad (11.10)$$

where the ith row answers the ith document and the jth column answers the jth document.

A hierarchy of partitions for requisite documents is formed with these clustering methods. During calculations, a cluster surface is formed. Points are joined to the cluster on this surface.

Aglomerative hierarchal clustering methods mainly belong to the sequential agglomerative hierarchical no-overlapping (SAHN) method. It holds true that two clusters formed with this method do not contain the same object [20]. These methods differ in the way in which their similarity matrix is initially calculated (point 4 following Algorithm 11.1). These methods usually have $O(n^2)$ for memory space complexity and $O(n^3)$ for time complexity, where n is the number of data points. This conversion is derived from Lance–Williams' formula for matrix conversions [20]:

$$prox[t, (p,q)] = \alpha_p \, prox[t, p] + \alpha_q \, prox[t, q]$$
$$+ \beta \, prox[p, q] + \gamma \, |prox[t, p] - prox[t, q]| \qquad (11.11)$$

where $prox[t, (p,q)]$ determines the cluster similarity c_t and cluster $c_{(pq)}$ is formed by clusters c_p joined with cluster c_q. Value parameters α_p, α_q, β a γ define various cluster SAHN methods. We list some of these methods in the Table 11.1. The Algorithm 11.1 describes calculations for hierarchal agglomerative clustering. In the following paragraphs, N_i is the amount of documents in a cluster c_i.

Algorithm 11.1 Hierarchal agglomerative clustering

---

1. We form a document similarity matrix.
2. When clustering begins, each document represents one cluster. In other words, we have as many clusters as we have documents. Gradually, as each individual cluster is joined, clusters dwindle away until we are left with one cluster.
3. We locate the two most similar clusters p a q and identify this similarity as $prox_s[p, q]$.
4. We reduce the amount of joined clusters p and q. We identify the new cluster as t (replaces row and column q) and recalculates the similarity ($prox_s[t, r]$) of the newly formed cluster t to other clusters r. Further, we identify $prox_l[p, q]$ as the similarity to which p a q clusters have been joined. This similarity is equal to $prox_s[p, q]$ in most methods. Then we delete the row and column corresponding to cluster p from the similarity matrix.
5. We repeat the previous two steps until only one cluster remains.

Table 11.1 SAHN matrix similarity conversion methods

SAHN method	α_p	α_q	β	γ
Single link	$\dfrac{1}{2}$	$\dfrac{1}{2}$	0	$-\dfrac{1}{2}$
Complete link	$\dfrac{1}{2}$	$\dfrac{1}{2}$	0	$\dfrac{1}{2}$
Centroid method	$\dfrac{N_p}{N_p + N_q}$	$\dfrac{N_q}{N_p + N_q}$	$\dfrac{-N_p\,N_q}{(N_p + N_q)^2}$	0
Ward's method	$\dfrac{N_p + N_t}{N_p + N_q + N_t}$	$\dfrac{N_q + N_t}{N_p + N_q + N_t}$	$\dfrac{-N_t}{N_p + N_q + N_t}$	0
Median method	$\dfrac{1}{2}$	$\dfrac{1}{2}$	$-\dfrac{1}{4}$	0

The results of the aforementioned algorithm differ in accordance with the similarity matrix conversion method used. Today, other specialized hierarchical clustering methods exist. Thanks to these new methods, we can reduce time and memory complexity and work with large document collections more effectively. Some of these new methods include [32]: SLINK, Single-link algorithm based on minimum spanning tree, CLINK, BIRCH, CURE, etc.

With the increasing importance of visualization methods being used in cluster analysis, a wide range of these methods has been created. Some of these methods include [32]: Sammon's mapping, MDS, SOM, class-preserving projections, parallel coordinates, methods for visualized categorical data, distance base mapping, FastMap, etc.

Tree maps [32] present a visualized tree structure created by a hierarchal cluster. We take the defined rectangular space and recursively share it based on the tree's structure. Its main advantage is that it can be use for large amounts of nodes (in this situation we cannot use a dendogram).

11.3 Learning Management Systems

eLearning is a method of education that utilizes a wide spectrum of technologies, mainly Internet or computer-based technology, in the learning process. Learning management systems (LMS) – also called course management systems (CMS) or Virtual learning environment (VLE) systems – provide effective maintenance of particular courses and facilitate communication between educators and students and within the student community. These systems usually support the distribution of study materials to students; content building of courses, preparation of quizzes and assignments, discussions, and distance management of classes. In addition, these systems provide a number of collaborative learning tools such as forums, chats, news, file storage, etc.

Unlike conventional face-to-face education methods, computer and Web-based education environments provide storage of large amounts of accessible information. These systems record all the information about students' actions and interactions onto log files or databases. Within these records, data about students learning habits can be found including favored reading materials, note taking styles, tests and quizzes, ways of carrying out various tasks, communicating with other students in virtual classes using chat, forum, etc. Other common data, such as personal information about students and educators (user profiles), student results and user interaction data, are also available in the systems' databases.

This collected data is essential for analyzing students' behavior and can be very useful in providing feedback both to students and educators. For students, this can be achieved through various recommended systems and through course adaptation based on student learning behavior. For teachers, some benefits would include the ability to evaluate the courses and the learning materials, as well as to detect the typical learning behaviors.

Regardless of its benefits, the huge amount of information generated by learning management systems makes it too difficult to manage these data collections and to extract useful information from them. To overcome this problem, some LMS offer basic reporting tools, but with such large amounts of information, the outputs become quite obscure and unclear. In addition, they do not provide specific information of student activities while evaluating the structure and contents of the course and its effectiveness for the learning process [130]. The most effective solution to this problem is to use data mining techniques.

11.3.1 Data Mining and eLearning

Data mining is a multidisciplinary area. It uses several methods to build analytic models that discover interesting patterns and tendencies from obtained data collections. The eLearning data mining process consists of the same phases as found in the general data mining processes [88]:

- Data collection – LMS produce a large amount of information about student activities and interaction during the learning process. These data collections are stored using databases or log files.
- Data preprocessing – Data collections are cleaned and transformed into an appropriate format to be used in the data mining application phase.
- Data mining application – Usage of data mining techniques and algorithms to obtain the required information, data summaries of discovered knowledge and visualizations of mined information or data models in relation to the requirements of users (instructors, students, system administrators).

- Data interpretation and result implementation – Data mining results are interpreted and used by educators or students to improve student learning processes (LMS).

The application of data mining in eLearning is an iterative cycle [87]. This thought is based on the fact that creating an eLearning entails a complicated and demanding process. The course developer (teacher or instructor) must design a course structure and its components in a way that ensures suitability of a given course's character while fulfilling student study requirements and providing different means for communication during lessons. Based on data obtained from LMS, student activity during the term may be monitored. At the end of a term, study results and course effectivity may be evaluated and any necessary improvements may be made. Data mining results are often applied for adapting courses to user profiles and study assessments. Another area of applying data mining techniques involves the collaborative learning process, in which students create a community for sharing information about criteria for completing courses successfully [18].

The classification of data mining techniques and computational intelligence methods is well known and has been mentioned in several publications [2, 15, 89].

11.4 Social Networks

Social networking is a complex, large and expanding sector of the information economy. Researchers' interest in this field is growing rapidly. It has been studied extensively since the beginning of the twentieth century. The first normative contributions in this area were proposed in the 1940s by sociologist Mark Granovetter and mathematician Freeman. The basic theory "The Strength of Weak Ties" was mentioned in 1973 [37]. Granovetter argued that within a social network, weak ties are more powerful than strong ties. Another significant principle was published in 1979 by Linton C. Freeman [31]. In his work he presented the definition of centrality, which is one node's relationship to other nodes in the network. He defined basic metrics such as degree, control, and independence, from which reason researchers proceed in their present works.

Social network researchers have acquired data for their studies using various methods. In the past, these studies were only based on questionnaire data, which typically reached some hundreds of individuals [123]. In the late 1990s, new technologies such as Internet and cellular phones enabled researchers to construct large-scale networks using emails [24], phone records [78] or Web search engines [61].

Social network is a set of people or groups of people with similar pattern of contacts or interactions such as friendship, co-working, or information exchange [33]. The World Wide Web, citation networks, human activity on the Internet (email exchange, consumer behavior in e-commerce), physical and biochemical networks are some examples of social networks. Social networks are usually represented by using graphs, where nodes represent individuals or groups and lines represent contacts among them. The configuration of relations among network members identifies a specific network structure, and this structure can vary from isolated structures where no members are connected, to saturated structures in which everyone is interconnected.

Social network analysis was defined by Barry Wellman as "social network analysts work at describing underlying patterns of social structure, explaining the impact of such patterns on behavior and attitudes" [56, 126]. Therefore, researchers are not only interested in describing the different social structures, but also emphasize on investigating the consequences of this variation on the member's behavior.

11.4.1 Recent Work

Social network analysis can be very useful and applicable in many spheres. Among others in the commercial sphere viral marketing is used to explore relations between existing and potential customers for increasing sales of products and services; social network analysis is used in biology and medical diagnostics for application of viral prevention; in law enforcement, knowledge of social networks can be useful in criminal investigation concerning organized crimes (terrorism, money laundering, drugs, etc.). With the increasing amount of people using mobile phones, the point of research view also turned to this domain. For example, information of social network obtained from call logs is presented in [83]. In this work, an end-to-end system for inferring social networks based on call logs using kernel-based naive Bayesian learning is proposed.

With the growing information medium – Internet and World Wide Web as well as – online advertising markets and other Web services such as online recommendation systems and online auction markets in e-business sphere are developed. In e-commerce, Web adaptation on the basis of users' behavior or online supply of goods and services coming out from previous purchases is used on the basis of log analysis, Webs and social networks.

Recently many researchers focused on analyzing the growth of social communities on the Web and Internet world. We can observe the occurrence and great expansion of various social bookmarking systems based on recommendation and sharing of various types of information like URLs (del.icio.us [106]), multimedia files – photos, videos, etc. (Flickr [107], YouTube [117]), music, blogs, etc. (MySpace [114], LiveJournal [112], citation Webs). The structure behind these social systems (called folksonomies) can be represented as a collection of users, tags and resource nodes. These collections of data can be viewed using graphs or visualization software and can be analyzed with orientation to structural properties to show the growth and exploration of social networks.

11.4.2 Online Social Networks

Environment of LMS is usually built on the basis of Web and Internet technologies. Hence, social networks found in this environment have similar characteristics and behavior such as common social network in World Wide Web. Members in this network can use conformable components for communication (blogs, forums, chats), create conformable on-line communities and have similar characteristics as Web social networks.

Web mining techniques used for online social network analysis are similar to other mining techniques. There are many traditional techniques used such as classification, clustering, association rule mining, etc. For data interpretation and analysis of results, visualization techniques such as graphs are usually used. Web mining techniques can be divided (according to the analysis target) to Web content mining (text data and natural language processing, analysis focuses on other multimedia sources, semantic Web, group analysis), Web structure mining oriented to the structure of Web sites (implementation of crawlers, deep-Web research) and Web usage mining which focuses on how Web sites are used (clickstream data analysis, navigation behavior, recommendation systems).

Many researchers focus on identifying and analyzing community structures in networks growing from Web users. Analysis of topological characteristics of the tripartite hyper graph of queries, users and bookmarks on a large snapshot of del.icio.us Web site and on query logs of two large search engines is described in [59]. The extensive analysis of characteristics of large online social network MySpace was published in [16]. Study was oriented to the socialibility of users based on relationship, messaging, and group participation, on the demographic characteristics of users with an emphasis on correlation with their privacy references, and on text analysis with an intention to construct language models used by MySpace users. In [63], researchers analyzed 70 large sparse real-world networks and defined network community profile plot which characterizes the "best" profile community. They compare and contrast several methods to approximately optimize metric, based on conductance measure.

Another study [17] is oriented to the analysis of social networks in relation to similarity and social ties. Authors developed techniques for identifying and modeling interactions between social influence and selection and consider the relative value of similarity and social influence in modeling the future behavior of social network. The problem of defining proximity measure between groups (communities) in online social networks is presented in [91]. This measure is used in recommendation systems for helping the users in selecting the groups of their interest.

11.4.3 Evolution of Social Networks

Structure analysis of social networks provide large amount of worthy information about interactions between nodes (users) in the network. Understanding the evolution of obtained network can serve more additional information of network behavior in progress. These findings can help to protect such networks from various attacks or can contribute in research of data distribution throughout the network. Several models of network evolution were proposed. In [60], analysis of large social Web networks like Flickr and Yahoo is presented. Authors analyzed the network evolution, and defined three types of network components on the basis of their activity – singletons, giant components and middle region. Approaches to link prediction of new interactions among members in a social network based on measures for analyzing the proximity of nodes was developed in [65]. Theoretical model which explains the evolution of communities in social networks where new friends are formed by looking at friends of friends was published in [38]. Group analysis of information in large social networks like Live Journal in relation to its growth and evolution is mentioned in [6], DBLP database is studied in [13]. Authors published that network cannot be analyzed independently, but need to be studied in the context of other networks.

11.4.4 Sequential Pattern Mining

Discovering social networks from event logs was mostly used in the business sphere in business information systems like ERP systems, CRM systems, B2B systems, call center applications, and others as well, e.g., hospital information systems or reviewing systems record transactions and other information in a systematic way. Recently this research area became significant in education as well.

LMS produce large amount of information maintained in databases or recorded to log files. Information in these data collections consist of various types of information. Besides typical information like event, type of event, device, or time when event was performed, we can find the information of the person, who initiated the event (activity). Using this information, we can obtain social network on the basis of similar attributes of persons and, in consequence, we can construct models that explain some aspects of behavior.

Many researchers were oriented to this sphere. Sequential pattern mining is used to evaluate a learner's progress in [128]. Generation of personalized activities for different groups of learners is presented in [121]. Identification of interaction sequences for suggesting questionable or successful patterns is proposed in [53]. Analysis of student's individual sessions is presented in [81] and the definition of learning period and searching for session patterns and time series are also described.

11.5 Social Network Analysis

Social network is the set of relationships among members of a team. To understand the dynamics of team structure and performances, social network analysis is used as an excellent tool to capture the underlying interaction processes within teams. This process is associated with some group characteristics such as centrality, cohesion and conflict.

Many of the approaches to understand the structure of a network emphasize on how dense connections are built-up from simpler dyads and triads to more extended dense clusters such as cliques. This view of social structure focuses on how solidarity and connection of large social structures can be built up out of small and tight components. Divisions of actors into groups and sub-structures can be a very important aspect of social structure. It can be important in understanding the behavior of the whole network [120].

Central to the theoretical and methodological agenda of network analysis is identifying, measuring and testing hypotheses about the structural forms and substantive contents of relations among actors. The central objectives of network analysis are to measure and represent these structural relations accurately, and to explain both why they occur and what their consequences are. The scientific objectives in social network analysis are generally to understand the processes that determine the topology, or structure, of the network, and to understand the extent and mechanisms behind any interpersonal effects within the network.

11.5.1 Patterns Mining

Substructure boosting methods, [93, 102], have been applied to various domains. With this algorithm, a pattern mining algorithm is called upon over and over again to form a feature space. In the first calling, patterns with high relevancy are collected. In ensuing callings, more focus is placed in identifying irrelevancy. This method results in less useless cases when compared to mine-at-once methods [76]. Experiments have proven that gPLS is more efficient than gBOOST. gBoost cannot be entirely replaced, however, due to the flexibility factor.

Several significant applications, i.e., network traffic monitoring, research citation network analysis, social network analysis, and regulatory networks in genes, can act as models for large sparse graphs. SVD and CUR are reliable methods for uncovering hidden variables and relevant patterns in high dimensional data. A new method, compact matrix decomposition (CMD), has been introduced, however, to compute sparse, low-rank approximations, while saving both cost and space, and to compensate for the fact that these methods often do not take the sparse property of graphs into consideration. CMD has been proven more efficient than SVD and CUR in many cases as it is 10× faster while requiring 1/10 of the space of its predecessors. CMD is also useful for detecting anomalies and monitoring time-evolving graphs, where worm-like, hierarchical, scanning patterns can be detected.

11.5.2 Measures in Social Network Analysis

A primary use of graph theory in social network analysis is to identify the important or prominent actors at both the individual and group levels of analysis. Centrality and prestige concepts and measures seek to quantify graph theoretic ideas about an actor's prominence within a complete network by summarizing the structural relations among all nodes. Centrality is when a prominent actor has high involvement in many relations, regardless of whether sending or receiving ties. Prestige is when a prominent actor initiates few relations but receives many directed ties. Knoke and Yang defined the above-mentioned terms in [56].

For the destiny of actor degree centrality,applications of the matrix algebra notation are required. Unlike actor degree centrality, group degree centralization measures the extent to which the actors in a social network differ from one another and the extent to which the actors in a social network differ from one another in their individual degree centralities.

Actor closeness centrality was developed to reflect how near a node is to the other nodes in a social network [90]. Closeness and distance refer to how quickly an actor can interact with others, for example, by communicating directly or through very few intermediaries. An actor's closeness centrality is a function of its geodesic distance (length of the shortest path connecting a two nodes) to all other nodes.

In [77], existing methods on calculating exact values and approximate values of closeness centrality is combined and new algorithms presented to rank the top-k vertices with the highest closeness centrality.

Betweenness concept of centrality concerns how other actors control or mediate the relations between two nodes that are not directly connected. Actor betweenness centrality measures the extent to which other actors lie on the geodesic path between pairs of actors in the network.

In [5], a faster algorithm is presented for betweenness centrality focused on large, yet very sparse networks. The algorithms is based on a new accumulation technique that integrates well with traversal algorithms solving the single-source shortest-paths problem, and thus exploiting the sparsity of typical instances.

Prestige is defined as the extent to which a social actor in a network "receives" or "serves as the object" of relations sent by others in the network. The sender-receiver or source-target distinction strongly emphasizes inequalities in control over resources, as well as authority and deference accompanying such inequalities [55].

And for centrality in egocentric networks with g alters is defined ego i's actor degree centrality as the maximum possible value of actor degree centrality, g-1.

One measure in networks is the global clustering coefficient. The local clustering coefficient of a vertex in a graph is based on ego's network density or local density. Duncan J. Watts and Steven Strogatz introduced the measure in 1998. And the global clustering coefficient is concerned with the density of triplets of nodes in a network. A triplet can be defined as three nodes that are connected by either two (open triplet) or three (closed triplet) ties. A triangle consists of three closed triplets, each centered on one node. The global clustering coefficient is defined as the number of closed triplets over the total number of triplets. In [79], a generalization of this coefficient that retains the information encoded in the weights of ties is proposed.

To understand networks and their participants, we provide the location of actors in the network. Measuring the network location is finding the centrality of a node.

These measures determine the various roles and groupings in a network, which are the connectors, specialists, leaders, bridges, isolates, where are the clusters and who is in them, who is in the core of the network, and who is on the periphery.

11.5.3 eTutors

In eLearning systems instructors/tutors/mentors undertake a vital teaching role that differs from that of a traditional classroom teacher. It is frequently asserted that the use of tutors is a major factor in achieving high student satisfaction, and low drop-out rates. Online tutors support e-learners through different roles [8, 69], these roles can be classified as:

- Pedagogical roles: tutors support the learning process itself by providing instructions, stimulating questions, examples, feedback, motivation, etc. to the learners.
- Managerial roles: The managerial role requires the tutor to perform basic course administration, track student progress and data, etc.
- Social roles: the tutor's social role includes the efforts to establish a friendly and comfortable environment and a community that stimulates learning.
- Technical roles: the technical role requires the tutor to acquaint the students and himself or herself with the ICT that is used for eLearning, and also to provide some technical support to the students.

To be successful in all the required roles, an online tutor has to possess certain skills. Thomas made a 4P checklist according to which a good online tutor should be: positive, proactive, patient and persistent (in [96]). Many authors emphasize the need for tutors to be experts in the field they are tutoring. Tutors should also have highly developed online communication skills, be ICT literate and familiar with the eLearning technology and have a positive attitude toward students and learning [96].

One of eLearning systems' purposes is to encourage knowledge sharing so that valuable knowledge embedded in the network can be effectively explored. Most of the learners participate in this type of education with the expectations that they can acquire and share valuable knowledge to fulfill their needs.

Wachter et al. pointed out that an enhanced learning environment is possible only if one goes beyond online course delivery and creates a community of learners and other related resource groups [118, 119]. Wasko and Faraj found that knowledge sharing has been a motivation for participation in virtual communities [118, 122].

In collaborative learning the students are engaged in an open-ended effort to advance their collective understanding. They are encouraged to rely on each other as sources of information and assistance. In addition, interactions among the students facilitate learning directly by encouraging them to explain the subject matter to each other and revealing in a constructive way the inconsistencies and limitations in their knowledge. This participation that takes place in a meaningful social context enables a group of students to acquire the skills of the eTutor and play his roles when he or she is not available. However, in some eLearning systems, it is difficult to achieve efficient and effective knowledge sharing due to the following two barriers: (1) the difficulty in finding quality knowledge and (2) the difficulty in finding trustworthy learning collaborators to interact with.

An important difference between user-generated content and traditional content is the variance in the quality of the content. In social media the distribution of quality has high variance from very high-quality items to low-quality; this makes the tasks of filtering and ranking in such systems more complex than in other domains. In that case, models of credibility, which are used extensively on search engine research and information retrieval, can be used in order to evaluate the trustworthiness of the students' knowledge.

Several graph theoretic models of credibility rely strongly on the consideration of the indegree of the node (the sum of the incoming arcs of a node in a directed graph) so as to extract importance and trustworthiness. However, there are social activities (e.g., collaborative authoring) that derive much of their credibility by their productions (e.g., authorship). In that case, the in-degree cannot provide input to evaluate the importance of that entity and therefore an alternative evaluation is needed, which has to consider the outputs of the entity (productions) [57].

PageRank and HITS were the pioneering approaches that introduced link analysis ranking, in which hyperlink structures are used to determine the relative authority of a Web page. PageRank assumes that a node transfers its PageRank values evenly to all the nodes it connects to. A node has a high rank if the sum of the ranks of its in-links is high. This covers both the case where a node has many in-links and that where a node has a few highly ranked in-links. This can be clarified by the following example given in c [11, 129]. If B is able to answer A's questions, and C is able to answer B's questions, then C should receive a high authority score, since he or she is able to answer the questions of someone who himself or herself has some expertise. PageRank provides interesting results when the interactions between users are around one specific subject only. The study in [129] illustrates this by using a PageRank-like algorithm called ExpertiseRank on data from the Java forum, in which the interactions between users are exclusively about Java programming.

The fundamental assumption of HITS is that in a graph there are special nodes that act as hubs. Hubs contain collections of links to authorities (nodes that contain good information). A good hub is a node that points to good authorities, while a good authority is a node pointed to by good hubs [54]. So, askers can act as hubs and best answerers can act as authorities. HITS associates two scores to each node: a hub score and an authority score.

11.5.4 Software for Social Network Analysis

This part reviews some well-known software for the analysis of social networks. Some software were developed for network visualization, and now contain analysis procedures (NetDraw, [10]).

Table 11.2 Software for
Social Network Analysis

Program	Characteristic
InFlow	Network mapping
NetDraw	Visualization
NetMiner	Visual analysis
Pajek	Large data visualization
StOCNET	Statistical analysis
UCINET	Comprehensive

The choice of social network analysis routines is based on the categorization of methods given by [124] (Table 11.2):

- Structure and location: centrality [26] and cohesive subgroups (cliques)
- Roles and positions: structural equivalence, blockmodeling [19], eigendecompositions
- Dyadic and triadic methods
- Statistical methods: exponential random graph models [125], QAP correlation, statistical analysis of network evolution [97]

11.6 Visualization of Social Networks

Creating visual images of networks can serve important heuristic purpose; visual images are powerful complements to quantitative analyses. Network images supplement statistical analyses and allow the identification of groups of people for targeting, the identification of central and peripheral individuals, and the clarification of the macro-structure of the network.

All graphs and also social networks can be represented as node-link graphs or as adjacency matrices. While graphs present visualizations of social networks, matrices use mathematical algebraic representations of network relations. Both this methods have their advantages and disadvantages. Graphs provide better visual illustrations of network structures but do not support mathematical manipulations. On the other hand, matrices are less user-friendly, but they facilitate sophisticated mathematical and computer analyses of social network data.

Networks can be arranged on a map to represent the geographic distribution of a population. Alternatively, algorithmically generated layouts have useful spatial properties: a force-directed layout can be quite effective for spatially grouping connected communities, while a radial layout intuitively portrays network distances from a central actor. Color, size, and shape have been used to encode both topological and non-topological properties such as centrality, categorization, and gender. In recent years, such approaches have been effectively used in the analysis of domains such as e-mail communication [29], early online social networks [3], and co-authorship networks in scientific publications [72]. There are a number of systems for generating social network visualizations and performing statistical analyses for the purpose of sociological research, such as UCINet [103], JUNG [111], GUESS [4] and NetMiner [113].

11.6.1 Node-Link Diagram or Matrix Representation of Network

The majority of network visualization systems use the node-link representation. This representation is well suited to show sparse networks, but social networks are known to be globally sparse and locally dense. Therefore, social network visualization faces a major challenge, obtaining a readable representation for both the overall sparse structure of social network and its dense communities.

One possibility of hybrid visualization is MatLink [45], an enhanced matrixbased graph visualization that overlays a linear node-link diagram on the edges and adds dynamic feedback of relationship between nodes.

The other possibility is NodeTrix [44]. This representation integrates the best of two traditional network representations: node-link diagrams and adjacency matrix-based representations. The strength of this representation for analyzing social networks is in combining the familiarity of node-link diagrams to understand the global structure of the network with the readability of matrices for detailed community analysis.

11.6.2 Clustered Graph Representation

Clustered graph representations reduce the visual complexity of graphs by grouping nodes, and are well suited to social networks as they highlight important structures, like communities and central actors linking them. Authors of MatLink and Node-Trix used NodeTrix for representation of clusters as visual adjacency matrices – each node is placed as a column and row in matrix, and links between nodes are marked in the matrix. They improved the readability of clustered social networks using duplication of nodes [43].

Social analysts often need to adjust the level of clustering. Eades et al. proposed several solutions to draw clustered graphs [22], eventually showing several levels of clustering at the same time [23].

The other possibility to visualize clustered graph (hierarchical structures), is Treemap [116]. It is very effective in showing attributes of leaf nodes using size and color coding. Treemap enables users to compare nodes and sub-trees even at varying depth in the tree, and help them spot patterns and exceptions.

11.6.3 Software for Visualization

The function of the software for social network visualization makes complicated types of analysis and data handling transparent, intuitive, and more readily accessible. We can visualize a whole system or subsystem to explore the architecture to apply visual data mining, visual analytics techniques for defect discovery or manually discover anomalies.

Software for visualization:

- Node-Link representation: Graphviz [110], Guess [4], Igraph [105], InFlow [115], Pajek [75], Ucinet [103], Vizster [46]
- Hybrid: MatLink [45], NodeTrix [44]
- Clusters (blockmodeling): Treemap [116]

11.7 Experimental Design

The main objective of this experiment is to analyze a data set obtained from the log files of the Moodle learning management system used at Silesian University and extract social network communities from it. These data were used to construct a number of weighted graphs , which represented the structure and relationship among students. Students were considered as vertices in the graph; while the relations between students were used as the weighted edges.

A group of students in a Moodle system course creates vertices in a social network. The relationship among students investigated in this chapter is not defined on the basis of their acquaintance or similar interests. In contrast to common social networks, this relationship is defined using the different study activities performed by students. When two students perform the same (or sufficiently similar) activities in the system, we can determine the relation between them. This relation is represented by edges assigned to each set of students. The main objective of this work is to define the relationship among Moodle students in terms of their activities, and to analyze the structure of different intensity levels of this relationship.

11.7.1 Definitions

First, a definition for the activity sequences for each student in relation to each subject was given.

Definition 11.1. Student activity is the activity in the Moodle system which includes a "resource view" (reading study materials), "forum view" (and other forum activities), "choice view" (questionnaires), "quiz attempt", etc.

Each student is assigned an activity sequence based on his or her activities in the Moodle system.

Table 11.3 Information about tested collection from Moodle system

	Input records	Students	Analyzed records
Microeconomy	63745	303	63541
Computer science	50216	286	49839
English	63064	250	62838

Definition 11.2. The type of activity is an activity sequence divided into a 30 min time period (In our experiments, 30 min time periods have been proven to be the most effective).

To define student similarity, the oversized activity sequence was reduced to smaller sets of student activity.

Furthermore, data correction was implemented; students who executed only one activity were removed from the set. This type of activity misrepresented the intensity of a relationship; many of these students log into the Moodle system only once and do not pursue their study. In contrast to full-time studies, in this type of education, there is a larger number of students who do not finish their studies (for various reasons connected with this type of education). For example, the number of eLearning students who did not register for the next term (after the term being analyzed) was 83 out of 285 from the first year (they did not complete their studies).

A number of activity types were obtained which were executed in the Moodle system (see Table 11.3) for each student. This can be represented as the matrix A (students X activity types). Matrix S (students X students), created from matrix A, defines student relationships using similar activity types. The similarity of activity types is defined by the Cosine measure [92]. The similarity between two vectors of activity types is defined by the angle which is formed by these vectors.

11.7.2   Division of a Students Group into Subgroups

In our previous article [67], a number of graphs were obtained, these graphs describe the entire group of students and depict the relationships among all students in one course. In this experiment this group will be divided into subgroups using the agglomerative hierarchical clustering method. And these subgroups will be analyzed to measure the similarity of study behavior among their members.

11.7.3   Experiment Results

The graphs represent the findings of the English course analysis.

Figure 11.1 shows a graph of all students relationships in one course.

Figure 11.2 represents a tree map (see [32]) with clusters of students. This tree map was generated on the $level = 0.6$. The numbers in the squares represent the number of students in each cluster.

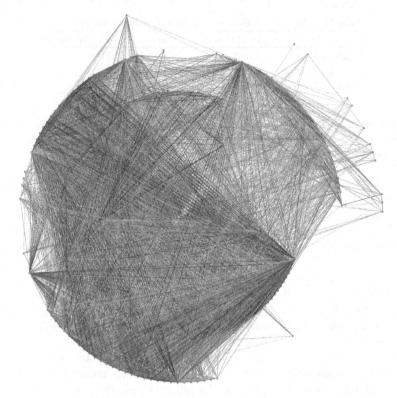

Fig. 11.1 Graph of all students

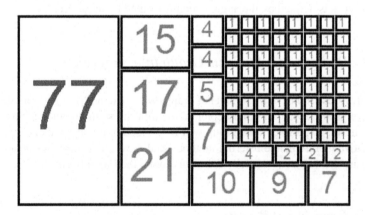

Fig. 11.2 A tree map with clusters of students

Figure 11.3 depicts a cluster with 17 students having various edge weights (presented by their grayscale).

Figure 11.4 describes another cluster, having 10 students and a smaller number of edges.

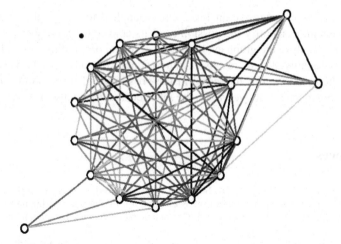

Fig. 11.3   A cluster with 17 students

Fig. 11.4   A cluster with
10 students

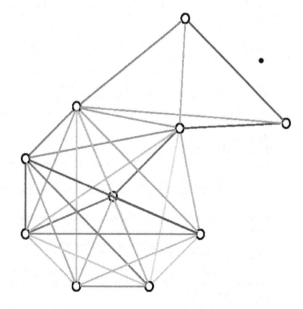

11.8   Conclusion

The result of the agglomerative hierarchical clustering method is a set of subgroups.
All students in one subgroup are somewhat similar.

The graph representation of the relationship between students shows that at the
specific level of relation intensity we can find clusters of students with similar activity types. They can be represented as the behavior models of study activities in the
Moodle system.

In the future, an intensive analysis will be applied to the graphs obtained by this experiment, to identify the possibility of its connection with social networks. We intend to analyze the graph evolution and compare our findings with eLearning information (quality of study results, recommendation of study models in eLearning, etc.). Furthermore, we are interested in the possibility of using similar behavior models in other spheres as well as on the Internet, and especially in search engines.

References

1. van der Aalst WMP, Reijers HA, Song M (2005) Discovering social networks from event logs. Computer Supported Cooperative Work (CSCW), 14. Springer, Berlin, pp 549–593
2. Abonyi J, Balasz F, Abraham A (2005) Computational intelligence in data mining. Informatica 29:3–12
3. Adamic LA, Buyukkokten O, Adar E (2003) A social network caught in the Web. First Monday 8(6)
4. Adar E, Kim M (2007) SoftGUESS: Visualization and exploration of code clones in context. In: Proceedings of the 29th international conference on software engineering (ICSE'07), pp 762–766
5. Brandes U (2001) A faster algorithm for betweenness centrality. J Math Sociol 25:163–177
6. Backstrom L, Huttenlocher D, Kleinberg J, Lan X (2006) Group formation in large social networks: Membership, growth, and evolution. In: Proceedings of the 12th ACM SIGKDD international conference on knowledge discovery and data Mining. ACM, Philadelphia, PA, pp 44–54
7. Benoit G (2002) Data Mining. In: Chronin B (ed) Annual review of information science and technology, vol 36. American Society for Information Science and Technology, Silver Spring, pp 265–310
8. Berge ZL (1995) Facilitating computer conferencing: Recommendations from the field. Educ Technol 35(1):22–30
9. Berkhin P (2006) A survey of clustering data mining techniques. Group multidimensional data, pp 25–71
10. Borgatti SP. NetDraw 1.0: Network visualization software, Version 1.0.0.21. Analytic Technologies, Harvard
11. Bouguessa M, Dumoulin B, Wang S (2008) Identifying authoritative actors in question-answering forums: The case of Yahoo! answers. KDD 2008, pp 866–874
12. Brusilovsky P (2003) Adaptive and intelligent Web-based educational systems. Int J Artif Intel Educ 13:159–169
13. Cai D, Shao Z, He X, Yan X, Han J (2005) Mining hidden community in heterogeneous social networks. In: Proceedings of the 3rd international workshop on link discovery. ACM, Chicago, IL, pp 58–65
14. Carrington PJ, Scott J, Wasserman S (2005) Models and methods in social network analysis. Cambridge university press, pp 57–62
15. Castro F, Vellido A, Nebot A, Mugica F (2007) Applying data mining techniques to e-learning problems. Stud Comput Intel (SCI) 62:183–221
16. Caverlee J, Webb S (2008) A large-scale study of myspace: Observations and implications for online social networks. Association for the advancement of artificial intelligence
17. Crandall D, et al. (2008) Feedback effects between similarity and social influence in online communities. KDD 2008, pp 160–168
18. Daradoumis T, Martines-Mones A, Xhafa F (2006) A layered framework for evaluating online collaborative learning interactions. Int J Hum Comput Stud 64:622–635

19. Doreian P, Batagelj V, Ferligoj A (2004) Positional analysis of sociomatric data. In: Carrington PJ, Scott J, Wasserman S (eds) Models and methods in social network analysis. Cambridge University Press, Cmabridge, pp 77–97
20. Downs GM, Barnard JM (2003) Reviews in computational chemistry, vol 18. Wiley-VCH
21. Dunham MH (2002) Data mining introductory and advanced topics. Pearson Education, Upper Saddle River, NJ
22. Eades P, Feng Q-W, Lin S (1997) Straight-line drawing algorithms for hierarchical graphs and clustered graphs. In: Proceedings of the syposium on graph drawing 96. Springer,London, UK, pp 113–128
23. Eades P, Feng Q-W (1996) Multilevel visualization of clustered graphs. In: Proceedings of the syposium on graph drawing. Springer, Berlin, Germany, pp 101–112
24. Eckmann J-P, Moses E, Sergi D (2004) Entropy of dialogues creates coherent structures in e-mail traffic. Proc Natl Acad Sci USA 101:14333–14337
25. Elden L (2007) Matrix methods in data mining and pattern recognition. SIAM
26. Everett MG, Borgatti SP (2004) Extending centrality. In: Carrington PJ, Scott J, Wasserman S (eds) Models and methods in social network analysis. Cambridge University Press, Cmabridge, pp 57–76
27. Faloutsos C (1995) Fast searching by content in multimedia databases. IEEE Data Eng Bull 18(4):31–40
28. Fayyad UM, et al. (1996) From data mining to knowledge discovery in databases. AI Mag 17(3):37–54
29. Fisher D, Dourish P (2004) Social and temporal structures in everyday collaboration. Vienna, Austria, pp 551–558
30. Frawley W, Piatetsky-Shapiro G, Matheus C (1992) Knowledge discovery in databases: An overview. AI Mag 213–228
31. Freeman LC (1979) Centrality in social networks: Conceptual clarification. Soc Networks 1:215–239
32. Gan G, Ma C, Wu J (2007) Data clustering: Theory, algorithms, and applications ASA-SIAM series on statistics and applied probability. SIAM, MAY
33. Garton L, Haythornthwaite C, Wellman B (1997) Studying online social networks. J Comput Mediat Commun 3(1)
34. Golub GH, van Loan CF (1996) Matrix computation. The John Hopkins University Press
35. Ghoniem M, Fekete JD, Castagliola P (2005) On the readability of graphs using node-link and matrix-based representations: A controlled experiment and statistical analysis. Info Vis 4(2):114–135
36. Granovetter M (1992) Decesion making: Alternatives to rational choice models economic action and social structure: The problem of embeddedness. SAGE, Newbury Park, CA pp 3304–33
37. Granovetter MS (1973) The strength of weak ties. Am J Psychol 78(6):1360–1380
38. Gollapudi S, Kenthapadi K, Panigrahy R (2008) Threshold phenomena in the evolution of communities in social networks. 17th International World Wide Web conference (WWW2008), Workshop on social web search and mining (swsM2008)
39. Guimerà R, Danon L, Díaz-Guilera A, Giralt F, Arenas A (2003) Self-similar community structure in a network of human interactions. Phys Rev 68:065103
40. Han J, Kamber M (2001) Data mining: Concepts and techniques (Morgan-Kaufman series of data management systems). Academic Press, San Diego
41. Hand DJ, Mannila H, Smyth P (2001) Principles of data mining (adaptive computation and machine learning). MIT
42. Hanneman RA, Riddle M (2005) Introduction to social network methods. Published in digital form at http://faculty.ucr.edu/ hanneman/
43. Henry N, Bezerianos A, Fekete J-D (2008) Improving the readability of clustered social networks using node duplication. IEEE Trans Vis Comput Graph 14(6):1317–1324
44. Henry N, Fekete J-D, McGuffin MJ (2007) NodeTrix: A hybrid visualization of social networks. IEEE Trans Vis Comp Graph 13(6):1302–1309

45. Henry N, Fekete J-D (2007) MatLink: Enhanced matrix visualization for analyzing social networks. In: Proceedings of the international conference interact
46. Heer J, Boyd D (2005) Vizster: Visualizing online social networks. In: Proceedings of the IEEE symposium on information visualization
47. Indyk P Stable distributions, pseudorandom generators, embeddings and data stream computation. JACM 53:307–323
48. Jain AK, Dubes RC (1988) Algorithms for clustering data. Prentice-Hall, Upper Saddle River, NJ
49. Jain AK, Murty MN, Flynn PJ (1999) Data clustering: A review. ACM Comput Surv 31(3):264–323
50. Johnson SC (1967) Hierarchical Clustering Schemes. Psychometrika 32:241–254
51. Jolliffe I (2002) Principal component analysis. Springer
52. Juan AA, Daradoumis T, Faulin J, Xhafa F (2008) Developing an information system for monitoring student's activity in online collaborative learning. International conference on complex, Inteligent and software intensive systems, pp 270–275
53. Kay J, Maisonneuve N, Yacef K, Zaiane OR (1999) Mining patterns of events in Students' teamwork data. Educational data mining workshop, Taiwan, pp 1–8
54. Kleinberg JM (1999) Authoritative sources in a hyperlinked environment. J ACM 46(5): 604–632
55. Knoke D, Burt RS (1983) Prominence. In Burt RS, Minor MJ (eds) Sage Publications, pp 195–222
56. Knoke D, Yang S (2008) Social network analysis. Sage Publications
57. Korfiatis N, Poulos M, Bokos G (2006) Evaluating authoritative sources using social networks: An insight from Wikipedia. Online Info Rev 30(3):252–262
58. Kossinets G, Kleinberg J, Watts D (2008) The structure of information pathways in a social communication network. KDD '08: Proceeding of the 14th ACM SIGKDD international conference on knowledge discovery and data mining, pp 435–443
59. Krause B, et al. (2008) Logsonomy – Social informatik Retrieval with Logdata. In: Proceedings of the 19th ACM conference on hypertext and hypermedia. Pittsburgh, PA, pp 157–166
60. Kumar R, Novak J, Tomkins A (2006) Structure and evolution of online social networks. Proceedings of the 12th ACM SIGKDD international conference on knowledge discovery and data mining. ACM, Philadelphia, PA, pp 611–617
61. Lee SH, Kim P-J, Ahn Y-Y, Jeong H (2008) Googling social interactions: Web search engine based social network construction. arXiv, 0710.3268v1
62. Lee SH, et al. (2007) Googling social interactions: Web search engine based social network construction. E-print, arXiv:0710.3268v1
63. Leskovec J, et al. (2008) Statistical properties of community structure in large social and information networks. WWW 2008, Beijing, China, pp 695–704
64. Leskovec J, Lang K, Dasgupta A, Mahoney M (2008) Community structure in real graphs: The "negative dimensionality" paradox. International World Wide Web conference
65. Liben-Nowell D, Kleinberg J (2007) The link prediction problem for social networks. J Am Soc Info Sci Technol (Wiley Periodicals) 58(7):1019–1031
66. Liljeros F, Edling CR, Amaral LA, Stanley HD, Aberg Y (2001) The web of human sexual contacts. Nature 411:907–908
67. Martinovic J, Drazdilova P, Slaninova K, Snasel V (2008) Relation analysis in elearning. Comput Info Syst Ind Manage Appl CISIM '08. 7th, pp 133–138
68. McGlohon M, Akoglu L, Faloutsos CH (2008) Weighted graphs and disconnected components: Patterns and a generator. KDD '08. In: Proceeding of the 14th ACM SIGKDD international conference on knowledge discovery and data mining, pp 524–532
69. McPherson M, Nunes MB (2004) The role of tutors as an integral part of online learning support. Eur J Open Dist Learn
70. Newman MEJ (2003) Fast algorithm for detecting community structure in networks. Phys Rev E 69
71. Newman MEJ (2003) The structure and function of complex networks, SIAM Rev 45: 167–256

72. Newman MEJ (2004) Co-authorship networks and patterns of scientific collaboration. Proc Natl Acad Sci USA 101:5200–5205
73. Newman MEJ, Girwan M (2004) Finding and evaluating community structure in networks. Phys Rev E 69
74. Newman MEJ, Balthrop J, Forrest S, Williamson MM (2004) Technological networks and the spread of computer viruses. Science 304:527–529
75. de Nooy W, Mrvar A, Batagelj V (2005) Exploratory social network analysis with Pajek. Structural analysis in the social sciences. Cambridge University Press
76. Nowozin S, Tsuda K, Kudo T, Bakir G (2007) Weighted substructure mining for image analysis. In: IEEE computer society conference on computer vision and patern recognition, pp 1–8
77. Okamoto K, Chen W, Li X (2008) Ranking of closeness centrality for large-scale social networks. Frontiers in algorithmics. Springer, Heidelberg, pp 186–195
78. Onnela J-P, Saramaki J, Hyvonen J, Szabo G, de Menezes AM, Kaski K, Barabasi A-L, Kertesz J (2007) Analysis of large-scale weighted network of one-to-one human communication. New J Phys 9
79. Opsahl T, Panzarasaa P (2009) Clustering in weighted networks. Soc Networks 31(2): 155–163
80. Otsuka LL, Kitsuregawa SM (2008) Query recommendation using large-scale web access logs and web page archive. In: Proceedings of the 19th international conference on database and expert system applications. Springer, Berlin/Heidelberg, pp 134–141
81. Pahl C, Donnelan C (2003) Data mining technology for the evaluation of web-based teaching and learning systems. In: Procceedings of the congress e-learning, Montreal, Canada
82. Peng W, Li T, Ma S (2005) Mining logs files for data-driven system management. ACM SIGKDD Explor Newslett 7(1) (June 2005). ACM, NY, pp 44–51
83. Phithakkitnukoon S, Dantu R (2008) Inferring social groups using call logs in on the move to meaningful Internet systems. OTM 2008 Workshops, LNCS 5333. Springer, Berlin/Heidelberg, pp 200–210
84. Pokorný J, Snášel V, Kopecký M (2005) Dokumentografické informační systémy. Vydavatelství Karolinum Praha, MFF UK Praha
85. Radicchi F, Castellano C, Cecconi F, Loreto V, Parisi D (2004) Defining and identifying communities in networks. Proc Natl Acad Sci USA
86. Ravasz E, Barabasi A-L (2003) Hierarchical organization in complex networks. Phys Rev E 67
87. Romero C, Ventura S (2006) Data mining in e-learning. Southampton. Wit Press, UK
88. Romero C, Ventura S, Garcia E (2007) Data mining in course management systems: Moodle case study and tutorial. Comput Educ
89. Rutkowski L (2008) Computational intelligence. Springer
90. Sabidussi G (1966) The centrality index of a graph. Psychometrika (Springer) 31(4):581–603
91. Saha B, Getoor L (2008) Group proximity for recommending groups in online social networks. SNA-KDD
92. Salton G, Buckley C (1988) Term-weighting approaches in automatic text retrieval. Info Proces Manage 513–523
93. Saigo H, Kadowadi T, Tsuda K (2006) A linear programming approach for molecular QSAR analysis. In: International workshop on mining and learning with graphs, pp 85–96
94. Saigo H, Kramer N, Tsuda K (2008) Partial least squares regression for graph mining, 14th ACM SIGKDD international conference on knowledge discovery and data mining, pp 578–586
95. Schommer CH (2008) An unified definition of data mining. arXiv:0809.2696v1
96. Shepherd C (2002) In search of the perfect e-tutor
97. Snijders TAB (2004) Models for longitudinal network data. In: Carrington PJ, Scott J, Wasserman S (eds) Models and methods in social network analysis. Cambridge University Press, Cmabridge, pp 215–247
98. Sun J, Xie Y, Zhang H, Faloutsos CH (2007) Less is more: Compact matrix decomposition for large sparse graphs. SIAM

99. Ting I-H (2008) Web mining techniques for on-line social networks analysis. Serv Syst Serv Manage 1–5
100. Tsuda K, Kudo T (2006) Clustering graphs by weighted substructure mining. 23rd international conference on machine learning, pp 953–960
101. Tsuda K, Kurihara K (2008) Graph mining with variational dirichlet process mixture models. In: SIAM conference on data mining, pp 432–442
102. Tsudo K, Maeda E, Matsumoto Y (2005) An application of boosting to graph classification. Adv Neural Info Proces Syst 17:729–736
103. URL: http://www.analytictech.com (04-12-2009)
104. URL: http://sp.ask.com/en/docs/iq/iq.shtml (04-12-2009)
105. URL: http://cneurocvs.rmki.kfki.hu/igraph (04-12-2009)
106. URL: http://delicious.com (04-12-2009)
107. URL: http://www.flickr.com (04-12-2009)
108. URL: http://www.google.com (04-12-2009)
109. URL: http://www.google.com/trends (04-12-2009)
110. URL: http://www.graphviz.org (04-12-2009)
111. URL: http://jung.sourceforge.net (04-12-2009)
112. URL: http://www.livejournal.com (04-12-2009)
113. URL: http://www.netminer.com (04-12-2009)
114. URL: http://www.myspace.com (04-12-2009)
115. URL: http://www.orgnet.com (04-12-2009)
116. URL: http://www.cs.umd.edu/hcil/treemap (04-12-2009)
117. URL: http://www.youtube.com (04-12-2009)
118. Yang SJH, Chen IYL, Kinshuk N-S (2007) Enhancing the quality of e-learning in virtual learning communities by finding quality learning content and trustworthy collaborators. Educ Technol Soc 10(2):84–95
119. Wachter RM, Gupta JND, Quaddus MA (2000) It takes a village: Virtual communities in supporting of education. Int J Info Manag 20(6):473–489
120. Wakita K, Tsurumi T (2007) Finding community structure in mega-scale social networks. arXiv, cs/0702048v1
121. Wang W, Weng J, Su J, Tseng S (2004) Learning portfolio analysis and mining in SCORM compliant environment. In: Proceedings of ASEE/IEEE frontiers in education conference, Savannah, Georgia, pp 17–24
122. Wasko MM, Faraj S (2005) Why should I share? Examining social capital and knowledge contribution in electronic networks of practice. MIS Quart 29(1):35–57
123. Wasserman S, Faust K (1994) Social network analysis: Methods and applications structural analysis in the social sciences. Cambridge University Press, Cambridge
124. Wasserman S, Faus K (1994) Social network analysis: Methods and applications. Cambridge University Press, Cambridge
125. Wasserman S, Robins G (2004) An introduction to random graphs, dependence graphs, and p^*. In: Carrington PJ, Scott J, Wasserman S (eds) Models and methods in social network analysis. Cambridge University Press, Cambridge, pp 148–161
126. Wellman B (1999) From little boxes to loosely bounded networks : The privatization and domestication of community. In: Abu Lughod JL (ed) Sociology for the twenty-first century. University of Chicago Press, pp 94–114
127. Wills GJ (1999) NicheWorks – Interactive visualization of very large graphs. J Comput Graph Statist pp 190–212
128. Zaiane O, Luo J (2001) Web usage mining for a better web-based learning environment. In: Procceedings of conference of advanced technology for education, Banff, Alberta, pp 60–64
129. Zhang J, Ackerman MS, Adamic L (2007) Expertise networks in online communities: Structure and algorithms. In: Proceedings of the 16th ACM international World Wide Web conference (WWW'07), pp 221–230
130. Zorilla ME, Menasalvas E, Marin D, Mora E, Segovia J. (2005) Web usage mining project for improving web-based learning sites. In: Web mining workshop, Cataluna, pp 1–22

Chapter 12
Interdisciplinary Matchmaking: Choosing Collaborators by Skill, Acquaintance and Trust

Albert Hupa, Krzysztof Rzadca, Adam Wierzbicki, and Anwitaman Datta

Abstract Social networks are commonly used to enhance recommender systems. Most of such systems recommend a single resource or a person. However, complex problems or projects usually require a team of experts that must work together on a solution. Team recommendation is much more challenging, mostly because of the complex interpersonal relations between members. This chapter presents fundamental concepts on how to score a team based on members' social context and their suitability for a particular project. We represent the social context of an individual as a three-dimensional social network (3DSN) composed of a knowledge dimension expressing skills, a trust dimension and an acquaintance dimension. Dimensions of a 3DSN are used to mathematically formalize the criteria for prediction of the team's performance. We use these criteria to formulate the team recommendation problem as a multi-criteria optimization problem. We demonstrate our approach on empirical data crawled from two web2.0 sites: onephoto.net and a social networking site. We construct 3DSNs and analyze properties of team's performance criteria.

12.1 Introduction

Human knowledge grows faster than it ever had. As the total volume of available knowledge definitely exceeds the capacity of any human being, it is necessary to represent knowledge in an abstract, but persistent way. There are many successful ways in which knowledge can be represented, stored and accessed, starting from the

A. Hupa
Institute of Applied Social Sciences, University of Warsaw, Warsaw, Poland
e-mail: albert.hupa@gmail.com

K. Rzadca and A. Datta
School of Computer Engineering, Nanyang Technological University, Singapore
e-mail: krz@ntu.edu.sg

A. Wierzbicki
Polish-Japanese Institute of Information Technology, Warsaw, Poland
e-mail: adamw@pjwstk.edu.pl

A. Abraham et al. (eds.), *Computational Social Network Analysis*, Computer
Communications and Networks, DOI 10.1007/978-1-84882-229-0_12,
© Springer-Verlag London Limited 2010

invention of writing through ancient libraries, then print, up to modern databases, wiki pages and search engines. However, there are many situations in which learning from these repositories and then applying the knowledge are impossible. For instance, the task may be too vast for one person. Or, mastering one of the skills needed for the task requires a university degree and many years of industrial experience. In many similar situations, the oldest version of knowledge passing – asking another human being for help – is indispensable.

However, with flexible, team- and project-oriented organization of the enterprises, our social environment also grows faster than it ever had. While we are usually aware what is the field of expertise of our friends and colleagues, knowing what their friends do is more difficult. Even if we know the skill we are looking for, it is thus hard to find an expert.

Social matching is the process of recommending an individual (an expert) to another individual (the seeker) based on seeker's criteria [60]. Social matching (or social recommender) software becomes popular especially in the context of large corporations, that employ tens or hundreds of thousands of experts [21]. The goal of such software is to assist in finding an expert, facilitate introduction, and sometimes help in interaction. Such systems need explicit information both on social ties linking the employees and on their domain of expertise. In order to get these information, social recommender systems typically analyze mailboxes, chat logs, documents and other products and by-products of employees.

The goal of our research is to build a social recommender system for independent professionals, such as programmers, system administrators, graphic designers, marketing specialists and tradesmen. These people have deep knowledge about their own domain. However, the projects they undertake usually require collaboration of experts from many different fields. For instance, in order to prepare and run a large web service, one needs many different professionals, including graphic artists, interaction designers, programmers, system administrators and web marketing experts. The goal of our system is, given a project, to find an appropriate group of people to realize it.

The purpose of this chapter is to review the relevant related work on social recommender systems and propose the architecture of our system. We start by reviewing related work on social recommender systems in Section 12.2.1. Most of these systems focus on the task of seeking an expert in the context of an enterprise. Such solutions are then compared to the general issue of teams in social networks in Section 12.2.2 and trust in Section 12.2.4. We point out the lack of a framework that allows to recommend teams of people, and not single individuals.

We base the general architecture for team recommendation on social network analysis (SNA). A social network is a graph that represents social relationships between individuals or other entities existing in the social world. Evolution of this concept has led to a multilevel analysis allowing to consider different kinds of relations at the same time. Our solution is focused on three social dimensions represented as different levels of relational analysis: acquaintance, trust and knowledge. In Section 12.3, we outline and define 3DSN, a graph representing relations between individuals, knowledge and tasks.

Framework of 3DSN allows not only to perceive teams as mere aggregations of individuals but also as entities possessing different traits depending on their composition in relation to potential tasks. These characteristics can be based on standard measures one can find in social network analysis but also can be inferred from the purpose of team recommendation. In Section 12.4, we propose measures of different aspects of the quality of a team: acquaintance, trust and knowledge. The idea of acquaintance is embedded in the classical approach to SNA and therefore draws from the idea of closeness – but is adjusted to teams instead of individuals. The measure of trust comes from [35, 46] that demonstrates the importance of dependency trust for cooperation of individuals in organizations and teams. Knowledge is perceived from the perspective of both social networks and semantic networks which are combined by multi-mode networks allowing for the comparison of people, tasks and related skills.

Section 12.5 presents possible application of these quality predictors on empirical data coming from online social networking sites.

The system described in this chapter is an early proposal for a team recommendation system. Certainly, there are a few important features that have to be considered in our future work. First, we do not explicitly consider limited availability of certain people during certain time periods, or other constraints, like geographic closeness. Second, the system has a static view of the social interactions. In future, our system has to continuously "learn" the social and knowledge environment of the users – either by querying the user; or, if the user does not explicitly define his or her social ties, by mining them, given the users' interaction patterns (such as emails or chat logs) with other people.

12.2 Related Work: Concepts, Approaches and Techniques for Team Recommendation

12.2.1 Recommendation Systems

The main task of a recommender system is to help an individual in the process of making a choice by reducing and ranking the set of items from which the choice is made. There are various recommender systems for recommending, e.g., books in an online bookstore or movies. Social matching systems (or social recommender systems) essentially recommend people to people. Typically, such systems are used in (possibly on-line) dating agencies, such as match.com. There are important differences between a general recommender system and a social matching system. See [60] for an excellent survey that underlines the fact that a social recommender should not only find appropriate people, but also profile people in an appropriate way, facilitate introduction (for instance, by providing the chain of referral), interaction and feedback. There are also some important issues, such as ensuring privacy of users, at the same time having fairly complete information in the system.

Most similar approaches to our context are *social recommender systems for information needs* that, given a topic of interest, match an individual with an expert on that topic, that is, moreover, socially close to the individual. ReferralWeb [38] creates a social network by analyzing what names appeared in documents returned by queries about an individual to a generic search engine. The domain area of each individual is mined similarly, though no details are provided.

Expertise recommender [47] is an enterprise-oriented social recommender system. It profiles each individual in an organization by analyzing his or her work products and by-products. For instance, in collaborative software development, if an individual has a problem with a certain source file, a simple heuristics, called the *history rule*, states that the last person who edited this file should be queried first. In another usage scenario, when an individual faces a problem, the system tries to find a person who dealt with the similar problems in the past (this heuristics is called the *tech support heuristics*). Having obtained a list of competent persons by similar heuristics, the system selects the expert whom the individual should ask by simple filters (like working in the same department or being close in the social network).

SmallBlue [21] describes a similar system for enterprise-oriented expert seeking that infers the complete social network from the individuals' email and chat logs. To preserve privacy, the system relies on aggregated and inferred information. Expertise is inferred from users' email and chat logs. Shami et al. [57] provide a systematic analysis of how people interact with SmallBlue. The main conclusion is that people prefer friends-of-friends to complete strangers and that the information about the shared friend is important.

Keim [39] proposes a decision support system for a human resource department that recommends candidates for a given job description. The system works by matching CVs with job descriptions and by mining candidates' job preferences. The system also considers descriptive and predictive trust. Descriptive trust models historic trust, assessed, e.g, during previous encounters with the candidate. Predictive trust infers the possible trust levels by propagating trust between common trusted friends.

12.2.2 Social Networks

Our approach to team recommendation uses the notion of a *social network* extensively. This section provides basic notions and definitions (see [49] for a more complete text).

A social network is a graph that models social interactions between individuals from a certain population. *Individuals* (also called *agents* or *actors*) are modelled by nodes in such a graph. Certain types of *interactions* or relations between individuals form *edges*.

The semantics of modeled relations or concepts may add further restrictions on the graph. For instance, a graph can be either undirected or directed. Some relations may assign weights to edges, representing the strength of the relation.

It is usually hard to construct a complete social network for the whole population because of the limited amount of information any agent has. An *ego network* is a localized view of the network from the perspective of one agent, called the *ego*. More formally, an *ego network* is defined as a network composed of a focal actor, termed the *ego*, a set of *alters* who have ties to ego and a set of relations among the ego and the alters [65, p. 42]. We assume that an ego network consists of all the alters being either directly connected to an ego or having at most one intermediate alter (*friend-of-friend* relationship).

12.2.3 Theories of Team Recommendation

Recommendation systems make use of different theoretical approaches to their engines but most of them are based on the notion of graphs [60, p. 417]. However, graphs are used differently – for instance, one can take all the relations in a given network or only some selected ones. The choice depends on social and/or psychological theories or mathematical approaches to problem optimization.

On one hand, social network analysis has designed intrinsic theories easily applicable to the issue of recommendation which in general can be grasped by the concept of social capital, grounded in the relation of acquaintance. Some of these concepts are tacitly assumed by managers or IT specialists. On the other hand, individuals can also be compared in terms of other relations, such as trust, whose role is often underestimated in the issue of recommendation. We argue that using trust improves understanding of matching individuals. Moreover, we also explicitly consider expertise knowledge of individuals.

12.2.3.1 Social Capital

According to classic theories of capital, the social capital is an effect of inequality between social classes. A group possessing the means of production accumulates capital by exploiting groups not possessing the means of production. In effect, the possessing group is able to invest the capital in further means of production [45]. Subsequent theories have not focused on the class division and tried to grasp the potential capital accessible across the whole society. Lin [41] suggested to call these approaches neocapital theories, because they still perceive social capital as a surplus value and represent an investment with expected returns, but refrain from focusing on social stratification and assigning purely monetary value to it.

Social capital is thus perceived as assets or resources for the performance in society, and can be approached from many perspectives. Among various kinds of social capital, human capital, i.e., accumulation of a surplus value of a labourer, such as education, certificates and experience, is invested in view of prospective incomes [34, 56]. The human capital reflects individuals' capabilities in potential cooperation. The identification of human capital is thus crucial in matching individuals to groups in which experts in certain areas of expertise are demanded.

Capital can also be perceived from a cultural point of view, where it represents investments on the part of the dominant class in reproducing a set of symbols and meanings, which are misrecognized and internalized by the dominated class as their own [9]. This approach focuses on the differentiation between classes (unlike all other modern theories) and is not useful in the context of social matching. However, other cultural approaches exist which introduce the notion of social capital. Among them Robert Putnam and Francis Fukuyama [26,51,52] identify capital as an investment in civic values and norms aiming at maintaining the society as a whole.

Apart from human and cultural capital, along with the development of social network analysis, another interpretation of social capital evolved, focusing on social relations (see also [7]). This interpretation identifies contacts maintained by individuals or groups as assets in their social performance. According to a static description, this social capital can be described as the sum of the resources, actual or virtual, that accrue to an individual or a group by the fact of possessing a durable network of more or less institutionalised relationships of mutual acquaintances and recognition [8, p. 119]. According to a dynamical description, this social capital is the investment in social relations by individuals through which they gain access to embedded resources to enhance expected returns of instrumental or expressive actions [41]. Regardless of the assumption, whether social capital can be perceived as the scope of potential resources or an action (process) aiming at getting access to these resources, both these perspectives reveal the possibility of accessing the resources.

The network resources are understood as both human resources embedded in the network (i.e., possessed by acquaintances) and network resources resulting from particular location in the network of acquaintances.

One of the most important divisions in the theories of social capital distinguishes social capital as a quality of a group [51] and as a quality of an individual [11]. The first approach focuses on the internal condition of the group, both the capital embedded in the structure of a group and the structure itself conditioning the flux of capital between members, while the second looks at the external capability of the individual to access, use and control the resources embedded in the personal network.

12.2.3.2 Individual Social Capital

Individual social capital can be perceived as an external capability of an individual to access, use and control resources embedded in the personal network. It measures the potential effectiveness of an individual in prospective collaboration project.

The measure of social capital understood as an ego's access to resources embedded in the network should include three factors: the amount and heterogeneity of resources of ego's alters and efficiency in contacts leading to these resources.

The following measures may be successfully applied to egonetworks with distance up to 3 from the ego (the focal point). Basic measures of individual social capital include the following:

Size/Degree The degree of a node, or the number of alters that an ego is directly connected to, possibly weighted by strength of tie. The relation to social capital is positive. The more alters ego has relationships with, the greater the chance that one of them has the resource ego needs. Level of analysis: directed or undirected graphs [10].

Clustering Coefficient/Density Clustering coefficient represents the proportion of pairs of alters that are connected. Its relation to social capital is negative. If all alters are tied to each other, they are redundant, and the contact's redundancy is negatively correlated with ego's social capital. Level of analysis: undirected graphs [10].

Weak Ties The number of weak ties ego possesses. A weak tie is a weighted edge with weight relatively smaller than edges representing contacts maintained on a regular basis. Granovetter, who researched the flow of information, discovered that the weak ties enable reaching populations and audiences that are not accessible via strong ties. For egos with larger number of weak ties, it is easier to access novel information. Level of analysis: weighted graphs [28, 31].

Closeness The total distance from a node to all other nodes in the network. Its relation to social capital is negative: the greater the distance (thus the smaller the closeness centrality) to other nodes, the less the chance of receiving information in a timely way. Level of analysis: undirected or directed graphs [25].

Betweenness The number of times that ego falls along the shortest path between two other actors. Its relation to social capital is positive: actors with high betweenness link together actors who are otherwise unconnected, creating opportunities for exploitation of information and control benefits [11].

Eigenvector Eigenvector of the largest possible eigenvalue of a measure of centrality expresses the extent to which ego is connected to alters who have high eigenvector centrality. Its relation to social capital is positive. An actor has high eigenvector score when he is connected to other well-connected actors. Level of analysis: undirected graphs [4]. Bonacich [5] also suggests a measure of eigenvector centrality which takes into account positive and negative links, which may be useful in the account of trust network.

Network Heterogeneity The variety of alters with respect to relevant dimensions (e.g., sex, age, race, occupation, talents). Its relation to social capital is positive (except when it conflicts with compositional quality) [10]. Level of analysis: nodes' attributes.

Knowledge Heterogeneity Measure directly connected with network heterogeneity, but aimed at measurement of the knowledge embedded in alters connected with ego. Its relation to social capital is positive. The more the various knowledge alters possesses, the more ego is valuable for cooperation [55]. Its measurement depends on the construction of knowledge network.

Structural Equivalence Structurally equivalent contacts posses the same sources of information and therefore provide redundant information benefits. In a network, the social capital is higher if there are few structurally equivalent contacts. Burt argues that structurally diverse networks (low in cohesion and redundancy) are good predictors of performance [12, p. 35]. Structural equivalence of two actors can be measured as the Euclidean distance of their contact vectors. Euclidean distance measures the square root of the sum of squared distances between two contact vectors, or the degree to which contacts are connected to the same people [2].

Network Constraint Measure resembling centrality measure, but constructed to count the extent to which an ego is embedded in a network [11, 51ff]. The higher the network constraint, the denser the network and more redundant is the information flow. According to research conducted by Burt and others, network constraint is negatively correlated with team performance, TQM team achievement, job promotion, job compensation and the level of production outputs [12].

Effective Size Describes the number of alters, weighted by strength of the tie minus a "redundancy" factor [11, p. 51]. This measure is positively correlated with ego's performance in accessing the information. That is, the more different regions of the network an ego has tie with, the greater the potential information and control benefits. The information access, timing, and referrals ego gets through alter are redundant to the extent of its substantial investment of time and energy in a relationship with alters.

Bandwidth Understood as diversity of information flows within ties. While it is positive for the social capital, if the total number of topics communicated across the entire network is large, some researchers argue that individual communication channels with alters should be low in bandwidth. While in other papers there are presented ideas on measuring bandwidth, it is essential to build such a measure according to the construction of a particular communication network [2].

12.2.3.3 Group Social Capital

Group social capital may consider both the internal and the external structure of the group's network. Internal structure corresponds to the members of a team and their efficient relations. External structure also considers the environment in which the group works.

Internal group social capital measures are not as efficient as measures for individuals. They focus on team performance, and they are well suited for maintaining a group, not its creation.

Some common measures of the social capital of a group include the following:

Density Density is the proportion of pairs of alters that are connected. According to [13], density within a group should be large, and endorse quick and efficient access to information, creation of common norms and sanctions resulting in higher efficiency. Others [12] argue that high density is negatively correlated with group efficiency or endorses personal conflicts [33]. That is why Burt suggests that internal group networks should possess *effective size* and feature small *network constraint* [11]. Effective size of a group, controlled by the position of a manager, is positively correlated with team performance [11]. Cummings [16] confirms this results, but also points that hierarchical structure is negatively correlated with the team performance.

External Contacts External contacts should supply necessary resources, thus they should be heterogeneous. Burt [11] argues that a team possessing homogeneous contacts narrows its perspectives and resources. Cummings [15] also confirms that a group may take full advantage of external knowledge when possessing diverse structure of contacts with managers, business units and assignment. Hansen [31] adds that these external contacts should be weak.

Average or Maximum Distance The average (or maximum) graph-theoretic distance between all pairs of members is negatively correlated with groups' social capital. Smaller distances mean faster communication among members, which is considered as an asset [33].

Centralization/Core-Periphery Structure The extent to which the network is not divided into cliques that have few connections between groups is positively correlated with social capital. Controlling for density, core-periphery structures are easier to coordinate than clustered networks [6, 25].

Bandwidth This measure is positively correlated with information flow within a group and endorses creativity [2].

Homophily The extent to which members of the group have their closest ties to members who are similar to themselves is negatively correlated with social capital (similarly to network heterogeneity). Smaller homophily should result in greater exposure to a wider range of ideas [43].

12.2.4 Teams and Trust

Teamwork often requires collaboration, not just co-action of team members. This observation implies that team members often need to depend on their colleagues, when the results of their own work will also depend on the efforts of others. This dependence is the source of uncertainty, and trust is used by humans to cope with such uncertainty. McAllister and Jones and George argue that the required level of interpersonal cooperation in teamwork requires a high level of trust among the team members, thus noting that trust is a factor that cannot be neglected when composing teams [35, 46].

   Dependency trust can be defined as *the subjective, context-dependent extent to which the trustor is willing to depend on the trustee in a situation of uncertainty.* This definition is an adaptation of dependency trust definitions proposed by [36] and [44]. The trust theory of [19] also supports this definition. A similar definition has been used in sociology [58, 59]: trust has been defined there as the attitude that allows the trustor to accept a bet on the trustee's behavior. Accepting such a bet would mean a willingness to depend on the trustee.

Dependency trust is a definition of human trust, which is a mental state of humans. In many kinds of IT systems, computational trust is used to support various forms of human collaboration. Examples of such systems are Web2.0 services such as epinions.com, a website for sharing opinions on products, or YouTube, enabling to share and to recommend films. Computational trust can be thought of as a *subjective, context-dependent rating of individuals based on the dependency trust of the trustor*. In some trust management systems, computational trust is replaced by reputation, when users evaluate the past behavior of others, instead of rating other users directly. Computational trust is expressed in various forms: on a discrete scale; or on a continuous scale from 0 to 1. In this chapter, we assume that computational trust can be transformed to the interval [0, 1], where the value of 0 indicates a lack of trust, while the value of 1 indicates full trust. Many authors support this simplification of computational trust modeling [1, 54].

Trust is inherently subjective, and is therefore usually modeled as a relation. A related concept is that of *trustworthiness*, which is a property of a person, rather than of a relation between two persons. Trustworthiness is more difficult to assess in practice, as all information that can be used to establish trust in a stranger is usually that received from other persons and is therefore relational in nature.

12.2.5 Knowledge

12.2.5.1 Knowledge in Social Sciences

Knowledge can be perceived as an objective pool of information (*top-down approach*) or as human-dependent (*constructivist approach*). In social sciences, knowledge is perceived as derived from information (and its structure) but is bound to belief and commitment leading to action [50]. Data are the basic building blocks, but knowledge conveys the meaningful application of the information, thereby enhancing decision making [18], that is – a *skill*.

Knowledge is not a given relation between concepts independent from its users or applications, but a process of sharing understanding that emerge through social interaction – sharing constructions of reality [40]. Knowledge is always context dependent and cannot be separated from its carriers; thus, it can be defined as subjective and valuable information with additional properties [17] – there is no one objective knowledge. *Knowledge resource* is a combination of a skill matched with an individual knowing how to apply it.

12.2.5.2 Knowledge Representation

A great deal of research in computer science and information Systems is devoted to knowledge representation. There are various solutions for knowledge representation, such as natural languages, data bases, mathematical logic, rough sets or neural networks. In the remainder of the review, we will, however, concentrate on the most "popular" forms of knowledge representation: ontologies and folksonomies.

An ontology is an explicit specification of a conceptualization [29] of a certain domain. An ontology is composed of a set of *objects* and *relations* between these objects. Both objects and relations are usually expressed using a controlled vocabulary. A relation provides an additional way to express semantics of objects. Common relations include "isA" (e.g., "laptop isA computer") and "isPartOf" (e.g., "keyboard isPartOf laptop"). Ontologies are expressed in an ontology description language, such as OWL or KIF [27]. Formally, an ontology is a statement of logical theory [29]. Consequently, it is a complex problem to design an ontology for a domain, involving both domain and logic experts. Note that hierarchies can be ontologies, but ontologies are not restricted to hierarchies.

A folksonomy is a result of associating tags to object in a shared environment [64]. A *tag* is an effort of an individual to label or categorise a given object. Folksonomy emerges when these individuals interact in a shared environment. Shared environments are usually open, thus the used vocabulary is not controlled. The resulting folksonomy is harder to process by an automated reasoning tool [30], by proposing a common ontology for folksonomy, attempts to define a formalized meaning for a folksonomy. The core relation is a tuple matching an object, a tag, a tagger (the one who is tagging) and a source (the shared environment from which the relation comes).

12.2.5.3 Knowledge in Social Networks

Although social network analysis focused on communication at its early stages, one of the first approaches to combination of social networks and knowledge was conceived as a semantic network [22] (*not to be confused with ontologies*). It focused on shared interpretations that people have for message content, such as corporate goals, slogans, myths and stories [20, 23] (see [48] for a summary).

Later on, most studies focused on either the diffusion of innovation [63] and information; or communication aimed at augmenting cooperation. Knowledge may be merged with social networks as the following:

Nodes The nodes in a knowledge network include individuals, their aggregations and knowledge repositories. In these networks, there are, both the social relations and relations from cognitive social networks. The links in a knowledge network describe *who knows what*. Cognitive knowledge links refer to *who knows who knows what* [14] and aim at representation of people's belief on knowledge of their acquaintances.

Vertexes' Attributes Several studies examine how characteristics of dyadic relationships, like the strength of ties, impact the effectiveness of knowledge transfer, and how knowledge transfer processes in turn affect performance [28, 31, 61, 62]. These studies infer the impact of network structure on the effectiveness of knowledge sharing from the strength of individual dyadic relationships. Reagens and McEvily [53] extends this work by simultaneously examining the effects of tie strength and network structure on the ease of transferring knowledge between individuals. These studies either examine the strength of dyadic ties or the impact of network structure on discrete dyadic information transfer events, rather than on the information actors receive from all their network contacts in concert.

Edges' Attributes Some studies examine characteristics of the information transferred across different types of ties. For example, Hansen et al. [31, 32, 61, 62] explore the degree to which knowledge being transferred is tacit or codifiable, simple or complex, and related or unrelated to a focal actor's knowledge. Fleming et al. [24] examine brokerage and cohesion in patent collaboration and knowledge in patent content.

12.2.6 Summary

Most of social recommendation systems usually focus, on one hand, on recommendation of individuals on basis of their several features, or, on the other, on single descriptive categories enrooted in a particular theory or approach to a problem. However, there are many theories, e.g., regarding contacts, trust or knowledge, which may help in team recommendations. Application of more perspectives can improve both the understanding of team performance and its prediction. That is why we present our proposal on multidimensional social network, where each dimension represent different human relations and is embedded in relevant theoretical approaches.

12.3 Three-Dimensional Social Network: A Model for a Social Environment

We propose to present the relevant social structure of collaborators with the means of multi-relational social network analysis [65].

We will use the following notation. A social network is represented by a graph $G = (V, E)$, where V is the set of n vertexes (also called nodes or egos in context of social networks) $V = \{v_i\}$ and E is the set of edges (also called links) $E = \{(u, v) : u, v \in V\}$.

We will use the term *seeker* to describe the focal ego who is the center of the ego networks (normally, the user of the recommender system).

In order to represent different aspects of social structure relevant to team performance, i.e., acquaintance, trust and knowledge, we define three different social networks.

Definition 12.1. Acquaintance Network is a graph $G_A(V_A, E_A)$ modeling the relations of acquaintance between individuals $V_A = V$. The acquaintance is defined as the intensity of interaction between two individuals u, v and is represented by an edge (u, v) weighted by the intensity of interaction $w_A(u, v)$ (edges are undirected).

Note that the "intensity of interaction" does not constitute the cognitive relation of "knowing somebody", although it shares some common characteristics.

The dimension of trust expresses the importance of dependency trust for cooperation in organizations and teams [35, 46].

Definition 12.2. Trust Network is a graph $G_T(V_T, E_T)$ modeling the relation of trust between individuals $V_T = V$. A directed edge $(u, v) \in E_T$ represents non-zero dependency trust between u and v. (u, v) is weighted by the degree $t(u, v)$ in which u trusts v.

Definition 12.3. Knowledge Network is a two-mode graph $G_K(V_V \cup S, E_K)$ with edges (v, s) linking individual $v \in V_v = V$ with skill $s \in S$. Edges are weighted by the degree $w_K(v, s)$ in which v masters skill s.

The 3DSN is a tuple of these three networks.

Definition 12.4. Three-Dimensional Social Network $3DSN = (G_A, G_K, G_T)$ is a tuple of three graphs where relations between team members $v, u \in \{V_A = V_T = V_v\}$ represent their acquaintance $E_A(v, u)$ and trust $E_T(v, u)$, while their relation to knowledge is represented by their competence $E_K(i, s)$.

This data structure serves as a source of information for matching individuals so that they accomplish a given project in the best way.

12.4 Predicting Quality of Team Performance

The goal of team recommendation is to propose a set of individuals in the seeker's ego network that will complete the given project efficiently.

Team performance may be very hard to define as a single, closed form expression, even using all the information from the 3DSN. Thus, the most straightforward approach is to consider each dimension of team performance individually. For each aspect of team performance, we propose a utility function, based on established results from social sciences. Then, we combine the criteria with a generic multiobjective optimization method, called the *reference point method*.

The reference point method goal is to produce a solution that has an acceptable performance regarding all the criteria. "Acceptable" is defined using two "levels" for each criterion: a minimal acceptable value (called the *reservation* point); and a value beyond which further improvement is unnecessary (called the *aspiration* point). For each criterion, we show how to determine these values using empirical data.

12.4.1 Social Capital

The issue of relation between work performance and social interaction has been mostly scrutinized in the perspective of the theory of social capital developed mostly by Ronald Burt, who saw this notion in terms of participation in, and control of, information diffusion [11]. Individual social capital can be perceived as external capability of an individual to access, use and control resources embedded in one's personal network [41]. In order to perform efficiently, ego v should be as close to all the others in a network as possible. Ego's *closeness centrality* measures the lengths of shortest paths γ to all other individuals in the network, scaled by the number of vertexes $n = |V|$ [3]:

$$CC(v) = \frac{n - 1}{\sum_{u \in V} \gamma(v, u)} \tag{12.1}$$

$CC(v)$ ranges from 0, if some of the vertexes are not reachable from v, to 1 when vertex v is adjacent to all other vertexes. CC is usually measured for individuals, but it can also be applied to teams. In team $M \subset V$, consisting of team members $v_i \in M$, every v_i features a particular γ to $u \notin M$. Then *closeness centrality* of a team $CC(M)$ is the sum of minimal γ's from the team to all other individuals:

$$CC(T) = \frac{|V| - |M| - 1}{\sum_{u \notin M} \min_{v \in M} \gamma(v, u)} \tag{12.2}$$

Note that this predictor does not take into consideration contacts' heterogeneity and redundancy.

In order to settle reservation and aspiration points, we generated 1,000 random scale-free graphs. Every graph has $V = 1,000$ vertexes, an average degree $k = 4$, scale-free distribution with weight of a vertex v degree $\alpha_{NOTslope} = 3$.

Figure 12.1 summarizes the results. The observed range of CC is in $[0.107, 0.388]$ with mean $\overline{CC} = 0.224$, median 0.223 and standard deviation $\sigma(CC) = 0.030$. The distribution of CC is positively skewed with skewness $\gamma = 0.266$, but the lack of symmetry occurs in outcomes higher than 2σ from the mean.

We propose to use $\overline{CC} - 2\sigma$ (0.164) as the reservation point and $\overline{CC} + 2\sigma$ (0.284) as the aspiration point. The reservation point $\overline{CC} - 2\sigma$ sets the minimum target CC to be higher than CC of (approximately) 3% of the worst random teams. Similarly, the aspiration point $\overline{CC} + 2\sigma$ means that it is not necessarily to improve CC beyond the value higher than in (approximately) 97% random teams. Moreover, CC seems to be symmetric on $[\overline{CC} - 2\sigma, \overline{CC} + 2\sigma]$ as skewness equals 0.12 in this range.

12.4.2 Intra-Group Trust

We assume that trust can propagate in a transitive way in social networks, i.e., for any $i, j, k \in V$, if there is relation of trust $t(i, j)$ and $t(j, k)$, then a new relation

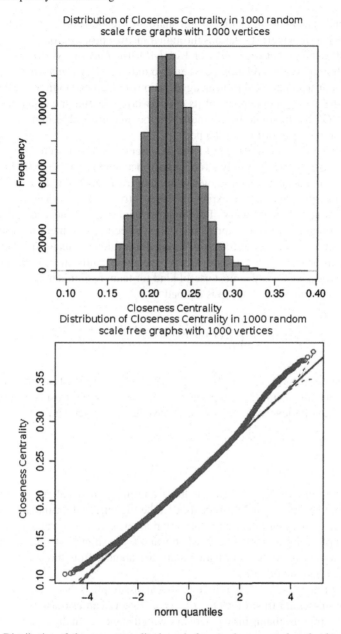

Fig. 12.1 Distribution of closeness centrality in scale free graphs generated randomly

$t(i, k)$ may be established [65]. Transitive propagation can occur under the condition that the trustee (i) will *know* that j trusts k. We make the assumption that in a recommended team, team members will share information about trust, allowing the establishment of new trust relations through transitive propagation.

We differentiate between *local* and *global* trust. *Local trust* $\theta(i, j)$ is defined as a function of a direct relation between two individuals. *Global trust* $t(i, j)$ is an attribute of an agent derived from an aggregation of direct and indirect trust relations between the agent and members of its egonetwork reflecting the experiences of all the alters. Global trust can be computed by the eigentrust algorithm [37] and is a measure of the trustworthiness of a peer.

We define the relation $\theta(i, j)$ of local trust between v_i that occurs if v_i trusts v_j. Positive values of $\theta(i, j)$ imply stronger trust between v_i and v_j. $\theta(i, j)$ equals 0 when the available data do not show a relation of trust between v_i and v_j. The information about trust that will be expressed using θ (our computational trust measure) can be obtained in many ways. The simplest (and perhaps most reliable, even if hardest to obtain) way is an expression of trust directly from interested users. Such an expression can be in the form of ratings that evaluate a team member's work. Then, the information used to construct θ concerns cognitive trust in the context of common work, which is the most useful kind for team recommendation.

Normalized local trust $c(i, j)$ is defined as

$$
c(i, j) = \begin{cases} \frac{\max(\theta(i,j),0)}{\sum_k \max(\theta(i,k),0)} & \text{if } \exists k : \theta(i, k) > 0 \\ 0 & \text{otherwise} \end{cases}
\tag{12.3}
$$

which ensures that $c(i, j) \in [0, 1]$ and $\sum_j c(i, j) = 1$ (if i trusts at least one agent).

Eigentrust algorithm [37] proposes to estimate the initial trust of v_i towards v_k by using the experiences of alters v_j who have had a contact with v_k:

$$
t_{i,k} = c_{i,k} + \sum_{j \neq k} c_{i,j} c_{j,k}.
\tag{12.4}
$$

Note that our equation for trust includes a term for the local, direct relation between i and k. The original formula used in the Eigentrust algorithm has been used for the situation when i had no information about k (indeed, trust propagation is usually applied in just such a case: when i and k are strangers). Our modified formula allows to extend the information that i has about k from direct experience, by asking the opinion of others.

It is kept that $t \in [0, 1]$, but there is also an assumption that every individual v_i can spare maximum trust of 1: $\sum_j t_{i,j} = 1$. Ego v_i can also ask the opinions of his friends' friends, that is his egonetwork with distance 2. In this manner this value can be obtained for any egonetwork with any distance n. However, human trust is not propagated without constraint, and humans tend to avoid accepting trust that is propagated too far. Therefore, a limitation of the radius of the trust propagation to two or three is reasonable.

Propagated trust can be used in a criterion of team quality that depends on trust. When considering the role of trust in a team, unless we can distinguish a particular team member that plays a special role, we need to consider all possible trust relations among team members. Thus, it becomes necessary to base the criterion on the propagated trust values between all pairs of team members. It should also be noted that trust is not symmetric, and thus we need to consider ordered pairs. In order to aggregate the trust values between all ordered pairs of team members, an average can be used. Then, the trust criterion (that can be called an average interpersonal trust measure, AITM) will have the form:

$$AITM = \frac{1}{|M|(|M|-1)} \sum_{i,k \in M, i \neq k} t_{i,k} \qquad (12.5)$$

for a team M of size $|M|$.

The AITM criterion has been proposed in [42]. The criterion has the desirable property that a team can be constructed in a greedy, stepwise manner, by adding one new candidate at a time. When a new candidate v_c is added to the team, the average trust measure between ordered pairs of all current team members and v_c should be maximized, in order to maximize AITM.

In order to settle reservation and aspiration points for the recommendation system one should realize that the distribution of trust probably follows the power law [68]. Thus, the reservation point equal to the global average $\bar{t} = \sum_{i,j} t(i,j)/(|V|(|V|-1))$ taken as reservation point will cut off too many vertexes. We assume that agent's v_i reservation point should be relative to the average value of its own trust $\bar{t}_i = (\sum_j t(i,j))/|n'(i)|$ (where $n'(i)$ is the number of agents and j is such that $t(i,j) > 0$). Consequently, we suggest that the reservation point for ego i should be equal to $\min(\bar{t}_i, \bar{t})$. On the other hand, we assume that a project should be conducted by people featuring maximum possible trust and in due fact the aspiration point should be set to the maximum possible value of trust t in the population (ego network) $\max(t)$.

12.4.3 Matching Team's Knowledge with Project Requirements

In order to measure how well a team is expected to succeed in a given project, we start with a more formal definition of a project.

Definition 12.5. **Project** P is described by a set of n_P skills $S_P \subset S$. Each skill $s \in S_P$ has a weight $w_P(s)$ representing the required level of its mastering for the project.

Regarding predictors of knowledge, two approaches can be distinguished. First, the measure can assess the average level of competence in the required skills. We suggest using a simplified version of Euclidean distance introduced in social network analysis in [10]. The knowledge network G_K of a team M represents the levels of competence $w_K(v,s)$ of a member $v \in M$ for a skill $s \in S$ (we will denote as S_M the sum of skills individual members of team M have). Similarly, project P

requires S_P skills, each of them must be performed with minimum required level of competence $w_P(s)$.

Assume that the level of competence $w_K(v, s)$ and $w_P(s)$ is represented on a scale $\{0, 1, 2, 3, 4, 5\}$, where 0 means no competence at all and 5 represents the maximum possible competence. Given the required skills S_P for a project, sum of relevant skills of team M can be computed as $\sum_{v \in M, s \in S_M \cap S_P} w_K(v, s)$. A similar sum can be computed for project P $\sum_{s \in S_P} w_P(s)$. Because project specification does not define the required number of individuals, in order to compare sums of skills between a team and a task it is convenient to scale $\sum_{s \in S_P} w_P(s)$ by the number of individuals $|M|$ in a matched team, resulting in $|M| \sum_{s \in S_P} w_P(s)$. Then, the skill difference SD between team M and project P is

$$SD = \sum_{v \in M, s \in S_M \cap S_P} w_K(v, s) - |M| \sum_{s \in S_P} w_P(s). \tag{12.6}$$

In order to represent the skill difference on a scale comparable with range of possible competence, aggregated skill difference ASD can be obtained by dividing the skill difference by the number of individuals $|M|$ and skills $|S_M|$ in a compared team t:

$$ASD = \frac{\sum_{v \in M, s \in S_M \cap S_P} w_K(v, s) - |M| \sum_{s \in S_P} w_P(s)}{|M||S_M|}. \tag{12.7}$$

Such a structure assumes that $ASD \in \{-5..5\}$, where -5 means maximum possible incompetence of a team, while 5 is the maximum possible competence. 0, on the other hand, means that the average competence of a team equals the aggregated average of competence required by a task. Thus, we suggest that $ASD = 0$ can be assumed as the reservation point, while the $ASD = 5$ constitutes the aspiration point for the recommendation of knowledge dimension.

Alternatively, one can also measure whether the required skills are distributed evenly in a team. The purpose is to restrict teams formed by an universal expert and a group of laymen. The measure is expressed by taking into account both, for every individual, the maximum competence of any of his or her skill, and, for every skill, the maximum competence of any team member. If one considers a team as matrix G_{vxn} representing values of S_M skills possessed by M individuals, then maximum values E of raw marginals $\max\{e_{i+}\}$ represent maximum competence of every individual and column marginals $\max\{e_{j+}\}$ represent maximum competence for every skill. Arithmetic product of these values for every skill and individual represents the distribution of maximum skills in a team. If the level of competence is $E \in \{0..5\}$, then at its best it may equal to 5^{V+N}. It equals 0 if there is at least one skill or individual not featuring any competence at all. We suggest that knowledge distribution in a team, that is *maximum skill distribution*, can be calculated as

$$MSD = \frac{\prod_M \max\{e_{i+}\} \prod_{S_M} \max\{e_{j+}\}}{5^{|M|+|S_M|}} \tag{12.8}$$

MSD is an internal value for a group and does not take into account levels of competence required by a project. However, it is a useful value when constrained to skills S_P required by a project P.

12.4.4 Multicriteria Optimization

Once we have a set of team performance criteria, it remains to combine them into a single function that can be optimized.

We combine the team performance criteria using the *reference point method* [66, 67]. Compared with the weighted average, the reference point method has two main advantages: parameters for each criterion are determined individually; and the method can deliver any Pareto-optimal solution.

In order to combine various criteria, they must be first transformed on a single scale. This transformation is done by a *scaling function* that depends on two parameters (called *reference points*): the *reservation and aspiration points*. The values of scaling functions for all criteria are comparable. The reservation and aspiration points are chosen individually for each criterion.

The scaling function σ_k can be interpreted as a measure of the decision maker's satisfaction with the current value (outcome) of the k-th criterion, η_k. The simplest form of a scaling function is a piecewise linear, increasing function of a criterion's values that changes slopes when it reaches the reservation point η_k^r and aspiration point η_k^a. The value of the scaling function when the criterion is equal to the reservation point is zero ($\sigma_k = 0$ for $\eta_k = \eta_k^r$). When the criterion is less than the reservation point, the scaling function is negative. The value of the scaling function when the criterion is equal to the aspiration point is one ($\sigma_k = 1$ if $\eta_k = \eta_k^a$). The slopes of the pieces of the scaling function decrease as the criterion reaches the reservation point and then the aspiration point.

Thus, the scaling function is given by

$$\sigma_k(\eta_k) = \begin{cases} \gamma(\eta_k - \eta_k^r)/(\eta_k^a - \eta_k^r) & \text{for } \eta_k \leq \eta_k^r \\ (\eta_k - \eta_k^r)/(\eta_k^a - \eta_k^r) & \text{for } \eta_k^r < \eta_k < \eta_k^a \\ \beta(\eta_k - \eta_k^a)/(\eta_k^a - \eta_k^r) + 1 & \text{for } \eta_k \geq \eta_k^a \end{cases} \tag{12.9}$$

where β and γ are arbitrarily defined parameters satisfying $0 < \beta < 1 < \gamma$. (For example, $\beta = 0.5$ and $\gamma = 2$.) This partial achievement function is strictly increasing and concave which guarantees its LP computability with respect to outcomes η_k.

The reservation point can be interpreted as a value of the criterion that should be reached even at a high cost or effort. Once the criterion exceeds the reservation point, the importance of maximizing this criterion decreases relative to other criteria that have not yet reached their reservation points. The aspiration point can be interpreted as a value of the criterion that, when reached, further reduces the importance of this criterion when compared to other criteria that have not yet reached their reservation or aspiration levels. It is a value of the criterion that is "good enough" for most purposes. Of course, increasing a criterion that has already exceeded its aspiration level will still improve the overall result, but will be less important than increasing this and other criteria above their reservation levels.

The individual scaling functions of the reference point method can be combined using a simple sum. However, a better method is to combine the sum with a minimum of the scaling functions. This method guarantees that all Pareto-optimal solutions can be found by optimizing the combined scaling function and changing the parameters (the reference points). The final objective function σ (maximized) that combines all criteria η_k, taking into account the decision maker's preferences as expressed by the reference points, is given by

$$\sigma(\eta) = \min_{k \in K}\{\sigma_k(\eta_k)\} + \varepsilon \sum_{k \in K} \sigma_k(\eta_k) \qquad (12.10)$$

where ε is an arbitrary small positive number and σ_k, for $k \in K$, are the partial achievement functions measuring actual achievement of the individual outcome η_k with respect to the corresponding aspiration and reservation levels (η_k^a and η_k^r, respectively).

12.5 Experiments

12.5.1 3DSN in onephoto.net

The first empirical data set we took into consideration comes from onephoto.net, a Web site aiming at augmenting cooperation of photographers who try to improve their competence by sharing their photos and commenting and rating other photos. We chose this site because it offers information resembling a 3DSN. First of all, users of OnePhoto share photos. Some of them put their works on the Web site, which are afterwards rated and commented by the rest of the community. One of the features offered by OnePhoto is the possibility of recommending other authors to all OnePhoto users. In due course, it is possible to track works of people who are considered to be good photographers. Works of recommended users are more probable to be appreciated than others. We consider this information as a relation of trust. As it is impossible to keep track of all the works in the service, users focus on works recommended by others, i.e., they trust, that works of recommended people are valuable. Another feature of OnePhoto is the possibility of putting one's work into 1 of 21 thematic categories. We assumed that good photographers focus on works of a particular type, e.g., architecture or nature. Such a division is not far from areas of expertise existing in other professional communities. That is why we considered possessing photos in particular categories as a relation of knowledge – reflecting number of works in different categories. In consequence, the relation of knowledge allows for finding people who most of the time take photos in selected areas.

We have gathered data about 101,554 photos of 45,394 users of onephoto.net (all the photos available at the time of crawling). Authors categorize each of their photos into 1 of 21 thematic categories.

The *trust* graph is based on the relation of "favs", or user v_i marking a user v_j as a favourite. Such a "fav" corresponds to the local trust $\theta(i, j)$. Using local trust, we derive the normalized local trust and then the transitive trust following the procedure in Section 12.2.4. The resulting graph is very sparse. Only 10,252 vertexes possessed a degree greater than 0 and 229,540 arcs. Degrees of nodes are not distributed according to the power law, but with normal distribution.

The knowledge graph is a two mode network representing the relation between persons V_v and categories V_s used to describe the individual photos. We regard every category as a skill and the (normalized) number of works in a category as the competence level. The 101,554 edges $E_{v,s}$ represented normalized numbers of photos in each category and are ranked $E_{v,s} \in \{1..5\}$ (based on a statistical bounded percentile rank). OnePhoto users use categories much more than that considered by others as favourites – this network possessed the density on the level of 0.106.

Note that we do not infer an acquaintance graph from the crawled data.

We wanted to see whether in the network of OnePhoto users there can be derived groups of people who would be able to conduct a joint project of taking photos in given categories. We assume that they should value works of each other and possess experience in taking photos in required categories. In order to apply our measures to possible teams we have chosen 15 different tasks taking into consideration two factors: task difficulty, i.e., average weight of every task ranging from 3 (medium difficulty) to 5 (extreme difficulty) and the number of skills required by a task (from 3 to 7). We wanted to find out what are the distributions of quality predictors and what is their level of interdependence in regard to different task structures.

We generated $N = 2,000$ random teams in a following way. First, we took the last percentile of users according to their in-degree of trust relation (i.e., users whose in-degree is in the top 1% of in-degree distribution). For every team, we chose randomly its size (from 2 to 6). Then, the team is constructed by choosing appropriate number of random individuals from egonetwork of size 2. For every team we have calculated predictors of trust according to equation 12.5 and knowledge according to equations 12.7 and 12.8. There were 314 teams not connected at all in either of the analyzed dimensions and were therefore excluded from further calculations.

The distribution of AITM in regard to the size of teams is presented on Fig. 12.2. It diminishes along with the size of a team, although medium 50% of the distributions remains on the similar level. One has to remember, though, that members were picked from egonetworks by people possessing highest in-degree of trust in the whole population. It is spread at its maximum for teams consisting of four members, which may suggest the team's optimal size regarding this factor. Adding more members potentially decreases the value of trust for the whole team.

Teams are in general less suitable to conduct a task along with the increase of both average task difficulty and its size, which is presented in Table 12.1 and Fig. 12.3. The average value of average skill distance remains above 0 only for tasks consisting of three skills required for performance. The level of difficulty is a

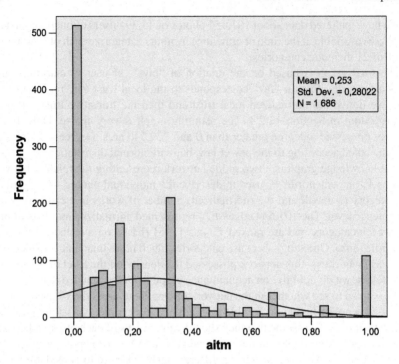

Fig. 12.2 AITM distribution

better predictor of the value of *ASD* than the number or required skills. The more difficult are the tasks, the harder they are to conduct.

Table 12.1 Average skill difference in different tasks in Onephoto

Task size	Task difficulty			Distribution	
	3	4	5	Skewness	Kurtosis
3	0.114	−0.282	−0.171	−0.458	−0.268
4	0.172	−0.183	−0.208	−0.538	−0.14
5	0.164	−0.736	−0.311	−0.394	−0.172
6	0.174	−0.111	−0.397	−0.308	−0.242
7	0.181	−0.151	−0.484	−0.272	−0.251

In case of OnePhoto, the distribution of *ASD* is negatively skewed, which suggests that only the small part of the teams is not suitable to perform given tasks,

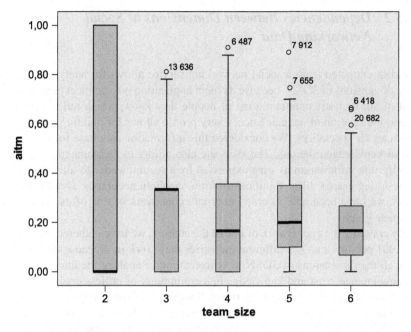

Fig. 12.3 AITM distribution in teams of different sizes

Table 12.2 Maximum skill
difference in different tasks
in OnePhoto

Team size	Mean	Skewness	Kurtosis
2	0.78	−1.358	0.665
3	0.72	−0.986	−0.375
4	0.64	−0.592	−1.077
5	0.597	−0.464	−1.227
6	0.503	−0.05	−1.484

while the rest remains on the similar level. In case of photographers, there is a huge competition of equal rivals. The competition diminishes along with the increase of the number of tasks required.

The internal measure of maximum knowledge distribution is dependent on the number of skills in the given case. It increases along with the number of skills taken into consideration. The measure of *MSD* is also dependent on the team size (Table 12.2) – in case of OnePhoto it decreases along with the number of individuals in a team, which shows that the skills in given teams are very diversified. As far as number of skills is considered, a team is much more competitive, when it possesses more individuals.

12.5.2 Dependencies Between Dimensions in Social Networking Data

The data extracted from a social networking service allows for analysis of all the three dimensions of 3DSN, because its main application is to connect professionals. First of all, its users maintain a list of people they know, which reflects (to some extent) the relation of acquaintance. Every profile allows for pointing industries in which a user specializes. We considered this information as a base for reconstruction of knowledge relations. The Web site also allows to recommend others – we identify this information as trust expressed by a recommender to alter. Moreover, the resulting graphs differ significantly from onephoto.net graphs. Due to Web site limits, we have been able to crawl only an egonetwork of one of us, and not the complete graph.

By crawling the egonetwork of one of the authors, we have gathered information on 3,981 persons and 725 different industries they work in. Because the data contains all the dimensions of 3DSN, it is interesting to analyze the interdependency of acquaintance, trust and knowledge in a community of professionals. For means of comparison all arcs in the trust network were converted to edges, while the bimodal knowledge network was converted to a one-mode binary network of actors. The resulting 3DSN is a multi-mode network with 3,981 vertexes V_v and 3,088 edges representing acquaintance $E_A(v, u)$, 725 edges representing trust $E_T(v, u)$ and 1,391,052 edges revealing relations of knowledge $E_K(v, u)$ among the vertexes (Table 12.3). Figure 12.4 shows the distribution of closeness centrality in the network. . In the next step, we counted the edges which represented all possible combinations of E_A, E_T and E_K.

In this experiment, we study the correlations between performance measures. We conducted a three way log-linear analysis. The likelihood ratio of the whole model is $\chi^2 = 0, p = 1$. This indicates that the highest-order interaction $(A x T x K)$ was significant, $\chi^2 = 2599.78, p < 0.001$. It should be noted, however, that this effect comes out of supremacy of knowledge relations. Because 3,981 actors in the network share only 142 skills, there is ample probability that although they know the same things, they neither know, nor trust each other.

This relation looks different from the point of view of acquaintance and trust. Knowing somebody does not assume possessing the same skills: odds ratio indicate

Table 12.3 Co-occurrence of A, T and K dimensions in social networking website

E_A	E_T	E_K	Frequency
1	0	0	1,687
0	1	0	219
0	0	1	1,389,204
1	1	0	20
0	1	1	467
1	0	1	1,362
1	1	1	19

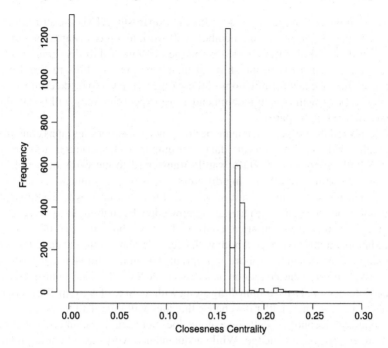

Fig. 12.4 Distribution of closeness centrality in social networking website egonetwork

that people are 1.24 more likely to be acquainted with users featuring other skills than their own ($p < 0.001$). Probably the relation of acquaintance does not come from strictly professional terms. On the other hand, actors are 2.02 times more likely to trust people who they share knowledge with than to trust experts in other areas ($p < 0.001$). They also do not tend to recommend people whom they know: the chances of recommending somebody from one's contacts are only 0.013 ($p < 0.001$). In general, one may draw a conclusion, that the network combines professional connections embedded in knowledge and trust and an informal network of people who interact with each other from time to time.

12.6 Concluding Remarks and Future Work

This chapter has presented the 3DSN an universal framework for storing information about the social context of an individual. A 3DSN is defined by: an acquaintance network that models interactions between individuals; a trust network that expresses direct and transitive trust between individuals; and a knowledge network that represents skills of individuals. Using information from these dimensions, we defined criteria that predict team performance from different perspectives. Team's social capital (CC) uses acquaintance network to estimate how good the group connected to the rest of the network is. Intra-group trust (AITM) uses trust network to estimate how smoothly group members will work together towards the common goal. Finally, the skill difference (SD) and the maximum skill distribution (MSD) measure the match between the skills of members and the skills required by the project. While the exact formulations of these criteria are yet to be determined when we validate them with a team recommender, we expect that they will be similar to the ones derived in the paper.

We analyzed the properties of team performance measures on graphs constructed from real-world social networking data. Our empirical data come from web communities and cannot be straightforwardly transferred to networks of people who communicate with each other using different means of communication. This problem is particularly obvious in case of the social network data, where acquaintance seems not to be connected with trust and knowledge. Even though, we have derived several conclusions from empirical analysis. First, we have realized that our quality predictors are interconnected both with each other and with real data. For easier tasks bigger teams seem to be more appropriate, but along with increasing difficulty of the task, team size should remain on a reasonable level. It is also confirmed by the average interpersonal trust diminishing along with the size of a group: the more individuals in a group, the smaller the chance that they will regard all the rest as skillful and proficient. Second, acquaintance alone does not seem to be an efficient predictor of either trust or knowledge. While acquaintance works as a bonding relation, professional teams should be constructed around other relations. That fact confirms our choice of multidimensional networks as structures for recommendation.

The 3DSN is not a new concept among social network scientists. Multi-mode networks have been an area of interest for quite a long time. What is interesting is that social recommendation systems have not been applying this idea in its full advantage, i.e., in relations to teams.

When looking at a team one should consider different structural factors. The first one is the internal structure of a team itself. As was shown, members of a team should trust and know themselves, as well as possess heterogeneous knowledge. On the other hand, a team is not alone. There are other teams that can be compared to each other using numerical attributes. Social networks enable comparing structural characteristics of teams with a special focus of embeddings of a team in the whole population of individuals. Different team members should possess different contacts with alters outside a team, relatively differentiated knowledge and feature maximum trust with important brokers in the population. We will focus on measures grasping these characteristics.

Note that it may be possible to formulate better criteria that depend on information from two or more dimensions of the 3DSN. However, at this stage of work, we focus on the simpler approach, leaving more complex team performance criteria for future work.

Another problem is the construction and representation of knowledge in social networks. So far, knowledge has been usually presented as a two mode network representing only the relations between individuals and skills. However, one should not forget that there are different relations of skills for every individual. Skills should not be considered regardless of contexts in which they are used. Such ontologies should be taken into consideration when looking at teams and distribution of knowledge inside them.

In construction of our social recommendation systems, we will try to apply real, network data. The development of research on team recommendation has been so far hampered by the lack of data about good teams that can be used as benchmarks or for training team recommendation systems. These data are increasingly available now. Mining the Internet is a powerful source of information, but it always requires operationalization and depends on the willingness of Internet users to provide relevant information. In our opinion, one cannot refrain from asking real people real questions about their subjective opinions on others and their relations. In the future, the team recommendation methods proposed here will be tested against data that describe good teams, and perhaps new team recommendation criteria will be proposed. The results presented in this chapter represent insight into the 3DSN that is a good framework for taking into consideration many differentiated points of view, and will be a basis for the development of comprehensive team recommendation methods.

Acknowledgements This project has been supported by research grants no: 69/N-SINGAPUR/ 2007/0 and no: N N516 4307 33 of the Polish Ministry of Science and Higher Education and by Singapore A-STAR grant no: 072 134 0055.

References

1. Abdul-Rahman A, Hailes S (2000) Supporting trust in virtual communities. In: System sciences, 2000. Proceedings of the 33rd annual Hawaii international conference in 2000
2. Aral S, Van Alstyne MW (2008) Networks, information & social capital (formerly titled 'network structure & information advantage). SSRN eLibrary
3. Beauchamp M (1965) An improved index of centrality. Behav Sci 10:161–163
4. Bonacich P (1972) Factoring and weighting approaches to status scores and clique identification. J Math Sociol 2:113–120
5. Bonacich P, Lloyd P (2004) Calculating status wih negative relations. Soc Networks 26:331–338
6. Borgatti S, Everett M (1996) Models of core/periphery structures. In: Sunbelt international social networks conference, Charleston, SC
7. Borgatti SP (2004) Social network measures of social capital. A methodological perspective. PDF via WWW
8. Bourdieu P, Wacquant LJ (1992) An invitation to reflexive sociology. University of Chicago Press, Chicago, IL
9. Bourdieu P, Passeron JC (1977) Reproduction in education, society, culture. Sage, Beverly Hills, CA
10. Burt RS (1983) Sage, Beverly Hills, CA, pp 176–194
11. Burt RS (1992) Structural holes. Cambridge University Press, New York
12. Burt RS (2001) Structural holes versus network closure as social capital. In: Lin N, Cook K, Burt RS (eds) Social capital. Theory and research, chap. 2, Aldine Transaction, New York, pp 31–56
13. Coleman J (1990) Foundations of social theory. Harvard University Press, Cambridge, MA

14. Contractor N, Monge P (2002) Managing knowledge networks. Manage Commun Quart 16:249–258
15. Cummings J (2004) Work groups, structural diversity, and knowledge sharing in a global organization. Manage Sci 50:352–364
16. Cummings J, Cross R (2003) Structural properties of work groups and their consequences for performance. Soc Networks 25:197–210
17. Dalkir K (2005) Knowledge management in theory and practice. Butterworth-Heinemann, Boston, MA
18. Davis S, Botkin J (1998) The coming of knowledge-based business. In: Neef D (ed) The knowledge economy. Butterworth-Heinemann, Boston, MA
19. Deutsch M (1973) The resolution of conflict. Yale University Press, New Haven
20. Dunn W, Ginnsberg A (1986) A sociogonitive network approach to organizational analysis. Hum Relat 40:955–976
21. Ehrlich K, Lin C, Griffiths-Fisher V (2007) Searching for experts in the enterprise: Combining text and social network analysis. In: Proceedings of the 2007 international ACM conference on conference on supporting group work. ACM, pp 117–126
22. Eisenberg E, Monge P (1987) Handbook of organizational communication, chap. Emergence communication networks. Sage, Newbury Park, CA, pp 304–342
23. Fiol C (1989) A semantic analysis of corporate language: Organizational boudaries and joint venturing. Admin Sci Quart 34:277–303
24. Fleming L, Mingo S, Chen D (2007) Collaborative brokerage, generative creativity & creative success. Admin Sci Quart 52:443–475
25. Freeman LC (1977) A set of measures of centrality based on betweenness. Sociometry 40:35–40
26. Fukuyama F (1996) Trust: The social virtus and the creation of prosperity. Free Press, Pigden, NY
27. Genesereth M, Fikes R, et al (1992) Knowledge Interchange Format, Version 3.0 Reference Manual
28. Granovetter M (1973) The strength of weak ties. Am J Sociol 78:1360–80
29. Gruber T (1993) A translation approach to portable ontology specifications. Knowledge Acquis 5(2):199–220
30. Gruber T (2007) Ontology of folksonomy: A mash-up of apples and oranges. Int J Semantic Web Info Syst 3(2)
31. Hansen M (1999) The search-transfer problem: The role of weak ties in sharing knowledge across organization subunits. Admin Sci Quart 44:82–111
32. Hansen M (2002) Knowledge networks: Explaining effective knowledge sharing in multiunit companies. Organ Sci 13:232–248
33. Harary F (1969) Graph theory. Addison-Wesley, Reading, MA
34. Johnson HG (1960) The political economy of opulence. Can J Econ Polit Sci 26:552–564
35. Jones G, George J (1998) The experience and evolution of trust: Implications for co-operation and teamwork. Acad Manage Rev 23(3):531–546
36. Josang A, Keser C, Dimitrakos T (2005) Can we manage trust? In: Trust Management (iTrust 2005), LNCS, vol 3477. Springer
37. Kamvar S, Schlosser M, Garcia-Molina H (2003) The eigentrust algorithm for reputation management in p2p networks. In: WWW2003. ACM, pp 20–24
38. Kautz H, Selman B, Shah M (1997) Referral Web: Combining social networks and collaborative filtering. Commun ACM 40(3):63–65
39. Keim T (2007) Extending the applicability of recommender systems: A multilayer framework for matching human resources. In: Proceedings of the 40th annual Hawaii international conference on system sciences. IEEE Computer Society Washington, DC
40. Klimecki R, Lassleben H () What causes organizations to learn? In: Third international conference on organizational learning, 6–8th June 1999, Lancaster University, UK
41. Lin N (2001) Building a network theory of social capital. In: Lin N, Cook K, Burt RS (eds) Social capital. Theory and research, chap. 1, Aldine Transaction, pp 3–29

42. Malinowski J, Weitzel T, Keim T (2008) Decision support for team staffing: An automated relational recommendation approach. Decis Support Syst 45(3):429–447 DOI http://dx.doi.org/10.1016/j.dss.2007.05.005
43. Marsden P (1988) Homogeneity in confiding relations. Soc Networks 10:57–76
44. Marsh SP (1994) Formalising trust as a computational concept. PhD thesis, University of Stirling
45. Marx K (1995) In: McLellan D (ed) Capital: A new abridgement. Oxfod University Press
46. McAllister D (1995) Affect- and cognition-based trust as foundations for interpersonal cooperation in organizations. Acad Manage J 38:24–59
47. McDonald D, Ackerman M (2000) Expertise recommender: A flexible recommendation system and architecture. In: Proceedings of the 2000 ACM conference on computer supported cooperative work. ACM, pp 231–240
48. Monge P, Contractor N (2003) Theories of communication networks. Oxford University Press
49. Newman M, Barabasi A, Watts D (2006) The structure and dynamics of networks. Princeton University Press, Princeton, NJ
50. Nonaka I, Takeuchi H (1995) The knowledge-creating company: How Japanesee companies create the dynamics of innovation. Oxfod University Press, New York
51. Putnam R (2000) Bowling alone: The collapse and revival of American community. Simon & Schuster
52. Putnam R (2003) Better together: Restoring the American community. Simon & Schuster
53. Reagans R, McEvily B (2003) Network structure & knowledge transfer: The effects of cohesion & range. Admin Sci Quart 48:240–267
54. Richardson M, Agrawal R, Domingos P (2003) Trust management for the semantic web. In: Proceedings of the second international semantic web conference, pp 351–368
55. Rodan S, Galunic D () More than network structure: How knowledge heterogeneity influences managerial performance & innovativeness. Strategic Manage J 25:541–562
56. Schultz TW (1961) Investment in human capital. Am Econ Rev LI(1):1–17
57. Shami N, Ehrlich K, Millen D (2008) Pick me!: link selection in expertise search results. In: Proceeding of the twenty-sixth annual SIGCHI conference on Human factors in computing systems. ACM
58. Sztompka P (1999) Trust: A sociological theory. Cambridge University Press, Cambridge
59. Sztompka P (2007) Zaufanie. Fundament Spoeczestwa (Trust. A foundation of society). Wydawnictwo Znak
60. Terveen L, McDonald DW (2005) Social matching: A framework and research agenda. ACM Trans Comput Hum Interact 12(3):401–434 DOI http://doi.acm.org/10.1145/1096737.1096740
61. Uzzi B (1996) The sources and consequences of embeddedness for the economic performance of organizations: The network effect. Am Sociol Rev 61:674–698
62. Uzzi B (1997) Social structure and competition in interfirm networks: The paradox of embeddedness. Admin Sci Quart 42:35–67
63. Valente T (1995) Network models of the diffusion of information. Hampton Pres, Cresskill, NJ
64. Wal TV Folksonomy coinage and definition. http://vanderwal.net/folksonomy.html
65. Wasserman S, Faust K (1999) Social network analysis. Cambridge University Press, New York
66. Wierzbicki AP (1984) A mathematical basis for satisficing decision making. Math Model 3:391–405
67. Wierzbicki AP, Makowski M, Wessels J (2000) Model based decision support methodology with environmental applications. Kluwer, Doordrecht
68. Zhou R, Hwang K (2007) Powertrust: A robust and scalable reputation system for trusted peer-to-peer computing. IEEE Trans Parallel Distrib Syst 18(4):460–473

Chapter 13
Web Communities Defined by Web Page Content

Miloš Kudělka, Václav Snášel, Zdeněk Horák, Aboul Ella Hassanien,
and Ajith Abraham

Abstract In this chapter, we are looking for a relationship between the intent
of Web pages, their architecture and the communities who take part in their usage and creation. For us, the Web page is entity carrying information around these
communities. Our chapter describes techniques which can be used to extract the
mentioned information as well as tools usable in the analysis of this information. Information about communities could be used in several ways thanks to our approach.
Finally, we present experiments which prove the feasibility of our approach. These
experiments also show a possible way as to how to measure the similarity of Web
pages and Web sites using microgenres. We define the microgenre as a building
block of Web pages which is based on the social interaction.

13.1 Introduction

The current Web – due its dimensions, number of Web pages and Web sites –
starts to exceed the scope of human perception. The problem with orientation in the
Web space is a consequence of this. As evidenced, we can consider the problems
of contemporary search engines with giving the relevant answers to user queries.
Therefore, new tools are still arising, and their authors come with new approaches
supporting interaction between users and computers in the Internet environment.
On one hand, in our chapter, we traverse through the field of Web content mining.

M. Kudělka (✉), V. Snášel, and Z. Horák
VSB Technical University Ostrava, Czech Republic
e-mail: milos.kudelka@inflex.cz; [vaclav.snasel;zdenek.horak.st4]@vsb.cz

A.E. Hassanien
Faculty of Computer and Information, Information Technology Department,
Cairo University, Egypt
e-mail: abo@cba.edu.kw

A. Abraham
Machine Intelligence Research Labs (MIR Labs), Scientific Network for Innovation
and Research Excellence, USA
e-mail: ajith.abraham@ieee.org

A. Abraham et al. (eds.), *Computational Social Network Analysis*, Computer
Communications and Networks, DOI 10.1007/978-1-84882-229-0_13,
© Springer-Verlag London Limited 2010

On the other hand, we try to consider the content mined from Web pages as a result of interaction between different social groups of people in the Web environment.

Metaphor A Web page is like a family house. Each of its parts has its purpose, determined by a function which it serves. Every part can be named so that all users envision approximately the same thing under that name (living room, bathroom, lobby, bedroom, kitchen, and balcony). In order for the inhabitants to orientate well in the house, certain rules are kept. From the point of view of these rules, all houses are similar. That is why it is usually not a problem for first time visitors to orientate in the house. We can describe the house quite precisely, thanks to names. If we add information about a more detailed location such as sizes, colors, furnishings and further details to the description, then the future visitor can get an almost perfect notion of what he, will see in the house when he or she comes in for the first time. We can also take an approach similar to the description of a building other than a family house (school, supermarket, office, etc.). Also in this case, the same applies for visitors, and it is usually not a problem to orientate (of course, it does not always have to be the case, as there are bad Web pages, there are also bad buildings).

In the case of buildings, we can naturally define three groups of people, who are somehow involved in the course of events. The first group is the people defining the intent and the purpose (those who pay and later expect some profit), the second group is those who construct the building (and are getting paid for it), and the third group is "users" of the building. These groups fade into another and change as society and technology evolve.

As we describe in the subsequent text, the presented metaphor can – up to certain point – serve as an inspiration to seize the Web pages content and also the whole Web environment.

This text is organized as follows. In the second section, we describe the Web page from the view of groups of people sharing the Web page existence. We also define the notion of the microgenre as a buliding block of Web page. The name of microgenre on Web page can serve as a linking element between groups of people with different intentions. In the third section, we provide an overview of related approaches and methods mostly from the area of Web genres identification and detection, Web design patterns and information extraction methods. The fourth section describes tools and techniques required for our experiments. In particular, our own Pattrio method, which is designed to detect microgenres within Web pages, and FCA are used for clustering. In the fifth section, we describe two experiments dealing with Web site description. The last section contains chapter recapitulation and focuses on possible directions of further research.

13.2 From Web Pages to Web Communities

The situation is similar with Web pages and communities. Every single Web page (or group of Web pages) can be perceived from three different points of view. When considering the individual points of view we were inspired by specialists on Web

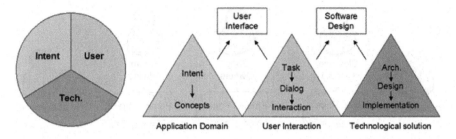

Fig. 13.1   Views of three different groups

design [33] and the communication of humans with computers [5]. These points of view represent the views of three different groups of communities who take part in the formation of the Web page (Fig. 13.1).

(1) The first group consists of those whose intention is that the user finds what he expects on the Web page. The intention which the Web page is supposed to fulfill is consequently represented by this group. (2) The second group consists of developers responsible for the creation of the Web page. They are therefore consequently responsible for fulfilling the goals of the two other groups. (3) The third group consists of users who work with the Web page. This group consequently represents how the Web page should appear outwardly to the user. It is important that this performance satisfies a particular need of the user.

As an example, we can mention blogs. The first community consists of the companies that offer the environment and the technological background for blog authors and to some extent also define the formal aspects of blogs. The second community consists of the developers who implement the task given by the previous group. The visible attribute of this group is that they – to a certain degree – share their techniques and policies. The third group consists of blog authors (in the sense of content creation). They influence the previous two groups retroactively. The second example can be the product pages – the intention of the e-shop is to sell items (concretely to have Web pages where you can find and buy the products), and the intention of the developers is to satisfy the e-shop owners as well as the Web page visitors. The intention of the visitors is to buy products, and so they expect clearly stated and well-defined functionality. From this point of view, the Web pages are elements around which the social networks are formed (Fig. 13.2). For further details and references, please see [1, 15] (which considers also the aspect of network evolution).

Under the term *Web community* we usually think of a group of related Web pages, sharing some common interests (see [22, 23, 32]). As a Web community we may also consider a Web site or groups of Web sites, on which people with common interests interact. It is apparent, that all three aforementioned groups participate in the Web page life cycle. The evolution of a page is directly or indirectly controlled by these groups. As a consequence, we can understand the Web page as a projection of the interaction among these three groups. The analysis of the page content may uncover significant information, which can be used to assign the Web page to a Web community.

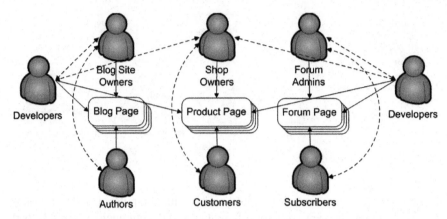

Fig. 13.2 Social network around Web pages

Our aim is to automatically discover such information about Web pages that comes out of intentions of particular groups. Using these information we can find the relations between the communities and describe them (on the technical level). The key element for Web page description is the name of the object, which represents the intention of the page or part of the page. It can be "Home page", "Blog" or "Product Page". In the detailed description, we can distinguish, for example, between "Discussion", "Article" or "Technical Features". We can also use more general description, such as "Something to Read" or "Menu" (see [14]).

13.2.1 Microgenres

According to Wikipedia.org, the genre is the division of concrete forms of art using the criteria relevant to the given form (e.g. film genre, music genre and literature genre). In all sectors of the arts, the genres are vague categories without fixed boundaries and are especially formed by the sets of conventions.

Many artworks are cross-genre and employ and combine these conventions. Probably the most deeply theoretically studied genres are the literary ones. It allows us to systematize the world of literature and consider it as a subject of scientific examination. We can find the term microgenre in this field. For example, in [21] the microgenre is seen as part of a combined text. This term has been introduced to identify the contribution of inserted genres to the overall organization of text. The motivation to use the term "microgenre" is because it is used as a building block of the analytic descriptive system. On the other hand, Web design patterns are used more technically and provide means for good solution of Web pages.

From our point of view the Web page is structured similarly to the literature text using parts which are relatively independent and have their own purpose (see Fig. 13.3). On the other side, the architecture of the Web page (individual parts)

Fig. 13.3 Structure of Web page

is based on Web design patterns. For these parts, we have chosen the term "microgenre". Contemporary Web pages are often very complex, nevertheless they can usually be described using several microgenres. This kind of description can be more flexible than the genre description (which usually represents the whole page). Genre and design patterns have a social background. On this background, there are different groups of people with the same interests.

Definition 13.1. (Web) microgenre is a part of a Web page,

1. Whose purpose is general and repeats frequently
2. Which can be named intelligibly and more or less unambiguously so that the name is understandable for the Web page user (developer, designer, etc.)
3. Which is detectable on a Web page using computer algorithm

The microgenre can, but does not have to, strictly relate to the structure of a Web page in a technical sense, e.g. it does not necessarily have to apply that it is represented by one subtree in the DOM tree of the page or by one block in the sense of the visual layout of the page. Rather it can be represented by one or more segments of a page, which form it together (see Fig. 13.4).

Remark 13.1. Microgenres are also contexts which encapsulate related information. In paper [14] we show the way we extract snippets from individual microgenres.

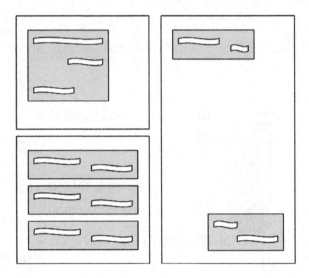

Fig. 13.4 Microgenres formed by Web page segments

We use these snippets in our Web application as an additional information for Web page description. The detection of microgenres can be considered in a similar way as the first step for using Web information extraction methods (see [8]).

13.2.1.1 Microgenre Recognition

It follows the previous description that in order to be able to speak about the microgenre, this element has to be distinguishable by the user. From what attributes should the user recognize, if and what the Microgenre is in question? We work with up to three levels of view:

1. The first view is purely semantic in the sense of the textual content of a page. It does not always need to have to be a meaning in a sense of natural language such as sentences or paragraphs with a meaningful content. Logically coherent data blocks can still lack in grammar (see [35]).

   For example, price information can be only a group of words and symbols ('price', 'vat', symbol $) of a data type (price, number). For similar approach see [27].

2. The second view is visual in the sense of page perception as a whole. Here individual segments of perception or groups of segments of the page are in question. It is dependent on the use of colors, font and auxiliary elements (lines, horizontal and vertical gaps between the segments, etc.) Approaches based on visual analysis of Web pages can be found in [6, 30].

3. The third view is a structural one in a technical sense. It is about the use of special structures, such as tables, links, navigation trees, etc. There are approaches based on the analysis of the DOM tree and special structures as tables [20, 25].

The first view is dependent on the user's understanding of the text stated on a Web page. The second and third views are independent of this user ability. However, it can be expected that an Arabic or Chinese product page will be recognized also by an English-speaking user who does not have a command of those languages. It is determined by the fact that for the implementation of certain intentions there are habitual procedures which provide very similar results regardless of the language. On the other hand, if the user understands the page, he or she can focus more on the semantic content of the microgenre. For example, in the case of "product info", the user can read what the product in question is, what its price is and on what conditions it can be purchased.

13.2.2 Web Page Description

Using mentioned views, we can describe every Web page by genre or a group of microgenres. This description, in principle, defines the communities mentioned in the preface of our chapter. On the other side, each defined community contributes somehow to the development of the Web and simultaneously to the behavior of the related communities (e.g., communities involved in blogging as mentioned earlier). Consequently, these contemplations lead to reduction of the Web to some particular types of pages and communities. This can be very useful, for example, in searching. Knowing that the user prefers product pages (or review pages, discussion pages, etc.), we can help him or her on – namely on the basis of knowledge – how the community of developers in a given domain (Web design patterns) works and what is the prevailing intent of the pages (genres).

13.3 Related Work

When we perceive the Web page as whole, the purpose is represented by a so-called Web genre. Similarly, the view of individual segments of the Web page is closely related to Web design patterns. A Web genre is a taxonomy that incorporates the style, form and content of a document which is orthogonal to the topic, with fuzzy classification to multiple Web genres [4]. For classification, there are many approaches and also many methods for genre identification. Kennedy and Shepherd [12] analyzed home page genres (personal home page, corporate home page or organization home page). Chaker and Habib [7] proposed a flexible approach for Web page genre categorization. Flexibility means that the approach assigns a document to all predefined genres with different weights. Dong et al. [10] described a set of experiments to examine the effect of various attributes of Web genre for the automatic identification of the genre of Web pages. Four different genres were used in the data set (FAQ, News, E-Shopping and Personal Home Pages).

Rosso [26] explored the use of genre as a document descriptor in order to improve the effectiveness of Web searching. Author formulated three hypotheses: (1) Users of the system must possess sufficient knowledge of the genre. (2) Searchers must be able to relate the genres to their information needs. (3) Genre must be predictable by a machine-applied algorithm because it is not typically explicitly contained in the document.

Design patterns and pattern languages came from the architecture in the work of Christopher Alexander et al. [2]. From the mid sixties to mid seventies, Alexander et al. defined a new approach to architectural design. The new approach centered on the concept of pattern languages is described in a series of books [2]. Alexander's definition of pattern is as follows: "Each pattern describes a problem, which occurs over and over again in our environment, and then describes the core of the solution to that problem, in such a way that you can use this solution a million times over, without ever doing it the same way twice."

According to Tidwell [31], patterns are structural and behavioral features that improve the applicability of software architecture, a user interface, a Web site or something or another in some domain. They make things more usable and easier to understand. Patterns are descriptions of best practices within a given design domain. They capture common and widely accepted solutions, and their validity is empirically proved. Patterns are not novel, patterns are captured experiences and each of their implementation is a little different.

Good examples are also the "Web design patterns", which are patterns for design related to the web. A typical example of a Web design pattern can be the forum pattern (see Fig. 13.5). This pattern is meant for designers who need to implement this element on an independent Web page or as a part of another Web page. The pattern describes key solution features without implementation details.

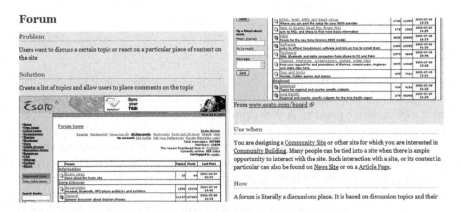

Fig. 13.5 Sample of Forum pattern (www.welie.com)

Generally, the design patterns describe a proven experience of repeated problem solving in the area of software solution design. From this point of view, the design patterns belong to key artifacts securing efficient reuse. While the design patterns have been proven in real projects, their usage increases the solution quality and reduces the time of their implementation.

There is a wide area of methods, which aim to detect objects related to patterns and extract their semantic details (e.g., opinion extraction [16], news extraction [34], Web discussion extraction [19], product detail extraction [24], and technical features extraction [28]).

13.4   Tools and Techniques

In the beginning of this chapter, we have presented our motivation, goals and thoughts. Now we mention some basic notions of useful technologies. The subsequent experiments illustrate the concrete application of proposed approach.

13.4.1   Pattrio Method

In our approach, we were inspired by the design pattern use for the analysis of Web page content. If we look for microgenres on Web pages, we need detailed technical information. That is why we have created our own catalog, in which we describe those repeated microgenres, which we manage to detect on Web pages by our method. For description we use a description similar to a pattern description, but its intention is different and it aims at understanding what characteristics are important for detection algorithm design. However, our view has a lot in common with patterns. It is mainly because also for us, in the same way as for a pattern, the most important characteristic is the name of the thing described. Our approach is different on the level of the general view and target. Simply said, we understand microgenre used by us as a projection of a Web design pattern . This projection does not always have to be unambiguous, e.g. one pattern can be projected to more microgenres.

13.4.1.1   Pattrio Catalog

Patterns are designed for Web designers who work with them and use them in production. A pattern description is composed from parts and each part describes a specific pattern feature. Authors usually use the pattern structure introduced in [2]. In the description, there is a pattern name, problem description, context, solution and examples of use. Usually, these are also consequences of the use of the pattern and related patterns which relate somehow with the pattern being used. For our description of microgenre we use the similar section-oriented structure.

13.4.1.2 Example – Discussion (Forum)

Problem How can a discussion about a certain topic be held? How can a summary of comments and opinions be displayed?

Context Social field, community sites, blogs, etc. Discussions about products and service sales. Review discussions. News story discussion.

Forces A page fragment with a headline and repeating segments containing individual comments. Keywords to labeling discussion on the page (discussion, forum, re, author, ...). Keywords to labeling persons (first names, nicknames). Date and time. There may be a form to enter a new comment. Segments with the discussion contributions are similar to the mentioned elements view, in form.

Solution Usually, an implementation using a table layout with an indentation for replies (or similar technology leading to the same-looking result) is used. The discussion is often together with the login. If discussion is on selling a product on Web site, there are usually purchase possibility, price information. The discussion can be alone on the page. In other case, there is also the something to read. In different domains the discussion can be displayed with review, news, etc. See Fig. 13.6.

Fig. 13.6 Discussion

13.4.1.3 Detection Algorithm

We have defined sets of elements mentioned above for each microgenre that are characteristic for this microgenre (words, data types, technical elements). These elements have been obtained on the basis of deeper analysis of a high volume of Web pages. This analysis also included the calculation of the weight of individual microgenre elements that defines the level of relevance for the microgenre. Besides, we have implemented a set of partial algorithms whose results are the extracted data types and also the score for the quality of fulfillment of individual rules of microgenres.

In our approach, there are elements with semantic contents (words or simple phrases and data types) and elements with importance for the structure of the Web page where the microgenre instance can be found (technical elements). The rules are the way that individual elements take part in the microgenre display. While defining these rules, we have been inspired by the Gestalt principles (see Fig. 13.7 and [31]). We formulated four rules based on these principles. The first one (proximity) defines the acceptable measurable distances of individual elements from each other. The second one (closure) defines the way to create of independent closed segments containing the elements. One or more segments then create the microgenre instance on the Web page. The third one (similarity) defines that the microgenre includes more related similar segments. The forth one (continuity) defines that the microgenre contains various segments that together create the Web pattern instance. The relations among microgenres can be on various levels similar as classes in OOP (especially simple association and aggregation).

The basic algorithm for detection of microgenres then implements the pre-processing of the code of the HTML page (only selected elements are preserved – e.g. block elements as table, div, lines, etc., see Table 13.1), segmentation and evaluation of rules and associations. The result for the page is the score of

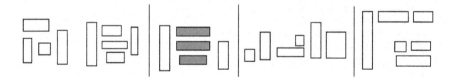

Fig. 13.7 Gestalt principles (proximity, similarity, continuity, closer)

Table 13.1 HTML tags – classification for analysis	Types	Tags
	Headings	H1, H2, H3, H4, H5, H6
	Text containers	P, PRE, BLOCKQUOTE, ADDRESS
	Lists	UL, OL, LI, DL, DIR, MENU
	Blocks	DIV, CENTER, FORM, HR, TABLE, BR
	Tables	TR, TD, TH, DD, DT
	Markups	A, IMG
	Forms	LABEL, INPUT, OPTION

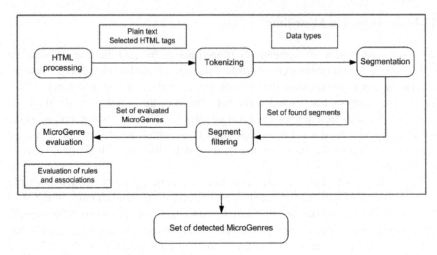

Fig. 13.8 Microgenre detection process

Algorithm 13.1 Microgenres score (pseudocode)

---

input : Set of PageEntities, set of microgenres
output : MicroGenresScore
foreach *PageEntity in PageEntities* **do**
    if *PageEntity is MicroGenreEntity* **then**
        if *does not exist segment* **then**
            create new segment in list of segment;
            to add page entity to segment;
        end
        add page entity to segment;
    end
end
foreach *segment in list of segments* **do**
    compute proximity of segment;
    compute closure of segment;
    compute Score(proximity, closure) of segment;
    if *Score is not good enough* **then**
        remove segment from list of segments;
    end
end
compute similarity of list of segments;
compute continuity of list of segments;
compute Score(similarity, continuity) of microgenre;
return Score

---

microgenres that are present on the page. The score then says what is the probability of expecting the microgenre instance on the page for the user. The entire process, including microgenre detection, is displayed in Fig. 13.8 and Algorithm 13.1.

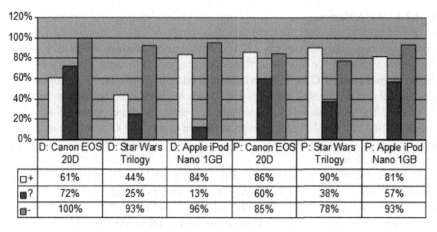

	D: Canon EOS 20D	D: Star Wars Trilogy	D: Apple iPod Nano 1GB	P: Canon EOS 20D	P: Star Wars Trilogy	P: Apple iPod Nano 1GB
□+	61%	44%	84%	86%	90%	81%
■?	72%	25%	13%	60%	38%	57%
▨-	100%	93%	96%	85%	78%	93%

Fig. 13.9 Accuracy of Pattrio method

13.4.1.4 Method Accuracy

The accuracy of the proposed method is about 80% (see [13]). Figure 13.9 shows the accuracy of the Pattrio method for three selected products (Apple iPod Nano 1 GB, Canon EOS 20D, Star Wars Trilogy film) and for the *discussion* and the *purchase possibility* microgenres. We used only the first 100 pages for each product. We manually, and using Pattrio method, evaluated the pages using a three-degree scale [9]:

+ Page does not contain required microgenre.
? Unable to evaluate results.
− Page do not contain required microgenre.

Then we compared these evaluations. For example the first value 61% expresses the accuracy for the pages with Canon EOS 20D product where there was a discussion.

13.4.2 Formal Concept Analysis

As one of the suitable tools for analyzing this kind of data we consider Formal concept analysis. When preprocessing Web pages, we often cannot clearly state the presence of a microgenre in the page content. We are able to describe the amount of its presence at some ref:CSNA-13-09le and this information can be captured using fuzzy methods and analyzed using a fuzzy extension of formal concept analysis [3]. But since we are dealing with a large volume of data [9] and a very imprecise environment, we should consider several practical issues, which have to be solved prior to the first application. Methods of matrix decomposition have succeeded in reducing the dimensions of input data (see [29] for application connected with formal concept analysis and [17, 18] for overview).

13.4.2.1 FCA Basics

Formal concept analysis (shortly FCA, introduced by **Rudolf Wille** in 1980) is well-known method for object–attribute data analysis. The input data for FCA is called **formal context** C, which can be described as $C = (G, M, I)$ – a triplet consisting of a set of objects G and set of attributes M, with I as the relation between G and M. The elements of G are defined as objects and the elements of M as attributes of the context. In order to express that an object $g \in G$ is related to I with the attribute $m \in M$, we record it as gIm or $(g, m) \in I$ and read that the object g has the attribute m.

For a set $A \subseteq G$ of objects we define $A' = \{m \in M \mid gIm \; for \; all \; g \in A\}$ (the set of attributes, common to the objects in A). Correspondingly, for a set $B \subseteq M$ of attributes we define $B' = \{g \in G \mid gIm \; for \; all \; m \in B\}$ (the set of objects which have all attributes in B). A **formal concept** of the context (G, M, I) is a pair (A, B) with $A \subseteq G$, $B \subseteq M$, $A' = B$ and $B' = A$. We call A the extent and B the intent of the concept $(A, B) \cdot \mathcal{B}(G, M, I)$ denotes the set of all concepts of context (G, M, I) and forms a complete lattice (so called **Gallois lattice**). For more details, see [11].

Now we give only a brief overview of FCA in fuzzy environment (approach of Bělohlávek et al.). Instead of classical binary case, we can consider the so-called complete residuated lattice $\mathbf{L} = \langle L, \vee, \wedge, \otimes, \rightarrow, 0, 1 \rangle$, where $\langle L, \vee, \wedge, 0, 1 \rangle$ is a complete lattice (with 0 and 1 being the smallest and biggest element), $\langle L, \otimes, 1 \rangle$ is a commutative monoid and $\langle \otimes, \rightarrow \rangle$ is an adjoint pair of binary operations (truth functions of fuzzy conjunction and fuzzy implication). The notion of being the element of a set can be replaced by the degree in which the element is contained in the set $(A(x))$. The notion of subset can be inferred in a similar way.

Now we can define the fuzzy **L-context** as $\mathbf{L} = \langle X, Y, I \rangle$ with X as a set of objects, Y as a set of attributes and I as a fuzzy relation $I : X \times Y \rightarrow L$. For a fuzzy set $A \in \mathbf{L}^X$, $B \in \mathbf{L}^Y$ (A is a fuzzy set of objects, B is a fuzzy set of attributes), we define fuzzy set of attributes $A' \in \mathbf{L}^Y$ and fuzzy set of objects $B' \in \mathbf{L}^X$ as

$$A'(y) = \bigwedge_{x \in X} \left(A(x)^{*_X} \rightarrow I(x, y) \right),$$

$$B'(x) = \bigwedge_{y \in Y} \left(B(y)^{*_Y} \rightarrow I(x, y) \right).$$

The $*_X$ and $*_X$ are the so-called truth-stressing functions or simple hedges which allows us to control the size of the resulting lattice.

Formal fuzzy concept is a pair $\langle A, B \rangle$, $A \in \mathbf{L}^X$, $B \in \mathbf{L}^Y$, such that $A' = B$ and $B' = A$. In this case, we will call A as the extent of the concept, and B as its intent. As $\langle \mathcal{B}(X^{*_X}, Y^{*_Y}, I), \leq \rangle$, we denote the set of all concepts, which when accompanied by the induced order is called **fuzzy concept lattice**. For further details and comparison with other approaches please see [3]. As you can see, the key terms from classical FCA have their parallel in the fuzzy environment. So the key algorithms have.

13.5   Experiments

In this chapter, we attempt to find such a description of a Web site that comes from the analysis of the architecture of pages belonging to this Web site. We treat the microgenres as the basis of this architecture, because they encapsulate those parts of the page content that have partial intent. We use our Pattrio method for microgenre identification. Our Web site description indicates the intent and purpose of the Web site. From this point of view the description provides interesting information about Web sites and as a consequence we can consider it as a description of the Web community.

As a Web site we consider a collection of Web pages placed together on one or more servers available via Internet. Web pages from one Web site share the same URL prefix and link to themselves. URL addresses of individual pages are organized into a hierarchy which allow users to orient themselves in a Web site. The root of this hierarchy is usually a special Web page known as the home page. From a technical point of view we understand a Web site as an Internet domain. This view can be inaccurate on a certain level, especially for Internet domains providing Web hosting. However, such domains are also usually specialized in some way, e.g. blogs, corporate and personal pages or small e-shops.

Various Web sites exist for various reasons. As typical examples, we can consider e-shops, news servers, social-related Web sites, corporate and academic Web sites, personal Web sites, etc. Web sites have different content and size. For example personal Web site can contain a small collection of Web pages, but a social-related Web site can have more than a million of Web pages.

From an external view, one Web site can appear differently to different users. Also the reasons to visit the Web site may vary. Let us take an e-shop as an example. It is sure that the aim of the e-shop owner is to sell the most goods. The aims of visitors may vary. A user can visit the e-shop to explore the kinds and prices of goods and read the terms of sale. The main target is the price information and maybe the price comparison. Another user wants to directly buy the goods. In that case, he or she will be interested in pages with a purchasing possibility. A third user may be interested in product parameters and the opinions of other users. Therefore, he or she will prefer pages containing technical features of products, discussion, FAQ, customer reviews and ratings. Web developers may have also another goal. Successful solutions and typically used compositions appear on Web pages in different Web sites. Therefore, some kind of unification can be seen in the development of Web pages with usual intent. This unification is based on principles which come out of simple consideration: "Let's do the things like others do successfully." Developers can follow the progress of their competitors. They can incorporate the new and successful techniques they have seen at their rivals.

It is hard to imagine that in the era of Internet search engines, users would always search Web pages by direct visit and navigation from a home page. One expects them to use one of the search engines to find the page. In that case, they will probably avoid the home page and will be navigating only through a limited part of the Web site, offered by the search engine in the first step. On the other hand, they can miss some pages completely.

We implemented a Web application with user interface connected to the API of different search engines (google.com, msn.com, yahoo.com and the Czech search engine jyxo.cz). Users from a group of students and teachers of high schools and VŠB – Technical University Ostrava, Czech Republic – were using this application for more than one year to search for everyday information. We have not influenced the process of searching in any way. The purpose of this part of the experiment was to view the World Wide Web using the perspective of users (as the search engines play key role in World Wide Web navigation). In the end, we obtained data set with more than 115,000 Web pages. After cleaning up, 77,850 unique Czech pages remained. For every single Web page we have performed the detection of 16 microgenres. The page did not have to contain any microgenre, as well as it may have theoretically contained 16 microgenres (price information, purchase possibility, special offer, hire sale, second hand, discussion and comments, review and opinion, technical features, news, enquire, login, something to read, link group, price per item, date per item, unit per item). The names of microgenres emerged from the discussions between us and students that took part in our experiments. They are therefore outcomes of social interaction. We used such preprocessed data sets for all the experiments.

13.5.1 Web Site Visualization

For the visualization of extracted information we have adopted one common graph drawing method, which works as follows: in the center of Fig. 13.10 you can see the circle representing the Web site. The size of the circle is determined by the relative size (number of pages) in the data set. The circles around the Web site correspond to individual microgenres. The size of circles is again determined by their relative presence in the data set.

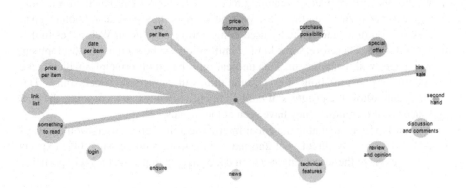

Fig. 13.10 Typical Web site aimed at selling products

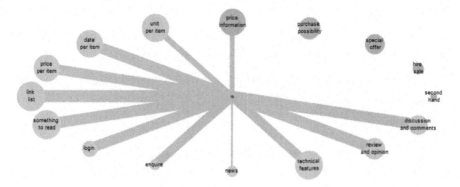

Fig. 13.11 Typical Web site aimed at information sharing

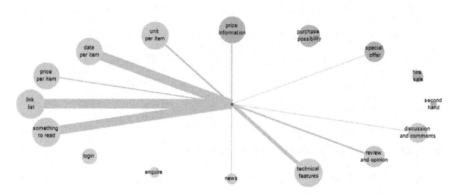

Fig. 13.12 Typical university Web site

The Web site is connected to microgenres using a straight line. The strength of this connection (represented by the line width) corresponds to the detected degree of microgenres present in the Web site.

Figures 13.10, 13.11, and 13.12 contain the described visualization of some Web sites from the Czech Republic – typical Web sites aimed at selling products, sharing information and education.

Figure 13.13 depicts two Web sites with similar intent – selling products. The second one differs in allowing users to share information in addition to a purchase possibility.

The presented view on Web sites allows comprehensive insight into the Web site essence. As a result, it also allows us to measure the similarity of Web sites. Similar Web sites can be understood as members of the same community.

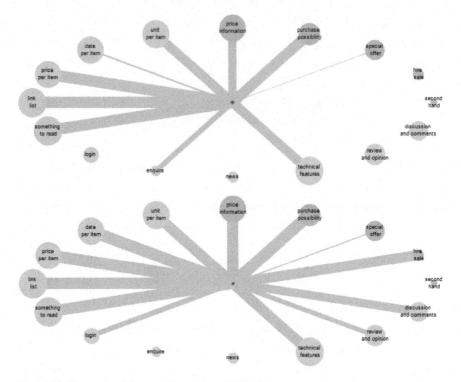

Fig. 13.13 Comparison of two product-oriented Web sites

13.5.2 Web Site Clustering

In the next experiment, we have tried to visualize the structure and relations of Web sites (and as a result also Web communities) referring to one specific topic. As an input, we have used the list of domains created in the previous experiment. Only Web sites with more than 20 pages in the data set have been taken into consideration. Each domain is accompanied by detected microgenres. This list is transformed into a binary matrix and considered as a formal context. Using methods of FCA we have computed a conceptual lattice which can be seen in Fig. 13.14. The resulting matrix has 516 rows (objects) and 16 columns (attributes) and the computed conceptual lattice contains 378 concepts.

From the computed lattice we have selected a sub-lattice containing 18 Web sites dealing with cell phones. Only five attributes have been selected and the visualization was created in a slightly different manner (see Fig. 13.15 and attached legend). Each node of the graph corresponds to one formal concept. To increase the visualization value, the attributes are represented by icons and the set of objects (Web sites) is depicted using small filled/empty squares in the lower part. It can be easily seen that the whole set of Web sites can be divided into two groups – the first one

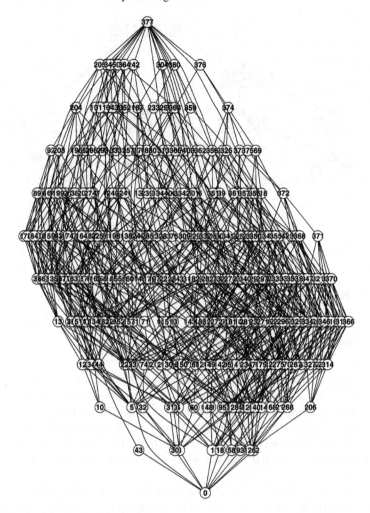

Fig. 13.14 Lattice calculated from whole dataset

contains sites where users are enabled to buy cell phones and the second one where the users are allowed to have a discussion. Deeper insight gives you more detailed information about Web site structures and relations.

The conceptual lattice forms a graph, which can be interpreted as an expression of relation between different Web sites. As a result, it describes the relation between different Web communities.

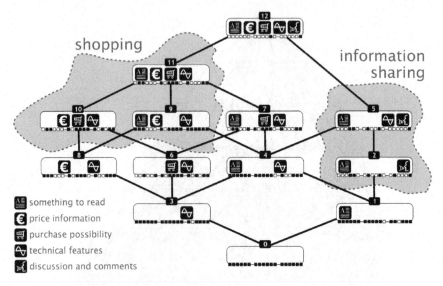

shopping

information
sharing

something to read
price information
purchase possibility
technical features
discussion and comments

Fig. 13.15 Part of lattice

13.6 Conclusions and Future Work

In this chapter, we have described three kinds of social groups which take part in Web page creation and usage. We distinguish these groups using their relation to the Web page – whether they define the intent of the page, whether they create the page or whether they use the page. By using this analysis, we can follow the evolution of the communities and observe the expectancies, rules and behavior they share. From this point of view, Web 2.0 is only a result of the existence and interaction of these social groups.

Our experiments illustrate that if we focus on Web sites and the Web page content they provide, we might come across a variety of interesting questions. These questions may bear upon the Web sites' similarity and the similarity of social groups involved in these pages, which could formulate interesting future research directions. The identification of additional microgenres and design of specific algorithms for their detection will be the matter of our future research.

References

1. Adamic L, Adar E (2005) How to search a social network. J Soc Networks 27:187–203
2. Alexander Ch (1977) A pattern language: towns, buildings, construction. Oxford University Press, New York
3. Belohlavek R, Vychodil V (2005) What is a fuzzy concept lattice. In: Proceedings of the CLA, 3rd international conference on concept lattices and their applications, Olomouc, Czech Republic, pp 34–45

4. Boese ES (2005) Stereotyping the web: genre classification of Web documents. Colorado State University
5. Borchers JO (2000) Interaction design patterns: twelve theses, workshop, vol 2. The Hague, The Netherlands
6. Cai D, Yu S, Wen JR, Ma WY (2003) Extracting content structure for Web pages based on visual representation. In: Fifth Asia Pacific Web conference, Xian, China, pp 406–417
7. Chaker J, Habib O (2007) Genre categorization of Web pages. In: Proceedings of the 7th IEEE international conference on data mining workshops, Omaha, Nebraska, USA, pp 455–464
8. Chang H Ch, Kayed M, Girgis MR, Shaalan KF (2006) A survey of Web information extraction systems. IEEE Trans Knowl Data Eng 18:1411–1428
9. Cole RJ, Eklund PW (1999) Scalability in formal concept analysis. Comput Intell 15:11–27
10. Dong L, Watters C, Duffy J, Shepherd M (2008) An examination of genre attributes for Web page classification. In: Proceedings of the 41st annual Hawaii international conference on system sciences, Big Island, HI, USA, pp 133–143
11. Ganter B, Wille R (1997) Formal concept analysis: mathematical foundations. Springer, New York
12. Kennedy A, Shepherd M (2005) Automatic identification of home pages on the Web. In: Proceedings of the 38th Hawaii international conference on system sciences, Big Island, HI, USA
13. Kocibova J, Klos K, Lehecka O, Kudelka M, Snasel V (2007) Web page analysis: experiments based on discussion and purchase Web patterns. In: Web intelligence and intelligent agent technology workshops, Silicon Valley, CA, USA, pp 221–225
14. Kudelka M, Snasel V, Lehecka O, El-Qawasmeh E, Pokorny J (2008) Web pages reordering and clustering based on Web patterns, SOFSEM 2008: Conference on current trends in theory and practice of computer science, Novy Smokovec, Slovakia, pp 731–742
15. Kumar R, Novak J, Tomkins A (2006) Structure and evolution of online social networks. In: Proceedings of the 12th ACM SIGKDD international conference on Knowledge discovery and data mining, Philadelphia, PA, USA, pp 611–617
16. Lee D, Jeong OR, Lee S (2008) Opinion mining of customer feedback data on the web. In: Proceedings of the 2nd international conference on Ubiquitous information management and communication, Suwon, Korea, pp 230–235
17. Lee D, Seung H (1999) Learning the parts of objects by non-negative matrix factorization. Nature 401:788–791
18. Letsche T, Berry MW, Dumais ST (1995) Computational methods for intelligent information access. In: Proceedings of the 1995 ACM/IEEE supercomputing conference, San Diego, CA, USA
19. Limanto HY, Giang NN, Trung VT, Zhang J, He Q, Huy NQ (2005) An information extraction engine for web discussion forums. In: International World Wide Web conference, Chiba, Japan, pp 978–979
20. Liu B, Grossman R, Zhai Y (2003) Mining data records in Web pages. KDD 2003, ACM SIGKDD international conference on knowledge discovery and data mining, Washington, DC, USA, pp 601–606
21. Martin JR (1995) Text and clause: fractal resonance. Text 15:5–42
22. Murata T (2004) Discovery of user communities from Web audience measurement data. Web Intelligence 2004, pp 673–676
23. Murata T, Takeichi K (2007) Discovering and visualizing network communities. Web intelligence/IAT workshops 2007, pp 217–220
24. Nie Z, Wen JR, Ma WY (2007) Object-level vertical search. In: Third biennial conference on innovative data systems research, Asilomar, CA, USA, pp 235–246
25. Pivk A, Cimiano P, Sure Y, Gams M, Rajkovic V, Studer R (2007) Transforming arbitrary tables into logical form with TARTAR. Data Knowl Eng 60:567–595
26. Rosso MA (2008) User-based identification of Web genres. JASIST (JASIS) 59(7):1053–1072
27. Santini M (2009) Description of 3 feature sets for automatic identification of genres in web pages. www.nltg.brighton.ac.uk/home/Marina.Santini/three_feature_sets.pdf. Accessed on 30 April 2009

28. Schmidt S, Stoyan H (2005) Web-based extraction of technical features of products. Beiträge der 35. Jahrestagung der Gesellschaft für Informatik, pp 256–261
29. Snasel V, Polovincak M, Dahwa HM, Horak Z (2008) On concept lattices and implication bases from reduced contexts. In: Supplementary proceedings of the 16th international conference on conceptual structures. ICCS 2008, pp 83–90
30. Takama Y, Mitsuhashi N (2005) Visual similarity comparison for Web page retrieval. In: Web intelligence, Compiegne, France, pp 301–304
31. Tidwell J (2005) Designing interfaces: patterns for effective interaction design. O'Reilly, Sebastopol, CA, USA, pp 0–596
32. Toyoda M, Kitsuregawa M (2001) Creating a Web community chart for navigating related communities. Hypertext 2001, Aarhus, Denmark, pp 103–112
33. Van Duyne DK, Landay JA, Hong JI (2003) The design of sites: patterns, principles, and processes for crafting a customer-centered Web experience. Addison-Wesley Professional, USA
34. Zheng S, Song R, Wen JR (2007) Template-independent news extraction based on visual consistency. In: Proceedings of the 22nd AAAI conference on artificial intelligence, Vancouver, British Columbia, Canada, pp 1507–1513
35. Zhu J, Zhang B, Nie Z, Wen JR, Hon HW (2007) Webpage understanding: an integrated approach. In: Conference on knowledge discovery in data, San Jose, California, USA, pp 903–912

Chapter 14
Extended Generalized Blockmodeling for Compound Communities and External Actors

Radoslaw Brendel and Henryk Krawczyk

Abstract Some social communities evident their own unique internal structure. In this chapter, we consider social communities composed of several cohesive subgroups which we call compound communities. For such communities, an extended generalized blockmodeling is proposed, taking into account the structure of compound communities and their relations with external actors. Using the extension, the community protection approach is proposed and used in detection of spam directed toward an e-mail local society.

14.1 Introduction

Social communities, such as groups of people or organizations that are joined by social interactions, form unique internal nets of ties that usually approve a formal organization of the community. Analysis of the structure of these ties could reveal an internal complex structure of such communities. In this chapter, we consider a group of communities composed internally of several cohesive subgroups. Although these subgroups are to some extent independent and "live on their own," they do exchange some information with other subgroups belonging to the same community, forming an internal net of ties. On the other side, every community as a whole also interacts with external actors, building with them another (external) net of ties. However, the communication with the external "world" is driven by different requirements regarding exchange of information other than the internal ones. That is why, if we consider internal and external patterns of communication ties, usually we find them different. Internal ties indicate the flow of information inside the community, whereas the external ties determine the way the community interacts with its neighborhood, i.e., other communities or external actors. A community whose internal structure is composed of several cohesive subgroups is called a compound community.

R. Brendel and H. Krawczyk
Gdansk University of Technology, Poland
e-mail: [radoslaw.brendel;henryk.krawczyk]@eti.pg.gda.pl

A. Abraham et al. (eds.), *Computational Social Network Analysis*, Computer
Communications and Networks, DOI 10.1007/978-1-84882-229-0_14,
© Springer-Verlag London Limited 2010

Observing the behavior (i.e., flow of information) of a compound community and external actors for a long enough time, it is possible to create a blockmodel describing typical relations between the components of the compound communities (i.e., cohesive subgroups) themselves and the components and external actors. The proposed blockmodel is composed of positions representing every community and external groups of actors (showing up similar behavior in respect to the communities) and relations between them (strictly, between external actors and components of compound communities). Additionally, the model can be used later in support of building a protection system of such communities. If we suppose that the model describes typical relations between communities and external actors, every new relation that is coming into being and that does not fit in the model is suspected because it shows exceptions from typical behavior and requires intervention from a security point of view. Moreover, if we are able to foresee some abnormal behavior of external actors, it is possible to include them in the blockmodel, letting the fitting process (in practice, clustering algorithm) immediately classify them as causing a certain, predefined type of threat to the communities. However, the efficiency of this method depends on whether we are able to detect the imminent threats from an external actor from anomalies in ties between the actors and the compound communities, saying more precisely between the external actors and cohesive subgroups of communities (Fig. 14.1).

In this chapter, we propose an extended generalized blockmodeling and the community protection approach by taking advantage of the extension. As an example of a compound community, we consider an e-mail network of one of the faculties of the Gdansk University of Technology. We define a prespecified extended blockmodel that helps us to detect unsolicited bulk e-mails directed toward the community of the faculty.

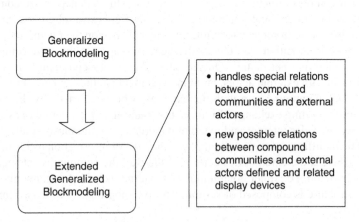

Fig. 14.1 Extended generalized blockmodeling

14.2   The Community Protection Approach

The community protection approach proposed in this chapter is assumed on the following foundations:

- The community (or communities) to be protected is a compound community, i.e., its components can be described as cohesive subgroups that do represent social groups.
- We know the typical flow of information between the following:
    - The community(-ies) components
    - The community components and external actors

- Threats (caused by abnormal behavior of external actors) we want to detect are discoverable through the analysis of anomalies in the information flow between external and internal actors.
- External actors have no or little knowledge about internal structure of the compound community and its typical relations with "friendly" external actors.

To begin with let us define sets of actors and relations that we are going to consider. Let $\mathbf{I} = \bigcup_{k=1}^{n} I^k$ be a set of compound communities; where each community is composed of several cohesive subgroups $I^k = \bigcup_i S_i^k$. The set $\mathcal{U}$ of all the actors we consider is then divided into two subsets: internal actors $\mathcal{U}_I = \{x : \exists_{k,i} \ x \in S_i^k \subset I^k \subset \mathbf{I}\}$ and external actors $\mathcal{U}_O = \mathcal{U}\backslash\mathcal{U}_I$. Then, we define the relations (see Fig. 14.2):

R: relation between external and internal (of a community) actors $R \subseteq \mathcal{U} \times \mathcal{U}$

R_S: relation between cohesive subgroups of the community: $\mathrm{den}(\gamma)(S_i^k, S_j^k; R)$
    $> \gamma_S \Rightarrow S_i^k R_S S_j^k$, where γ_S is an arbitrary set value

R_X: relation between external actors and cohesive subgroups: $xRy : x \in \mathcal{U}_O, y \in S_i^k \Rightarrow xR_X S_i^k$, thus: $R_X \subset \mathcal{U}_O \times \bigcup_{\substack{I^k \in \mathbf{I} \\ S_i^k \in I^k}} S_i^k$

The community protection approach can be presented as a three-step process, as shown in Fig. 14.3. The first stage deals with identification of cohesive subgroups inside the community. At this stage, we can use organizational data. However, it

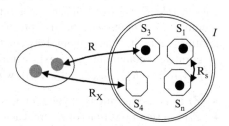

Fig. 14.2 Relations concerning compound community and external actors

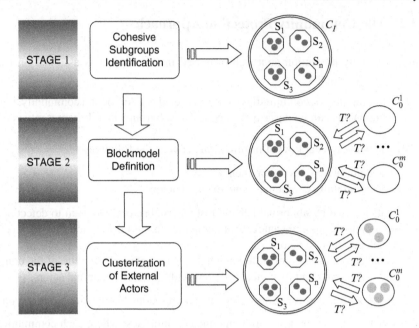

Fig. 14.3 Three step community protection approach

is advisable to approve the identification of cohesive subgroups by other relational data (see example later where we used affiliation data of our faculty to prespecified departments and e-mail exchange data).

In the second step, the proper blockmodel is constructed based on our knowledge regarding typical flow of information between compound communities and external actors. The proposed blockmodel is an extension of the blockmodel defined in [3] (p. 220). Let $\mathcal{Z}_I$ and $\mathcal{Z}_O$ be sets of positions of clusters of the communities and external actors adequately. Let $\mu_I : \mathcal{U}_I \rightarrow \mathcal{Z}_I \, \big| \forall_{x,y \in \mathcal{U}_I} x, y \in \mathcal{U}_I^k \Leftrightarrow \mu(x) = \mu(y)$ denote a mapping that maps each unit (community) to its position. Analogically, for external actors, let $\mu_O : \mathcal{U}_O \rightarrow \mathcal{Z}_O$. The cluster of communities $C_I(t_I)$ with the same position $t_I \in \mathcal{Z}_I$ is $C_I(t_I) = \mu_I^{-1}(t_I) = \{x \in \mathcal{U}_I : \mu_I(x) = t_I\}$ and for external actors: $C_O(t_O) = \mu_O^{-1}(t_O) = \{x \in \mathcal{U}_O : \mu_O(x) = t_O\}$.

The clustering (partition) can be expressed as follows: $\mathbf{C}(\mu_I; \mu_O) = \{C_I(t_I), C_O(t_O) : t_I \in \mathcal{Z}_I, t_O \in \mathcal{Z}_O\}$ or $\mathbf{C} = \{C_I^k, C_O^l : k = 1..n, l = 1..m\}$. The corresponding model matrix is shown in Table 14.1.

As we can see, the blockmodel is constrained because we know the number of clusters (classes) of external actors and internal actors (equals to a number of communities). The model will be also prespecified if we are able to provide types of relations (at least some of them) between the communities and external actors.

Formally, communities – ext. actors blockmodel is defined as $\mathbf{M}_{IO} = (\mathcal{Z}_I, \mathcal{Z}_O, K_{OI}, K_{IO}, \mathcal{T}_{OI}, \mathcal{T}_{IO}, \pi_{OI}, \pi_{IO})$, where:

- $\mathcal{Z}_I$ is a set of positions of communities actors.
- $\mathcal{Z}_O$ is a set of positions of external actors.

Table 14.1 Model matrix for compound communities and external actors. Gray fields indicate relations described by blockmodel M_{IO}

		C_I^1			...	C_I^n			C_o^1	...	C_o^m
		S_1	S_2	...		S_1	S_2	...			
C_I^1	S_1										
	S_2										
	...										
...	...										
C_I^n	S_1										
	S_2										
	...										
C_o^1											
...											
C_o^m											

- $K_{OI} \subseteq \mathcal{Z}_O \times \mathcal{Z}_I$ is a set of connections between positions of external and internal actors.
- $K_{IO} \subseteq \mathcal{Z}_I \times \mathcal{Z}_O$ is a set of connections between positions of internal and external actors.
- $\mathcal{T}_{OI}$ is a set of predicates used to describe the types of connections between clusters of external and internal actors (we assume that null $\in \mathcal{T}_{OI}$).
- $\mathcal{T}_{IO}$ is a set of predicates used to describe the types of connections between clusters of internal and external actors (we assume that null $\in \mathcal{T}_{IO}$).
- Mapping $\pi_{OI} : K_{OI} \rightarrow \mathcal{T}_{OI}\backslash\{null\}$ and $\pi_{IO} : K_{IO} \rightarrow \mathcal{T}_{IO}\backslash\{null\}$ assign predicates to connections.

To complete the specification of the communities – external actors blockmodel we defined a set of predicates that describe types of connections between clusters of internal and external actors. In Tables 14.2 and 14.3, we give some examples of such predicates for sets $\mathcal{T}_{OI}$ and $\mathcal{T}_{IO}$ adequately (for clarity, we substituted C_O with O and C_I with I).

For each new predicate (block type), we defined new display devices for letting the blocks be visualized. In Table 14.4, we proposed display devices defined for two types of connections from Tables 14.2 and 14.3. Table 14.5 captures deviation measures for the predefined types of blocks. These measures allow us to calculate the "distance" between an ideal block and the corresponding real block in a blockmodel. The measures are used in a clustering algorithm to calculate a criterion function.

The quantities used in the expressions for deviations have the following meaning:

$n_r = card\,O$ – number of rows in a block

$n_c = |I|$ – number of cohesive subgroups in the community

$s_i = \sum\limits_{S \in I} sig(card(R_X(e_i, S)))$ – number of cohesive subgroups with which an

external actor $e_i \in O$ has at least one relation; in other words: a number of nonnull blocks of type $R_X(e_i, S)$ for each cohesive subgroup and the external actor e_i

Table 14.2 Types of connections: external actors $\rightarrow$ communities actors (T_{OI})

O2I null	$oi - null(O, I; R)$	$\equiv R(O, I) = \emptyset$
O2I complete	$oi - com(O, I; R)$	$\equiv \forall x \in O \forall S \in I : xR_X S$
O2I row regular	$oi - rreg(O, I; R)$	$\equiv \forall x \in O \exists S \in I : xR_X S$
O2I row degree $> n$	$oi - rdeg(> n)(O, I; R)$	$\equiv \forall x \in O :$ $\sum\limits_{S \in I} card(R_X(x, S)) > n$
O2I row degree $< n$	$oi - rdeg(< n)(O, I; R)$	$\equiv \forall x \in O :$ $\sum\limits_{S \in I} card(R_X(x, S)) < n$
O2I not related	$oi - nrel(O, I; R)$	$\equiv \forall x \in O \forall S_1, S_2 :$ $R_X(x, S_1), R_X(x, S_2), S_1 \neq S_2$ $\Rightarrow \neg S_1 R_S S_2$
O2I not related $> n$	$oi - nrel(> n)(O, I; R)$	$\equiv oi - nrel(O, I; R)$ and $oi - rdeg(> n)(O, I; R)$
O2I not related $< n$	$oi - nrel(< n)(O, I; R)$	$\equiv oi - nrel(O, I; R)$ and $oi - rdeg(< n)(O, I; R)$
O2I related	$oi - rel(O, I; R)$	$\equiv \forall x \in O \forall S_1, S_2 :$ $xR_S S_1, xR_S S_2, S_1 \neq S_2$ $\Rightarrow S_1 R_S S_2$
O2I related $> n$	$oi - rel(> n)(O, I; R)$	$\equiv oi - rel(O, I; R)$ and $oi - rdeg(> n)(O, I; R)$
O2I related $< n$	$oi - rel(< n)(O, I; R)$	$\equiv oi - rel(O, I; R)$ and $oi - rdeg(< n)(O, I; R)$

Table 14.3 Types of connections: communities $\rightarrow$ external actors (T_{IO})

I2O null	$io - null(I, O; R)$	$\equiv R(I, O) = \emptyset$
I2O complete	$io - com(I, O; R)$	$\equiv \forall x \in O \forall S \in I : SR_x^{-1} x$
I2O column regular	$io - creg(I, O; R)$	$\equiv \forall x \in O \exists S \in I : SR_x^{-1} x$
I2O column degree $> n$	$io - cdeg (>n)$ $(I, O; R)$	$\equiv \forall x \in O :$ $\sum\limits_{S \in I} card(R_x^{-1}(S, x)) > n$
I2O column degree $< n$	$io - cdeg(<n)$ $(I, O; R)$	$\equiv \forall x \in O :$ $\sum\limits_{S \in I} card(R_x^{-1}(S, x)) < n$

$s_t = \sum\limits_{i=1}^{n_r} s_i$ – total number of cohesive subgroups and external actors in a block that developed at least one relation

p_r – number of nonnull rows in a block; in other words: number of external actors in a block that do have at least one relation with any cohesive subgroup

$p_r(n+)$ – number of rows in a block that correspond to external actors that have more than n relations with different cohesive subgroups

$p_r(-n)$ – number of rows in a block that correspond to external actors that have less than n relations with different cohesive subgroups

s_{ir} – number of cohesive subgroups an external actor e_i relates to that are also related to themselves

Table 14.4 Block types

O2I null	oi − null	All 0	
O2I complete	oi − com	∃ at least one 1 in each row for each subgroup S	
O2I row regular	oi − rreg	∃ at least one 1 in each row	
O2I row degree $> n$	oi − rdeg($> n$)	∃ at least one 1 in each row for at least $(n + 1)$ subgroups	n+
O2I row degree $< n$	oi − rdeg($< n$)	∃ at least one 1 in each row for at most $(n − 1)$ subgroups	−n
O2I not related	oi − nrel	!∃ two 1s in any row corresponding to different subgroups that relate	
O2I not related $> n$	oi − nrel($> n$)	∃ more then n 1s in any row corresponding to different subgroups that do not relate	n+
O2I not related $< n$	oi − nrel($< n$)	∃ less then n 1s in any row corresponding to different subgroups that do not relate	−n
O2I related	oi − rel	∀ two 1s in each row, if they correspond to different subgroups, the subgroups relate	
O2I related $> n$	oi − rel($> n$)	∃ more then n 1s in any row corresponding to different subgroups that all relate	n+
O2I related $< n$	oi − rel($< n$)	∃ less then n 1s in any row corresponding to different subgroups that do not relate	−n
I2O null	io − null	all 0	
I2O complete	io − com	∃ at least one 1 in each column for each subgroup	
I2O column regular	io − creg	∃ at least one 1 in each column	
I2O column degree $> n$	io − cdeg($> n$)	∃ at least one 1 in each column for at least $(n + 1)$ subgroups	n+
I2O column degree $< n$	io − cdeg($< n$)	∃ at least one 1 in each column for at most $(n − 1)$ subgroups	−n

Table 14.5 Deviations measures for types of blocks

Connection	$\delta(O, I; T)$
O2I null	s_t
O2I complete	$n_r^* n_c - s_t$
O2I row regular	$(n_r - p_r)^* n_c$
O2I row degree $> n$	$(n_r - p_r(n+))^* n_c$
O2I row degree $< n$	$(n_r - p_r(-n))^* n_c$
O2I not related	$p_{rr}^* n_c$
O2I not related $> n$	$(n_r - p_{rn}(n+))^* n_c$
O2I not related $< n$	$(n_r - p_{rn}(-n))^* n_c$
O2I related	$(n_r - p_{rr})^* n_c$
O2I related $> n$	$(n_r - p_{rr}(n+))^* n_c$
O2I related $< n$	$(n_r - p_{rr}(-n))^* n_c$
Connection	$\delta(I, O; T)$
I2O null	s_w
I2O complete	$n_r^* n_c - s_w$
I2O column regular	$(n_c - p_c)^* n_r$
I2O column degree $> n$	$(n_c - p_c(n+))^* n_r$
I2O column degree $< n$	$(n_c - p_c(-n))^* n_r$

$s_{tr} = \sum_{i=1}^{n_r} s_{ir}$ – total number of cohesive subgroups that are related to themselves and to external actors counted separately for every external actor

p_{rr} – number of rows in a block for which $s_{ir} > 0$

$p_{rr}(n+)$ – number of rows in a block for which $s_{ir} > n$

$p_{rr}(-n)$ – number of rows in a block for which $s_{ir} < n$

s_{in} – number of not related cohesive subgroups an external actor e_i relates to

$s_{tn} = \sum_{i=1}^{n_r} s_{in}$ – total number of not related cohesive subgroups an external actor relates to, counted separately for every external actor

p_{rn} – number of rows in a block for which $s_{in} > 0$

$p_{rn}(n+)$ – number of rows in a block for which $s_{in} > n$

$p_{rn}(-n)$ – number of rows in a block for which $s_{in} < n$

$s_j = \sum_{S \in I} sig(card(R_X^{-1}(S, e_i)))$ – number of cohesive subgroups that relate to an external actor $e_i \in O$; in other words: a number of nonnull blocks of type $R_X^{-1}(S, e_i)$ for each cohesive subgroup and the external actor e_i

$s_w = \sum_{i=1}^{n_c} s_w$ – total number of cohesive subgroups and external actors in a block that developed at least one relation

p_c – number of nonnull columns in a block; in other words: number of external actors with which at least one cohesive subgroup has a relation

$p_c(n+)$ – number of columns in a block that correspond to external actors with which more than n cohesive subgroups have a relation, and

$p_c(-n)$ – number of columns in a block that correspond to external actors with which less than n cohesive subgroups have a relation

Having defined the blockmodel for communities–external actors, types of connections T_{OI} and T_{IO} and deviations measures of types of blocks $\delta(O, I; T)$ and $\delta(I, O; T)$, we need a method for clusterings external actors according to the blockmodel. Generally, the clustering problem can be expressed as an optimization problem. The clustering problem $(\Phi, P, \min)$ can be expressed as follows: Determine the clustering $\mathbf{C}^* \in \Phi$, for which

$$P(\mathbf{C}^*) = \min_{C \in \Phi} P(\mathbf{C}) \qquad (14.1)$$

where Φ is a set of feasible clusterings and $P : \Phi \to \mathbb{R}_0^+$ is a clustering criterion function [2].

A criterion function that we use is as follows:

$$P(\mathbf{C}) = P(\mathbf{C}; T_{OI}) + P(\mathbf{C}; T_{IO}) \qquad (14.2)$$

where:

$$P(\mathbf{C}; T_{OI}) = \sum_{(t,w) \in \mathcal{Z}_O \times \mathcal{Z}_I} \min_{T \in T_{OI}} \omega(T)\delta(C(t), C(w); T) \qquad (14.3)$$

$$P(\mathbf{C}; T_{IO}) = \sum_{(w,t) \in \mathcal{Z}_I \times \mathcal{Z}_O} \min_{T \in T_{IO}} \omega(T)\delta(C(w), C(t); T) \qquad (14.4)$$

Finally, having the blockmodel specified, one of the clustering algorithms can be used to cluster external actors into partitions thus fitting the blockmodel to the considered social network.

14.3 Short Description of Algorithms

The proposed community protection approach assumes that we deal with compound communities. To check whether the condition is satisfied, we have to use one of the formal methods that allows us to divide all actors into groups with characteristics that actors belonging to the same group exchange information more often with each other than with actors from another group. There are several techniques to detect cohesive subgroups based on density and connectedness, three of which are components, k-cores, and cliques or complete subnetworks. All the three techniques assume relatively dense patterns of connections within subgroups, but they differ in the minimal density required, which varies from at least one connection (weak components) to all possible connections (cliques). However, the most important is that the obtained result (cohesive subgroups) has to be verified whether it really represents social group because not every cohesive subgroup does it. If it does not, the proposed method may fail because it would mistakenly classify "enemies" as "friendly" actors.

In the case of the direct blockmodeling approach, where an appropriate criterion function to capture the selected equivalence is constructed, one of the local optimization clustering procedures can be used to solve the given blockmodeling problems. For general blockmodeling the relocation algorithm is usually proposed (see [7], pp. 188).

14.4 Example

In this chapter we propose the community protection approach. Below, we show how this approach can be used to model an e-mail network community and other e-mail users – external in respect to the community.

Stage 1 As an example of a compound community we analyzed a structure of one of the faculties of the Gdansk University of Technology. We expected the departments of the faculty to form social cohesive subgroups. To some extent, e-mail traffic generated by members of the departments should reveal these social properties. To prove it, we collected e-mail traffic generated by all the members of the faculty and grouped them into clusters according to the affiliation of every e-mail sender to an adequate department. The results are presented in Fig. 14.4 (for the clarity of the image, six representative departments are shown; we removed interdepartmental links and summarized the network).

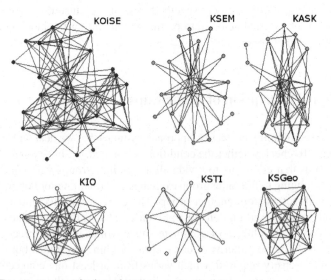

Fig. 14.4 Departments as cohesive subgroups

Fig. 14.5 E-mail network
between two departments

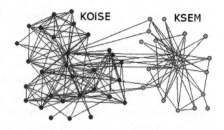

Table 14.6 Densities of
departmental networks

Dept.	KOiSE	KSEM	KASK	KIO	KSTI	KSGeo
KOiSE	0.33	0.02	0.02	0.02	0.01	0.03
KSEM	–	0.27	0.01	0.02	0.01	0.03
KASK	–	–	0.44	0.04	0.02	0.03
KIO	–	–	–	0.68	0.02	0.03
KSTI	–	–	–	–	0.27	0.01
KSGeo	–	–	–	–	–	0.79

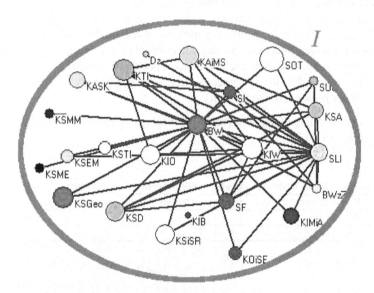

Fig. 14.6 Identified cohesive subgroups (stage 1)

In Fig. 14.5 we showed two example departments along with relations between
them. We can see that connections between the departments are much weaker in
comparison to intradepartmental connections.

To verify whether the departments of the faculty do form cohesive subgroups,
we calculated densities of the departmental and interdepartmental subnetworks. The
results for the six departments are shown in Table 14.6.

As a result, we can model the e-mail community of the faculty as shown in
Fig. 14.6. The circles represent departments (cohesive subgroups) and lines show

departments that cooperate (we assumed cooperation if $\gamma_S > 0.05$). Sizes of the circles are proportional to the density of the departmental network.

Stage 2 At this stage, we define the proper blockmodel. In our case, the model should help us to capture one of the most important problems of today's e-mail service – spamming. To protect e-mail users from being flooded by spam, we proposed a prespecified constrained blockmodel. We distinguished five clusters: one for the identified (stage 1) compound community and four classes of external actors representing spammers and regular users. Additionally, we defined relations between the clusters (positions) representing external groups of actors (spammers and regular users) and the compound community. The constrained prespecified blockmodel is presented in Table 14.7.

We defined the following external groups of actors:

- G_1 – a class of regular users that received at least one e-mail from the members of the community (io-cdeg(> 0))
- G_2 – a class of regular users that send e-mails to people from c different departments and that do relate to each other (oi-rel($> c$))
- S_1 – a class of spammers that send a substantive amount of e-mails to different components of the community (departments of the faculty) (oi-rdeg($> a$)) and nobody from the protected community responded to it (io-null)
- S_2 – a class of spammers that send e-mails to people from b different departments and that do not relate to each other (oi-nrel($> b$)) and nobody from the protected community responded to it (io-null)

The corresponding blockmodel using the display devices defined in Table 14.4 is presented in Fig. 14.7.

Table 14.7 Model matrix for a faculty compound community and external actors

| | E-mail Network Cluster | Spammers Clusters | | Regular users clusters | |
	I	S_1	S_2	G_1	G_2
I	–	io-null	io-null	io-cdeg(>0)	?
S_1	oi-rdeg($> a$)	–	–	–	–
S_2	oi-nrel($> b$)	–	–	–	–
G_1	?	–	–	–	–
G_2	oi-rel($> c$)	–	–	–	–

Fig. 14.7 A blockmodel for a compound community and external e-mail users

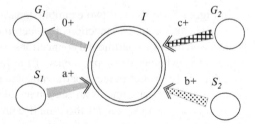

Stage 3 In the last step of the proposed approach, we should run the proper clusterization and optimization process. According to the blockmodel defined at stage 2 (Table 14.7), we classified external e-mail users assigning them to one of the four predefined roles (positions): G_1 or G_2 (regular users) and S_1 or S_2 (spammers). In our test, we assumed parameters having the following values: $a = 6, b = 1, c = 1$. We collected the e-mail exchange data between the faculty and external e-mail actors for a period of 2 months building an e-mail exchange graph. After that, we did proper classification. The summary results are shown in Table 14.8. Figure 14.8 shows a part of the e-mail exchange graph where external users are grouped according to their assigned roles.

The classification shows that considering nonspammers clusters (G_1 and G_2), 7% of e-mail users classified as nonspammers were spammers in reality (false negatives). All users from G_1 were classified correctly. Indeed, we answer spammers rather by mistake. However, it happened that 7% of spammers succeeded in sending e-mail toward people belonging to community's subgroups that cooperate. They were just lucky unless they knew the internal structure of the community at the faculty. Looking at the spammers clusters (S_1 and S_2) almost 16% of regular users left unrecognized. Considering a cluster containing users that sent mass e-mail 6.7% of them turned out to be regular users. However, it is rather something strange in a way of communication between these users and a community because normally we do

Table 14.8 Classification of e-mail external users

	Spammers		Nonspammers	
	Percent class'd as spammers	Percent classified as nonspammers	Percent classified as spammers	Percent classified as nonspammers
G1	–	0.0	–	100.0
G2	–	18.8	–	81.3
S1	93.3	–	6.7	–
S2	64.3	–	35.7	–
Total G	–	7.0	–	93.0
Total S	84.1	–	15.9	–
Total	92.5	7.5	14.9	85.1

Fig. 14.8 E-mail users grouped by assigned roles (stage 3)

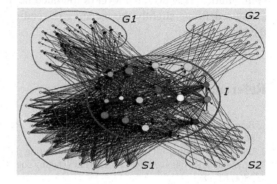

not send business letters to a significant amount of users of one organization. Lastly, a reason for the significant amount of 35% of misclassified users in cluster S_2 is that these users represent somebody that is not business related with a compound community. Mostly, these "users" represent mailing lists of various hobby services the company users belong to. So, it is rather natural that relations between these users and the community are rather casual.

14.5 Conclusions

In this chapter, we proposed the extension of generalized blockmodeling that captures relations between communities composed of several cohesive subgroups (compound communities) and external actors. We proposed new types of connections and new display devices as well. For each new type of relation we defined deviation measures that are used in a clustering algorithm, letting us properly evaluate criterion functions. The new blockmodelling approach was then used to model relations between departments of one faculty of the University and external users based on e-mail traffic. Then, according to this model, external e-mail users that started relations with any of e-mail faculty users were classified as spammer or non-spammer with considerable success. Faults in the classification resulted from the fact that some faculty e-mail users use their account for non-company issues, thus relations they develop are not related to company structure hence compromising the prerequisites of the proposed approach.

The proposed extention of general blockmodeling can also be useful in modeling an environment composed of several compound communities. In this case, it is possible to group external actors according to specific relations they developed toward every compound community. However, this situation requires cooperation of the communities, i.e., one community knows relations between external actors, and the other communities included in the blockmodel. Another possible usage can be identification of plagiary in published papers.

It seems that the main drawback of this method is that it assumes (maybe too far) an inflexible model of communication between external users and compound communities. However, the level of tolerated flexibility can be "regulated" to some extent redefining slightly the meaning of relation between cohesive subgroups of the communities.

References

1. Batagelj V, Mrvar A Pajek – Program for large network analysis. Home page http://vlado.fmf.uni-lj.si/pub/networks/pajek/
2. Batagelj V, Ferligoj A (1998) Constrained clustering problems. IFCS'98, Rome
3. Boykin PO, Roychowdhury VP (2005) Leveraging social networks to fight spam. IEEE Comput 38(4):61–68

4. Brandes U, Erlebach T (2005) Network analysis. Methodological foundations. Springer, New York
5. Brendel R, Krawczyk H (2006) Spam classification methods based on users' e-mail communication graphs. In: Proceedings of the second IEEE international conference on technologies for homeland security and safety. Kadir Has University, pp 81–86
6. Carrington PJ, Scott J, Wasserman S (2007) Models and methods in social network analysis, Cambridge University Press, New York
7. Doreian P, Batagelj V, Ferligoj A (2005) General blockmodeling. Cambridge Univeristy Press, New York
8. de Nooy W, Mrvar A, Batagelj V (2005) Exploratory social network analysis with Pajek. Structural analysis in the social sciences 27. Cambridge University Press, New York
9. Wasserman S, Faust K (2007) Social network analysis. Cambridge Univeristy Press, Cambridge

Chapter 15
Analyzing Collaborations Through Content-Based Social Networks

Alessandro Cucchiarelli, Fulvio D'Antonio, and Paola Velardi

Abstract This chapter presents a methodology and a software application to support the analysis of collaborations and collaboration content in scientific communities. High-quality terminology extraction, semantic graphs, and clustering techniques are used to identify the relevant research topics. Traditional and novel social analysis tools are then used to study the emergence of interests around certain topics, the evolution of collaborations around these themes, and to identify potential for better cooperation.

15.1 Introduction

This chapter presents a novel model for social network analysis in which, rather than analyzing the quantity of relationships (co-authorships, business relations, friendship, etc.), we analyze their communicative content. Text mining and clustering techniques are used to capture the content of communication and to identify the most popular themes. The social analyst is then able to perform a study of the network evolution in terms of the relevant themes of collaboration, the detection of new concepts gaining popularity, and the existence of popular themes that could benefit from better cooperation.

The idea of modeling the content of social relationships with clusters of terms is not entirely new. In [6], a method is proposed to discover "semantic clusters" in Google news, i.e., groups of people sharing the same topics of discussion. In [9], the authors propose the Author–Recipient–Topic model, a Bayesian network that captures topics and the directed social network of senders and recipients

A. Cucchiarelli and F. D'Antonio
Polytechnic University of Marche, Italy
e-mail: [cucchiarelli;dantonio]@diiga.univpm.it

P. Velardi
"Sapienza Università di Roma", Italy
e-mail: velardi@di.uniroma1.it

A. Abraham et al. (eds.), *Computational Social Network Analysis*, Computer
Communications and Networks, DOI 10.1007/978-1-84882-229-0_15,
© Springer-Verlag London Limited 2010

in a message-exchange context. In [21] the objective is reversed: they introduce consideration of social factors (e.g., the fact that two authors begin to cooperate) into traditional content analysis, in order to provide social justification to topic evolution in time; similarly, in [11], topic models and citations are combined. On a similar perspective is also the work of [10], in which content mining and co-authorship analysis are combined for topical community discovery in document collections. To learn topics, the latter three papers use variations of Latent Dirichlet Allocation (LDA), a generative probabilistic model for collection of discrete data such as text corpora [3]. Statistical methods for topic detection (and in particular LDA) require complex parameter estimation over a large training set. Another problem with state-of-the-art literature on topic detection is the rather naif bag-of-words model used for extracting content from documents. For example, in [6] one of the topics around which groups of people are created is *"said, bomb, police, London, attack"*, an example from [9] is: *"section, party, language, contract, [...]"*, and from [10] is: *"web, services, semantic, service, poor, ontology, rdf, management"*. In many domains, the significance of topics could be more evident using key phrases (e.g., *"web"* + *"services"* in the third example). As a matter of fact, this problem is pervasive in the term clustering literature (see, e.g., clusters in [16]), regardless of the application. Authors are more concerned with the design of powerful clustering models than with the data used to feed these models. Unfortunately, it has been experimentally demonstrated (see, e.g., [8]) that clustering performance strongly depends on how well input data can be separated, an issue which makes the selection of input features a central one. In our view, the usefulness of a content-based social analysis is strongly related to the informative level and semantic cohesion of the learned topics. A simple bag-of-words model seems rather inadequate at capturing the content of social communications, especially in specialized domains[1] wherein terminology is central.

Other related work in the area of social networks concerns the so-called *Semantic Social Web (SSW)*. Recently, several papers [5, 7] and initiatives (e.g., the SIOC *"Semantically-Interlinked Online Communities"* project[2]) proposed the integration of online community information through the use of ontologies, such as the FOAF, for expressing personal profiles and social networking information. Through the use of ontologies and ontology languages, user-generated content can be expressed formally, and innovative semantic applications can be built on top of the existing Social Web. Research efforts in this area focus primarily on the specification of ontology standards and ontology matching procedures, assuming a "Semantic Web-like" reality in which documents are annotated with the concepts of a domain ontology. This is a rather demanding postulate, since in real SN, the information exchanged between actors is mostly unstructured, or we can imagine that, given the

---

[1] Note that specialized domains are those with higher potential of application for social analysts: thematic blogs, research communities, networked companies, etc.

[2] http://www.sioc-project.org

variegated social nature of many communities, these will eventually entrust a knowledge engineer to manage the job of ontology building and semantic annotation. Therefore, we believe that the success of the SSW vision also depends on the availability of automated tools to extract and formalize the information from unstructured documents, restricting human intervention to verification and post-editing.

The contribution of this chapter is twofold:

- First, we propose a methodology to capture the relevant topics of a communication, which is based on natural language processing and semantic techniques. High-quality terminology extraction, ontological, and co-occurrence relation analysis allow it to improve the significance of topic clustering, by virtue of a more clearly separable feature space.
- Second, a social network analysis (SNA)is conducted (supported by a dedicated interface) to study the evolution of collaborations around topics, the topic shift in time, and to detect potential or active collaborations among groups sharing the same interests. We show that the SN model we propose enables a rather deeper and informative analysis of a community of interest.

These capabilities were found particularly useful in the analysis of a research group born during the EC-funded INTEROP Network of Excellence (NoE), now continuing its mission within a permanent institution named "Virtual Laboratory on Enterprise Interoperability."[3] The networks of excellence have the main purpose of reducing research de-fragmentation; therefore, the availability of diagnostic tools such as those presented in this chapter provides valuable support to monitor the increase of cooperation, the emergence of new research themes, and the definition of targeted actions aimed at improving research collaboration on a given theme. The following are relevant types of information, enabled by our model, to support the governance of research networks:

- Potential areas for collaboration between groups that share similar interests (but do not cooperate), to avoid duplication of results
- Popularity of research topics, to redirect, if necessary, the effort on potentially relevant but poorly covered topics
- Evolution of collaborations over time, to verify that governance actions produce the desired progress toward research de-fragmentation

These data cannot be gathered by the mere study of co-authorships.

The chapter is organized as follows: Sect. 15.2 summarizes the methodology and algorithms used for concept extraction and topic clustering. Section 15.3 presents the Content-Based Social Network (CB-SN) model and measures, and it provides detailed examples of the type of analysis supported, applied to the case of the INTEROP NOE. Finally, Sect. 15.3 is dedicated to concluding remarks and presentation of future work.

---

[3] http://www.interop-vlab.eu

15.2   Identification of Themes of Interest in a Social Network

The first objective of our SN analysis is to identify the relevant topics that depict
at best the content of communications among network members. As remarked in
the introduction, we use a novel methodology, aimed at extracting truly informative
clusters, not simply based on bag of words. The methodology relies on our previous
work on automated terminology [14], glossary [12], and taxonomy [18] learning in
specialized domains.

15.2.1   Summary of the Topic Extraction Methodology

Figure 15.1 summarizes the processing steps to extract research themes. Examples
of input–output data in Fig. 15.1 belong to the INTEROP domain.

1. **Concept extraction** First, the document corpus D characterizing the scientific
   domain is processed, using our freely available terminology extraction system[4]
   [14] to detect the relevant domain terms. Let T be the extracted terminology:
   notice that, in restricted domains, it is commonly assumed that terms are unambiguous; therefore, we can denote them also as "concepts."

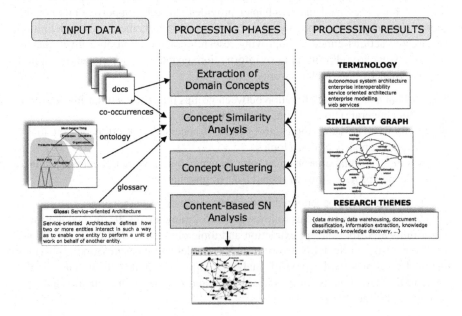

Fig. 15.1   Processing phases for research themes extraction

---

[4] http://lcl.uniroma1.it./termextractor

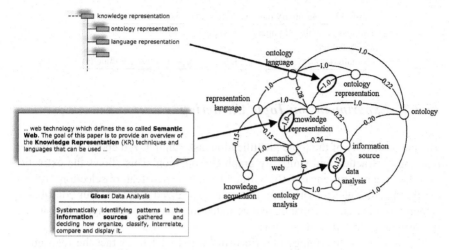

Fig. 15.2 Different sources used to draw edges in the similarity graph

2. **Concept Similarity Analysis** A graph G is generated, wherein nodes are the concepts in T, and edges represent statistically weighted relations between node pairs. Relations are extracted from three sources: co-occurrences in the domain corpus D and in a domain glossary, and semantic relations encoded in a domain ontology. Glossary[5] and ontology have been semiautomatically learned, as described in [12, 18]. Figure 15.2 shows an excerpt of a similarity graph G: the figure provides examples of different sources of evidence contributing to the creation of edges. Though the nature of these sources is different, they all suggest that related concepts are semantically close in the analyzed domain. The graph G is used to compute similarity vectors x_i for each $t_i \in G$. The element (i, j) of x_i is the similarity between t_i and t_j, $\text{sim}(t_i, t_j)$, estimated as a function of the minimum path connecting t_i and t_j in G.

3. **Detection of Research Themes** The similarity matrix X (x_i are the rows of X) is clustered using two recently introduced clustering algorithms, *K-means++* [1] and *Repeated Bisections* [20]. We defined a novel clustering evaluation measure[6] to select the "best" clustering $\mathscr{C}^{BEST}$: within a set of results obtained when varying the algorithm, the number k of generated clusters, and range reduction[7] of the matrix X. The clusters $C_i \in \mathscr{C}^{BEST}$ are considered to represent the relevant research themes, or *topics*, of the analyzed community.

---

[5] http://lcl.uniroma1.it/glossextractor

[6] The measure is described in detail in [4].

[7] Singular value decomposition (SVD) is used to reduce data sparseness of the similarity matrix X.

Table 15.1 Summary data on corpus analysis

Number of analyzed papers	1,452
Extracted terms	728
Domain ontology used	http://interop-vlab.eu/backoffice/tav

15.2.2 Experiments on Topic Clustering

The major novelty of the topic identification task summarized above lies in the terminology extraction and similarity graph computation. This allows the extraction of rather meaningful clusters (by virtue of an improved feature selection), reflecting the specific interests of communities in specialized domains. Our contribution is therefore focused on semantic feature induction, not on clustering; in fact, we use two available clustering algorithms.

We used the methodology described in Sect. 15.2.1 to extract the relevant research topics of the INTEROP community. We collected 1,452 full papers or abstracts authored by the INTEROP project members belonging to 46 organizations. Table 15.1 summarizes the relevant results and data of the corpus analysis phase.

The similarity graph-based methodology was then applied to the extracted concepts, using the semantic relations encoded in the INTEROP ontology, and the co-occurrence relations extracted from the domain corpus and from the INTEROP glossary. An example of similarity vector x_i (in which we show only the highest-rated arguments) is:

activity_diagram = (class_diagram (1), process_analysis (0.630), software_engineering (0.493), enterprise_software (0.488), deployment_diagram (0.468), bpms_paradigm (0.467), workflow_model (0.444), model-driven_architecture (0.442), workflow_management (0.418)).

Finally, the similarity matrix X was used to feed the two clustering algorithms. We generated over 100 clustering results by changing the clustering algorithm (*k-means++* or *Repeated Bisections*), the matrix range reduction, and the number k of generated clusters. There are no straightforward ways for an objective evaluation of different clustering results: external evaluation criteria (i.e., evaluation on standard datasets) are not possible, since no benchmarks are available on term clustering[8] but only on document clustering. As for internal evaluation criteria, it has been experimentally evidenced that none of the proposed validity indices reliably identifies the best clusters, unless these are clearly separated [8, 17]. To obtain a ranking of the clustering results, we defined a novel evaluation measure,

---

[8] Evaluation on data sets in different applications makes no sense, since k-means++ and Repeated Bisections have been already evaluated in the literature. What matters here is to measure the added value of the feature extraction methodology.

Table 15.2 Some best clusters with $k = 50$

C6: {social interaction, inter-enterprise collaboration, database interaction, business interaction, interaction, multimedia interaction}
C9: {e-service, service-based architecture, e-finance, web mining, e-banking, e-government, e-booking}
C11: {conformance requirement, engineering requirement, business requirement, configuration requirement, traceability, testing requirement, class-based representation formalism, language specification, integration requirement, production cycle, organisation requirement, requirement, testability, security service, user requirement, tolerance, manufacturing planning, consistency checking}
C29: {interoperability barrier, representation interoperability, interoperability problem, ERP interoperability, organisation interoperability, interoperability measurement, financial institution, intra organisation integration, knowledge interchange format, e-government interoperability, enterprise integration framework, organizational barriers, enterprise integration}

based on adjusting the cluster granularity by using what we called the "wise librarian" metaphor: a librarian would want to more or less evenly distribute books across shelves, while also managing not to add shelves as new books arrive. Similarly, topics (shelves) should be identified such that the documents (books) group nicely into topics. We developed quantitative metrics to model such criteria. Details on the "wise librarian" evaluation metrics are found in [4]. In summary, we found that clustering results with $k = 50$ and the Repeated Bisection algorithm show the best global values. Table 15.2 shows some best-rated clusters according to our validity measure.

We then performed a qualitative evaluation of these best-performing clustering results, based on our experience and knowledge of the INTEROP community and research domains.[9] Though this is not a common practice in clustering literature, we still believe that no numerical evaluation can fully exclude the need for manual validation by domain experts, whenever available. Inspecting the data, the relevant phenomena for the best-rated clustering results according to our "wise librarian" procedure remain more or less the same:

- The "central" research themes of the INTEROP community constantly emerge: for example, it is always possible to find an "interoperability" topic (such as C29 in Table 15.2), but, as k grows, an initially large cluster is split into more fine-grained subtopics. Similar is the case for the central research themes of the INTEROP community, such as enterprise modelling, e-services, semantic techniques, and architectures.
- About 20–25% of the extracted concepts aggregate in a rather variable manner, eventually contributing to singleton clusters as k grows. This was expected, since, in natural language applications, a certain degree of data sparseness is indeed

---

[9] All the authors had direct responsibilities in the research network monitoring and management tasks.

unavoidable, and even predictable.[10] However, to the extent that a significant number of relevant topics clearly emerge, this phenomenon does not affect the subsequent SNA.

In general, we found the quality and informative power of extracted topics far more evident than with a naive bag-of-words model.

15.3 The Content-Based Social Network

The results of the methodology to capture the relevant research themes within a scientific community presented in the previous sections are then used to perform a new type of SNA, the *Content Based-Social Network Analysis*, which is described in this section. To enable *CB-SN* analysis, we used both well-established and novel SN measures. Furthermore, we developed a visualization tool to support the analysis and to verify its efficacy in real domains. We refer here to the analysis conducted on the INTEROP NoE, but the approach is general, while written material is available to model the relationships among the actors.

This section is organized as follows: Section 3.1 describes how we model the *CB-SN*. Section 3.2 explains how we introduce and motivate the SN measures that will be used to perform the network study. Then, in Sect. 3.3 we briefly introduce the graphic tool that we have developed and present several examples of analyses that are enabled by our model. Finally, Sect. 15.3.3.2 summarizes our findings. The efficacy of the methodology is evaluated with reference to the main network monitoring objectives of the INTEROP NoE (objectives which are common to all EC NoEs). Furthermore, the correspondence of our findings with the reality – whenever not immediately verifiable by looking in the INTEROP knowledge repository[11] – was assessed through a comparison with known, manually derived, information reported in the INTEROP deliverables concerning network analysis.

15.3.1 Modeling the Content-Based Social Network

We model a content-based social network as a graph $G_{SN} = (V_{SN}, E_{SN}, w)$, whose vertices V_{SN} are the community research groups g_i and whose edges E_{SN} represent the content-based social relations between groups, weighted by a function

---

[10] The clustering tendency of concepts is measurable by computing the entropy of the related similarity vectors. Sparse distribution of values over the vector's dimensions indicates low clustering tendency.

[11] For example, if the analysis reveals that partner X and partner Y have common research interests but do not cooperate, this can easily be verified by looking at the partners' publications and activities in the INTEROP knowledge-base, the KMap [18].

$w : E_{SN} \rightarrow [0, 1]$. In this section we describe how to populate the set E_{SN} and define the weight function w of a Content-Based Social Network G_{SN}.

First, we need to model the knowledge of a research group in terms of the research topics (i.e., the clusters $C_h \in C$) that better characterize the group activity. With C, we now denote for simplicity the $\mathscr{C}^{BEST}$ selected according to the third step in Sect. 15.2.1. The objective is to associate with each research group g_i, based on its publications (documents) and on C, a k-dimensional vector whose hth component represents the relevance of topic C_h with respect to the group's scientific interests. For each document d_i in the collection D, we consider the k-dimensional vectors v_{ih} whose elements are computed as

$$v_{ih} = \frac{y_{ih}}{\sum_{j=1}^{k} y_{ij}} \qquad (15.1)$$

where

- $y_{ih} = \sum_{j:x_j \in C_h} ntf \cdot idf(t_j, d_i)$.
- x_j is the similarity vector associated with concept t_j (as defined in Sect. 15.2.1).
- $ntf \cdot idf$ is the normalized term frequency-inverse document frequency, a standard measure for computing the relevance of a term t_j in a document d_i of a collection D [2].

Given a research group $g \in V_{SN}$, we define a k-dimensional vector p_g, which is the centroid of all document vectors associated with the publications of group g.[12] We determine the similarity between pairs of groups g, g' by the cosine function [13]:

$$\text{cos-sim}(g, g') = \cos(p_g, p_{g'}) = \frac{p_g \cdot p_{g'}}{|p_g||p_{g'}|} \qquad (15.2)$$

For each pair of groups $g, g' \in V_{SN}$, if $\text{cos-sim}(g, g') > 0$, we add an edge (g, g') to E_{SN} with a corresponding weight $w(g, g') = \text{cos-sim}(g, g')$.

As a result, we are now able to characterize the scientific interests of research groups, as well as interest similarity among groups. To perform an SN analysis of the G_{SN} network, we now need a set of appropriate social network measures.

15.3.2 Social Network Measures

In the SNA field, different measures have been defined to delve into the networks' characteristics. They are generally focused on density, dimension and structure (mainly in terms of relevant subelements) of a network, and on the role and centrality

---

[12] Clearly, if a document (a paper) is authored by members of different groups, it contributes to more than one centroid calculation.

of its nodes [15]. For the purposes of the analyses we intend to carry out, the following SNA measures, defined in [19], have been selected:

- *Degree Centrality of a Vertex* A measure of the connectivity of each node (i.e., research group) $g \in V_{SN}$:

$$DC(g) = \deg(g) \qquad (15.3)$$

  where $\deg(g)$ is the degree of g, i.e., the number of incident edges.
- *Weighted Degree Centrality of a Vertex* A measure of the connectivity of each node, that takes into account the edges' weight:

$$DC_w(g) = \sum_{e \in E_g} w(e) \qquad (15.4)$$

where $E_g \subset E_{SN}$ is the set of edges incident to the node v, and $w(e)$ is the weight of the edge e, as defined in the previous section.

In addition to the previous ones, we have defined a new measure to trace the evolution of a network over time through the analysis of its connected components. Let us now introduce the concepts on which this measure is based. Given two nodes of a network, a and b, b is reachable from a if a path from a to b exists. If the edges are not directed the reachability relation is symmetric. An undirected network is connected if, for every pair of its nodes a and b, b is reachable from a. If a network is not connected, a number of maximal connected subnetworks can be identified: such sub-networks are called *connected components* and NCC denotes their number in a given network. Strictly related to the connected components is the concept of *bridge*. A bridge is an edge in the network that joins two different connected components. By removing a bridge, the number of connected components NCC of a network increases by one unit.

If we represent the set of connected components of the network after the removal of a bridge e as $NewCC(e)$, the following measure can be defined for our network G_{SN}:

- *Bridge Strength* The dimension, associated with each bridge e, of the smallest connected component in the graph obtained by removing e from G_{SN}:

$$BS(e) = \underset{cc \in NewCC(e)}{\arg\min} \ |Nodes(cc)| \qquad (15.5)$$

where $Nodes(cc)$ is the set of nodes in G_{SN} belonging to the connected components

With respect to our social network, the $DC(g)$ and $DC_w(g)$ measure the potential for collaboration of each community member: in the first case, by considering only the presence of common interests between nodes, and in the second, by taking into account also the similarity values. $BS(e)$ can be used to estimate how the community is "resilient," i.e., formed of members that widely share research interests and that are not part of sub-communities loosely interconnected and focused on specific topics. This can be done by characterizing and tracing over time the evolution of those subnets that are coupled to the rest of the network through a single bridge.

To analyze deeply the relevant phenomena inside the research community modeled by the social network defined above, we enriched the graph components (i.e., nodes and edges) in G_{SN} both with the values of the *SN* measures defined in this section, and with other data useful for their characterization. Each node representing a research group has an associated data set including, beyond its unique identifier, the number of its researchers, of the publications produced in a given time interval and the number of them co-authored by other members of the research community. In the same way each edge, along with the value of the similarity between the nodes it connects, is associated with the set of concepts that contribute to the similarity value. This additional information has no direct influence on the network topology (in its basic formulation, only similarity relations between nodes have been considered), but it can be used for the analysis of the dependencies among the network structure and the data associated with its elements. In this way, for example, the correlation between the number of publications of a group and the properties of its direct neighbors can be investigated, or a filter by topic can be applied to the similarity relations of a single group, as detailed later.

Before actually providing an in-depth example of *CB-SN* analysis using the model described so far, we briefly introduce a graphic tool that we developed to support visual analysis of a *CB-SN*.

15.3.3   Analysis of a Research Network

The purpose of this section is to show that our content-based SN model allows it to perform an analysis that is far more informative and useful than in traditional network models. The previously defined SN measures were applied to analyze different network configurations, each focused on a different aspect of the research community. They have been built by using various sets of partners' publications, relations, and attributes associated with nodes and edges. These measures can be used both to highlight any relevant phenomena emerging from the social structure of a research community and to analyze its evolution.

In order to analyze the networks produced, we built up *Graph VIewer* (*GVI*), a JUNG[13] library-based software tool able to support the incremental analysis of a network by acting directly on its graphic representation. The core of *GVI* is the mechanism of incremental filtering: at each step of the analysis, some elements of the network (nodes and edges) can be selected according to some filter conditions on the values of the elements' attributes. The selected items can then be hidden, if not relevant for the analysis to be made, or highlighted, by changing their graphic representation (shape and color). *GVI* allows both the creation of simple filters on

---

[13] http://jung.sourceforge.net

a single attribute, and their combination through AND/OR operators. Another relevant feature of the application is the capability to set the dimensions of the nodes and the edges according to the value of one of their attributes. For example, the thickness of the edges can be a function of the similarity value between the nodes (the thicker the line, the higher the similarity), or the size of the circle representing a node can be related to the associated DC measure (the greater the size, the higher the DC). This feature is extremely useful for the analysis of a network, because it gives a graphic representation of the distribution of relevant parameters selected by the analyst in the entire set of network elements.

The example of analysis provided in the next sections is taken from the INTEROP NoE. As already remarked, detailed data on the community members and publications are available on the NoE collaboration platform; hence we could verify the actual correspondence of any phenomenon highlighted in the next sections with respect to the reality. The results, described in what follows, clearly show the ability of the CB-SN model to reveal the shared interests, the active and potential collaborations among the community members, and their evolution over time.

15.3.3.1 Facilitating Governance of Research Networks

To monitor the evolution of Networks of Excellence and verify that collaboration targets are indeed met, precise types of indicators are usually manually extracted from available data by the network governance committee. We show here that these types of indicators can be automatically and more precisely extracted by our CB-SN model and tools.

As already pointed out in the introduction, the following data are extremely useful to monitor a research network and introduce, if needed, corrective actions to improve cooperation results:

- **Potential Areas for Collaboration** Between groups that share similar interests (but do not cooperate), to avoid fragmentation and duplication of results
- **Popularity of Research Topics** To redirect, if necessary, the effort on potentially relevant but poorly covered topics
- **Evolution of Collaborations** Over time, to verify that governance actions actually produce progress toward research de-fragmentation

Potential Research Collaboration on All Topics To evaluate the fields of potential research collaboration between groups, the network of similarity was built by considering all the 1,452 documents, and the $DC_w(g)$ for each node was calculated. Figure 15.3 is a graph that shows the subnet of the global network obtained by selecting only the edges with cos-sim$(g_i, g_j) \geq 0.97$.

This threshold was experimentally set to show the subnet of strongly interconnected nodes (i.e., the ones having the higher similarity of interests). In the figure, the dimension of the nodes and the thickness of the edges are related, respectively, to the $DC_w(g)$ and the cos-sim values. The biggest nodes represent the community

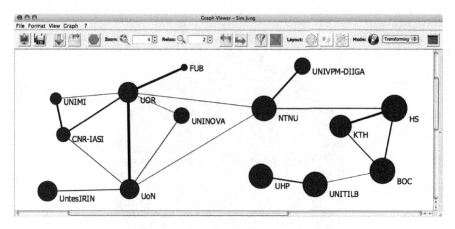

Fig. 15.3 Graphic representation of DC_w in a subnet of strongly related nodes

members that have the highest potential in joint researches, whereas the thickest edges reveal the best potential partners. The *GVI* allows also the visualization of the topics involved in the similarity relations by clicking on the corresponding edges.

Potential Research Collaboration on a Given Topic   Another analysis we carried out by using the *GVI* application was the selection of a topic and the visualization of all groups with research interests involving that topic. Starting from the global network of the previous experiment, we selected the subnet of all nodes sharing the cluster $C9$ of $\mathscr{C}^{BEST}$.

> **C9**: {e-service, service-based architecture, e-finance, web mining, e-banking, e-government, e-booking}

We filtered the resulting graph by selecting the edges with cos-sim$(g_i, g_j) \geq$ 0.97 to highlight the higher potential collaboration between groups involving that topic. Figure 15.4 shows the complete graph obtained after the topic selection, and Fig. 15.5 represents the subnet of filtered potential collaborations wherein the thickest edges reveal the best potential links.

Co-authorship Relations   We used the SNA approach to give an insight into the real research partnerships among the groups. We modeled such relations through a "traditional" co-authorship network, wherein the edge between each pair of nodes has an associated weight that is the normalized number of papers co-authored by the members of the two groups. This value $CP_{norm}(i, j)$, is defined as

$$CP_{norm}(i, j) = \frac{CP(i, j)}{\min(P(i), P(j))} \tag{15.6}$$

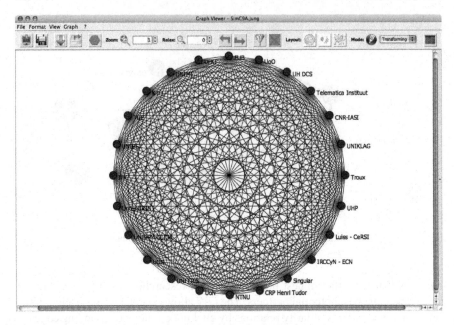

Fig. 15.4 A subnet of groups sharing the same research interests

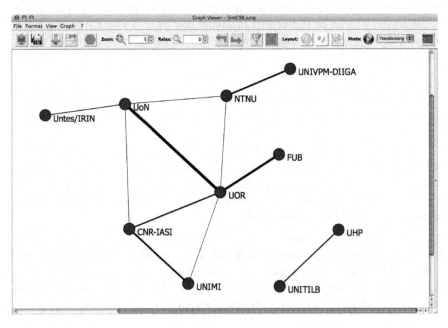

Fig. 15.5 A highlight of the highest potential collaborations among groups sharing the same research interest

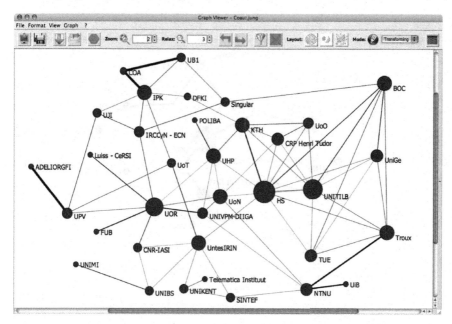

Fig. 15.6 The co-authorship network

where $CP(i, j)$ is the number of publication co-authored by the members of groups i and j, $P(j)$ is the number of publication of group j, and $\min(P(i), P(j))$ is the minimum value between $P(i)$ and $P(j)$. In this way, $CP_{\text{norm}}(i, j) = 1$ expresses the condition of maximum possible co-authorship between two groups (i.e., one group has all its publications co-authored by the other). Figure 15.6 shows the network obtained by considering the papers co-authored by researchers belonging to different groups, in which the thickness of the edges is proportional to the $CP_{\text{norm}}(i, j)$ and the dimension of the nodes to the $DC(g)$. In the figure, it is possible to see "at a glance" (biggest nodes) the groups that have the highest number of co-authorship relations with the others, and the pairs of groups that have a large number of papers co-authored (thickest edges), i.e., groups that have a strong collaboration in research activities.

Real versus Potential Collaborations By comparing co-authorship and interest similarity data (e.g., network types such as those in Figs. 15.3 and 15.6), the network analyst can identify those groups that have many research topics in common, but do not cooperate. This kind of analysis has proven to be very useful in the diagnosis of the research networks, like INTEROP, where one of the main goal was to improve collaboration and result sharing among partners. We conducted the analysis on a variant of the network used for potential research collaboration (Fig. 15.3), which was built by adding a second type of edge representing the number of papers co-authored by the groups' members. Figure 15.7 shows the network as visualized by GVI, after the application of a filter that selects the similarity edges having

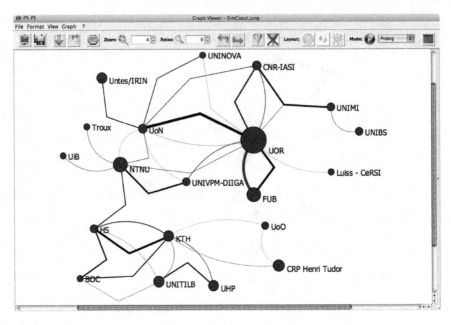

Fig. 15.7 The co-authorship + similarity network

cos-sim$(g_i, g_j) \geq 0.97$ and the co-authorship edges with co-authored papers ≥ 3. These two thresholds have been experimentally selected to focus the analysis on the strongest correlations between groups. In the figure, the curved lines are used for the co-authorship relation and the bent lines for the similarity relation. Moreover, the line thickness is proportional to the value of the corresponding relation and the node dimension to the number of publications of the associated group. The graph clearly shows the groups that have many common interests (high similarity value) but few papers co-authored (CNR-IASI and UNIMI, HS and BOC, UNITILB and UHP, etc.), as well as the groups that have few common interests but many co-authored papers (KTH and UNITILB, KTH and UHP, UOR and UNIVPM-DIIGA, etc.). In the second case, we must remember that the absence of a similarity link between two nodes does not mean that the similarity value between them equals 0, but that the value is lower than 0.97. If we remove the similarity threshold, the network of similarity is fully connected (46 nodes and 1,035 edges). Another element that justifies this apparent incongruence is that nodes in a graph represent research groups of variable dimensions. Large groups have variegated interests; therefore, they might have strong cooperations concerning only a small subset of their competences.

For the activity of monitoring and stimulating the integration of the members of a research network such as INTEROP, this analysis is very interesting. It reveals the set of groups that have good potential to collaborate, but who probably do not have enough knowledge of their common interests, and the set of groups that are very clever at maximizing the chances of partnership.

Another interesting phenomenon shown by the graph is the presence of a *clique*, a well-known concept in graph theory defined as "a subset of graph nodes in which every node is directly connected to the others in the subset, and that is not contained in any other clique" [19]. If we focus on similarity relations (the bent lines in the graph), for example, the groups KTH, HS, and BOC form a clique. Each of them has some research topics in common with the others, so that the clique can be seen as a sort of research subgroup. On the contrary, observing the co-authorship relations, we see that BOC is not related to the other nodes, and this is a strong evidence of a poor collaboration between groups having a strong similarity in their research interests.

Delving into Groups Competences The *GVI* capability to display and give support to the analysis of bipartite graphs (i.e., graphs having nodes belonging to two disjoint sets) gave the analyst the opportunity to delve deeply into the groups competences. Consider the case in which the analyst is interested in studying the impact of a specific argument, e.g., *information systems*. In $\mathscr{C}^{BEST}$, there is no single cluster that groups all the concepts related to *information systems* (e.g., *information system development, enterprise information system, etc.*). It is rather obvious that there is no single way to group concepts together: our clustering algorithm uses co-occurrence and hierarchical relations as a cue for creating topics, but a social analyst may wish to investigate the relevance of a research area that is not necessarily represented in a compact way by a single cluster.

To support this analysis, the *GVI* is able to hide all the nodes associated to those topics not having any component concept with a name that contains *information system* as a substring. The result is shown in Fig. 15.8. The network contains four topics, $C20$, $C26$, $C44$, and $C46$ (the nodes with different shapes on the right side of the figure), the only ones including concepts related to *information system*:

- **C20**: {..., *mobile information system, information system validation, information system language, information system analysis, information system interface, information system reengineering, ...*}
- **C26**: {..., *information system specification, mobile web information system, information system integration, information system model, information system verification, information system, information system development, multilingual information system, ...*}
- **C44**: {..., *cooperative information system, ...*}
- **C46**: {..., *enterprise information system, ...*}

In this way, by using the GVI filtering capability, it was possible to highlight all the groups that have competences related to the information systems field. By using the GVI options that make the thickness of the edges proportional to the value of the associated weights and the dimension of the nodes representing groups to their $DC(g)$, one more consideration can be made observing Fig. 15.8. Two groups

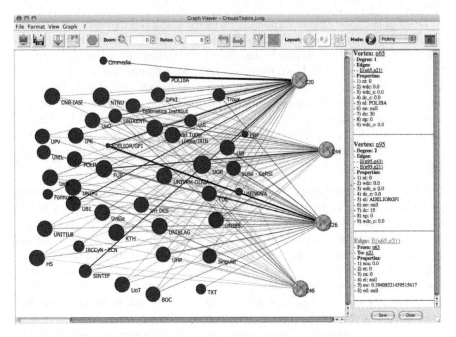

Fig. 15.8 Groups involved in "information system"-related research

(POLIBA and ADELIOR/GFI) have a strong competence in topic $C20$ (the weight of the edge between POLIBA and $C20$ is 0.394085, as reported in the text pane on the rightside of the figure, which shows the characteristics of any graph element selected by the user), but ADELIOR/GFI has a narrow set of competences with respect to POLIBA (its node size is smaller, corresponding to a $DC(g)$ of 15, the node's dc property in the text pane), and it is probably more focused on the topic.

15.3.3.2 Network Evolution over Time

Research Groups Defragmentation A good indicator to take into account for the analysis of a network over time is the evolution of the number of connected components NCC (see Sect. 15.3.2). If the network grows properly, we expect that initially isolated groups (or clusters of groups) establish connections among them. This was one of the stated goals of INTEROP: to join groups coming from different research areas or from different fields (industry vs academia). To analyze the NCC evolution, we defined four similarity networks, obtained by grouping the 1,452 papers written by the community members into four incremental sets, each of which contains, respectively, the documents produced before the end of 2003, 2004, 2005, and up to the end of the project

In Table 15.3 the NCC values referred to the four networks are shown, together with the dimension of the various connected components (CC Dim.). For example,

Table 15.3 Connected
components evolution

Set	# of Docs	NCC	CC Dim.
1	595	9	38,1,1,1,1,1,1,1,1
2	859	8	39,1,1,1,1,1,1,1
3	1,127	4	43,1,1,1
4	1,452	3	44,1,1

the network associated with the first set of documents (595 papers published before
2003) has nine connected components: one with 38 nodes and eight made by a
single node. In the reality, when the INTEROP project was launched, most of the
participating organizations had common research interests, but not all.[14] The values
in the table show the reduction of NCC over time due to an aggregation of the
isolated groups into the larger component.

Research Community Resilience A research community having members that share
their research interests with many others is a "robust" community, in which the cohesion of the researchers is based on a wide network of relations. One of the main
goals of an NoE is to spread knowledge about researchers activities and interests,
thus fostering potentially new collaborations and relations among the members. In
some cases, the aggregation of the community begins with a relation between single members of different, well-established, small groups of researchers, focused on
specific domains of interest. In this situation, the network modeling the community
is connected (there are chains of interests that connect any pair of members), but the
removal of a single link can split the network into two separated components. This
phenomenon, strictly related to the presence of bridges (as defined in Sect. 15.3.2),
is known as network *resilience*, and can be considered as a measure of community
robustness. In an NoE, this measure is expected to increase over time, as a consequence of sharing knowledge and interests.

We evaluated the *resilience* of the INTEROP NoE by adding the $BS(e)$ measure
to the edges of the social networks described in the previous analysis. The networks
have been filtered by selecting only the edges with cos-sim$(g_i, g_j) \geq 0.85$, in order
to focus on the strongest potential collaborations. A total of six bridges were found
in the network modeling the second period of the project: one with $BS(e) = 5$, two
with $BS(e) = 2$, and the remaining with $BS(e) = 1$. Considering the first bridge
(the only one representing an interconnection between potential sub-communities
formed by a significant number of research groups) we can see that it is no longer
present in the following period. Figures 15.9 and 15.10 show the GVI plots of the
networks corresponding to the second and third year of the project.

---

[14] As a practical example, the partners from Ancona (UNIVPM-DIIGA) and Roma (UoR) were
more oriented on research on natural language processing and on information retrieval, initially
not a shared theme in the INTEROP community. During the project, a fruitful application of our
techniques to interoperability problems has led to a better integration of our organizations within
the NoE, as well as to the emergence of NLP-related concepts among the "hot" INTEROP research
themes.

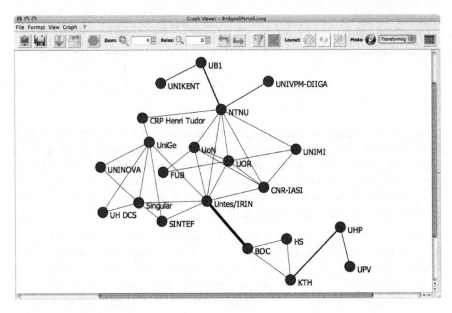

Fig. 15.9 Similarity network of year 2004

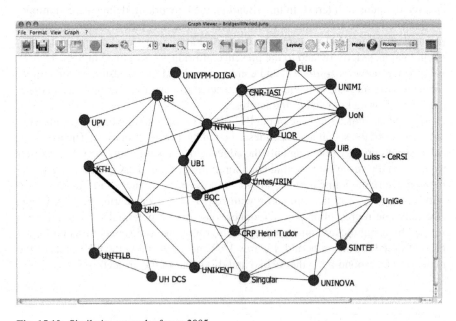

Fig. 15.10 Similarity network of year 2005

In Fig. 15.9, in which the thickness of the edges is proportional to the $BS(e)$ value, the thickest edges (between Untes/IRIN and BOC) is the bridge with $BS(e) = 5$, and the sub-communities it connects are clearly represented. In the following year, (Fig. 15.10) the edge (highlighted, along with the other bridges of Fig. 15.9, with a thicker line to be more easily located) has lost its previous role, because the shared potential interests among the researchers belonging to the original sub-communities have increased. This provides evidence that the NoE activities have strengthened the robustness of the community.

15.3.4   Summary of Findings

By using different combinations of the SNA measures, as defined in Sect. 15.3.2, to analyze in depth the different types of phenomena related to the research community modeled as a social network, and supported by the GVI application to evaluate the community members involved in the conducted analyses at a glance, we have highlighted some relevant aspects of the INTEROP NoE and its evolution over time.

We have been able to identify potential collaborations among the research groups on the basis of their competence regarding interoperability, and to focus attention on a subset of them, related to a specific subarea of the research domain. Moreover, through the co-authorship relation, an analysis of the established joint research activities has been conducted, and the strongest partnerships as well as the more active groups in the community have been pointed out. Then, by using evidence both of potential and real collaborations between groups, the partnerships to be strengthened have been revealed. Lastly, it has been possible to discover how the competences of the community members are distributed over the different topics of the interoperability research field. A deeper characterization of the NoE was carried out through the analysis of its evolution over time. It showed that there was a constant de-fragmentation of the community and that it has become more "robust" with respect to its initial structure. As stated at the beginning of section, a great part of the described results have been assessed through a comparison with the information contained in the INTEROP deliverables concerning the NoE monitoring activity.

15.4   Conclusions

In this chapter, we presented a novel SNA methodology, which deals with the *semantic content* of social relations, rather than their surface realization as in traditional SNA. The motivation behind this work lies in the fact that network analysts are typically interested in the *communicative content* exchanged by the community members, not merely in the number of relationships. Especially in the analysis of research networks, the use of semantics allows it to discover topics shared by otherwise unrelated research entities, emerging themes together with their most active research entities, and so on. To the best of our knowledge, no similar methodology in the social network literature provides such a refined capability of analysis, as we showed in the previous section.

While our work builds on top of well-established techniques such as clustering and social networks, and on previous results by the authors on terminology and glossary extraction, the chapter provides several novel contributions to the implementation and analysis of content-based social networks:

- We extend the notion of term co-occurrences to that of semantic co-occurrences, with the aid of a novel graph-based similarity measure, which combines lexical co-occurrences with ontological information.
- We provide a novel criterion for evaluating the clustering results based on the intuitive notions of compactness, even dimensionality and generalization power.
- We experiment with traditional and novel SN measures, that we use to support the study and evolution of collaboration themes in a research network.

Our methodology has been fully implemented, including a visualization interface, which facilitates the study of the community by a social analyst. Some interesting aspects and extensions of CB-SN have been left for future work. First, we aim to model in a more refined way, with respect to the graph of Fig. 15.8, a social network with two types of nodes: topics and researchers. By so doing, we can better analyze topic evolution across time, a promising extension deferred to future publications. Second, we remark that the literature on Social Networks does not provide formal, quantitative criteria to *evaluate* an SN model, but simply presents examples of usage of the various SN measures. Accordingly, in this chapter, the actual efficacy of the content-based SN model was supported by a *qualitative* evaluation of its utility when applied to a well-studied case, the INTEROP NoE, for which a diagnosis was already manually conducted, and reported in the appropriate project deliverables.[15] These documents, along with available network databases, served as a comparison to establish whether the information pinpointed by our SNA tools was indeed reasonable and corresponded to what was already known about the network. This type of evaluation, though commonly adopted in the SN literature, is not entirely satisfactory, therefore another future target for our research will be to investigate quantitative methodologies for SN evaluation.

References

1. Arthur D, Vassilvitskii S (2007) k-Means++: The advantages of careful seeding. In: SODA '07: Proceedings of the eighteenth annual ACM-SIAM symposium on discrete algorithms Society for Industrial and Applied Mathematics, Philadelphia, PA, USA, pp 1027–1035
2. Baeza-Yates R, Ribeiro-Neto B (1999) Modern information retrieval. Addison-Wesley
3. Blei DM, Ng AY, Jordan MI, Lafferty J (2003) Latent dirichlet allocation. J Machine Learn Res 3

---

[15] http://interop-vlab.eu/ei_public_deliverables/interop-noe-deliverables/

4. Cucchiarelli A, D'Antonio F, Navigli R, Velardi P (2009) Semantically interconnected social networks. TKDD (submitted)
5. Finin T, Ding L, Zhou L, Joshi A (2005) Social networking on the semantic web. Learn Organ 12(5):418–435
6. Joshi D, Gatica-Perez D (2006) Discovering groups of people in google news. In: HCM '06: Proceedings of the 1st ACM international workshop on Human-centered multimedia. ACM, New York, NY, pp 55–64
7. Jung JJ, Euzenat J (2007) Towards semantic social networks. In: ESWC '07: Proceedings of the 4th European conference on the semantic web. Springer, Berlin, pp 267–280
8. Legány C, Juhász S, Babos A (2006) Cluster validity measurement techniques. In: AIKED'06: Proceedings of the 5th WSEAS international conference on artificial intelligence, knowledge engineering and data bases. World Scientific and Engineering Academy and Society (WSEAS), Stevens Point, WI, pp 388–393
9. Mccallum A, Corrada-Emmanuel A, Wang X (2005) Topic and role discovery in social networks, pp 786–791
10. Mei Q, Cai D, Zhang D, Zhai C (2008) Topic modeling with network regularization. In: WWW '08: Proceeding of the 17th international conference on World Wide Web. ACM, New York, NY, pp 101–110
11. Nallapati RM, Ahmed A, Xing EP, Cohen WW (2008) Joint latent topic models for text and citations. In: KDD '08: Proceeding of the 14th ACM SIGKDD international conference on Knowledge discovery and data mining. ACM, New York, NY, pp 542–550
12. Navigli R, Velardi P (2007) Glossextractor: A web application to automatically create a domain glossary. In: AI*IA '07: Proceedings of the 10th congress of the Italian association for artificial intelligence on AI*IA 2007. Springer, Berlin, pp 339–349
13. Salton G, McGill MJ (1986) Introduction to modern information retrieval. McGraw-Hill, New York, NY
14. Sclano F, Velardi P (2007) Termextractor: A web application to learn the shared terminology of emergent web communities. In: Proceedings of the 3rd international conference on interoperability for enterprise software and applications (I-ESA 2007), Funchal, Portugal
15. Scott JP (2000) Social network analysis: A handbook. Sage Publications
16. Tagarelli A, Karypis G (2008) A segment-based approach to clustering multi-topic documents. In: Text mining workshop, SIAM datamining conference
17. Steinbach KT (2006) Introduction to data mining. Addison-Wesley
18. Velardi P, Cucchiarelli A, Petit M (2007) A taxonomy learning method and its application to characterize a scientific web community. IEEE Trans Knowl Data Eng 19(2):180–191
19. Wasserman S, Faust K, Iacobucci D (1994) Social network analysis : Methods and applications (structural analysis in the social sciences). Cambridge University Press
20. Zhao Y, Karypis G (2004) Empirical and theoretical comparisons of selected criterion functions for document clustering. Mach. Learn. 55(3):311–331
21. Zhou D, Ji X, Zha H, Lee Giles C (2006) Topic evolution and social interactions: How authors effect research. In: CIKM '06: Proceedings of the 15th ACM international conference on Information and knowledge management. ACM, New York, NY, pp 248–257

Part III
Social Network Applications

Chapter 16
IA-Regional-Radio – Social Network for Radio Recommendation

Grzegorz Dziczkowski, Lamine Bougueroua, and Katarzyna Wegrzyn-Wolska

Abstract This chapter describes the functions of a system proposed for the music hit recommendation from social network data base. This system carries out the automatic collection, evaluation and rating of music reviewers and the possibility for listeners to rate musical hits and recommendations deduced from auditor's profiles in the form of regional Internet radio. First, the system searches and retrieves probable music reviews from the Internet. Subsequently, the system carries out an evaluation and rating of those reviews. From this list of music hits, the system directly allows notation from our application. Finally, the system automatically creates the record list diffused each day depending on the region, the year season, the day hours and the age of listeners. Our system uses linguistics and statistic methods for classifying music opinions and data mining techniques for recommendation part needed for recorded list creation. The principal task is the creation of popular intelligent radio adaptive on auditor's age and region – IA-Regional-Radio.

16.1 Introduction and Issue

Social networking sites are a global phenomenon. For the hundreds of millions of people worldwide who belong to sites such as MySpace, Facebook and YouTube, social interaction in cyberspace has become an indispensable part of their lives.

Nowadays the Internet is an essential tool for the exchange of information on a personal and professional level. The Web offers us a world of prodigious information and has evolved from simple sets of static information to services that are more and more complex. With the growth of the Web, Internet radio, recommendation

G. Dziczkowski (✉)
Ecole des Mines de Douai, Departement Informatique et Automatique
941, rue Charles Bourseul, BP 10838 59-500 Doaui
e-mail: dziczkowski@ensm-douai.fr; g.dziczkowski@gmail.com

L. Bougueroua and K. Wegrzyn-Wolska
Ecole Superieur d'Ingenieurs en Informatique et Genie des Telecommunication,
77-215 Avon-Fontainebleau Cedex, France
e-mail: [lamine.bougueroua;katarzyna.wolska]@esigetel.fr

A. Abraham et al. (eds.), *Computational Social Network Analysis*, Computer
Communications and Networks, DOI 10.1007/978-1-84882-229-0_16,
© Springer-Verlag London Limited 2010

tools and e-commerce have become popular. Many Web sites offer online services or sales and propose object ratings to their users, for music, films, and products, for example. With globalization, the product choice is too much diversified; therefore, users are not aware of the availability of products. For this reason, prediction engines were developed to offer the user alternative products. Generally, the influences of others are important for opinion making.

Prediction engines' algorithms are based on the experience and opinion of other users. In order to develop those engines, we need to have an extremely large user profile base. In our case – Internet radio, products furnished by our system are musical hits. In this case, auditors are not supposed to make the validation process of listened musical hit. The need of such a system is justified by increasing the value of radio auditors. For example, in France, there are 42 millions of auditors each day, which represents that eight people out of 10 are older than 13 years old [19]. The value of Internet radio listener drew over 1.2 additional millions of listeners aged 13 and over last year [Mediametrie 126,000 Radio 2007–2008] [19].

The general objective of our system is to furnish the intelligent Internet radio, which needs to be programmed first but which interacts with the taste of listeners from the same region and of the same age. The vote of the listeners will directly affect the single rotation frequency. Another advantage of our system is that the predictions are not made for each auditor but for the group of auditors from the same region and of the same age. Like this, we also present musical hits that have not been discovered yet by singular listeners. In addition, our method is more useful for new auditors who did not evaluate too many musical hits. The time at which auditors connect to the Internet to listen to the music is arbitrary. It is possible that a musical hit is very much appreciated in the morning but not at night. Therefore, we look at voting time to understand better the tastes of users.

Most of radios are using automation radio software. In fact, it gives the possibility to make playlists, to play all types of song (jingles, advertisement, music, interviews, live, ...) and that with just a simple computer. In France for example, we have a radio totally automated, "Chante France". There are no speakers, but only a computer which plays songs. Some products exist in radio automation software. These products are used by associative or personal radios. There is also a little list of professional products used by national radios.

The player Zarasoft has no database; there is no possibility to program and regroup into categories. But there is the possibility to program events at specific time. It detects silence at the end of track. It is every time necessary to manually add the playlist, or to select a directory, and zararadio selects randomly the songs to play, but there is no possibility to show the time remaining for introduction. We can describe this software as semi-automatic.

Zradio is a freeware, developed by a local radio RMZ at Poitier before 2003. It has the possibility to play jingles, advertisements and to be programmed in a format by using a database. Winamp is a simple free media player developed since 1997. Contrary to Zararadio, it cannot select randomly a song from the directory. There is no automation because we need to manually program all the songs we want to hear. Radugo exists since before October 2001. We need to manually add all the songs. There is a possibility to create list, automatically generate log files, protect passwords, schedule events and silence detection.

The player DRS2006 includes an automatic playlist editor. With the plug-in broadcast, it is possible to directly broadcast the stream on the Internet. It includes a database, a playlist editor, a studio radio and a studio DJ, and some tolls about database. Easyradio exists since 1998. It is the most complete software in radio automation for little radios. It is simple to use, it has the possibility to define some time formats, and the playlists are generated automatically. This software is very complete and is recommended for DJs, radios, and expositions. The editor of Sam Broadcaster has been created in 1999. It seems to be a complete software. It integrates a Web broadcaster. We can make some graphs with the statistical number of listeners. It gives an html output that allows the update of the song play, for example, for a Web site.

All softwares have its own advantages and disadvantages. But all the advanced solutions do not include an automatic update of the song frequency based on the vote of the listeners.

The system presented in this chapter searches and retrieves probable music reviews from the Internet. Subsequently, the system carries out an evaluation and rating of those reviews. From this list of musical hits, the system directly allows notation from our application. Finally, the system automatically creates the record list diffused each day depending on the region, the year season, the day hours and the age of listeners. Our system uses linguistics and statistic methods for classifying music opinions and data mining techniques for recommending parts needed for recorded list creation. The principal task is the creation of popular intelligent radio adaptive on auditor's age and region – IA-Regional-Radio.

16.2   General System Architecture

In this section, we make a description of the architecture. Our objective is to make an Internet radio that interacts with the taste of listeners. Principal modules of our architecture are (Fig. 16.1) research and collection of reviewers on Internet, attribution of a mark for each review, and storage of interesting information in the database. We also store mark collected from Internet radio Web sites. The most important part of our modular architecture system is the *Opinion marking module* described in Sect. 16.6. The recommendation system is based on information from *opinion marking module* to understand better tastes of users.

The last module is used to generate lists of songs depending on several criteria: region and age of listener, recommendation results, and hours of broadcasting.

The first part will be to make a database and an interface to add songs on it. The fields in the database will essentially be the title of the song, the artist name, the category, the frequency, the listener's age, the listener's region and some others information (Fig. 16.2).

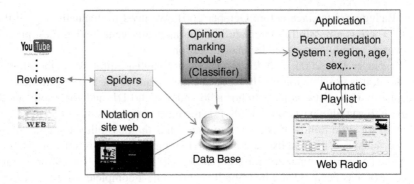

Fig. 16.1 Application architecture

Fig. 16.2 Data base

The next part is to collect information about musical hits on Internet (youtube, ...). In fact, we use spider, which is the automated and methodological traverse and index of Web pages, for subsequent search purposes. The application has a Web site to receive requests from Web listeners, which result in a note or comment on musical hits.

All relevant information are, then, recovered either directly from the application, or by the spiders. Finally, information is stored in a database.

After collecting the reviews, we will assign notes by using the classifiers. The classifiers provide ratings from the user's feelings. The classifier uses three different methods for assigning a mark to the reviews. Those methods are based on different approaches of corpus classification. The notes of the classification will be stored in a database.

The recommendation system, relying on the notes in the database and region, sex, and age of the user, determines the most appropriate musical hits to broadcast. Each day, the application auto-generates playlists by using the playlist scheme generator model (Fig. 16.3). It selects the sound to play by respecting the restrictions and the playlist scheme according to the song frequency in the database.

The Web radio is composed of two parts. The first part is the studio player interface. It represents the server side. It displays the list during playback and the remaining time to start playing musical hits.

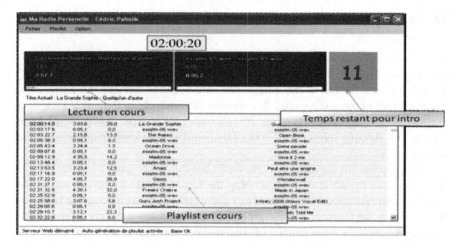

Fig. 16.3   Web radio application – server

The second part is the Web interface. It represents the listener interface. It allows listeners to view the jacket and title name being circulated, the last five titles available, the vote for the title currently broadcast, and the possibility to obtain additional information on a title.

16.3   Text Mining

The text categorization *TC* is now applicable in many different contexts. Document indexation is based on a lexicon, a document filtration, an automatic generation of metadata, a suppression of words ambiguity, the settlement of hierarchical catalogues of Web resources, and, in general, every application, which needs document organization or selective processing and document adaptation [16, 23].

The machine learning *ML* describes a general inductive process, which automatically constructs a text classifier via the learning, from a series of pre-classified documents or from characteristics of interest categories. Text mining *TM* is a set of informatics processing, which consists of extracting knowledge in terms of innovative criteria or in terms of similarities in texts produced by human beings for human beings. A field using *TC*, *ML* or *TM* techniques is, in particular, the field of sentimental analysis [4], known as opinion mining [5]. The research in this field covers different subjects, in particular the learning of words' or expressions' semantic orientation, the sentimental analysis of documents and opinions and attitudes analysis regarding some subjects or products [15, 18].

16.3.1 Representation of Documentary Corpus

Texts in natural language cannot be directly interpreted by a classifier or by classification algorithms. The first linguistic unit representing the sense is the words' lemma. The recognition of those linguistic units requires carrying out a linguistic preprocessing of the text's words. The number of words characterizing a document corpus can be really wide. Therefore, it is necessary to conserve a subgroup of those words. This filtering relies on the root of the word's occurrence frequencies in the corpus.

Other approaches are using not just words but a group of words, eventually sentences such as linguistic units, describing the sense. Thanks to this approach, we have an order relationship between words and words' co-occurrences. The inconvenience is that the frequency of the group of words apparition cannot offer reliable statistics because the great number of combinations between words creates frequencies which are too weak to be exploited.

Another approach to represent the documentary corpus is the utilization of the n-grams technique [26]. Those methods are independent from the language; however, neither the segmentation in linguistic units nor pre-treatments as filtration and lemmatization are necessary.

If we are using words such as linguistic unit, we notice that different words have acommon sense or are simply another form of conjugation. Therefore, a processing named stemming has to be carried out. It is a processing that proceeds at a morphologic analysis of the text [24]. The processing that needs a more complex analysis than stemming is lemmatization, which is based on a lexicon. A lexicon is a set of lemmas with which we can refer to the dictionary. Lemmatization needs to carry out in addition a syntax analysis in order to resolved ambiguities. Therefore, it conducts a morphosyntactic analysis [25].

The role of textual representation is represented mathematically in a way that we can carry out the analytic processing, meanwhile, conserving at a maximum the semantic one. The indexation process itself consists in conducting a simple complete inventory of all corpus lemmas. The next step is the selection process of the lemma, which will constitute linguistic units of the field or vector space dimension of the representation of documentary corpus.

16.3.2 Classification Techniques

The classification procedure is automatically generated from a set of examples. An example consists of a description of a case with the corresponding classification. We dispose, for example, a database of patients' symptoms with the status of their respective health state, as well as the medical diagnostic of their sickness. The training system must then, from this set of examples, extract a classification procedure, which will, with a view of patients' symptoms, establish a medical diagnostic. It is a matter of inducing a general classification procedure taken from examples. The problem is therefore an inductive problem. It is a matter of extracting a general rule from observed data.

Bayes' Classifier

The probabilistic classifier interprets the function $CSV_i(d_j)$ in terms of $P(c_i|\mathbf{d_j})$, which represents the probability that a document is represented by a vector $\mathbf{d_j} =< w_1, j, \ldots, w_{|T|j} >$ of terms, which belongs to c_i, and determines this probability by using the Bayes' theorem, defined by

$$P(c_i|\mathbf{d_j}) = \frac{P(c_i)P(\mathbf{d_j}|c_i)}{P(\mathbf{d_j})}. \tag{16.1}$$

where $P(\mathbf{d_j})$ is the probability that a document chosen at random has the vector $\mathbf{d_j}$ for its representation; and $P(c_i)$ is the probability that a document chosen at random belongs to c_i. The probability estimation $P(c_i|\mathbf{d_j})$ is problematic, since the vector number $\mathbf{d_j}$ possible is too high. For this reason, it is common to make the hypothesis that all vector coordinates are statistically independent. Therefore:

$$P(\mathbf{d_j}|c_i) = \Pi_{k=1}^{|T|} P(w_{kj}|c_i). \tag{16.2}$$

Probabilistic classifiers, which are using this hypothesis are named Nave Bayes' classifiers and find their usage in most of the probabilistic approaches in the field of text categorization [17, 29].

Calculation of a Classifier by the SVM Method

Support vector machine methods (SVM) have been introduced by Joachims [6, 13, 14, 35]. The geometrical SVM method can be considered as an attempt to find out between surfaces $\sigma_1, \sigma_2, \ldots$ of a dimension space $|T|$, what is separating examples of positive training from negative ones. The set of training is defined by a set of vectors associated to the belonging category: $(X_1, y_1), \ldots, (X_u, y_u)$, $X_j \in R^n, y_j \in \{+1, -1\}$ with:

- y_j represents the belonging category. In a problem with two categories, the first one corresponds to a positive answer ($y_j = +1$) and the second one corresponds to a negative answer ($y_j = -1$).
- X_j represents the vector of the text number j of the training set.

The SVM method distinguishes vectors of positive category from those of negative category by a hyperplane defined by the following equation: $W \otimes X + b = 0, W \in R^n, b \in R$.

Generally, such a hyperplane is not unique. The SVM method determines the optimal hyperplane by maximizing the margin: the margin is the distance between vectors labeled positively and those labeled negatively.

Calculation of a Classifier by the Tree Decision Method

A text classifier based on the tree decision method is a tree of intern nodes, which are marked by terms; branches getting out of the node are tests on terms, and the leaves are marked by categories [20]. This classifier classifies the document of the test d_j by testing recursively the weight of the intern node of the vector d_j, until a leaf is reached. The knot's label is then attributed to d_j. Most of those classifiers use a binary document representation and therefore are created by binary trees.

A method to conduct the training of a decision tree for the category c_i consists in verifying if every training example has the same label (c_i or $\bar{c}_i$). If not, we will select a term t_k, and we will break down the training set in document categories, which have the same value for t_k. Finally, we create sub-trees until each leaf of the tree generated this way contains training examples attributed at the same category c_i, which is then chosen as the leaf label. The most important stage is the choice of the term of t_k to carry out the partition [20].

Neural Network

A text classifier based on neural network *NN* is a unit network, wherein entry units represent terms, exit units represent the category or interest categories, and the weight of the side-relating units represents dependency relationships. In order to classify a document of test d_j, its weights w_{kj} are loaded in entry units; the activation of those units is propagating through the network, and the value of the exit unit determines the classification decision. A typical way of training neural network is retro propagation, which consist of retro propagating the error done by a neuron at its synapses and to related neurons. For neural networks, we usually use retro propagation of the error gradient [3], which consists of correcting error according to the importance of the elements, which have participated to the realization of those errors.

16.4 Sentiment Analysis

16.4.1 The Complexity of Opinion Marking

In order to determine the complexity of opinion marking, we are going to take an example of a review. The example is

> Yeah, Beautiful girl. I've only met 2 people in real life and 1 person on the net who hates this musical hit. My favorite song ever!

As we have noticed, the review is composed of three phrases, which have opposite polarity. Even though, we can easily deduct that the first sentence is the movie title, *Beautiful girl*, we will have two subjective phrases but hard to mark correctly. The last phrase is rather easy to mark: *"My favorite song ever!"*. However, there is a problem for the marking of the phrase: *I've only met... who hates this musical hit*, because a statistical study shows us that the polarity is negative for this phrase but in fact the polarity is positive and with high intensity.

Sentiments can often be expressed in a subtle manner, which creates a difficulty in the identification of the document units when considering them separately. If we consider a phrase, which indicates a strong opinion, it is hard to associate this opinion with keywords or expressions in this phrase. In general, sentiments and subjectivity are highly sensitive to the context and dependent on the field.

Moreover, on Internet, everyone is using their own vocabulary, which adds difficulties to the task; even though it is in the same field. Furthermore, it is very hard to correctly allocate the weight of phrases in the review.

It is not yet possible to find out an ideal case of sentiment marking in a text written by different users because it does not follow a rule and it is impossible to schedule every possible case. Moreover, frequently the same phrase can be considered as positive for one person and negative for another one.

16.4.2 Detection of Subjective Phrases

For many applications, we have to decide if a document contains subjective or objective data and identify which parts of the document are subjective in order to be able, then, to process only the subjective part.

Hatzivassiloglou and Wiebe [12] have demonstrated that the phrases' orientation is based on the adjectives' orientation. The objective was to establish if a given phrase is subjective or not by evaluating adjectives of this phrases [34], [1]. Wiebe et al. [31] present a complete study of the recognition of subjectivity by using different indications and characteristics (the results are compared by using adjectives, adverbs and verbs in taking into account the syntax' structure like for example the words' location).

Another approach made by Wilson et al. [33] has proposed an opinion classification according to their intensity (the opinion strength) and according to other subjective elements. When other researches have been made on the distinction between subjectivity and objectivity or on the difference between positive and negative phrases, Wilson et al. have classified the opinion and emotion strength expressed in individual clauses. The strength is known as neutral when it corresponds to the absence of opinion and subjectivity.

Recent works consider as well the relationship between the ambiguity in the words sense and in the subjectivity [32]. The subjectivity detection can also be done, thanks to classification techniques.

16.4.3 The Opinion Polarity and Intensity

The classification of the opinion polarity consists of a document classification between positive and negative status. A value called semantic orientation has been created in order to demonstrate the words' polarity. It varies between two values: positive and negative; and it can have different intensity levels. There are several calculation methods for the word's semantic orientation. Generally, the semantic orientation method of the associations SO-A is calculated as a measure of positive words association less the measure of negative words association:

$$SO - A(word) = \Sigma_{p \in P} A(word, p) - \Sigma_{n \in N} A(word, n) \qquad (16.3)$$

where A(word,pword) is the association of a studied word with the positive word (equivalent negative).

If the sum is positive, the word is oriented positively, and if the sum is negative, the orientation is negative. The sum absolute value indicates the orientation intensity. In order to calculate the association measure between words – A, there are several possibilities. One of them is called the pointwise mutual information – SO-PMI (proposed by Church and Hanks).

$$PMI(mot_1, mot_2) = log_2 \frac{p(word_1 \& word_2)}{p(word_1) p(word_1)} \qquad (16.4)$$

The $p(word_1 \& word_2)$ defines the probability that the two words coexist together.

Another possibility to analyze the statistical relationship between words in the corpus is the utilization of the technique: the singular value decomposition (SVD).

16.4.4 Different Approaches for the Sentiment Analysis

Turney's Approach

The semantic orientation of words has been elaborated first of all for the adjectives [11, 30]. The works on the subjectivity detection have revealed a high correlation between the adjective presence and the subjectivity of phrases [12]. This observation has often been considered as the proof that some adjectives are good sentiment indicators. A certain number of approaches based on the adjectives presence or polarity have been created in order to deduct the text subjectivity or polarity. One of the first approaches has been proposed by Turney [27] and can be presented in four stages:

- First of all, there is a need to make phrase segmentation (part-of-speech).
- Then, we put together adjectives and adverbs in a series of two words.

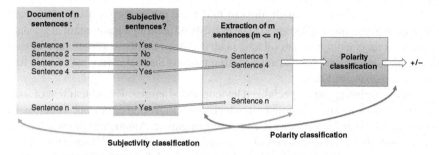

Fig. 16.4 Pang's approach – utilisation of the same classification technique for the detection of subjectivity and afterwards of phrases polarity labeled as subjective

- Afterwards we apply SO-PMI in order to calculate the semantic orientation of each detected series.
- Finally, we carry out a review classification as positive or negative by calculating the average of all the find orientations.

Results obtained by this approach are different compared to the field: for cars = 84%, for banking documents = 80% and for cinematographic reviews = 65%. The fact that adjectives are good opinion preachers is not diminishing the other words signification. Pang et al. [21], in the polarity study of cinematographic criteria, have demonstrated that using only adjectives as characteristics gives result less relevant than using the same number of unigrams.

Pang's Approach

Pang and Lee [22] are proposing another approach for the polarity classification of cinematographic reviews. The approach is composed of two stages (Fig. 16.4). The first goal is to detect the document's parts, which are subjective. Then, they are using the same statistical classifier to detect the polarity only on subjective fragments detected previously. Instead of doing the subjectivity classification for each phrase separately, they admit that they can see a certain degree of continuity in the phrases subjectivity – a writer generally is not changing often between the fact to be subjective or objective. They give preferences in order to have proximity phrases, which have the same level of subjectivity. Every phrase in the document is then labeled as subjective or objective in the process of collective classification.

16.5 Linguistic Analysis

Sentiment detection and marking can also be carried out by NLP techniques – natural language processing. Information extraction consist of identifying precise data of a text in natural language and representing it in a structured form [23]. It is a documentary research, which aims to find back in the corpus a set of relevant documents regarding a question [28]. It consists of building up automatically a data bank from texts written in natural language. It is not a matter of giving unprocessed text to use, but to give precise answers to questions that have been asked by a formula or database padding.

The extraction requires specialized lexicon and grammar. The adjustment of such resources is a long and tiresome task, which needs most of the time and expertise in the tackled field and knowledge in computing linguistic. Among this knowledge, we can mention filtration techniques of document categorization and data extraction.

Systems of text understanding have been conceived, for most of them, as generic systems of understanding, but it has been revealed that they are not much usable in real applications. Understanding is seen as a transduction, which transforms a linear structure. It means that the text (i.e., the linear structure) is transformed in an intermediary logical–conceptual representation. The final objective is then to create inferences on those representations in order to conduct different processing, for example, answering questions.

In order to understand the whole text, there is a need to carry out the syntactic and the semantic analysis. The syntactic analysis is the largest possible because of the ambiguity problem. The semantic analysis aims to produce a structure representing, the most reliable possible, entire sentence, with its nuances and its complexity, and then to integrate all produced structures in a textual structure. At the end, we obtain a logical–conceptual representation of the text. The semantic representation varies from one system to another.

This has driven an important number of researchers to describe natural languages in the same way as formal languages. Maurice Gross to precede, with his LADL team, has done an exhaustive examination of simple French phrases, in order to dispose of reliable and calculated data, on which it will be possible to conduct meticulous scientific experiences. To reach this result, each verb has been studied so as to test if it verifies or not syntactical proprieties as the fact to admit a completive proposition as a subject emplacement. We will see that we cannot describe French with general rules. The same situation applies to all other languages. Results of this research have been encoded in matrices called lexical-grammar tables. This table shows a precise description of the syntactic behavior of each French word. The aim is to use all the resources of the lexical-grammar tables in order to obtain a system able to analyze any simple phrase structure. The sense minimal unit, according to Maurice Gross, is the sentence not the word. The principle is therefore to study the transformation that simple sentence can have. Simple sentences have been indexed via their verbs. For a verb, we can have several different usages. Thanks to syntactical proprieties, we can distinguish the usage of a verb. There are no verbs, which possess exactly the same syntactical behavior. We cannot express, therefore, general rules, which could explain the language.

The text corpuses are represented by automates, in which each path corresponds to a lexical analysis. Linguistic phenomena are represented by local grammar, which is translated into automates in a final stage in order to be easily confronted to the text corpuses. A local grammar [10] is an automatic representation of the linguistic structures, difficult to formalize in lexical-grammar tables or in dictionaries. Local grammars represented by graphs describe elements that are part of the same syntactic or semantic field.

Linguistic descriptions described in local grammar form are used for a huge variety of automatic applied processing on the text corpus. Thus, different methods of lexical disambiguates have been developed in order to carry out grammatical constraints described with the help of this type of graph.

16.6   Opinion Marking Module

Our system possesses a modular architecture. Its principal tasks are the following: research and collection of reviews on Internet, attribution of a mark for each review and presentation of the findings. Each task is done by a specialized module (Fig. 16.5).

First of all, for the opinion marking part, we have developed three different methods for the attribution of a mark to a review:

- The group behavior classifier (Sect. 16.6.1)
- The statistical classifier (Sect. 16.6.2)
- The linguistic classifier (Sect. 16.6.3)

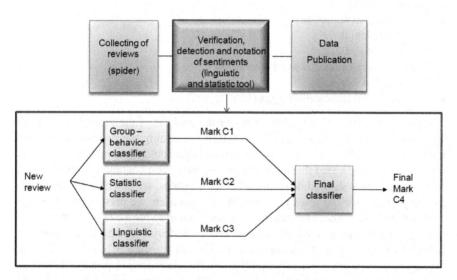

Fig. 16.5 General architecture of the system (the three principal modules and cinematographic reviews marking)

Those measures are based on different approaches of document classification. Second, we have developed, for each method, a classifier, which assign separately the mark [7, 9]. We have obtained, therefore, three marks for each review, which can be different. We have used, finally, another classifier, which assigns the final mark for the review, based only on the three marks attributed previously in the classification process [8]. For the calculation of the final mark, we have used the values of the three marks previously attributed and their probabilities.

On a research point of view, the most important part of the system conceived is the opinion marking module.

16.6.1   The Group Behavior Classifier

In this section, we present the classifier used for the opinion marking. The general approach is based on the verification that reviews, having the same associated mark, have common characteristics. Then, we determine a reviews behavior, for those having the same mark. We determine, therefore, the general behavior of each review group (five groups corresponding to five different opinion marks). We have a huge number of reviews already marked. We have gathered together all the reviews according to their mark. We obtain, then, five different groups of music marks. Afterwards, we have tried to determine typical characteristics of each group. We have defined all parameters, which can characterize the group behavior such as:

- Characteristic words
- Characteristic expressions
- The phrase length
- The opinion size
- The frequency of several words repetition
- The negation
- The number of punctuation signs (!, :), ?)

The choice of criteria that we have kept for the analysis of the group behavior has been done in an empirical way. Fist of all, by analyzing the reviews corpus, we have defined criteria that seems interesting and that could determine group behavior. Then, we have tested those criteria on a training base containing a thousand of reviews. If results showed differences between groups, we consider those criteria as valid criteria for our research work. In this approach, we present the statistical study on linguistic data. The training base has been used for the review analysis, of those having the same mark, in order to find characteristics, which determine the behavior of each group. Each approach used in our research is based on different characteristics, in order not to repeat them in the classification process. However, we have borrowed semantic classes from the linguistic approach for the creation of the words list characteristics. The utilization of those data is different in those two groups. After having selected criteria that characterize mark groups, we have analyzed the corpus in order to obtain statistical results. Results show huge differences between the characteristics of those groups. The creation of the global behavior of each group enables to determine the group in which a new review is. We have calculated for new reviews, the distance between its characteristics and those of the groups.

16.6.2   The Statistical Classifier

In this section, we propose a general approach used in the sentiment analysis. We use this method to compare results of our approaches with the same training base. The way to carry out a classification is to find a characteristic of each category and to associate a belonging function. Among known methods, we can mention Bayes' classifiers and the SVM method. As we have obtained better results for the classifier of Nave Bayes, we are going to base ourselves on this classifier. In our research work, we have used this classifier first of all to determine the subjectivity or objectivity of phrases, then in order to attribute a mark to subjective phrases of the review. The general process needs the preparation of a training base for two classifiers to attribute a mark. The intermediate stages are the followings:

- Preprocessing and lemmatization
- Vectorization and calculation of complete index
- Constitution of training base for each classifier
- Reduction of the index dedicate to the classifier
- Addition of synonyms
- Classification of texts

We are using, for the attribution of a mark to the sentiment of the review via a statistical approach, two classifiers: first one to filter the objective and the subjective phrases and second one to mark the review. The marking is done only on subjective phrases. Those classifiers rely on a vectorial representation of the text of the training base. This vectorial representation needs for the first time a linguistic preprocessing for the segmentation of the phrase, lemmatization and suppression of all words, which has no impact on the sense of the document. This preprocessing has been carried out for the linguistic classifier.

We carry out the preprocessing, thanks to the application Unitex. We are already disposing of linguistic resources prepared for this task as, for example, the grammar of the phrase segmentation or dictionaries. Then, we take off term with no sense, such as defined or undefined articles or prepositions. We can conduct this task because those grammatical elements have a low impact on the text sense as, for example, on the opinion described in reviews, contrary to adverbs, which give a high contribution to value judgment. Afterwards, on a training corpus, we calculate the dimension of the vectorial space of the text representation in order to carry out all lemma enumeration – the entire index. Each document is then represented by a vector, which contains the number of occurrences of each lemma present in the document. Every document of the training base is represented by a vector, wherein dimension corresponds to the whole index and components are occurrence frequencies of the index units in the document. Therefore, at this stage of the process, texts are seen as a set of phrases. Now, each phrase is labeled according to the construction of classifiers (the subjective classifier and the marking classifier). Labels correspond to subjective phrases (PS) or objective ones (PO) and the estimating mark attributed to those phrases (N from 1 to 5). A phrase j of the document i is marked as followed:

$$\mathbf{V}_{\mathbf{D_i P_j}} = (f_{D_i P_j 1}, \ldots, f_{D_i P_j k}, \ldots, f_{D_i P_j |D|}, PS/PO, N) \qquad (16.5)$$

where $f_{D_i P_j k}$ represents the number of occurrences in the lemma k in the phrase j of the document i. The stage of the labeling was based on the reviews' marks of the training base, and subjective phrases have been labeled manually. This is how we have built the set of training necessary to the determination of classifiers of subjectivity and sentiment marking.

The last stage of the vectorial representation of the document corpus is the reduction of the entire index dedicated to the classifier. The reduction of the complete index consists of eliminating from the vectorial space of the training base, vectors, which have many components always null. This task enables us to eliminate the noise in the classifier calculation [2]. We have used the method of mutual information associated to each vectorial space dimension.

In our works, we have used two classifiers: the classification based on Bayes' model and the classification using SVM. The two methods have been tested and the best results (F-score) have been obtained by the Bayes' classifiers. It is, as a result, Bayes' classifier which was used in the system. In the process of the statistical classification, we have, at first, classified subjective phrases and then we have attributed a mark.

Interesting phrases to carry out the opinion marking are subjective phrases because they are the only ones which contain the author's point of view. For this reason, we have first of all carried out the filtration of subjective phrases. The diagram, which represents those tasks, is shown in the Fig. 16.6.

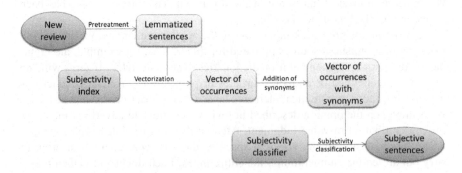

Fig. 16.6 Subjectivity classification – the classification steps

The process presented enables to filter only subjective phrases, those expressing an opinion. The different stages are as follows:

- The preprocessing consists of carrying out the phrase segmentation, the lemmatization and the elimination in our research of words without sense.
- The vectorization consists of putting all phrases in the form of a vector of occurrences and reducing the complete index.
- The addition of synonym consists of adding terms (synonyms) in the vector of occurrences, thanks to the linguistic analysis.
- The subjectivity classification consists of gathering together phrases in subjective or objective phrases. The classification is based on Bayes' theorem. For the rest of the classification (marking), we keep only subjective phrases.

After carrying out the subjectivity classification, we only keep subjective phrases. We conduct a classification in order to be able to attribute a mark to those phrases of each analyzed review. The diagram representing those tasks is presented in Fig. 16.7. The process presented enables to attribute a mark to phrases classified in the subjective phrases. The marking varies between 1 and 5. The stages are the following ones:

- The vectorization and the reduction of the complete index dedicated to the classification of the marking.
- The addition of synonyms.
- The marking classification, which consists of putting together phrases according to the sentiment intensity. Marks are between 1 and 5.

At this stage of the process, we obtain marks associated to every subjective phrase. The global mark of a review of the statistical classification is the arithmetical average of all the phrases of this review.

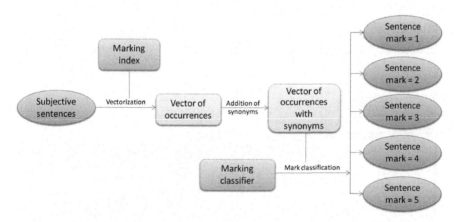

Fig. 16.7 Subjectivity classification – the classification steps

16.6.3   The Linguistic Classifier

We carry out reviews marking on a scale going from 1 to 5. We have created for
the linguistic approach a grammar rule for each of those groups. This grammar is
based on reviews' analysis of the training base, which contains approximately 2,000
phrases for each mark (the same database than for the other classifiers). For this
part, we have used a linguistic processing, which demands specialized lexicon and
grammar. The development of those resources is a long and tiresome task, which
generally needs an expertise in the field and knowledge of linguistic information
processing such as filtration techniques, documents categorization and data extraction. This part of the system has been developed with the application Unitex. We are
using a linguistic analyzer Unitex to conduct a preprocessing and a lemmatization
of words and finally, for the most important part of our research work, the construction of complex local grammar. The example of application is shown in Fig. 16.8
We have introduced, in order to fragment words in different opinion intensity levels,
words semantic categories, which are associated to words and show polarity and intensity. We have used, in order to associate words semantic categories, a subjective
dictionary named general inquirer dictionary.

The principal goal of the linguistic classifier is the attribution of a mark according to sentiment described in the review. The marking is done phrase by phrase.

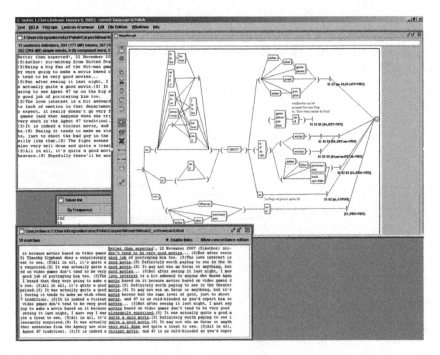

Fig. 16.8 Example of linguistics resources

The reviews' study of the training base has been carried out with the aim of creating grammar rules for each mark (in this case, the mark is between 1 and 5). Five grammars have been therefore created, one for each mark. Each grammar contains a huge number of rules taken from local grammar. For each grammar, more than thirty local grammars have been created. The analysis is done phrase by phrase to attribute a mark to a new review in order to find a rule (from our rules base) corresponding to the studied phrase. At the end of this processing, we obtain the phase of the newly studied review with matching grammar rules. The final mark of this classification is the average of marks corresponding to general grammars.

The construction of local grammar has been carried out manually via phrases analysis of the reviews having the same associated mark. Local grammar cannot be too general because this tends to add ambiguity to results. However, if the grammar is too specific and complex, the use of this grammar is indeterminate because silence grows in a significant way. Grammars have been created to detect the opinion polarity and intensity in a phrase, thanks to the local grammar forms, which constitute a general grammar for each marking group. Research works are based only on local grammars form. Other characteristics purely statistical like words or characteristic expressions, phrase size, words frequency, words repetition, the number of punctuation signs and so on, are not taken into account. Of course, characteristic words are in dictionaries with semantic categories and in local grammar, but this approach is a linguistic processing (grammar is necessary) not a statistical one (like the two other classifiers).

The creation of local grammar is a tiresome task. Grammars used in our system have been created in an empirical way. We have carried out in the following way: first of all, we have constructed general grammars, then we added a complexity level to the linguistic analysis and we have made tests. After those tests, we have repeated the process (addition of a complexity level). For each level, we have conducted tests and calculated the F-score. The final result of grammar rule forms have been chosen to obtain the best result of F-score. Unfortunately, we cannot be sure of the fact that our choice is the most coherent one. We have taken into account the fact that each classifier presented in our system should have its own criteria and characteristics. It is important to mention that the linguistic classifier provides the best results. We can observe, in particular, that the precision parameter is better than the one obtained by using other approaches.

This part of the system has been conducted with the text analyzer Unitex. Unitex enables to process in real time texts of several megabytes for the indexation of morphosyntactic patterns, the research of hard or semi-hard expressions, the production of concordance and the statistical study of results.

16.6.4   The Final Classifier

Until now, we have presented three different methods to attribute a mark to a review. Thus, we obtain three different estimations (one for each classifier). The marking is

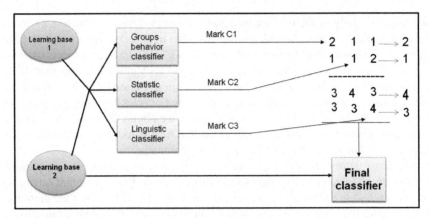

Fig. 16.9 Final classification – the marks behavior shows the presence of a determinant classifier in some situations

carried out each time in a different way. Marks are therefore not always the same. As we are obtaining three different marks, another problem consists of conducting the final marking in order to attribute only one mark to the review. We need a final classification to obtain the final mark, which will be retransmitted to our radio. We have observed that, if we are calculating the final average obtained by the three classifiers, results are less efficient than those obtained by the linguistic classifier.

We have also observed that often a classifier in specific situations gives best results, whereas in other circumstances, it would be another one. For example (Fig. 16.9), we have observed that often when the first classifier gives a mark equal to 2 and the last two give a mark of 1, the correct results is 2. As a consequence, the first classifier is the determinant in this case. By implementing neural networks for this stage and by taking into consideration each probability for each score for each classifier, we improved our results from 3% to 7% depending on the class.

We are using, for this reason, a final classifier. For this classification we are applying a neural network. The choice of this classifier is justified by the presence of a wide review base, already annotated, which will be useful for the training base. Moreover, it is easy to implement those data, for it to be used in the training base. The classifier takes into account only the probability of the mark of each classifier. No other characteristics are taken into consideration. This choice is acceptable because we think that we have used all other possible characteristics in the marking process (by using the three classifiers mentioned previously), and we do not wish to repeat those characteristics in the classifications. Furthermore, the utilization of a characteristic of an opinion marking classifier in the final classification can influence the choice of this classifier.

For the entries of the final classifier, we have used marks of the previous classifiers. The marks of each classifier are represented by the belonging probability of one of the five marks categories. For example, the linguistic classifier attributes the mark in the following way: the probability that the mark is:

- Equal to 5 is $p_5 = 0,6$

- Equal to 4 is $p_4 = 0, 2$
- Equal to 3 is $p_3 = 0, 1$
- Equal to 2 is $p_2 = 0, 1$
- Equal to 1 is $p_1 = 0$

We have used a neural network to determine the correlation between marks obtained by the three classifiers. We are using the neural network of multilayer perceptron (PMC) with the algorithm of retro propagation of gradient.

16.7 Results

We have observed for the base of cinematographic reviews that we obtain the best results with the linguistic classifier (especially for the precision). The worst results are those of the statistical classifier of Nave Bayes (the playback is correct but the precision is too low). This is to demonstrate that it is necessary to carry out a deep linguistic analysis. We have observed that the best results found for the three approaches were those expressing extreme opinions (Fig. 16.10).

Knowing the principle that it is an obligation to dispose of grammars more complex, we have demonstrate that the linguistic classifier gives better results than the statistical or the group behavior ones (Table 16.1).

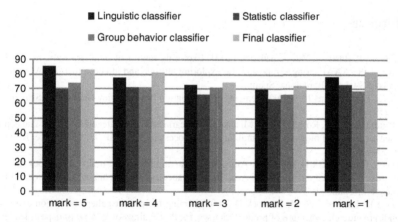

Fig. 16.10 Final classification – the marks behavior shows the presence of a determinant classifier in some situations

Table 16.1 Classifiers results

	Mark 5 (%)	Mark 4(%)	Mark 3(%)	Mark 2(%)	Mark 1(%)
Linguistic classifier	85	77.6	72.9	69.6	77.8
Group behavior classifier	73.8	71	70.8	66.1	68.3
Statistic classifier	70	70.7	66.1	63.3	73
Final classifier	83.1	81.2	74.5	72.2	81.4

16.8 Conclusion

In this chapter, we presented an entire system based on social network for radio application. Our radio will update a playlist depending on the votes of auditors. Users can express their selves via forums, blogs, or directly by adding a mark to the song. In the goal of understanding the opinions written in natural language, an opinion mining knowledge was necessary to implement. For this reason, we presented, in this chapter, new approaches to automatically detect opinion from the text. The two classifications (group conduct and linguistic) have been proposed by us. Then, we have compared our approaches with the approach generally used in this field (the statistical classification, which is based on Nave Bayes' classifiers).

After carrying out tests, we can observe that we have succeeded to implement the first innovative method based on a linguistic classifier. The results obtained after this classification give us satisfaction. We can, therefore, conclude that the linguistic analysis, which is deeper, is an important research path in the field of sentiment analysis.

Despite the fact that the linguistic classifier enables to obtain the best results, its utilization cannot be universal. Its application to a new field requires the creation of a new linguistic resource base, and it is necessary to carry out the deep linguistic analysis again. These processing are unavoidable because the language is highly dependent on the field.

References

1. Beineke P, Hastie T, Vaithyanathan S (2004) Exploring sentiment summarization. In: Proceedings of the AAAI spring symposium on exploring attitude and affect in text, AAAI technical report SS-04-07, Barcelona, Spain
2. Cover TM, Thomas JA (1991) Elements of information theory. Wiley New York (ISBN 0-471-06259-6)
3. Dagan I, Karov Y, Roth D (1997) Mistakedriven learning in text categorization. In: 2nd conference on empirical methods in natural language processing, EMNLP-97, Providence, RI, USA, pp 55–63
4. Das S, Chen M (2001) Yahoo! for Amazon : Extracting market sentiment from stock message boards. In: Proceedings of the 8th Asia Pacific finance association annual conference (APFA), Bangkok, Thailand
5. Dave K, Lawrence S, M, Pennock D (2003) Mining the peanut gallery : Opinion extraction and semantic classification of product reviews. In: Proceedings of WWW, Budapest, Hungary, pp 519–528
6. Drucker H, Vapnik V, Wu D (1999) Automatic text categorization and its applications to text retrieval. IEEE Trans Neural Netw 10:1048–1054
7. Dziczkowski G, Wegrzyn-Wolska K (2007) Rcss – Rating critics support system purpose built for movies recommendation. In: Advances in intelligent web mastering. Springer, Verlag France
8. Dziczkowski G, Wegrzyn-Wolska K (2008) An autonomous system designed for automatic detection and rating of film. Extraction and linguistic analysis of sentiments. In: Proceedings of IEEE/WIC/ACM inter conference on web intelligence and intelligent agent technology, Sydney, pp 847–850

9. Dziczkowski G, Wegrzyn-Wolska K (2008) Tool of the intelligence economic: Recognition function of reviews critics. In: ICSOFT 2008 proceedings. INSTICC Press, Setúbal Portugal, pp 218–223

10. Gross M (1997) The construction of local grammars. Finite-state languauge processing. The MIT Press, Cambridge, Mass, pp 329–354

11. Hatzivassiloglou V, McKeown K (1997) Predicting the semantic orientation of adjectives. In: Proceedings of the of the joint ACL/EACL conference, Madrid, Spain, pp 174–181

12. Hatzivassiloglou V, Wiebe, J (2000) Effects of Adjective Orientation and Gradability on Sentence Subjectivity. In: Proceedings of the international conference on computational linguistics (COLING), Universitat des Saarlandes, Saarbrucken, Germany

13. Joachims T (1998) Text categorization with support vector machines: Learning with many relevant features. In: 10th European conference on machine learning, ECML-98, Chemnitz, Germany, pp 137–142

14. Joachims T (1999) Transductive inference for text classification using support vector machines. In: 16th international conference on machine learning, ICML-99, Bled, Slovenia, pp 200–209

15. Joachims T, Sebastiani F (2002) Guest editors introduction to the special issue on automated text categorization. J Intell Inform Syst, 18:103–105

16. Knight K (1999) Mining online tex. Commun ACM 42(1):58–61

17. Lewis DD, Gale WA (1994) A sequential algorithm for training text classifiers. In: 17th ACM international conference on research and development in information retrieval, SIGIR-94, Special Issue of the SIGIR Forum, Dublin, Ireland, pp 3–12

18. Lewis DD, Haues PJ (1994) Guest editorial for the special issue on text categorization. ACM Trans Inform Syst

19. Mediametrie (2008)www.mediametrie.fr/new.php?rubrique = rad&news$_i$d = 229

20. Mitchell TM (1996) Machine learning. McGraw Hill

21. Pang B, Lee L, Vaithyanathan S (2002) Thumbs up? Sentiment classification using machine learning techniques. In: Proceedings of the conference on empirical methods in natural language processing (EMNLP), University of Pennsylvania, Philadelphia, USA, pp 79–86

22. Pang B, Lee L (2004) A sentimental education: Sentiment analysis using subjectivity summarization based on minimum cuts. In: Proceedings of the association for computational linguistics (ACL), Barcelona, Spain, pp 271–278

23. Pazienza MT (1997) Information extraction. In: Lecture notes in computer science, vol 1299, Springer, Frascati, Italy

24. Porter WA (1980) Synthesis of polynomic systems. J-SIAM-J-MATH-ANA 11:308–315

25. Schmid H (1994) Part-of-speech tagging with neural network. In: 15th conference on computational linguistics, Kyoto, Japan, 1:172–176

26. Shannon C (1948) A mathematical theory of communication. Bell Syst Tech J 27:379–423

27. Turney P (2002) Thumbs up or thumbs down? Semantic orientation applied to unsupervised classification of reviews. In: Proceedings of the association for computational linguistics (ACL), pp 417–424

28. Voorhess EM (1999) Natural language processing and information retrieval. Information extraction, toward scalable, adaptable systems, Lecture notes in computer science, pp 32–48

29. Wang Y, Hodges J, Tang B (2005) Classification of web documents using naive bayes method. In: Proceedings of the 15th IEEE international conference on tools with artificial intelligence, pp 560–564

30. Whitelaw C, Garg N, Argamon S (2005) Using appraisal groups for sentiment analysis. In: Proceedings of the ACM SIGIR conference on information and knowledge management (CIKM), Bremen, Germany, pp 625–631

31. Wiebe JM, Wilson T, Bruce R, Bell M, Martin M (2004) Learning subjective language. Computat Linguist 30(3):277–308

32. Wiebe J, Mihalcea R (2006) Word sense and subjectivity. In: Proceedings of the 21st conference on computational linguistics/association for computational linguistics (COLING/ACL), Sydney, Australia, pp 1065–1072

33. Wilson T, Wiebe J, Hwa R (2006) Just how mad are you? Finding strong and weak opinion clauses. In: Proceedings of the AAAI, pp 761–769. Ext. version in Computat Intell 22(2 Special Issue on Sentiment Analysis):73–99
34. Wilson T, Wiebe J, Hoffmann P (2005) Recognizing contextual polarity in phrase-level sentiment analysis. In: Proceedings of the human language technology conference and the conference on empirical methods in natural language processing (HLT/EMNLP), pp 347–354
35. Yang Y, Liu X (1999) A re-examination of text categorization methods. In: 22nd ACM international conference on research and development in information retrieval, SIGIR-99, Berkeley, CA, USA, pp 42–49

Chapter 17
On the Use of Social Networks in Web Services: Application to the Discovery Stage

Zakaria Maamar, Leandro Krug Wives, and Khouloud Boukadi

Abstract This chapter discusses the use of social networks in Web services with focus on the discovery stage that characterizes the life cycle of these Web services. Other stages in this life cycle include description, publication, invocation, and composition. Web services are software applications that end users or other peers can invoke and compose to satisfy different needs such as hotel booking and car rental. Discovering the relevant Web services is, and continues to be, a major challenge due to the dynamic nature of these Web services. Indeed, Web services appear/disappear or suspend/resume operations without prior notice. Traditional discovery techniques are based on registries such as Universal Description, Discovery and Integration (UDDI) and Electronic Business using eXtensible Markup Language (ebXML). Unfortunately, despite the different improvements that these techniques have been subject to, they still suffer from various limitations that could slow down the acceptance trend of Web services by the IT community. Social networks seem to offer solutions to some of these limitations but raise, at the same time, some issues that are discussed in this chapter. The contributions of this chapter are three: social network definition in the particular context of Web services; mechanisms that support Web services build, use, and maintain their respective social networks; and social networks adoption to discover Web services.

Z. Maamar (✉)
Zayed University, PO Box 19282, Dubai, United Arab Emirates
e-mail: zakaria.maamar@zu.ac.ae

L.K. Wives
Instituto de Informtica, UFRGS, Porto Alegre, Brazil
e-mail: wives@inf.ufrgs.br

K. Boukadi
École des Mines, Saint-Etienne, France
e-mail: boukadi@emse.fr

A. Abraham et al. (eds.), *Computational Social Network Analysis*, Computer
Communications and Networks, DOI 10.1007/978-1-84882-229-0_17,

17.1 Introduction

Web services are paving the way for a new generation of large-scale, loosely coupled business applications. This can be noticed from the large number of standards and initiatives related to Web services [1, 22, 24, 27, 30, 37], which tackle a variety of issues such as security, fault tolerance, and high availability. These issues, in fact, hinder the smooth automatic composition of Web services, which constitutes the basis of this new generation of business applications. Composition, which is one of Web services' selling points, handles the situation of a user's request that cannot be satisfied by any single, available Web service, whereas a composite Web service obtained by combining available Web services may be used.

Despite the tremendous capabilities that Web services offer for the development of loosely coupled, cross-enterprise business applications, they still lack some capabilities that would propel them to a higher level of adoption by the IT community and make them compete with other traditional integration middleware such as the Common Object Request Broker Architecture (CORBA) and the Distributed Component Object Model (DCOM). Due to this lack of capabilities, there is a risk of seeing the adoption of Web services slow down, if some persistent issues such as the complexity of their discovery are not properly addressed [17]. For the particular issue of discovery, we examine, in this chapter, the use of recommendation-based techniques with focus on *social networks* [8, 36]. Such networks permit to establish between people relationships of different natures such as friendship, kinship, conflict, and competitiveness. These relationships are dynamic and hence adjusted (or re-evaluated) over time depending on different factors such as outcomes of previous interaction experiences, types of partners dealt with, and penalties incurred following the execution of prohibitive actions. A person who stops trusting a peer either breaks or reviews the trust relationship with this peer and then reflects this change (in terms of breaking or review) on his or her social network. Replacing people with Web services is doable since Web services are constantly engaged in different types of interaction sessions with users and peers as well [18, 21]. For example, Manuel Serra da Cruz et al. identified interaction patterns between Web services and users [21]. The purpose is to offer users better interaction patterns in the future.

Roughly speaking, the purpose of the discovery process is to find a suitable Web service for a given consumer's request. A consumer could be a user or another Web service. This process relies a lot on the Web Services Description Language (WSDL) documents that providers of Web services post on various registries such as Universal Description, Discovery and Integration (UDDI) and Electronic Business using eXtensible Markup Language (ebXML). Unfortunately, the current registries still struggle with different limitations (e.g., lack of semantics, consistency, security) despite the multiple extensions and improvements that are reported in the literature [15, 28, 33]. A social network could help address some of these limitations. The idea is simple; let Web services consider the previous composition scenarios in which they took part so that they can establish relationships with the peers that were involved in the same composition scenarios.

The followings are our contributions: (i) define social network in the context of Web services; (ii) support Web services build, use, and maintain their respective social networks; and (iii) adopt these social networks to discover Web services. The rest of this chapter is organized as follows. Section 17.2 suggests some introductory materials on Web services, social networks, and the multiple application domains that adopted social networks. Section 17.3 discusses the use of social networks for Web services discovery. Prior to concluding in Sect. 17.5, some experimental results are reported in Sect. 17.4.

17.2   Background

This section consists of two parts. The first part suggests definitions on some concepts such as Web service and UDDI (selected as an example of registry). The second part provides a brief literature review on the use of social networks in different application domains such as artificial intelligence and recommendation.

17.2.1   Definitions

Web Service It is *"a software application identified by a URI, whose interfaces and binding are capable of being defined, described, and discovered by XML artifacts, and supports direct interactions with other software applications using XML-based messages via Internet-based applications"* (W3C). A Web service implements a functionality (e.g., BookOrder and WeatherForecast) that users and other peers invoke by submitting appropriate messages to this Web service. The life cycle of a Web service could be summarized with five stages namely description, publication, discovery, invocation, and composition. Briefly, providers describe their Web services and publish them on dedicated registries. Potential consumers (i.e., requesters) interact with these registries to discover relevant Web services, so that they could invoke them. In case the discovery fails, i.e., requests cannot be satisfied by any single Web service, the available Web services may be composed to satisfy the consumer's request.

Composite Web Service Composition targets users' requests that cannot be satisfied by any single, available Web service, whereas a composite Web service obtained by combining available Web services may be used. Several specification languages to compose Web services exist, for example, WS-BPEL [7] (*de facto* standard), WS-CDL [14], and XLANG [34]. In [6], Chakraborty and Joshi differentiate between proactive and reactive composition. The former is an off-line process that gathers available component Web services in advance to form a composite Web service. This one is precompiled and ready for execution upon users' requests. The latter creates a composite Web service on-the-fly upon users' requests. Because of the on-the-fly property, a dedicated module is in charge of identifying the needed component Web services, making them collaborate, tracking their execution, and resolving their conflicts if they arise.

Universal Description, Discovery, and Integration UDDI specifications define how Web services should be published and discovered by providers and users, respectively. At the conceptual level, information provided in an UDDI registry consists of three components [35]. First, white pages include address, contact, and known identifiers of Web services. Second, yellow pages include industrial categories based on standardized taxonomies. Finally, green pages include the technical information that a provider would like to offer on its Web services. At the business level, an UDDI registry can be used for checking whether a given provider has particular Web services, finding companies in a certain industry with a given type of Web service, and locating information about how a provider has exposed a Web service.

17.2.2 Some Works on Social Networks

Social networks have been used in different domains ranging from social sciences to artificial intelligence and e-business. According to Ethier, *"the study of social networks is important since it helps us to better understand how and why we interact with each other, as well as how technology can alter this interaction. The field of social network theory has grown considerably during the past few years as advanced computing technology has opened the door for new research"* [8]. According to Raab and Milward, social network research falls into two categories [32]: bright networks wherein the outcomes are considered beneficial for individuals, groups, businesses, and society at large; and dark networks wherein the objectives are achieved at great cost to individuals, groups, businesses, and social welfare.

Generally, a network consists of nodes and edges. The nodes refer to any type of object or entity such as individuals or organizations, and the edges refer to relationships (or associations) between these nodes such as degree of friendship between two persons or distance between two cities. Relationships are sometimes directional, bidirectional, with weight, or a mixture of all of these. Research in a number of academic fields has revealed that social networks operate on many levels, from families up to the level of nations, and play a critical role in determining the way problems are solved, organizations are run, and the degree to which individuals succeed in achieving their goals [10, 26]. Another use of social networks is to determine the social capital of individual actors. According to Kadushin, *"social capital refers to the network position of the object or node and consists of the ability to draw on the resources contained by members of the network"* [12].

In the field of distributed artificial intelligence, social networks have been extensively used in the specification of coordination, cooperation, and negotiation mechanisms of software agents. For Castelfranchi, *"an agent can be helped or damaged, favored or threatened, it can compete or co-operate"* [5]. The idea of using social networks in distributed artificial intelligence stems out of the fact that an agent does not form an independent world, but is part of a society. Agents can engage in interactions with peers from the same society or different societies, which require specific mechanisms to sustain the progress of these interactions. An example of the use of social networks is discussed in [31]; the reputation of an agent is assessed with respect to the position it holds in a society/community.

In the field of recommender systems, Donovan and Smyth propose two computational models of trust and show how these models could be incorporated into collaborative-based recommender systems [29]. The authors report that users tend to ask friends (i.e., persons they normally trust and are part of their social networks) for advices prior to taking actions or making decisions. To address the reliability problem that could undermine the provided recommendations, Donovan and Smyth consider historical evaluations that users give to these recommendations. If a user is behind a good number of accurate recommendations over time, his or her level of trust as a reliable partner increases compared to the one who makes poor (or misleading) recommendations.

In [39], Zhang and Pu use different recursive algorithms to predict the evaluations that users should give to specific items by analyzing their nearest-neighbor users. Because collaborative-based recommender systems need neighbors' evaluations to generate recommendations, some neighbors may not have yet evaluated the item to recommend, while others already have. Thus, by traversing the network of neighbors in a recursive way a prediction for a neighbor's evaluation of the item in question is computed.

In [23], McDonald analyzes the application of social networks to recommend individuals for possible collaboration based on their offered or needed expertise. A similar process may be performed using ReferralWeb [13], which is a system that analyzes paper co-citation and co-authoring relationships. In [38], Zhang and Ackerman go beyond this type of analysis and consider search strategies designed to provide help in expertise location in social networks. This is particularly useful to find the right people who can give the right answer to a specific problem.

Though the aforementioned paragraphs offer a good snapshot of the different initiatives that have embraced social networks, there is a lack of initiatives which are directly related to Web services. Numerous questions such as how Web services build their social networks, thanks to composition scenarios, and how Web services are discovered using these networks, are left unanswered, and thus, responses are provided on a case-by-case basis.

17.3   Social Network-Based Web Services Discovery

Web services discovery is critical to the success of users' requests satisfaction. A plethora of Web services exist on the Internet and identifying the right ones is not always straightforward. Moreover, independent providers develop almost the same set of Web services with different non-functional properties, which increases the complexity of this discovery process a little bit. Bui and Gacher point out that despite the heterogeneity of Web services, their functionalities are sufficiently well-defined and homogeneous enough to allow for market competition to happen [4]. For example, the US National Digital Forecast Database XML Web Service (www.weather.gov/xml) and the US National Weather Service Forecast Office (www.srh.noaa.gov/mfl) each propose weather forecast Web services. In this section, we discuss the development of social networks for Web services discovery by answering three questions: how to build, use, and maintain social networks.

Building a social network is an incremental and continuous process that begins when a Web service takes part in a composition scenario for the first time. Dependency interactions[1] between this Web service and other peers in this scenario permit to at least form the initial edges of this network. Future participations of this Web service in additional composition scenarios would permit to extend its social network, but at the same time would call for a possible review of the already-established edges as new edges might have to be added for example. Another reason to review a social network is when a Web service ceases functioning following its withdrawal. The node and incoming and outgoing edges associated with this Web service are to be checked out, which will affect the shape of the social network.

17.3.1 Social Networks Building

Building a social network means identifying the nature of nodes and edges that will constitute this network. In terms of nodes, Web services would be the sole constituents. In terms of edges, we would suggest three types of associations namely *Recommendation* (R), *Similarity* (S), and *Collaboration* (C).

Formally, a $\mathcal{S}$ocial $\mathcal{N}$etwork $\mathcal{SN}$ of a $\mathcal{W}$eb $\mathcal{S}$ervice $\mathcal{WS}$ is a couple: $\mathcal{SN}_{\mathcal{WS}} = (\mathcal{N}, \mathcal{E})$ where $\mathcal{N}$ and $\mathcal{E}$ are the set of $\mathcal{N}$odes and $\mathcal{E}$dges, respectively. Each edge $e \in \mathcal{E}$ is a tuple of the form $< \mathcal{WS}_i, t, w, \mathcal{WS}_j >$, where the edge is directed from $\mathcal{WS}_i$ to $\mathcal{WS}_j$, t denotes the type of association (or name) between $\mathcal{WS}_i$ and $\mathcal{WS}_j$, and w denotes the weight affected to the association. This weight is a calculated numerical value with a range from 0 to 1.

Recommendation-Based Association (R) In [16], we discuss the combination of recommender systems and Web services in terms of what recommender systems can do for Web services and what Web services can do for recommender systems. We, hereafter, rely on the first dimension of this combination to show the recommendation cases that could stem out of the interactions between Web services. We identify two cases namely *partnership* and *robustness* that should help in specializing the recommendation-based association of the future social networks to build.

---

[1] These interactions are part of the business logic that underpins the specification of a composite Web service. For example, following hotel confirmation, a person could now purchase his or her air ticket.

1. Partnership Case (Rp) A component Web service that participates in a composition scenario could propose that new peers should be appended into this scenario. Though these new peers are not required in satisfying a user's request, they could yield extra responses for the user. For instance, a speaker attending an overseas conference could be interested in some sightseeing activities according to his or her profile, though this speaker did not explicitly express this interest. The new component Web services (or peers) are subject to the speaker's approval prior to their execution.

   - *Example* <RoomBookingWS, t_{Rp}, $w_{t_{Rp}}$, SightSeeingWS>:
     if RoomBookingWS is part of a composition scenario, then this Web service will recommend that SightSeeingWS should be part of this scenario subject to checking and seeking the requestor's profile and approval, respectively.
   - *Properties Rp* is asymmetric and transitive (transitivity may be limited in terms of transition cycles/paths by a threshold that a Web service's owner could set[2]).
   - Association weight for recommendation based on partnership $w_{t_{Rp}}$ is given by the following equation:

   $$w_{t_{Rp(WS_i, WS_j)}} = \frac{|WS_j \ selection|}{|WS_i \ participation|} \quad (17.1)$$

   where $|WS_i \ participation|$ and $|WS_j \ selection|$ stand for the number of times WS_i participated in composition scenarios and the number of times that WS_j accepted to participate in these composition scenarios based on the recommendation of WS_i. The higher the weight, the better for WS_j.

2. *Robustness Case (Rr)* A Web service could suggest peers that will substitute for it in case of failure. These peers are identified based on the functional and non-functional characteristics they have in common with the Web service that needs to be made robust. Reasons for substitution are multiple including Web service failure to respond to a client's requests or inability of meeting a certain level of quality of service.

   - *Example* <RoomBookingWS, t_{Rr}, $w_{t_{Rr}}$, HotelReservationWS>: if RoomBookingWS fails in a composition scenario at run-time, then HotelReservationWS will substitute for this Web service subject to the approval of the user and other peers in this scenario. Peers' providers could refuse interacting with a certain Web service in case of some unsuccessful previous experiences.
   - *Properties R_r* is asymmetric and transitive (like R_p, R_r is limited in terms of transition cycles/paths by a threshold that a Web service's owner could set).

---

[2] Another way to limit transitivity would be the application of a function that controls the propagation of recommendation. Such a function should introduce a minimization rate per transition performed, somehow similar to what Google's PageRank [3] algorithm does. It propagates the "reputation" of a page to the rest of pages that it refers to.

- Association weight for recommendation based on robustness $w_{t_{Rr}}$ is given by the following equation:

$$w_{t_{Rr(WS_i,WS_j)}} = \frac{|WS_j \ selection|}{|WS_i \ failure|} \qquad (17.2)$$

where $|WS_i \ failure|$ and $|WS_j \ selection|$ stand for the number of times that WS_i failed in composition scenarios and the number of times that WS_j was called to substitute for WS_i in these composition scenarios upon the recommendation of WS_i, and obviously did not fail as well. The higher the weight, the better for WS_j.

Similarity-Based Association (S) In [2] we report on the role of communities as a structure that gathers Web services with the same functionality independently of many factors such as origins, locations, nonfunctional properties, and functioning. A community is dynamic by nature: new Web services join, other Web services leave, some Web services become temporarily unavailable, and some Web services resume operation after suspension. By letting Web services join communities, it would be possible to form similarity associations between them, which could be useful for the process of building social networks. Similarity could permit to reduce the search space of Web services in case the first-discovered Web service does not accept to satisfy a user's request for multiple reasons that we report in [19]. Therefore, the discovery could continue with the Web services that are similar with the discovered Web service in a community without screening registries (e.g., UDDI) from scratch.

- *Example* <RoomBookingWS,t_S,w_{t_S},RookReservationWS>: RoomBookingWS and RookReservationWS are similar at the functionality level. However, this does not guarantee that both Web services have similar nonfunctional properties, which is a prerequisite to their substitution in the robustness case.
- *Properties* S is symmetric and transitive.
- Association weight for similarity w_{t_S} is given by the following equation:

$$w_{t_{S(WS_i,WS_j)}} = \frac{|WS_j \ selection|}{|WS_i \ similar|} \qquad (17.3)$$

where $|WS_i \ similar|$ and $|WS_j \ selection|$ stand for the number of Web services that are similar to WS_i and the number of times that WS_j was selected out of the set of Web services that are similar to WS_i. The higher the weight, the better is for WS_j.

Similarity has a great value added to the robustness case that was presented earlier. Similarity could guarantee the compatibility property to a composition scenario by avoiding the conflicts or deadlocks that could arise between the new component Web services (already added to a scenario) and the existing component Web services in this scenario.

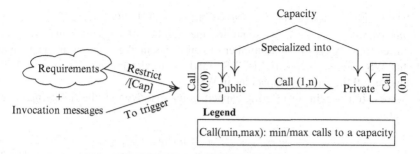

Fig. 17.1 Capacity categorization into public and private types

Collaboration-Based Association (C) In [20], we discuss *capacity-driven Web services* as a new type of Web services that are sensible to context. Capacity, which is a set of actions, represents the ability of a Web service to appropriately act in response to some requirements in the environment. These requirements could be related to network throughput, threat level, data quality, and peer reliability. Like access modifiers in object-oriented programming, we classify the capacity in a Web service into public and private (Fig. 17.1). On the one hand, public capacities are exposed to the external environment that consists of users and Web services. Submitting invocation messages from users or Web services to public capacities is subject to satisfying requirements in the environment. On the other hand, private capacities are hidden as their names hint and only public capacities can call them. Contrarily to private capacities that might call each other if needed, public capacities do not, since they all implement the unique functionality of a Web service.

A capacity-driven Web service offers public capacities to other peers for invocation and requires public capacities of other peers for the same purpose. Offering and requiring public capacities allow to create links of type collaboration between Web services. It should be noted that not all public capacities in a Web service could be made available to peers. Security or access rights reasons could motivate these restrictions.

- *Examples* `<AirTicketPurchaseWS,`$t_{Cr_{capacity_1}}$`,`w_{tCr}`,`
  `RoomBookingWS>`
  and
  `<AirTicketPurchaseWS,`$t_{Cr_{capacity_2}}$`,`w_{tCr}`,RoomBookingWS>`:
  `AirTicketPurchaseWS` requires two capacities from `RoomBookingWS`.
  `<AirTicketPurchaseWS,`$t_{Co_{capacity_3}}$`,`w_{tCo}`,TicketDeliveryWS>`:
  `AirTicketPurchaseWS` offers a capacity to `TicketDeliveryWS`.
- *Properties* C is asymmetric and non-transitive.
- Association weight for requiring capacities w_{tCr} is given by the following equation:

$$w_{tCr(WS_i,WS_j)} = \frac{|Cr_{capacities(WS_i,WS_j)}|}{|capacity_{WS_j}|} \times \frac{|invocation_{capacity_{x(WS_i,WS_j)}}|}{|invocation_{capacities(WS_i,WS_j)}|} \quad (17.4)$$

where $|Cr_{capacities(WS_i,WS_j)}|$, $|capacity_{WS_j}|$, $|invocation_{capacity_x(WS_i,WS_j)}|$, and $|invocation_{capacities(WS_i,WS_j)}|$ stand for the number of capacities that WS_i requires from WS_j, the total number of capacities in WS_j, the number of times that WS_i invoked $capacity_x$ in WS_j, and the total number of times that WS_i invoked all the required capacities in WS_j.

- Association weight for offering capacities $w_{t_{C_o}}$ is given by the following equation:

$$w_{t_{C_o(WS_i,WS_j)}} = \frac{|Co_{capacities(WS_i,WS_j)}|}{|capacity_{WS_i}|} \times \frac{|invocation_{capacity_x(WS_j,WS_i)}|}{|invocation_{capacities(WS_j,WS_i)}|} \quad (17.5)$$

where $|Co_{capacities(WS_i,WS_j)}|$, $|capacity_{WS_i}|$, $|invocation_{capacity_x(WS_j,WS_i)}|$, and $|invocation_{capacities(WS_j,WS_i)}|$ stand for the number of capacities that WS_i offers to WS_j, the total number of capacities in WS_i, the number of times that WS_j invoked $capacity_i$ in WS_x, and the total number of times that WS_j invoked all the offered capacities in WS_i.

17.3.2 Social Networks Use

The purpose of a social network is to help, first, identify additional Web services based on the Web services that are already selected, and second, reinforce (or measure) the associations that connect all these Web services together based on the recommendation-, similarity-, and collaboration-based associations (Sect. 17.3.1). The idea is to combine traditional Web services discovery mechanisms (such as UDDI) with the details that social networks carry on. Any Web service that is discovered using these mechanisms constitutes an entry point to its own social network and probably to the social networks of other peers if navigation (or graph traversal) rights are granted to this Web service. We identify, hereafter, some cases where social networks could be used:

1. In case of composition, the recommendation-based association with focus on partnership would enrich a composition scenario with additional Web services that were not initially taken into consideration during the specification exercise of this scenario. Starting from a Web service that is already part of this scenario, this Web service could recommend a *number* of other Web services that have got the highest weights $w_{t_{R_p}}$ (Eq. 17.1). This number should be specified by the user or composition designer. If this number is set to zero, this means that neither the user nor the designer is interested in expanding or reviewing the specification of the established composition scenario. This could simply be motivated by the extra financial charges that the user does not want to bear, or the lack of computing resources upon which the recommended Web services will be deployed for performance. Otherwise (i.e., number not set to zero) and upon approval of either user or composition designer, the additional Web services are appended into

the composition scenario. We recall that Web services can refuse to participate in composition scenarios as per our work in [19].

2. In case of failure, the recommendation-based association with focus on robustness would enable a direct (and probably automatic) selection of the Web service that will smoothly substitute for the failed Web service. Furthermore, to guarantee the success of this selection, the similarity-based association would ensure that this Web service is compatible with the peers (specially the next ones) that are supposed to interact with the failed Web service, but need now to interact with this Web service. In these two steps, the selection of the new Web service would depend on the weights for robustness ($w_{t_{R_r}}$, Eq. 17.2) and similarity (w_{t_S}, Eq. 17.3), respectively.

3. In case of monitoring, the collaboration-based association would permit to identify the peers that a Web service interacted with at run-time because of the capacities it requires from these peers or it offers to these peers. If the weight for requirement capacities $w_{t_{C_r}}$ (Eq. 17.4) is extremely high (close to one), this means that the interactions between Web services were intense. This could be a good indicator of where to physically locate these Web services in the future so that communication costs among others could be reduced [25]. For the offered capacities, this would permit to identify the peers that sought the help of a Web service and to reveal some potential cases of misuses that affected this Web service. For instance, some offered capacities in a Web service were invoked despite the peek hours.

17.3.3   Social Networks Maintenance

The initial establishment of social networks falls within the responsibilities of providers of Web services. They set up associations between their respective Web services and other peers, prior to letting some (semi-) automated techniques take over the maintenance responsibilities. A provider could use the period of posting a Web service on a registry (or making this Web service join a certain community) to establish some associations. For instance, the provider could screen this registry to look for the Web services that are similar to the Web service it just posted.

In Sect. 17.3.1, three types of associations are described. Some associations could be established at the time of announcing Web services, while others could be established at the time of composing (and invoking) Web services.

Announcement Time Similarity- and recommendation-based associations could be established to maintain a social network. Different techniques that assess the similarity between Web services are reported in the literature [9] and could be adopted in our work. However, because these techniques primarily focus on the similarity at the functionality level, we judge some of them inappropriate for the recommendation-based association with focus on partnership. When Web services participate in the same composition scenario, they in fact complement each other, so they cannot be treated as similar. To address this lack of techniques, previous composition scenarios in which Web services participated could be used. This makes a provider establish the recommendation-based association with focus on partnership at composition and not announcement times.

Composition Time   In addition to the recommendation-based association with focus on partnership, collaboration-based association could be established at this stage of maintaining a social network. Because a composite Web service could be either proactively or reactively designed, establishing such an association varies. In the first case, a designer could easily identify the Web services that will collaborate with its own Web service. These Web services are already known and included in the composite Web service. In the second case, the designer will have to wait until the composite Web service is formed and executed to find more about the Web services that interacted with its Web service.

In Fig. 17.2 we illustrate how the three types of associations can be connected together. For this purpose, we split functionality into two types: similar, which makes Web services compete for participation in composition scenarios, and complementary,[3] which makes Web services take part in the same composition scenarios. In the same figure, we show (i) how a similarity-based social network supports a recommendation-based social network with focus on robustness by identifying the Web services that would be compatible with the rest of the Web services that are already in the composition scenario and (ii) how a recommendation-based social network with focus on partnership results in a collaboration-based social network through the capacities that Web services require from and offer to the peers who are identified out of this recommendation-based social network with focus on partnership.

On top of the announcement and composition times that illustrate when social networks are maintained, these networks could turn out to be useful in the specification of new composite Web services. On the one hand, recommendation- and similarity-based social networks are used at design time by identifying extra Web services and not screening registries. On the other hand, collaboration-based social network is used and updated at run-time by keeping track of all the interactions between Web services.

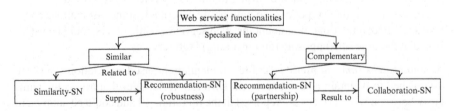

Fig. 17.2 Social networks in interaction

---

[3] Complementary notion is reported in [11]. Jureta et al. gather Web services into groups called service centers that are dedicated to specific types of functionalities and hence, facilitate the development of composite Web services.

17.4 Experiments as Ongoing Efforts

To test the viability of our proposed approach, we have implemented a social network-based prototype for Web services using `Java` and integrated into `Eclipse 3.2`. The prototype provides a tool for social networks building and execution through two modules known as *social network modeler* and *social network simulator*. The first module is complete while the second one is still under development.

The first module is about building social networks in terms of identifying the Web services and the associations between them. Service engineers access the system via a dedicated user interface. The social network modeler assists these engineers in specifying the social networks. In particular, we developed a visual interface for editing such networks using graphs (Fig. 17.3). Moreover, the social network modeler helps the designers of composite Web services to suggest some association types between the Web services that constitute this network.

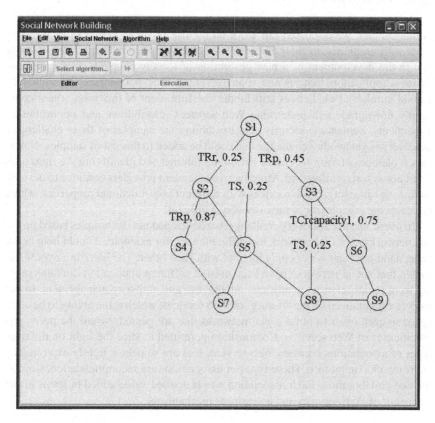

Fig. 17.3 Main interface of the prototype

The second module is responsible for simulating social networks functioning such as adding new nodes and updating some associations' weights. The social network simulator proposes some simulation scenarios that help first identify additional Web services based on the Web services that are already selected, and second, reinforce the associations that connect all these Web services together based on the recommendation-, similarity-, and collaboration-based associations. For example, in case of composition, the social network simulator should use the recommendation-based association with focus on partnership in order to enrich the composition scenario with additional Web services that were not initially taken into consideration during the specification. Another example can be in the case of failure, when the recommendation-based association with focus on robustness would enable an automatic selection of the Web service that will smoothly substitute for the failed Web service.

17.5 Conclusion

In this chapter, we discussed our work on the use of social networks in Web services with emphasis on their discovery. Web services are poised to play a major role in the development of a new generation of loosely coupled, cross-enterprise business applications that can now span over enterprises' boundaries. Unfortunately, a good number of challenges still hinder the fulfilment of this role, which could simply downgrade and undermine Web services' capabilities and opportunities, respectively. Semantics, security, and trustability are samples of these challenges. Discovery is yet another challenge that could be added to this list of samples. Nowadays a plethora of Web services exist on the Internet and identifying the right ones is not always straightforward. Moreover, independent providers continue to develop almost the same set of Web services with different non-functional properties, which increases the complexity of the discovery a little bit.

To overcome the discovery challenge, we developed new techniques based on social networks. A social network has different uses, for example, it could help better understand how and why people interact with each other. The literature review has shown that social networks have been used in different application domains ranging from social sciences to artificial intelligence and authority management. In our work, we capitalized on the "beauty" of Web services, which is the ability to be composed to each other to build social networks that are geared toward the needs and specificities of Web services. Composition permitted to shed the light on different types of associations between Web services that are somehow lightly exploited by the research community. These types of associations are recommendation, similarity, and collaboration. Each association was described value-added in terms of the discovery of Web services and assessment mechanisms.

Acknowledgements This work was partially supported by a grant to Leandro Krug Wives from the CAPES-COFECUB project AdContext (057/07), and Conselho Nacional de Desenvolvimento Cientfico e Tecnolgico (CNPq), Brazil.

References

1. Bentahar J, Maamar Z, Benslimane D, Thiran PH (2007) An argumentation framework for communities of web services. IEEE Intell Syst 22(6):1541–1672
2. Bentahar J, Maamar Z, Wan W, Benslimane D, Thiran PH, Sattanathan S (2008) Agent-based communities of web services: An argumentation-driven approach. Serv Oriented Comput Appl 2(4):219–238 .
3. Brin S, Page L (1998) The anatomy of a large-scale hypertextual web search engine. Comput Network [and ISDN System] 30(1–7):107–117
4. Bui T, Gacher A (2005) Web services for negotiation and bargaining in electronic markets: Design requirements and implementation framework. In: Proceedings of the 38th Hawaii international conference on system sciences (HICSS'2005), Big Island, HI, pp 38–38
5. Castelfranchi C (1995) Commitments: From individual intentions to groups and organizations. In: Proceedings of the international conference on multiagent systems (ICMAS'1995), San Francisco, CA, pp 41–48
6. Chakraborty D, Joshi A (2001) Dynamic service composition: State-of-the-art and research directions. Technical report, TR-CS-01-19, Department of Computer Science and Electrical Engineering, University of Maryland, Baltimore County, MD
7. Curbera F, Goland Y, Klein J et al (2003) Business process execution language for web services (BPEL4WS) Version 1.1
8. Ethier J (2008) Current research in social network theory, Visited September 2008. http://www.ccs.neu.edu/home/perrolle/archive/Ethier-SocialNetworks.html
9. Hameurlain N (2007) Flexible behavioural compatibility and substitutability for component protocols: a formal specification. In: Proceedings of the fifth IEEE international conference on software engineering and formal methods (SEFM'2007), London, UK, 391–400
10. Jackson MO, Wolinsky A (1996) A strategic model of social and economic networks. J Econ Theor 71(44):44–74
11. Jureta I, Faulkner S, Achbany Y, Saerens M (2007) Dynamic web service composition within a service-oriented architecture. In: Proceedings of the IEEE international conference on web services (ICWS'2007), Salt Lake City, UT, pp 304–311
12. Kadushin C (2008) A short introduction to social networks: A non-technical elementary primer, Visited September 2008. http://construct.haifa.ac.il/ cerpe/papers/kadushin.html
13. Kautz H, Selman B, Shah M (1997) Referral web: Combining social networks and collaborative filtering. Communun ACM 40(3):63–65
14. Kavantzas N, Burdett D, Ritzinger G, Fletcher T, Lafon Y, Barreto C (2005) Web services choreography description language version 1.0. W3C Candidate Recommendation, November 2005. http://www.w3.org/TR/ws-cdl-10/
15. Kawamura T, De Blasio JA, Hasegawa T, Paolucci M, Sycara K (2004) Public deployment of semantic service matchmaker with UDDI business registry. In: Proceedings of the international semantic web conference (ISWC'2004), Hiroshima, Japan, pp 752–766
16. Krug Wives L, Maamar Z, Tata S, Sellami M, Defude B, Moreira de Oliveira JP (2008) Towards a marraige between recommender systems & web services. Technical report, College of Information Technology, Zayed University, Dubai
17. Langdom C (2003) The state of web services. IEEE Comput 36(7):93–94
18. Maamar Z, Kouadri Mostéfaoui S, Lahkim M (2005) Web services composition using software agents and conversations. Ingénierie des Systèmes d'Information 10(3):49–66
19. Maamar Z, Kouadri Mostéfaoui S, Yahyaoui H (2005) Towards an agent-based and context-oriented approach for web services composition. IEEE Trans Knowl Data Eng 17(5):686–697

20. Maamar Z, Tata S, Belaïd D (2009) Towards an approach to defining capacity-driven Web services. In: Proceedings of the 23rd international conference on advanced information networking and applications (AINA'2009), Bradford, UK
21. Manuel Serra da Cruz S, Maris Campos L, Luiza Machado Campos M, Pires PF (2003) A data mart approach for monitoring web services usage and evaluating quality of service. In: Proceedings of the XVIII Brazilian symposium on databases (SBBD'2003), Manaus, Brazil
22. Margaria T (2007) Service is in the eyes of the beholder. IEEE Comput 40(11):33–37
23. McDonald DW (2003) Recommending collaboration with social networks: A comparative evaluation. In: Proceedings of the SIGCHI conference on human factors in computing systems (CHI'2003), Ft. Lauderdale, FL, pp 593–600
24. Medjahed B, Atif Y (2007) Context-based matching for web service composition. Distrib Parallel Dat 21(1):5–37
25. Messer A, Greeberg I, Bernadat P, Milojicic D (2002) Towards a distributed platform for resource-constrained devices. In: Proceedings of the IEEE 22nd international conference on distributed computing systems (ICDCS'2002), Vienna, Austria, pp 43–51
26. Moody J, White DR (2003) Structural cohesion and embeddedness: A hierarchical concept of social groups. Am Sociol Rev 68(1):103–127
27. Mrissa M, Ghedira C, Benslimane D, Maamar Z, Rosenberg F, Dustdar S (2007) A context-based mediation approach to compose semantic web services. ACM Trans Internet Technol (Special Issue on Semantic Web Services: Issues, Solutions and Applications) 8(1)
28. Nasirifard P (2003) Web services security overview and security proposal for UDDI framework. In: Proceedings of the international conference on security and management (SAM'2003), Las Vegas, NV
29. O'Donovan J, Smyth B (2005) Trust in recommender systems. In: Proceedings of the 10th international conference on intelligent user interfaces (IUI'2005), San Diego, CA, pages 167–174
30. Papazoglou M, Traverso P, Dustdar S, Leymann F (2007) Service-oriented computing: State of the art and research challenges. IEEE Comput 40(11):38–45
31. Pujol JM, Sangüesa R, Delgado J (2002) Extracting reputation in multi agent systems by means of social network topology. In: Proceedings of the first international joint conference on autonomous agents & Multiagent Systems (AAMAS'2002), Bologna, Italy, pp 467–474
32. Raab J, Milward HB (2003) Dark networks as problems. J Publ Admin Res Theor 13(4):413–439
33. Sun C, Lin Y, Kemme B (2004) Comparison of UDDI registry replication strategies. In: Proceedings of The IEEE international conference on web services (ICWS'2004), San-Diego, CA, pp 218–225
34. Thatte S XLANG: Web services for business process design, 2001. http://www.gotdotnet.com/team/xml_wsspecs/xlang-c/default.htm
35. uddi.org (2003) UDDI technical white paper. http://www.uddi.org/, 2003. Visited August 2003
36. Wasserman S, Glaskiewics J (1994) Advances in social network analysis: Research in the social and behavioral sciences. Sage
37. Yu Q, Bouguettaya A, Medjahed B (2008) Deploying and managing web services: Issues, solutions, and directions. VLDB J 17(3):537–572
38. Zhang J, Ackerman MS (2005) Searching for expertise in social networks: A simulation of potential strategies. In: Proceedings of the 2005 international ACM SIGGROUP conference on supporting group work (GROUP'2005), Sanibel Island, FL, pp 71–80
39. Zhang J, Pu P (2007) A recursive prediction algorithm for collaborative filtering recommender systems. In: Proceedings of the 2007 ACM conference on recommender systems (RecSys'2007), Minneapolis, MN, pp 57–64

Chapter 18
Friends with Faces: How Social Networks Can Enhance Face Recognition and Vice Versa

Nikolaos Mavridis, Wajahat Kazmi, and Panos Toulis

Abstract The "friendship" relation, a social relation among individuals, is one of the primary relations modeled in some of the world's largest online social networking sites, such as "FaceBook." On the other hand, the "co-occurrence" relation, as a relation among faces appearing in pictures, is one that is easily detectable using modern face detection techniques. These two relations, though appearing in different realms (social vs. visual sensory), have a strong correlation: faces that co-occur in photos often belong to individuals who are friends. Using real-world data gathered from "Facebook," which were gathered as part of the "FaceBots" project, the world's first physical face-recognizing and conversing robot that can utilize and publish information on "Facebook" was established. We present here methods as well as results for utilizing this correlation in both directions. Both algorithms for utilizing knowledge of the social context for faster and better face recognition are given, as well as algorithms for estimating the friendship network of a number of individuals given photos containing their faces. The results are quite encouraging. In the primary example, doubling of the recognition accuracy as well as a sixfold improvement in speed is demonstrated. Various improvements, interesting statistics, as well as an empirical investigation leading to predictions of scalability to much bigger data sets are discussed.

18.1 Introduction

The work presented here was carried out as part of the "FaceBots" research project,[1] whose original purpose was to show that references to shared memories as well as to shared friends can enhance long-term human robot relationships. Towards that

N. Mavridis (✉) and W. Kazmi
Interactive Robots and Media Lab, United Arab Emirates University, 17551 Al Ain, United Arab Emirates
e-mail: irmluaeu@gmail.com; wajahat.kazmi@em-a.eu

P. Toulis
ISSEL laboratory, Aristotle University of Thessaloniki, Greece
e-mail: ptoulis@issel.ee.auth.gr

[1] We thank Microsoft External Research for providing seed funding for this project through its Human-Robot Interaction CFP.

A. Abraham et al. (eds.), *Computational Social Network Analysis*, Computer Communications and Networks, DOI 10.1007/978-1-84882-229-0_18, purpose, a special physical robot was created, with face recognition (FR) as well as spoken natural-language dialogue capabilities, which was also equipped with an interaction as well as a social database [1]. Furthermore, this robot ("Sarah Mobileiro the FaceBot") is able to connect in real time to the FaceBook online networking web site, and thus was the world's first robot that was able to utilize and publish online social information. Sarah is able to perform training as well as recognition not only from its camera-derived photos, but also from online photos, posted on FaceBook, which might also contain tags. Thus, all the ingredients were there in order to explore the idea of trying to utilize social context towards better FR, as well as trying to find out who might be friends with whom on the basis of photos.

18.1.1 Background

Context-assisted visual recognition is a highly promising research area, and some attempts already exist, as we shall see. In contrast, very few attempts exist towards utilizing FR on images belonging to online social networking (SN) web sites (for example [2], without the utilization of context). On the other hand, as noted above, some methods for context-assisted object recognition have appeared in the literature recently: Torralba [3] provides an example of contextual priming for object recognition, based on holistic context representations, while Hoiem et al. [4] perform object detection by modeling the interdependence of objects, surface orientations, and camera viewpoint. However, none of these papers addresses the utilization of social context for FR; the only noteworthy exception is [5]. There is an important difference though between this paper and the methods we are presenting here as Stone et al. [5] only use the identity of the person contributing the photo to the online networking web site in order to enhance the recognition and the method only works if this is known. In contrast, our method does not require this information. It can be seeded by the social context created through postulated or recognized participants in the photo, and is much more flexible in that respect, and can thus be used also on photos with no submitting author information, arising anywhere on the Internet or live. Finally, it is worth noting that apart from the mutual benefits between FR and online networks, there exists a whole triangle of synergies between the two and interactive robotics, as demonstrated on Sarah the FaceBot, and discussed in [6]. And from a wider viewpoint, we hope for this chapter to also act as a concrete demonstration that very promising avenues exist at the crossroads between social networks and numerous other areas, many of which remain yet unexplored.

18.1.2 Overview

This chapter is structured around two sections: Section 18.2 addresses the enhancement of FR through social knowledge, whereas Sect. 18.3 discusses the acquisition of social knowledge through photos containing faces. In the first section, we introduce basic concepts, problems and classes of algorithms, describe the algorithms in detail, and provide thorough coverage of a real world empirical investigation of the performance of the proposed methods on a data set arising from the friends of our robot and their facebook profiles. We present interesting statistics, results, and conclusions, as well as a further investigation of the expected performance of the algorithm as the size of the friendship network grows, that is, a prediction of scalability-related issues. In Sect. 18.2, we discuss the converse problem of estimating friendship through photos, propose algorithms, and provide real-world results. A conclusion closes the chapter, together with appendices regarding notation and proofs.

18.2   Utilizing Social Context Towards Face Recognition

18.2.1   Basic Concepts

Our *purpose* here is to illustrate how social context can help towards enabling faster as well as more accurate FR in photos. We will do so by presenting a number of basic problems, algorithms and variations, and finally concrete results for a real-world example concerned with facebook photos accessible through a conversational interactive physical robot. The *salient idea* behind our illustration is simple to state: *co-occurrence* of faces in photos and *friendship* have a strong correlation between them. As we shall see, in our real-world experiments, two random tagged faces within a facebook photo had a probability of almost 80% of being faces of declared first-level friends within facebook. Thus, one can expect that knowledge of the friendship relationships among individuals can assist towards predicting co-occurrence of them in photos, and consequently towards better FR in photos with more than one faces.

From a higher-level viewpoint, one can conjecture *three realms* implicated in the setting of this discussion: first, a *social realm*, in which identities are entities, and friendship a relation; second, a *visual sensory realm*, of which faces are entities, and co-occurrence in images a relation; and third, a *physical realm*, in which bodies belong, with physical proximity being a relation. The frequent physical proximity of bodies of friends, as they engage in activities and interactions together, is imprinted in photos and correlates with co-occurrence of their faces; and thus photo co-occurrence (a sensory-domain relation among regions in images) correlates with friendship (a social relation among individuals).[2]

---

[2] When viewed from a slightly different viewpoint, here we have a *sensory grounding* not of a conceptual *entity* (as is often the case in language grounding research), but of a social-level *relation* among entities, in a manner similar to grounding ontologies. Also, one might conjecture that the actual grounding of the social-level relation of friendship, might start during development initially from a restricted tangible meaning: that of the bodies of two individuals often being close and interacting. This restricted meaning is later extended during development in order to include social-level attributes that might include co-operation, sincerity, etc.

Before we proceed, let us introduce some *basic notation* in order to clarify our exposition:

Identity (*Id*) An individual, which might or might not have a facebook Id, and whose name might or might not appear as a tag in a facebook photo.

Face (*F*) A region of an image corresponding to a human face, having ultimately been generated through the visual sensory effect of an underlying Identity.

Photo (*Ph*) An image potentially containing multiple faces, which might or might not be a photo available within facebook.

Tag (*T*) A string which has been entered by a facebook user in order to identify a face in a photo. This might or might not be equal to the facebook name of an identity, if the identity belongs to facebook.

Classifier (*Cl*) A black-box abstraction of a pattern recognizer, whose input is an image region (detected as having been a face in our case) and output a measure of likelihood of this face having been the sensible emission of an identity. Each classifier is trained through a training set consisting of faces, which are conjectured to belong to the target identity to be classified.

Friendship Relation (*FR*) A relationship among two identities.

Friendship Matrix (*FM*) A square matrix whose rows and columns are identities, and whose entries $FM_{i,j}$ are

$$
\begin{aligned}
&1 \text{ (knowledge of friendship among identities } i \text{ and } j) \\
&0 \text{ (knowledge of non-friendship among } i \text{ and } j) \\
&-1 \text{ (lack of knowledge about friendship of } i \text{ and } j)
\end{aligned}
\tag{18.1}
$$

18.2.2 Basic Problems and Classes of Algorithms

Here, let us first introduce *three basic problems* that we will deal with in this section. In all three, our purpose is to recover the identities of the faces in the photo, but the number of available tagged faces differs:

Pr1) *Seeded Face-Rec* A photo is given, in which exactly one face is assumed to have a tag attached to it.

Pr2) *Unseeded Face-Rec* A photo is given, in which no faces are assumed to have a tag attached to them.

Pr3) *Multi-seed Face-Rec* A photo is given, in which more than one faces are assumed to have a tag attached to them.

Regarding evaluation of the effectiveness of solutions to the above problems, we distinguish between *two types of real-world usage* of the system: *fully-automated recognition (AR)*, with no human intervention, as well as *semi-automated recognition (SAR)*, in which the system, instead of offering a unique solution regarding the postulated identity of a face, offers a number of alternatives, which are presented to a human, who finally picks up the one he or she thinks is correct. The requirements of classification accuracy for the latter case are more relaxed; although we require the postulated identity to be equal to the actual identity for the case of AR (i.e., only one guess is possible and it should be correct), we only require the postulated identity to belong to a small set of identities proposed by the system for the case of SAR. A practically tractable size for the set of identities proposed by a SAR system is here taken to be 10 photos, which can be glanced upon by a human and selected within 10 s or less. Thus, we will quantify performance using primarily two metrics:

Rank1 Accuracy (for the Case of AR) The percentage of times during which the postulated identity of a face by a classifier is correct.

Rank10 Accuracy (for the Case of SAR) The percentage of times during which the correct identity of a face belongs to the ten most probable identities as postulated by a classifier.

Towards the solution of the basic problems introduced above, we will later provide more details on the following four basic classes of algorithms:

Alg0 Face-by-face recognition without use of social context
Alg1 Whole-photo rec utilizing social context (Pr1, single seed id known)
Alg2 As Alg1 but for problem Pr2, i.e. no known seed identity
Alg3 As Alg1 for Pr3 (multiple seed identities known)

18.2.3 The Proposed Algorithms in Detail

For the *four basic classes of algorithms* that we have defined above, here we provide a detailed description and discuss possible *variations*.

18.2.3.1 Algorithm 0

A photo is given containing multiple faces, but no knowledge of any friendship matrix is assumed. Each face is subsequently passed through the set of available classifiers, and scores are recorded. The identity giving the best score is reported (for the rank1 case for AR), or the identities of the top ten scores (for the rank10 case for SAR). Summing up:

Input A photo *(Ph)* containing n faces $F1 \cdots Fn$.
Output A vector of postulated identities (for the AR version of Alg1):

$$[Id(F1) \cdots Id(Fn)] \tag{18.2}$$

or a vector of 10-D vectors of postulated best-10 identities (SAR version):

$$[\{Id1(F1), Id2(F1) \cdots Id10(F1)\} \cdots \{Id1(Fn), Id2(Fn) \cdots Id10(Fn)\}] \tag{18.3}$$

18.2.3.2 Algorithm 1

A seed is already given, as well as some knowledge of the friendship matrix *(FM)* is assumed. Then, the first-level friends of the Id of the seed are recovered from the corresponding column of the friendship matrix, in the form of a friendship vector:

$$FV = [FR(i, 1), FR(i, 2), FR(i, 3) \cdots FR(i, m)] \tag{18.4}$$

where

$$FR(i, j) = \begin{cases} 1 \\ 0 \\ -1 & \text{(as explained in Sect. 18.2.1)} \end{cases} \tag{18.5}$$

At this stage, two possible variants of the algorithm exist:

Alg1H: *(Hard biasing)* For each face F_i in the photo *Ph*, scores are taken only for those classifiers whose entries at the friendship vector are 1, i.e. only for the classifiers whose identities are the known friends of the seed. Then, the rank1 or rank10 best identities are chosen, among the classifiers of the first level friends of the seed (for AR and SAR, respectively).

Alg1S: *(Soft biasing)* For each face F_i in the photo *Ph*, the scores at the output of all the known classifiers are taken, say *(S1··· Sm)*. Then, biasing is accomplished through a biasing vector added to the score vector; this vector *BV* is calculated as a function of the friendship vector *FV* in the following way:

$$BV(i) = \begin{cases} \alpha_1 & \text{if } FV(i) = 1 \\ 0 & \text{if FV(i) = 0} \\ \alpha_{-1} & \text{if } FV(i) = -1 \end{cases} \tag{18.6}$$

Thus, the two constant parameters a1 and a-1 determine the relative contribution to biasing for the known friendship relationships, as well as the unknown relationships. The optimal values of these parameters can be determined empirically, as discussed later in this paper. Finally, the rank1 or rank10 best identities are chosen, among the classifiers of the first-level friends of the seed (for AR and SAR, respectively).

Alg1TS: *(Biasing According to Training Set Size)* An extra term is added to the biasing vector, to account for variance in the training set sizes of different classifiers. As the classifiers are trained through the facebook photos which contain tags for the classifier's identity, there is considerable variance in the number of photos available for training for each identity (as quantified later in this paper). Identities with larger training sets generally result to classifiers with more reliable outputs; and the converse holds for those identities that have small training sets. The biasing term has the form:

$$BSV(i) = \beta log(size(Tr(Id_i))) \tag{18.7}$$

where
$$Tr(Id_i) = \text{the available training set for Identity } i \qquad (18.8)$$

This extra biasing term is added to the social biasing vector BV.

Input A photo Ph containing n faces $F1\cdots Fn$, as well as a seed (i: seed is face F_i, and $Id(F_i)$)
Output Rank1 and Rank10 scores, as described in Alg0.

18.2.3.3 Algorithm 2

As in Algorithm1, but with no seed. Thus, a seed should be selected, then Alg1 carried out, and then possible results evaluated and potentially a different seed reselected. Thus, here we distinguish three of the possible variations:

Alg2RS Here, out of the n faces in the picture, one is randomly selected to serve as the seed (alternatively, the first face always serves as the seed). Its postulated identity is given by choosing the identity of the classifier that has the highest score on this face, out of all existing classifiers. Then, Alg1 is run, i.e., the friendship vector is created, hard or soft biasing takes place, etc. The problem with this approach is that, as we shall see, any mistake in the identity of the seed might have devastating consequences for correct recognition on the rest of the faces of the photo.

Alg2BS Here, the seed is not randomly selected; all the faces are taken in turn, and classified as belonging to one of all existing classifiers. The face which has the biggest score is then selected as the seed (i.e., the one for whose identity we appear to be more certain).

Alg2PE Here, the seed is not randomly selected; all the faces are taken in turn, and classified as belonging to one of all existing classifiers. Then each of these faces is taken as a possible seed, and Alg1 is applied n times in total, giving n total whole-photo classifications. Then, one is chosen out of all these n whole-photo hypothesis, through maximization of a suitable "total match" metric. The metric chosen could be, for example, the sum of square of the scores of the chosen identities across all faces in the photo.

18.2.3.4 Algorithm 3

In the class of algorithms referred to as *Alg3*, multiple seed photos might exist at a given time. Thus, these extend upon *Alg2* and consequently *Alg1*, in the following respects:

Higher-Level Friendships and Mutual Friendships Once more than one seed photo is postulated, there exist multiple radii of social circles (first-level friends of seed 1, first-level friends of seed 2, second-level friends of seed 1, etc.) as well as of intersections of circles (mutual friends of seed 1 and seed 2, mutual friends of seed 1 and seed 3, etc.) that can be taken into account. Each one of these is taking into account, for example, through a different weighing parameter when adding a soft bias. As an example, for maximum two seeds, and maximum radius 1, we get a wealth of combinations of possibilities: $\{-1, 0, 1\} \times \{-1, 0, 1\}$, i.e. the set of all classifiers is partitioned into nine possible subsets according to each classifier identity's friendship relationship with the two seeds.

Ongoing Rebiasing Instead of just biasing initially, and then classifying all remaining faces at once, with ongoing rebiasing one can successively increase the number of seeds while classifying, by incorporating as a new seed each new face that has been classified with highest confidence. For example, we might start with problem 2; i.e. no known seed faces. Then, we might chose as a seed the face that was classified with highest confidence without social information (say seed 1); and bias through it. Then, we might again chose the new face that was classified with highest confidence (among the remaining yet unclassified faces – let us call it seed 2), and add this to the seed set. Now, at this stage we can perform mutual biasing from the two seeds, as described in the above paragraph. The next classified face with highest confidence will also be added to the constantly expanding seed set, and mutual biasing will be performed again, until no more unclassified faces remain.

Backtracking The primary problem of ongoing rebiasing is that any wrong choice in the postulated identity of the face might have destructive effects for the next faces, as through social biasing with the wrong seed it might avert their correct recognition. One possible solution for this is the introduction of backtracking; for each face, at each stage, multiple, say n, possible identities are kept (the *rankN* best solutions). Also, either at the end (whole photo classified), or at intermediate stages (k photos classified so far), an overall photo-so-far confidence metric is evaluated. If the overall confidence metric is low, then the identity choices for faces so far that have been made are partially retracted, and the next possible identity (for example, *rank2*) is considered for the faces in question, as well as their combinations.

18.2.4   Empirical Investigation

18.2.4.1   Data Acquisition

Aspects of the Facebots project [6] required accessing and processing, a large amount of data, contributed by people in the "Facebook" networking site. Generally, these include friendship relations, photos, news updates and also data generated through user-to-user communication (messages, chats, etc.). The ranging sensitivity of personal information is, in most cases, directly equivalent to its degree of accessibility, and this rule holds also on how much of this information, our robot was able to access. The idea of a robot crawling information pages on Facebook is quite an interesting one, and is tightly intertwined with issues regarding access and openness, and so this section is devoted to further details regarding how our information gathering was achieved, described at the programming level.

18.2.4.2 Facebook Site Mechanism and Security

Facebook [7] is a popular SN, which currently (2009), allows around 200 million people to interact with each other [8]. The site has been built with strict security mechanisms that protect users' data from unprivileged access, which in part accounts for its big popularity. In what follows, we provide with some information about the inner workings of Facebook as an application, that enabled us to build the first social networked robot. However, the reader should keep in mind, that this information became available to the authors only by means of experimentation and reverse engineering, and that it is due to constant changes. Nevertheless, it is still an outline of how related research efforts can be performed.

To start with, Facebook is itself very strict with accounts that seem suspicious for spamming or for other than personal use. As an example, it is not possible to create accounts with names containing the distinct words "spam" or "bot" or reporting an age less than 18. Communication with the site is being carried through SSL, with the familiar cookie-based authentication. The benefits and vulnerabilities of this scheme are well known and the reader can refer to [9].

Upon login to the SN site, the user's browser is receiving two important id's : the post-form Id and a channel Id, the former being an hexadecimal number and the latter being actually a host name, while both of them are being used for enabling the communication of the user with the web site. In specific, almost any POST action will require for the post-form Id (e.g., updating user status, sending messages, etc.), while the channel Id identifies a Facebook server which provides with all of the instant messaging functionality : updating online friends' list, sending instant(chat) message, receiving chat messages, and others.

All sensitive information and operations, such as messages exchanged or new friendship connections, are not available or accessible by any means. Provided that the intrinsic Facebook cookie-mechanism remains un-compromised, an automated software entity cannot access data that has not been published by their owners. In addition, a bot cannot perform any bulk activities, such as sending messages, or sending friendship requests, without being able to solve known computationally hard problems (e.g., captchas).

18.2.4.3 Facebots Data Access

What data does our robot actually have access to and what operations does it perform for the purposes of our research? In order to answer this question, we will present in brief, but in a technical manner, what and how our robot accesses the information needed.

Our robot, the first FaceBot [1], Sarah Mobilero, has currently 76 first-level friends in its Facebook account, and the following functions related to Facebook have been implemented:

login Logins into Facebook and retrieves basic information, such as robot's Id, post-form Id and channel Id *get(status, friends, posted_photos, joined_groups, status_updates)* Gets a number of available information such as friend lists or status updates, all related to the robot's friends.

set(status, String STATUS) Sets the robot's status to STATUS

composeMessage(String MESSAGE, int FID) Composes a new message to the friend with a Facebook Id equal to FID

chat(int FID, St ring CHAT_MESSAGE) Sends the instant message CHAT_ MESSAGE to user FID

The mechanism for obtaining data and performing the aforementioned actions is uniform and in fact it is described by the term "HTML scraping," [10] which has been a known technique for network programming. The structured format of new Web 2.0 applications, relying heavily on frameworks such as the CSS or JSON, makes them consumable with a reasonable effort, by regular expressions, without the use of further messaging protocols on top of HTML (e.g. Web Services/SOAP). The use of the Facebook API [11], was not considered due to latency problems and functionality limitations. The idea is to basically emulate ordinary user-browser sessions through the automated use of the underlying HTML GET/POST requests. This way, a software entity can replay the interactions with a browser, and parse their output using predefined regular expressions, to generate the desired data structures (e.g. friend lists, photo updates). This way, the robot is able to do what a normal user can do using a regular browser when interacting with Facebook.

18.2.5 A First Look at the Data Sets

In order to access a big pool of photos that were contributed by Sarah's friends or photos in which these friends were tagged, we used the following methodology: first, we acquired the first-level-friends set of Sarah. Then, for each first-level friend, we downloaded all photos in which he or she was tagged. After a purging process for discarding erroneous pictures, available photos summed up to a total of 7,597. This set was split into two different sets, one for training and one for testing, which contained 3,752 and 3,845 images, respectively. In order to extract faces from the photos, a Viola-Jones HAAR-based face detector [14] was used for detecting frontal faces only. Upon successful detection, a face was only accepted for training or testing if a compatible tag match was found. From the training set of photos, a total of 1,306 classifiers (based on Embedded HMM's [15]) were obtained out of which, for only 840 we could find social information and for the remaining 446 we could not (they did have their friends information private or the tag names did not correspond to a valid Facebook account). The testing set, after the face detection phase, produced a total of 5,258 total faces. Sarah was able to acquire the tags from these photos, each consisting of a pair of the following information:

Name of person tagged
Position of face in photo (X,Y coordinates in percentages of dimensions)

Along with the tag information, our robot, would try to explore the friendship relationships within the picture, even for people who were not her friends. This could be partially accomplished through a special Facebook AJAX call which is essentially equivalent to following the link "View Friends", which appears in the Facebook Search Results. By doing the same procedure iteratively, we were able to build a database of 2,637 people along with their friendship information, which accounted for the number of people that were reachable through the photos that the robot explored, and who had their friends list publicly open. The total size of the data, including the images, the classifiers' output and the social information, was around 640 MB fragmented in 15.920 files. These files were then used for experimenting with the algorithms described in Sect. 18.2.3.

18.2.5.1 A Closer Look at the Data Sets

The given name of the first Facebot that we have built is Sarah Mobileiro, which is also her online name. There exist three kinds of friends of the robot: first, those that have been physically encountered, but are not on facebook, second, those that have been physically encountered, and are also on facebook, and third, those that have not yet been physically encountered, but are facebook friends. It is also worth noting here that there is a highly dynamic nature in figures related to the network – facebook profiles are being added and retracted or become restricted every day; thus, here, we will chose to report approximate numbers, which are based on data gathered during three snapshots, in the last 6 months.

First-Level Friends The robot at this moment has 76 Facebook friends,[3] out of which 14 she has met physically, and has also acquired camera pictures of.[4] The robot also has another 80 friends who are not on Facebook, and also has camera pictures of them. The set of the first-level friends (direct friends) of the robot in Facebook is depicted in Fig. 18.1.

Higher-Level Friends and Mutual Friends Upon moving from the first-level friends to the second-level, i.e. the friends of the first-level friends of the robot who are not first-level friends, there is, as expected, a huge increase: the set FL2 (of friends with minimum distance 2) of Sarah the Facebot contains almost 14,000 members. By a simple division, one gets the figure of on average approximately 175 new second-level friends for each first-level friend. Of course, the average number of second-level friends corresponding to each first-level friend is higher (on the order of 210 as compared to 175, i.e. on average 35 friends are shared, i.e. approximately 15% of the friends are shared). This is due to the existence of mutual second-level friends between any two first-level friends. Also, it is worth noting that the variance

---

[3] The robot accepts friendships only from a selected circle at the moment.

[4] which we are not including in the experiments reported in this chapter. Interesting results regarding the transferability of training from camera- to facebook-photos and vice versa can be found in [6]. Also, results for hybrid training sets are included there.

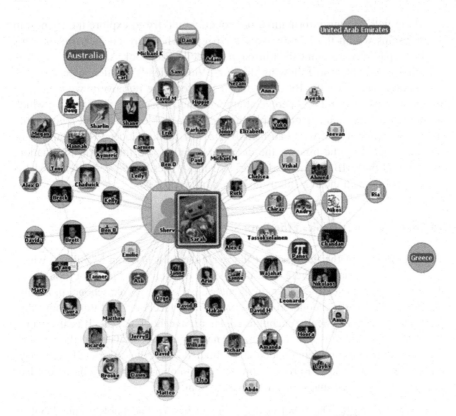

Fig. 18.1 A **Touchgraph** depiction of the 1st-level friends of our robot, 03/09

of the number of friends of each member of FL1 is quite high too almost 120 in this case.

Number of Friends for Which We Can Create Classifiers All the above statistics are related to the social network of Sarah, at maximum distance two. Now, having briefly explored this, let us move on to the next question in sequence: How many of the first and second level friends of Sarah can we create classifiers for, towards FR?

The total number of tagged photos of the members of *FL1* and *FL2* which are directly accessible to Sarah is on the order of 11,000. This number arises as the sum of the number of tagged photos across each first-level friends tagged photos of second-level friends is not generally accessible due to visibility constraints. The distribution of the number of available tagged photos for the 76 first-level friends is in Fig. 18.2.

The average number of tagged photos per first-level friend is approximately 140, with a standard deviation of 180 easily explicable through the 4 outliers with more than 300 tagged photos. Thus, we expect to have a wide variety of training set sizes as numerous friends have only 1 photo available, while a significant number might have 100 or more.

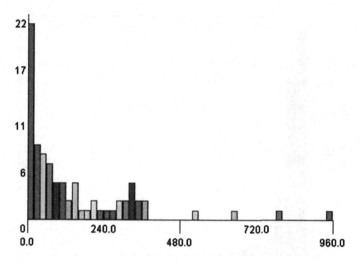

Fig. 18.2 Histogram of number of available tagged photos per first-level friend of the robot (these tagged to be potentially utilized as a training set)

Now, although as we mentioned there is a sum on the order of 11,000 photos when tagged photos are summed across the 76 first-level friends, not all of these are unique. Out of these, given the possibility of a photo having more than one person tagged, the number of unique photos is around 7,650, including 50 or so problematic images, leaving about 7,600 usable. Furthermore some of these will have only a single face tagged and some more than one face. Indeed, more than two thirds out of the 7,600 unique photos have more than one tagged face, as can be seen from the histogram of number of photos containing n tagged faces in Fig. 18.3. And now the question arises: for how many of the first- and second-level friends of the robot do we have adequate training sets to create classifiers out of? If we restrict ourselves to gathering training data through these tagged photos (the simplest and safest solution, as described in [6]), then we have at least one tagged photo for only approximately 3,600 out of the 14,000 or so first- and second-level friends of Sarah, i.e. roughly 25% of the union of first- and second-level friends.

Relationship of Co-occurrence with Friendship Now, let us provide a first quantification of the relationship between face co-occurrence and friendship, as manifested in our data set. Consider the following three questions:

Q1: Given a person A in a photo, what is the probability of any other person B in the photo being a first-level friend of A? Let us call this P1.

Q2: Given a person A in a photo, what is the probability of any other person B in the photo being a second level friend of A? Let us call this P2.

Q3: Given two persons A and B in a photo, what is the probability of any other person C in the photo being a mutual friend of A and B (where it is not necessary that A is a first level friend of B)? Let us call this P3.

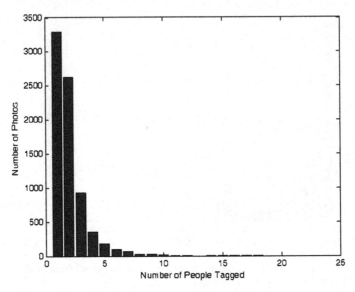

Fig. 18.3 Histogram of number of photos containing exactly n tagged faces

By examining all the approximately 5,000 unique tagged photos with more than one tagged face that Sarah has direct access to, we obtain the following estimates for the three above probabilities (measured across tagged photos with > 1 face):

$$P1 = 0.785, \ P2 = 0.024 \text{ and } P3 = 0.278$$

Notice that P1 is strikingly high: almost 80% of any two faces in photos are first-level friends, and this very strong correlation underlies the high effectiveness of the incorporation of social context in our algorithms, which we will be illustrating by quantitative results in the next section. Finally, a very important point not discussed yet deals with the amount of overlap between the identities (people) included in the training set and having formed classifiers, and those tagged in the testing set. As mentioned above, there were approximately 1,300 classifiers and 1,400 unique tags in the testing photos; however, only approximately 400 people had classifiers and appeared in the testing photos, i.e., only roughly a third or so of the people appearing in the testing set we had classifiers for.

Demographics According to Friendship The demographics of the identities (people) are also quite interesting in their own right. As mentioned above, the intersection of training and testing set identities is approximately 400, and the union of the training and testing set identities is straightforward to calculate: $1,300 + 1,400 - 400 = 2,300$ people. These can be divided into five categories: those belonging to the first-level friends of the robot *(F1)*, those belonging to the second-level friends of the robot *(F2)*, those who are on facebook but not first- or second-level friends

(F4), and those who are not on facebook *(F5)*. Rough percentages of these categories within the union and intersection follow:

> Union: *F1* 3%, *F2* 55%, *F3* 28%, *F4* 14%
> Intersection: *F1* 16%, *F2* 69%, *F3* 10%, *F4* 5%

Now, having examined various interesting statistics regarding our data set, we will proceed to presenting results from our algorithms and comments.

18.2.6 Results and Commentary

Here we present results quantifying the performance of the previously described algorithms on our acquired data set. Later, in a separate section, experiments investigating the effect of training set size and consequently providing predictions of scalability are provided.

Initial Comparison of Algorithms The plots of the recognition results for the three algorithms are presented in Figs. 18.4, 18.5 and 18.6, i.e. Alg0 without social info, and Alg1 and Alg2 with social info respectively. In each of these figures, there are two curves: one corresponding to the correct recognition percentage as a function of training set size and the other corresponding to participation in the Rank10 subset of the classifier, again as a function of training set size. It is obvious that the latter curve should always be above the former. Two linear fits are also presented above the curves. Correct recognition is in practice useful for an AR system; while Rank10

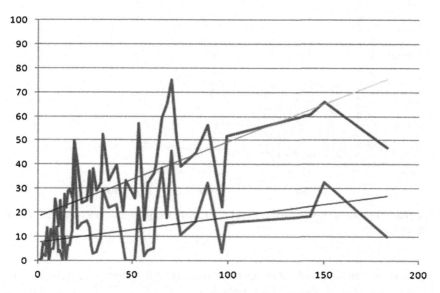

Fig. 18.4 Alg0 (no social info) Rank1 and Rank10 recognition accuracy, as a function of training set size

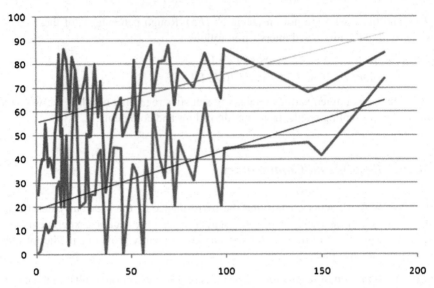

Fig. 18.5 Alg1 (social info, single seed known) Rank1 and Rank10 recognition accuracy, as a function of training set size

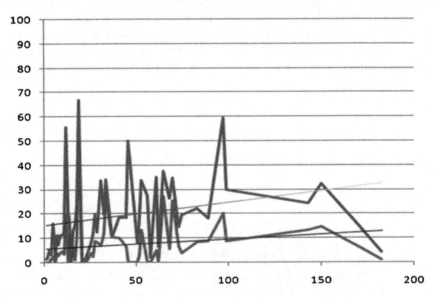

Fig. 18.6 Alg2 (social info, unseeded) Rank1 and Rank10 recognition accuracy, as a function of training set size

participation can be useful for an operator-assisted SAR system, where the Rank10 list is presented to an operator for selection.

The *first conclusion* to be reached by the figures is that clearly there is a *significant increase in recognition performance through the utilization of social information* (e.g., compare Figs. 18.4 and 18.5). In practice, without social info, classifiers made from training sets of size 1–50 or so were totally unusable for both AR as well as SAR; and only remotely helpful in the case of SAR in the case of larger sets (Fig. 18.4). However, with social info, one can start using SAR even with training sets of 10 or so, and can definitely use SAR with bigger sets and AR becomes useful with sets over 50. In quantitative terms, across all training set sizes, the Rank1 percentage is 11.5% with Alg0 and 20.3% with Alg1, while the Rank10 percentage grows from 30% to 52.4% (almost a twofold increase). If we restrict ourselves to only those training sets that have more than four photos, then Rank1 grows from 14.5% to 30%, and Rank10 from 38.5% to 64.4%.

The *second conclusion to be reached* is that although social information can really help, by comparing Fig. 18.6 with Fig. 18.5 or Fig. 18.4, it becomes clear that *a reliable seed is required* for this to take place. Alg2 (a very simple algorithm, multiple extensions of which exist as noted) just picks a face at random, calculates recognition scores for it and chooses the identity that has the highest score as its true identity, and then seeds Alg1 from this. However, if the seed is unreliable, then the social-context-driven boost cannot be so simply utilized. For Alg2, Rank1 and Rank10 percentages are of the order of 4.5% and 12.8% on average; which is even worse than Alg0. Things do not change with larger training sets, too. However, the other variants of Alg2 provide improvements, as we shall see later.

Finally, there is a *third conclusion* which is very important. The total testing time without utilizing social info is on the order of 23 s per face without parallelization. With social info, through the option of hard-restriction of the hypothesis space, this moves down to 4 s, i.e. a *sixfold improvement in recognition time*, quite important in real-time scenarios.

Thus, in conclusion: *social information helped us achieve a twofold increase in Rank1 and Rank10 accuracies, and has turned unusable results into usable ones. However, one should be very careful when seeding; an unreliable seed can revert the above situation, and a more complicated algorithm than Alg3 has to be used if no seed exists. Finally, social info can also enable a sevenfold speedup.*

18.2.6.1 Tuning Alphas and Betas

An investigation of the tuning of the parameters α_1, α_{-1}, and β, which appear in the soft versions of Algorithm 1, i.e. *Alg1S* and *Alg1TS*. Initially, a number of values were hand-picked and tried. Then, a non-linear optimization was performed, using the *Nelder-Mead method* [13]. The resulting optimum was found to be at

$$(\alpha_1, \alpha_{-1}, \beta) = (25, 0, 0.3) \tag{18.9}$$

The interpretation of this result is the following: We found that performance was increasing with α_1 increasing; however, no further increase took place after $\alpha_1 = 25$

(no further decrease too). In essence, such a huge value of α_1 (our variance of classifier score output is much lower), practically makes all first-level friend classifier biased scores to be bigger even than the biggest non-first level friend classifier output (i.e., equivalent to hard biasing if more than 10 friends of the seed exist). On the other hand, α_{-1} was found to be optimally at zero; i.e. for the purpose of FR, no distinction needs to be made between a '0' in the friendship matrix (knowing that somebody is not a friend of the seed), and -1 (having no knowledge whether the person is a friend of the seed), hence both categories are equivalent when it comes to their treatment. Finally, it was found that biasing according to training set size could indeed improve results, as we had a non-zero value for the optimum β. The optimum beta for our classifier score statistics was approximately 0.3. For the optimal α, the increase in *Rank*1 accuracy by the optimal β was on the order of 1% (additive over the baseline of roughly 20%) and the increase of *Rank*10 accuracy roughly was double at 2% (additive over the 50% or so, baseline).

Summing Up To achieve optimal recognition for *Alg*1, it is enough to first perform hard biasing and then to just add a training-set-size biasing term to the remaining classifiers, after having optimized for a value of β (for our classifiers this was $\beta = 0.3$). This extra term has a noticeable, however, not significantly large effect on recognition accuracy.

Effect of Random versus Best Seed A quantitative comparison of Alg2RS and Alg2BS was carried out. It was found that the latter, which was chosing as the seed the face that we had most confidence regarding its identity, was superior, giving an increase of 2% or so for *Rank*1, and 5% or so for *Rank*10 accuracy. Still, however, the overall performance of the algorithm was quite prohibitive.

Effect of Overall Match Metric Initial experiments on cycling around all possible seeds (i.e., the *Rank*1 postulated identities of each of the faces in the photos), performing seeded classification, evaluating the overall confidence of the resulting solution and selecting as seed, the one that gave maximum overall confidence took place. For a simple sum square metric, it was found that the results were worse than *Alg2BS* (a priori choose best seed) and close to random seed results.

18.2.7 Predicting Scalability

In this section, we attempt to explore the relation of recognition accuracy with the size of the available friendship network. In order to achieve this, our method, which we are going to present formally in what follows, was to randomly create subsets of various sizes, of the robot's friends and then repeat the recognition process based on data derived from this subset.

At this stage, we will start using the extra notation which is introduced in Appendix A.

Using these extra notations, we generate randomly a subset of Sarah's friends of predefined size, denoted by F', in each run of our experiments. This subset is then used to create new photo sets denoted by P', $P'tr$ and $P'te$ for total photos, the training photos and the testing photos, respectively. Finally, from these sets, only a subset of the original DFN can be created, denoted by DFN', and fewer classifiers can be built denoted by C'.

Formally, these sets, satisfy the following relations:

$$F' < F, \text{ random subset of size-}n \tag{18.10}$$

$$P' = \{p \in P | tags(p) \cap F' \neq 0\} \tag{18.11}$$

$$P'tr = \{p \in Ptr | tags(p) \cap F' \neq 0\} \tag{18.12}$$

$$P'te = \{p \in Pte | tags(p) \cap F' \neq 0\} \tag{18.13}$$

$$DFN' = \{t, t \in tags(p) \cap Fr(t) \neq 0, p \in P'tr\} \tag{18.14}$$

$$C' = \{U\,tags(p) | p \in P'tr\} \tag{18.15}$$

All these equations are straightforward and actually answer to the question of what portion of any data set would be accessible provided that the friends set was actually equal to F'. It is important to note that, every classifier in C' is not trained with the exact same set of photos, with which the same classifier in C was trained with, or mathematically the respective sets $P'tr_i$ and Ptr_i are not identically equal for every I in C'. Remember that the i-set of a set of photos Po, denoted by Po_i is defined by

$$Po_i = \{p \in Po | I \in tags(p)\} \tag{18.16}$$

However, the following lemma holds.

Lemma 18.1.

$$P'tr_i = Ptr_i, \forall I \in C' \cap F' \tag{18.17}$$

A proof of this lemma can be found in Appendix B.

18.2.7.1 The Testbed

For the purposes of the research presented in this section, we devised a testbed in which, random subsets of various sizes were created for the complete set of friends of our robot (denoted as F). This yielded new sets of photos for training and testing and new sets for DFN and for the classifiers (P', $P'tr$, $P'te$, DFN', C'), using the process described in Eqs. 18.10 to 18.15. In specific, the subset size was ranging from 0 to $|F|$, incremented by 2 in each run, taking four samples for each. Actually F' is subset of F, so it is actually a $|F'|$-combination of F, meaning that there are exactly $\frac{N!}{(N-k)!k!}$, if we denote $|F|$ by N and $|F'|$ by k. The sample size we take is small, but from the one hand, a single run of the testbed is computationally expensive (25 s and 50 Mbs for each sample), which puts a significant constraint on how many samples we can actually take, and from the other hand taking almost 160 samples in total is enough to perform a quick analysis of how the accuracy is affected by the total number of people in the social information seed and finally check how our social algorithms scale to the amount of social information at hand.

In the Table in Fig. 18.7 the sizes of the aforementioned sets are being presented for subset size that are multiples of 10. It is easy to see that all metrics quickly converge to a linear relation with the size of the friend s' subset (F'). A linear regression on these values might yield the following results

$$|P'| = 79.|F'| + 451 \tag{18.18}$$

$$|P'tr| = 39.|F'| + 231 \tag{18.19}$$

$$|P'te| = 23.|F'| + 134 \tag{18.20}$$

$$|DNF'| = 18.|F'| + 102 \tag{18.21}$$

$$|C'| = 13.|F'| + 90 \tag{18.22}$$

The above equations do reveal some interesting attributes of the Facebook data set we are analyzing, from which we distinguish the most important to be the relation of the *DFN* and the set P of photos as compared to the friends subset size. All other metrics (testing/training sets and classifiers) are in fact dependent on these sets.

We begin by taking into consideration the case in which a new person joins our friendship network and try to examine its effect on the photos that we can access (P') and the identities we can be aware of (DFN'). First of all, for every new person coming into a social friendship network, new resources are added, such as 79 new photos, 19 new tags (from these photos) and 13 more classifiers can be built for our system. These numbers are referring to mean values (Fig. 18.7) and might vary greatly depending on the social attributes of the new person added. In our data set, the big majority of our photos contained only one face, which seems also to be true for the entire Facebook data set based on our experience. This in part explains the

Number of Friends (F')	Set of photos (P')	Set of training photos ($P'tr$)	Set of testing photos ($P'te$)	Discoverable friendship network (DFN')	New classifiers(C')
10	1241	621	364	282	220
20	1848	919	505	466	355
30	2828	1406	820	706	526
40	3701	1834	1079	869	643
50	4692	2326	1342	1158	861
60	5188	2576	1510	1167	863
70	6133	3034	1801	1412	1049

Fig. 18.7 Effect of increasing the number of first-level friends

relatively large number of photos added for each new person added in the social circle, since these photos most probably contain only the face of this person, so they were previously unknown.

The total number of distinct tags of these new photos, add new identities in the DFN. The total number of these new identities obtained from the tags are mostly affected by two factors:

1. The likelihood of this person being a friend of someone in our initial network, and the transitivity of this network
2. The type of images that the new person has available in his profile

For example, if the new person is already a friend of someone in our initial network and the transitivity of this network is high, the new person will most probably have many of his friends already in it. As a consequence, there is again a high probability that his or most of his photos have already been available from through those friends. In addition, the number of faces in a photo greatly depends on the type of the photo (e.g., personal, friends, events, etc.) which in turn defines how many new identities can be inserted into *DFN*.

From our results, this number is approximately 19, which means that for any new person, 19 more people are discovered whose social information (just the list of 1st level friends) can be accessed. A simple analysis reveals that we get approximately one new identity for almost four new pictures added in the photo set. This ratio is yet another testament on the fact that the personal photos (photos with one face) is the prevailing type of our photo data set.

18.2.7.2 Recognition Performance and Training Set Size

Another important aspect is how recognition performance changes according the size of the friendship network that we use as a basis. For example, currently our robot has around 80 friends; what would be the expected performance of the methods described above if she had 1,000 or 5,000? An initial layman's thought might be that we might not be able to make strong estimations of what this relation might be, since accuracy improvement using social information is largely dependent on the type of photos that were used both in the training and the testing set (e.g., applying social information on a testing set with personal photos only, i.e. photos with one face, would be useless).

Nevertheless, the results of the previous section indicate a strong and stable correlation among the various data sets that are the focus of our research, which can be used to a certain extent for obtaining some insight over the extent of how useful the social information-based algorithms can be, for bigger numbers of first-level friends and larger sets in general. For this, one has to first identify the circumstances under which, applying social algorithms on the testing photos, provide the best results.

A very important observation to be made at this stage is the following: in Alg0 (w/o social ctxt), the larger the set of classifiers we have, the smaller we expect our recognition performance to be, as there are more possibilities for false identification.

This is indeed the case, as can be verified by the lower curves in Fig. 18.8. On the other hand, for Alg1 (with social ctxt), one should notice that in the hard-bias case we are effectively restricting our hypothesis space (number of effective classifiers) to the first-level friends of the seed face (and not to the first-level friends of the robot, and all the classifiers that are created through our process of getting their tagged photos and using other tags too). That is to make things clearer: as the number of first-level friends of our robot increases, so does the number of classifiers that it can create. However, if using Alg1 for recognition, the effective hypothesis space of classifiers does not grow; because it depends on the number of friends of the seed faces, and not of the robot. That is even if the number of friends of the robot increases dramatically, in which case the recognition performance of Alg0 (w/o social ctxt) will fall, we do not expect the same to be the case for Alg1 (w social ctxt), given that its performance depends on the average number of friends of the seed faces, and not on the actual number of friends of the robot. Thus, as the number of friends of the robot increases dramatically, *we expect Alg 1 to sustain its performance*; and this seems to be, at first glance at least, the case in Fig. 18.8.

In conclusion: We saw how various quantities related to our problem vary as a function of the number of first-level friends of our robot. Many of these grow linearly, as we have seen. Recognition performance without social information (Alg0) falls as this number grows, as expected. However, recognition performance with social information (Alg1) is expected to *remain stable* after a while, due to the argument given above: i.e., the effective constraining of the hypothesis space to size equal to the average number of first-level friends of the seed. This, at first sight,

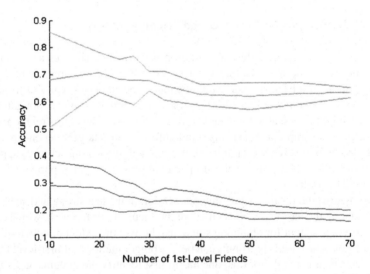

Fig. 18.8 Recognition performance as a function of increasing number of first-level friends of the robot, estimated using the multiple subsets technique described here. *Upper curves*: Alg1 (with social ctxt). *Lower curves*: Alg0 (no social ctxt). The *three curves* in each group correspond to the mean value as well as mean+std and mean−std.

seems to also agree with the results of our empirical investigation, and is a very encouraging result, promising very good scalability of our method.

18.3 Using Co-occurrence in Photos Towards Estimation of The Friendship Network

18.3.1 Introduction and Problem Setting

After having seen how social context (and more specifically knowledge of the friendship relation among individuals) can help enhance FR, through exploitation of the correlation of friendship with face co-occurrence in photos, now we will discuss the inverse problem, i.e., how we can estimate the friendship relations of a number of individuals, by having many photos of them.[5] Again, the key is obviously the correlation of co-occurrence of faces in photos with friendship. More precisely, we define the following problem:

Pr4 Given a number of photos containing tagged faces, estimate the friendship matrix $(\hat{FM})$ of a number of individuals. Metrics for comparing the success of different approaches usually measure the differences between the estimated $(\hat{FM})$ and original friendship matrix (FM). One possibility is to employ signal detection theoretic metrics and investigate false positive rates, sensitivities, confusion matrices, and ROC curves. This is the approach being followed here.

18.3.2 Proposed Algorithms

We propose a basic class of algorithms for solving **Pr4**.

18.3.2.1 Algorithm 4

Input A set of tagged photos
Output A friendship matrix estimate

First, we create a co-occurrence count matrix CM, in the following manner, starting from a zero matrix: for each photo in the input set, take all possible pairs of faces (F_i, F_j), including the case for $i = j$, and increase the count in the co-occurrence matrix in $CM(i, j)$. At the end of the process, the resulting symmetric matrix will have the number of occurrences of an identity's face in the diagonal of the matrix,

---

[5] To our knowledge, Hiroshi Ishiguro first mentioned a similar problem for the case of a robot observing people [12].

and the number of co-occurrences of two identities i *and* j in the off-diagonal element $CM(i, j)$. Now, the co-occurrence matrix has to be converted to an estimate of the friendship matrix. The following two approaches are proposed, and results will be presented below.

Alg4T Here, simple thresholding is employed. The friendship matrix is to be filled with $\{1, 0 \ or \ -1\}$, corresponding to the three cases (are friends, are not friends, do not know). If our ultimate purpose is to later reuse the matrix for social-context assisted FR, then as we saw above in the results section for the algorithm2, we do not need to differentiate between the cases of $(-1 = donot\,know)$ and $(0 = not\,friends)$, because for the case of optimal recognition results the weight a_{-1} is zero. Thus, we move across the diagonal of the co-occurrence matrix CM and if the diagonal element is zero, we fill row i and column j of $\hat{FM}$ with -1. If it is non-zero, then we copy the corresponding row and column from CM to $\hat{FM}$ after transferring through the following rule:

R1

$$\hat{FM}(i, j) = \begin{cases} -1 & \text{if } \dfrac{CM(i, j)}{CM(i, i) \cdot CM(j, j)} \leq Th1 \\ 1 & \text{if } \dfrac{CM(i, j)}{CM(i, i) \cdot CM(j, j)} > Th1 \end{cases} \qquad (18.23)$$

If we are interested in also creating a friendship matrix containing not only 1 and -1 but zeros, then a variation of the above rule could be:

R2

$$\hat{FM}(i, j) = \begin{cases} -1 \text{ if } CM(i, i) \cdot CM(j, j) < Th2^6 \\ 0 \ \text{ if } \{ \dfrac{CM(i, j)}{CM(i, i) \cdot CM(j, j)} \leq Th1 \} \wedge \{ CM(i,i) \cdot CM(j,j) > Th2 \} \\ 1 \ \text{ if } \{ \dfrac{CM(i, j)}{CM(i, i) \cdot CM(j, j)} > Th1 \} \wedge \{ CM(i, i) \cdot CM(j, j) > Th2 \} \end{cases}$$
$$(18.24)$$

The appropriate thresholds are chosen through signal detection theory, given a criterion for choosing the operating point.

Alg4TE Here we employ transitive extensions (TE) instead of thresholding. The underlying idea that when the set of photo observations is small, if $Id1$ and $Id2$ appear in a photo, and $Id2$ and $Id3$ appear in another, then chances are they are all first-level friends with each other. Thus, we quantize the co-occurrence matrix CM to contain only 0 (no co-occurrence) and 1 (for non-zero co-occurrence count). Then, we multiply CM with itself m times, and quantize again. The appropriate value of m is again determined through a signal detection theoretic criterion. We

---

[6] Not enough observations for adequate knowledge.

expect to reach transitive closure (TC) after a specific m, and after this no further changes arise if we further multiply and quantize.

18.3.3   Results

Results of the two cases of *R1* (with and without TEs) will be described here. In our experiments, the data set as described in Sect. 18.2.5.1 was used and we compared our resulting estimated friendship matrix $\hat{FM}$ against the original friendship matrix *FM* described in Sect. 18.2.1. In more detail, we were able to reach a total 2,637 people (following the tags accompanying the facebook photos) through the friends of our robot Sarah's facebook profile. Hence the dimensions of *CM*, *FM* and $\hat{FM}$ matrices are the same (i.e., 2637 × 2637). As already discussed in Sect. 18.3.1, in R1, we do not differentiate between relation levels -1 and 0, the resultant confusion matrix reduces to Fig. 18.9. Receiver Operating Characteristics (ROCs: True Positive Rate versus False Positive Rate) are presented in Figs. 18.10 and 18.11.

When *FM* is constructed using R1 without transitive extensions, the ROC of Fig. 18.10 is obtained.

Using R1 with TEs, TPR (True Positive Rate) and FPR (False Positive Rate) stabilize after nine iterations ($m = 9$). By looking at the graph in Fig. 18.11, one can observe that with TEs, the TPR almost saturates at 23%, meanwhile the FPR gradually grows. On the other hand, in the case without TEs, the TPR and FPR remain almost constant at 11% and 0% (Fig. 18.10 which are both lower than the former. Therefore, it is quite obvious that using simple TEs increases the TPR rate by approximately double meanwhile the corresponding increase in FPR remains insignificant. Thus, we have seen how with computationally very less expensive methods that are easy to implement one can easily recover a significant amount of the friendship network from photos; and one can chose among many possible operating points depending on the tolerance of different FP and FN.

	−1	0	1
−1	TN	TN	FP
0	TN	TN	FP
1	FN	FN	TP

Fig. 18.9 Confusion Matrix for R1

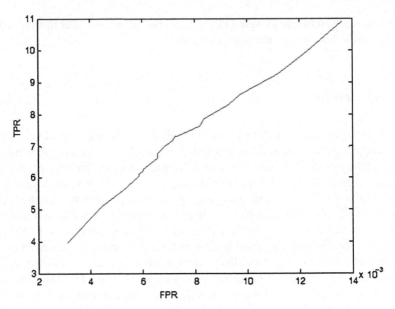

Fig. 18.10 ROC: TPR × 100 (Y) vs FPR × 100 (X) for 50 iterations (Th1=0:0.01:0.5), no TE

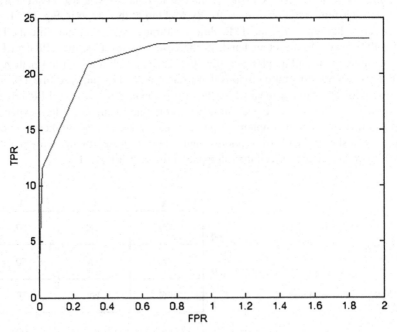

Fig. 18.11 ROC: TPR × 100 (Y) vs FPR × 100 (X) for 50 iterations (Th1=0:0.01:0.5), TC at $m = 9$

18.4   Conclusion

In this chapter, we have discussed proposed algorithms and demonstrated through real-world results *how knowledge of the "friendship" social relation can help create faster and better face recognition, and how sets of photos with recognized faces can help estimate the friendship relationships existing among individuals.* This was possible, because the two relations of friendship (among individuals) and co-occurrence (of faces in photos), though appearing in different realms (social vs. visual sensory), have a strong correlation: faces that co-occur in photos often belong to individuals that are friends. Using real-world data gathered from "facebook", which were gathered as part of the "FaceBots" project, the world's first physical face-recognizing and conversing robot that can utilize and publish information on "Facebook", we presented novel methods as well as results for utilizing this correlation in both directions. The results were quite encouraging: in our primary example, we were able to demonstrate doubling of the recognition accuracy as well as a sixfold improvement in speed. Various improvements, interesting statistics, as well as an empirical investigation leading to predictions of scalability to much bigger data sets were also discussed. Finally, we hope that apart from the specifics presented here, this chapter has also acted as a concrete demonstration that very promising avenues exist at the crossroads between social networks and numerous other areas, many of which are open to future exploration.

Appendix A

Formal Notation   Here we introduce a notational system in order to formalize our basic concepts and enable a succinct and precise exposition of the rationale behind using social algorithms. This system should be considered complimentary to the notation introduced in Sect. 18.2.1 which was more a verbose explanation of the algorithms. In order to be able to enumerate identities, we are assigning to an identity, a unique positive integer (not necessarily the same with the facebook identity, for those identities that are on facebook). If the maximum assigned *id* is denoted by M, we can define a total set of our assigned *ids* as:

$$D = \{1 \ldots M\} \tag{18.25}$$

Next, we denote the set of all tagged facebook photos as P_b.

$$P_b = \{\text{Total set of facebook photos}\} \tag{18.26}$$

We assume that there is a function which maps a photo to the set of id's of its corresponding tags:

$$tags() = P_b \overset{maps\ to}{\rightarrow} D^k \tag{18.27}$$

We also assume that there exists a procedure *Fr*:

$$Fr(x) : D^k \stackrel{maps\ to}{\rightarrow} D^k = \{\text{ids of friends of } x\} \tag{18.28}$$

For convenience, we assume $x \in Fr(x)$. Based on Fr we can define:

$$FR = \text{Friendship Relationship} = D \times D \stackrel{maps\ to}{\rightarrow} \{-1, 0, 1\} \tag{18.29}$$

for which it holds

$$FR(i, j) = \begin{cases} 1, & \text{iff } i \in Fr(j) \text{ or } j \in Fr(i) \\ 0, & \text{iff } i \notin Fr(j) \text{ and } Fr(j) \neq 0 \text{ or } j \notin Fr(i) \text{ and } Fr(i) \neq 0 \\ -1, & \text{otherwise} \end{cases} \tag{18.30}$$

Notice that $FR(i, j) = -1$, only when we do not have social information for neither i nor j. Also notice that $FR(i, j) = FR(j, i)$, i.e., FR is a symmetric relation and also non-transitive. The FR relation is the same as presented in Sect. 18.2.1. We further define notation to account for our Robot's Id, for the first-level friends of an Id, and for the available tagged photos containing a set of ids:

$$s = \text{Our Robot's Id} \tag{18.31}$$

$$F = Fr(s) \tag{18.32}$$

$$P = \{p \in P_b | tags(p) \cap F \neq 0\} \tag{18.33}$$

where the member p of P is the same as Ph in Sect. 18.2.1. Equation 18.32 provides a set of our robot's friends. Equation 18.33 is the set of all photos that are accessible by our robot through its friend network (F). By dichotomizing this, we are able to build two sets of photos, for training and testing Ptr, Pte, respectively. A classifier (denoted as Cl in Sect. 18.2.1 is an HMM (Hidden Markov Model) of the facial characteristics of an identity. Therefore, the set of classifiers can be mapped on the set of ids (D)

$$C = \{\text{set of classifier ids derived from the training set } \forall p \in Ptr\} \tag{18.34}$$

We then proceed by defining the discoverable friendship network DFN as the total set of tagged ids on every photo of the training set:

$$DFN = \{t | \forall p \in Ptr, t \in tags(p) \text{ and } Fr(t) \neq 0\} \tag{18.35}$$

We then create a new set which will be the basis of our social information:

$$D_e = \text{extended id set} = \{C \cup DFN\} \tag{18.36}$$

Finally, we then define the friendship matrix (already introduced in Sect. 18.2.1) which holds information for friendship relationship among all accessible ids (as available in D_e):

$$FM = \text{Friendship matrix} = D_e \times D_e \to \{-1, 0, 1\} \qquad (18.37)$$

for which

$$FM(i, j) = FR(i, j), \; \forall (i, j) \in Fe \qquad (18.38)$$

the tuple (F, P, DFN, FM, C) defines completely an instance of the problem we are investigating. This completes the set of notational machinery required.

Appendix B

Lemma 18.2. *The training sets of the classifiers in C' (the new set of classifiers produced by starting from the reduced friends set F'), and specifically those classifiers in C' with Id's belonging to F', will be identical with the training set of the original classifiers in the full problem (i.e., those arising for $F' = F$, the full friend set).*

$$P'tr_i = Ptr_i, \forall I \in C' \cap F' \qquad (18.39)$$

Proof. First notice that:

$$P'tr_i \leq Ptr_i \qquad (18.40)$$

This is true since for any p in $P'tr_i$, it holds that:

$$I \in tags(p) \forall p \in P'tr \Rightarrow I \in tags(p) \forall p \in Ptr \Rightarrow p \in P'tr_i \qquad (18.41)$$

Now assume that $P'tr_i < Ptr_i$, then there exists a photo p such that

$$p \in Ptr_i \qquad (18.42)$$

$$p \notin P'tr_i \qquad (18.43)$$

From (18.43) we get that

$$p \notin P'tr \text{ since } I \in tags(p) \qquad (18.44)$$

From (18.42) we get that

$$p \in Ptr \qquad (18.45)$$

Therefore from the definition of $P'tr$, we get that

$$tags(p) \cap F' = 0 \qquad (18.46)$$

However, it holds that

$$I \in tags(p) \qquad (18.47)$$

$$I \in F' \cap C' \tag{18.48}$$

therefore:

$$tags(p) \cap F' \geq \{I\} \neq 0 \tag{18.49}$$

The initial assumption has led us to a contradiction, and the training sets for the classifiers that also belong to the new F' friend subset are identically the same. In the special case, in which, $|tags(p)| = 1$, for every $p \in P$, (photos with one face), which is also the vast majority of our own photos, it is easy to prove the equality of the training sets for any classifier in the entire set C'. In brief, (18.46) in the above Lemma $\Rightarrow I \notin F'$, while $C' \cap F' \leq F', \Rightarrow I \in F'$, which is also a contradiction. Therefore, the entire set of classifiers C' will be trained with the same set of training images.

References

1. Mavridis N, Datta C, Emami S, BenAbdelkader C, Tanoto A, Rabie T (2009) FaceBots: social robots utilizing facebook. In: Proceedings of the 4th ACM/IEEE HRI '09. ACM, New York, NY
2. Michelson J, Ortiz J (2006) Auto-tagging the Facebook. http://www.stanford.edu/class/cs229/proj2006/MichelsonOrtiz
AutoTaggingTheFacebook.pdf
3. Torralba A (2003) Contextual priming for object detection. Int J Comput Vision 53(2)(Jul 2003): 169–191
4. Hoiem D, Efros AA, Hebert M (2006) Putting objects in perspective. In: Proceedings of the 2006 IEEE computer society conference on computer vision and pattern recognition, Vol 2 (17–22 June 2006). CVPR. IEEE Computer Society, Washington, DC, pp 2137–2144
5. Stone Z, Zickler T, Darrell T (2008) Autotagging facebook: social network context improves photo annotation. IEEE computer society conference on computer vision and pattern recognition workshops, Anchorage, Alaska, USA, June 2008
6. Mavridis N, Kazmi W, Toulis P, Ben-AbdelKader C (2009) On the synergies between online social networking. Face recognition, and interactive robotics, CaSoN 2009
7. Facebook online social networking website. http://www.facebook.com
8. Facebook statistics. http://www.facebook.com/press/info.php?statistics
9. Samar V (1999) A single sign-on using cookies for Web applications. In: Proceedings of the 8th workshop on enabling technologies on infrastructure for collaborative enterprises table of contents, pp 158–163, ISBN:0-7695-0365-9
10. Nelson ML, Maly K (2001) Buckets: Smart objects for digital libraries. Commun. ACM 44, 5 (May 2001) 60–62
11. Facebook API. http://wiki.developers.facebook.com/index.php/Mainpage
12. Kanda T, Ishiguro H (2006) An approach for a social robot to understand human relationships: friendship estimation through interaction with robots. Interact Stud 7:369
13. Nelder JA, Mead R (1965) A simplex method for function minimization. Comput J 7:308–313
14. Viola P, Jones M (2004) Robust real-time object detection. Int J Comput Vision 57(2):137–154
15. Nefian AV, Hayes MH (1998) Hidden markov models for face detection and recognition, in International Conference on Image Processing, Chicago, Illinois, USA

Index